Shakespeare's Patterns
of Self-Knowledge

Rolf Soellner

SHAKESPEARE'S
PATTERNS OF
SELF-KNOWLEDGE

Ohio State University Press

Library of Congress Cataloging in Publication Data

Soellner, Rolf.
Shakespeare's patterns of self-knowledge.

1. Shakespeare, William, 1564–1616—Criticism and
interpretation. 2. Self-knowledge in literature.
I. Title.
PR3069.S4R6   822.3'3   72–5804
ISBN 0–8142–0171–7

TO

THOMAS WHITFIELD BALDWIN

who to me as to many Shakespeareans

is the master of those who know

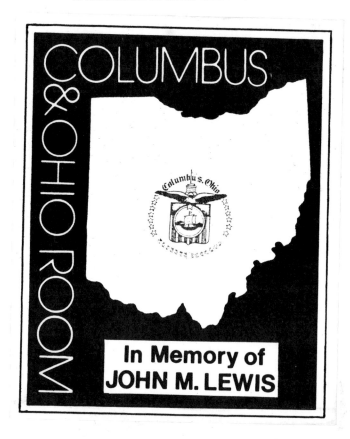

CONTENTS

Preface   *ix*
Introduction   *xi*

1 HUMANISM AND ANTIHUMANISM

1 *Nosce Teipsum:* Learning the Method   *3*
2 *Nosce Teipsum:* Charting New Courses   *26*

2 THEORY AND ADAPTATION

3 Microcosm and Macrocosm: Framing the Picture of Man   *43*
4 *The Comedy of Errors:* Losing and Finding Oneself   *62*
5 *Love's Labor's Lost:* Seeking Oneself   *78*
6 *Richard II:* Looking into the Mirror of Grief   *97*
7 *Henry V:* Patterning after Perfection   *113*

3 PROBLEMS AND AMBIGUITIES

8 The Real versus the Ideal: Taking a Skeptic View   *131*
9 *Julius Caesar:* Taking an Uncertain Road   *150*
10 *Hamlet:* Probing a Restless Self   *172*
11 *Troilus and Cressida:* Fragmenting a Divided Self   *195*
12 *Measure for Measure:* Looking into Oneself   *215*

4 ACHIEVEMENT AND SYNTHESIS

13 Will and Passion: Heightening the Self   *239*
14 *Othello:* Subjecting the Self   *259*
15 *King Lear:* Valuing the Self   *281*
16 *King Lear:* Stripping the Self   *305*

17 *Macbeth:* Losing the Self   *327*

18 *The Tempest:* The Mastered Self   *356*

APPENDIXES

A *Hamlet:* "What is a man?"   *387*

B *Lucrece:* "Why should the worm intrude the maiden bud?"   *390*

C *Hamlet:* "What a piece of work is a man!"   *399*

    Notes   *405*

    Index   *437*

Preface

I have sought in the following study to quote primary rather than secondary sources wherever feasible. I have modernized the spellings in the titles and in the quotations taken from sixteenth- and seventeenth-century books and also modified the punctuation so as to make it better conform to modern usage. In a study of ideas like mine, the old spellings would have hindered more than helped. We do, of course, generally quote Shakespeare from modernized texts; not to grant the same advantage to his contemporaries means to provide them with an even greater handicap than they already have by intrinsic merit. In quoting from the Bible, I have used the versions of Shakespeare's time, that is, the Bishops' Bible, the Genevan, and its variant, the Genevan-Tomson; but in most cases I have had the Genevan closer at hand, and it is the version referred to unless specified differently. It also offers ample, even if at times rather doctrinal, notes. The Shakespeare edition used is that of *The Complete Works,* edited by Peter Alexander (American edition: New York, 1952). In a few instances, indicated in my notes, I have preferred readings different from Alexander when they are supported by the Folio or an authoritative quarto; and in Appendix C I have retained the spelling and punctuation of the sources because they are substantive to my argument. The abbreviations of the titles of periodicals in the notes conform to *PMLA* practice.

Whatever I can say in expressing my gratitude for what I owe to others in conceiving and writing this book is, to speak with Shakespeare's Kate, "too little payment for so great a debt." In many cases I shall not be able to acknowledge particular debts since it is impossible for a Shakespeare scholar to remain aware of the myriad influences his predecessors have exerted on him. But I am gratefully conscious of the abiding effect that two masters of Shakespeare scholarship have had on me: Levin L. Schücking, my mentor during my German student days, and T. W. Baldwin, my adviser during my graduate studies at the University of Illinois. To the latter, this book is affectionately dedicated. I began my exploration of Renaissance moral philosophy while I held a Guggenheim fellowship, and I am most appreciative of the personal encouragement I received from the president of the foundation, Gordon N. Ray. Professor Paul Jorgensen, who in his study of *Lear* was the first to bring Renaissance *nosce teipsum* concepts to bear on the interpretation of a Shakespeare play, was most generous in giving up his plans of extending this approach and in leaving the field to me when he heard that I had a similar intention. A travel grant by my former institution, Kansas State University, aided my work; but I would not have been able to complete it if it had not been for the kindness and help I received from my colleagues in the English Department of the Ohio State University, then under the leadership of Albert J. Kuhn, who guided my weary steps and revived my hope. For reading and criticizing parts of my manuscript at various stages, I am indebted to Ruth Hughey, Joan Webber, Jewell Vroonland, John Gabel, Julian Markels, and Charles Wheeler; to Edwin Robbins I am grateful for reading the whole and for making some excellent suggestions. Samuel Schoenbaum of Northwestern University scrupulously read the penultimate version; I have benefited immensely from his great learning, critical discernment, and editorial know-how. Where I stubbornly stuck to arguments he criticized, I have at least tried to strengthen them.

My research was done at the British Museum in London, the Henry Clay Folger Library in Washington, D.C., and the Henry E. Huntington Library in San Marino, California; the latter library awarded me a grant-in-aid, and the personnel of all three were most understanding and helpful. Mrs. June Johnson painstakingly typed the manuscript; and my student Mr. Dan Atwood acted as both proofreader and stylistic critic. Finally, I am grateful to Mr. Weldon A. Kefauver, director of the Ohio State University Press, for his interest and encouragement, and to Mr. Robert S. Demorest, the editor, for his care in guiding the manuscript through its final stages. Whatever in this book (to speak with Kate again, in her triumph of self-knowledge) is still "muddy, ill-seeming, thick, and bereft of beauty," I must acknowledge as undeniably my own.

Introduction

T HE RENAISSANCE, particularly the humanistic Renaissance, evinced a strong interest in self-knowledge. The
ancients' slogan *nosce teipsum,* or γνῶθι σαυτόν, became a
universal watchword. It was, it is true, not unknown in the Middle
Ages, when self-knowledge was thought desirable by some thinkers,
especially the mystics, as a prerequisite to the knowledge of God;
but at no time was there the same fascination with the study of the
self as in the Renaissance.[1] Sir Philip Sidney's was then one of the
many voices to acclaim its significance and to do so with the characteristic admonition of making the results of self-study fruitful for the
moral conduct of life. In *An Apology for Poetry,* he said that all
sciences were "directed to the highest end of the mistress-knowledge,
by the Greeks called ἀρχιτεκτονική, which stands, as I think, in the
knowledge of a man's self, in the ethic and politic consideration,
with the end of well-doing and not of well-knowing only. . . ."[2]
Sidney saw the poet, ahead of even the moralist and the historian,
as the best guide toward this goal.

The idealistic hope expressed by Sidney that much can be gained
for the conduct of life from the study of literature has in some form
always been one of the major attractions of that part of literature
which we consider great (but we must remember that great literature shares this attraction with much artistically inferior work). And
this hope was and is one of the major reasons for the appeal of
Shakespeare. Even of the activity of modern Shakespeare critics,
averse as they are to being thought subjective and moralistic, more
may be motivated by this feeling than appears at first sight. For
instance, we have become fond of saying that Shakespeare's tragic
heroes are destroyed because they do not know themselves. Surely,
the indistinct hope that we can learn something from their failures is

a major reason for the popularity of this phrase. By saying that Shakespeare's tragic heroes do not know themselves, we can think of them as negative examples for us without being too obviously moralistic; we need not pose and answer the vexing question of what, if any, moral commitment Shakespeare had. We can use the phrase to mean vaguely that the tragic heroes have weaknesses that make it impossible for them to cope with their fate. Since all of Shakespeare's tragic heroes, with the possible exception of Romeo, have some responsibility for their downfall and destruction, we make a safe, even if hardly very meaningful, statement about them when accusing them of lack of self-knowledge.

The present study is not concerned with what we moderns think self-knowledge is, or with what Shakespeare may be able to contribute to our much-needed ethical amelioration, although perhaps I have not altogether been able to conceal my feelings on these matters. The subject of this book is what the Elizabethans and Jacobeans thought self-knowledge was and what dramatic patterns Shakespeare created from this thought. If the concept of self-knowledge is to become useful in the criticism of Shakespeare, it will have to be given a more specific content than it has had; and I believe that little will be gained by asking our contemporary psychologists, philosophers, and theologians, vitally interested in ideas of self-knowledge as they are, for help. What they have to say differs widely, determined as it is by the special concern of the definers; and it differs even more from what the Renaissance theorists, particularly the Christian humanists, had to say. Neither do I think that much can be gained by asking the literary critics, ancient or modern.

This last point may require some illustration. Aristotle, whose *Poetics* has given rise to many clichés about tragedy, held a concept that superficially resembles the statement of modern critics that the tragic heroes do not know themselves. This is the famous *hamartia,* vulgarly translated in its application to Shakespeare as "the tragic flaw." But for Aristotle, the term did not have the psychological or moral implications it has in modern use, but meant merely something like "miscalculation." What he had in mind is perhaps best illustrated by *King Oedipus,* to which he repeatedly referred. The *hamartia* of Oedipus is his inquiry into his own background, not in itself blamable, particularly in view of the Greeks' intellectual curiosity. No more does that other often-invoked term *anagnorisis,* discovery or recognition, parallel what we mean when we say that at some points during the action Shakespeare's tragic heroes get to know themselves or discover themselves or have a tragic illumination. According to Aristotle, *anagnorisis* is an external identification, whether of things, events, or persons, that is dramatically most effective when it occurs together with *peripeteia,* the change of fortune from good to ill or the reverse. The *anagnorisis* in *Oedipus* is the King's recognition that he has killed his father and married his mother as the oracle predicted he would. Thus Aristotle's *anagnorisis* reflects the Greeks' sympathy with human errors and their belief in the inexorable nature of fate. Aristotle did not have Shakespeare's interest in individual character; he was not concerned with the psychic constitution of particular men that makes them prone to failure. Neither did he have Shakespeare's Christian consciousness that some failures are different from others because they are sins rather than mistakes and that much more is at stake in committing the former than the latter. If we use the Aristotelian term for Shakespeare—and like others from the *Poetics* it has become too much a part of our critical vocabulary to do without it—we must redefine it with an awareness that concepts of self-knowledge are not independent of cultural contexts.

The idea of self-knowledge as a modern critic of drama may conceive it cannot be applied to Shakespeare without such an awareness. For instance, in an essay on the common man as tragic hero, Arthur Miller has said that tragedy is the consequence of man's total compulsion to evaluate himself justly.[3] What Miller may mean by this statement can presumably be illustrated by his own dramatic practice—best seen, perhaps, in his *Death of a Salesman,* when he has Willy Loman lose himself in the spiritual emptiness of his dream of success. This is the tragedy of a common man who abandons his individuality and humanity by listening to the siren songs of his age. Obviously, Shakespeare's tragic heroes are not common men, and he knew nothing of salesmen. He did not have Miller's sociological orientation or his heightened belief that an individual must build his own value system. Miller's, as well as Aristotle's, ideas of self-knowledge are too deeply rooted in their respective cultures to aid us in establishing Shakespeare's concept.

Our first and primary source for this purpose is, of course, Shakespeare himself. Direct allusions to self-knowledge through phrases denoting knowing oneself and not knowing oneself occur with some frequency in his dramas and poems—fifteen times altogether,[4] and considerably more often if variations are included, such as finding oneself, being oneself, being true to oneself, and losing oneself, not being oneself, and forgetting oneself. The context of these occurrences makes it clear that self-knowledge had for Shakespeare and his audience a different emphasis from what it has for us. In most cases, the primary reference is to the control of passion by reason. But this is generally more than the simple act of keeping one's temper. When, for instance, Regan says so unkindly of her father that "he hath ever but slenderly known himself" (I.i.293), she is referring to his recent outbreak of anger; but when she goes on to predict that his infirm and choleric years will increase this weakness, she is alluding to assumptions about the behavior of men according to their age of life made by Shakespeare and his audience, but not by us. A few scenes later, Goneril accuses Lear of neglecting to check the "Epicurism and lust" of his retainers and demands that he restrict himself to "such men as may besort your age, / Which know themselves and you" (I.iv.250–51). Here again the reference is to proper behavior according to age, but Goneril's exhortation—we are, of course, not concerned with the question of whether it is justified—also points to a code of manners, to proper knightly behavior. As another illustration in which the reference to self-knowledge extends beyond its primary meaning of control of passion, we may note an instance in a comedy, *As You Like It*. When Rosalind lectures Phoebe on her disdainful rejection of Silvius's wooing, she concludes: "But, mistress, know yourself" (III.v.57). Here the allusion, as is evident from the context, points beyond the censure of pride to Elizabethan notions of the relationship of wooer and wooed, undeserving maid and deserving lover, man and woman.

In other allusions to self-knowledge in Shakespeare's plays, control of the emotions does not appear to be the main issue or is not involved at all. When Macbeth, after murdering Duncan, says "To know my deed, 'twere best not know myself" (II.ii.73), he seems in some way to associate self-knowledge with a moral way of life. Elsewhere the context of the reference does not give any satisfactory explanation of its meaning. When Hamlet says of Osric that "to know a man well were to know himself" (V.ii.139), the turn of the phrase and the prince's enigmatic intellectuality suggest that something is meant in addition to the fencing skills that are the immediate reference; but the text gives no clue at all.

Shakespeare evidently used the concept of self-knowledge with some vagueness, just as we do, but his vagueness differed from ours. Or we might say that the field of reference, a shifting one, differed in his time from that in ours. For him, as for us, the advantage of references to self-knowledge lay in their very vagueness and allusiveness. "Know thyself" was a signpost to a variety of ideas he and his audience considered important for man's behavior and character development. If we wish to identify and define these ideas, we must follow the signs into the territory to which they point, and this can best be done by reading Renaissance moral literature. But whatever explicit definitions we may find here are not likely to be very helpful since Renaissance definitions were notoriously unscientific, repeating generally what ancient or Christian authorities said on the subject. The meaning of self-knowledge in Shakespeare's time must be established in the same way in which Shakespeare acquired it, that is, contextually.

In following this procedure, I have undertaken something of a source study although I have not inflicted all my evidence on the reader. Even so, I have had to quote passages from Renaissance moral literature and, sometimes, extensively so. But my intention has been not to prove that Shakespeare read this or that book but that he received from somewhere similar currents of intellectual stimulation. One cannot, of course, read through many Renaissance tracts without lighting here and there on passages that give one the feeling that Shakespeare knew them. But it is not important whether my reader shares this feeling, provided I can convince him that these parallels prove that Shakespeare was interested in theories of self-knowledge and that he knew much about them. I hope to show that he was strongly and vitally interested in these theories by discussing a number of plays in which they are prominent in the dramatic patterns, be it in thought, theme, or character portrayal. Seeing these patterns in the Renaissance context of *nosce teipsum* notions, I believe, is a valuable and heretofore little-used means for Shakespeare interpretation.[5]

No study of this kind is free from assumptions based on what one confidently believes he knows clearly. As to the Renaissance intellectual background, my main assumptions, as far as I am aware, are two: first, that the Renaissance began as an educational movement, and, second, that it led to an increasing diversity in men's conceptions of themselves and of the world. Shakespeare's patterns of self-knowledge, I believe, reflect both this educational concern and this increasing diversity. I have devoted the first part of the book and the introductory chapters of the other parts to general considerations of how the movement of the Renaissance, from its Christian humanist basis in the direction of greater individualization, influenced Shakespeare's patterns.

As to the Christian humanist aspect, I believe that the role of formal education is too often neglected in studies of Shakespeare's intellectual background. We sometimes talk vaguely about Shakespeare's inheritance of medieval or humanistic ideas and forget that the first and, I think, lasting stimulus came in grammar school, the institution designed by the Christian humanists to teach both good Latin and good morals. I have followed Professor T. W. Baldwin's footsteps over part of this terrain in search of the influence of school indoctrination on Shakespeare's moral ideas, and my reader will find some reflections on this matter in my first chapter.[6] Insofar as the humanism into which Shakespeare grew was Christian, we must not forget the religious ingredients, contained as they were sometimes in such literary exercises as translations of biblical passages from Latin into English and from English into Latin. However, the Christianization of pagan *nosce teipsum* concepts can best be seen in some English moral tracts that I have used throughout and whose nature I have briefly examined in the first chapter.

My second assumption, that the Renaissance led to an increasing diversification of ideas (and that the Reformation, child of the Renaissance, contributed to that), is one of the oldest assumptions concerning the period; but it has been drawn into doubt so as to require some defense, at least in its validity for sixteenth-century England. When Jakob Burckhardt defined the Renaissance as the discovery of man and nature, he saw its ethos in the emancipation from medieval unity and in the development of individual impulses that shaped man's conception of art and his attitude toward nature. Nobody today is likely to accept this thesis *in toto*. The change from the Middle Ages to the Renaissance was not a revolution; many of the old ideas and attitudes persisted and became in Christian humanism the core of a new attempt at an old synthesis. Yet the sixteenth century was different from the fourteenth and fifteenth, and Shakespeare was not Chaucer. There is, I believe, much that is persuasive in the view of an early Burckhardtian like Wilhelm Dilthey that Renaissance literature arose from a change in *Lebensgefühl* and *Lebensführung,* which gave the individual greater scope by acquainting him with choices of conduct and philosophy.[7] Although this individualization was a slow process, it did reach England in Shakespeare's time. In my second chapter, I have analyzed what I think were the major impulses on changes in the concepts of the self and self-knowledge owing to this development.

As I studied the patterns of self-knowledge in Shakespeare's whole dramatic work, I distinguished three major periods: an early one in which he took the patterns as he found them and adapted them to his dramatic designs; a middle one, in which he showed an increasing awareness of their rigidity and occasional incongruity with experience; and a final one, in which he accepted diversity as a fact of life and overcame his earlier hesitations in an emphatic synthesis of theory and life. The first period is that of his early and middle plays up to and including *Henry V* and the great romantic comedies. The second, overlapping with the first, is dominated by plays that, by various critics, have been called "problem plays": *Julius Caesar, Hamlet, Troilus and Cressida, All's Well That Ends Well,* and *Measure for Measure.* The third period begins with *Othello* and includes the major tragedies and the romances. I have examined four plays from each of these periods, plays in which the patterns of self-knowledge are particularly prominent.

In selecting these I have not been guided by considerations of genre, and I have included examples from comedy, history, tragedy, and romance not in order to have a sample of Shakespeare's work in each of these categories but because I saw strong patterns of self-knowledge in the particular plays. I came to the conclusion that for Shakespeare there was no separate comic, tragic, or historical man, nor were there different kinds of self-knowledge; for him, man was one and the same being whether he exulted in victory or writhed in defeat. I admit that I was temporarily drawn to a provocative distinction made by L. J. Potts:

> I connect the essential distinction between tragedy and comedy with two opposing impulses deeply rooted in human nature. Until we can find a way of reconciling the antinomy in our nature, we are all torn between the desire to *find* ourselves and the desire to *lose* ourselves.[8]

I believe that Shakespeare very much addresses himself to the antinomy of our desire to find ourselves and to lose ourselves and also to the antinomy of our fear of finding ourselves and of losing ourselves; but I do not think that a real distinction can be made on this basis between Shakespeare's comedy and tragedy, or between his comical and tragical history. The patterns of self-loss and self-recovery pervade all of Shakespeare's dramas regardless of genre. Even if it is true that some kind of "finding" must take place at the end of the comedies and tragicomedies, in some of these the losses cannot be eradicated from our minds. Not all characters in Shakespeare's comedies find themselves in the end—consider Malvolio, for instance—and not all endings lead to unconditional findings—consider, for instance, the very conditional happiness of Bertram and Helena at the end of *All's Well*. No more do the tragedies present merely self-loss: Edgar at the end of *King Lear* emerges as a character who has made one of the most spectacular self-discoveries. For that matter, all losing is not tragic or potentially so; the kind of self-loss in romantic love that leads to marriage in the comedies and in *Romeo and Juliet* is an eminently desirable state, a paradoxical finding-in-losing. Shakespeare holds the mirror up to nature in not separating completely the tragic and comic worlds, which, we know, cannot be separated in life.

I should say that my principle for selecting plays and my way of discussing them owes something to my twofold assumption concerning the Renaissance as an educational and individualizing movement. In the second part of the book, which is devoted to Shakespeare's first period, I have concentrated on those earlier plays that seemed to me to demonstrate best Shakespeare's technical familiarity with the humanistic lore of self-knowledge; and I have discussed these with an eye on what was to come, particularly in the later tragedies. For that very reason, I have felt that it was more valuable to examine two early comedies like *Love's Labor's Lost* and *The Comedy of Errors,* which deal with the antinomy of losing and finding in an almost formulaic way, rather than to examine Shakespeare's two early tragedies, *Titus Andronicus* and *Romeo and Juliet,* which have less explicit patterns of self-loss and self-recovery. Of the histories, *Richard II* was an obvious choice since in the fate of its hero, the royal failure and sufferer, it foreshadows the self-loss of Shakespeare's later tragic heroes. The last chapter of this part, on *Henry V,* examines the hero-king as Shakespeare's embodiment of conventional humanistic ideals and thus as a norm by which to measure Shakespeare's later approaches to, and deviations from, the recognized Renaissance pattern of perfection. My later comparisons of the portrait of Henry with modifications of the pattern—Brutus in *Julius Caesar,* Duke Vincentio in *Measure for Measure,* and Prospero in *The Tempest*—will, I hope, be instructive demonstrations of Shakespeare's developing concepts of self-knowledge.

I have chosen to include all plays that belong to the second period with the exception of the artistically least satisfactory *All's Well.* The two tragedies *Julius Caesar* and *Hamlet* are, of course, masterworks that had to be included; but I have discussed them as well as the difficult-to-classify *Troilus and Cressida* and the problematic comedy *Measure for Measure* for the transitional, searching, and sometimes tentative patterns of self-knowledge they contain. The relatively prominent place they have in my study comes from their significance in showing the interplay of tradition and a new spirit. The very tentativeness of the questions posed and answered in these plays has made them so congenial to our own age, which has lost many certainties, as to warrant greater interest in them.

The selection of plays for individual discussion from Shakespeare's third period has been painful. Since everybody's interest in Shakespeare's patterns of self-knowledge centers on the tragic heroes, I have chosen the three major tragedies, *Othello, King Lear,* and *Macbeth.* I regret the omission of *Timon of Athens, Antony and Cleopatra,* and *Coriolanus,* dictated by considerations of time and prudence. In discussing the tragedies, I have interpreted from the patterns of self-knowledge outward to attempt a whole critical assessment of the plays. I have also dealt thus with *The Tempest,* the one romance included. The patterns of self-knowledge in this play form a natural culmination of those that preceded, and this chapter is therefore a fitting conclusion to the book.

Inevitably, I have had to concern myself throughout with the analysis of Shakespeare's dramatic characters; it is primarily through character that self-knowledge is sought, expressed, and achieved. But character analysis is at present somewhat out of fashion—a recent critic of *Hamlet* calls it "a valetudinarian topic." [9] This attitude is an understandable and largely wholesome reaction to the excrescences of romantic, impressionistic, and Bradleyan psychological criticism of the nineteenth and early twentieth centuries, which often treated Shakespeare's characters as if they had a life independent of their parts in the dramas. But the main reactors to character analysis, the historical critics, have in turn become passé; and alternative critical modes, such as the close reading of the poetic fabric of the plays, valuable as they are, have not succeeded in totally suppressing the universal and, I think, legitimate interest in what makes Shakespeare's characters behave as they do. The time may have come to return to character analysis, chastened by the valid critique of the post-Bradleyans.

If the thought of having engaged in a *démodé* subject does not really disturb me, the realization does that I may have contributed somewhat to the more questionable endeavor of searching in Shakespeare's plays for his own philosophy. His infinite variety and the temptation of passing off one's own thoughts for Shakespeare's make this a notoriously perilous enterprise, but paying heed to dramatic and historical conditions can be something of a check to the threatening subjectivism. I have examined Shakespeare's words and not my feelings about them, and I have tried to be sensitive to the poetic texture and to the plot situations. We may, on the whole, assume that Shakespeare gave his views to sympathetic characters, but this is certainly not a uniform rule; even a villainous Iago can cite scripture to his purpose, and an unselfish idealist like Brutus can be dead wrong. We must see the ideas expressed by Shakespeare's characters in the total context, and we should use only legitimate means to interpret their relevance to Shakespeare's philosophy. Such means are comparisons with sources and with moral attitudes as they can be identified by the study of the intellectual background. Even so, we can often achieve only probability. Shakespeare was not a propagandist; his attitudes were subtle and qualified. But he was certainly not morally indifferent; if an idea is repeated in his plays by sympathetic characters and is underlined by theme and dramatic structure, we can, with some assurance, say that it was part of his philosophic credo, at least at the time he stated it.

Shakespeare was not, of course, a philosopher in the sense of an inventor or propagator of a coherent and consistent system. In any case, such synthesis would have been difficult to achieve in the fermenting and changing climate of the Renaissance. Even Bacon, who did not have Shakespeare's need to present dramatic tensions and conflicts, was more a herald of a new system than its instigator. If Shakespeare had aspired to the single-minded eminence of founding a philosophic system, he could not have been "myriad-minded"; he could not have looked at the world through the devilish soul of an Iago as well as the freedom-loving mind of a Brutus.

Shakespeare had a "philosophy" in the sense in which all thinking men have one: a body of ideas, not totally consistent and very much subject to revisions, on man, life, and the world. This was a changing and growing structure of thought, as his was a growing and changing art. His philosophy was sometimes articulated and more often merely intimated, but it was almost always subordinated to dramatic purposes. Shakespeare so skillfully infused ideas—moral and immoral—into the thoughts of his characters that we tend to forget that these ideas were in some sense conceived by him, that is, acquired or invented, and in any case deeply understood in their bearing on life. How else could he have made them so powerfully appropriate?

In the course of my study I have come to appreciate increasingly Shakespeare's philosophical acumen, both in the way he used traditional ethical concepts and modified them or supplanted them with newer ones or with his own ideas. In the conflict between tradition and innovation, Shakespeare gradually came to realize his inner resources; he learned to know himself. And as he learned to know himself, he came to master his art.

PART ONE

Humanism and Antihumanism

CHAPTER ONE

Nosce Teipsum:
Learning the Method

L IKE MANY ANOTHER Elizabethan, William Shakespeare presumably first heard the slogan *nosce teipsum,* "know thyself," which he was to hear many times afterward, in the grammar school of Stratford-on-Avon. He may have been told to memorize it together with other *sententiae* in one of the anthologies used in Elizabethan schools, such as *Sententiae Pueriles* or *Disticha Catonis.* In the latter collection, it appeared among the sayings of the seven wise men of Greece and was attributed, as traditionally, to Chilon, the Lacedaemonian. Whether already at this point or later, Shakespeare must have been told something about the meaning of self-knowledge. He would thus have learned that *nosce teipsum* was inscribed on the entrance to the temple of Apollo at Delphi. He may have been shown the composite emblem of the seven wise men, in which *nosce teipsum* was illustrated by a mirror.[1] In any case, he would have met the phrase in such Latin authors as Ovid, Persius, and Cicero, and his schoolmaster would then very likely have taken the opportunity to instruct him on its significance and application.

Such explanation would have been an introduction to the Christian humanists' philosophy of man. The reference books that a schoolmaster had at his disposal were compiled by them and conveyed their views. Erasmus's *Adagia* was here a very obvious choice. It contained the traditional remarks on the origin of the saying, defined it as an advice for humility and moderation, and supplied various other definitions and explanations from classical and Christian writers. Several of these stressed the difficulty of knowing oneself, the obligation to improve oneself, and the need to observe others in order to understand oneself.

Erasmus was more explicit on these matters in his *Enchiridion Militis Christiani* (1502), a book that was still very influential up to

3

and during the time Shakespeare went to grammar school. The English Reformers had liked its insistence on purity of faith and its attacks on ceremonies. A translation ascribed to William Tyndale went through nine editions between 1533 and 1576, and Miles Coverdale made an abridged version in 1545. If there were no further English editions after 1576, the reason was surely that the Erasmian arguments had become common property in moral and religious thought.

The metaphor that unifies and illuminates Erasmus's *Enchiridion* is that of life as warfare, a metaphor that was familiar to medieval and Renaissance Christians through Job 7:1 in the military terminology of the Vulgate: "Militia est hominis vita super terram." For Erasmus, this warfare was primarily man's struggle against internal enemies, the disturbing and destructive passions, which, leagued with the temptations of the world, led man to vice and sin. To conquer his archenemies, the flesh and the devil, man must know himself; this, Erasmus said, was the first point of wisdom. The ancients believed that the injunction *nosce teipsum* came from heaven; but the saying also agreed with Christian religion, since the mystical lover in the Song of Solomon asked his bride to leave the house (i.e., the Church) unless she understood herself: "O, thou beautiful among all women, if thou know not thyself, go out of doors, and walk after the steps of thy flock and sort." [2]

The derivation of the injunction for self-knowledge from both pagan literature and the Bible was characteristic of Erasmus's *philosophia Christi*. Although his *Enchiridion* had a more specifically religious purpose than the works he composed for school use, it too attempted to balance Socrates and Christ, earth and heaven, mind and spirit. Erasmus struck a similar balance when he spoke of the self, which, for him, was both good and bad, reasonable and passionate, divinely inspired and humanly corrupted. The problem of self-knowledge was to reconcile the warring elements in man; outer and inner man, body and soul, flesh and spirit, passion and reason must be given their due, and all must serve Christ. What was against nature was as bad as what was against God. Faith alone was not a guarantee of salvation; self-discipline and self-control also must be used.

Sometimes, it is true, Erasmus spoke of the self as if it were the enemy. He demanded conquering oneself, getting out of oneself, and losing oneself. But, as the context shows, he meant here only the baser parts of the self, the flesh and the passions, and he did not really think that these could or should be completely suppressed. The passions were not to be eradicated, Stoic fashion; they must be tempered in the way Aristotle and the Fathers recommended by using the better emotions for ennobling life and by controlling the baser ones. The man who knows himself is temperate.

Erasmus saw the self as having a reassuring organic and hierarchical structure. He adopted the Platonic analogy of man to a monarchy, with reason enthroned in the head; the higher passions, such as love and shamefulness, located beneath it in the chest; the destructive ones, such as lust and ambition, exiled below the diaphragm. The ethical health of man depended on the preservation of this order; a revolt of the lower forces meant passion, vice, and sin, and threatened the immortal substance of the soul. To combat this danger, man must use his reason according to God's instruction. But he must not fall prey to the allurement of this faculty; he must remain conscious of his human limitations. With a touch of *contemptus mundi,* Erasmus recalled the misery of man's entrance into life, the precariousness of his existence, and the certainty of his death.

Erasmus and the Christian humanists gave *nosce teipsum* an active meaning; the injunction not only implied an assessment of the human condition but also constituted an exhortation to a morally oriented life. And they were optimistic about translating this meaning into pedagogy; they put great faith in the efficacy of morality couched in grammatical and rhetorical instruction. In his programmatic tract *De Ratione Studii,* Erasmus demanded that the schoolboy should learn *verba* in order to acquire, even if not immediately, *res,* that is, concepts and ideas. The school curricula were planned so as to make the boys assimilate the ideas that the humanists considered right, that is, conforming to their moral outlook, and to enable them to express these according to formal principles derived from the ancients.

An Elizabethan schoolboy like William Shakespeare thus was exposed to a great deal of moral advice of the *nosce teipsum* kind. Even before reaching grammar school, he was likely to have memorized some verses on manners and morals, such as those which constituted Francis Seager's *The School of Virtue* (1557, several times reprinted). It included the following admonition:

>Let reason thee rule and not will thee lead
>To follow thy fancy a wrong trace to tread.
>But subdue thy lust and conquer thy will
>If it move thee to do that is ill.[3]

And the schoolboy's Catechism and Psalter gave similar advice; it warned him to bridle "the inward affections" of his heart and thus enjoined the temperance that the Christian humanists thought central to self-control and self-knowledge. His little grammar, the Erasmus-Colet-Lily collaboration, probably was prefixed by some English moral sentences like the "Precepts of Living," which enjoined subduing his appetites, thrusting down pride, and refraining from wrath, and it contained similar instructions in its illustrative Latin sentences.[4] And the schoolboy was inundated with such material in the Latin phrase books for parsing and memorization: "cognosce teipsum . . . iracundiam tempera . . . ne cui invideas . . . invidia suum torquet auctorem . . . ingratitudo viciorum caput . . . perturbato corde nihil jucundum . . . gravior inimicus qui latet sub pectore . . . teipsum ne negligas . . . vive memor mortis."[5] One understands the sententiousness and the morality of the Elizabethans better when he sits down with them, for a while, on a school bench.

Erasmus himself devoted a considerable part of his Herculean labors to making it easier for the schoolboy to learn both Latin and self-knowledge. Many of the sentences, figures, parables, and apothegms in his *De Copia Verborum ac Rerum, De Conscribendis Epistolis,* and *Parabolae Sive Similia* served clearly this dual purpose. In two of the dialogues of his *Colloquia,* "Puerpera" and "Convivium Religiosum," he provided for the children's need to understand the body-soul relationship fundamental to their self-knowledge by weaving into the conversation a list of appropriate metaphors: the body was the vessel, the garment, the house, the instrument, the tabernacle, the grave, the prison, the inn, and the fortress of the soul. By these metaphors, the boy was taught the soul's integrity, preciousness, purity, and immortality as well as the body's frailty, impermanence, impurity, and burdensomeness. Shakespeare, like the other Elizabethan poets, never forgot the lesson; he used all the metaphors on Erasmus's list and similar ones; he knew how to express moral ideas in the way the Christian humanists thought they should be expressed—only, of course, he did so in the vernacular rather than in Latin. But, directly or indirectly, he was indebted to Erasmus for formulating basic moral ideas of self-knowledge as the knowledge of body and soul.

Many of Shakespeare's fundamental patterns of self-knowledge must have derived ultimately from what he learned in grammar school. One needs to take in hand some of the annotated Renaissance editions of the classics to understand how the Christian humanists introduced moral ideas aimed at teaching self-knowledge into their commentaries. The injunction *nosce teipsum* appeared only occasionally in these notes, but the precepts that were thought implied in it were numerous. The variorum editions of Terence with their full commentaries offer some of the best examples of the method. The plays were examined not only for the author's language and the comic types portrayed but also for the psychological and moral instruction they were assumed to convey. A notable humanistic commentator, Jodocus Willichius, thus observed in minute detail Terence's depiction of the passions with some regard for their place in the play's structure but primarily from a physician's, rhetorician's, and moralist's point of view. In analyzing Geta's outbreak of anger in *Adelphoe,* III.ii, he claimed, for instance, that physicians could use this example to teach the causes, symptoms, reasons, and results of anger as a passion.[6] The claim and the method remind one of modern psychologists and psychiatrists who would use Shakespeare's plays as textbooks of their science; like these, Willichius read much into the text that it does not imply. But what some humanists like Willichius were reading into Terence reached Elizabethan schoolboys as certainly as what some Freudians have read into Shakespeare is reaching the modern student. Even Montaigne, emancipated as he was from the Christian humanists' preceptorial methods of teaching self-knowledge, allowed their claims for Terence, judging him "wonderful conceited and apt lively to represent the motions and the passions of the mind and the condition of our manners; our actions make me often remember him." [7]

With a method similar to that applied to Terence, other ancient authors were made to demonstrate the advantages of self-knowledge and the consequences of its lack: Virgil, whose Aeneas furnished a model of manhood; Horace, whose odes were called "medicinal" by his Elizabethan translator, Thomas Drant; and Ovid, whose *Metamorphoses* was recommended to the reader by its translator, Arthur Golding, as "a mirror for thyself thine own estate to see." [8]

Two other authors deserve special attention here, the neo-Latin
Palingenius and the classical Cicero; they needed no humanistic commentaries to make them into *nosce teipsum* authors, and they were
more influential than any of the others in forming Elizabethan notions of self-knowledge.

Palingenius's didactic poem *Zodiacus Vitae* (ca. 1531) had what
seems to us an inordinate place in the curricula, where it appeared
almost universally as a text in the lower forms of grammar school,
hardly because of its questionable aesthetic quality, but because it
poeticized a Christian-humanist philosophy of life and helped to
immunize the student against whatever paganism he might be exposed to elsewhere. Besides, the book conveyed some information on
mythology, natural philosophy, and astrology, all made subservient
to a theologically tinged philosophy of man. In his Seventh Book,
"Libra," Palingenius specifically expounded the meaning of *nosce
teipsum*. As he explained, self-knowledge must be combined with a
search for the knowledge of God. Man must consider the nature of
the Creator before examining His creation, man. So prepared, he
will understand why God created man of two substances, body and
soul, the one mortal, the other immortal. Just as his reason will show
him that God is eternal, it will prove that the soul does not die. It
follows that the soul must rule the body and the passions that tend to
ally themselves with it. Self-knowledge makes man capable of controlling these by reason, God's grace assisting.

Thus Palingenius went over the same ground as did Sir John
Davies in *Nosce Teipsum* (1599), with which students of Elizabethan literature are likely to be more familiar. Yet *Zodiacus Vitae,*
which received an unattractive English translation by Barnabe Googe
(1565), was a seminal book in Shakespeare's time, certainly one of
Shakespeare's sources and, I suspect, one of Davies's.[9]

Palingenius prepared the Elizabethan schoolboy for the moral
philosophy of Cicero, to which he would be exposed in upper grammar school. Cicero's eminence in the curricula, as well as his general
esteem as a philosopher in the Renaissance, stemmed from the rhetorical rotundity and the religious emphasis of his eclectic ethics. In
Cicero, Petrarch had read long before much of what he thought and
felt, and the Christian humanists continued to find the Roman
philosopher and orator most like themselves among the pagan
writers. Cicero's divine felicity of speech, Erasmus said in his Preface
to *Tusculan Disputations,* came from the sanctity of an erudite heart.

man is he, and not that figure and shape which may be pointed and showed with the finger." Newton's marginal gloss put it succinctly: "A man is his mind." [10] This equation could be brought into harmony with Christian theology, particularly with Paul's insistence on the hegemony of the spirit over the flesh. As Bullinger asserted in his sermon "Of the Reasonable Soul of Man," *"Anima,* the soul, is taken in the Scripture for the thing itself that hath life, yea, even for any, or rather for the whole, man." [11] William Shakespeare had good precedent in identifying man with his mind or soul, as he did repeatedly, often in order to underline man's special claim to perfection: ideal men were for him "dear," "noble," "true," and "strong" minds or souls. In this sense, mind and soul were synonymous with "self," for which he used such epithets as "dear," "noble," "great," "high," "precious," and "worthiest." [12]

But both *Tusculan Disputations* and *Somnium Scipionis* gave self-knowledge a meaning that transcended the individual soul. *Tusculan Disputations* interpreted the injunction of Apollo as including the soul's contemplation of the divine essence: man mediates on the world order and realizes that the psychic substance is part of the deity. Thus he can solve the problem posed by his destructive emotions, cleanse himself of them, and acquire tranquillity and happiness. Cicero's First Book, which borrowed from Plato, gave instructions for overcoming the fear of death; the remaining four books, heavily indebted to the Stoics, presented rules on how to conquer pain, distress, and other passions and to achieve the happy life of a virtuous man. *Tusculan Disputations* was influential in establishing control of the emotions as a priority for self-knowledge. In *Somnium Scipionis,* Cicero extended *nosce teipsum* to the political sphere by asking the statesman to strive for immortality through glorious service to the state. Drawn into a Christian context, this demand appealed to the Elizabethan moralists, who bid the prince or magistrate realize that to know himself meant bringing his exercise of power in line with the divine plan.

But it was Cicero's description of the *humanitas* ideal in *De Officiis* that became most influential. Whenever man's place in the creation and his duties were invoked in the Renaissance, there was likely to be an echo of Cicero. Thus, when Hamlet asks the question "What is a man, / If the chief good and market of his time / Be but to sleep and feed?" (I.iv.33 ff.), he reflects, as has long ago been noted, a key passage from the beginning of *De Officiis* (I.11). [13] The resemblance,

Renaissance commentators, such as Georgius Valla, Joachimus Camerarius, and Philippus Beroaldus, brought their learning and bias to bear on Cicero's text, thus constructing an eclectic humanistic moral philosophy by explaining Cicero in Platonic, Aristotelian, and, in particular, Christian theological terms. Some of this lore was likely to have reached the schoolboy William Shakespeare; if so, it helped to make him aware of what the humanists considered the "right" ideas of Cicero, but it would not have given him a feeling of the scope and variety of ancient philosophy.

Of Cicero's moral philosophy, the works most widely used in the schools were *De Officiis* and four small tracts, *De Amicitia, De Senectute, Paradoxa,* and *Somnium Scipionis* (from the sixth book of *De Republica*), all of which were often printed together in an octavo edition. Of Cicero's other philosophical works, the one most favored in the schools was *Tusculan Disputations.* Shakespeare could also read these books in English; they had been translated long before he went to London. *De Officiis* was rendered by Robert Whittington in 1534 and again, much better, by Nicholas Grimald in 1553. Grimald's version, accompanied by his remarkable Preface, which stresses Cicero's value for attaining self-knowledge, was reprinted a number of times before 1600. John Dolman issued a translation of *Tusculan Disputations* in 1561, and in 1577 Thomas Newton added the small treatises in the octavo volume, that is, *De Amicitia, De Senectute, Paradoxa,* and *Somnium Scipionis,* under the title of *Four Several Treatises.* Newton, incidentally, is a witness to the humanists' scholarly versatility arising from a concern with self-knowledge; a divine, physician, and poet, he translated several theological and medical tracts, two of them of the *nosce teipsum* kind (Levinus Lemnius's *The Touchstone of Complexions* [1565] and Philip de Mornay's *The True Trial and Examination of a Man's Own Self* [1586]), and edited the influential translation of Seneca's ten tragedies (1581), contributing to it his own version of *Thebais.*

Both *Tusculan Disputations* and *Somnium Scipionis* contained definitions of self-knowledge influenced by Plato, who equated it with an understanding of the nature of the mind or soul. In *Tusculan Disputations* (I.52), Cicero said that to know oneself meant to know one's soul; in *Somnium Scipionis,* he put it more emphatically (I quote Newton's translation): "Neither art thou that which thy outward form and shape declareth; but the mind and soul of every

I believe, becomes much closer when Hamlet's argument is compared to that in sixteenth-century editions of *De Officiis* with the headings, marginal notes, and commentaries supplied by humanist commentators. (See Appendix A.) As I have shown elsewhere, the debate in the Trojan camp in *Troilus and Cressida* (II.ii) also uses arguments from *De Officiis* when it touches on man's moral role in society and the universe.[14]

Cicero, following Plato, saw all moral action falling under the four cardinal virtues of justice, prudence, fortitude, and temperance. Of these, temperance was most closely associated with self-knowledge. *Temperantia* was a comprehensive virtue which, according to *De Officiis,* included *verecundia, modestia, sedatio perturbationum,* and *decorum.* The Renaissance commentators noted that in *De Inventione* (II.53–54), Cicero called *continentia, clementia,* and *modestia* qualities of *temperantia,* and they added the testimony of other philosophers and of Christian writers to Cicero's on the meaning of temperance. In this fashion, Cicero's discussion was supplemented with Aristotle's doctrine of virtue as the temperate mean between excess and defect, with the Stoics' warnings against all passions, with Saint Paul's demand for sobriety in word and deed, with the rhetoricians' notions of the moderation and control of the passions in speech, and with the physicians' analysis of temperance as the right mixture of the humors.

This conglomeration of elements tended to make temperance a composite and an almost chaotic concept. We need to think of the Renaissance idea of temperance as a cluster of vaguely related virtues, most of them more positive than what we have in mind when we use the term. It included not only the suppression of the appetites, particularly of desire and lust, but also the active use of reason in leading an orderly life; it encompassed the health of man in his entirety, body and soul. Intemperance thus meant all violations of virtue through the submission of reason to the lower forces of the soul and any disorder of body and mind; it was equivalent to lack of self-knowledge, and the moralists and theologians saw in it a threat to the God-given order of the universe.

In Cicero's discussion of *temperantia,* the commentators and thus the writers of moral tracts after them were particularly attracted to the concept of *decorum.* The term also played a considerable role in dramatic criticism, where it meant something rather different: the behavior of a character in conformity with the type, age, and characteristics of the person portrayed.[15] But in *De Officiis* (I.93–151), Cicero expounded a theory of moral *decorum,* proper ethical behavior. Of this, he distinguished two major kinds, *decorum generale* and *speciale.* The *decorum generale,* he said, required man to control his appetites; by observing it, man differed from the beasts. The *decorum speciale* allowed man to develop his individual talents; by assuming it, man differed from other men. In order to observe the *decorum speciale,* Cicero declared, man must watch himself and others. He must make a balanced estimate of his own ability, show himself a critical judge of his merits and defects, and know his disposition in order to play the role most suited to himself: nothing that runs against the grain of one's nature can be right, and a man's nature fits him best when it is the most characteristically his own.[16] As Grimald translated the core of this argument, "In the pointing out the whole life, much more regard thereof must be had that in the continuing of our life we may agree with ourselves, and never halt in any duty." This stipulation was given special emphasis in Grimald's 1556 edition by the marginal note "know yourself." [17] Thus to *know* oneself became to *be* oneself or to *be true* to oneself, or, as Grimald put it in his Preface, to "use" oneself.

However, it should be understood that the *decorum speciale* did not imply an invitation for man to become an unrestrained individualist. Cicero modified his *decorum speciale* by the *decora* of circumstances and choice; that is, he asked that every individual be aware of the requirements of his profession, status, age, and other external conditions. Most importantly, he considered individual *decorum* limited by general *decorum,* which prescribed man's proper moral behavior as a rational being, fundamentally different from the animals. Thus the classical concept of *decorum* was a useful weapon in the Christian humanists' fight against the flesh and the devil, who always took advantage of men who did not know what it truly meant to be man.

Shakespeare knew exactly how to use the arguments on *decorum* in this fashion. In *Lucrece,* he made his heroine engage in a lengthy attempt to dissuade Tarquin from his nefarious intention by appealing to his "likeness" or identity as a man and a prince. In the former role, she argues, he must control his appetites; in the latter, he must be a model to his subjects (568 ff.). She thus implores Tarquin to observe *decorum.* Quite properly she bases individual *decorum* on general *decorum* and sees it as modified by the circumstantial kind:

Tarquin cannot assume his likeness without behaving as he must as a human being and the son of a king. And Lucrece speaks very much to the point because, as the wiser sort of Shakespeare's readers must have known, his Tarquin is not only a rapist but also a horrible perverter of *decorum*. When he tries to excuse his desire for Lucrece to himself, he claims the privileges of a young lover and declares "sad pause and deep regard" to be the qualities that 'beseem" an old sage (274 ff.). Tarquin thus injects a rule of artistic *decorum* into an argument that requires the application of moral *decorum*—it is symptomatic that he visualizes his situation as if it were that of young lover in a comedy who "beats these [i.e., sad pause and deep regard] from the stage." Shakespeare's moralizing in *Lucrece* may be obtrusive, but it has the advantage of showing up a basic scheme that underlies the humanistic patterns of self-knowledge and demonstrates their indebtedness to the concepts of temperance and moral *decorum* based on Ciceronian ethics. (See Appendix B.)

The preceding summary of the role that instruction on self-knowledge played in grammar school will have shown that it provided Shakespeare with some basic patterns that, coming mainly from the ancients, were selected and given emphasis by the Christian humanists. Before Shakespeare ever read an English tract on the significance of self-knowledge, he had been taught much about it. Whether he had an ardent desire to read such English moral tracts may be doubted, but it is reasonable to suppose that he would at least have dipped into some of them. He was, after all, a country boy with no university education, and it was for such as him that the authors and (since many tracts were translated from Latin or modern foreign languages) the translators provided.

A general account of sixteenth-century English *nosce teipsum* literature is thus in order. We may begin it with works that, in the tradition of Cicero and Plato, equated self-knowledge with the soul's knowledge of itself. Foremost in this category was *A Treatise of the Immortality of the Soul* by John Woolton (1576). Woolton, a divine who later became bishop of Exeter, claimed to be the first to write in English on the subject of the soul's immortality, a claim that is hardly tenable but is symptomatic of the humanists' conviction of doing something new even when, like Woolton, they were heavily indebted to the medieval moral and theological tradition.[18] The humanistic *de anima* treatises, of which Woolton's book was a descendant, continued a medieval Christian genre, which in turn derived from Aristotle's work on the soul. Like his predecessors, Woolton defined, divided, and subdivided the soul; he located it in particular parts of the body; he established a hierarchy of operational elements that subordinated the senses and the passions to reason and made the ultimate functioning of this system dependent on divine grace. As was customary, Woolton saw the danger to man's physical, emotional, and spiritual well-being in the rebellion of the lower forces of the soul, a rebellion that had become endemic since the Fall. Man's moral problem was the conflict of his reason with his passions; his hope for overcoming it lay in achieving, with the help of God, control over himself. The key to this control was self-knowledge; as Woolton said in his Introduction, the greatest wisdom was to know oneself, the greatest folly, not to know oneself.

Woolton equated self-knowledge with the soul's knowing itself and therefore knowing other things, but most writers in the *de anima* tradition declared it to include an understanding of the body and its functions as well; in this case, too, soul and body were seen to be essentially different and the hegemony of the soul was thought to be divinely established. In the same year in which Woolton published his *Treatise,* Thomas Rogers, admittedly using his university notes, sent to press a work making these points, *A Philosophical Discourse Entitled The Anatomy of the Mind.*[19] Like Woolton, Rogers explained the nature of the passions, classified them, and gave instructions on their pacification. He added a brief treatment of the cardinal virtues so that Christians might learn from pagans to become more virtuous. Like many *nosce teipsum* writers, Rogers emphasized the significance of man by describing him as a little world reflecting in himself the larger world of the universe.

The concept of the microcosm played as important a role in the humanistic thought of the Renaissance as it did in the Middle Ages. It was generally fathered on Aristotle, who was indeed, as far as is known, the first to use the term μικρὸς κόσμος—he used it only once —but who neither invented the macrocosmic analogies, which are much older, nor stated the concept in explicit terms.[20] Its formulation seems to have been the work of Philo and other neo-Platonists, from whom medieval theologians appropriated it. The Christian humanists liked the concept because it agreed with their emphasis by attracting attention to man as both the epitome of the universe and its favored member. Man's recognition of himself as a microcosm was one of their basic postulates for achieving self-knowledge. Shakespeare's

Richard II is aware of this requirement; when he makes a final attempt to understand himself and his situation, he tries to create in his "little world" an image of the greater one (V.v.1 ff.).

Next to theologians, doctors were most in evidence as *nosce teipsum* authors. According to what Thomas Wright, himself a divine, said in the Preface to his *The Passions of the Mind* (1601), the subject of self-knowledge was the particular province of both the theologians, the curers of the soul, and the physicians, the curers of the body. Actually, the members of the two professions did not always confine themselves to their particular sphere of competence; there was much about the body in the theologians' treatises and much about the soul in the physicians'. The latter, however, were more apt to concern themselves with the physiological humors, which had evolved from the microcosm concept. They ascribed to them man's diseases as well as his emotional disturbances and thought man's health and happiness to depend on the right mixture of the humors or *crasis,* although they were not unanimous on the exact nature of that state. As we have already noted, the moral aspects of this equilibrium were also called "temperance"; the humoral balance constituted the physical side of that cardinal virtue central to self-knowledge and self-control. The ideal man of the physicians was of a temperament "exactly and perfectly temperate," as Levinus Lemnius described him in *The Touchstone of Complexions* (translated in 1565 and several times reprinted); he was the fortunate being in whom the elements, as in Shakespeare's Brutus, were so mixed as to make Nature stand up and say, "This is a man."

In basing mental stability and moral behavior on man's physical composition, the physicians were in danger of taking a materialistic position, which to the Elizabethans was equivalent to atheism; and indeed, the suspicion of harboring atheistic notions hovered about them as it did in the Middle Ages when Chaucer's Physician studied but little in the Bible.[21] However, in their *nosce teipsum* tracts, this materialistic tendency was counteracted by theological references and arguments. The balanced man of Lemnius, for instance, was an ideal completely realized only in Christ.

Although the ultimate effect of the constant admonitions that man should know himself may have been secularizing, the tracts themselves spread a strongly religious aura with occasional shadings of *contemptus mundi.* The seminal work of this tradition, the eleventh-century *De Humanae Miseriae Conditione* of Pope Innocent III, was

still popular in sixteenth-century England; George Gascoigne incor-
porated a large section of this work in his *The Drum of Doomsday*
(1576; reprinted, 1586), and there was a full English version by
Humphrey Kerton, entitled *The Mirror of Man's Life* (1576; reprinted, 1577, 1586). Pope Innocent described in gloomy colors the
beginning, progress, and ending of life; the misery, presumption,
vanity, and pride of man on earth; and the uncertainty of existence
contrasted with the certainty of death. Innocent took a much more
pessimistic view of man than did the Christian humanists; but since
he too dwelt on the antithesis of body and soul, depicting the former
in its horror and hideousness and the latter in its potential heavenly
glory, *contemptus mundi* touched *nosce teipsum* on an important
point. So, for that matter, did a related medieval convention, the
consideratio, a penitential exercise. It took its cue from biblical passages in which the notion of "considering" man is associated with
repentance for evildoing.[22] In works like Bernard of Clairvaux's *De
Consideratione,* an examination of man's miserable state was proclaimed to be medicinal and purifying. This penitential strain of
consideratio was continued in sixteenth- and seventeenth-century
religious literature, where it was sometimes identified with self-
knowledge, as, for instance, in *De Contemptu Mundi,* by the Spanish
Jesuit Diego de Estella, which was twice translated, once in 1584
(Douay?) by Geoffrey Coulton and again in 1586 by none other than
the Protestant clergyman and *nosce teipsum* author Thomas Rogers.
In one of the book's most eloquent chapters, "The knowledge of ourselves bringeth us to the knowledge of God," Diego took his cue from
Saint Augustine and argued that God was reflected merely darkly in
the human mind; in order to see his image more clearly, man needed
to humble himself by considering the misery of his body. The best
glass for a man to see himself in was another man; but this man had
to be considered not in the uncertain glory of his life but in the
misery of his death. The mirror of self-knowledge was not the flattering glass of life but the true image of death; man must prepare himself for the moment of facing it. This idea is vividly illustrated by an
early seventeenth-century emblem that shows death as a terminus
figure, holding a mirror, and a man's footprints tracing by him on
the ground; a banner above reads: "He has considered himself and
has departed." [23]

These somber tones sounded in Elizabethan and Jacobean times no
less than in the Middle Ages. The dust into which man's body disin-

tegrated at death and the worms, the inheritors of this decay, were so demonstratively evoked as to jar sometimes our modern sensibilities that would rather evade this aspect of self-knowledge. But we cannot escape its power in some of Shakespeare's great passages, such as the pessimistic speeches of the dethroned Richard II or the Duke's preparation of Claudio for death in *Measure for Measure* (III.i.5 ff.). Even a character like Percy Hotspur, unreflective in nature, stammers a memorable *memento mori* in his last words, being mindful that he is nothing but dust. In the storm on the heath, as Lear strips himself and considers man in his nakedness, the *consideratio* achieves its ultimate expression; the thematic statement is accentuated by the king's violent gesture and fortissimo of pain.

Even if, as seems plausible, Shakespeare was not an avid reader of *contemptus mundi* literature, he was affected by the religious tone and by the otherworldly implications given to *nosce teipsum*. His was an age of universal church attendance, and self-knowledge, as he must have been told in many a sermon, involved a combat against earthly pride and a preparation for salvation. In the official Elizabethan homilies, appointed to be read in churches, these points were repeatedly made in the two introductory sermons, dealing with the salvation and the misery of mankind. Knowing oneself, the argument went, meant humbling oneself, acknowledging oneself to be but dust and ashes, and confessing to being a miserable sinner. When man submitted himself to the will of God, he recognized his dependence on Him and could thus hope to understand His nature: "The true knowledge of ourselves is very necessary to come to the right knowledge of God." [24] Man was endowed with a mortal body and an immortal soul in order to feel his sinfulness and misery and to be advised of the grace and goodness of God. His self-examination proved his capacity to choose between good and evil, between God and the devil.

The Calvinists, it is true, granted less to man's power of choice and more to God's. Calvinism was a major ingredient in the religious climate of Shakespeare's time and must not be neglected in this review of the theological implications of *nosce teipsum*.[25] It is, of course, impossible here to do justice to Calvin's philosophy of man, but we may at least note some of the main points in which it differed from the Erasmian synthesis as well as from the evolving Anglican theology as represented by Richard Hooker's *Of the Laws of Ecclesiastical Polity*.

Like the Elizabethan homily, which took a Christian-humanist
point of view, John Calvin connected the knowledge of the self with
the knowledge of God. There were only two kinds of knowledge, as
Calvin said at the opening of the *Institutes,* and these were the knowledge of the self and the knowledge of God. But for him, self-knowledge had no independent value at all; one could know the self only by
knowing God. Self-knowledge, for Calvin as for Saint Augustine,
was merely God's light shining upon man. It is true that, much like
the humanists, Calvin extolled the beauty of what he called "the philosophers' microcosm," that is, the symmetric form and the organic
function of man's body and the excellence and acuity of his mind.[26]
But he referred here to prelapsarian man, to man as he might have
been but no longer was. Calvin's concern was not with this ideal but
with sinful and fallen mankind. Thus self-knowledge became for him,
much as with the *contemptus mundi* writers, a recognition of man's
ignorance, vanity, poverty, infamy, depravity, and corruption; it was
the condition for accepting God as the only true wisdom, solid
strength, perfect goodness, and complete righteousness. Although
man was God's noblest work, his fall had made him a most lamentable
ruin. Man's endeavor must be to restore the divine image in himself.

Calvin tended to disparage the role of reason in this process. He
accused the philosophers of arrogance in prescribing rational rules
for leading a virtuous and contented life. In unregenerated man, reason had been reduced to only a few weak sparks, insufficient to serve
as a light to salvation. The self was not a balanced antithesis of body
and soul, flesh and spirit, passion and reason, in which the latter elements could control the former. The whole of fallen man, body and
soul, had become corrupt; not merely were the inferior appetites ensnared by the devil, but abominable impiety had also seized the citadel
of the mind (II.i.9). For Calvin, we might say, man had already lost
the warfare of life, which Erasmus thought he could win. His hope
for regeneration lay only in the grace of God. But it was fortunate in
this respect that God had put man in a turbulent, unquiet, and uncertain world. Thus man could realize that heaven and not earth was his
real home. Calvin, however, did not conclude that one should therefore withdraw from life; in fact, he argued that Christians could
prove God's grace as effective in themselves by laboring in their voca-
tions and aiming at improvement. Thus *contemptus mundi* paradoxically proved the need for *activitas mundi.*

Calvinism's insistence that the whole man, including his reason, was corrupt might have led to a total rejection of traditional pre-scriptions of self-knowledge. When reason and will are assumed to be as degenerate as the senses and the emotions, it will hardly do to establish rational rules for self-control. Yet *nosce teipsum* authors whose Calvinist leanings were like those of John Davies of Hereford drew no such conclusion. Davies's *Microcosmos* (1603) differed from similar works only through a somewhat more skeptical attitude toward the mind's ability to discern the truth and a greater emphasis on the misery of man and the inscrutability of God. And the conduct books of the Puritans pursued the moral pulse-takings of the Christian humanists even more systematically than they.[27]

The major influence of Calvinism on the meaning of self-knowl-edge in Shakespeare's time appears to have been an emphasis on the dependence of man on the grace of God, a dependence that was also recognized at least in some form by non-Calvinists. As Berowne says in *Love's Labor's Lost* (I.i.148–51) concerning control of the emo-tions, "every man with his affects is born, / Not by might mast'red, but by special grace." According to Friar Lawrence in *Romeo and Juliet* (II.iii.27–28), there are "two opposed camps" in man's psyche, "rude will" and "grace," that is, the passions leagued with the human will and reason aided by divine grace. The problem of self-knowledge and self-control in Shakespeare is never the simple one of the use of reason. In the theological overtones in his plays, even Calvinists might have found much to commend.

If it is likely that Shakespeare furthered his education by reading some books that propagated religious aspects of self-knowledge, it is also probable that he, who came to designate himself a gentleman and wrote plays about princes and noblemen, would seek to learn about the specific application of self-knowledge to the nobility. But whether he ever read aristocratic conduct books or not, he could not help observing the ideals and practices of the nobility with which he came in contact. His Christian-humanist education had taught him to expect that *nosce teipsum* applied to all classes and estates. Thomas Wright, who singled out divines and physicians as most apt to benefit by his *Passions of the Mind,* in typically humanistic fashion went on to generalize that also "the good Christian that attendeth to mortifi-cation and the prudent civil gentleman that procureth a graceful con-versation may reap some commodity touching their professions and, in fine, every man may by this come to a knowledge of himself, which ought to be preferred before all treasures and riches."[28] It must be

said, however, that by and large the courtesy books written for the
nobility did not provide much of the commodity Wright so highly
acclaimed; those clearly in the tradition of Christian humanism were
exceptions.[29] The most notable in this respect was Sir Thomas
Elyot's *Governor* (1531), which applied the Delphic maxim to the
gentleman's need to recognize that he had a body and a soul like any
other man, and that of liberty of will as much or as little was given to
an emperor as to a poor carter.[30] Another humanistically oriented
book, greatly influential in England, was Pierre de la Primaudaye's
French Academy, the four parts of which were translated between
1586 and 1618. Ostensibly written to record a conversation among
four young noblemen engaged in founding a courtly academy at
Anjou, *The French Academy* was actually a compendium of knowledge radiating from the concept of self-knowledge. It has often been
drawn upon for studies of the intellectual history of the Renaissance
and for the background of Shakespeare's ideas, and I have also made
considerable use of it. Yet it must be said that the Huguenot author's
view of the aristocracy was colored by his Christian humanism and
that his value system did not reflect that of the nobility in general.
Even more of an outsider's view was that of Laurence Humphrey in
The Nobles and of Nobility (1563), which teemed with demands that
noblemen must rule themselves, consider themselves, solitarily reverence themselves, and, above all, know themselves. But then, Humphrey was a clergyman and university educator inclined to Calvinism,
and he was not especially close to the aristocrats. The self-negation he
demanded of the noblemen clashed with their desire for self-expansion
and with the honor code. Elizabethan noblemen were certainly not
generally reputed for patience and humility.

　　In aristocratic circles, these restrictive virtues were thought to be
more appropriate for the gentlewoman than for the gentleman, and
the courtesy books recommended them as such.[31] For instance, Giovanni Bruto, in a tract translated in 1598, wanted a noble girl's education to be primarily one in humility and piety: "For that humility
is not only a Christian and civil vertue, but the foundation and pillar
of all Christian and civil vertues; and, because it engendereth in us
the knowledge of ourselves, as much as her weak mind may comprehend, she [the matron in charge of the girl's education] shall show
her the wisdom of God, of his goodness and power."[32] Only the gen-
tlewomen who knew themselves, that is, humbled themselves, could,
according to Bruto, be exalted.

Shakespeare's attitude in these matters owed as much to observation as to theory. He had the advantage of seeing aristocrats at close range, and he knew that some of them thought that what in mean men was entitled patience was cowardice in noble hearts. But his humanistic education had also prepared him to understand deeply and sympathetically the democratic equality of all flesh. Clay and clay might differ in dignity, but their dust was all alike. As to the noble-women, some of his heroines are indeed endowed with the patience and humility that the courtesy books ordained for them, but they also are refreshingly more active and vital than one might expect those to have been who had gone through the kind of submissive training prescribed by Bruto. Here as elsewhere, Shakespeare's characterizations show, most of all, a sure sense for human values.

Among the books from which an Elizabethan could learn the meaning and significance of self-knowledge, we should finally not forget those that purported to address themselves to rulers. Since the princes were "the glass, the school, the book, / Where subjects' eyes do learn, do read, do look," as Shakespeare's Lucrece puts it (615–16), they had a particular obligation to know themselves thoroughly, and their subjects had a corresponding duty to study them as models. Although Machiavelli's portrait of the prince may have been more relevant to actual political practices in Tudor England than the moral tracts of the Christian humanists, the intellectual and spiritual climate favored the latter's theories. In drawing pictures of model rulers, the Christian humanists continued the tradition of medieval *specula principis,* adding their own educational programs. The seminal work here was Erasmus's *Institutio Principis Christiani* (1516). For Erasmus, the prince had to be, first of all, a good Christian and a good man, even though not every good man would necessarily make a good prince. But Erasmus believed that a balanced diet of classical and moral-religious instruction had a beneficial effect on the prince's ethical conduct of affairs. Similar, even if less urbanely phrased, arguments were voiced in *The Institution and First Beginning of a Christian Prince* (1571), which Sir James Chillester translated from the French and dedicated to Queen Elizabeth. The prince's first prerequisite, said *The Institution,* was self-mastery. The fourth chapter expounded, "How that those which shall command others ought first to master themselves and so to suppress and moderate their affections and passions that, by their good lives, they may induce those that be subject to them to virtue and goodliness." Princes were asked to lay away pride, insolence, and ambition and to acknowledge the common condition of mankind. If they were subject to moral infirmities, they were to subdue their imperfections by reason and frame themselves to gentleness, modesty, and humanity. To do so, they must "enter into themselves and have good consideration of their own proper natures and withal continually remember that they are but men, formed and made of the slime of the earth as others." [33] This is the same moral as that of the *de casibus* tragedies narrated in *The Mirror for Magistrates* and dramatized in the plaintive speeches of Shakespeare's Richard II; it echoes still in Lear's self-discovery.

It would be tedious to examine all possible ways in which Shakespeare could have learned the significance and meaning of self-knowledge. The preceding survey is sufficient to demonstrate that admonitions to self-knowledge and prescriptions on achieving it were his regular moral and religious diet and that they had a Christian-humanist flavor. They were in the books he read in school and out of it, and they were in the sermons he heard. This moral indoctrination was lasting enough to have left impressions all through his works. Shakespeare was, and remained in some sort, a disciple of the Christian humanists. But his exquisite sense for what is truly human made him realize that human nature was recalcitrant and unpredictable and that all theory was inferior to reality. Some of his early plays, particularly *Love's Labor's Lost* and *The Comedy of Errors,* give evidence of his ironic amusement about being told so insistently to know himself. And the plays of his middle period give some indications that he saw weaknesses in the Christian-humanist picture of man. But I think there is proof that he never completely disowned Christian humanism and that he thought of self-knowledge always in terms at least related to it.

Although the Christian humanists' approach to self-knowledge was too theoretical and idealistic to lead to new discoveries about the nature of man, it offered, I think, some distinct advantages for dramatizing the human condition, advantages that Shakespeare consciously or instinctively realized. These fall into three major categories: first, the humanistic ideas of self-knowledge contained a method for self-examination; second, they provided a body of ideas on man that balanced favorable and unfavorable traits; and, third, they presented a viable ideal for mankind.

As to the first advantage, Christian humanism established a method for asking certain questions about man and his purpose that

Shakespeare could translate into dramatic terms. Although the *nosce teipsum* instructions were generally hortatory, they implied a program of self-questioning and sometimes put it into catechistic form. One of the best examples of this program was Sir James Perrott's *The First Part of the Consideration of Human Condition* (1600), a short and, except for the form, quite traditional treatise.[34] Sir James was stimulated by the Delphic maxim to dispense strong doses of *contemptus mundi, consideratio,* and *memento mori.* He presented this advice in a question-and-answer pattern by stipulating that a man who wants to know himself must ask himself certain questions, which fall under three headings, that is, questions on what man is, who he is, and what manner of man he is. To answer these, he claimed, other questions must be asked. Thus the answer to what man is requires an examination of what he is according to his creation, his life, and his death. Perrott's method made self-search a quasi-dramatic event, a dispute of the soul with itself. In a general way it thus provides a pattern for the struggle of Shakespeare's heroes for clarity about themselves in the crisis of their lives; it resembles Richard II's anguished introspection, Angelo's confrontation with his true character, Hamlet's existential probing of his mind, and, most of all, Lear's agonizing ruminations on the human condition and his own. Of course, we need not therefore assume that Shakespeare read *The Consideration;* but certainly he was familiar with its general method of self-questioning, which reflects both Ciceronian prescriptions of *decorum* and the introspection of the medieval *consideratio* and gives them a humanistic emphasis.

A second advantage of the humanistic interpretation of *nosce teipsum* derived from its balance of optimism and pessimism concerning man's earthly existence. Even a writer as much addicted to *contemptus mundi* as Pierre Boaistuau felt evidently, after having written his *Théâtre du monde* (1558), that he needed to counterbalance the misery of man with his greatness. He thus added to his book a *Bref discours de l'excellence et dignité de l'homme* (1558), and it was this composite volume that, translated by John Alday as *Theatrum Mundi* (1566, 1574, 1581), attained a considerable popularity in England. According to the first part of the work, man is deplorably ignorant of himself: "He is so masked and disguised that he knoweth not himself; he is the beginner and foreshower of things contained in the circuit of this world, and yet he is blind and dumb in his own doings." [35] According to the second part, however, he is

god-like in his erectness, endowed with a divine mind, and capable
of greatness. The same paradoxical assessment of man is presented
in a stanza, more morally edifying than poetically pleasing, added
during one of the numerous augmentations of the ever popular
Treatise of Moral Philosophy by William Baldwin (1564; first
edition, 1547):

> Man, that consisteth of body and of soul,
> Is God's own creature, specially made
> To know his maker, also to control
> Such lusts in flesh as elements persuade—
> A beast, if that his life be beastly trade,
> An earthly God, if void of hope and hate
> He live content and know his own estate.[36]

Here is the basic Christian-humanist paradox, which we know
best through Hamlet's splendid résumé "What a piece of work is
a man!" This piece of work, which Hamlet knows how to praise
even if he does not like it, is a quintessence of dust that, in apprehension, is like a god. (See Appendix C.) Shakespeare's tragic heroes
embody this precarious dignity of man; it is their main claim to
human greatness.

Third, and perhaps most important, the Christian humanists'
prescriptions for self-knowledge provided Shakespeare with a feeling
that men were, in essence, very much alike. An anecdote in the
dedication of John Woolton's *Immortality of the Soul* illustrates this
pervasive humanistic feeling. This is a story about a visit by the
painter Apelles to the shop of his colleague Protogenes. Apelles
found there only an old woman who did not recognize him and
asked him for his name. In answer, Apelles drew an extremely fine
and small line on the table, remarking that it would reveal his
identity. And, indeed, on his return, Protogenes immediately realized
who had been the caller. A modern reader of this anecdote would
probably surmise that it demonstrates how one man differs from
the other just as the line of one artist differs from that of another;
but that, characteristically, was not Woolton's conclusion. Rather,
Woolton moralized, the fact that Protogenes recognized the line
shows that all creation testifies to its creator; the wonderful composition of man is therefore proof of the greatness of God. Man is God's
finest creation; if he knows himself, he sees himself as a little world
that reflects the larger world, both created by God.

Obviously, such prescriptions for self-knowledge could not lead to psychological discoveries; they could not really demonstrate why men draw infinitely varied lines. Shakespeare, from his own observation, knew better, and he also must have become aware of other theoretical ways to consider men, ways that promised to show them as they really were. These new approaches and their conflict with the traditional methods will be the subject of the following chapter. But it would be erroneous to think of the humanists' approach as a mere blind alley. The general picture of man that they established provided Shakespeare at the outset of his career with a feeling of norms that he could use and imitate, just as he could use the figures of speech and other devices of rhetoric. When he was asked to hold a mirror up to himself, he was expected to see a double image, his own superimposed upon an ideal image of man, and to adjust his own features as much as possible to the ideal portrait. In such fashion, Shakespeare was given human norms that helped him to classify and describe the bewildering variety of human characters, to create deviations from the ideal pattern, like Richard II, or close approaches to it, like Henry V. As Shakespeare came to realize, the Christian humanists' explanation of human behavior was in need of revision, but their ideals remained admirable.

CHAPTER TWO

Nosce Teipsum:
Charting New Courses

WHEN JOHN DAVIES of Hereford published in 1603 his didactic poem on man, *Microcosmos,* he gave it the auspicious subtitle "The Discovery of the Little World, With the Government Thereof." One of the minor poets who contributed commendatory verses to Davies's learned and labored effort rose to this challenge by comparing him with Columbus and Sir Francis Drake; *Microcosmos* was the "paper bark" that would convey the reader to the *terra incognita* of himself.

Since *Microcosmos* was very much in the tradition of Christian humanism, the promise of new discoveries with which the poem was launched was specious. Like other products of the *nosce teipsum* vogue, Davies's work was circumscribed by its theological view of the soul, confused by its inconsistent definitions and descriptions of psychological faculties, and barred by the humors theory from giving a sensible account of the working of the body. Symptomatic of the reductive nature of Davies's approach was the redundancy of such reflexive constructions as the unwarranted promise that in his pages "we ourselves ourselves may find." No new discoveries could be made by presumably looking into oneself but coming up with the same old commonplaces. Real progress could come only from charting courses different from those of the Christian humanists; and all the great artists and writers of the Renaissance who sought to illuminate the condition of man had to venture at some points beyond the familiar waters. Shakespeare was no exception.

In the present chapter I should like to survey briefly the major directions taken by major Renaissance writers who were new and independent explorers of the self and to show the similarities and differences between their courses and Shakespeare's. I do not think Shakespeare was ever a disciple of these writers, but he was aware

26

of the intellectual currents they set in motion and took some cognizance of them. These currents ran away from—occasionally, counter to—Christian humanism, although all of them can be said to have in some way originated in it. I shall not try to unravel here the mingled yarn of what one could call "counter-humanism" or "antihumanism"; I shall merely single out a few of its strands, those that contained new conceptions of the self and of self-knowledge.[1]

I have in the preceding chapter simplified somewhat the formative influences on Shakespeare's conception of the self by treating the Renaissance and the Reformation as more closely related than they were. Although the Reformers appreciated Erasmus's criticism of religious formalism, few of them were pleased with his attempt to balance faith and reason. In one of his more virulent moments, Luther called reason a whore; and in another, he said that there was nothing that an Erasmus, that is, reason, would not ridicule. But it was Calvin's theology more than Luther's polemics that militated against the Erasmian balance. As we noted in the preceding chapter, Calvin declared fallen man to be disastrously corrupted in mind as well as body. How then could man use the depraved instrument of his reason to achieve self-knowledge in the way the humanists said he could? Interestingly, this very question did occur to a certain Robert Chambers, evidently an austere Calvinist, while reading the confident assertion in Sir John Davies's *Nosce Teipsum* that he knew himself as that proud and wretched thing, a man, and had certainty about the composition of his body and soul and their respective functions. Chambers felt compelled to write a poetic commentary on, and refutation of, Davies's poem, which is extant in a British Museum manuscript. Chambers was incensed by Davies's claim that self-knowledge could be gained by rational self-examination:

> The law writ in our hearts works not so high
> To teach ourselves in all to know;
> That skill, to souls, grace only sure doth tie,
> And, to ourselves, ourselves doth plainly show.

Chambers argued that the soul, when conjoined with the body, was too frightened to see its own image truly and that reason was too corrupt to separate itself from the senses and passions to make a correct estimate of the human condition. The soul could see clearly only when dissolved from the body, and then "manhood," that is, the self, ceased to exist. Therefore, the hope of gaining self-knowledge in Sir John Davies's way was unchristian; as Chambers put it in a prose appendix to his uncouth verses, "Know thyself was an oracle delivered by the devil to the heathens and infidels, of whose knowledge he was so well assured." [2]

Even though Shakespeare surely did not think of man as the child of hell as did Chambers, it is worth noting that self-knowledge and self-discovery are never merely rational processes in his plays; "grace," as he repeatedly insisted, was needed to control the will and the passions. In the later plays in particular, reason appears as much a hindrance as an aid to self-knowledge. King Lear in or near madness learns more about himself than he ever knew before in full sanity. Conversely, Macbeth loses himself in spite of understanding his predicament and the danger to his soul well enough. Shakespeare gives us no comforting belief that man can perfect himself if he only uses his reason.

In disparaging the role of reason as an aid to self-knowledge, the Calvinists were joined by the Renaissance skeptics, who, like them, were fideists. [3] But, while going even further than the Calvinists in showing the weakness of human reason, they restored self-knowledge, although a differently oriented kind, to a high place in their arguments. Calvin at least granted that the "philosophers' microcosm" described accurately prelapsarian man; Montaigne ridiculed the whole concept. In "An Apology for Raymond Sebond," he attacked not only the medieval theologians (and thus Raymond Sebond, whom he purported to defend) but, with them, the Christian humanists who had put together their picture of man from the philosophers' fragments: "Verily they have thence had reason to name it *microcosmos,* or little world; so many several parts and visages have they employed to fashion and frame the same." [4] The nature of man was opaque and freakish, and "where I seek myself, I find not myself." Thus self-knowledge could not be achieved by methodical and theoretical exploration but had to be gained experimentally, even haphazardly, "and I find myself more by chance than by the search of mine own judgment." [5] Although he was an assiduous collector of commonplaces, he saw no such medicinal value in them as did the Christian humanists: "Should I have died less merrily before I read the *Tusculans?* I think not." [6] He preferred a pragmatically acquired self-knowledge to a derived and doctrinaire one: "I had rather understand myself well in myself than in Cicero." [7]

Obviously, Montaigne's experimental approach to himself and to mankind was very different from the humanists' methodology. Montaigne saw the peculiar nature of the self emerging in the subjective, unpredictable, and even irrational moments that Erasmus disregarded. Although he was deeply concerned with self-knowledge, which he called his "supernatural metaphysics" and his "natural philosophy," the subject and object of his inquiry was not, as tacitly understood by the Christian humanists, a generalized man but the individual, Michel de Montaigne. He proceeded pragmatically to explore this fascinating individual in all sorts of situations and catch him unawares and unexpectedly. It is true that Montaigne had still a humanistic picture of man in the back of his mind to which he compared himself and seemed at times anxious to adjust, but he was motivated more by nostalgia than belief. He felt at odds with the picture, and he found men in general too diverse to be classified satisfactorily. In viewing the whole human scene, he was struck by the discrepancies between act and effect and by events shaping themselves without, and counter to, human agencies.

Of course, this was only one side, the more disturbing one, of Montaigne's thought. And at least he himself was not greatly disturbed; the recognition of the insufficiencies of medieval and humanistic pictures of man did not induce in him a metaphysical anxiety but led him to develop a new and tentative ideal of the self, epitomized in the concept of the "honnête homme," a more personal, more versatile, and adaptable ideal. But it was the Montaigne of the "skeptic crisis," of "The Apology of Raymond Sebond," whose influence was strongly felt in England.

I shall, in Part III, argue that Shakespeare went through a similar phase of development as did Montaigne, a phase in which he took a skeptical view of the received portrait of man. He seems from the outset to have been inclined to a gentle skepticism; a kind of ethical and historical relativism is notable even in some of his earlier plays. The self adopts the coloring of its environment and threatens to become submerged in the shifting situations of *The Comedy of Errors* and *A Midsummer Night's Dream.* Even generally sympathetic figures like Antonio and Bassanio in *The Merchant of Venice* reveal tendencies that make us think of them at least on occasion as less than ideal when, for instance, the former spits at Jews and the latter mentions Portia's legacy before her beauty and virtue. And Shakespeare's moral judgments appear sometimes divided or suspended in situations where men are as much victims as makers of political crises, such as in *Richard II* and *King John*. This relativism increased markedly in the plays of Shakespeare's middle period, from *Julius Caesar* on, reaching its height in *Hamlet* and in the "problem comedies," *Troilus and Cressida, All's Well That Ends Well,* and *Measure for Measure,* whereupon it subsided. But this relativistic phase must be judged not merely from a philosophical and moral point of view but also from an artistic one, since it brought with it aesthetic as well as ethical and psychological perplexities and appears to have been the result of Shakespeare's changing attitude toward his art as much as toward man. For this reason (on which I shall be more explicit later), I prefer to think of this phase as "mannerist." It is, I believe, best to consider the influence of skepticism on Shakespeare, an influence that is by no means restricted to Montaigne, when discussing the plays in which it is most prevalent.

It should be said that the individualizing trend in the meaning of the injunction "know thyself," which distinguished Montaigne from the earlier Christian humanists, did not begin with him. Actually, most humanists thought that the Delphic maxim contained the advice to play the role best suited to oneself, to observe what Cicero called individual *decorum*. Roger Ascham declared it the main duty of parents to recognize the special talents of their children and encourage them in using these.[8] But such admonitions were not accompanied by helpful descriptions on how to develop individual attitudes, and they became submerged in traditional statements on the nature of the human soul and on the difference between men and animals. Individual *decorum* was circumscribed by general *decorum,* the demand to adjust to the *humanitas* ideal.

However, in aristocratic conduct books this ideal often took second place or was ignored for class standards that favored a more individualized and greatly expanded self. The courtier was encouraged to examine his endowments and make the most of them. Castiglione, whose *Il Cortegiano* was translated in 1561, thought that a nobleman should try to win his prince's grace in the ways most natural to himself. A witty courtier would do well to use his humor; a serious one, his gravity. To try an approach unsuited to the individual disposition was foolish and unsuccessful. As Castiglione said, "It is meet each man know himself and his own disposition and apply himself thereto and consider what things are meet for him to follow and what are not." [9] Castiglione, it is true, thought that the courtier would use the acquired grace to influence his prince morally. But the idea of extending the potentiality of the self lent itself to vulgarization and was vulgarized in many aristocratic conduct books. Self-knowledge here served a purpose very different from that it had served for either Erasmus or Montaigne: it was not the condition for leading a pure and holy life or the final result of an inquiry into the individual psyche; rather, it had the utilitarian and sometimes arriviste function of achieving material gratifications. But even in its purer form, the ideal of the courtier emphasized the assertion and expansion of the self rather than its limitation, and it conflicted thus with the Christian-humanist attitude. The Platonizing philosophy of love and beauty, expounded eloquently in the fourth book of *Il Cortegiano,* advocated a flight very different from the flight on the wings of contemplation that Erasmus described in a passage of his *Enchiridion.* Romantic love and humanistic self-knowledge were in the final analysis irreconcilable, but their conflict animates some of Shakespeare's plays as it does many an Elizabethan sonnet.

The book that did most to promote the Renaissance drive for egotistic self-assertion, Machiavelli's *Il Principe* (1532), was also the one that most terrified the humanistic conscience. The pseudo-Machiavellian villains of Kyd, Marlowe, Shakespeare, and others owed their existence to the horror of a generation educated in humanistic and Reformation morality that saw its assumptions challenged. But the fact that characters who recognized no limitations for their selves, such as Tamburlaine and Doctor Faustus, were created also proves that Machiavellian virtù appealed to the Elizabethan imagination. We can now safely discard the previously held belief that all this repulsion and attraction came merely from misconceptions about Machiavelli's actual arguments through their distortions in hostile reactions such as in Innocent Gentillet's *Contre-Machiavel* (1576; translated by Simon Patrick in 1602). Although there was no printed translation of *The Prince* until that of Edward Dacres in 1640, the book was read in England, as extant Elizabethan manuscript translations testify.[10] Moreover, Machiavelli's *Art of War* and his *Florentine History,* which in some points parallel *The Prince,* were available in English versions (1560 and 1595 respectively). The dedications of these latter translations to Queen Elizabeth and Sir Christopher Hatton demonstrate that the name of Machiavelli possessed a certain respectability in some circles. There is sufficient indication that at least from the last decade of the sixteenth century on Machiavelli was read and admired in England by a great many advanced spirits, and the number of those who were willing to say that he was right concerning politics and morals increased in the seventeenth century.

In view of the present fashion of reading *The Prince* as a political tract for Machiavelli's time or a theoretical defense of *Realpolitik* in general, it is surprising that the Elizabethans seem to have thought of it as a treatise on ethics and psychology as much as on politics.[11] It is only by realizing this fact that one understands the enormous emotional reaction as well as the growing influence it had on Shakespeare's contemporaries. It was not for them an Italian historian's blueprint for achieving unity in Italy or a realistic assessment of the instruments available to absolutist governments, but a conduct book for man's life in the state. Machiavelli's way of presenting his arguments actually lent support to such interpretation. He said in his Epistle Dedicatory that his intention was to regulate, that is, give rules to, princely governments; and he generalized, often incisively, on human nature and behavior. Thus the book approached at least outwardly the pattern of the *specula principis* or *institutiones principis Christiani* and therefore was liable to be read as proposing a model not only for princes but also for other men. Both Gentillet, who detested it, and Gabriel Harvey, who cherished it, read it as a general conduct book, the former to warn against the godlessness of its author, a devil incarnate, the latter to strengthen himself in the privacy of his study for the battle of life.

And, indeed, Machiavelli thought of life as a warfare, a fundamentally different one, it is true, from that in Erasmus's *Enchiridion*. For the Christian humanist, man had to fight his baser instincts, his vices and passions; for Machiavelli, he had to fight against other men, body against body, mind against mind. Only by preparing himself for this combat could the prince (and, by implication, any other man) hope to succeed:

> A prince then ought to have no other aim, nor other thought, nor take anything else for his proper art but war and the orders and discipline thereof; for that is the sole art which belongs to him that commands, and that is of so great excellence that not only those that are born princes it maintains so, but many times raises men of private fortune to that dignity.[12]

Victory in the battle of life described by Machiavelli required self-expansion rather than the self-limitation of Erasmus's *militia Christiani*. Physical force was an indispensable means for survival, and individual success depended on the conquest of other, antagonistic selves rather than on the control of one's own self. Rules could be stretched or broken in emergency. There were two kinds of fighting, said Machiavelli, the one by right of laws, the other by force. The former was proper to men and the other common to beasts, but "because the first many times sufficeth not, there is a necessity to make recourse to the second." [13] Machiavelli's view of life was not very far from the Hobbesian state of nature as a warfare of everybody against everybody.

It was Machiavelli's attitude toward conventional moral virtues that most incensed his enemies, an attitude based on the premise that the prince must assert himself in a hostile world full of inconstant, ungrateful, and dissembling men. Machiavelli treated with contempt the humanistic view that men and princes were allied in the pursuit of virtue and goodness; the cleavage between how men live and how they ought to live was unbridgeable. To assert himself in this tough world, the prince had to be a lion and a fox—metaphors that became immediately famous. Machiavelli still accepted the humanists' assessment of men as composed of a rational and a beastly part; but contrary to them he founded his political and ethical philosophy on the supposition that animal instincts guided man's moral and social behavior. "Conscience" and "soul" are not words to be found in *The Prince;* they would be out of place in arguments arising from a materialistic view of life governed by self-interest. Whenever Machiavelli referred to self-knowledge, he gave the concept a utilitarian and egoistic meaning. Thus he argued that both cruelty and wiliness were necessary for a prince's success: "Those that stand wholly upon the lion understand not well themselves." [14] Such general maxims encouraged the application not merely to princes but also to men in general.

Machiavelli's fox metaphor implied that knowing oneself was not equivalent to being oneself, as humanistic theory maintained. Since the prince was seen by many, but intimately known only by few, the image he projected mattered more than the reality he represented. As Machiavelli generalized in another of those maxims that invited application to men at large, "Every man may come to see what thou seemest, few come to perceive and understand what thou art." [15] For

Machiavelli, knowing oneself meant, at least at times, not to be one-self.

Although Machiavelli's assessment of humanity may strike one as more pessimistic than the humanists', it was more optimistic about men's chances for success in this world, and it was felt to be so by those who agreed with him. The world was a battleground on which one could hope to win victories if he adopted the proper strategy and tactics, as Harvey noted in a lengthy passage of his *marginalia* with repeated reference to Machiavelli. In the most telling phrases, he applied the biblical metaphor of the warfare of life in the new, Ma-chiavellian sense:

> Machiavel and Aretine [Pietro Aretino] knew their lessons by heart and were not to seek how to use the wicked world, the flesh, and the devil. They had learned cunning enough and had seen fashions enough and could and would use both with advantage enough. . . . *Vita militia, vel togata, vel armata.* First cast to shoot right, then be sure to shoot home.[16]

Machiavelli's effect on his disciples was to bring about something of a Nietzschean transvaluation of ideals in which good was what contributed to power. In the exercise of force man proves himself a man, as Harvey implied in adapting the Roman quality of *virtus* to the Machiavellian virtù: "Quicquid est in deo, est deus; quicquid est in viro, sit virtus et vis." [17] When the man endowed with this quality —ironically Harvey was not—said that he knew himself, he did not mean, as did the Christian humanists, that he had probed his con-science in order to improve himself morally or to earn the transcen-dent glory of salvation; he meant that he had assessed himself criti-cally in order to strengthen himself for a battle in which victory meant the enjoyment of material rewards, promotion, wealth, and authority. Marlowe's Tamburlaine fully accepts this Machiavellian view of the human condition:

> Nature, that framed us of four elements
> Warring within our breast for regiment,
> Doth teach us all to have aspiring minds.
> Our souls, whose faculties can comprehend
> The wondrous architecture of the world
> And measure every wandering planet's course,
> Still climbing after knowledge infinite,
> And always moving as the restless spheres,

> Wills us to wear ourselves and never rest,
> Until we reach the ripest fruit of all,
> That perfect bliss and sole felicity,
> The sweet fruition of an earthly crown.[18]

Stripped of the soaring poetry and of the glittering symbolism of the crown, this Machiavellian philosophy could become the excuse of scramblers for office and rewards as well as of those who sought to defend their tyranny over others. Self-knowledge in this sense was a different thing from what it ever had been before, as Thomas Hobbes well realized when he said disapprovingly in his Introduction to *Leviathan* (1651):

> But there is another saying of late understood, by which they [those that think they can learn more from life than from books] might truly read one another if they would take pains; that is, *nosce teipsum,* read thyself; which was not meant, as it is now used, to countenance either the barbarous state of men in power toward their inferiors or to encourage men of low degree to a saucy behavior towards their betters. . . .[19]

This passage serves as a preamble to Hobbes's investigation of man's psyche; the true meaning of *nosce teipsum,* he claimed, was that self-knowledge must begin with a rational examination of the nature of the human mind and the passions. Like the humanists, Hobbes thought that individual self-inquiry would lead to a general concept of man; but the concept he arrived at was totally different—it was not ethical or religious but materialistic and mechanical. And Hobbes's view of the commonwealth as the result of a social contract that ended the state of nature in which life was solitary, short, and brutish indicates that he thought of man as a political animal much as did Machiavelli. But then Hobbes, like the Machiavelli of *The Prince,* was an apologist of absolutism.

Clearly, Shakespeare never adopted the vulgarization of self-knowledge censured by Hobbes; the one character that represents it most is his darkest villain, Iago, and there are indications in his great tragedies, in *Othello, Lear,* and *Macbeth,* that he was disturbed about the change in the meaning of self-knowledge for some of his contemporaries. Although Jacobean pessimism left its traces on his major tragedies and is surely a prime reason for their gloom and ethical severity, Shakespeare never leaves us with the impression that we must accept the evil world as a given and unchangeable fact or that we ought to make the best of it. The representatives of the world as it is at its worst are contrasted with those that show it as it ought to be. The Iagos, Edmunds, and Antonios are the antitheses of the Desdemonas, Cordelias, and Prosperos, and our sympathies clearly lie with the latter. Thus Shakespeare reasserted the validity of the humanistic search for an ideal humanity at a time when his artistic power had developed to its full strength. But this is a matter that must be dealt with later, in the discussions of the great tragedies and *The Tempest*. As is true for the second phase of Shakespeare's art, the conception of the self that emerges in the plays of this third period gains its configuration from a change in his artistic style, a change that, for reasons I shall give in Part IV, I think to be one toward the baroque.

Although the inquiry into the patterns of self-knowledge in this greatest of Shakespeare's periods must be postponed, I think it will be instructive to glance at the patterns of one of his contemporaries who came to the fore during this time, Sir Francis Bacon.[20] Of the great Renaissance writers who charted new courses for exploring the self, he is one of the most interesting to consider, not for the reason that he influenced Shakespeare, which he almost certainly did not, but because he demonstrates the pervasive influence of Machiavelli and provides a contrast with Shakespeare's own course. It is certainly odd, for this reason and others, that Bacon should have become the main candidate of the "Anti-Stratfordians."

Like Machiavelli, Bacon approached man and society with toughmindedness, and his concept of self-knowledge drew something from the Florentine's utilitarian and egoistic emphasis. Bacon's statement that "we are beholden to Machiavel and others that write what men do and not what they ought to do" is symptomatic of an intellectual kinship. But this was a cautiously acknowledged one, and it was never complete. In *Advancement of Learning* (1605), in which Bacon offered his tribute to Machiavelli, he hastened to accompany it with the proviso that the "serpentine wisdom" of a realistic assessment of men must be joined with the "columbine innocency" of a virtuous disposition in the assessor.[21] Nor did Bacon wish to abandon all humanistic recipes for self-knowledge. For instance, he acclaimed learning as a remedy to the diseases of the mind; the unlearned man, he said, did not know "what it is to descend into himself or to call himself to account, nor the pleasure of that *suavissima vita, in dies sentire se fieri meliorem"* (p. 72). Like the Christian humanists, Bacon thought that in the study of man a balance should be made of the positive and negative aspects, and he referred to "those delightful and elegant discourses which have been made of the dignity of man, of his miseries, of his state and life, and the like adjuncts of his common and undivided nature" (p. 102).[22] On the relationship of body and soul, a central issue of *nosce teipsum,* Bacon had nothing new to add to the Christian humanists' analysis.

It is in placing self-knowledge in relation to other human knowledge that Bacon differed completely from Christian humanism. In his proposed universal system of sciences, *nosce teipsum* was no longer a general introduction and guidepost to all man's endeavors, nor was it associated with a knowledge of God. Instead of being the beginning of all science, self-knowledge was only the object of one of the "three beams of man's knowledge; that is, *Radius Directus,* which is referred to nature, *Radius Refractus,* which is referred to God . . . , *Radius Reflexus,* whereby man beholdeth and contemplateth himself." Although Bacon acknowledged that the self-knowledge resulting from this beam was "the end and term of natural philosophy in the intention of man," he immediately added that it was "but a portion of natural philosophy in the continent of nature" (p. 101). For Bacon, the study of the self was subsumed in the study of nature.

In spite of his nod to the pleasures of contemplation, Bacon did not really believe that self-knowledge could come from turning inward; withdrawal from the observation of nature and experience appeared to him a grievous error: "Upon those intellectualists, which are notwithstanding commonly taken for the most sublime and divine philosophers, Heraclitus gave a just censure, saying Men sought truth in their own little worlds, and not in the great and common world; for they disdain to spell and so by degrees to read in the volume of God's works" (p. 59).

If Bacon thus wanted to integrate the study of the self into the study of nature, he also sought to make a closer connection between the self and the social milieu. Human philosophy or humanity, he said, had two parts, "the one considereth man segregate, or distributively; the other congregate, or in society" (p. 101). Although admitting some of the humanists' claims for the uses of self-knowledge to man segregate, Bacon completely departed from the humanistic basis of a disinterested concern with virtue when turning to man congregate. It is here that he paid his compliment to Machiavelli and

recommended studying the "conditions of the serpent." The advice
of the old *nosce teipsum* tracts, he felt, could not stand the pressure of
the actual world: "For men of corrupted minds presuppose that
honesty groweth out of simplicity of manners and believing of
preachers, schoolmasters, and men's exterior language" (p. 140).

For Bacon, the mirror of self-knowledge rendered a picture totally
different from that of the Christian humanists. For these, it showed
a not too clearly individualized man against the background of a
timeless and idealized humanity; for Bacon, it presented a distinct
psychological portrait of an individual against the sharp contours of
his time. He said that "the window of Momus," that is, the window
to look into men's hearts, was to give a view not of the state of men's
souls and their chances of salvation but

> of their natures, their desires and ends, their customs and fashions,
> their helps and advantages, and whereby they chiefly stand; so
> again, their weaknesses and disadvantages, and where they lie most
> open and obnoxious; their friends, factions, dependencies; and
> again, their opposites, enviers, competitors, their moods and times
> . . . ; their principles, rules, and observations, and the like; and
> this not only of persons, but of actions; what are on foot from time
> to time, and how they are conducted, favored, opposed; and how
> they import, and the like. (p. 155)

Those that wished really to know themselves must look into a "politic
glass," that is, into "the state of the world or times wherein we live"
(p. 158).

When Bacon was writing his *Advancement of Learning,* he looked
deeply into this glass, a look to which he owed his subsequent mete-
oric career. The shrewd advice he had for others like him, "architects
of their own fortune," was quite often a practical Machiavellism appropriate not only for Bacon's age but for all times. He recommended
taking an impartial view of personal abilities and virtues as well as of
debilities and impediments and then considering the appropriateness
of one's constitution and temperament for the times. With deliberate
regard for both the self and the age, profession and course of life must
be chosen, competitors observed, a wise choice of friends and ac-
quaintances made, successful models followed, strength displayed
advantageously, virtues made out of weaknesses, and flexibility
shown according to the occasion (pp. 158–67). The long list of these
sagacious recommendations could be supplemented and illustrated by

equally keen observations, weighted with shrewd self-interest, from his *Essays.* Bacon's prescriptions for self-knowledge are not as edifying morally as those of the Christian humanists, but they are more practical and, as one discovers with a shock, more modern. They make self-knowledge a means to an end and not an end itself, and they are totally secular and morally indifferent, advocating self-expansion rather than self-limitation.

Bacon thus had much better reason than John Davies of Hereford, with whom we began this chapter, to appropriate for himself the discovery metaphor, and he did so with his characteristic heraldic manner. He said in his *Novum Organum* (Aphorism 92) that the scientific method he had drawn up was analogous to the declaration, made by Columbus before crossing the Atlantic, of why and how new lands were to be discovered (p. 287). This scientific method included rules for the study of man, and here, as well as in those applicable to the study of nature, Bacon anticipated much that was to come in the future. Man could not have increased his knowledge of himself unless he was willing to sail routes different from those charted in *Microcosmos,* which led only to regions already known and explored.

But the analogy to discovery and exploration in the study of man is in some ways misleading. Columbus did not leave a moral territory for a scientific one, but one continent for another. The kind of venture on which Bacon set out meant to leave the old humanistic ground irrevocably behind even though, in caution or perhaps in sincerity, he paid his respects to some humanistic arguments. There could be no return of his Santa Maria. Serpentine wisdom cannot serve columbine innocence without in the end swallowing it.

It is not my purpose to moralize but to point up sharply the distance between Bacon and the Christian humanists and to see Shakespeare in some relation to the two. This is not a simple matter, since Shakespeare was not a moralist or philosopher but a dramatist, and a rather impersonal one at that, who had no one system or truth to communicate. He had what Keats called "negative capability"; he could live with the uncertainties, mysteries, and doubts that surround the great questions of life. He could and did look at the world through the eyes of characters with the most diverse attitudes and philosophies. But he was also a moral artist with a deep sympathy for man. It is surely significant that those among his characters who hold views that have anything in common with Bacon's definition of self-knowledge are villains like Iago and Edmund. The equation of self-knowledge with self-interest, self-assertion, and self-expansion was and remained antipathetic to Shakespeare.

There is in all his plays a residual humanism; it is as strong or stronger in the late *Tempest* as in the early *Love's Labor's Lost*. His contemporaries' espousal of the world as it is does not seem to have lessened Shakespeare's concern for the world as it ought to be. If he makes us feel the tension between the real and the ideal, he also makes us feel the pity of the tension. However, we may consider it fortunate that he was born into an age in which this tension was sensed more acutely than at other times because, even though Baconian empiricism is now as much behind us as Christian humanism, the conflict has proved archetypal for much that was to come; it can be thought to have both historical and general significance.

PART TWO

Theory and Adaptation

CHAPTER THREE

Microcosm and Macrocosm: Framing The Picture of Man

T HE CHRISTIAN HUMANISTS were emphatic in their demand that a man who wishes to know himself must realize that he is a little world that reflects on a smaller scale the larger world of the universe. Thus, for instance, said Du Bartas in the influential account he gave of the Creation and the beginnings of man in *The Divine Weeks* (Sir Joshua Sylvester's translation) :

> There's under sun, as Delphos' god did show,
> No better knowledge than ourselves to know.
> There's no theme more plentiful to scan
> Than is the glorious, goodly frame of man ;
> For in man's self is fire, air, earth, and sea.
> Man's, in a word, the world's epitome
> Or little map, which here my Muse doth try
> By the grand pattern to exemplify.[1]

The twin theme of microcosm and macrocosm was indeed scanned plentifully in the sixteenth and seventeenth centuries, when poets and moralists were notoriously fond of drawing all sorts of parallels between the smaller frame and the larger. On the other hand, the whole idea of man as a microcosm was questioned by those who were not in sympathy with the medieval-classical synthesis created by the Christian humanists. Calvin found "the philosophers' microcosm" irrelevant to fallen man; Montaigne ridiculed it as a patchwork of brain-conceived illusions; and Bacon asked his contemporaries to turn away from studying the microcosm and apply themselves to unraveling the mysteries of external nature.[2] Thus the concept of microcosm may be taken as central for the humanistic Renaissance, and the attacks on it as symptomatic of a dissatisfaction with this

43

kind of Renaissance. I should like to go further and suggest tentatively that this concept in its literal, humanistic form was central to the mentality that the art historians see behind the style they define as Renaissance and contrast with mannerism and baroque. However, I am not concerned with establishing absolute stylistic categories; I wish merely to explore the changing ideas about self-knowledge against the background of larger intellectual and artistic changes.

At any rate, a study of Renaissance patterns of self-knowledge requires an examination of the implications of the analogies between microcosm and macrocosm. This means glancing at some books that, like *The Divine Weeks,* deal as much or more with the universe than with man, and it means investigating the assumptions behind that set of medieval-Renaissance ideas that sometimes have been too exclusively identified with *the* Elizabethan world picture. Conventional forms of thought about man and the universe were being challenged in Shakespeare's time; yet certainly they were those that prevailed in his youth, and they provided him, at an impressionable age, with norms and standards. It is not amiss to investigate the assumptions of the traditional picture, provided that one remains aware that the picture was felt to be old-fashioned by some and irrelevant by others.

Du Bartas's verses are characteristic of what I think is the main feature of the humanistic appraisals of man as a microcosm: they appear to heighten and expand the self, but, in a deeper sense, they actually limit and circumscribe it. They do, of course, make man important in the whole pattern, and often, as is true for the context of the passage in *The Divine Weeks,* they depict him as the hero in the cosmic drama. But it is probably more significant that the analogies between man and the universe visualize both as well-defined entities. The beauteous pattern of the universe was to inspire man with confidence about the structure of his own frame, and the proportioned composition of his body was to reassure him of the purposeful pattern of the universe—the reasoning was circular, and therefore the desire for metaphysical assurance was bound to remain unfulfilled in the long run, the more so because the two frames were old models that new discoveries were making obsolete.[3] As the Renaissance skeptics observed, faith in merely verbal constructs could not be sustained.

But, for a while at least, the analogies did provide some assurance. It is, I believe, instructive to investigate the ubiquitous concept of the frame for the semantic associations that supported this faith. The word "frame" had not yet acquired—or was, at most, in the process of acquiring—its modern meaning of a border or case in which something is set; it generally denoted an underlying structure that upheld and shaped an object or idea.[4] It thus reflected the Aristotelian notion of reality as matter given form and configuration by a spiritual design, a notion propagated by the medieval scholasticism that avoided the extremes of realism and nominalism. As a medieval-Renaissance encyclopedia explained, the angels were pure form, that is, spirit; men below them were both matter, that is, body, and form, that is, soul; the created world beneath them was arranged in a descending order of purity and strength of form down to the dregs of the universe.[5]

One way to determine the connotations and denotations of "frame" in the meaning of "cosmos" for the Elizabethans is to investigate for what terms in other languages the word was used. One such term was *machina mundi*. In translations where "frame" was used in its place, the word sometimes conveyed the notion that the universe was an intricate engine in constant motion. So, for instance, in Ralph Robinson's translation of Sir Thomas More's *Utopia;* the Utopians study nature and expect from this endeavor the thanks and favor of God, "whom they think, according to the fashion of other artificers, to have set forth the marvelous and gorgeous frame of the world [*machina mundi*] for man with great affection intentively to behold." [6] But more often, the foreign words translated by "frame" signified architectural structures. Sir Joshua Sylvester rendered Du Bartas's *bastiment* as "frame," and as a look at Thomas Cooper's *Thesaurus* (1565) shows, "frame," "framing," and "framer" were the words with which the Elizabethans translated the Latin *fabrica, fabricatio,* and *fabricator.* These were thus the English terms they chose for the corresponding Latin ones in accounts of the Creation by classical writers. They are, for instance, used in Arthur Golding's translation of Ovid's *Metamorphoses;* but in his preceding Epistle, Golding made sure that the Christian God was properly credited with the "framing": it was "God, the Father, that / Made all things, framing out the world according to the plat / Conceived everlastingly in mind." [7]

The universe was often likened to a building. None of these comparisons is more familiar to students of the drama than that between the world and the theater. The public theater, such as the Globe, was a frame, that is, a structure, that was enclosed by another frame, the galleries of the spectators. As Nevill Coghill has noted, Hamlet's speech on "the goodly frame, the earth" had a direct relevance to the Globe Theater, named for the Renaissance *topos* that the stage is the world and the world the stage: the actor reciting Hamlet's speech could with a sweeping gesture draw in the circumference of the wooden O, which symbolized the world; he could point up to the "heavens," represented by the star-spangled ceiling of the stage above him, and at the elevated platform, the "promontory," beneath him. When he then gestured toward himself as he turned to the "piece of work" that is a man, he had placed the microcosm in its macrocosmic context.[8]

In descriptions of the earth itself, analogies to paintings prevailed. Du Bartas took delight in the "landscape, various, rich, and rare," painted on a large canvas by God. In admiring this work, man admired God, whom it reflected "as in a glass."[9] Castiglione waxed enthusiastic about "the ensign of this world that we behold with a large sky, so bright with shining stars, and, in the midst, the earth, environed with the seas, severed in parts with hills, dales, and rivers, and so decked with diverse trees, beautiful flowers and herbs—a man may say it to be a noble and great painting, drawn with the hand of nature and of God."[10] The divine achievement, Castiglione noted, reflected an indirect glory on the human art of painting. In narrative descriptions of the earth as a landscape, the brushstrokes of the divine painter were generally made visible by borrowing terms from biblical and theological accounts of the Creation. This is true for Hamlet's appraisal of "the goodly frame, the earth." Although the speech must have evoked in Shakespeare's theater some architectural associations of the cosmic frame, its details are the pictorial ones of the Creation.[11]

Related to pictorial and architectural conceptualizations of the universe were the geometrical ones. Renaissance art depended on line, perspective, and mathematical ratios. This geometrical mode of vision encouraged some moralists to give man a calculable place in the total design. In *Of the Knowledge Which Maketh a Wise Man* (1533), Sir Thomas Elyot based man's understanding of his position in nature on a kind of innate sense of perspective that enabled him to reconstruct the order of the universe. Self-knowledge, he argued, made it possible for man to know others and, through his immortal soul, the essence of God and the working of His providence. Through the order in himself, which reflects God's purposes, man could understand the order of nature, which "like a straight line issueth out of

providence, and passeth directly through all things that be created."
Man was set "in the highest degree of the line," and the place of
things and creatures on it depended on their usefulness to him; a
deviation from the line violated the divine order.[12]

Geometrical principles were sometimes thought to determine the
configuration of the microcosm similar to the way they determined
the proportions and outlines of the human figure in Renaissance
drawings. This visual mode was adopted, not surprisingly, by the
mathematician and astronomer John Dee in his Preface to a translation of Euclid (1570). Dee demanded that geometrical and numerological principles be applied to the study of man and that thus a science of "anthropography" be established, which is to provide "the description of the number, measure, weight, figure, situation, and color
of every diverse thing in the perfect body of man." Noting that there
were several sciences to describe the universe, such as astronomy,
geography, and cosmography, Dee asked why there was no single
science of man that was analogous to "the description of the whole
universal frame of the world": "Why should not the description of
him who is the less world and from the beginning called *microcosmus*
(that is, the less world) and for whose sake and service all bodily
creatures else where created, who participateth with the spirits and
angels, and [who] is made to the image and similitude of God, have
his peculiar art?" All sciences could contribute to this new science, an
"art of arts," and testify to man's "harmonious and microcosmical
constitution." Dee recommended to begin the study with Albrecht
Dürer's *De Symmetria Humani Corporis* and with Noah's ark (!)
and then to proceed further: "Remember the Delphical Oracle, *nosce
teipsum* (know thyself), so long ago pronounced, of so many philosophers repeated, and of the wisest attempted, and then you will perceive how long ago you have been called to the school where this art
might be learned." [13]

Shakespeare's sonnet 24 gives evidence of his apprenticeship to
the particular school of self-knowledge that attempted to establish
the ideal proportions of man and to place him in the perspective of a
structured frame. According to the sonnet's opening conceit, the
poet's eye "hath play'd the painter," delineating in his heart the
beauty of the friend: "My body is the frame wherin 'tis held, / And
perspective is best painter's art." The perspective, one might say, is
less of the eye and heart than of the geometrical intellect. Here and
in Hamlet's speech, Shakespeare adopted the Renaissance habit of

depicting man as a symmetrically constructed figure placed in an
orderly composition with coherent space. This placement gave him a
prominent, firm, and significant position with a clear orientation toward the universe, analogous to the manner in which the Elizabethan
actor of Hamlet was poised in full view on the promontory platform
surrounded by the frame of the theater.

A very similar conception of man's cosmic position is symbolized
by the early seventeenth-century emblem bearing the title *nosce teipsum:* the picture shows an erect human figure in the midst of a circle,
representing the earth; his lifted arm almost touches the circumference; two smaller circles above the larger one represent the sun and
the moon, which shed their lights on the center. The motto draws the
moral: "O man, you most worthy part of the world, do not diminish
your exalted position by servile behavior; in you is apparent a perfect image of the heavens and the earth. Learn from that your glory
and your endowments." [14]

The humanists' prescriptions for self-knowledge posited an anthropocentric universe, which it was man's duty to admire as divinely
created. The world was *cosmos* or *mundus,* that is, an ornament
glorifying the Creator but designed for man's reasonable use. Just as
he was asked to contemplate the world's beauty, so he was held to
admire the purposeful arrangement of the microcosm, Sylvester's
epitome of the world or Du Bartas's *tableau racourci.* Shakespeare
properly commended these two frames; he used epithets like "fine"
and "wondrous" for both. Man's frame was for him a "composed
wonder" and "framed in the prodigality of nature." [15] Even Hamlet
calls the larger frame "goodly" and knows that he is supposed to take
delight in both frames. His inability to do so can be attributed to his
melancholy, but it should also be said that the play in which he is the
hero belongs to a period in Shakespeare's work when the landscapes
take on gloomier hues and when the Renaissance certainties inspire
less confidence than they inspired earlier. We shall deal with this
problem later; for the present we need to recall merely that the speech
is constructed in the pattern of humanistic orations on the dignity
of man, a pattern with which the Elizabethans were familiar.

I do not wish to imply that most Elizabethans were Panglossian
optimists. Probably very few were. For one thing, the age was too
conscious of original sin and of the confusion and death it was
thought to have brought into man's life and into nature to indulge in
pagan glorifications of man and the world. The analogies between

microcosm and macrocosm were in fact quite often given a somber turn by focusing on the misery of man's life. An early seventeenth-century emblem, similar in appearance to that mentioned previously, symbolizes this darker view. In the picture, man is framed not merely by the circle of the universe but also by angry clouds that surround it; the motto is Job 14:1: "Man that is born of a woman is of short continuance and full of trouble." [16] All that was thought wrong with man could be seen reflected in the universe just as well as everything thought to be right. *Contemptus mundi* pessimism propagated the idea that the world, like man, was shrinking and decaying and that the orbits of sun and moon were drawing closer to the earth in a slow disintegration of the cosmic system.[17] Natural catastrophes and strange occurrences were apt to be interpreted as signs of the approaching end, as, for instance, by Abraham Fleming, who took them as "a token that the world was sick after the manner of man, who is therefore called a little world." [18] Man's wickedness was thought to be a symptom of this fatal illness or even a factor in bringing about a speedier demise. In this vein, Hamlet sees his mother's corruption reflected in a universe destined to perish by fire, as it was generally believed it would perish:

> Heaven's face does glow
> O'er this solidity and compound mass
> With heated visage, as against the doom—
> Is thought-sick at the act.
> (III.iv.48–51)

One cannot escape the feeling that Hamlet projects his own unwholesome mind into the universe. But if so, there were many Hamlets in the last years of Elizabeth and the early years of James, when the decay of the world was gloomily diagnosed by many prophets of doom.[19] This metaphysical pessimism was abetted by the political and religious discords that threatened to break the frame of order. It is hardly accidental that in Shakespeare's later plays references to a microcosmic or macrocosmic frame occur generally in a context that suggests its being twisted or broken. A huge passion "shakes" Othello's "frame" (V.ii.47). Lear's "frame of nature" is "like an engine, wrench'd . . . From the fix'd place" (I.iv.267–68), and Macbeth swears that he will let "the frame of things disjoint, both the worlds suffer" rather than endure the terrible dreams that shake him nightly (III.ii.16).

But even those who preached the decay of the world asserted the significance of man. The process of decay had been caused by man's transgression; because of him nature had been corrupted and had, so to speak, become human. In *A Discourse of the Felicity of Man* (1598), Richard Barckley described, in spite of the book's misleading title, an almost Timonesque world—in fact, his account of Timon's life, which may have been one of the sources of Shakespeare's tragedy, is one of the few that show some sympathy with the misanthrope's pessimism. For Barckley, wickedness and misery dominated the human scene, and all striving for felicity through worldly means, even through virtue and contemplation, was vanity. Yet even he declared that God had placed man "as the end of the whole frame of the world in this goodly theater." [20] Man did not yet need to fear that what was happening to him was not tragic but merely absurd.

It appears that the confidence in the significance of man drew some support from the Ptolemaic system of the universe, which prevailed in Elizabethan consciousness. Man was placed on the central body, the one sphere that was not turning but around which all the others, the moon, the sun, the individual planets, and the fixed stars, turned in regular circular orbits. Yet there was no automatic connection between metaphysical confidence and the geocentric theory since man also could be visualized as being farthest removed from God. Even in Shakespeare's beautiful evocation of the Ptolemaic system in Lorenzo's hymn to love (*Merchant of Venice,* V.i.54 ff.), man is depicted as being prevented from hearing the harmony of the spheres by his "muddy vesture of decay." [21] The geocentric theory at any rate encouraged looking for the key to the system of the universe in the earth. Here was "the center" where Polonius claimed he would dig out the truth no matter how deeply hidden (II.ii.157). But perhaps it is not fortuitous that in *Hamlet,* which shows much influence of philosophical skepticism, this geocentric self-confidence is that of Polonius, whose sensitivity to truth is weak. The old system also encouraged geometrical analogies between the frame of the world and the circle (for that matter, "frame" was regularly used to translate *sphaera*), analogies which were also applied to the microcosm. These could be spun *ad nauseam,* as was done by John Davies of Hereford, for whom man was a circle in the larger circles of the earth and the universe; he had a body that was also a circle and a soul that was a circle in it. But God, being perfection, was also symbolized by the circle, the most perfect figure, and when He dwelt in man's mind,

He was the innermost circle.[22] This geometrical madness was intended to instill in man a desire to achieve a perfection analogous to the symmetrical harmony of the universe; but by 1603, the date of Davies's *Microcosmos,* the *nosce teipsum* geometry was becoming an exercise in metaphor. Many elements in Shakespeare's world, as William Elton has noted, "point towards the incipient disordering or breakdown of the analogical and pre-Cartesian tradition." [23]

To this breakdown the spread of the Copernican theory was a contributing influence since it dislodged man from his favored place in the center. But it was not so immediately. The first acquaintance with the Copernican theory does not seem to have shaken the Renaissance belief in the anthropocentric order. Some of the astronomers in the vanguard of the revolution advertised the new cosmology as being so symmetrical and orderly as to inspire man with even greater awe and humility than the old. Its acceptance would enable him to control his beastly nature and rise to the height of the angels.[24] New philosophy called all in doubt only when, as in Donne, it became leagued with a skeptical epistemology and a *contemptus mundi* attitude.

The analogies included not only man and the universe but also the state. As Barckley had it, "There are three bodily worlds coupled together one with another as if it were with a chain of gold: the greater, the less, and man's commonwealth between them both." [25] The state could be looked upon as a microcosm of the universe or a macrocosm of man; or, for that matter, the universe could be viewed as a macrocosm, and man as a microcosm, of the state. In Shakespeare's political theorizing, the analogies between the state and the body prevailed; the sound state was a healthy body; the disordered state was a diseased one. The England of Henry V is a "little body with a mighty heart" (II. Prol. 17), that of his father a "foul" body in which "rank diseases grow" (*2 Henry IV,* III.i.39). The organic conception of the state explained temporary and even continued breakdowns.

Ultimately, the disorder in all organisms could be attributed to man's original sin and God's ensuing wrath. This was Barckley's explanation. God, he said, had originally created all things from heaven to earth "in such exact order and uniformity to the production of things in their most perfection and beauty so as it might be likened to that *aurea catena,* as Homer calleth it"; but after the Fall He withdrew his benign influence and cursed the earth so that it "doth so much degenerate from his former estate that it resembleth a chain rent in pieces, whose links are many lost and broken and the rest so slightly fastened as they will hardly hang together." [26] Here is one example of that elusive chain of being—the only example in Elizabethan literature I know in which the metaphor of the chain is used in this manner—but, alas, it happens to be a broken chain.

Yet even to pessimistic viewers of the human scene like Barckley it appeared that God's original order was at least in some sort reflected on earth. It showed itself, for instance, in the way certain units were linked and yet clearly demarcated from each other. As Luciana says in *The Comedy of Errors* (II.i.16–17), "There's nothing situate under heaven's eye / But hath his bound." It is a bound that, as she argues, links husband and wife but also separates them because man is the superior of woman. Renaissance paintings express a similar mode of perception, one that entails what has aptly been described as an "harmonious adjustment of clearly bounded units with absolute clarity of statement." [27] This way of looking at the world shows itself not only in the canvases of a Raphael or a Dürer, with their sharply outlined and proportioned details, but also in Du Bartas's and Castiglione's descriptions of the world as a painting. And it is also in evidence in Shakespeare's earlier plays.

The measured and limited units of the cosmic frame were governed in their relationship to each other by universal laws, the laws of God and of nature, on which all other laws depended. Basic to this system, of which Richard Hooker was the great Elizabethan apologist, was the philosophical concept of the law of nature. It had evolved from classical philosophers, such as Cicero, and medieval theologians, particularly Aquinas. This law regulated the relationship of men to each other and to nature on the assumption that God had created a rational and harmonious system with man as the central figure. On the psychological level, the law demanded the rule of passion by reason; on the governmental level, it sanctioned the rule of the queen and her officers; on the international level, it regulated the relationship of states to each other. Or, to put it from the perspective of man, the law asked him to curb his appetites; it demanded that he obey lawful authorities; and it enjoined him to respect the rights not only of men of his own nation but also those of other nations.[28] In short, it required him to "frame" himself to a moral and reasonable design. Thomas Cooper's *Thesaurus* quoted some of the pertinent key phrases from Cicero's *De Officiis* under *"Dirigo: . . .* to order, to direct: . . . *Ad rationem dirigere aliquid.* To frame or rule according to reason. . . . *Ad naturam leges hominum dirigun-tur.* Men's laws are framed and made agreeable to nature."

The humanistic view of the state and the world demanded that all ranks and professions, from the lowest to the highest, adjust themselves to this rational design. By referring to Cooper again, one finds that English "to frame" was used for the Latin *conformare* and *accommodare* and, when education was meant, *instituere.* Elizabethan society paid much attention to the framing of the upper classes, of the aristocracy and the royalty, and made some special stipulations for it; but the general process did include a son of a tradesman in Stratford-on-Avon, as was Shakespeare. When he went to grammar school, as one might expect from his father's status alone that he did, he faced a master who was hired to "frame" (*formare*) his pupils' manners and minds. The greatest effort, it is true, went into "framing" (*componere*) the young boys' Latin writing and speeches; but the Christian humanists' emphasis on grammar and rhetoric was connected with their moral and philosophical goals. They believed that any kind of composition, a sentence, a question, an answer, a letter, an essay, or a drama had to be invented, arranged, and structured to fit into the frame of a world ordered for the instruction of man. Shakespeare's Henry V knows this, even though his education is by no means orthodox; once a king, he knows how to frame his life (*dirigere vitam*) and his speeches (*componere orationem*) in the way expected of him—for which some critics have not forgiven him. By contrast, the melancholy and maddened Richard II does not know how to put his discourse in some frame—for which some critics have declared him to be a great poet.

The order to be achieved in all major frames—man, the state, and the universe—was not thought to be one of equals. It was assumed to be God's design that the head ruled the belly, the soul the body, the king the state; that fire was above air, air above water, and water above earth; that the sun was enthroned above the moon; and that beyond these spheres there was a heavenly region in which the angels kept their exemplary hierarchical order. The usual term for the superiority of one part of the created world over another was the biblical "preeminence." Shakespeare's Luciana uses it in her speech on the husband's control over his wife: he is preeminent over her just as men are preeminent over animals. Elizabethan lawyers were apt to argue the subjection of women in such fashion and to prove male prerogatives by analogies to the preeminences at different levels of the cosmic system.[29]

Yet it should be noted that the Elizabethans did not think of the cosmic system as static; they did not deny the presence of tension and strife. The harmony established by God, said Sir John Davies, included "disagreeing strings." [30] Palingenius had said similarly that

> The world in such a wondrous sort the almighty Lord did frame
> That many things do well agree as joined in the same.
> And many things do disagree and keep continual fight,
> Whereby some men have surely thought that strife and friendship might
> Be justly called beginnings chief, by which all things are wrought.[31]

In a Platonic vein, Spenser in "An Hymn of Love" allegorized the beginning of the world as the linking of the "contrary dislikes" of the four elements through the power of love. For the Renaissance as for the Middle Ages, the world was framed of opposites (*conjunctus*), physical, psychic, societal, and cosmic. These were tied together in a harmony that was often symbolized by a golden chain; of the varied uses to which the *aurea catena* was put, this was by far the most frequent.[32]

Humanistic self-knowledge required that man understand the universal *conjunctio oppositorum,* beginning with the *discordia concors* of himself, a creature of body and soul, so that he might lead a life that ratified God's harmonious design. As La Primaudaye said, "during this conjunction, as all things that move within this general globe are maintained by agreeing discords, even so, of necessity, there must be such a harmony between the body and the soul that by the help of the one the other subsisteth and abideth, and that through their continual striving sometimes the one and then the other in the end be obeyed." [33] To be aware of the nature of the two opposites and to use them accordingly was a fundamental postulate of *nosce teipsum.* In his Epistle to the Reader of *The Anatomy of the Mind,* Thomas Rogers declared it evident that

> he which thoroughly would know himself must as well know his body as his mind; the body to put him in mind of his slavery, the mind of his sovereignty; the body of his misery, the mind of his felicity, the body of his mortality, the mind of his eternity. For by the one we participate the nature of beasts; by the other, of angels. By the one we are for a time; by the other we continue for ever.[34]

On this confidence in a purposive antithesis of man's composition, a confidence anchored in a belief of a universal *discordia concors,* the Christian humanists founded their conviction that man could know himself better than he could know anything else. Palingenius, for instance, was skeptical about man's ability to unravel the divine mysteries, but he was confident that man understood his exact place in the universal scheme of things: he was a conjunction of slime, mud, and earth with an invisible, immortal, and celestial substance.[35] And Sir John Davies's *Nosce Teipsum* opens with an account of the vanity and uncertainty of knowledge, which leads up to several emphatic stanzas that overcome all doubt by the triumphant assertion that he knows himself a man, that is, a linkage of body and soul.

This realization was thought to imply the acknowledgment that the mind must rule over the body; to put this rule into effect was practical self-knowledge. The task was difficult because, since the Fall, when man had permitted his body and the lower parts of his soul to dominate his reason, he inclined to disobedience. He had delivered himself to death through sin; preeminent above the animals, he had tried to rise even higher by attempting to become a god; capable of ranging himself through his immortal soul with the angels, he had polluted it with the filth of his body, and he was in constant danger of reenacting this rebellion. We know all this from Milton, whose concept of self-knowledge puts him in line with the Christian humanists as perhaps their last great representative.[36]

That Shakespeare also based self-knowledge on the realization that man was a *conjunctio oppositorum* proceeds from the way in which some of his good and self-possessed characters demonstrate their knowledge of the doctrine. Viola in *Twelfth Night,* for instance, decides to trust the Captain's offer to help her although she is quite aware how deceptive outward appearance is; the difference between the two substances joined in man, she knows, can be great:

> There is a fair behaviour in thee, Captain;
> And though that nature with a beauteous wall
> Doth oft close in pollution, yet of thee
> I will believe thou hast a mind that suits
> With this thy fair and outward character.
> (I.ii.47–51)

But Viola's brother, Sebastian, demonstrates his knowledge of the relationship of body and soul even more effectively than his sister.

When he appears at the end of the play, Viola, who had thought him drowned, cannot believe her eyes: "If spirits can assume both form and suit, / You come to fright us." Whereupon Sebastian properly identifies himself as a man:

> A spirit I am indeed,
> But am in that dimension grossly clad
> Which from the womb I did participate.
> (V.i.227–30)

It may not be amiss to point out how very technical these few lines are in indicating Sebastian's knowledge of his composition as a man. In *Tusculan Disputations* (I.54 ff.), Cicero had argued that self-knowledge, that is, the soul's knowledge of itself, depended on realizing that its beginning was different from a birth. As Beroaldus commented on this passage, Cicero meant that one should examine such questions on the nature of the soul as the following: Was it physical or nonphysical? Was it simple or composed of several elements? Was it created from something or nothing? Was it transmitted together with the body or did it come from the outside in finished form to be clothed with a body in the mother's womb?[37] Sebastian chooses to reassure his sister on his identity as if she had asked some such question as Beroaldus. He affirms that he is primarily a soul and thus an incorporal spirit, "clad" (*induatur*) with the body "from the womb" (*inter visca muliebra*). When he says that he "did participate" the body from the womb, he asserts the dominance and preexistence of the soul.[38] He is theologically sound in knowing that the soul is infused in the body rather than inherited ("traduced") from the parents. Moreover, Sebastian knows that, unlike other spirits, he has a body that has a "dimension" (and not "dimensions" as some would emend); Bartholomaeus Anglicus noted very similarly that incorporal spirits differed from man by not having a "dimension."[39]

The opposites in man to be harmonized were not only body and soul but also the forces of the soul itself. Its lower elements tended to league themselves with the body and threaten the soul's immortality. Although Shakespeare and the Elizabethans were familiar with the tripartition of the soul into rational, sensible, and nutritive parts, in common practice they reduced it to a bipartition in conformity with the Pauline dichotomy of spirit and flesh. The rational part, sometimes called "mind" and more often simply "soul," was contrasted with the irrational part, generally called "sense." [40] In the theological language of Friar Lawrence, the components are "grace" and "rude will"; in Brutus's Roman idiom, they are "the Genius" and "the mortal instruments.[41] Regardless of the terms chosen for these elements, strife between them was thought inevitable. The danger to man's stability lay in the lower elements, the senses and the passions, rebelling against the higher part, reason, and thus bringing about sin and damnation. Like man, the soul was a junction of opposites; its health depended on the organic cooperation of its discordant elements. But this harmony had to be achieved by the direction of the mind, and, because the soul was the vitalizing principle of the whole human organism, the mind also was responsible for the total harmony of man. It *was* harmony, and thus it could not contain the disharmony that threatened the breakup of other substances. As Sir John Davies said, "what can be contrary to the mind, / Which holds all contraries in concord still?" [42] This was one of Davies's arguments for the essential immortality of the mind or rational soul.

Shakespeare was familiar with such reasoning and based on it his sonnet 146, his most explicit statement on self-knowledge as knowledge and control of the human *conjunctio oppositorum*. In a sort of dramatic monologue, the poet addresses his "poor soul, the centre of my sinful earth," which is "arrayed," that is, dressed (and presumably also threatened with battle) by "these rebel pow'rs." He asks the soul why it has suffered internal want and painted its "outward walls so costly gay." To prevent it from spending too much on the fading mansion of the body, he evokes the worms that will inherit "this excess" and contrasts the body's end with the survival of the soul after its servant's loss. He enjoins upon himself to feed his soul, which feeds on Death, who feeds on man. Thus, punningly, Death will be removed and only the immortal soul will remain: "And, Death once dead, there's no more dying then."

This sonnet is hardly a favorite of modern critics, who tend to read it as a relapse into a medieval commonplace and hurry on to the poet's passionate outcry in the next: "My love is as a fever." Yet sonnet 146 must have struck Shakespeare's contemporaries (and why not Shakespeare?) as essential for the story. The episode of the dark lady, to which it belongs, dramatizes and particularizes the discord between reason and passion, soul and body; it is a record of

the poet's failures to make the former prevail over the latter. Sonnet
146 dramatizes and generalizes the ideal concord of man; it is the
poet's assertion as a Christian and Renaissance humanist that man
must identify himself with his better part, his mind. The moral
should not be missed.

In summarizing this discussion of the cosmic and metaphysical
implications of the humanists' concept of self-knowledge, we may
recall that this concept required man to be aware of his central
position and to acknowledge that he was framed according to principles analogous to those of the universe. His health, character,
success, happiness, even his salvation could in some sense be said to
be determined by the effect these principles had on him or by the
way he made them work. It will be appropriate to restate them and
characterize their role in Shakespeare's play worlds.

The principles that have emerged in the preceding pages can be
grouped under four major headings: strife or tension, hierarchy or
degree, measure or proportion, and balance or harmony. According
to their predisposition and particular purpose, Renaissance writers
tended to stress one or the other of these, with the result sometimes
of breaking up the humanistic synthesis. All four principles occur in
Shakespeare's play worlds, but which of them is dominant is a
question not easy to answer. One must resist the temptation to answer
it according to the relative regard in which these principles are
held in one's own time, and one must not assume that Shakespeare's
emphasis was necessarily the same from play to play. Yet I believe
that a general answer can be given for Shakespeare's works and a
more specific one for the earlier plays even when observing these
precautions. A good way of showing the relative importance of the
structural principles of the frame of order is to compare Shakespeare
with some signal exponents of each of the four.

The first principle, that of strife or tension, was perhaps most
boldly espoused by the French humanist Louis Leroy (Regius) in
De la Vicissitude, which was translated by Robert Ashley as *Of the
Interchangeable Course or Variety of Things* (1594). Leroy saw
in nature a continuing conflict of forces. These had, throughout history, effected political and cultural changes, which Leroy welcomed
as vicissitude or variety. The greatest variety could be brought
about by the utmost development of arms and letters, the two opposite qualities that determined the excellence of a state. Man, by
making himself an instrument of this change, could aspire to perfec-

tion. His own age was for Leroy one of maximum change and variety because it flourished in arms as well as in letters. He considered Tamburlaine to have been the warrior who ushered in this glorious period, and he described his career; therefore it has been plausibly argued that Marlowe evolved his character of the Scythian conqueror and particularly the speech on the warring elements in nature and man from *De la Vicissitude*.[43] But such glorification of the aspiring mind was, as we noted, akin to Machiavellism. In its joyous affirmation of earthly warfare and its total disregard of human depravity, it led away from Christian humanism.

The second organizing principle of the frame, that of degree or hierarchy, was, as noted, usually evoked by the Elizabethans when they argued the subjection of women. Its other frequent application was political. Some Tudor moralists and theologians, afraid of new political unrest and perhaps also eager to please their sovereigns, who had good reason for fearing disorder, appealed to the principle of degree as forbidding revolt and usurpation. The sermons on disobedience and rebellion in the official homilies proclaimed preeminence as the rule of macrocosmic order. But it also should be noted that there was a rival to this Christian-Platonic conception of order in the pragmatic Aristotelian approach to politics that recognized several constitutional models as justifiable and concerned itself primarily with their organic functioning and with changes from one political system to another.[44] Also, too strong an emphasis disagreed with the humanistic premise of the basic equality of all flesh; in practice, of course, it led to out-and-out absolutism. This is what happened under James. Unlike her successor, Queen Elizabeth was wise enough not to evoke the royal prerogative too often to alienate those who looked to Parliament for political, and to Puritan preachers for religious, direction.

Richard Hooker may be cited as a witness for the third principle, that of measure and proportion. His was a finite and limited world. It was full of "riches," but it did not achieve "plenitude" in the sense of being so full of objects and creatures as to make a more comprehensive world inconceivable. Like other Elizabethan theologians, Hooker felt that a world of plenitude was irreconcilable with the idea of an all-powerful God that could create as he wished—the advocates of plenitude had argued that a totally full world was the only possible one for an all-good God to create.[45] As Hooker discusses this matter, his Renaissance sense of measure and proportion asserts itself:

> If it therefore be demanded why God, having power and ability
> infinite, the effects notwithstanding of that power are all so limited
> as they are, the reason hereof is the end which He has proposed
> and the law whereby His wisdom hath stinted the effects of His
> power in such sort that it does not work infinitely, but correspond-
> ently unto that end for which it worketh even all things, χρηστῶς,
> in most decent and comely sort, "all things in measure, number, and
> weight." [46]

Hooker's admiration for the proportioned world contrasts with the
contempt for it by those who saw nothing but universal decay; but
it does not go as far as the uninhibited glorification of universal
beauty one finds in some Platonizing tracts like Annibale Romei's
The Courtier's Academy (translated by J. Kepler in 1598), where
one of the discussants calls proportion the principal cause in creating
and preserving the physical and the spiritual worlds.[47] Hooker stayed
with the humanistic mean.

Hooker can serve also as an exponent of the fourth principle of
Renaissance natural order, that of harmony. In a time that was
growing more and more contentious, he sought to reestablish the
Erasmian balance of reason and faith. Unlike Calvin, he did not see
human reason as deeply corrupted by the Fall. Reason could still
ascertain the laws of nature and determine their congruence with the
laws of God. Hooker's concept of order, it is true, included a "gradual disposition," but it was intended to produce an organic unity:
"The very Deity itself both keepeth and requireth for ever this to be
kept as a law that, wheresoever there is a coagmentation of many,
the lowest be knit to the highest, by that which is interjacent may
cause each to cleave to the other, and so all continue one." [48] The
principle of balance and harmony can be traced also in Hooker's
ideas of political and ecclesiastical order: he saw the essence of the
former in government by the sovereign in conjunction with Parliament, that of the latter in assent between the sovereign and the Con-
vocation. Although few of Hooker's contemporaries were willing to
accept this kind of balance in church and state government, Hooker's
general insistence on political and religious harmony places him in
the mainstream of Christian humanism and Elizabethan thought.

In assessing the relative importance Shakespeare gave to the four
principles of order, it is immediately obvious that he did not glorify
strife in the fashion of Leroy and Marlowe. He accepted it as a
reality—in some plays, particularly the later tragedies, it may appear

to be the dominant reality—but never as a joyful one. And when he created an aspiring mind like Coriolanus, he took a critical attitude toward him.

The second principle, degree or hierarchy, does appear occasionally in Shakespeare's theoretical formulations. He certainly was a man of his time in being a royalist and in believing that nature had ordained some for commanding and others for obeying. But, a few humorous passages on the subjection of women aside, he does not appear to me to have argued this principle strongly; and he certainly did not emphasize it to the exclusion of other principles as did the homilies. The reading of the history plays as apologies of the Tudor myth has become suspect, and justly so, and the often-quoted apotheosis of degree and obedience by Ulysses in *Troilus and Cressida* (I.iii.78 ff.) has been shown to be suffused with ambiguities and ironies.[49] Ulysses lacks credentials for being considered a mouthpiece of Shakespeare, and the satirical and skeptical tone of the play makes it difficult to evaluate the validity of any concept it examines.

This leaves the principles of measure or proportion and balance or harmony, the principles most prominent in Renaissance artistic composition. My reader will not be unaware that I consider these strongly present in Shakespeare's early plays. I shall in the following chapters argue that the search for self-knowledge in these plays proceeds in a universe that by its proportioned measure and harmonious balance resembles Hooker's ideal model. I shall be concerned only incidentally with the ways in which these principles are reflected in the rhetorical and dramatic structures of the plays; my intention is to show primarily how they support the search for self-knowledge on the part of their heroes and other characters by positing an intelligible universe in which man can hope to find himself by properly framing the picture of man. The universe or—as I think we had better say—universes of the later plays are more opaque, and they do not offer the seeker for self-knowledge a readable cosmic map; they appear indifferent and even hostile toward this search. But this need not concern us at present.

CHAPTER FOUR

The Comedy of Errors:
Losing and Finding Oneself

VYING FOR THE CLAIM of having been Shakespeare's earliest comedies are *The Comedy of Errors* and *Love's Labor's Lost.* Although both have had some success on the stage, neither can be counted among Shakespeare's great comic achievements. Yet, I believe, the two plays warrant more than passing consideration because of the patterns of self-knowledge embedded in them, patterns that reappear, with variations, not merely in Shakespeare's subsequent comedies but also in his histories, tragedies, and romances.

The Comedy of Errors, the subject of the present chapter, is a boisterous farce full of buffoonery and horseplay, surely one of Shakespeare's happiest comedies; but it nevertheless contains incidents and themes out of which more serious drama can be and has been made, that is, errors and misidentifications that, aggravated by unfortunate accidents, lead to disruptions of family relationships and to general social disorders.[1] The play's first scene casts an ominous shadow that does not fully vanish until the very end: Aegeon, a grief-stricken father in search of his son—the only family member remaining to him after the earlier apparent loss of his wife and first son—is condemned to die at sunset for entering hostile territory. This melancholy beginning was Shakespeare's invention; his basic source, Plautus's *Menaechmi,* had no such searching and suffering father. Shakespeare introduced him from another story, that of Apollonius of Tyre, and with him the idea of the storm and the shipwreck. The second scene, it is true, lightens the shadow by bringing on the stage the son for whom Aegeon has been searching and, through the resulting confusion in Ephesus, indicates that the other son may also be alive—a supposition soon to be confirmed. As the reader or auditor of the play senses that he is experiencing a comedy, his anxiety about the unresolved fate of Aegeon lessens, but it is not removed totally until the very end.

This grave beginning emphasizes the serious theme of searching and finding, which Shakespeare developed much beyond anything he found in Plautus. In *The Comedy of Errors,* there is not only a son who risks his life in search of a brother but also a father who endangers it for his sons, and father and sons are subjected to much pain before they gain happiness in the end, a greater happiness than could have been imagined by any of them because it encompasses and unites the whole family. Further, the movement from initial disruption to final recovery affects in various ways all major characters: Adriana, wife of Antipholus of Ephesus; Luciana, her sister; the Dromios, twin servants to the twin masters; and it even touches some minor figures, such as the schoolmaster, the merchant, the goldsmith, and the sergeant.

Before the happy turn of events occurs, the search to reestablish the severed family ties leads to one error and misidentification after another, each of which brings increasing pain and anxiety and loosens the natural bonds further. But with the help of Aegeon's wife, the Abbess, a kind of *dea ex machina,* the errors are explained, the identities restored, and a more meaningful order is evolved. When in the end she invites all to a "gossips' feast"—a celebration of baptism—family and society are, as it were, reborn. Those who came into the world as brother and brother—so Shakespeare has Antipholus of Ephesus sum up the meaning of the ending—now go hand in hand, not one before the other. The play thus moves from grief to joy, from disunity to unity, from loss of identity to reidentification, from the confusion of souls to the clarity of minds.

This general movement from threatening self-loss to self-recovery is, of course, common to all of Shakespeare's comedies and tragicomedies. Yet, I think there are some differences in the degree of the danger and in the completeness of the recoveries between Shakespeare's "happy" or "romantic" comedies and his "dark" or "problem" comedies, and there are differences in this respect between these two kinds of comedies and the tragicomedies. In the comedies from *The Comedy of Errors* through *Twelfth Night,* the threat of self-loss is much less ominous and the efficacy of the final recoveries can hardly be questioned, but in *Troilus and Cressida, All's Well That Ends Well,* and *Measure for Measure,* the heroes come close to losing themselves irrevocably and find themselves either imperfectly or make us question their staying power. In the tragicomedies, from *Pericles* through *The Tempest,* the self-losses go even beyond the stage of these comedies, and it is not clearly apparent in the course of the plays that there will be recoveries; it takes extraordinary, in some cases supernatural, means to bring them about. On the basis of this theme alone, one could put Shakespeare's comedies into the three categories that have become conventional for them.

Although in *The Comedy of Errors* self-loss is a relatively harmless matter, the theme is clearly struck. It is adumbrated by "the griefs unspeakable" of Aegeon, with which the play opens, and it is unmistakably formulated in the first soliloquy of Antipholus of Syracuse, who feels submerged in the strange and unhospitable city of Ephesus:

> I to the world am like a drop of water
> That in the ocean seeks another drop,
> Who, falling there to find his fellow forth,
> Unseen, inquisitive, confounds himself.
> So I, to find a mother and a brother,
> In quest of them, unhappy, lose myself.
>   (I.ii.35–40)

This figure of the waterdrop is a memorable one since it echoes through the play. Shakespeare, as Professor Baldwin has shown, developed it from Plautus's image of looking for a needle; he gave it the maritime turn perhaps with Aegeon's story of the storm in mind or because of Plautus's remark that the two Menaechmi resembled each other as water resembles water (l. 1089). It should, however, be noted that Plautus spoke only of seeking a needle, not of losing and finding one; the antithetical figure was Shakespeare's dilation. With it he gained an allusion to the paradox of salvation in Matthew 16:25: "For whosoever will save his life shall lose it, and whosoever shall lose his life for my sake shall find it" (similarly, Matthew 10:39, Luke 9:24, John 12:25). The side-note of the Genevan-Tomson version marked the paradox as a specific warning against self-loss, saying that those who "would save themselves do not only gain that which they look for, but also lose the thing they would have kept, that is, themselves, which loss is the greatest of all. . . ."

The biblical formula is so simple and artless as to have induced a modern poet to say that it lacks poetic glamor; according to A. E.

Housman, the paradox of salvation is "the most important truth that has ever been uttered, and the greatest discovery in the moral world; but I do not find in it anything that I should call poetical." [2] But for Shakespeare, this most important of all truths belonged to the vocabulary of self-knowledge; just like the Christian humanists, he found it both significant and poetical, and he gave it to Antipholus of Syracuse, who is the more important of the two brothers, the hero of the play, if it can be said to have one, and the character most conscious of the identity problem.

This focus on the searching brother was Shaksepeare's own idea. In Plautus, the citizen Menaechmus was the main character, the first to appear and the most frequently present of the two brothers. And not only is Shakespeare's stranger-brother a more important character than Plautus's, he also becomes a recognizable individual, capable of not merely drawing laughter but also of attracting some sympathy. He is a thoughtful, somewhat melancholy man, who would wander in the streets to "lose himself" (I.ii.30) with no idea as yet how thoroughly this desire will be fulfilled. He is at first puzzled about the misidentifications and confusions and then becomes sincerely worried about his identity. It is merely the belief that he is in a city of witches, as Ephesus was assumed to be, that prevents him from completely succumbing to his feeling of alienation.

The strangers around him do their best to thrust on him an identity that he cannot recognize as his own and does not want. First it is the servant who treats him as if he were somebody else; then it is Adriana and Luciana who conspire to make him into the former's husband. He becomes baffled and uncertain: "What, was I married to her in my dream? / Or sleep I now, and think I hear all this?" (II.ii.181–82). He is shaken enough in his self-knowledge to accept the dinner invitation and to feel at least temporarily a stranger to himself, as much an alien on earth as one of Kafka's heroes:

> Am I in earth, in heaven, or in hell?
> Sleeping or waking, mad or well-advis'd?
> Known unto these, and to myself disguis'd!
> (211–13)

But he decides that in this case self-alienation has its compensation because it offers him not only an unexpected dinner but also a woman, Luciana, who excites his amorous desire. Were it not for her insistence that he is married to her sister, he would be willing to accept a kind of Pythagorean transformation into an Ephesian. As he says to Luciana,

> Transform me, then, and to your pow'r I'll yield.
> But if that I am I, then well I know
> Your weeping sister is no wife of mine,
> Nor to her bed no homage do I owe.
>
> (III.ii.40–43)

He is ready to drown his identity—one remembers the image of the waterdrop associated with him—but not through merging into Adriana:

> O, train me not, sweet mermaid, with thy note,
> To drown me in thy sister's flood of tears.
> Sing, siren, for thyself, and I will dote.
>
> (45–47)

True love is the kind of self-loss he will accept even if it means death: "Let Love, being light, be drowned if she sink" (52). And when Luciana attempts to redirect his ardors by asking him to turn his straying eyes to her sister, Antipholus waxes even more eloquent:

> It is thyself, mine own self's better part;
> Mine eye's clear eye, my dear heart's dearer heart,
> My food, my fortune, and my sweet hope's aim,
> My sole earth's heaven, and my heaven's claim.
>
> (61–64)

We may stop here for a moment and consider Antipholus's terms of endearment because they are part of an image cluster evolving from the Platonic lore of self-knowledge as the knowledge of the soul. Antipholus identifies his beloved as his "better part," that is, his soul.[3] She is dearer to him than he is to himself, a notion that Cicero in De Amicitia (xxi.80) mentioned as a pardonable lover's exaggeration and that became part of the convention "one soul in bodies twain." [4] Antipholus's amplifying epithets—eye, heart, and heaven—belong to the terminology of the soul as much as they do to lovers' language: the eye was held to be analogous to the soul;[5] the heart, of course, was one of its organs in the body; and "sole" in "my sole earth's heaven" puns on "soul." Antipholus knows how to identify himself with his most important substance, and he knows how to identify himself analogously with his beloved; rather than loving her sister as she demands, he asks her, "Call thyself sister, sweet, for I am thee" (66).

But Luciana rejects him, and he is thus prevented from transforming himself into her husband, a transformation he sees now as dangerous; she "hath almost made me traitor to myself" (160). He recalls the reputation of Ephesus for witchcraft. As a melancholy man, he has the more reason to be afraid, for it was believed in Shakespeare's time that men of this type were susceptible to being transformed by their exuberant imagination. John Woolton, among others, warned that a kind of Pythagorean metempsychosis could come to pass "by means of witchcraft and abundance of melancholy humors in man's body, wherewith the devil conjoineth himself often times." [6] But the decision to depart from the bewitched city restores Antipholus's self-confidence; he suffers no more self-alienation although the confusions continue. His and Dromio's departure, however, is frustrated by their being taken for the other pair; they flee to the priory, where they take sanctuary—a fortunate circumstance because it will bring them face to face with the other set of twins, who are to arrive at the same location shortly.

When we turn to examining the role of Antipholus of Ephesus and compare it to Plautus's citizen-brother, we note that it is both diminished and changed because of Shakespeare's emphasis on the theme of search. Antipholus of Syracuse does not appear until the third act and takes second place to his brother the searcher. But he is a better man than his Plautine counterpart, and he is more pitifully victimized. Antipholus does not plan to deceive his wife; when he goes to the courtesan for dinner, it is in pardonable anger: he has just been subjected to terrible treatment. He has been excluded from his own house in the presence of a friend whom he had invited, and his wife, while entertaining company inside, has denied being married to him: "Your wife, sir knave! Go get you from the door" (III.i.64). Everybody he meets acts as if Antipholus did not know himself. The goldsmith asks him for payment of a chain he ordered but did not receive and has him arrested; the courtesan thinks him insane and convinces his wife that he is; worst of indignities, he is exorcised by the odious Pinch. These cumulative irritations produce in Antipholus an understandable but excessive reaction. He "trembles in his ecstasy" (IV.iv.47) as he beats the servant and the schoolmaster and vehemently insults his wife.

It is interesting to note that this passionate outbreak of the Ephesian Menaechmus was Shakespeare's revision. In Plautus, it is the stranger-Menaechmus who is characterized as a man of ungovernable temper (1.269: "ego autem homo iracundus, animi perditi") whereas the citizen-Menaechmus is and remains fairly even-tempered. When he plays the madman, he does so merely to frighten his wife. By investing the Ephesian brother with the temper of Plautus's stranger-Menaechmus, Shakespeare combined in the *summa epitasis* of his play both the climax of confusion and the climax of emotion. The Terentian five-act formula as evolved by Renaissance commentators favored such construction of the emotional curve because it demanded the highest of perturbations for this part of the structure.[7] Moreover and most importantly, Shakespeare thus created another moment of threatening self-loss, the most dangerous of the play. Antipholus comes near to suffering the direst transformation of all, that from man to animal through passion, a transformation against which the moralists never ceased to warn. Because anger was often defined as a "short madness," his being declared insane symbolizes the danger. Without their fair judgment, as Claudius says of the mad Ophelia, men are "pictures, or mere beasts." But in a comedy, the *summa epitasis,* no matter how turbulent, must bring forth the occasion of the catastrophe; and it does so in *The Comedy of Errors:* the violence of Antipholus of Ephesus makes it possible for him to break away from his captors and escape to the abbey, where the reunion of all characters takes place and everybody finds unhoped-for joy.

In concentrating on the main plot, I have undoubtedly overstressed the serious aspects of the play. All through, the strand of the action involving the two Dromios neutralizes the potential dangers by reminding us that we are witnessing a farce, and an improbable one at that. The servant subplot, it has been said with slight overstatement, keeps *The Comedy of Errors* from becoming a tragedy.[8] However, it is not generally noted how beautifully this subplot echoes and varies the semi-serious themes of self-loss and self-transformation in a scherzo mood. As one master suffers an identity crisis, so does his servant, and both comic convention and the way in which these crises are expressed keep them from having the same weight as the masters' anguish. Just as Antipholus of Ephesus comes close to losing his reason and thus to transforming himself into an animal, so his servant suffers a painful metamorphosis of his own. First beaten by one master for inviting him to dinner, he is called an ass by the other and beaten again for merely truthfully claiming to have been beaten before. As he says, it appears he is becoming an ass, and thus he should be free to kick when being kicked so that "you would keep from my heels, and beware of an ass" (III.i.15–18). Mistaking and mistiming play another painful trick on him when the man he supposes to be his master sends him for a rope; he delivers it only to find his master now asking for a sum of money of which he knows nothing since the other Dromio was dispatched for it. Beaten and called "senseless," Dromio protests:

> I would I were senseless, sir, that I
>   might not feel your blows.
> E. Ant.   Thou art sensible in nothing but blows,
>   and so is an ass.
> E. Dro.   I am an ass indeed; you may prove it by my long ears.
>   I have served him from the hour of my nativity to this
>   instant, and have nothing at his hands for my service but
>   blows.
>   (IV.iv.25–31)

By saying that Dromio is sensible in nothing but blows, Antipholus grants Dromio only a sensitive soul and denies him the distinctive mark of a human being. Antipholus thus degrades Dromio into an animal, just at the moment he is in danger of becoming one himself. Both incidents derive their meaning from the Renaissance pride in human identity and from the Renaissance fear of human self-loss. However, the servant's travesty helps to lessen the serious implications in the master's change.

Dromio of Syracuse too suffers a pseudo-Ovidian metamorphosis. Just after his master has declared that he is willing to change his identity if he can thereby gain Luciana, the latter, whom he had never seen before, addresses him by his own name. What else can he do except to believe in a metamorphosis:

> I am transformed, master, am not I?
> S. Ant.   I think thou art in mind, and so am I.
> S. Dro.   Nay, master, both in mind and in my shape.
> S. Ant.   Thou hast thine own form.

S. Dro.	No, I am an ape.
Luc.	If thou art chang'd to aught, 'tis to an ass.
S. Dro.	'Tis true; she rides me, and I long for grass.
	'Tis so, I am an ass; else it could never be.
	But I should know her as well as she knows me.

(II.ii.194–201)

In an even more notable parallel to his master's plight, Dromio of Syracuse is claimed as a husband by a woman he does not know, and that by the spherical and unappetizing kitchen wench Nell! He cries out in despair: "Do you know me, sir? Am I Dromio? Am I your man? Am I myself?" (III.ii.73). Although Antipholus tries to reassure Dromio, the latter feels he has lost his identity altogether: "I am an ass, I am a woman's man, and besides myself" (76).

The scene makes its point by itself; to elaborate on it is to run the risk of making an obvious joke a matter of great profundity. But one cannot escape the feeling that Shakespeare suggests here that such "errors" as happen in this play could on a more serious level bring about more dangerous transformations. The denial of man's identity can lead to self-loss in ignorance, passion, and madness. *The Comedy of Errors,* it is true, does not permit the characters to experience states of metaphysical anxiety as do the later dark comedies and the tragedies, but it does make them visible in the distance. Dromio of Syracuse's amazed question, "Do you know me, sir? . . . Am I your man? Am I myself?" anticipates at least faintly the identity question asked by the tortured Lear: "Does any here know me? . . . Who is it that can tell me who I am?" (I.iv.225 ff.). But it is no accident that in *The Comedy of Errors* the identity question is asked in its most impressive form by a servant, whom, according to comic convention, we cannot take altogether seriously. We never cease to laugh even when we feel his plight.

Both the Dromios' and the Antipholuses' identity problems are solved when they are confronted with their mirror images, and they are solved in a way of which Plautus knew nothing. Shakespeare's happy comedies not only provide joyous endings but they also reassert social norms. It is presumably for this reason that *The Comedy of Errors* has an elaborate domestic-romantic setting. Shakespeare was not merely interested in the external confusions and their potential threat to identity; he was also concerned with making his characters find themselves in the end in a proper human and social context. Self-knowledge is achieved only when the positioning of each self toward the other selves has taken place.

There are in *The Comedy of Errors* also some indications that such a reestablishment of relationships must proceed in the kind of framed and articulated Renaissance universe described in the preceding chapter. The confusions have "tangled" the chain that had previously linked the characters to family and society and have even threatened to break the links, but the recovery brings about the kind of organic unity idealized by the Elizabethan moralists. Notably, Shakespeare chose a chain (rather than, as in Plautus, a coat) for the main prop of misidentification and reidentification; and images of tying, attaching, and fastening flowed from his pen.[9] The chain is delivered to the wrong Antipholus, and the rope is about to land on the back of one of the Dromios. But in the happy catastrophe, the chaos is avoided. To speak with the moralists, everybody is again properly linked to society, and the knot of friendship is retied.

The theme of the individual's bonds with the larger units, with family and city, is developed primarily in the domestic-romantic subplot, which was entirely Shakespeare's own. Its central character, Luciana, has no equivalent in Plautus, and her part-time occupation as marriage counselor and *nosce teipsum* preacher make her into a figure inconceivable in Roman comedy. But even Adriana assumes a more important role than does the Citizen's wife in Plautus. She is a loving spouse rather than a mere shrew, and she would like to make her husband cherish her. But by harassing him, she goes about it the wrong way and creates family disunity. Luciana serves as her confidante, as recipient of her laments, and as her adviser. Primarily, however, she is the object of the amorous attention of Antipholus of Syracuse, making a romantic love intrigue possible and offering an opportunity for the bachelor Antipholus to find himself in the haven of marriage. And, like the princess in *Love's Labor's Lost,* she is an early, if slight, sketch of Shakespeare's later romantic heroines, of Rosalind and Viola, who, though involved in the confusions, have enough self-knowledge to help others to find themselves.

In a manner quite foreign to Plautus but resembling the debates of some Tudor interludes, Adriana and Luciana are introduced in a discussion about a marriage problem. Adriana is angry with her husband for not returning home promptly after being sent for. She is something of a rebel against the social order that subordinates her to him. Luciana becomes her marriage counselor, a role in which she must have seemed most competent to Shakespeare's audience, for she preaches the official Elizabethan position on marital order as given in "An Homily of the State of Matrimony" when she admonishes Adriana to let her husband be the bridle of her will.[10] When Adriana perversely rejoins, "There's none but asses will be bridled so," Luciana lectures her on the duties of a true wife:

> Why, headstrong liberty is lash'd with woe.
> There's nothing situate under heaven's eye
> But hath his bound, in earth, in sea, in sky.
> The beasts, the fishes, and the winged fowls,
> Are their males' subjects, and at their controls.
> Man, more divine, the master of all these,
> Lord of the wide world and wild wat'ry seas,
> Indu'd with intellectual sense and souls,
> Of more pre-eminence than fish and fowls,
> Are masters to their females, and their lords;
> Then let your will attend on their accords.
>   (II.i.15–25)

This is the same theory the remorseful Kate in *The Taming of the Shrew* proclaims unexpectedly in the end: the wife's duty to obey her husband is the divine law of the universe that prescribes a hierarchical order. Luciana appropriately evokes the subjection of animals to men as an analogy because it had established the general principle of subordination in the orderly Christian world: God created man to "have rule of the fish of the sea and the fowl of the air, and of cattle, and of earth, and of every creeping thing that creepeth upon the earth" (Genesis 1:26). Also, God "put all things in subjection under their feet; all sheep and oxen; yea, and the beasts of the field, the fowls of the air, and the fish of the sea; and whatsoever walketh through the paths of the seas" (Psalms 8:6–8). Luciana properly refers to this triplicity of subjected animals: "the beasts, the fishes, and the winged fowls."

Luciana takes a Renaissance view of the world that is theologically sound when she sees every creature's place in the universal order as allocated and circumscribed; each, she says, has its "bound." In a paraphrase of a passage in Cicero on the law of nature, Woolton noted similarly that all animals, "for that they cannot usurp the trade and conditions of other kinds, do contain themselves within the enclosures of their own natures."[11] The general argument that the subjection of female to male was the plan of Creation had formidable theological and legal authority.[12] Luciana expounds what generally passed for an account of order based on the Creation even though she may be overdoing the praise of the masculine species by calling it "more divine," for that epithet (although certainly not the *idea* of greater divinity) seems to have been reserved for man in the generic sense—Shakespeare may well have been having his fun with the male chauvinists of his time.

But for generic man it was quite correct to claim that he was, as Arthur Golding put it, "far more divine, of nobler mind," and that he was a creature that passed all others "in depth of knowledge, reason, wit, and high capacity, / And which of all the residue should the lord and ruler be." [13] The greater divinity of men, according to Luciana, depends on their possession of "intellectual sense and souls" —a phrase that demonstrates a careful and technical terminology. Luciana appropriately divides the psychic apparatus by which man excels into a superior sensory mechanism ("intellectual sense") and the strictly human and immortal soul. John Woolton similarly explained that "there was also in this image of God in man a preeminence and superiority above all other inferior creatures, whom he excelled in many ways, both in reason and quickness of senses." [14] And Luciana, like Woolton, knows the proper biblical term for male and human superiority when she speaks of "preeminence." Altogether, her lecture is good advice to a wayward wife and a competent disquisition on the Renaissance frame of the world in which the marriage unit was a clearly defined and bounded part of the structure.

Even if one can, to some degree, sympathize with Adriana's retort that, after all, Luciana knows about these matters only through theory, Shakespeare made it abundantly clear that Luciana points out a weakness in her sister. Adriana does not know herself and wishes to assume a hegemony in marriage that she cannot properly claim. When she lectures Antipholus (it happens to be the wrong one) on his "estrangement," she betrays that she does not really understand her place in the scheme of things:

> How comes it now, my husband, O, how comes it,
> That thou art then estranged from thyself?
> Thyself I call it, being strange to me,
> That, undividable, incorporate,
> Am better than thy dear self's better part.
>
> (II.ii.118–22)

In a way, Adriana is not wrong when she seeks to identify herself with her husband; their marriage vows have made them "incorporate," that is, one flesh.[15] She might even be forgiven for claiming to be his "better part," that is, his soul—a claim that is underlined by "undividable" and "incorporate," for indivisibility and noncorporality were common attributes of the soul. But Adriana says to Antipholus she is *"better* than thy dear self's better part"; she claims superiority, a reversal of roles particularly reprehensible in a society that believed, in Guazzo's words, that the husband was united with his wife to rule over her in the same manner as does "the mind over the body, which are linked together by a certain natural amity." [16] By making herself into the super-soul of the Antipholus family, she would establish a *discordia discors;* it is not he but she who suffers from self-estrangement.

Adriana goes on to depict herself as the soul of the Antipholus family in a metaphor that recalls Antipholus of Syracuse's earlier self-characterization as a waterdrop lost in the sea (I.ii.35 ff.)—the similarity should be enough to make him wince:

> Ah, do not tear away thyself from me;
> For know, my love, as easy mayst thou fall
> A drop of water in the breaking gulf,
> And take unmingled thence that drop again
> Without addition or diminishing,
> As take from me thyself, and not me too.
> (II.ii.123–28)

Here again, Adriana presumes; the "breaking gulf" toward which the "drop," that is, her husband, has fallen stands not only for her own person but also metaphorically for the soul of the incorporate Antipholus family she fancies herself to be. Palingenius illustrated the indivisibility of the soul in very similar terms:

> But soul is indivisible and of no gross degree;
> But as a center does she seem, where many lines do meet,
> Which senses do convey to her, as floods to seas do fleet.[17]

Adriana's desire to fasten herself to Antipholus's sleeve (175), however, is evidence that her wish to be the soul of the Antipholus family is not based on independence and self-reliance. She resembles more a body knitting itself to a soul than a soul to a body. Her next metaphor emphasizes this weakness:

> Thou art an elm, my husband, I a vine,
> Whose weakness, married to thy stronger state,
> Makes me with thy strength to communicate.
>
> (173–75)

Adriana here adapts a common *topos* for the soul; in Sir John Davies's version, "She [i.e., the soul] is a vine which doth no propping neede / To make her spread herself or spring upright." [18] Clearly, Adriana lacks comprehension of her destined role in marriage. In the end, she finds herself; she is subdued enough even to accept responsibility for her husband's madness and to acknowledge the Abbess's harsh sermon against the "venomous clamours of a jealous woman" as justified: "She did betray me to my own reproof" (V.i.90). A new Adriana has emerged. She understands her proper relationship to her husband just at the moment when Antipholus of Syracuse finally finds Luciana, the Abbess is miraculously revealed as the wife of Aegeon, and all self-estrangements and self-transformations come to an end.

Thus the ending is something more than the happy resolution of classically conceived comedy. We are made to feel, as we always are at the end of Shakespeare's happy and romantic comedies—my reader will be aware that I think of them as specifically his *Renaissance* comedies—that a benevolent world order has reasserted itself. The frame is rebuilt. The clearly defined selves are put into an equally clearly structured society that reflects the order of the universe. In the end, both masters recognize each other and so do both servants, but they go out hand in hand not only as brother and brother but also as masters and servants according to their proper role. And besides the restored relationships, in particular the restored marriages, a new alliance is soon to take place between Luciana and Antipholus of Syracuse. Thus the stability and continuity of man and society are asserted.

There is, I believe, in this respect a fundamental difference between *The Comedy of Errors* and the plays of Shakespeare's later periods. I shall be more explicit on this difference when discussing these plays; at present I wish merely to suggest it. It is not only that in watching them we do not have the same kind of assurance we have in *The Comedy of Errors* that all will be right with the world even when a great many things are temporarily wrong, but also that we are never assured during and after the plays that the heroes' selves can find their proper places in a firmly structured societal and cosmic frame or could have found them if they or the circumstances had been somewhat different. After the Forest of Arden and Illyria, Shakespeare never returned to Ephesus.

Actually, the skies may already have been darkening during the time Shakespeare wrote his high comedies if I am correct in seeing in *Julius Caesar* signs of his distress about the incongruity between a hero's self-knowledge and the functioning of state and universe. And the change is evident in *Hamlet,* which may have been written no later than the high comedies. It takes, I think, some very strained interpretation of the play and particularly of its ending to attribute to the prince an insight into who and what he is in the frame of the universe; and for us to be certain about the answer is hazardous— critics who are certain use their own assumptions and value systems for those of Hamlet and the play. If it be objected that *Julius Caesar* and *Hamlet* are tragedies and cannot be compared with comedies, it should be said that Shakespeare's early tragedies—we may, for the purposes of this argument, disregard the artistically inferior *Titus Andronicus*—are quite different from the later tragedies but resemble *The Comedy of Errors* in providing a clear orientation of the main characters toward the societal and cosmic frame, even when, as in *Romeo and Juliet,* the frame is in temporary disorder. That the disorder *is* temporary we are told in the prologue to the play, and both prologue and ending carry explicit statements on the restoration of order and the improvement of life in Verona. In *Richard II,* which is both a history and a tragedy, Richard's road to self-knowledge is firmly entered on the map even though he walks it only part of the way, and, as I shall argue, the play holds out a distinct hope of future harmony. By contrast, the later comedies *All's Well* and *Measure for Measure* (not to speak about *Troilus and Cressida*) are distress- ing and puzzling plays that, like *Hamlet,* pose questions on whether things will ever be right in the world. The heroes, Bertram and Angelo, as well as some of the other characters, are released in the end into a quite undeserved but also strangely conditional happiness.

It is true that some of the later tragedies make the road to self- knowledge clearer and the goal more desirable, but they also dis- connect road and goal from the cosmic frame or draw into question the existence of a design. It is obvious that Lear achieves some insight into himself, but it is quite difficult to say whether this includes an understanding of "the mystery of things" if by that is meant the way of God with men; one cannot even be sure that God's in his heaven. Attempts at attributing a cathartic quality to the ending of these tragedies seem doomed to failure. Few critics are nowadays willing to accept Bradley's benevolent and, to some at least, comforting idea that Lear "dies into joy." And although the ending of *Antony and Cleopatra* is often said to have a "transcendence," those who use this term generally mean by it an aesthetic gratification rather than a reassurance about the universe or the future of Rome and Egypt. The romances do indeed have joyful endings, brought about by more or less miraculous means, endings which like those of *All's Well* and *Measure for Measure* are more forced than those sanctioned by the comic convention and practiced in Shakespeare's earlier comedies. For this and other reasons, I do not think that the romances comfort us about the existence of a rational cosmic design as does *The Comedy of Errors*. If they make us believe in a design at all, it is because of a certain faith they create in the triumph of goodness—a faith, not an expectation stemming from a knowledge of how things generally are. When at the end of *The Tempest* Prospero returns to Milan, it is to a city fraught with uncertainties, and he is accompanied by a villainous brother who gives no clear indication that he will, from now on, walk in hand with him. Most of us trust that Prospero will succeed in Milan; but we must take it, as in fact he does himself, on faith. Prospero does not return to a city, a state, and a universe that have reassumed their God-given order as has Ephesus.

CHAPTER FIVE

Love's Labor's Lost:
Seeking Oneself

A S IT DOES in *The Comedy of Errors*, the losing-finding antithesis forms the structure of *Love's Labor's Lost*. The formula is clearly stated in the *summa epitasis* in Act IV, when
the King of Navarre and his three courtiers have fallen in love and
find it impossible to keep the part of their oaths that forbids them
to see women. In their quandary, they turn to Berowne, their greatest
wit, for a way out of the dilemma, and he responds with a masterpiece
of oratory. We shall analyze it later in detail; we need to note here
only the final paradox in Berowne's string of paradoxes, offered as
excuses to giving in to the promptings of nature: "Let us once lose
our oaths to find ourselves, / Or else we lose ourselves to keep our
oaths" (IV.iii.357–58). Even though Berowne's argument is fashioned on the paradox of salvation, it is a piece of palpable sophistry.
In this respect it resembles Proteus's attempt in *The Two Gentlemen
of Verona* to rationalize his treachery toward his friend and his
beloved into an act of self-discovery:

> Julia I lose, and Valentine I lose;
> If I keep them, I needs must lose myself;
> If I lose them, thus find I by their loss:
> For Valentine, myself; for Julia, Sylvia.
> (II.vi.19–22)

Berowne's and Proteus's protests underline the danger of self-loss
through disloyalty, but the comforting feeling that we are watching
"happy comedies" reassures us that appropriate findings will take
place in the end. Proteus will, after all, marry his Julia, and Valen-
tine will get his Sylvia just as Berowne will win his Rosalind (even
though it happens that in the latter case marriage will have to be
delayed).

Love's Labor's Lost adds to the movement from losing to finding a related theme that was new for Shakespeare and proved fruitful for his later patterns of self-knowledge, the theme of the quest for the self. King Ferdinand of Navarre and his courtiers have founded an academy devoted to the pursuit of learning; but it turns out that what they are most in need of knowing is themselves, and, in a confused way, they set out to gain this knowledge. Theirs is an ill-considered quest, demonstrating mainly how not to go about it; but through their errors and through some hints at how self-discovery can take place, the play gives us, as long ago Edward Dowden noted, an insight into Shakespeare's ideas of self-culture.[1]

The idea of a learned academy provides an appropriate context for the theme of self-quest. Although academies were in vogue in the Renaissance, it is tempting to think that Shakespeare was stimulated to write a play on this subject by reading Pierre de La Primaudaye's *French Academy*.[2] Shakespeare could have found in this book both the theme of the quest and the traditional humanistic recipes for achieving self-knowledge. La Primaudaye quoted in an early chapter the saying of Heraclitus, "I have sought myself," and went on to point out how man could seek himself by studying his body and soul and their natures. Self-knowledge was for La Primaudaye as for Shakespeare the prerequisite for all other knowledge. But there are more differences than similarities in the behavior and goal of the four young men of Anjou and the four aristocrats of Navarre. The former begin their enterprise with a sense of its difficulty and with humility, the latter with overeagerness and overconfidence (except for Berowne, who joins the others reluctantly and against his better knowledge). La Primaudaye's courtiers are aware of the need for moderation in learning and interrupt their intellectual pursuits for a considerable time; Shakespeare's academicians devote themselves immoderately to learning, seclude themselves, and attempt, unsuccessfully, to live ascetically.

I believe that there was a more important source for the theme of the quest for self-knowledge in *Love's Labor's Lost* than La Primaudaye, whose influence on Shakespeare must, after all, remain doubtful. This source was the general convention of the warfare of the Christian knight. We have noted earlier the seminal book of this tradition, Erasmus's *Enchiridion Militis Christiani;* and it may also be helpful to call to mind its most notable artistic product, Albrecht Dürer's famous engraving *Knight, Death, and Devil* (1513). Erasmus's book, be it recalled, strikes a characteristic balance of religion and philosophy and brings both under the heading of *nosce teipsum:* self-knowledge is the first point of wisdom for the Christian knight. Equipped with the humility derived from it, the spiritual warrior may hope to reach the castle of knowledge and faith, which in Dürer's drawing towers above the dim glen haunted by death and devil. But Shakespeare needed no direct acquaintance with either *Enchiridion* or Dürer's engraving to know the convention. He was indoctrinated with it from his early youth, and he may have associated it, in particular, with the only academy he ever attended, the grammar school. Here he would have found it, for instance, in Palingenius's *Zodiacus Vitae,* the moral-didactic poem that appears in most Elizabethan curricula. In his poeticized version of the warfare of life in the sixth book, "Virgo," Palingenius specifically singled out the hardship of scholars: fasting, lack of sleep, and sexual abstention. But even if Shakespeare should never have read *Zodiacus Vitae,* he was still intimately acquainted with the slogans and the strategy of the spiritual battle through Saint Paul's various exhortations, which the Book of Common Prayer had made part of church ritual. From birth to death, the Elizabethans were reminded that they needed to fight devil and flesh. At baptism, the minister received the child into "the congregation of Christ's flock" and signed him with the cross in order "manfully to fight under His banner against sin, the world, and the devil, and to continue Christ's faithful soldier and servant unto his life's end." The Catechism in particular reminded the children of their duties as Christian soldiers. It informed them that their godfathers and godmothers had promised in their name that they would "forsake the devil and all his works and pomps, the vanities of the wicked world, and all the sinful lusts of the flesh." As the Preamble explained, they must be confirmed so that "they may receive strength and defence against all temptations to sin and the assaults of the world and the devil," for they had now come "to that age that, partly by the frailty of their own flesh, partly by the assaults of the world and the devil, they begin to be in danger to fall into sundry kinds of sin." We can be assured that William Shakespeare, who at a later time took the vow of a godfather himself when his godson William Walker was baptized in 1608, was enrolled in the army of the combatants against the devil and the flesh.

In *Love's Labor's Lost,* the spiritual warfare convention, of course, is made subservient to the purposes of comedy as is everything else.

One may well suspect that in using so many of the slogans of the convention and showing their ineffectiveness, Shakespeare may have had a satirical purpose. He may have taken his revenge for some of the overdoses of moral advice he received. But he did not poke fun at this advice as such; he did not satirize the idea of spiritual warfare, only its inopportune, immature, and ill-considered application. Berowne, unprincipled as he is in joining an enterprise he recognizes as doomed to failure, points out well his colleagues' naïveté in believing that the devil and the flesh can be easily conquered. Even the pedagogues in Shakespeare's audience could have taken some satisfaction from the fact that the play proved one of their favorite axioms, that "the study of love letteth and turneth away every other study." [3] If they had looked on this development with a jaundiced eye, they would have missed, of course, that other, more important point of the play, that it is natural for young men to fall in love and that nature must not be suppressed by an unnatural asceticism.

In order to fully understand the thought and the humor of *Love's Labor's Lost,* one needs some acquaintance with the strategy of spiritual warfare and a familiarity with its vocabulary. It forms a major part of the religious terminology with which, as critics have noted, the play is saturated.[4] Only if one knows what is behind this saturation—a surprising phenomenon at first sight—does he understand the irony in the courtiers' speeches at the turn of events: the disciples of philosophy merge their slogans of spiritual warfare, which sanctifies their pursuit of learning, into a pseudo-religious idiom of courtly love, which glorifies their pursuit of ladies. Shakespeare's best verbal effects come from his clever juggling of the words and ideas of the two contradictory conventions.

In the idiom of learning, the vocabulary of spiritual warfare is prominent from the beginning. It is unmistakable in the king's opening speech, more a trumpet call than an inaugural address:

> Let fame, that all hunt after in their lives,
> Live regist'red upon our brazen tombs,
> And then grace us in the disgrace of death;
> When, spite of cormorant devouring Time,
> Th' endeavour of this present breath may buy
> That honour which shall bate his scythe's keen edge,
> And make us heirs of all eternity.
> Therefore, brave conquerors—for so you are
> That war against your own affections

> And the huge army of the world's desires—
> Our late edict shall strongly stand in force:
> Navarre shall be the wonder of the world;
> Our court shall be a little Academe,
> Still and contemplative in living art.
>
> (I.i.1–14)

Ferdinand calls for battle against enemies more dangerous than a mysterious "School of Night" or a dictionary maker and translator named Florio: his foes are the two waylayers of the Knight in Dürer's engraving, Death and Devil. Ferdinand pledges himself and his three followers to do battle for honor by overcoming the "scythe's keen edge" of death and time in despite of their allies, the "affections" and the "world's desires," that is, the fleshly temptations, usually symbolized in the spiritual warfare convention by the devil. Ferdinand's speech has a general resemblance to exhortations for spiritual warfare, such as, for instance, the opening of Erasmus's *Enchiridion:*

> The first point is: we must needs have in mind continually that the life of mortal men is nothing but a certain perpetual exercise of war, as Job witnesseth, a warrior proved to the uttermost and never overcome; and that the most part of men be overmuch deceived whose minds this world, as a juggler, holdeth occupied with delicious and flattering pleasures, which also, as though they had conquered all their enemies, make holiday out of season none otherwise verily than in a very assured peace. It is a marvelous thing to behold how without care and circumspection we live, how idly we sleep, now upon one side and now upon the other, when without ceasing we are besieged with so great a number of armed vices, sought and hunted for with so great craft.[5]

Against these enemies, Erasmus enjoined never-ending watchfulness; he warned in the words of the heading of the first chapter, "We must watch and look about us evermore while we be in this life." He found those particularly prone to defeat who acted "as though they had conquered all their enemies"—men who have the overconfidence displayed by Ferdinand. The Erasmian model warrior prayed for victory in the awareness that his own power and strength were insufficient and that he needed the help of God; he did not claim already to have conquered.

In the context of the spiritual warfare convention the king uses in his opening speech, his sentiment on acquiring honor is incongruous. Erasmus thought that the Christian warrior should seek his reward in heaven; he expressly decried the quest of earthly glory ("Against ambition or desire of honor and authority"). For Palingenius, the whole success of spiritual warfare hinged on the right attitude toward honor; he broached the subject by answering an imaginary gentleman's contention that all virtue aimed at gaining honor: "for her own self is virtue sought, and not for honor's sake." [6] Palingenius here opposed the Christian humanists' ideal of a humble and limited self to the expansive selves of the courtiers and gentlemen. But King Ferdinand's heroic expansiveness bursts through the shell of the spiritual idiom when he proclaims that the academy will make him and his friends "heirs of all eternity"—the sentiment echoes rather immodestly the hope of the baptismal service that the infants enlisted in Christ's army "be made heirs of everlasting salvation."

The more discerning in Shakespeare's audience also must have noted a basic confusion in Ferdinand's philosophic terminology when they heard him acclaim the academy as "still and contemplative in living art." "Living art" appears to be a translation of *ars vitae* or *ars vivendi,* the Stoics' and Cicero's terms for moral philosophy.[7] But as such it could not be "still and contemplative" since it belonged to the "active" part of philosophy that was distinct from the contemplative part. La Primaudaye, like other Renaissance moralists, separated philosophy "into two parts only: into the contemplative part and into the moral, which some call active." A few sentences later, La Primaudaye described this active part as the "art and mistress of life"—a phrase similar to Ferdinand's "living art," but he also expressly associated with this art the rising above fortune "by despising glory and enduring contempt." [8] Ferdinand's confusion of basic philosophic terminology is symptomatic of his ignorance of the goals of both moral philosophy and Christian warfare. In seeking glory through establishing an academy of warriors of the spirit, Ferdinand violates these goals; his lack of self-knowledge threatens to make him lose the labor of love from the very beginning.

The oath-taking ceremony again evokes vividly the warfare convention as Ferdinand charges his courtiers: "If you are arm'd to do as sworn to do, / Subscribe to your deep oaths, and keep it too" (I.i.22–23). The very idea of taking oaths evokes the confirmation ceremony and perhaps also the vow of the Nazarites, which Erasmus held up as exemplary (sig. D8ᵛ). But most important, the rhythm in which the courtiers reaffirm their oaths is reminiscent of the baptismal service with its threefold vows of the godparents as well as of the exhortation-and-response method of the Catechism. Somewhat like children repeating the promise their godparents had given in their steads about fighting the devil and the flesh, Ferdinand's subjects dedicate themselves to their oaths—Berowne, it is true, with some reluctance. First Longaville affirms his resolution for a three-year fast:

> The mind shall banquet, though the body pine.
> Fat paunches have lean pates; and dainty bits
> Make rich the ribs, but bankrupt quite the wits.
>   (25–27)

This variation of the familiar proverb *plenus venter non studet libenter* fits into the warfare convention; in Erasmus's words, "The body waxeth lean, but the mind waxeth fat. The beauty of the skin vanisheth away, but the beauty of the mind appeareth bright" (sig. G4ʳ).

When Dumain adds to this renunciation a touch of humanistic *contemptus vulgi* by throwing "the grosser manner of these world's delights / . . . upon the gross world's baser slaves" (29–30), he agrees quite with Erasmus's demand to forsake the pleasures of the world, to change silver for gold, flint for jewels, and to please the fewer but the better (G3ᵛ). Dumain confidently declares himself "mortified": "To love, to wealth, to pomp, I pine and die, / With all these living in philosophy" (31–32). His "mortification" echoes Paul's orders to the Christian soldier to mortify the body and the affections.[9] In dying to "love, to wealth, to pomp," Dumain seems to answer the minister's question and prayer in the baptismal service: "Dost thou forsake the devil and all his works, the vain pomp and glory of the world . . . ? . . . All carnal affections may die in them [i.e., the children], and . . . all things belonging to the spirit may live and grow in them." In joining those "living in philosophy," Dumain parallels this latter sentiment and also the minister's prayer at baptism that the child, "being dead unto sin and living unto righteousness, . . . may crucify the old man." Ferdinand's courtier vies with him for the prize of all eternity.

Only Berowne has sufficient self-knowledge to realize that "the old man" cannot be so easily mortified. He understands the nature of his affections and of those of man in general, and he knows that

the academy is doomed to failure. In the face of the altitudinal protestations of the others, he plays the advocate of the devil, but he
does so being very much aware of the purposes of philosophy and of
the fine print in the contracts of spiritual warfare. It is almost as if
the devil in Dürer's engraving had come to life and started citing
scripture against the confident, armed knight. First, Berowne interrogates the king about the aim of the studies to which the academicians are pledged and elicits the answer that it is to seek "things hid
and barr'd . . . from common sense" (57). The Elizabethans, like
their teachers the humanists, no enemies of the *sensus communis,*
were accustomed to judge such highly speculative endeavors in the
light of the criticism by activist philosophers like Cicero who objected to those who "devote too much industry and too deep studies
to matters that are obscure and difficult and useless as well." [10]
When Berowne singles out book astronomers, the "continual plotters" and "earthly godfathers of heaven's light," as examples of the
aridity of mere theory, he sides with Cicero and the humanists. Palingenius ridiculed those who "search the secret things" and "headlong
fall, and prove themselves a laughing-stock thereby." [11] Astronomer-
astrologists were natural examples for the foolishness of a study that
searches for things removed from common sense; we surely need
not assume that Berowne aimed a satirical arrow at Sir Walter
Raleigh's astronomer! Berowne's two references to astronomers as
godfathers, who do no more than give names to stars (89, 93), recall
again the baptismal service; and when Berowne says that "Too much
to know is to know nought but fame" (92), that is, nothing but ru-
mors, he needles the king for his glorification of fame, of honor.
Berowne realizes the astral as well as the earthly weaknesses of the
philosophic spirit.

Berowne is, of course, quite the advocate of the devil when he
recommends study of such secret matters as where one may dine or
find where "mistresses from common sense are hid" (61 ff.), but
he has a splendid answer from the pages of spiritual warfare when
the king calls these pursuits "vain delight":

> Why, all delights are vain; but that most vain
> Which, with pain purchas'd, doth inherit pain,
> As painfully to pore upon a book. . . .
>
> (72–74)

Even Palingenius admitted the masochism of scholarship:

> The other part of virtue that doth search with studious pain,
> And, for to know, the causes hid of nature doth obtain,
> And truth to learn that scarce you can at any time come by:
> How hard and full of pain it is, they know that it do try . . .
> By which he many books can make, what good gets he thereby? [12]

Obviously, both Berowne and Palingenius have glanced at Eccles.
12: 12: "there is none end in making many books, and much reading
is a weariness of the flesh." In *The Praise of Folly,* Erasmus had
Stultitia turn this reminder of the vanity of making and reading
books against the scholars as Berowne does; awareness of the ultimate vanity of one's own scholarly effort was the kind of folly that
resembled saintliness.

Berowne, however, becomes quite the sinner when he advocates
supplanting useless book learning by the study of ladies' eyes; yet
the twist in which he equates the pursuit of truth with the pursuit
of love is a clever application of a religious tradition that exalted
heavenly love above study. As Erasmus put it, "Then prepare thyself unto the study of sciences, but no further than thou mayst think
them profitable to good living. . . . It is better to have less knowledge and more of love than to have more knowledge and not to love"
(sig. G6^{r-v}). Berowne, of course, equates "love" with *eros* and not,
like Erasmus, with *caritas*. The interchangeability of the two, to
which the courtly love tradition tended, later serves the courtier as
an ingenious defense for oath-breaking:

> It is religion to be thus forsworn;
> For charity itself fulfils the law,
> And who can sever love from charity?
> (IV.iii.359–61)

In castigating the vanity of book learning, Berowne acclaims the
superiority of love in a humorous conceit which also is evolved
from the warfare convention. It is, he says, in vain for man

> To seek the light of truth; while truth the while
> Doth falsely blind the eyesight of his look.
> Light, seeking light, doth light of light beguile;
> So, ere you find where light in darkness lies,
> Your light grows dark by losing of your eyes.
> Study me how to please the eye indeed,
> By fixing it upon a fairer eye;

Who dazzling so, that eye shall be his heed
And give him light that it was blinded by.
Study is like the heaven's glorious sun,
That will not be deep-search'd with saucy looks.

(I.i.75–85)

The nucleus for this conceit is in *Zodiacus Vitae*. Palingenius said more prosaically than Berowne that, in reading, light beguiles light: "Of many, whilst so much they read, both sight and eyes decay." And like Berowne, he found the light of truth neither in the pages of books nor in the course of the stars:

Like as the owl of night
Can not behold the shining sun with clear and perfect sight,
So fares the mind of man; as oft as it intends to fly
Aloft to search the secret things, falls headlong straight from high.[13]

For Palingenius, however, the sunlight of truth was not reflected in ladies' eyes but in "the inner eye" that saw God with the same spiritual certainty that brightened the eye of Dürer's lonely knight in his ascent through the dark glen. Yet Berowne's ladies' eyes make a nice contrast to the stars of the astronomers, and there was some warrant in the secular Platonism of the Renaissance to search for illumination in the beauty of women. Castiglione's Bembo acknowledged the admiration of feminine beauty as the first step in the stair of love by which the soul ascends until "it seeth in herself a shining beam of that light which is the true image of the angelic beauty partened with her." [14] Berowne's conceit proves so much more ingenious when seen against this background than if it were aimed at an alleged "School of Night," as it has been held to be.

The sensible Berowne knows that his lord's ascetic rules cannot and will not work; the need to accommodate the French ladies that have come on embassy already points up the necessities that will vitiate the courtiers' oaths. As he puts it, slightly twisting a phrase in Nowell's *Catechism,* "Necessity will make us all forsworn / Three thousand times within this three years' space" (147–148).[15] And he backs up this prophecy by what is, I believe, one of the most fundamental tenets of self-knowledge held by Shakespeare: "For every man with his affects is born, / Not by might mast'red, but by special grace" (149–50).

Berowne here espouses the orthodox anti-Stoic position of the

humanists and theologians when he insists that emotions cannot be
completely suppressed. In *Enchiridion,* Erasmus sided in this question with Aristotle and the Peripatetics, who taught that the emotions
were given to man by nature and could not be destroyed, but merely
controlled. Such conventional arguments against the Stoics offer
close parallels to Berowne's argument on necessity; Beroaldus, for
instance, defended the Peripatetics against Cicero's attack in *Tusculan Disputations* (IV.xix.42), asserting with Horace that "nobody
is born without faults" and agreeing with the Peripatetics that the
emotions are implanted in man by providence and necessity.[16] By
attributing the final control of the emotions to "special grace," Berowne echoes the Catechism as well as the literature of self-knowledge
and spiritual warfare.[17]

Thus, clearly, if assurance is needed, Berowne's insight into human
nature does not actually derive from women's eyes—"How well he's
read, to reason against reading!" the king comments appropriately
(94). Berowne can claim that he has said more for barbarism than
the others can say for that "angel knowledge" (113), the reason
being that some of his best arguments use angelic vocabulary. It is
therefore natural for the king and the courtiers to turn to him for an
ideological defense when, defeated by the temptations of the flesh,
they have broken their oaths: "O, some authority how to proceed; /
Some tricks, some quillets, how to cheat the devil!" (IV.iii.283–84).

We are now in a position to see how Shakespeare structured
Love's Labor's Lost on the losing-finding formula and the spiritual
warfare convention, letting the language of the former gradually
slide into the idiom of courtly love. It is on this plan that Shakespeare
related the subplot to the main plot by making it into a scherzo variation of the dominant themes. The fantastic Spaniard, Armado, on
whom the subplot centers, has come to provide "recreation" for the
academicians by relating "in high-born words, the worth of many a
knight / From tawny Spain lost in the world's debate" (I.i.170–71).
But his first contribution to the academy is a literary masterpiece
about a lost soul of a lower kind: his inimitable letter about the
amorous transgressions of the clown Costard, caught with "a child
of our grandmother Eve, a female" in the park (250). Even the
clown, however, knows his enemy in the warfare of life; says Costard: "Such is the simplicity of man to hearken after the flesh"
(212). Amusingly we learn promptly that Costard's accuser, Armado, too has lost himself in the world's debates: he also has fallen

in love with that female, Jaquenetta. In the manner of a *miles glori-osus,* he tries to cover up this lamentable defeat by boasting his prowess: "If drawing my sword against the humour of affection would deliver me from the reprobate thought of it, I would take Desire prisoner, and ransom him to any French courtier for a new-devis'd curtsy" (I.ii.58 ff.). But Armado at least knows that he has succumbed to a mighty enemy: "Love is a familiar; Love is a devil. There is no evil angel but Love." Unlike King Ferdinand, he does not underestimate the strength of the foe; and he rehearses, together with that "tender juvenal," the satirical page Moth, the fates of Her-cules, Samson, and Solomon, famous conquerors conquered by Love, whose "disgrace is to be called boy, but his glory is to subdue men" (176 ff.).

Armado's resistance is from the beginning merely verbal. Shake-speare may well have intended the name "Armado" to highlight the bearer's lack of military prowess and of philosophical resilience. Iron-ically, Armado is the least "armed" of the inhabitants of Navarre. His martial accomplishment is a legend, and he wears, quite literally, an inadequate armor: when Costard challenges him to a wrestling match in shirts, he has to admit that he wears none (V.ii.697)— surely because of poverty rather than for penitence! And how in-gloriously Armado has succumbed to the enemy in his own chest is demonstrated graphically by Jaquenetta's condition at the end of the play. If the name Armado evoked the idea of the Spanish Armada in Shakespeare's audience, as has been suggested, it must have been by way of seeing him as a comic symbol of this fleet's disaster.

Thus the first act has introduced the argument in both main and subplots: the gentlemen of Navarre have foolishly founded an academy and dedicated themselves to it on the basis of ill-understood principles. The astute criticism of Berowne has exposed the weak-nesses of the plan, and the defeats of Costard and Armado by Cupid foreshadow its inevitable failure; the academy has begun to crumble at the edges.

The second act confronts the knights with their temptations, the French maidens, and thus begins the action proper. The girls imme-diately show themselves as formidable adversaries by their intellects as well as their charm. They have much more self-knowledge than the men: the princess' first words in dispraise of beauty contrast favorably with the king's initial glorification of fame. Since the no-woman rule forbids their entrance into court, they must pitch their tents outside. The scene becomes thus quasi-emblematic, contrasting the army of the world's desires with the beleaguered souls of the courtiers. But these do not quite hold to their resolved course like Dürer's constant knight; the end of the act shows that their resolution is breaking down when the ladies' counselor, Boyet, notices in Navarre's eyes the gleam not of philosophy but of love.

The suspiration of Armado, with which the third act opens, is the overture to the utter defeat and confusion of the philosophic army. Berowne, never a wholehearted combatant, is the first to defect, confessing his overthrow by "Dan Cupid," the boy over whom he was erstwhile a "domineering pedant." The former soldier of philosophy has become a "corporal" in Cupid's army; he has signed up in service of "a whitely wanton with a velvet brow, / With two pitch balls stuck in her face for eyes" (III.i.186–87). Since Berowne's love letter gets crossed with Armado's, these two defectors are uncovered in the following act.

The fourth act increases the perturbations by the lamentable rout of the philosophers and the revelation of the sad state of their auxiliary forces. The act opens with a report of the king's spurring his horse against the rising hill—an attempt, it appears, to sublimate his rising affections. The maidens in turn practice archery, an appropriate occupation for an army ordained by Cupid to battle philosophers. The girls' half-serious, half-bantering conversation on salvation by merit or mercy, a subject important for spiritual warfare, shows them better equipped than the courtiers. Unlike shrewish wives, whose desire to win glory over their husbands the maidens deride, and thus also unlike the courtiers, these amazons fight not for fame.

Armado is appropriately the first whose defection is revealed as the ladies receive his miscarried letter to Jaquenetta. His quixotic genius compares his attraction to her with King Cophetua's to the beggar maid; but not even his Caesarian boast of "veni, vidi, vici" nor his poetic roaring in the vein of the Nemean lion can make this defeat into the victory he claims it is. The parallel disaster of the philosophers is delayed by a scene devoted to the intellectual extravaganzas of the pedant, Holofernes, and the curate, Sir Nathaniel, literary and spiritual advisers of the academy. Although their professions should have conditioned them to know themselves, they are in their own ways subject to the weakness of the flesh that debilitates the spirit. Holofernes, in magisterial presumption, poses as a judge of good Latin and poetic taste; but in misquoting the beginning of an eclogue by the familiar grammar-school author "good old Mantuan," he shows his Achilles' heel.[18] And Sir Nathaniel falls prey to arrogance when he dissects the ignorance of Dull and claims for himself and Holofernes superior sense and feeling (IV.ii.22). Exhorting the spiritual warrior to know himself, Erasmus warned against such "swelling of the mind" and recommended that he use the reverse procedure by comparing himself with those who excel him and make him look like a complete ignoramus (sig. S2ʳ). If Nathaniel and Holofernes have no talent for humility, neither do they for fasting: both are strongly attracted to the pleasures of dining, a most notable weakness of the flesh that the academicians would like to eliminate.

Before any actual combat between the courtiers and the ladies takes place, the former defect from philosophy's army. In the climactic scene of the play (IV.iii), the king, Longaville, and Dumain enter successively, declaim their love sonnets, accuse each other of betrayal, and are promptly exposed to ridicule by the discovery of their own treason. They are now truly lost. Confused as they are, they seek to endow their passion with the sublimity of their former aspiration. Longaville's syncretism is in this respect the most ludicrous when he argues that his earlier oath against women really did not apply to the lady of his present affection, who is a goddess: "My vow was earthly, thou a heavenly love; / Thy grace being gain'd cures all disgrace in me" (IV.iii.62–63). The argument sounds like a travesty of Erasmus's injunction to compare "the two Venuses and two Cupids of Plato, that is to say, honest love and filthy love, holy pleasure and unclean pastime; compare together the unlike matter of either other" (sig. Kʳ). Berowne comments appropriately that Longaville's sonnet is in "the liver-vein, which makes flesh a deity, / A green goose a goddess—pure, pure idolatry" (70–71). However, Longaville, who is blind to his own aberration, clearly sees his friend's: "Dumain, thy love is far from charity" (123).

The fusion and confusion of love and charity provides for scintillating wit as the renegade soldiers of philosophy repeat with only slight variations their earlier vows of service. But, alas, they carry now the frivolous banner of Cupid! In more serious times, they decried the darkness of ignorance and sought the light of truth. Now they quarrel merely on whether dark- or light-complexioned ladies are preferable. It is in this context that the king utters his much-commented-upon denigration of Berowne's Rosaline: "O paradox! Black is the badge of hell, / The hue of dungeons, and the school of

night" (250–51).[19] Berowne, forced to defend his love, reminds the
king of temptation—not, as formerly, by the flesh and the devil but
—by light-complexioned ladies like the princess: "Devils soonest
tempt, resembling spirits of light" (253). The allusion is to 2 Cor.
11:14, which Erasmus also used as a warning.

The quandary of the courtiers is that the demands of their natures
prevent them from keeping their oaths. "As true we are," says
Berowne, "as flesh and blood can be" (211), recalling Eph. 6:12,
one of the passages of spiritual warfare ("for we wrestle not against
flesh and blood . . ."). And, evoking the humor of blood, whose
heating-up in the liver was thought to engender appetite, Berowne
continues: "Young blood doth not obey an old decree. / We cannot
cross the cause why we were born" (213–14).[20] Erasmus might even
have agreed to this statement since he warned in *Enchiridion* against
striving "with God and things more mighty than thou," and recommended to every man "that thou oughtst to abstain from such studies
as nature abhorreth, and that thou shouldst set thy mind unto these
things—if they be honest—whereunto thou art most apt naturally"
(sig. H6ᵛ–H7ʳ).

It is at this point that the others demand from Berowne "some
authority how to proceed," and he comes forward with his ingenious
"tricks and quillets" to cheat the devil. Berowne understands how to
adapt the articles of self-knowledge to the new situation. As in his
earlier objections to the rules of the academy, he draws on the
spiritual warfare convention, applying it to that very different one of
the war of the sexes. He begins with a line that reminds one of the
king's initial battle address to his spiritual warriors: "Have at you,
then, affection's men-at-arms." (IV.iii.286). He goes on to repeat
his earlier criticism of the rules of the academy—to fast, to study, and
to see no women: such rules are treason against the "kingly state of
youth," and they make true learning impossible.

> For when would you, my lord, or you, or you,
> Have found the ground of study's excellence
> Without the beauty of a woman's face?
> From women's eyes this doctrine I derive:
> They are the ground, the books, the academes,
> From whence doth spring the true Promethean fire.
>   (295–300) [21]

Love, says Berowne, contrasting it with the slow labors of book learning,

> Lives not alone immured in the brain,
> But with the motion of all elements
> Courses as swift as thought in every power,
> And gives to every power a double power,
> Above their functions and their offices.
>
> (324–28)

Berowne's opposition between "leaden contemplation" and the invigorating speed of love resembles Erasmus's contrast in the fourteenth chapter of *Enchiridion* between the absorption in the visible—that is, rules and empty rituals including merely mechanical obedience to monastic rules, such as fasting—and the devotion to the invisible, to love. Erasmus admonished man not to be bound to the earth by unnecessary and aggravating labors, but to lift himself up, "always sustained with those wings which Plato believeth to spring ever fresh through the heat of love in the mind of men." He who does ascends "from the body to the spirit, from the visible world unto the invisible, from the letter to the mystery, from things sensible to things intelligible, from things gross and compound unto things single and pure" (sigs. L4ᵛ–L5ʳ). Erasmus borrowed this image from the winged flight of the soul in Plato's *Phaedrus,* an image that served both theologians and idealizers of love. Berowne's particular application of this idea to love, racing "with the motion of all elements," traces back to ancient theories on the nature of the soul as being fire and air, carried by their lightness to higher regions.[22] Berowne illustrates this power of love by a metaphor that may have been stimulated by Erasmus: "It [i.e., love] adds a precious seeing to the eye: / A lover's eyes will gaze an eagle blind" (229–30). Erasmus attributes to love, that is, to holy love, the same vision: "If it were so that thou hadst eyes much sharper of sight than hath a beast called lynx or much clearer than hath the eagle, yet with these eyes, in the most clearest light that could be, couldst thou not behold more surely that thing which a man doth before thee than all the privy and secret parts of the mind be open unto the sight of God and his angels" (sig. Rʳ).

Yet in spite of Berowne's ingenuity, the courtiers have not won a battle but lost one, and they have not really found themselves but incurred new self-loss—one undoubtedly less perilous than their immature asceticism, but a self-loss nevertheless, romantic love. Even more seriously, they have broken oaths. Shakespeare therefore saw to it that their self-loss is not remedied by the easy means in which it usually is in the comedies, that is, by quick marriage. First, the men of Navarre are subjected to indignities; they who ingloriously left Holy Philosophy for Saint Cupid prove to be no more successful under their new banner than they were under the old. At the beginning of the last act they are routed by the ladies, who easily outdo them in wit encounters. The ladies now refuse to take the love vows any more seriously than they took the philosophic oaths. The subplot mirrors the courtiers' disaster when the pageant of the Nine Worthies turns into a lamentable spectacle of great men conquered.

But considering the seriousness of the courtiers' offense, Shakespeare evidently thought even these debacles not enough of a lesson. He introduced what I think is a brilliant ending, regardless of whether it was his original plan or, as is possible, an afterthought. The ending once more evokes the "scythe's keen edge" of death, against which Ferdinand had sought to erect his academy, forgetting that self-knowledge included a realization that there is no such stronghold. The news of the death of the princess' father makes all merrymaking impossible. Yet, ironically, this very change of conditions also brings about the solution to the courtiers' dilemma and, for that matter, to that posed by the action of the play. The period of mourning is ingeniously used to furnish the period of expiation for the courtiers. The ladies, who have proved conquerors in the battle against the stormy affections of their suitors, wisely decide that self-knowledge decrees they too must obey the law of necessity: they will marry the knights after a year if these are still inclined to matrimony. But appropriately, the knights must do penance by obeying the laws of the spirit they have violated, although the penitential period of one year is more reasonable than the three-year term they had pledged themselves to live ascetically. The knights, who have lost themselves, have, after all, a chance to reach the castle that towers above the dark glen of Dürer's knight. As Erasmus said, "The only way therefore to felicity is first that thou know thyself." But the path is not easy: "Nothing is more hard than that a man should overcome himself; but then is there no greater reward than is felicity" (sig. D7ᵛ).

For Berowne, whom we have come to like so well, the path may seem to us unduly arduous. But his imposed task of entertaining the sick in a hospital is in keeping with his trespass. Although Shakespeare used Berowne partly to comment on the difficulty of trying to master the "affects" with which every man is born, he made him also an example of the need to do so; the merry-madcap courtier, who took the oath against his better knowledge and became the equally lighthearted apologist of love madness, must swear off the taffeta phrases and spruce affectation in which he so delighted. He will have to cheer the sick rather than confound the healthy by paradoxes. There is poetic justice in the special penitence imposed on the king, head of the bankrupt academy, who must live in a hermitage to cure his mind through his soul. And equally appropriate is Armado's voluntary penitence in which he gives up his pseudosophistication in favor of holding the plow to sustain Jaquenetta and her expected offspring. All who have lost themselves are given a chance to find themselves properly.

Thus we can see that even in one of his gayest comedies Shakespeare was concerned with the problem of self-culture. The central theme of *Love's Labor's Lost* is the quest for the self, a quest in which man, with the best of intentions, can go astray. Every man is born with his passions and must in some way control them or risk being lost forever. One cannot simply rule them out; nature will take its revenge. Yet dangerous as they are, they are part of the glory of being human. We delight in the courtiers' losing themselves in love; it springs naturally from their hearts and justly wins out over the merely brain-conceived devotion to study. The ideal of conduct, however, does not lie in permanent abandonment to this most delightful of self-losses, but in a balanced, antipedantic, and humanistic way of life. It is a path that Berowne sees clearly even if the warm blood of his youth makes it difficult for him to walk it steadily. But *Love's Labor's Lost* is not a problem play or a tragedy. We never really fear that the knights of Navarre will lose themselves so thoroughly as to make recovery questionable or impossible. Their asceticism, ostentatious as it is, is a temporary aberration and not the unnatural and deeply ingrained suppression of human desires of an Angelo in *Measure for Measure*, and their self-abandonment in love is only a brief interlude and not the all-embracing and destructive passion of an Othello.

Although *Love's Labor's Lost* is not a disturbing play, it does show that the man who wishes to know himself has difficult choices to make and threatening dangers to face. The more formidable man's temptation, the harder his struggle through the valley of life; and the less grace available to him, the more likely is his failure. The action of *Love's Labor's Lost* at least implies that a man may lose himself so thoroughly as to make full recovery impossible. And this is the fate of Richard II, about whom Shakespeare wrote a tragedy not too long after his gay comedy. Shakespeare's tragic heroes, different as their individual features are from those of the courtiers of Navarre, have yet a recognizable kinship with them; these heroes too are possessed of a human nature that is tempted by the world, the flesh, and the devil. They fall, of course, more deeply; and their suffering is excruciating, their defeat irredeemable. Their self-search is not granted success; they cannot escape the scythe's keen edge of death. The predicament of the heroes of Shakespeare's later tragedies is the more painful because not only are they in a darker valley—this is true for Richard—but the region above it also is shrouded in mist or darkness.

CHAPTER SIX

Richard II:
Looking into the Mirror of Grief

O F ALL SHAKESPEARE'S earlier tragedies and histories, *Richard II* has the most interesting and, for Shakespeare's dramatic progress, most significant patterns of self-knowledge. The themes of losing and finding and of the search for the self are focused on a hero who shows a most conspicuous lack of self-knowledge, but who also elicits our tragic sympathy as no other hero does whom Shakespeare created before him.

When, probably in 1594 or 1595, Shakespeare decided to write a play about the reign of Richard II, he may have been drawn to this subject because he wished to depict the source of the troubles he had dramatized in the Henry VI plays. He also may have thought the forced abdication of Richard II and the usurpation of the throne by Henry Bolingbroke topical because of the Elizabethans' interest in, and anxiety about, succession.[1] But if Shakespeare was induced to write a play about the fall of Richard because of its political relevance, he underplayed this aspect when he actually came to write the play. Whether considerations of political prudence persuaded him to concentrate on the human side of the conflict rather than on the clash of forces or whether he was stimulated by the pathos of the tortured king in Marlowe's *Edward II,* he poured his poetic and dramatic powers into depicting the suffering of Richard. The weak king, who falls and suffers, is in the front of the stage; the strong man, who rises and conquers, is hardly more than a background figure, generally doing only what the occasion requires.

To acclaim this reticence in word and action as the master strategy of a Machiavellian schemer is to deny the requirements of the stage, particularly of the Elizabethan stage, according to which characters live by what they do, say about themselves, and what others say about them, not by what they fail to do and say, and what others fail to say about them. The interest of *Richard II* certainly does not derive from seeing Bolingbroke outmaneuver Richard because, as has often been said, Richard really defeats himself. In a sense, Bolingbroke is not only Richard's conqueror but also his victim, as is England in general. Bolingbroke too suffers from the grief that Richard inflicts on his country and comes to feel, most of all, himself. Bolingbroke loses his legacy and is banished; he returns indeed to become king, but as such, he inherits fear of rebellion and, in the end, is left with sorrow and remorse.

The early quartos and Francis Meres called *Richard II* (as well as other history plays) a tragedy, and the play has a better claim to the title as we have come to apply it by abstraction from Shakespeare's later tragedies than any other of his early dramas. *Richard II* focuses on one passion, grief, and makes it the prime mover of tragic sympathy. Some characters, such as the Duchess of Gloucester, Gaunt, and Richard's queen, Isabel, have the primary function of showing the grief that comes to all, first to the victims of Richard's misrule, then to his family and adherents. Grief imagery penetrates the play, and the passion itself is constantly varied with fear and contrasted with joy and hope; no play of Shakespeare offers better illustration for his use of these four primary passions.[2]

Lack of self-knowledge and intemperance are the roots of Richard's tragedy just as they are of Tarquin's in *Lucrece,* and the subject matter of the history play would have lent itself to a treatment very similar to that which Shakespeare accorded to the passion and disgrace of Tarquin. Shakespeare's sources presented a king who did not know himself, or, as Holinshed had it, who "forgot himself and began to rule by will more than by reason, threatening death to each one that obeyed not his inordinate desires."[3] Shakespeare did not altogether deny this Richard; his guilt in the murder of his great-uncle, Woodstock, is alluded to in the second scene and throws a shadow over his seemingly impartial effort to make peace between Mowbray and Bolingbroke. We also learn in the protasis of the play that Richard is "not himself, but basely led / By flatterers" (II.i.241–42); yet the Richard we remember most is that of epitasis and catastrophe: the man intemperate in grief, who loses himself in paroxysms of lament; the extraordinary sufferer, who knows the hollowness of the crown but cannot live a mere man; the poet of pain, who in his deepest humiliation yet gains an inkling of the common condition of man, a glimmer of tragic self-knowledge. Richard is not merely an exemplum of a bad ruler; he is also a man who comes, even if too late, to seek himself.

In making Richard into this kind of character, Shakespeare could build on some hints in his sources, which depicted Richard's tragedy as a *de casibus* story, a fall from a high place in the manner of the examples in the *Mirror for Magistrates,* and which showed some sympathy to him.[4] Said Holinshed:

> This surely is a very notable example and not unworthy of all princes to be well weighed and diligently marked that this Henry, Duke of Lancaster, should thus be called to a kingdom and have the help and assistance almost of all the whole realm, which perchance never thereof thought or yet dreamed, and that King Richard should thus be left desolate, void, and in despair of all hope and comfort, in whom, if there be any offence, it ought rather to be imputed to the frailty of wanton youth than to the malice of his heart.[5]

At first Richard sees himself exclusively in the light of a victim of fortune's wheel; only very slowly does he accept the moral of the *specula principis* that kings must be virtuous or they may be punished, even deposed, by the vengeance of God. Richard sees his fall almost to the very end as primarily a *de casibus* tragedy, but we understand it from the beginning as a tragedy of character.

For creating as sorrowful a king as he did, Shakespeare had little precedent. Holinshed recorded only that Richard, returning from Ireland and advised of Bolingbroke's progress, "became so greatly discomforted that, sorrowfully lamenting his miserable state, he utterly despaired of his own safety and, calling his army together, which was not small, licensed every man to depart to his home." [6] The passage must have struck Shakespeare's eye by the marginal gloss: "K. Richard in utter despair." Shakespeare made, at any rate, this incident into the apex of Richard's emotional curve: up to this point he is a carefree youth; after it, he is a care-worn sufferer.

This is not to say that there are two Richards as there are two Edwards in Marlowe's *Edward II,* from which Shakespeare appears to have learned both positively and negatively. Marlowe's Edward is at first a pitiful, lascivious, and cruel boy, willing to hand over his kingdom, lock, stock, and barrel, to the patently immoral Gaveston; later, Edward is a suffering, tortured victim of his wife's and Mortimer's cruelties. The earlier Richard never sinks as deeply as the earlier Edward, and the later Richard is still recognizably the same

man as the earlier one. Richard before his fall is insolent and insouci-
ant; he is callous to the exhortations of Gaunt and York; he is irre-
sponsible, to say the least, in confiscating Gaunt's property. On the
whole, however, he is a somewhat better man than Holinshed's
Richard; he threatens no death to others; he does not manifest his
addiction to pleasure or to lust so patently as to lose our sympathy.
He wears his crown with just enough dignity to make his later consciousness of its halo believable and pitiable.[7]

Essentially, the predicaments of Marlowe's and Shakespeare's
kings are alike: they both suffer for their human inadequacies, and
they suffer from their inability to separate the injuries done to them
from the indignities inflicted on the crown. Like Edward, Richard
is ignorant of the meaning of the injunction "know thyself" as Sir
Thomas Elyot applied it to the man of authority:

> If thou be a governor, or hast over other sovereignty, know thyself,
> that is to say, know that thou art verily a man compact of soul and
> body and that all other men be equal unto thee. Also that every man
> taketh with thee equal benefit of the spirit of life, nor hast thou any
> more of the dew of heaven or the brightness of the sun than any
> other person. Thy dignity or authority wherein thou differest from
> other is, as it were, but a weighty or heavy cloak, freshly glittering
> in the eyes of them that be purblind, where unto thee it is painful
> if thou wear him in his right fashion and as it shall best become
> thee.[8]

As a king, Richard wears the robe of authority too lightly even if
he does not wear it as unbecomingly as Edward; he never dreams
that it can be taken away, as Elyot warned, if used negligently. Gaunt
calls him "possess'd . . . to depose thyself" (II.i.108). And York
despairingly comments on his rash confiscation of Gaunt's property:
"Be not thyself—for how art thou a king / But by fair sequence and
succession?" (II.i.198–99).

Although Richard is unaware of the heaviness of his robe, he is
dazzled by its glitter. He is obsessed with his "preeminence," with
his privileged place in the hierarchy of being and with the symbolism
of his divine stewardship, but he neglects to balance this awareness
with a just understanding of his duties. In adversity, he intoxicates
himself with vain hopes and illusions, such as that the native stones
will prove soldiers on his side and that God will provide a glorious angel to make up for each of Bolingbroke's followers. There is
something extravagantly un-English about his imagination—possibly

Shakespeare thought of a remark of Holinshed's that Richard took pleasure in being addressed by one of his followers in the fashion of an oriental potentate. At any rate, his consciousness of his halo before and after the deposition transcends the conventional belief in the divinity of kings.

Although the earlier and the later Richard are recognizably the same man, Richard does change under the impact of suffering, and I believe that Shakespeare conceived this change as being accompanied by an alteration of humor. From reading Holinshed, he must have thought of the earlier Richard as of the sanguine complexion that turned into melancholy of the kind physicians thought to have come about by "adustion," that is, burning of the original humor. This melancholy was considered most serious, leading sometimes to madness and self-destruction.[9] Holinshed's characterization of the young Richard contained features that the Elizabethans would have ascribed to the sanguine disposition, such as wantonness, extravagance in entertainment and clothes, general good nature, and seemliness in shape and favor. The Richard of the beginning of the play shares with Holinshed's some general characteristics of the sanguine temperament as in *The Touchstone of Complexions* (1581) Levinus Lemnius described them: men of this type, Lemnius said, are easily drawn to folly and pursue what is worst; given to sensual fantasies, they are unconcerned about the state of their country; as rulers, they are subject to the influence of evil advisers. The sanguine humor was thought to afflict particularly the young; Lemnius compared the sanguine youths to calves that in spring "skip and leap up and down," [10] a phrase that recalls Bolingbroke's later speaking of Richard as "the skipping King, he ambled up and down" (*1 Henry IV*, III.ii.60). Lemnius's description of sanguine men as smooth-skinned, of ruddy or purple color, is paralleled in the Queen's characterization of Richard as a fair rose (V.i.8) and in Bolingbroke's as "a happy gentleman in blood and lineaments" until "unhappied and disfigured" by his followers (III.i.8 ff.). Shakespeare's Richard resembles the men of this humor who, as Lemnius said, although pleasant in company, know no measure in their affections. It is probably sentimentality rather than political strategy that makes him remit four years of banishment from Bolingbroke's sentence. He claims to be affected by the tears in Gaunt's eyes (I.iii.208), and I see no reason why this explanation (invented by Shakespeare) should be taken as hypocritical. But sentimentality is a different matter from goodness, and, among his favorites, Richard can be quite callous about Gaunt's plight (I.iv.59–60). His almost clinical interest in watching the display of emotions shows itself also in the curiosity with which, on this occasion, he inquires "what store of parting tears were shed" at Bolingbroke's leave-taking (I.iv.5 ff.). Richard remains an observer of the effect of grief on others even when it is his own grief that creates this effect: "thou weep'st, my tender-hearted cousin," he says to Aumerle at Flint Castle (III.iii.160). Melancholy, as Lemnius said, retains some traits of the faculty and nature from which it came; [11] the melancholic emoting of Richard evolves believably from that in his sanguine period.

The transition occurs at Richard's landing (III.ii) when he "weeps for joy" and "weeping-smiling" greets his native earth, and when, overwhelmed by messages of misfortune, he alternates violently between despair and hope. As Lemnius explained, such ups and downs are natural in the transition to melancholy, a humor that is not without heat: "And hereupon, in a manner all in one instant and without any time betwixt, do we see them suddenly changed from laughter and mirth into sorrow and pensiveness." [12] Richard's outward and inward change is repeatedly emphasized. One such instance is when, with his characteristic interest in his own grief, he studies the "external manner of laments" in his face during the mirror scene (IV.i.296). Another instance is the parting scene, when the Queen finds him "both in shape and mind / Transform'd and weak'ned" (V.i.26–27). In the series of house-grave images, which precedes this observation, Isabel calls him "the model where all Troy did stand," a "map of honor," "King Richard's tomb," and a "beauteous inn" in which now grief is lodged. Interestingly, Lemnius illustrated his argument that one can still discern the former state of a body that has suffered alteration by grief by a very similar comparison to "great, huge, and sumptuous houses, being fallen down and decayed, [which] show evidently . . . of what hugeness and magnificence they erst were, how curious and busy the frame was, how skillful and industrious the architect and workman was." [13]

In conceiving Richard as a victim of melancholy, Shakespeare appears to have had two purposes in mind. First of all, the symptoms of the humor as the physicians described them—such as doubt, diffidence, distrust, morbid ruminations, indulgence in monstrous fictions, solitariness, weeping, sighing, and quick changes from indolence to mental activity—made Richard a dramatically interesting character.[14]

But, more importantly, melancholy meant a concern with the earth, from which it was thought to arise, with dust, graves, worms, and death—in a word, with the *contemptus mundi,* and thus with the estate of man; "Melancholy," said Sir James Perrott, "is fittest for consideration." [15] Shakespeare's use of the *contemptus mundi* convention gave him an opportunity to endow Richard with an overpowering rhetoric that displays his vanity but also brings with it an ingredient of self-knowledge.

Richard's first long lament strikes the characteristic note (III.ii. 144 ff.). At the moment of danger, he loses his head; informed of the execution of Bushy, Green, and the Earl of Wiltshire, he rejects all comfort and wishes to talk only "of graves, of worms, and epitaphs." Nothing, he says,

> can we call our own but death
> And that small model of the barren earth
> Which serves as paste and cover to our bones.
> (III.ii.152–54)

Richard's subject is, in terms of the title of the second chapter of the Elizabethan translation of Pope Innocent's *De Humane Miseriae Conditione,* "The Vile and Base Matter Whereof Man is Made." It is a substance that determines his composition and his decay: "I am compared, saith holy Job, to clay and likened to embers and ashes. Clay is made of water and dust, both of them remaining, but ashes are made of wood and fire, both of them consuming and decaying." [16] Innocent's reference to Job points to the biblical associations of Richard's speech: the ground to which Richard wishes to bequeath his deposed body is Job's "slimy valley" (xxi.33), the "water and dust" of Innocent, or as Richard has it, the "paste and cover to our bones." [17] The Genevan side-note made the figure an appropriate reminder for royalty: "He shall be glad to lie in a slimy pit, which before could not be content with a royal palace." Richard's figure of the "model of the barren earth" recalls Job's elsewhere (iii.14) expressed desire to sleep and be "at rest with the kings and councilors of the earth, which have built themselves desolate places" ("barren places" in the variation of the Genevan side-note, which comes closer to Richard's words).

Richard sees himself as the epitome of "sad stories of the death of kings" that, *de casibus* fashion, he invites himself and others to tell, sitting upon the ground; he comes to the conclusion that the crown of a king is a hollow crown, in which death keeps his court. The similarity of this idea to Holbein's woodcuts of death, particularly to the one depicting the dying Emperor Maximilian, has been noted often: [18] a grinning Death, resembling Richard's "antic," his skeleton upreared behind Holbein's enthroned emperor, reaches for the crown. But Maximilian, unlike Richard, has not resigned himself to crying woe, death, destruction, and despair; although his sword is broken and his eyes are closing, he still metes out justice, turning severely toward the proud oppressor on the right and protecting the poor supplicant on the left: the Emperor, not Death, keeps his court. Richard's antic, who allows the king "a little scene, / To monarchize, be fear'd, and kill with looks" (164–65) recalls the commonplace that the world is a stage, which fits into the *contemptus mundi*,[19] but it is impossible not to associate the figure also with Richard's histrionics; his "self and vain conceit" (166) is infused into the image. And so it is when Richard takes up the equalitarian strains of *contemptus mundi* and of *consideratio*. Chelidonius wished princes to "consider the common beginning of all, the first matter whereof we are made and how we be all continued of like elements, bought with one blood, . . . nourished and fed all with like sacraments." [20] But Richard, who says more vividly that "I live with bread like you, feel want, / Taste grief, need friends" (175 ff.), does not really believe with Chelidonius that the consideration of his mortal body shows that "there is no difference between the vilest creatures of the earth" and himself; when he asks his followers to "throw away respect, / Tradition, form, and ceremonious duty," it is in a plaintive tone that highlights his perplexity about what he and the world have come to.[21]

There is a similar mixture of true grief and "self and vain conceit" in Richard's confrontation with Bolingbroke at Flint Castle. Desolate and bereft of friends, Richard takes consolation in the extravagant hope that the wrath of God, which the *contemptus mundi* predicted for sinful mankind, will avenge the injustice done to Richard; God "is mustering in his clouds on our behalf / Armies of pestilence" (III.iii.85 ff.). And when Richard appears to turn inward by offering to exchange his position with that of a hermit, he spoils the appeal to our sympathy with the theatrical effect of the idea of exchanging England with "a little little grave, an obscure grave—" an effect increased by the suggestion that he be buried "in the king's highway" (154 ff.). One looks here in vain for a recognition of his own responsibility for his fall. There are, at most, occasional dim realizations of his insufficiency, as when, descending to the "base court"—the punning adds a histrionic accent to the symbolic moment —he compares himself with "glist'ring Phaeton, / Wanting the manage of unruly jades" (178–79); it was Phaeton's presumption that made him want to drive his father's chariot, and it was his incompetence, not any particular unruliness of the horses, that brought him too close to the sun. Like Richard, Phaeton was responsible for his own disaster.

The abdication scene, the *summa epitasis* of the play, brings not only a significant turn of events but also an important stage in Richard's growth toward self-awareness. But if one may speak here of *anagnorisis,* it is in a sense different from Aristotle's; Richard's recognition is not really a "change from ignorance to knowledge." Hardly more than some glimmers of self-knowledge shine through Richard's display of vanity. Just before the symbolic transfer of the crown, Richard achieves a culmination in self-aggrandizement when he likens himself to Christ and degrades his enemies into Judases (IV.i.168 ff.). His public "undoing" of himself still betrays how deeply he "drinks" his griefs; it is a rhetorical showpiece with puns, antitheses, and anaphora, and even his announcement that he must "nothing be" is as much an appeal to the spectators' emotions as resignation; his feeling for the nothingness of man is overshadowed by the feeling of his nothingness due to deprivation from kingship (216 ff.). When Northumberland tries to force him to read the accusations against him and to confess to their truth, his eyes fill with tears; he cannot see, and he looks inward to find himself a "traitor with the rest" (245 ff.). He feels a total loss of identity and knows "not now what name to call myself" (259).

This, the moment of Richard's greatest self-loss, produces his first confrontation with the truth, which is given symbolic emphasis in the mirror scene. The idea is imaginatively prepared for earlier in the play by glass or mirror images symbolic of grief. Thus in his days of happy kingship, Richard read grief in the "glasses" of Gaunt's eyes. And when Bushy attempted to console Queen Isabel, he compared the view of sorrow's eyes to perspective glasses that "rightly gaz'd upon, / Show nothing but confusion—ey'd awry, / Distinguish form" (II.ii.14 ff.). In looking into the mirror during the abdication scene, Richard for the first time distinguishes form.

In this scene, Shakespeare availed himself of the multifaceted symbolism of the mirror. It was, first of all, the emblem of vanity and self-love, often associated in Shakespeare's time, as now, with femininity. The moralists sought to combat the allurement of the mirror with ethical considerations. One of the sayings in *Disticha Catonis,* the collection Shakespeare had in grammar school, recommended that man contemplate himself in the mirror and, if he appeared handsome, act in a way that expressed this *forma.* If he appeared ugly (*deformus*), he was asked to compensate for the lack of facial beauty by good manners.[22] The mirror was thus a medium for *vanitas* as well as *veritas,* as the Elizabethans often were reminded. In Diego de Estella's *De Contemptu Mundi,* translated by Thomas Rogers (1586), the Christian was told, "if thou have a desire to know who thou art, take a glass and behold thyself in it. . . . And that thou mayst not be deceived, behold not thyself in a glass that is hollow, which maketh a show of the thing represented therein clean contrary to that which it is indeed, but take unto thee a glass that is plain, which setteth out man according as he is in truth." The hollow glass, Estella said, is the glass of life; it makes men look lusty and strong; but it is a glass of vanity and lies; the true glass is the glass of death, which shows man his sinfulness and mortality.[23] The mirror of self-knowledge thus became the mirror of death. As Sir John Davies said, "Then she [the soul] which hath been hoodwinked from her birth, / Doth first herself within Death's mirror see." [24]

Richard's gaze into the mirror reveals all these symbolic facets. When he wishes to look into it rather than read the articles of abdication, he desires to study "the very book indeed / Where all my sins are writ, and that's myself" (IV.i.274–75).[25] It is the first mentioning of his sins—the mirror is to reflect Richard's "true" image. But a narcissistic self-fascination interferes momentarily; he sees a "brittle glory" in the face and wonders why it has not become deformed. Yet Richard's grief is too great to make him accept the image in the "flatt'ring glass"; the discrepancy between appearance and reality, between the outside of grief and its substance angers him, and he smashes the deceptive glass, quipping that his sorrow has destroyed his face—his face in the mirror, that is. Bolingbroke emends: "The shadow of your sorrow hath destroy'd / The shadow of your face" (292–93). Richard retorts that he is no longer interested in the outside look, in the "external manner of laments," which are "merely shadows to the unseen grief / That swells with silence in the tortur'd soul" (294–98). But even at this moment of inward turn, Richard cannot resist the temptation of displaying his vanity; he "thanks" Bolingbroke for not only giving him cause to wail but also for "teaching" him to lament his cause (300–302). Whether Richard here actually finds the refinement of his rhetoric by his adversary worthy of imitation or, more likely, is piqued by being upstaged even momentarily, Richard's interest in self-expression wins out over his desire for self-knowledge. The mirror of truth turns into a mirror of flattery.

Richard cannot help dramatizing himself even in that scene of intense pathos when he takes leave of his queen. One may read repentance into his exhortation to her and to himself that "Our holy lives must win a new world's crown" (V.i.24); but he is as much as ever intent on audience effect when he asks her to tell others after his death the lamentable tale of his misfortune "and send the hearers weeping to their beds" (45).

Only once before his death does Richard immerse himself in self-consideration without such side-interest in the effect of grief: in his long soliloquy that compares his prison at Pomfret Castle to the world (V.v.1 ff.). The speech begins as an exercise in self-delusion and ends in near-maddening grief, but in the process Richard penetrates to some understanding of his condition as a man and a king.

Richard's soliloquy hinges on concepts of body and soul and forms in this respect a climax to this *nosce teipsum* imagery prominent in the play. In the earlier acts, the images are associated primarily with grief and suffering, but also with the notion that in this experience lies a way to truth. As Bolingbroke accuses Mowbray of the treason that has its source in the king himself, he promises that "My body shall make good [the challenge] upon this earth, / Or my divine soul answer it in heaven" (I.i.37–38). When the king prevents the duel, Bolingbroke regrets that the issue cannot be settled; if it had been, either his or Mowbray's soul would have "wand'red in the air, / Banish'd this frail sepulchre of our flesh" (I.iii.195–96). The imagery becomes associated with Richard's party when the queen agonizes in his absence and finds her apprehensions confirmed; as her soul has "brought forth her prodigy," she feels like a new-delivered mother that has joined woe to woe and sorrow to sorrow (II.ii.64 ff.). From the time of the king's return, the body and soul images characterize his own attitudes and are either used by him or refer to him. "All souls that will be safe, fly from my side," he says at the first moment of danger as he abandons all hope and begins to talk of graves and the decomposition of the body (III.ii.80). But this morbid preoccupation demonstrates also that he understands now that kings are made of the same clay as other men. He realizes the vanity of the belief that "this flesh which walls about our life / Were brass impregnable," when a little pin can bore through this "castle wall" (166 ff.). The house-grave imagery the queen applies to his grief-wasted body at their parting adds further pathos to his own ruminations on the fact of human impermanence.

Richard's last long speech at Pomfret Castle gathers this imagery into a magnificent finale. His first sentence, "I have been studying how I may compare / This prison where I live unto the world" (V.v.1–2), strikes a characteristic *contemptus mundi* note. Pope Innocent's tract devoted a chapter to "The Lamentation of the Soul Being in Prison," [26] which took its cue from the cry of the penitent sinner of Psalm 142, "bring my soul out of prison," the latter being interpreted as the body. When Richard despairs of being able to compare his prison to the world because "the world is populous / And here is not a creature but myself," he laments his loneliness much like the Psalmist: "I looked also upon my right hand and saw there was no man that would know me." Richard's fantastic remedy of populating his prison world by begetting "a generation of still-breeding thoughts" recalls the queen's earlier conception of melancholy, the "unborn sorrow, ripe in fortune's womb" she felt coming toward her trembling soul (II.ii.10). And as much as the queen brings forth a "prodigy," Richard's mental issue is unnatural. His plan for engendering thoughts analogous to the people of his kingdom is to make his brain "the female to my soul, / My soul the father" (6–7). But there is disharmony in the kingdom of man, said John Woolton, when "notices or seeds and, as it were, sparks of knowledge . . . are together engendered with the body and soul." [27] The conjunction of the soul with understanding, said Plutarch, makes reason, but with the body, passion.[28] Richard's thoughts thus become microcosmic correspondences of the melancholy world he knows; his thoughts "people this little world, / In humours like the people of this world, / For no thought is contented" (9–11). And Richard's thoughts are at odds, like the people of his kingdom. Those thoughts "tending to ambition" plot "how these vain weak nails / May tear a passage through the flinty ribs / Of this hard world, my ragged prison walls"—the prison of Richard now becomes his body, from which he would like to escape (18 ff.). The idea recalls Richard's earlier realization of the vulnerability of kings whose "castle wall" can be pierced by a little pin (III.ii.169). The prison image betrays Richard's desire to be freed from the world and from his body; his murder thus becomes a kind of deliverance.

Richard's speech is fancy in Coleridge's term, not imagination; it is chaotic as his mind is chaotic. But, in an erratic way, the speech does explore Richard's condition not only as a king but also as a man. For the first time, he realizes the value of "nothing," a word with which he had played when he resigned his kingship. But then he still thought of nothingness as the state of non-kingship; now he desires, like the just man in "the lamentation of the soul being in prison" of Innocent's tract, to be released from life: "Suffer me that I may be refreshed before I go from hence and before I shall become nothing." [29] Richard knows now that, whether he is still king or not,

> Nor I, nor any man that but man is,
> With nothing shall be pleas'd till he be eas'd
> With being nothing.
> (39–41)

As he hears music that does not keep time, he realizes fully the disharmony in himself that led to his downfall:

> But, for the concord of my state and time,
> Had not an ear to hear my true time broke.
> I wasted time, and now doth time waste me.
> (47–49)

Thus, in the end, Richard gains an inkling of the cause and meaning of his tragedy.

But Richard's self-discovery is clearly limited. He does not, for instance, ever admit his guilt in Woodstock's murder. Neither does his new humility displace completely his old vanity, as is evidenced in the incident that follows the soliloquy. When he learns from the Groom of the Stable that Bolingbroke rode on coronation day on Richard's own roan, Barbary, he questions the servant about the behavior of the horse; and when he learns that it strode proudly, he rails against the ungrateful jade that "hath eat bread from my royal hand" (V.v.85). Even Richard's last words breathe as much an exaltation of royalty as of the hope of heaven: "Mount, mount, my soul! thy seat is up on high; / Whilst my gross flesh sinks downward, here to die" (V.v.III–I2).

Richard is all of a piece. He is portrayed as a man and a ruler who does not know himself and lacks a sense of moral *decorum,* but who gradually grows toward a limited self-awareness. Through his own misrule, he loses his crown and thus the only identity he knows, that of a divinely ordained king. From sanguine lightheartedness, he changes to melancholic dejection. Plunged into excessive and histrionic grief, he is the first of Shakespeare's tragic heroes to be dominated by an overwhelming passion, which is his undoing, the major reason for his fascination, and a stimulus to gain self-knowledge. In tasting, relishing, and exploring his grief, Richard assumes a *contemptus mundi* attitude, which is, at first, more of a posture than a conviction; but the attitude becomes increasingly sincere, and, though it drives him near to madness, Richard gains on the way some of the self-knowledge he so sadly lacked, but he does not totally lose his latent vanity. The particular charm of *Richard II,* as John Middleton Murry has said, lies in the "nascent self-awareness" with which it is pervaded.[30]

This nascent self-awareness, one might say, is not only Richard's but was also that of Shakespeare as a great tragic artist. In *Richard II,* Shakespeare found a way of integrating into a tragedy the themes of self-search, self-loss, and self-finding he had depicted in his early comedies. As in *Love's Labor's Lost,* the self-search of the hero is a confused and ill-planned quest that does not lead to one particular crowning insight.[31] If one can speak of self-discovery at all, it is in quite a different sense from Aristotle's *anagnorisis.* What Richard finds out about himself does not constitute a straight-line movement culminating in a *peripeteia*—Aristotle thought the connection between *anagnorisis* and *peripeteia* was the best solution—and Richard does not achieve a particular culminating discovery comparable to the full and devastating disclosure Oedipus receives of his true situation. Richard's self-discoveries are dispersed and even precede the first unmistakably tragic development, since they begin in the flashes of *contemptus mundi* that ignite when there is yet much hope of rescue; the discoveries continue intermittently until his death, punctuating both epitasis and catastrophe. Moreover, and most important, Richard's recognitions are much less intellectual than is Oedipus's *anagnorisis.* They include a confession of sins and are more often emotional than intellectual approaches to the truth, as in that memorable scene when Richard sees his own features and those of humanity more clearly by looking into the mirror of grief. Richard's slow, painful groping toward a sense of his character and situation reveals his potential worth as a human being while not denying his lack of suitability as a king. Richard's self-search and partial self-finding have moral and religious dimensions that Aristotle's *anagnorisis* does not have and could not have had.

Not for a long time did Shakespeare go beyond *Richard II* in the treatment of tragic self-loss and self-finding. The guilt-ridden Henry IV also lacks self-knowledge, but he never falls as deep or soars as high as Richard. Henry V, it is true, comes closer to achieving complete self-knowledge than any of Shakespeare's previous heroes, but he also never loses himself, not even as a prince, in the abyss of the soul, as does Richard. Only the great tragedies—in particular, *Lear* —provide parallels. And indeed, then Shakespeare gave a greater, richer meaning to the "all" that man has at stake in the struggle for self-knowledge, and of which Richard gains only an inkling; but he also made it a more elusive goal.

Like Shakespeare's earlier plays in general, *Richard II* delineates a road to self-knowledge and points up its potential rewards. Self-loss and self-finding take place in a cosmic frame the purposes of which are fairly evident. The play suggests not only a definable ideal of humanity but also of kingship—the ruler who is legitimate, moral, and strong. And though the play deals with disharmony, it shows harmony as attainable and indeed destined for England at a future time.

In hinting at such attainable ideals lies, I think, the main significance of two episodes that precede the catastrophe of Richard's death: the conspiracy of Aumerle, ending in pardon, and the new king's reference to his wayward but promising son. The small drama-within-the-drama of the Aumerle episode finds its happy resolution in the same scene in which Bolingbroke is induced to inquire about the dissolute prince who, as Shakespeare's audience knew, became the healer and harmonizer of England. York's betrayal of his son (or should we speak about York's loyalty to the only ruler who can rule?) points up the troubles of England in the frame of one family; but Bolingbroke's pardon of Aumerle turns a mother's grief to joy and moves, as do Shakespeare's early comedies, from confusion to its resolution, from disruption to unity. One small link of the broken chain is restored. And in Bolingbroke's words about Hal, we hear not merely a father's distress but see also the son's "sparks of better hope, which elder years / May happily bring forth" (V.iii.21–22). In evoking this future development and the concomitant rise of England surely lies the main interest of this speech and not in any reference to a play or plays about the life of the prince and king Shakespeare intended to write—of this intention Shakespeare's audience knew nothing. Thus the movement of grief is temporarily relieved by some, if muted, notes of joy and hope. Appropriately, even if one of these notes does come from Bolingbroke, it is struck before those of grief and fear associated with him in the end, notes that are the finale of the tragedy of Richard.

CHAPTER SEVEN

Henry V:
Patterning after Perfection

THE THESIS of this chapter, that in Henry V Shakespeare portrayed what was for him at the time an ideal or nearly ideal character—that is, a man and a king who thoroughly knows himself—is by no means revolutionary; but in view of the coldness and even hostility with which in particular twentieth-century critics have considered Henry, it is not a mere statement of the obvious.[1] And even if my main argument is not new, I believe some of the reasons I shall give in its support are; and, I hope, they will help to restore a badly needed objectivity about a character who is not as simple as some have thought but hardly deserves to be as controversial as he has become.

It is eminently reasonable to assume that Shakespeare, who in agreement with tradition had laid out the character of the future Henry V as developing from profligacy to reform in the two parts of *Henry IV*, wished to dramatize the triumph of this evolution in his new play. It is equally apparent that all of Shakespeare's previous history plays lead up to *Henry V*, which forms their culmination and, except for the afterthought of *Henry VIII*, their conclusion. So far, Shakespeare had dramatized the lives and reigns of kings who were, at best, partial successes as rulers and some of whom were unmitigated disasters for England: the saintly but ineffective Henry VI; the sardonic Machiavellian and killer Richard III; the willful and larmoyant Richard II; the strong but guilty Henry IV, whose reign was troubled by the conflicts arising from his usurpation of the throne. In *King John*, Shakespeare depicted another ruler whose title was flawed by broken succession and who brought misfortune to his country. But in this play, there also appears a popular hero, Faulconbridge, who becomes, in troubled times, the pillar and hope of England. A drama about a strong and victorious king who pos-

sessed Faulconbridge's popular virtues and who had not incurred
guilt by obtaining the crown illegally, as had John and Henry IV,
was the logical capstone of Shakespeare's history plays.

It is surely also plausible that, after depicting such conspicuous
exemplars of lack of humanistic self-knowledge as Tarquin, Richard
III, and Richard II, Shakespeare wished to dramatize the life of a
king who was what the moralists considered to be an ideal man, a
"pattern of perfection," as Levinus Lemnius called it in *The Touchstone of Complexions* (trans. 1565). Lemnius devoted a whole chapter to portraying just such a man, one who was, as he said in the
physicians' terminology, "of a complexion perfectly and exactly temperate." This ideal man has a body "featly framed" and a mind
"well settled and perfectly stayed"; he is balanced, quick-witted, industrious, cheerful, constant, but yet humane and gentle. In other
words, he possesses both a Galenic *crasis* and a humanistic moral
temperance. Lemnius admitted that absolute perfection existed only
in Christ, but mortal men might at least approach the ideal.[2] Other
theorists claimed that kings could come closest to it; their office, as
Huarte said in *Examen de Ingenios* (trans. 1594), made possible
the greatest wisdom and knowledge in the world, an assertion he
exemplified by Solomon and by Christ, the "King of the Jews"—
both were physiologically and morally temperate according to
Huarte.[3]

As we have noted earlier, there was a substantial humanistic literature on the subject of how princes could imitate these patterns of
perfection, a literature given direction by Erasmus's influential
Institutio Principis Christiani (1516).[4] Its premise was that the
good king must be a good man and a good Christian. Erasmus said
it was quite possible to find a good man who would not make a good
prince, but there could be no good prince who was not also a good
man.[5] The excellences of a king therefore derived largely from the
excellences of man. Just as a man needed to possess the four cardinal
virtues of fortitude, justice, prudence, and, in particular, temperance
—the virtue central to self-knowledge—so did the king, and to a
higher degree.

In portraying Henry, Shakespeare showed himself cognizant of
these humanistic requirements, as did the chroniclers on whom he
based the play. Both Hall and Holinshed conspicuously praised
Henry as a pattern of perfection. Edward Hall, whose history of the

War of the Roses Shakespeare appears to have consulted, called Henry "a blazing comet and apparent lantern in his days . . . the mirror of Christendom and the glory of his country, . . . the flower of kings past, and a glass of them that would succeed" [6]—from which series of laudatory epithets Shakespeare probably derived the Chorus's praise of Henry as "the mirror of all Christian kings" (II.6). Like Hall, and borrowing from him, Raphael Holinshed appended to his account of Henry's reign a formal praise, a *laus* in terms of humanistic classical rhetoric, which emphasized the King's possession of the four cardinal virtues. Henry, said Holinshed, was "a justicer both loved and obeyed, . . . a terror to rebels and a suppressor to sedition. . . ." He was "so manful of mind as never seen to flinch at a wound or to smart at a pain. . . . Of courage invincible, of purpose immutable. . . ." No man was "more moderate in eating and drinking. . . . Wantonness of life and thirst in avarice he had quite quenched in him." He possessed "such wit, such prudence, and such policy withall, that he never enterprised anything before he had fully debated and forecast all the main chances that might happen, which done, with all diligence and courage he set his purpose forward." [7]

Instances in which Shakespeare's Henry exemplifies these four cardinal virtues come easily to mind. He demonstrates his sense of justice through restraint as well as, when necessary, through severity: he pardons the drunken man who scorns him, and, in the same scene, he suppresses sedition by condemning the traitorous Scroop, Cambridge, and Grey to death—a punishment that they themselves unwittingly have declared appropriate for their crimes. In meting out this judgment, Shakespeare's Henry emphasizes that "Touching our person seek we no revenge; / But we our kingdom's safety must so tender, / . . . that to her laws / We do deliver you" (II.ii.174–77). Henry dispenses justice in the way Erasmus thought a prince should: he forgives most readily those crimes that affect him alone, and he seeks to punish rather than to take revenge.[8]

The fortitude of the victor of Agincourt hardly needs proof. Neither does his temperance, which is so strong as to have irritated some critics who have called it priggishness. Henry's plea to the French ambassadors not to fear that he might take a personal vengeance on them for any insult contained in their official messages proves temperance to be central to his ideal of kingship:

> We are no tyrant, but a Christian king,
> Unto whose grace our passion is as subject
> As are our wretches fett'red in our prisons.
>   (I.ii.241–43)

It is remarkable how technically accurate Shakespeare's portrayal of Henry's temperance is in terms of the humor physiology. Henry's appearance and behavior in the morning just before the battle of Agincourt approach so closely the description of the pattern of perfection in Levinus Lemnius's chapter "Of a Complexion Perfectly and Exactly Temperate" as to raise the suspicion of being modeled on it. Shakespeare had no warrant for this incident in his sources; in these, Henry had no need to show himself to his troops in the way he does in the play: the English, though outnumbered, were described as in good spirits. In the play, they sorely require the encouragement of the radiant king that walks among them:

> For forth he goes and visits all his host;
> Bids them good morrow with a modest smile,
> And calls them brothers, friends, and countrymen.
> Upon his royal face there is no note
> How dread an army hath enrounded him;
> Nor doth he dedicate one jot of colour
> Unto the weary and all-watched night;
> But freshly looks, and over-bears attaint
> With cheerful semblance and sweet majesty.
>   (IV. Prol. 32–40)

Henry here looks and acts quite like Lemnius's temperate man, who

> hath all his senses fresh and perfect, every of the faculties natural duly doing his office and function. . . . For in him plentifully appeareth, and is evidently descried: humanity, gentleness, frugality, equity, modesty, and a continent moderation of all affections. . . . [He] suffereth all the discommodities of life with a mind stout, cheerful, and invincible, and such a one as will not at any hand be drawn away from his constancy and settled determination. . . . For in the countenance, which is the image of the mind, in the eyes, which are the bewrayers and token-tellers of the inward conceits, in the color, lineaments, proportion and feature of the whole body, there appeareth a kind of heroical grace and amiableness in so much that the very view and sight thereof allureth and draweth everyone by a certain secret sympathy or consent of nature to love it without

any hope or profit or commodity thereby to be reaped or received. The body is decently made and featly framed, containing an absolute construction and comely frame of all the parts together. . . . The head . . . [is] greatly honored with a pair of amiable eyes, . . . the color fresh, sweet, and pleasant.[9]

Henry has the magnetic attraction of Lemnius's ideal; he becomes, therefore, a pattern for imitation by his troops, who, pining and pale before, "pluck comfort from his looks." In a "largess universal, like the sun," Henry gives "his liberal eye . . . to every one, / Thawing cold fear." As is true for Lemnius's ideal man, the temperance of Henry rubs off on all, low and high, who behold "a little touch of Harry in the night" (41 ff.).

Henry also possesses an extraordinary prudence, which manifests itself both in peace and war. Before embarking on the invasion of France, he assures himself circumspectly of the justice of his claim to the French crown, and he takes the necessary precautions to protect his kingdom from the rapacious Scots. The initiative to these measures comes from him, not, as in the sources, from his counselors. He can say justly that he has "all things thought upon / That may with reasonable swiftness add / More feathers to our wings" (I.ii.305–7). In warfare, Henry's prudence shows itself in stern words when he convinces the people of Harfleur that they must surrender; at other times, it proves itself in stern actions and at least once in an order that appears to be so severe as to be cruel, that of cutting the French prisoners' throats during the battle of Agincourt. This action—adopted by Shakespeare from Holinshed, who explained it as absolutely necessary—has cost Henry some sympathies; but we should note that it is not occasioned by willful ferocity: it comes at the moment of greatest peril, when the endangered and outnumbered English are threatened by a new attack just after the French, as Fluellen puts it, have "killed the poys and luggage." Both Gower and Fluellen think this action a cowardly violation of the law of arms, as did Holinshed and, one must assume, Shakespeare. At other times, when prudence permits it, Henry shows himself lenient, as when he forbids Harfleur to be sacked and pillaged—Shakespeare here directly contradicted Holinshed. Shakespeare's Henry, to say the least, is not unnecessarily cruel; he knows that "when lenity and cruelty play for a kingdom the gentler gamester is the soonest winner" (III.vi.108).

Henry's practical calculations in politics and strategy have created

the suspicion that he is, at heart, a "Machiavellian." [10] One might
say, of course, that in Shakespeare's time, as well as before and after,
every successful absolutist ruler, including so seemingly gentle and
certainly popular a monarch as Queen Elizabeth, was something of a
Machiavellian. But the epithet is as inappropriate for Henry as it is
for Elizabeth if it is taken in the Elizabethan sense. For ordinary
Elizabethans, although not for some advanced spirits, a Machiavellian prince was not merely shrewd, sometimes severe, and occasionally devious; he was a monster in human shape. That Shakespeare did not belong to the coterie of Machiavelli's admirers, I
have argued elsewhere. And a comparison of some essential features
of Henry's portrait with what the Elizabethans considered the key
chapters in *The Prince* shows that if Shakespeare read this book at
all—and I incline to think that he knew at least the argument of
these key chapters—he was motivated by it to make his Henry
different from Machiavelli's standard.

For Machiavelli, prudence was the only one of the conventional
humanistic virtues a prince needed to possess; he might, it is true,
outwardly display others as long as they did not impede his success.
In the famous eighteenth chapter of *The Prince,* Machiavelli contended that what mattered for a ruler was not that he should *be*
good but that he should be *thought* to be good—actual goodness
could even be harmful. Machiavelli reacted adversely to the stereotyped praises of princes' virtues, such as their temperance, clemency,
and justice, which in another famous chapter, the fifteenth, he criticized as irrelevant. This chapter is entitled (in the seventeenth-
century translation of Edward Dacres) "Of Those Things in Respect
Whereof Man, and Especially Princes, Are Praised or Dispraised."
Qualities of this kind, Machiavelli argued, were apt to bring about
the ruin rather than the success of princes. But *Henry V* contains, as
I shall show, a number of elaborate rhetorical praises of Henry's
humanistic virtues. To assume that they are insincere would make
the play a huge effort in irony—an irony that no Elizabethan could
have understood. If rhetoric is to be equated with insincerity, Renaissance literature as a whole is insincere.

But surely the conventional *laudes* in *Henry V* serve the function
of delineating an ideal man and king; praise and dispraise were,
after all, the traditional ways of rhetorical characterization. It has
been demonstrated that Shakespeare modeled his praises of Henry
closely on patterns in Aphthonius's *Progymnasmata,* the standard

schoolbook for such exercises[11]—an indication that he was intent
on creating a correct rhetorical frame for his portrait of perfection.
The several Aphthonian praises in the play specify Henry's nobility,
courage, temperance, knowledge, and piety, and they are not shown
to be inappropriate by the action that they introduce or on which
they comment.

The most significant formal praises are: the bishops' accolade of
Henry, preceding his first appearance; the Chorus's introduction
to the climactic battle of Agincourt, which praise we have noted as
primarily lauding Henry's temperance (IV.Prol.28 ff.); and Fluellen's comparison of Henry to Alexander (IV.vii.21), which is both
a military compliment and, as we shall see, another testimony to
Henry's temperance.

The first of these, the most elaborate *laus* and the one most revealing for Shakespeare's conception of Henry, warrants detailed
analysis. The bishops' conversation deals with "how things are
perfected" (68) in the character of Henry; it is a praise in the Aphthonian form of *narratio*. Understandably, the bishops are concerned
primarily with Henry's religious development into a "lover of the
holy Church"; they approve of his acquisition of "grace," but they
also acclaim his secular accomplishment, his "fair regard" (22–23).
This introduction to the person and his attainment (*persona faciens*,
in Aphthonian terms) is followed by an account of the time in
which it occurred (24–27, Aphthonius's *tempus circa quod*), of the
way in which it came about (28–37, *modus quo pacto*), and of the
specific qualities of mind acquired (38–52, *res gestas animi*); the
laus is concluded by a statement on the reason why this development
occurred (53–66, *causa propter quam*). The Bishop of Canterbury
determines the *tempus circa quod* as the time of Henry IV's death
and stresses the suddenness of the *modus quo pacto*: "The breath
no sooner left his father's body / But that his wildness, mortified in
him, / Seem'd to die too" (25–27). Henry's transformation was a
"reformation"; "consideration" came like an angel and whipped the
"offending Adam" out of him. A listing of his *res gestae animi*
shows the comprehensiveness of the change: the king is as good a
debater in theology as he is in commonwealth affairs and discourses
of war.[12] Only on the *causa propter quam* do the bishops differ. The
Bishop of Canterbury considers Henry's sudden scholarship miraculous, although he cannot call it a miracle because theology has
established that miracles have ceased; the Bishop of Ely thinks of it

as a hidden growth—and a typically English one at that: "The strawberry grows underneath the nettle . . ." (60 ff.). Thus Shakespeare glanced at the chronicler's claim that Henry's change partook of the nature of a religious conversion; but he also reinforced the impression he created in the *Henry IV* plays that under the veil of wildness the prince prepared himself for his future role as king. The praises of the bishops form an important link between the earlier plays and *Henry V* and testify to Shakespeare's consistent view of Henry's development.

The second elaborate *laus* is in the form of a strange *comparatio* between Henry and Alexander perpetrated by the brave, if long-winded and somewhat illogical, Fluellen (IV.vii.11 ff.). After finding much relevance in the fact that both conquerors were born in cities with rivers, Fluellen mentions a famous episode: "Alexander . . . in his rages, and his furies, and his wraths, and his cholers, and his moods, and his displeasures, and his indignations, and also being a little intoxicates in the prains, did, in his ales and his angers, look you, kill his best friend, Cleitus." On the protest of Gower that "our king is not like him in that," Fluellen continues with his "figures and comparisons": "As Alexander kill'd his friend Cleitus, being in his ales and his cups, so also Harry Monmouth, being in his right wits and his good judgments, turn'd away the fat knight with the great belly doublet. . . ." But, ironically, what Fluellen conceives as *similitudo* serves to underline the *dissimilitudo* of Henry and Alexander. Fluellen, although unwittingly, brings out the feature of Alexander the humanists thought objectionable, his intemperance, a feature which Henry does not share—witness his turning out that lovable embodiment of intemperance, Falstaff! Erasmus had admonished Christian kings to imitate the Macedonian conqueror's commendable valor but not to slide back to his deplorable intemperance.[13]

Only superficially does the situation in which Fluellen compares Henry and Alexander warrant the parallel. It is true that Henry has just given orders to kill the French prisoners and that he is about to enter the stage in fiery spirit: "I was not angry . . . / Until this instant" (IV.vii.52). As we noted before, the king's behavior is quite in accord with military prudence, Renaissance (and, deplorably, even modern) style, and his anger transfers itself to his troops as an incitement for renewed attack. Whenever Henry appears angry, as at Harfleur, it is to incite his countrymen. Whenever

Henry boasts, as before the battle of Agincourt, it is not to aggrandize himself but to glorify England. Outwardly, he may seem as obsessed with honor as Hotspur: "But if it be a sin to covet honour, / I am the most offending soul alive" (IV.iii.28–29). Henry's sense of honor, however, is not egotistic like that of Hotspur, nor does it demand the ostentatious reverence Richard II sought of his subjects. Henry rejects the idea of having his sword carried before him during his triumphal return to London; he is "free from vainness and self-glorious pride," as the Chorus says (V.20). For him, the greatest glory is that of heaven, attained in the flight of man's better part, his soul, upward; he tells Mountjoy that the fallen English will be "fam'd; for there the sun shall greet them / And draw their honours reeking up to heaven, / Leaving their earthly parts to choke your clime" (IV.iii.100–102). Whatever one may think of Henry's warrior spirit—he would be doomed without it—it is not an illusion based on a glamorous view of war. For him as for the humanists, war is a fearful thing, and the greatest honor is not of the earth but of heaven.

Whenever Shakespeare compares Henry to Alexander, he suggests, sometimes quite subtly, a difference between the two. At the beginning of the play, the bishops say in their praises that Henry knows how to untie the "Gordian knot" of policy; but what they have in mind requires the word rather than the sword. And when at Harfleur Henry evokes the name of Alexander, it is not to identify himself with the Macedonian conqueror but with his and his soldiers' ancestors:

> On, on, you noblest English,
> Whose blood is fet from fathers of warproof—
> Fathers that like so many Alexanders
> Have in these parts from morn till even fought,
> And sheath'd their swords for lack of argument.
>   (III.i.17–21)

Monmouth and Macedonia may be similar in that they have rivers, as Fluellen observes, but Henry and Alexander have little in common besides courage and soldiership. To have said *"we few, we happy few"* would have been quite out of character for the Alexander described by Plutarch or Erasmus.

Shakespeare, who is likely to have read Plutarch's *Life of Alexander* while composing *Henry V,* also appears to have glanced at

the *Life of Caesar,* set in parallel to that of the Macedonian conqueror. When the Chorus of the fifth act describes Henry as returning triumphantly to London, the mayor and the citizens are said to
swarm around him like the senators and plebeians of Rome, who
"go forth and fetch their conqu'ring Caesar in." But here again
Shakespeare was concerned with emphasizing contrast as well as
likeness: the Chorus's immediately preceding observation on Henry's
modesty in refusing to have his helmet and sword carried before him
offsets any suspicion that he shares the burning ambition that Plutarch and general tradition associated with Caesar.

Why is it then that this glorious and yet modest king whom
Shakespeare extolled above all others—"praise and glory on his
head" (IV.31)—has been so little admired by modern critics? An
accolade like that of Hudson is a rare phenomenon indeed:

> Henry is the most complex and many-sided of all Shakespeare's
> heroes with the one exception of Hamlet, if indeed Hamlet ought to
> be excepted. . . . The character of Shakespeare's Henry may al-
> most be said to consist of piety, honesty, and modesty. He embodies
> these qualities in their simplest form. He is honest in his piety,
> pious and modest in his honesty.[14]

The scarcity of such wholehearted eulogies of Henry's character
is, I believe, in large part due to the nature of the pattern of perfection
Shakespeare embodied in him. An appreciation of any idealization
depends on the viewer's sympathy with the ideals portrayed or at
least demands his willingness to respond to them aesthetically, and
we have grown far away from the ideals portrayed in Henry, those
of moderation and balance, which the humanists derived from Christian ideas of sobriety as well as from classical concepts of harmony
and self-control. Also, there are dramatic limitations to the portrayal
of a perfectly stable temperament. The king is in equilibrium; unlike
the dauphin's horse, to which the owner devotes an unusual *laus*
(III.vii.11 ff.). Henry is not just fire and air; but the "duller elements," earth and water, drag him, at times, down. (Henry's fire,
it must be said, also has proved bothersome to critics.) Even before
attaining his later perfection, in the *Henry IV* plays, Hal already
is weighed down somewhat by the duller elements when, for instance, his moderate attitude toward honor makes him look a little
pale compared to the gloriously obsessed Hotspur and the funnily
"discreet" Falstaff. There are elements of dullness in all moderation

even when it comes about, as in Henry's case, by control over a strong temperament. But to find fault with Shakespeare's portrait of him because he is not mad or insane or inspired with a divine afflatus is as foolish as to criticize a Holbein figure for not writhing in the agonies of El Greco's "Laocoon."

In order to account for their discomfort with Henry, critics have been driven to contradictory explanations and, in the process, have furnished proof that his character cannot be summarized in a simple formula. One critic dislikes him for being too formal—"he is never off the platform" [15]—and another finds him too brisk and folksy— "a hearty undergraduate with enormous initials on his chest." [16] The truth is that Henry can be either formal or folksy, and always at the right time. Generally, in speeches from the throne and in addresses to his troops, he speaks in a ceremonial and almost ritualistic language; but, as the Williams episode shows, he has not forgotten the idiom of the people he learned in the taverns of Eastcheap.

The formal aspects of Henry's character are enhanced by Shakespeare's casting him—in particular, through the praises of the choruses—in the role of a kind of epic hero.[17] Henry is given some of the traits Virgil lauds in his *vir perfectus,* Aeneas—*fortitudo, constantia, justitia, religio, pietas, industria, celeritas, prudentia,* and *ratio*—traits that are not apt to warm modern hearts for either hero. Yet Henry is certainly much less priggish than Aeneas; his self-awareness has dimensions and subtleties with which Virgil did not endow his Roman pattern of perfection. Henry knows the hollowness of his crown and reflects on it in a great soliloquy. He realizes that the paraphernalia of kingship are nothing but "place, degree, and form, / Creating awe and fear in other men" (IV.i.242 ff.). Unlike Richard II, he is not blinded by the glitter of his robe; he has the self-knowledge that, as Sir Thomas Elyot said, makes a man of authority realize that he has a body and soul like any other man.[18] When, incognito, he explains to the soldier that the king is but a man, his words have the concreteness of experience: "The violet smells to him as it doth to me; the element shows to him as it doth to me; all his senses have but human conditions; his ceremonies laid by, in his nakedness he appears but a man; and though his affections are higher mounted than ours, yet, when they stoop, they stoop with the like wing." Like Lemnius's pattern of perfection, Henry is a man of feeling, not a monument of stone and marble. He even knows fear; yet he will never show it, "lest he, by showing it,

should dishearten his army" (IV.i.102 ff.). In this sense of total
outward control, Henry is always on a platform; by accepting his
position and his duties as obligatory, he remains on a platform.

Because the king's public persona is prominent, some critics have
insisted that there is nothing left of the sophisticated and courtly
irony that marked the prince.[19] But I do not think this is a totally
fair appraisal. The king betrays—just at the moments when he is
most optimistic and approaches outwardly Mr. Van Doren's expansive undergraduate—a certain detachment from his role or, at least,
an engaging lack of illusion about it. So he does when, before his
troops on the morning of Agincourt, he breathes an infectious self-
confidence:

> There is some soul of goodness in things evil,
> Would men observingly distil it out;
> For our bad neighbour makes us early stirrers,
> Which is both healthful and good husbandry.
> Besides, they are our outward consciences
> And preachers to us all, admonishing
> That we should dress us fairly for our end.
> Thus may we gather honey from the weed,
> And make a moral of the devil himself.
>   (IV.i.4–12)

Henry expresses what must be one of the oldest of human consolations, that nothing is so bad but some good can be found in it; he
does so, however, in a way that points up the absurdity to which
a rationalizing optimism can be driven and sometimes was driven
in Shakespeare's time. Henry identifies the "outward consciences"
not merely with the "preachers" but also with the "bad neighbour"
who is responsible for making one rise early; thus, in effect, he
identifies the outward consciences with the enemy. Indeed, by the
quirk of the figure, the consciences—or, if one prefers, the preachers
—become the devil. Shakespeare must have heard similar oratorical
gems from the pulpit.[20] Shakespeare-Henry continues, I think, this
subtle parody into the immediately following "proof" that " 'Tis
good for men to love their present pains":

> Upon example; so the spirit is eased;
> And when the mind is quick'ned, out of doubt
> The organs, though defunct and dead before,

> Break up their drowsy grave and newly move
> With casted slough and fresh legerity.
>
> (IV.i.19–23)

These words form an odd echo to Renaissance doctors' recommendations of "reasonable exercise and convenient motion." This latter phrase is Lemnius's, whose proof very much resembles Henry's: "For by it [the exercise] the quickness and vigor of his mind is revived, the faint, drowsy spirits stirred up and awaked, the soul and mind cheered and exhilarated, all the parts of the body and all the senses both within and without made nimble, active, perfect, and ready to do their proper functions." [21] Henry's words, which resemble Lemnius's jargon, parody such advice on physical fitness. By applying it to readiness for deadly battles, the king demonstrates not only that he knows what is expected of patterns of perfection but also that he can detach himself ironically from the means he must employ as a leader.

He stops short of the frivolity he indulged as a prince; he feels too keenly his responsibility. He remains the shepherd and protector of his people that the Christian humanists demanded a king should be. But he does so in full awareness of the sacrifices his position entails. Erasmus said abstractly that a king must watch and spend sleepless nights over the welfare of his subjects,[22] but Henry knows concretely what it means to face "horrid night, the child of hell." The man who cheerfully greets his troops on the morning of the battle of Agincourt has slept little. Henry is, of course, not neurotic; to expect him to be so is to wish him to be less effective and more imperfect—an understandable wish. Even though Henry knows the abyss of the soul, he does not probe it lest he plunge his nation into it.

How simple is that Henry, then, who calls himself a "plain king" when he woos the French princess in terms that are indeed prosaic and artless? In this role, Henry does appear to come close to the blunt and somewhat coarse king of the popular tradition and of Shakespeare's source play, *The Famous Victories of Henry V*. But what is one to think when one critic finds him guilty here of "military grossness" [23] while another castigates him for his clever "Machiavellian" scheme of obtaining the inheritance of France through the hand of her princess? [24] The truth of the matter is surely that Henry's wooing has both a human and a political purpose and that for him the two purposes are not at variance; he pursues them with his usual ingenuity, sobriety, and success.

Henry's firm and unproblematic marriage to success is perhaps his greatest handicap for receiving sympathetic appreciation. Who could read without some uneasiness a statement such as that of H. A. Evans in the Old Arden Edition: "Conscientious, brave, just, capable, and tenacious, Henry stands before us as the embodiment of worldly success, and as such he is entitled to our unreserved admiration." Evans may have felt some discomfort with his own boldness, for he continued with a slight lapse in logic, "Such a character he [the reader] will accept with its inseparable limitations as Shakespeare intended it to be accepted; he will not look for those finer touches of the intellect or of the emotions which mark the hero of another sort; he will miss, as has been well said, the light that is upon the brow of a Hamlet or an Othello." [25] Henry surely does have some of these finer touches; if he lacks a "light upon his brow," whatever that exactly means, is it not because he is gloriously successful rather than radiantly doomed as are Hamlet and Othello?

Of course, Henry does not have the tragic heroes' penchant for passion; the very keys to his success are sobriety and temperance. When Shakespeare wrote *Henry V,* he is likely to have thought of these traits not only as fundamental for a pattern of perfection but also as conducive to success. So, for that matter, did the Puritans. But this Puritan ideal of a combination of morality and success, which after Shakespeare dominated the English middle class, owed something not only to Calvin but also to Christian humanism, which was the more powerful in its influence on life as it merged with a native piety. One can think of none better to exemplify these pre-Puritan virtues than Sir Thomas More. Henry has them too: he is sober, temperate, prudent, self-controlled, pious, and practical. He thus embodies features that historically have been associated with the English national character. He appears, perhaps even more to a non-English observer, eminently English—and, after all, Shakespeare conceived him as such. There is surely every reason to believe that it is a sympathetic portrait. Indeed, that side of Shakespeare's own character which led to his business success as a shareholder of the Globe and landowner of Stratford must have had something in common with Henry.

The dissatisfaction of some modern critics who declare Henry to be simple-minded derives not so much from the king's character as from his situation: he is not in the kind of problematic predicament we generally like our heroes to be in. But in Shakespeare's conception of the interplay of character and history, which underlay his *Henry V* as well as his other history plays, Henry could not be in such a predicament. Because he and England are in harmony, he cannot suffer the anguish of a Richard II that comes from disharmony. Henry expresses the spirit of England somewhat as Tolstoy's Marshall Kutuzov expresses that of Russia; he cannot, like a Dostoevskian character, plumb the depth of his mysterious soul. He is a pattern of perfection put in a perfect frame; but, unfortunately, we are not well attuned to the pattern and the frame. Henry is an authentic hero who challenges us in our age of anti-heroes; he is a military leader, whose acceptance of the conditions of war offends our pacifist leanings; he is a man of success, who makes us uneasy because we have come to distrust success. We are not used to plays that celebrate public figures of his kind. But it certainly will not do to make the play into something that it is not and cannot be, such as an accusation against war (it is, of course, not a defense) or an exposure of Machiavellian scheming.

In the context of this study, *Henry V* and the portrait of its hero indicate a culmination of one phase of Shakespeare's development. If clear placement, compositional perspective, and a system of proportions and balances that brings about a unified design can be taken to be characteristic principles of Renaissance art, as art historians say they can be, *Henry V* is a play that is most characteristic of the Renaissance. The principles are evident in the texture and the structure of the play, such as in the careful gradation of language and style according to the principles of artistic *decorum*, in the oratorical patterns of speeches suitable for the occasion, and in the clear act divisions, marked by choruses whose epic tone sets the mood for the particular dramatic action that follows. The play has the kind of "multiple unity" art historians discern in Renaissance paintings.[26] It celebrates the providential synthesis of character, nation, and destiny at an ideal moment of English history. Henry V is placed in the structural and ideological center of this play comparable to the way Renaissance painters placed the human figure on their canvases and the Christian humanists described man as the significant center of the harmonious cosmic circles. Henry is an ideal king according to the design that makes him the soul of his nation; he is himself symmetrically constructed, a balanced man, a pattern of perfection, the ideal creator and beneficiary of the ideal historical moment.

But *Henry V*, which marks a kind of culmination of one phase of Shakespeare's developing patterns of self-knowledge, is also near the end of this phase. The high comedies seem still to belong to this phase, to continue and perfect it in another genre. But when Shakespeare turned away from English histories and romantic comedies, he was subjected to the influence of different models and, at about this time, appears also to have felt the effect of new currents of thought, as I shall argue in the next chapter. It is possible that he was already in doubt whether the pattern he adopted in *Henry V* and brought to a successful conclusion was really relevant to his own time. I do not think one should read an uneasiness or dissatisfaction of Shakespeare with his subject into the apologies of the choruses for the inadequacies of the stage; the lines are poetic helps to give the viewer the feeling that he is watching what we like to call an event of epic proportions, for the presentation of which we moderns have technically more adequate but less poetic means. Perhaps more remarkable, because not conditioned by artistic requirements, is the way Henry distances himself psychologically from the role he superbly fills. And there is a small note at the very end, in the epilogue, that draws attention to the precarious nature of the synthesis celebrated in the play. This is the passing reference to Henry's son, the child-king Henry VI, under whom "the world's best garden" was brought again into disorder. This is not an orchestral movement that disturbs the present celebration; it is not comparable to the stronger and reverse effect noted in the discussion of *Richard II:* there a movement of joy in the form of the pardon of Aumerle and of the promise of hope in Hal preceded the finale of grief and provided some comfort. The celebration does not turn into anxious questioning; we are only reminded of fortune and the course of history. But the brittleness of all earthly achievements is at least implied. Perhaps for Shakespeare, too, the glory of kings had passed. In his work, at any rate, it was never again to shine as radiantly as it does in *Henry V*.

PART THREE

Problems and Ambiguities

CHAPTER EIGHT

The Real versus the Ideal:
Taking a Skeptic View

U
NUSUALLY TRUSTWORTHY EVIDENCE points to
Shakespeare's having written *Henry V* and *Julius Caesar* in
the same year, 1599. Yet the two plays have marked differences, which go beyond those that one expects between a history
and a tragedy. *Henry V* is a translucent play that centers on the
hero-king it celebrates; *Julius Caesar,* by contrast, is controversial in
all its aspects: in its structure, its theme, its thought, and the quality
of the major characters.[1] But the relevance of the two plays to our
time appears to be in an inverse ratio to their degree of clarity.
Henry V, at least when presented as a national celebration of a
heroic king, has seemed to many a twentieth-century critic peculiarly
dated and has been strongly popular only in times of a consciously
felt outward threat, such as existed in the forties, when patriotism
and heroism were in men's hearts. *Julius Caesar* is quite a different
case; its gripping account of power-play and its controversial major
character are congenial to our problem-oriented age. And so is the
group of plays Shakespeare wrote soon afterward, *Hamlet, Troilus
and Cressida, All's Well That Ends Well,* and *Measure for Measure.*
Hamlet, of course, has always been popular. But the three other
so-called problem plays have come into their own only in recent
years, when it has been proved that they can be effective on the
stage in spite of their complexities, ambiguities, and vexations and
when they have attracted critical interest for these very features.
They appear to have a special modernity that transcends whatever
artistic defects they may have, a modernity we do not quite experience in Shakespeare's earlier works.

   I believe we do best to understand the plays of this group, the two
tragedies and the three "problem comedies" (for simplicity's sake,
Troilus and Cressida may here be called a comedy) as constituting

in Shakespeare's creative work a special phase, one in which he
became highly sensitive to changing intellectual and cultural tendencies of an age that has a fascinating resemblance to our own age of
accelerated change. The five plays are united by a common "style"
in the art historians' sense of the word, that is, they share identifiable
features that give them a certain likeness and that can be seen as
responses to a particular mentality of an age. I would like to suggest
that we label this style "mannerist" in order to distinguish it from
the preceding, "Renaissance" period and the subsequent one, that
of the "baroque." This is not to deny that some features I have
isolated in the plays under discussion and called "mannerist" occur
sporadically in earlier or later plays, that other characteristics I have
considered "Renaissance" persist in the two later periods, and that
some baroque traits appear occasionally before *Othello,* the first play
that, I think, can be called "baroque." The point is that the respective features are conspicuous in the plays I have labeled accordingly.

All periodization of literature or art is the work of the classifying
and categorizing human mind and, of necessity, involves a certain
simplification. We are not bound to traditional groupings if they
prove unsatisfactory or oversimplified, as, I think, has been the
case with the use of "Renaissance" for that enormously long and
diverse period from the fourteenth (or, in the north, sixteenth)
century to the end of the seventeenth. The discussion on breaking up
this period into more meaningful units is in process, but, unfortunately, it has not yet led to generally accepted results. Moreover,
the division into Renaissance, mannerism, and baroque, though
widely used by art historians, is still controversial among literary
historians. Yet it appears to me a sensible one, for it allows one to
think of "style" as an artist's total response to the dominant concerns of his age, a response that includes not only diction, but also
structure, choice and treatment of subjects, preference of themes, and
much more. Shakespeare's own style is then an expression of his
individuality within the period style or styles. It is by no means an
attempt to limit his genius if one declares a particular play to be
"mannerist." The term is merely a shorthand symbol for certain
identifiable features in which his artistic response resembled that
of his contemporaries. I trust that my reader will not be impeded by
my choice of labels, and, I hope, he will be helped if, for the sake of
following my argument, he accepts them in the interpretation I shall
give them. This interpretation has some currency among scholars,

particularly in continental Europe. We cannot enter here into this on-going discussion; ample, although sometimes quite divergent, treatments are available elsewhere.[2]

The meaning of baroque and its application in this study will be discussed at a later point. As to mannerism, the term appears to me advantageous in denoting, as it does in the analysis of most art historians, a reaction to the classical Renaissance and, as such, a transitional phase as well as an authentic style that makes itself felt in the form and the content of a work of art. Changes in form are not a primary concern of this study, but we may at least note the changes in structural patterns because they make more obvious the differences between the five plays under discussion and the preceding plays and because they also have a considerable influence on the patterns of self-knowledge. There is something opaque or even unsatisfactory about the structure of each of the five plays, a fact that contributes much to the difficulty of their interpretation, but, on the other hand, has also attracted modern readers and audiences, who find the well-made play artificial. The structural opaqueness is least apparent in *Julius Caesar,* which connects in many ways with the preceding "Renaissance" plays. But even it has a structural problem by suffering from what one could call a mannerist tension between the apparent theme and the content of the play. Although Caesar is in the center of its forces, he is not its protagonist or, in the conventional sense of the word, the tragic hero; these designations fit only Brutus.[3] It could also be said, of course, that Prince Hal is the real hero of the Henry IV plays; but these are histories that dramatize the events of a reign and are therefore appropriately named. In the case of *Julius Caesar,* we ponder whether to attribute greater significance to the personal tragedy of Brutus, or to the dramatic struggle for power, or to the revenge tragedy of Caesar. As to *Hamlet,* Shakespeare's audience must have expected it to be a revenge tragedy, as was its predecessor, the *Ur-Hamlet;* yet it erupts into a drama of character and thought. Brutus is as unusual a conspirator as Hamlet is an avenger; both speak highly reflective and analytical idioms that contrast with the turbulent climate of their plays. The question of dramatic form is even more vexing in the case of the three comedies. W. W. Lawrence called them "bastard brothers of tragedy," [4] and, in fact, "tragedy" has seemed to some a better term than "comedy" for *Troilus and Cressida.*[5] These discrepancies between general form and major subject are very similar to those noted by art historians in mannerist paintings. The problematic structures of all five plays make applicable the concept of the "gestörten form" (disturbed form) that Gombrich coined for mannerist art.[6]

One reason for their structural imbalance is their heavy burden of thought. Except for *King Lear,* no earlier or later plays contain more theoretical statements on self-knowledge, or, for that matter, theories in general. Professor Tillyard considered this incumbrance with ideas a major reason for calling them problem plays (he did not include *Julius Caesar,* as he might have done). He said that they showed "an overriding concern with religious dogma or abstract speculation or both" and that these matters were "felt rather more for their own than for the drama's sake, as if, in this form at least, they were new and urgent to Shakespeare's mind, demanding at this point statement and articulation rather than solution and absorption into other materials." [7] Such preponderance of thought and theory in drama, which by conventional definition has its center in action and character, is comparable to the way certain elements, such as ornamentation and psychological content, which were thought secondary in Renaissance art, became primary during mannerism.

The best proof that change was in the air lies in the increased interest in the theme of change. In all five plays, Shakespeare, in varying degree, was concerned with the problem of innovation versus tradition. In *Julius Caesar,* Brutus's old-fashioned ideas of liberty are irreconcilable with the evolving new order, that of a dictatorship. In *Troilus and Cressida,* Ulysses appears to apotheosize a moribund social order based on priority and degree; but he himself violates it by stirring up against each other Ajax and Achilles, and he becomes a foremost champion of a new spirit of craft and force that is about to destroy the sentimental chivalric notions of the Trojans. In *All's Well,* Bertram rejects his dead father's old-fashioned virtues and turns to new habits and new vices until Helena regenerates him. A major issue of *Measure for Measure* is the question of what form of government is best in a state that has become corrupt as its duke has grown older.

But it is *Hamlet,* the play carrying the heaviest burden of thought, that concerns itself most explicitly with the theme of change. The prince cannot be categorized simply as a traditionalist or as an innovator; he is both. Young as he is, he is already rooted in the past, no longer at home in Denmark, before even the ghost's command pits him against the new order. To the courtiers at Elsinore, Hamlet seems a dangerously wild spirit, and they are right in a sense that transcends their comprehension. The very voice of the past assigns him to a role that requires him to abandon conventions. The new Hamlet, as we shall note, examines the whole range of traditional microcosmic and macrocosmic knowledge for its relevance to himself, and finds little. It is of interest in the present context that he takes a direct interest in Shakespeare's own profession, acting, and that he proves to be a decided conservative in this field. The matter is worth considering for indications of Shakespeare's attitude toward the one aspect of change that concerned him most.

Hamlet's remarks on acting and the theater have a tinge of bitterness one cannot help associating with Shakespeare. It is true, the only overt expression of irritation is Hamlet's response to the children's companies that "are now the fashion, and so berattle the common stages—so they call them—that many wearing rapiers are afraid of goose quills and dare scarce come thither" (II.ii.336 ff.). Shakespeare was concerned about the welfare of the children: he blamed the exploiters who made the children "exclaim against their own succession," that is, caused them to satirize the profession they might later elect. But there is also a touch of professional dissatisfaction here, a not negligible one in a dramatist reticent about personal matters, as was Shakespeare, and it is underlined by Hamlet's application of the incident to the situation in Denmark; the children's popularity reminds him of the adulation afforded his odious uncle since he became king.

Hamlet's specific instructions on acting (III.ii.1 ff.) also breathe an air of discomfort with the times. The prince bases his precepts on the rules of conventional Renaissance rhetoric; [8] he enjoins the players to use good "pronunciation," that is, appropriate oral delivery ("speak the speech . . . trippingly on the tongue") and fitting gestures ("suit the action to the word, the word to the action"); and he instructs them to acquire "in the very torrent, tempest, and, as I may say, whirlwind of your passion . . . a temperance that may give it smoothness." This is quite in the tradition of classical rhetoric, which demanded a temperance of πάθος by ἦθος, of the vehement emotions by the lighter ones.[9] Hamlet censures those who do not practice moderation but tear the passions to tatters and strut and bellow so "that I have thought some of Nature's journeymen had made men, and not made them well" (33). One should not

be misled by Hamlet's remark that these practitioners outdid Ter-
magant and out-heroded Herod; the actors Shakespeare had in mind
surely did not attempt to reintroduce the style of the old mystery
plays.[10] Hamlet's annoyance points to Shakespeare's irritation with
a new-fangled way of acting, a more impassioned, presumably a
more naturalistic one than that in which he had been trained. The
word "journeyman" is indicative: Shakespeare himself had as an
apprentice or journeyman been taught to suit the action to the word
and the word to the action. When he had Hamlet imply that the new
style was against nature, he surely meant that it was against the
theoretical norms of human nature as humanistic-classical theory
had formulated them.

Because the change in the style of acting was accompanied by a
change in dramatic fashions, it is justifiable to read into Hamlet's
strictures a reluctance of Shakespeare to adjust himself to a new
style of drama in general. The plays of some of Shakespeare's
younger contemporaries, such as Marston and, later, Beaumont and
Fletcher, tended to satirical extravagances and to stronger, sometimes perverse emotions, for which the acting style censured by
Hamlet is quite appropriate. Perhaps under the impact of these inno-
vations, Shakespeare rethought some of the principles on which his
art was founded; *Hamlet* contains Shakespeare's one definition of
drama in the prince's advice to the actors that the end of playing,
"both at the first and now, was and is to hold, as 'twere, the mirror
up to nature; to show virtue her own feature, scorn her own image,
and the very age and body of the time his form and pressure"
(III.ii.22–26). It must be said that the statement is vague; it reiter-
ates a classical commonplace on the imitation of nature and combines it with a moralistic definition of drama as the humanists
applied it generally to comedy; but in Hamlet's mouth, the remark
that the players should show the "very age and body of the time his
form and pressure" has a peculiar urgency. One recalls how the
prince himself holds constantly the mirror up to others; the reformer of the stage also would like to be the reformer of his time. In
either role, Hamlet leaves something to be desired; he has not
finished his thoughts, and, presumably, neither had Shakespeare.
Hamlet's strictures on acting and drama are symptomatic of Shakespeare's struggle with the problem of artistic change; they breathe a
nostalgic addiction to a fading tradition and an acute awareness of
a change. In practice, Shakespeare was already in the process of

adjusting himself to new fashions, particularly to the satiric mood. But he did not yet release the full power of passion in any of the characters he created. It is possible to pronounce the speeches of the tortured Hamlet in the mixture of passion and temperance he advocates; but it is impossible to utter those of the jealous Othello in the same fashion.

Hamlet's remarks on the theater point to a tension between theory and practice in Shakespeare, a tension characteristic of mannerist art, which sought to solve the problem of tradition versus innovation by rational means.[11] There is here an attempt to cling to the balanced certainties of the Renaissance; but they fail to satisfy. The heroes of the two tragedies of this period, Hamlet and Brutus, are confronted with tasks for which their theoretical training does not equip them. For them, what knowledge teaches differs from what experience shows, and Hamlet, at least, is pained by the discrepancy. The theme of seeming and being, of deception and truth, which always interested Shakespeare, is more strident in these plays. Troilus, even more unequipped to deal with reality than Brutus and Hamlet, fragments his psychological substance in a fruitless attempt to identify the real Cressida with the woman he seeks to idealize. Bertram and Angelo are men of deceptive and even engaging outsides, but both are deeply corrupt underneath.

And what is true of the characters is also true of their milieu. Rome, Denmark, Troy, and Vienna are more insidiously and perplexingly vicious than the locations of Shakespeare's previous dramas. It is not merely that they are corrupt—so is the Venice of *The Merchant of Venice* and the court of *As You Like It*—but that the corruption is ingrained and unrelieved by convincing alternatives. There is no Belmont to balance Venice, no Forest of Arden in which to take refuge from Duke Frederick's court. And it is not merely that much significant action takes place at night—so it does in earlier and later plays—but that darkness becomes a cloak for dubious and deceptive actions. Troilus's and Cressida's tryst, taking place under the aegis of the leering Pandarus, is a deliberate and satirical variation of Romeo's and Juliet's wedding night. In *All's Well* and *Measure for Measure,* the happy solutions are achieved by acts of darkness and deceit, the bed-tricks by which Helena and Mariana claim their husbands. In *Julius Caesar,* the conspirators gather in stormy nights, and Caesar's ghost appears to Brutus in a dark tent at Sardis. In *Hamlet,* two nocturnal appearances of a ghost open a play that is never perfectly lighted. A later tragedy, *Macbeth,* it is true, contains more night scenes than *Hamlet,* and they hold more terror, but they do not have the same atmosphere of uncertainty. There is in *Hamlet* and the plays of this period a fascination with night because it disguises the truth or makes it ambiguous.

The uncertainties, ambiguities, and unresolved problems that permeate these plays point to a shift in Shakespeare's world view away from the certainties of the Renaissance. The vision of reality that shaped his earlier dramas resembled that of a Renaissance painter who depicted persons and things as solid, tangible bodies, clearly bounded, proportioned, and situated in intelligible space. Now reality becomes fluid and problematic as it is in mannerist art: the lines twist and curve; proportion and spatial arrangements are freakish and vexing. Mannerist art, as Jacques Bousquet has noted, has sometimes a dreamlike quality: "In dreams, people and things are never exactly what they seem; they are either in contradiction with themselves, being one thing and its very opposite simultaneously; or, if they do achieve a moment of precise definition, it is only to change just as abruptly and become something else." [12] Hamlet's world approaches this oneiric state; he could be a king of infinite space if he had not bad dreams.

But when mannerist vision is awake and conscious, as it is generally in Shakespeare, the contradictions and ambiguities of the world are due to an eminently skeptic look at it: there is no clear demarcation of shadow and light, of truth and falsehood; opposites merge imperceptibly into each other and become indistinguishable. From being a comprehensive, structured frame, the world becomes a shifting semblance. As Justus Lipsius, a neo-Stoic touched by skepticism, said, acting prudently in this world was a very "diffused thing, confused, and obscure" because this world itself was very "diffused." [13] And Montaigne in "An Apology of Raymond Sebond" —although he purported to defend the *Theologia Naturalis,* an elaborate fifteenth-century defense of a rational universe—granted a little condescendingly to Sebond that it was likely "that this vast world's frame must bear the impression of some marks therein imprinted by the hand of this great, wondrous architect, and that even in all things therein created there must be some image somewhat resembling and having coherency with the workman that wrought and framed them." Montaigne went on to say that "our imbecility" is the cause that we cannot read or discover the marks imprinted by God in the visible world.[14] To a diffused world like that of Lipsius or an unreadable one like that of Montaigne, it is difficult to apply the existing standards. The nature of both macrocosm and microcosm, as well as their relation, are uncertain. When there are no longer definite answers to the question of what is true and false, right and wrong, it follows that there is no static system of values and that one must suspend judgment. Skepticism and mannerism come from the same world view and are interrelated. Montaigne has been called "the unofficial philosophic voice of mannerism" when he asked: "What do I know?" [15]

In all the plays of Shakespeare's mannerist period, there is a similar concern with questioning and even with rejecting the ability of the mind to see the truth. It was not a totally new interest for Shakespeare; it appeared, for instance, in *Richard II,* a play that anticipates some of the mannerist patterns. But now the heroes are not only ignorant of themselves and uncertain of the world in which they live; they also are placed in situations that make self-knowledge peculiarly difficult if not impossible. This begins with *Julius Caesar,* where already the story, as Shakespeare found it in Plutarch, turned on the irony that men make decisions whose moral significance they cannot foresee. Brutus is a man most studious of virtue; he ponders deeply whether to join the conspiracy or not; when he decides that he must do so if he is to remain himself, he, the selfless idealist, enters the world of political intrigue and assassination in alliance with the self-seeking Cassius, and, while he remains addicted to his high ideals, his actions become dubious and criminal. Hamlet's problem of determining the truth of the things he believes he knows is even more acute: first his mother's hasty and incestuous marriage, then the revelation of the ghost make him a stranger to the world and to himself. He loses his way more thoroughly than Brutus and can much less keep from doing so; he is astray in a universe of disintegrating and illusionary values, where an "uncle-father" murders his own brother, marries the latter's widow, and yet smiles; where school friends are enemy spies; and where it is impossible to say whether it is better to act or not to act, to be or not to be. And he finds it difficult to say clearly whether anything is good or bad— thinking makes it so. Troilus believes he knows Cressida, but finds out differently; his idealism and chivalric code make him incapable of understanding the real nature of his beloved. Nor does he judge his own nature better; some weakness, difficult to diagnose but connected with an endemic relativism and with a Trojan obsession with honor, prevents him from asking the question whether he is not himself responsible for his delusion. In *Measure for Measure,* Vincentio undertakes a governmental and human experiment that is to determine the best way to govern and to test the moral nature of Angelo; but the dangerous situation of his state obliges him to take the direction of events in his own hands to prevent misfortune. In the process, Angelo falls and asks the question "What dost thou and what art thou Angelo?" in a spirit of incomprehension about himself and human nature in general. Angelo appears indeed to achieve self-knowledge through repentance, but many of the ethical and political questions posed by the duke's experiment remain unanswered.

Clearly, Shakespeare during this period was particularly concerned with the problematic nature of knowledge and inclined to some sort of skeptical position. Of course, this is not, as such, proof of his interest in philosophic skepticism. Skepticism is an attitude as well as a philosophy, and one can be a skeptic without being a philosopher. In a sense, every dramatist must be something of a skeptic: he must be able to see more than one side of a question; he must take an experimental attitude toward the reality he wishes to dramatize; he must devise situations that make his characters react at variance and create different characters that react variously to one and the same situation. The growth of a relativistic and skeptic spirit in Shakespeare was surely related to his development into a mature artist.

It is also highly probable that personal experiences had something to do with Shakespeare's more skeptic look at the world from *Julius Caesar* on. When he wrote *Henry V,* he looked forward expectantly to the victorious return of the Earl of Essex, "bringing rebellion broached on his sword" (V.32). But soon after that, perhaps when Shakespeare was engaged in writing *Julius Caesar,* Essex's failure became apparent. In *Henry V,* Shakespeare had compared Essex to the victorious king, but his debacle must have given him a heightened feeling of the dubiousness of all political action, a feeling that pervades not only *Julius Caesar* but also *Hamlet, Troilus and Cressida,* and *Measure for Measure.*

Relativism and skepticism feed on the awareness of man's errors and contradictory actions, whether this awareness comes from life or theory. Plutarch's *Lives,* in which Shakespeare immersed himself when writing *Julius Caesar,* must have sharpened his view of man's subjection to errors and of the baffling discrepancies between intention and execution. That Shakespeare took a more detached attitude toward Brutus and toward Caesar than he had taken toward the characters of his history plays, can surely at least in part be attributed to his having graduated from the Tudor chroniclers to a wiser guide, one more sensitive to the weaknesses of human nature. And the satire in *Hamlet* and *Troilus and Cressida* undoubtedly owes much to Shakespeare's seeing the relativistic and debunking plays of some of his contemporaries like Marston and Jonson. As Shakespeare became acquainted with attacks on, and alternatives to, orthodoxy, his sense of the relativity of values grew even without any specific knowledge of skeptic philosophy. Relativism is encouraged by the realization of contradictions between world views, by the canceling-out of one supposed certitude by another. Hamlet's "nothing is either good or bad, but thinking makes it so" does not, as such, prove that Shakespeare was reading skeptic philosophy; the remark is symptomatic of the age's increasing disillusionment with norms and occurs in some form quite frequently.

But it still appears to me likely that Shakespeare was reading skeptic philosophy at some time during this period, perhaps not yet when he was writing *Julius Caesar,* but at least when he came to *Hamlet* and *Troilus and Cressida.* Hamlet tests some of the most cherished humanistic assumptions on the nature of man in ways that owe something to skeptic ideas, and *Troilus and Cressida* is pervaded by these.

This latter play also contains evidence that Shakespeare had a technical knowledge of the distinction between the moderate, academic skepticism of Cicero and its difference from the radical, "Pyrrhonic" school of which Sextus Empiricus's *Hypotyposes* was the classical model. The former skepticism was embraced by many Christian humanists; the latter was gaining ground in Shakespeare's England, particularly after the translation of Montaigne's "Apology of Raymond Sebond." [16] The proof of Shakespeare's knowledge of the two schools comes in the debate of the Trojans, when Hector assumes the moderate, and Troilus the radical, position. Hector, the mouthpiece of reason, proposes peace negotiations and the restoration of Helen to the Greeks because of the uncertainty the future holds; "modest doubt," he says, "is call'd / The beacon of the wise, the tent that searches / To th' bottom of the worst" (II.ii.15–17).

Hector thus sides with the wise man of Cicero's *Academica* who
doubts to the degree of not giving too easy an assent to the phenomena. Troilus, however, will have none of such caution, and puts his
argument for passion and war on the relativity of all values; the
Trojans can make Helen into a symbol of reward for their struggle
because "What's aught but as 'tis valued?" (52). Troilus here takes
a Pyrrhonic view much like Montaigne's: "That our opinion en-
deareth and encreaseth the price of things . . . and we call that
worth in them, not what they bring us, but what we bring to them.
According as it weighteth and is of consequence, so it serveth." [17]
Hector objects to this argument that "value dwells not in particular
will: / It holds his estimate and dignity / As well wherein 'tis precious of itself / As in the prizer" (53–56). This is quite the moderate humanistic position that things have value not only through the
appraiser but also in their own right.[18]

Although Montaigne's popularity in early seventeenth-century
England undoubtedly was great, the *Essays* were not the only source
of philosophical skepticism, and one should not make the mistake
of equating the influence of skepticism on Shakespeare with that of
Montaigne. Neither should one equate philosophic and religious
skepticism, although it is true that on the edges of philosophic doubt
agnosticism and atheism were spreading.[19] Skepticism in its simplest
form as doubt in the mind's ability to attain to the truth was a
respectable Christian attitude. Christianity, as the Elizabethans inherited it, contained many anti-intellectual, pietistic, and mystical
elements that were antipathetic to the rationalists' claim for the
efficacy of human knowledge. The skeptic passages in Shakespeare's
plays do not give any indication of religious doubt, and some emphasize that faith is superior to knowledge. Thus Hamlet reproaches
Horatio, who takes a rationalistic attitude toward the ghost and
will not let belief take hold on him:

> And therefore as a stranger give it welcome.
> There are more things in heaven and earth, Horatio,
> Than are dreamt of in your philosophy.
>   (I.v. 165–67)

The remark echoes many Christian objections to rationalism, beginning with Paul's deprecation of "philosophy and vain deceit"
(Col. 2:8) and his glorification of the mystery of God over human

wisdom (I Cor. 2:7). The Genevan side-note to the latter passage defines "mystery" as "that which men could not so much as dream of" and thus uses the same metaphor as does Hamlet and, for that matter, as did countless Renaissance theologians.[20] Another, even more pronounced fideistic declaration is in *All's Well* when the king's old counselor, Lafeu, expresses his master's seemingly miraculous cure by Helena:

> They say miracles are past; and we have our philosophical persons to make modern and familiar things supernatural and causeless. Hence is it that we make trifles of terrors, ensconcing ourselves into seeming knowledge when we should submit ourselves to an unknown fear.
>
> (II.iii.1 ff.)

Lafeu here opposes the "atheistic" position, as it was held for instance by Cicero in *De Divinatione* (II.60) that all natural events have natural causes. Except for taking the opposite viewpoint, Lafeu's words come close to Cicero's.[21]

Like Montaigne, Shakespeare was open-minded and undogmatic when it came to natural occurrences. But we must not press this and other affinities of thought even if they are occasionally combined with verbal resemblances; the arguments about truth developed often on classical and theological commonplaces that were all cultured men's property. It would be equally hazardous to assert on the basis of Hamlet's and Lafeu's words that Shakespeare had a sudden upsurge of faith or to claim him as being radically relativistic on the basis of the rampant skepticism in *Troilus and Cressida*. Positions taken in these plays are generally subjected to questioning through ironies, ambiguities, and paradoxes. Thus Lafeu's espousal of fideism occurs in a bantering conversation with Parolles, who echoes, apes, and contradicts the old counselor. We are left in doubt where Shakespeare stands because whatever seriousness Lafeu's words lose by the travesty, they regain in part by the fact that Parolles is an example of the "seeming knowledge" that the old counselor castigates.

Shakespeare generally did not let his philosophic interests damage his dramatic designs; yet these very designs breathe a conception of life as a hazardous venture. More noteworthy than the skeptic attitudes taken by Hamlet and Lafeu are the ways in which their statements highlight the dramatic uncertainties from which the actions of the two plays arise. The speeches, spoken in awe about most unusual occurrences, draw attention to the difficulty and dubiousness of the tasks that are central to both plays. In *Hamlet,* the ghost demands a course of action from the prince for which the latter has no map or plan; he must act on the command of a questionable agent, who may be his father's spirit or the devil. In *All's Well,* the healing of the king is the achievement on which Helena has staked her hope of winning and regenerating Bertram, a hazardous enterprise, considering the young count's nature.

The fideistic position with its low opinion about the mind's ability to decipher microcosm and macrocosm often entailed, as it does in Hamlet's and Lafeu's words, an attack on man's pride in his reason. The main thrust was aimed at such idealistic or rationalistic metaphysics as that of Plato and Aquinas, but fideism-skepticism also contradicted the more moderate Christian-humanist position as exemplified by Erasmus and Hooker. Not that either Aquinas or the Christian humanists neglected to list pride as a sin detrimental to self-knowledge—Erasmus castigated pride strongly in *Enchiridion* —but they did not direct their castigations at man's attempts to come to some rational conclusions about his role in the universe. Montaigne's sarcasm about such presumption was uninhibited:

> Is it possible to imagine anything so ridiculous as this miserable and wretched creature, which is not so much as master of himself, exposed and subject to offenses of all things; and yet dareth call himself master and emperor of this universe in whose power it is not to know the least part of it, much less to command the same? And the privilege, which he so fondly challengeth, to be the only absolute creature in this huge world's frame perfectly able to know the absolute beauty and several parts thereof, and that *he* is only of power to yield the great architect thereof due thanks for it, and keep account both of the receipts and layings-out of the world! Who hath sealed him this patent? Let him show us his letters of privilege for so noble and so great a charge.[22]

Montaigne, however, did not push this position to the logical conclusion that man could say nothing about the universe and his relationship to it. He was not averse to accepting the idea of a universe shrinking and degenerating like man when it could be made to show up man's absurd pride, the pride of an animal living on a shrinking planet "farthest from heaven's cope." [23]

For the mannerist-fideist, self-knowledge implied a realization of the absurdity of man's proud claim to rationally know himself and

God. This fideistic article is reflected iconographically in an early seventeenth-century emblem, mannerist in its paradoxical subtlety. Entitled *Nosce Teipsum,* it shows a peacock—symbolizing man—rearing a pearl-studded tail—symbolic of reason—proudly toward the sky; but the bird turns its crest toward its ugly feet—meditation, as the punning motto explained, bows man (*homo*) to the earth (*humus*).[24]

The exposure of man's pride in his reason was not a subject new to Shakespeare in his mannerist period—we may recall *Richard III* —but it becomes now more explicitly associated with the patterns of self-knowledge, as, for instance, in Brutus's persuasion by Cassius (I.ii.51 ff.) and in Ulysses's appeal to Achilles to rejoin the battle (III.iii.95 ff.). This exposure appears also in a much subtler form than in *Richard III* as the hard-to-discern defect of an essentially fine and sympathetic mind like that of Brutus. And, I think, there is a similar dram of pride in Duke Vincentio and Isabella; as I shall argue, it is, by implication, acknowledged by them in the end. And Hamlet, metaphysically, although not psychologically, the humblest of men, deflates the intellectual certitude of the Danish court, as when, most amusingly, he exposes Polonius's presumption in conceiving of himself as sane and of Hamlet as mad.

In their varied ways, all of Shakespeare's plays of this period demonstrate man's inability to discern rationally who he is and where he belongs. The plays take problematic attitudes toward the self, toward man in general, and toward society and the universe. The various frames of existence are shown to have fissures, and the possibility of harmonious relationships between them is drawn into question. Brutus, essentially harmonious man that he is, becomes disharmonious in a Rome that is changing from republic to dictatorship. Hamlet's agonized spirit cannot break through the prison bars of his Denmark even though he sees a light beyond. Troilus's debilitated idealism is deflated by the brutal sexual and military realities of Troy and Greece. Duke Vincentio never finds the answer to what it takes to be an ideal ruler in the corrupted currents of Vienna. As the characters' world becomes problematic, they turn inward to find other insoluble contradictions: Hamlet comes to a point where he questions the very possibility of self-knowledge, and Troilus thinks of himself in the end as being just as contradictory and fragmented as Cressida and the Trojan war appear to him.

When conventional ideas associated with self-knowledge are invoked, their relevance becomes sometimes ambiguous or disappears. The old humanistic conviction is lacking when Hamlet asks himself the question what man is if the chief goods and markets of his time are but to sleep and feed. And when, as in *Troilus and Cressida,* ethical norms are proclaimed, their application to the present situation is questionable, as is instanced by Ulysses's advocacy of degree that he conspicuously fails to translate into action. The old commonplace becomes a euphemism for power politics and for shoddy intrigue. There is here and elsewhere a cleavage between what was once and what is now as well as a contradiction between what there should be and what there is. Theory and practice, ideal and reality have a problematic relationship to each other.

The discrepancy between the humanistic theory and the reality of the self is expressed in Shakespeare's ambiguous attitude toward the "pattern of perfection," the ideal man he had embodied in his ideal king, Henry V. There is no character in Shakespeare's plays of this period who can be said to know himself in the manner of Henry. Brutus is indeed a man of virtue, but he falls prey to an appeal to his awareness of himself as a virtuous Roman; his errors and failures prove that it is not enough in this world to be a well-balanced man. Hamlet admires Horatio as a kind of pattern of perfection, a just man, who is neither the slave of fortune nor of passion; but Hamlet's attraction to the ideal appears an aesthetic and nostalgic aspiration that is drawn in question by the paleness of Horatio's actual character as it appears in the play. In this respect, Hamlet's attitude resembles that of Montaigne, who still was fond of patterns of perfection and flirted with the idea that they could be found among the poor. (Hamlet, too, notes Horatio's poverty when he commends him.) Montaigne also admitted that he was pleased when others said of him, "Lo, there a pattern of true fortitude; lo, there a mirror of matchless patience." [25] But the pinch of his kidney stone kept him from keeping up the pose, and he admitted that "there is nothing I so hardly believe to be in man as constancy and nothing so easy to be found in him as inconstancy." [26]

Inconstancy and inconsistency are characteristic of the heroes of four of the five plays under discussion. Brutus is the one exception; but his republican constancy is a corollary to his lacking sensitivity to the moral ambiguity of his action. Hamlet, whatever else he may be, is the spirit of inconsistency; the shallower Troilus, although he chants absolutes, is corroded by a pervasive relativism. Bertram has not enough psychic substance for us to expect constancy from him; that of Angelo, thought spectacular, proves an illusion. Even Duke Vincentio, the stablest of the major characters, has troubles in deciding what his actions should be. He has let the law lapse for many years, then experiments with restoring it through the agency of a deputy stricter than himself; but finally he takes the reins in his hands again. Although he is the most exemplary of Shakespeare's rulers after Henry V, he is far from being a signal pattern of perfection; but then, he also has to contend with more difficult psychological problems.

With the problematic moral orientation of the major characters is connected a disorientation of the minor ones. In Shakespeare's earlier plays, the heroes put themselves in a context of either morality or immorality and take the others with them in the one or the other direction. Henry V is a perfect king, and his follower Fluellen an admirable man and soldier; Richard III is a villain, and his friend and supporter Buckingham a traitor. Henry and his adherents opt for a moral world, Richard and his for an immoral one; but both sets act according to the choices offered to them in a world that they understand. For Brutus and Hamlet, there are no clear moral options; the world is an uncertain and hazardous place.

This is not to say that the characters in the earlier dramas are merely static. Prince Hal, for instance, is placed on a middle ground between evil and good and grows morally in each of the two parts of *Henry IV*. He is at first attracted to the fun-loving but duty-eschewing Falstaff and cold toward the political world of his father to which one day he must belong fully. But Hal's position does not have the baffling uncertainties of the call to political action Brutus receives or the soul-harrowing terror of the demand to avenge his father that comes to Hamlet. It is indeed clear from the beginning in which direction Hal will go; he will become England's hero-king rather than end in a tavern brawl in Eastcheap. Hal's attitude to others, to his father, to Falstaff, and to Hotspur, is at any time known to us even if not always to them. Hamlet's oddities and antics, as much as they fascinate us and as much as we accept them as part of his character, sometimes bewilder us as much as the characters on whom he practices them. He and some of the other heroes of this period seem to need a psychological disguise in a world which, like that portrayed by mannerist painters, is one of doubt and secret anxiety, which therefore requires an armor instead of a body, a mask instead of a face.[27] Brutus wears the armor; Hamlet and Duke Vincentio wear masks, the one a psychological one, the other an outward one; Troilus tries both the mask and the armor but is successful with neither.

In Shakespeare's mannerist plays, the feeling of uncertainty created by the characters' lack of direction carries through the dramatic designs from the beginning to the end. It is true that the hope of Romeo and Juliet to find themselves is as precarious after the death of Tybalt as is Hamlet's endeavor to restore his own and Denmark's health after the killing of Polonius; but the two lovers' certainty about themselves lessens our feeling that it is so. Also, they are placed in a symmetrical design between the hostile Montagues and Capulets, a design that allocates the tragic responsibility to fate and the hostile parties. They never lose themselves as inextricably as does Hamlet in the labyrinthine worlds of his soul and the universe. Although Romeo and Juliet die, they win a victory for Verona and humanity: this is a better world for their having lived and loved. It is not so in Denmark or in Rome: Hamlet's wounded name may be healed, but Denmark will be in the hands of the unknown Fortinbras, and the ideal of liberty is certainly not advanced by the death of Brutus. The endings of *Troilus and Cressida* and the two comedies are so dubious as to have made some critics attribute them to Shakespeare's artistic uncertainty. Nothing is really concluded in *Troilus and Cressida* except Troilus's love for Cressida. And there is something conditional about the happiness of the characters at the end of *All's Well* and *Measure for Measure:* we must trust in the sustained efficacy of the astonishing conversions, and more than one critic has found such trust difficult.

The complexities and ambiguities of these plays go deep, deeper than this and the following brief discussions can indicate. For instance, one may read the endings of some of the plays more positively than I have done. Hamlet's decision to abandon his attempts to analyze himself, his situation, Denmark, and the world is accompanied by his declaration that, from now on, he will trust in the providence that is present even in the fall of a sparrow. Similarly, the ending of *Measure for Measure* can be read as an apotheosis of faith.[28] Certainly, an appreciation of these endings requires more than the customary acceptance of improbable accidents at the end of conventional comedies; it does require faith. faith in the miraculous moral regeneration of a scoundrel like Bertram and a hypocrite like

Angelo. And *Measure for Measure* does make the point of the Sermon on the Mount that one should not mete out to others what one does not mete out to oneself. Admittedly, fideistic elements are present in these plays although, contrary to some theologically oriented critics, I believe that Shakespeare used them tentatively, hesitatingly, and with some mental reservations, not yet, as for instance in *The Winter's Tale* and in *The Tempest,* with force and artistic assurance.[29] Yet, the quality and role of fideism and, for that matter, many other problems of form and thought in these plays are difficult to evaluate. One may arrive at divergent, at times even opposite, conclusions if one chooses a perspective different from the one I have adopted in making the issue of man's knowledge of himself the focal point.

Shakespeare's mannerist plays are vexing and disturbing, and they make self-knowledge a more puzzling and hazardous quest than do any of his other works, but they also speak to us in a particularly provocative voice. We feel a keen and probing mind at work in an age that resembles so much our own. These tragedies and comedies point to a conflict in Shakespeare's mind and art between humanist and counter-humanist ideas; they are the product of an age that felt tentative, torn, and self-conscious in exploring man and the universe independently. The plays reflect Shakespeare's struggle with the ideas of the world in which he was brought up. At times they affirm them, at other times they reject them; but more often they probe and question them. Whatever blemishes some of the plays may have, they all render fascinating insights into extraordinary human predicaments. They have a quality of improvisation, of attempting statements that are not definite but demand revision and perhaps total restatement. Agitated by the winds of a cultural crisis, they strike a sympathetic chord in us, makers and victims of another cultural crisis.

CHAPTER NINE

Julius Caesar:
Taking an Uncertain Road

SHAKESPEARE'S REFERENCES to Alexander and Caesar in *Henry V* make it appear likely that he was reading Plutarch while writing the English history play that he followed up very shortly with his second Roman tragedy, the first to be based on Plutarch.[1] But whether Shakespeare was reading the Life of Brutus while he wrote *Henry V* or soon after it, he must have felt that Brutus, no less than Caesar and Alexander, resembled his ideal king in some important respects but differed from him in others. Brutus was Plutarch's pattern of perfection as much as Henry was Holinshed's; but in Holinshed, the pattern was equated with success, in Plutarch, with failure. Brutus was a man of moral excellence; yet he murdered the greatest man of the world.[2] In making him into the protagonist, Shakespeare could not take a simple and absolute approach; he had to accept the relativistic position that, under certain circumstances, ethical strength becomes ineffective and that what is good from one point of view is evil from another. He must have felt at this time, if not before, that neither man nor the universe was quite what, on the basis of his humanistic education, he had thought they were, and he must have been struck by the baffling discrepancies in human life between intention and execution, character and motive, action and result.

At any rate, to dramatize the story of the assassination of Julius Caesar meant for Shakespeare to take a new and uncertain road. In the present chapter, I shall examine Shakespeare's difficulties and his solution; in particular, I shall review in some detail how he created Brutus from Plutarch's facts and appraisals and what changes he made, changes that had considerable influence on the patterns of self-knowledge not only in *Julius Caesar* but also in *Hamlet,* which was to follow.

Plutarch characterized Brutus as an ideal personality, Roman style; but, since many features of this type were taken over by the humanists, Plutarch's Brutus resembled the humanists' pattern of perfection. Examples of his courage, magnanimity, constancy, gentleness, and justice abound in the Life of Brutus. He was for Plutarch, particularly in contrast with Cassius, a model of temperance, that virtue central to self-knowledge: Cassius, although skillful in war, was too choleric, too familiar with his friends, and too cruel with his enemies. Brutus, however, was esteemed by everybody, "because he was a marvelous lowly and gentle person, noble-minded, and would never be in any rage, nor carried away with pleasure and covetousness, but had ever an upright mind with him and would never yield to any wrong or injustice, the which was the chiefest cause of his fame, of his rising, and of the good will that every man bare him: for they were all persuaded that his intent was good." Plutarch certified this portrait by the testimony of Caesar's closest friend and Brutus's conqueror: "For it was said that Antonius spoke it openly diverse times that he thought that of all them that had slain Caesar there was none but Brutus only that was moved to do it as thinking the act commendable of itself, but that all the other conspirators did conspire his death for some private malice or envy that they otherwise did bear unto him." [3]

From this passage Shakespeare fashioned Antony's famous epitaph of Brutus:

> This was the noblest Roman of them all.
> All the conspirators save only he
> Did that they did in envy of great Caesar;
> He only in a general honest thought
> And common good to all made one of them.
>   (V.v.68–72)

To this paraphrase from Plutarch, Shakespeare added a characterization of Brutus in terms of Renaissance humor physiology by taking up the cue of temperance:

> His life was gentle; and the elements
> So mix'd in him that Nature might stand up
> And say to all the world "This was a man!"
>   (V.v.73–75)

We could have no better authority and no clearer formulation: Brutus is a harmonious, balanced man, a man who knows himself.[4]

Yet it is remarkable how little of this Brutus we ever actually see in the play. When he first appears, he is a deeply unhappy man, a lonely figure who takes no "gamesome" interest in the public competition at the feast of Lupercalia. He is absorbed with his own problems, "vexed . . . with passions of some difference . . . with himself at war" (I.ii.39–46). And this conflict in his soul grows as he ponders whether to join the conspiracy. He disquiets his wife by his musing and sighing, his "ungentle looks," his angry gestures, and his walking at night (II.i.237). After he has made his decision, it is true, he is resolute; but we still have indications, such as his irritability toward Cassius and his restlessness in the dark tent at Sardis, that all is not well with him.

Not that we ought to write off Antony's tribute to Brutus's internal harmony as posthumous glorification. We see sufficient vestiges of the earlier, balanced Brutus to accept the notion that he was once a completely harmonious man. This is most apparent in his private life. His tender care for his friends and servants shows him to be a man of exceptional humaneness. But, most of all, he has in Portia a companion whom he trusts and who in return enters into his life and gives it completion. The episode in which she proves her constancy by wounding herself in her thigh presents a picture of a marriage of two souls, who yet—in an image of which Shakespeare was fond—become one self. She implores him gently,

> By all your vows of love, and that great vow
> Which did incorporate and make us one,
> That you unfold to me, your self, your half,
> Why you are heavy . . .
>   Am I your self
> But, as it were, in sort or limitation?
> To keep with you at meals, comfort your bed,
> And talk to you sometimes?
>   (II.i.272–85)

Brutus's subsequent revelation of his plans to her shows that there are no impediments to this marriage.

Even in his public life, Brutus evinces something of his earlier harmony. His firm leadership of the conspiracy points to his basic stability and equanimity. Divided and disharmonious as he is internally, he braces himself outwardly and exerts a vivifying effect on the conspirators similar to that which Henry V has on his troops before Agincourt. Like the English king, he exhorts his followers to look "fresh and merrily" and to bear their burdens "with untir'd spirits and formal constancy" (II.i.224–27). His example has an inspirational effect on Caius Ligarius, who arrives at the conspiratorial meeting in the guise of a sick man:

> I here discard my sickness. Soul of Rome!
> Brave son, deriv'd from honourable loins!
> Thou, like an exorcist, hast conjur'd up
> My mortified spirit.
>
> (321–24)

Like Henry, Brutus can conjure up mortified spirits, but—the difference is essential—he cannot sound in harmony with the state, whose soul Caius thinks him to be. In the English history play, an harmonious king is in tune with an essentially harmonious kingdom; in the Roman tragedy, a potentially harmonious statesman is placed in a commonwealth which does not "keep in one consent, / Congreeing in a full and natural close, / Like music" (*Henry V,* I.ii.181–83).

As Brutus prepares himself for his deed, the microcosmic-macrocosmic analogy he draws suggests that the discord of the state is reflected in the dissonance of his soul:

> Between the acting of a dreadful thing
> And the first motion, all the interim is
> Like a phantasma or a hideous dream.
> The Genius and the mortal instruments
> Are then in council; and the state of man,
> Like to a little kingdom, suffers then
> The nature of an insurrection.
>
> (II.i.63–69)

The psychological lore on which Shakespeare drew for this passage is the organic and hierarchical conception of the microcosm as he used it in the history plays. The harmony of Brutus's soul is disturbed because the natural order has ceased to function; the king-like mind no longer rules; the psychic instruments refuse to play their proper advisory and executive functions. Instead, "the mortal instruments," [5] that is, the lower parts of the soul, the senses and passions, arrogate seats in the royal council to which they are not entitled. The soul of Brutus is in a state of crisis.

We should not be oversubtle and diagnose Brutus's "aristocratic" psychology as reflecting a subconscious desire to be king instead of Caesar. Shakespeare psychologized in the terminology of his time, as we do in ours, and the political analogy was natural to him. However, the passage is symptomatic of his general lack of interest in Brutus's republicanism and of his concern with a larger issue, that of the interaction between the order of the state and the individual's self-fulfillment. The psychological problem of Brutus is analogous to the political problem of Rome; it turns on the question of how to establish a legitimate and functioning order, and Brutus's psyche is affected by the perplexing situation that order in Rome is represented by the detestable system of Caesarism. There can be no such simple solution for him as there is for the heroes of the history plays, who realize their self by bringing it in harmony with a monarchical and organic conception of the state. In this respect, Shakespeare's choice of the unusual, Latinate word "Genius," meaning the mind, is of interest; it is a reminder that the particular mind now ruling Rome is Caesar. And in Elizabethan English, "Genius" denoted not only the rational soul but also the *daimon,* a spirit, good or evil, with which man had an inseparable and fateful connection. [6] Shakespeare used the word in this latter sense at the end of *The Comedy of Errors* when the duke wonders whether one of the Antipholuses is "genius to the other" (V.i.331). The clever Antony alludes to the same superstition when he calls Brutus "Caesar's angel" (III.ii.181), hinting ambiguously that Brutus was beloved by Caesar but turned into his evil spirit. But for the Brutus that ponders the conspiracy, the designation of "genius" applies to Caesar, and it does so in an even more sinister manner: Caesar is the evil angel that has usurped the state, and this usurpation is reflected in the disturbed order of Brutus's microcosm. The image of Caesar becomes the "genius" of the mind of Brutus. But, as he sees his problem, it is not the simple one of restoring harmony in the state and order in the soul by removal of the corruption in the former and the conquest of the passion in the latter; it is the task of liberating state and soul from the danger of being dominated by a demonic spirit. To say that Brutus invents the spirit of Caesar would be an exaggeration, for we see the spirit manifested in Caesar's frail body and later in his much stronger ghost; yet only Brutus among the conspirators conceives the issue in terms of a fight against an evil force rather than a tangible person or a definable system. Brutus can be said to exorcise the spirit that defeats him.

The dissonance in the soul of Brutus was altogether Shakespeare's idea. Plutarch's Brutus suffered no anxiety until he joined the conspiracy, and he was nervous then merely because of the danger of discovery. Nor was Plutarch's Rome as turbulent as Shakespeare's; although in transition from republic to monarchy, it was competently ruled and not particularly dissonant. In the play, the political atmosphere is as stormy as the nights in which the conspiracy gathers force; the transition that threatens is not one from a republic—it has ceased to exist—into a monarchy but from a dictatorship into a tyranny based on the low instincts of the crowd.

This, I believe, is the main point of the opening scene, in which the tribunes, Marullus and Flavius, oppose the populace by pulling the trophies off Caesar's images. The anecdote was in Plutarch's Life of Caesar, but its occasion and meaning were quite different. The incident followed rather than preceded the Lupercalia, and the people sided with the tribunes, who were adherents of Brutus rather than of Pompey. In the play, the opening conveys a feeling of a loosening order: the "mechanicals" are in the streets without the signs of their trades and make a holiday where none is called for. They have lost their sense of what is due to Rome and what to Caesar; they are sheep running after their leader. As Marullus pointedly reminds them, it was for Pompey's victory over external enemies that they cheered earlier; now they hail Caesar for triumphing over a personal, internal foe, this very Pompey. And Shakespeare's crowd is particularly fickle and shifty. Scolded by the tribunes, the people appear ready for another turnabout and "vanish tongue-tied in their guiltiness" (I.i.63).

This is the disturbing prelude to the intricate second scene in which Cassius accosts Brutus while Caesar takes part in the feast of Lupercalia, is offered the crown, and refuses. This scene is most important for an understanding of the character and situation of Brutus; but we will do well to turn first to Caesar, whose words and actions—partly presented on the stage and partly reported by the blunt and cynical Casca—are intertwined with the probing of Brutus by Cassius. In this play of conflicting personal and political loyalties, it is particularly difficult to isolate one figure from the other. One is

forced to piece together his opinion about a character from words
and actions that are partisan; sometimes these are spoken by some-
one bound to this character by friendship or separated from him by
enmity; at other times what is said subtly involves one's own political
bias. What one thinks of Brutus, in particular, rests very much on
what one holds of a Caesar and Caesarism.

I cannot attempt here to do justice to Shakespeare's subtle portrait
of Caesar. He is neither simply a hero nor clearly a villain. But I
think that in the second scene an unpleasant fact about Caesar
emerges, which, at this point, would have influenced favorably the
Elizabethans' attitude toward Brutus: Caesar shows himself as "ambitious"—a word they uniformly took in a bad sense. He wants
the crown, but does not dare to claim it yet because the people cheer
his feigned reluctance. His first words are almost all orders, and they
are promptly obeyed by the sycophants around him. As Antony puts
it euphemistically, "When Caesar says 'Do this', it is perform'd"
(I.ii.10). These and other features, such as his appeal to crowd
instincts and prejudices, his boastfulness, and his capricious insistence
that his every whim be gratified, would have made an Elizabethan
audience conclude that Caesar is, or aspires to be, a tyrant.[7] And that
is exactly what Plutarch said he was: when the Romans chose him
to be perpetual dictator, they chose "plain tyranny." [8] In Elizabethan
English, this word had strong emotional associations; it evoked fear
of misrule and of the vengeance of God. Shakespeare's audience would
transfer to Caesar some of the apprehension they felt about a tyrant
like Richard III.

But the second scene depicts also a curiously frail Caesar who
suffers from epilepsy and is deaf in one ear. The contrast between
his physical infirmity and his unquestioned political power is ironic,
and so is that between the sterility of his marriage and his attempt
to reach for the crown. In a way, Caesar's frailties serve to humanize
him. Although in that moment of *hybris* before his downfall he
sees himself as above the ranks of men of flesh and blood, he is
human enough to make one believe that Brutus loves him or loved
him once. But he is also the instigator of a new, tyrannical order,
which is ominously evoked by Casca's laconic report that the two
censorious tribunes "are put to silence" (284)—a much more sinister
remark than Plutarch's comment that they were deprived of their
tribuneship. This is the same order as that instituted after Caesar's
death, when men are "pricked to death" without trial—an order

triumphant in the coolly effective Octavius, who has no human handicaps. If Brutus has reason to love Caesar, he has even more reason to fear him; the behavior of the crowd, of Caesar, and of Caesar's entourage all support his apprehension. Shakespeare's ambiguous portrait of Caesar gives Brutus a cause to oppose him that is subtler and more difficult to define than the solid republicanism embraced by Brutus in Plutarch; he is a man of divided feelings who requires an internal struggle and clever outside persuasion before he joins the conspiracy.

The Cassius who approaches Brutus in the play is a much more skillful intriguer than Plutarch's. He uses even Machiavellian techniques: he has letters thrown into Brutus's window, reminding him of his noble ancestor who defeated tyranny (whereas in Plutarch, the friends of Brutus spontaneously urged him to oppose Caesar). Caesar judges Cassius shrewdly as a dangerous man who sees through the deeds of others and envies those greater than himself. Cassius's arguments to make Brutus join the conspiracy are artful and deceptive: they appeal astutely to Brutus's self-image and distort cleverly a text from the book of self-knowledge.

The cue for Cassius's appeal was in Plutarch, who had him demand that Brutus prove worthy of his name: "What, knowest thou not that thou art Brutus?" The Romans, said Plutarch's Cassius, would suffer any hardship for Brutus's sake "if thou wilt show thyself to be the man thou art taken for and that they hope thou art." [9] Shakespeare's Cassius couches this appeal in a figure traditionally associated with self-knowledge, that of the eye's inability (analogous to the soul's) to see itself.[10] Cassius's opening gambit— "Tell me, good Brutus, can you see your face?"—produces Brutus's expected answer: "No, Cassius; for the eye sees not itself / But by reflection, by some other things" (51–53). Cassius now offers himself as the convenient medium by which Brutus may look into his soul or, to use Cassius's conventional figure, as the glass, which "Will modestly discover to yourself / That of yourself which you yet know not of" (69–70). Brutus recognizes the drift of this argument even before it is made:

> Into what dangers would you lead me, Cassius,
> That you would have me seek into myself
> For that which is not in me?
>
> (63–65)

But by the end of the scene it is evident that Brutus will search his soul.

The persuasion of Brutus by Cassius introduces a problematic quality into Shakespeare's patterns of self-knowledge. In a way, it is true, the use of the mirror image has some resemblance to that in *Richard II;* the mirror is ambiguous, it is simultaneously one of truth and flattery. But truth and flattery become now inextricable. Caesar's power is dangerous; the freedom-loving, noble Brutus must oppose Caesar and Caesarism if his soul is to see itself clearly. But Cassius appeals covertly to the pride of Brutus in his honor and strength; Cassius's account of Caesar's weakness is surely not merely evidence of his envious nature but also a subtle blandishment of Brutus's self-conception as a strong man who fears the loss of honor more than death—unlike the Caesar who dared Cassius to a swimming match and then had to implore him for help. Brutus's sense of honor, justified by his reputation, provides an opening for Cassius to demand that Brutus take his fate into his hands and show that the name of Caesar is no more than that of Brutus (139 ff.). We are not told how much this argument influences Brutus; but certainly his attempt at gaining self-knowledge is polluted by elements of deception: by flattery and by an evil insinuation. Cassius's Iagoesque sneer that noble minds should ever be with their likes is a grim comment on the ambiguous image of Brutus as a virtuous seeker and a deluded victim.

It is worth noting that in the passage in Plato's *First Alcibiades* (132 ff.)—the *locus classicus* for the eye-mirror analogy—the comparison illustrates the argument of Socrates that the statesman requires self-knowledge. I wonder whether Shakespeare knew the passage, perhaps through some commentary on Cicero's *Tusculan Disputations;* if not, certainly he was familiar with the ubiquitous idea of the mirror for princes and magistrates. In direct contrast to these precedents, the mirror of Brutus promises no clarity. If Brutus is to seek in his soul "what is not there," he must seek to establish order, a different one from Caesar's, in himself and in the state. Yet the traditional self-examination advocated by the Renaissance moralists provided no help for a situation like his. We cannot say, as we can with Richard II, that disaster would have been avoided if he had considered himself in time; had known himself as a composite of body and soul; and had realized the presumption and weakness of the former, and the strength and glory of the latter. The kind of questions that Brutus should ask himself are much more practical and particular than those asked in the conventional *nosce teipsum* tracts. He should concern himself with his role in politics, with the suitability of his temperament and character for political leadership, with the justification of using questionable means to achieve desirable ends, and with the chances of predicting the outcome of violent action.

Brutus does examine himself, and he has no choice but to do so in uncharted ways. Nothing is more characteristic of his lack of convenient precedent than his great soliloquy, "It must be by his death" (II.i.10 ff.), which examines the motives that have made him decide to murder Caesar. The soliloquy follows that ominous scene of thunder and lightning and miraculous happenings, a scene that orchestrates the uncertainty in which the decision has to be made. In the words of the coolly skeptical Cicero, this is "a strange-disposed time." The conspirators, men of action, interpret without qualms the portents in a sense favorable to them; Brutus, man of action as well as of reflection, finds taking a position much harder. But three parts of him, we learn from Cassius during the storm, already are persuaded to join the conspiracy. The soliloquy shows that now the whole man is convinced. Rising before daybreak after the tempestuous night in which he has not slept, he goes over the reasons why Caesar must be killed. They are reasons of great significance for Brutus's attempt to assess his relation to Caesar, an attempt that begins with his fateful conversation with Cassius. Although they have been often examined by critics, who have come to diverging conclusions on the bearing these reasons have on the character of Brutus, we must look at them again. Much of what one thinks of Brutus depends on them.

Shakespeare's Brutus does not object to Caesar's becoming king as such; he seems in fact reconciled to this prospect. Any reference to the motivation of Plutarch's Brutus, that of restoring the republic, is avoided. Shakespeare's Brutus fears what Caesar, crowned, may become: "How that might change his nature, there's the question" (II.i.13). And he answers this question by finding Caesar's coronation potentially dangerous: it would "put a sting in him / That at his will he may do danger with" (16–17). He bases his hypothesis that Caesar may turn into a tyrant on the axiom of the corrupting influence of power: "Th' abuse of greatness is, when it disjoins / Remorse from power" (18–19). Admittedly, Brutus has not observed that Caesar's "affections sway'd / More than his reason" (20–21). However, he fears that Caesar's incipient ambition will grow. This surmise is based on another axiom, a "common proof" of the danger of the upstart's reach for power: "lowliness is young ambition's ladder" (22). Brutus admits that this is all hypothetical, founded on what Caesar *may* become rather than what he is. And since the quarrel cannot be based on what Caesar is, Brutus will kill him "as a serpent's egg, / Which, hatch'd, would as his kind grow mischievous" (32–33).

These are highly theoretical reasons, but they are surely not invented to support a foregone conclusion, as M. W. McCallum claimed, nor are they symptomatic of the muddleheaded idealism to which, according to John Palmer, all liberal politicians are given.[11] Brutus's soliloquy clearly follows a pattern of inner struggle; it is not a declaration of political principles, but a recapitulation of the reasons why Caesar must be killed. In his later speech to the people, Brutus's tone is decisive, his attribution of ambition to Caesar categorical. In the soliloquy, he goes out of his way to take the most favorable opinion of Caesar possible. It is worth noting that Plutarch (in the comparison of Dion and Brutus, the two conspirators paired in the *Lives*) spoke of the skillful way in which Caesar established his dictatorship so that, to well-meaning Romans, he appeared a benevolent healer of the state: "For there never followed any tyrannical nor cruel act, but contrarily it seemed that he was a merciful physician, whom God had ordained of special grace to be governor of the empire of Rome and to set all things again at quiet stay the which required the counsel and the authority of an absolute prince."[12] Having seen Caesar and his entourage in Shakespeare, we find it difficult to accept this estimate, and Brutus's benevolence appears akin to naïveté. But, although Brutus does not see or want to see fully the progress Rome has made toward tyranny, he does not engage in fantastic theorizing when he sees Caesar as a threat. After the experience of our own age, it would be hard to deny that such "lowliness" as Caesar's— how his fawning to the crowd contrasts with his usual presumption!—is "ambition's ladder" and perilous to any nation. Caesar and Caesarism, as J. Dover Wilson has well argued, represent perennial dangers.[13]

Brutus fails to satisfy us not so much in what he says but in what he omits to say. He should ask himself such questions as the following: Can I really cleanse the state by making common cause with an envious and selfish man like Cassius? Will not the act that I wish to make one of liberation become soiled by the hands of Machiavellian conspirators? And, most of all, he should ask: Does my cause justify murdering a man? Brutus does not ask these questions, and thus, scrupulous as he tries to be, he misses the mark. Brutus's soliloquy foreshadows the several overly analytical soliloquies of Hamlet, which, searching as they are, somehow do not go to the heart of the matter.

We should say, of course, that to ponder such questions as the above would have made Brutus an even more problematic leader of a conspiracy. And we must also say that the answers are not so simple as they appear. This is a difficult and confusing moral territory. All political action involves means over which the politician lacks full control. To adapt a maxim of Henry V, battles cannot be won with clean soldiers only. If Brutus's analysis of the political situation in Rome is accepted, as I think it must be, the state is in an emergency that requires an extraordinary solution. And most of us, as much as we deplore murder, sympathize with those who risk their lives to free their country from oppression. We rejoice in the fall of a tyrant and may even condone his killing if it appears the only way of his removal.

Brutus may not think hard enough; but that at least absolves him from the accusation of being too theoretical a man for leading a conspiracy. He is, admittedly, not the stock type of a conspirator; but that makes him, up to Caesar's death, not less, but more effective. He is an idealist, but he is also a man who can inspire others. Plutarch admired his leadership, and I see no reason to think that Shakespeare did not. Brutus injects fervor and a sense of purpose into what otherwise would be a merely brutal enterprise. When he takes the high road, he takes the best one—provided of course that we think he should go forward. When he dissuades the plotters from taking an oath and asks them to trust in "honesty to honesty engaged," he chooses a practical as well as a noble course: to assume loyalty is a good way to achieve it. Brutus's leadership up to and including the murder of Caesar is superior; by contrast, the others are nervous, and even Cassius turns to Brutus for reassurance and instruction when, at the last moment, he believes the plot betrayed.

But, good as Brutus's direction is, he cannot prevent the moral ambiguities of his action from asserting themselves at the murder. In his last minute, Caesar wins, as it were, a victory over Brutus. *"Et tu Brute!* Then fall, Caesar!" is the most brilliant utterance of that effective phrasemaker and steals the thunder from Cinna's simultaneous cries of liberty and freedom. The great actor Caesar understands how to make himself into a martyr and a victim of ingratitude; he does not accept the role of sacrificial lamb for the gods assigned to him by Brutus. And Caesar's murder also proves the delusion of Brutus's claim that "We all stand up against the spirit of Caesar, / And in the spirit of men there is no blood" (II.i.167–68). There is much blood in Caesar, as is manifest in the rite in which the conspirators wash their hands in this blood. The hands of Brutus, too, are now soiled. What he did, he did in honest thought; but he used the unclean hands of the others, and no more than they will he escape the consequences of the act. He was wrong when he believed that he could be a sacrificer without being a butcher. Yet in an ironic sense he was right when he said that the conspirators stood up against the spirit of Caesar. A spirit cannot be laid to rest through murder. Brutus's uncertain road has led to a certain crime that will be avenged.

Shakespeare's Brutus falls, as does Plutarch's, through a series of errors. Shakespeare was bound to have Brutus commit them, but he could and did create intellectual contexts that made them more plausible. The worst of these mistakes is to let Antony live and to permit him to make the funeral oration. On both counts, the conspiratorial instinct of Cassius, who opposes him, are right even though Brutus's is the nobler attitude. But it is an attitude abetted by the delusion that a man's spirit can be killed by killing his body. Antony may be but a limb of Caesar, but the limb becomes mighty indeed when directed by Caesar's spirit.

This spirit of Caesar was Shakespeare's most brilliant addition to the story. Plutarch had almost all the elements of which it is composed—Caesar's tremendous popularity, outlasting his death, the desire of the people to be ruled by a strong man, Caesar's magnetism, the adoption of his methods by his inheritors, and an evil spirit that appears to Brutus—but he had no spirit of Caesar. By creating it, Shakespeare read sense and purpose into the facts of history Plutarch recorded, and he established a dramatic counterforce to Brutus, which prevents the play from losing its balance in the last two acts. The conspirators' failure evolves logically and consistently from the murder and is presided over, from this very moment on, by Caesar's spirit.

We can go further and say that Caesar's spirit is actually the presiding genius from the beginning of the play when the disorderly crowd hangs trophies on Caesar's images. Brutus is up against an evil genius, in the modern and in the Elizabethan sense of the word, who exploits the disharmony in the state to create a new political system that mocks any kind of order in which men can live freely. Significantly, the one appeal to the principle of subordination on the basis of a universal order in the play is made by Caesar when he calls himself "constant as the northern star" (III.i.60), and it is conspicuously perverted by his claim of being far above humanity, "unshak'd of motion." The inhuman spirit of Caesar is in his people. As Max Lüthi has noted, it is in the seeds of violence Cassius sows in the mind of Brutus; the letter Cassius has thrown in Brutus's window incites him to "speak, strike, redress!" (II.i.47), which in its rhythm anticipates the crowd's later turn against the conspirators: "Seek! Burn! Fire! Kill! Slay!" (III.ii.204).[14] It is this spirit that makes Brutus's listeners shout "let him be Caesar," when he wins their approval for his action (49)—even this moment of his greatest triumph really belongs to Caesar. And the spirit of Caesar infuses strength into Antony when, left alone with Caesar's bleeding body, he prophesies that "Caesar's spirit, ranging for revenge, / With Até by his side come hot from hell" will "let slip the dogs of war" (III.i. 271 ff.). Antony can turn the crowd against Brutus not merely because of his well-appreciated oratorical skill and Brutus's prosaic deficiency but also because he is carried along by the Caesarism around him. When, at the opportune moment, he removes the covering mantle from the body of his master, the populace roars for revenge. The living Caesar caters to, and espouses the spirit of, violence that sets in motion currents that ignite and that, after his death, destroy the conspirators.

The spirit of Caesar, living and dead, prevents the essentially harmonious Brutus from recovering the stability he has lost. There is one moment in the play when it looks as if he might become fully himself again, in his tent at Sardis, when he is reconciled to Cassius; he feels that he has a chance of changing his fortunes for the better: "There is a tide in the affairs of men / Which, taken at the flood, leads on to fortune" (IV.iii.216–17). When his friends depart, he asks for music, that harmonizer of souls. The lute-playing boy falls asleep; Brutus gently takes the instrument from him and meditates, book in hand. Just then the ghost appears and announces that he will return at Philippi. The hope for harmony is gone.

Brutus does not concern himself here or later with the question of whether his decisions are and were morally right; after his soliloquy in the second act on the reasons for murdering Caesar, he has put this question aside. The moment he comes closest to asking it again, or perhaps we should say the moment at which we feel most that he ought to ask it, is during the quarrel scene with Cassius. He does here question his friend, "Did not great Julius bleed for justice' sake?" But Brutus's uncertainty—if there is uncertainty in his voice —comes only from his realizing the smaller contamination of his cause through Cassius's weakness for bribery, not from understanding the more serious wholesale contamination of the cause by the egotistically-motivated conspirators. Neither does he examine the question whether political assassination is ever justified. This lack of a sufficient self-examination goes far toward making us lose our tragic sympathy for him.

Not that we really expect him to voice regret about having killed Caesar or to realize fully the fallacies of his actions; we understand his motives well enough and, if we do not approve them, we take satisfaction in our wider view of his predicament (although our wider view is facilitated by our not really being in his predicament). Regardless of how we feel about the crime he has committed, we take him for a man whom fortune has treated most harshly; his hopes for a free Rome have proved an illusion, he has become an exile, he is disappointed in his main friend and ally, and he faces the possibility of being defeated in battle. Yet, we are disappointed when he gains no insight into his condition and remains almost totally immutable while his world crumbles. We can hardly expect Shakespeare to have made him into a neurotic victim of a harrowing ghost-spirit as he made Hamlet—the conception of Brutus's character in Plutarch and in Renaissance consciousness prevented this possibility—but, had he wished, he could surely have given him some awareness of the irony of committing an act whose consequences completely contradicted his expectations. He could have given him a realization of the cleavage between intention and execution, character and events, and he could have given him something of a momentary shudder. The absence of any such reaction is remarkable. Brutus's tragedy, as Ernest Schanzer has noted, is that of a denied *anagnorisis*.

In seeking for an explanation as to why Shakespeare did not give Brutus as least an inkling of his tragic situation, critics often attribute to the Roman hero a rigid Stoicism and make its insufficiency as a guide to human conduct responsible for his lack of insight. Brutus, we are told, has steeled himself against fate and refuses to fret about it; the training of his will has atrophied his sensibilities.[15] But I do not think that this is a fair judgment, and to the extent that it is based on Brutus's alleged Stoicism, it is quite false. Shakespeare did not characterize Brutus as a Stoic if the word is to be understood in any technical sense. My reader, I trust, will bear with me if I examine this matter in some detail; it is significant not only for the character of Brutus but also for Shakespeare's attitude toward Stoicism and philosophy in general.

Plutarch's Brutus was certainly not a Stoic. He had studied, as Plutarch noted at the beginning of his Life of Brutus, all sorts of Greek philosophers and liked them, "but above all the rest he loved Plato's sect best and did not much give himself to the New or Mean Academy, as they call it, but altogether to the Old Academy." [16] Like Plutarch's Brutus, that of Shakespeare criticizes the Stoic Cato for his suicide (V.i.101 ff.). But the clearest indication that Brutus is not to be taken as a Stoic is in the quarrel scene with Cassius, when he proves incapable of suppressing the emotions in the way the austere members of this school demanded.

This is a remarkable and pivotal scene that brings into focus the contrast between the idealistic and righteous Brutus, for whom a war fought for justice' sake must not be tainted by private corruption, and the pragmatic Cassius (philosophically he is an Epicurean), who fails to see why a little bribery can hurt the war-effort. But while the scene demonstrates that Brutus is a stranger to the thought of selfish plotters, it shows that he is no stranger to the inner life, the life of feelings. He is, in Edward Dowden's phrase, "studious of self-perfection," [17] but he is not inhumanly so. In the quarrel scene, he is close to losing his emotional control, and the real reason for that is not Cassius but Portia.

It is significant that Shakespeare connected and combined the quarrel scene with the news of Portia's death. In Plutarch, it came at a later juncture and produced no reaction from Brutus beyond making him write letters that reproached his friends for not having prevented her suicide. In combining the quarrel with the news of Portia's death, Shakespeare motivated Brutus's reaction not merely by his irritation about Cassius but also by his personal grief—a motivation, it appears, that was important enough for him to make it clearer by revising the scene as he had originally written it.

As the scene stands in the Folio and in modern editions, there are two mentions of Portia's death. In the first instance, Brutus himself breaks the news to Cassius when the latter accuses him of not making use of his philosophy (IV.iii.144 ff.). Cassius immediately apologizes for crossing his friend, calling the loss "insupportable" and "touching." Then Messala enters, and, in the course of questioning Brutus concerning other matters, asks him whether he has news about Portia (179). Strangely, Brutus answers in the negative, and Messala now announces hesitantly that Portia is dead. The reaction of Brutus is to assert his own patient readiness.

It has long ago been argued that in all probability the duplicate report of Portia's death was due to Shakespeare's revision of the scene, and that the canceled passage, presumably the messenger's report and Brutus's second reaction, remained accidentally in the text.[18] In what appears to be the original version, Brutus takes refuge in his philosophy—the strain is evident—as he is apprised of Portia's death. In the presumable revision, Brutus is aware of it from the beginning, and his irritation with Cassius is partly motivated by the sorrow he finds hard to master. In either version, but more poignantly in the revision, Brutus shows signs of strain. And, after he has settled his quarrel with Cassius, he freely admits that he was ill-tempered. Emotions, as he knows, do at least temporarily affect him:

> O Cassius, you are yoked with a lamb,
> That carries anger as the flint bears fire;
> Who, much enforced, shows a hasty spark,
> And straight is cold again.
>   (IV.iii.109–12)

In admitting that he was affected by passion, Brutus gives a characteristic twist to an image the Elizabethans associated with Stoicism. For claiming that the wise man is impervious to all emotion, the Stoics were, since Cicero, called men of wood or stone.[19] Antony, who surely knows that Brutus is no Stoic—as much as he knows that men's souls have not fled to beasts—seeks yet to attach to him the opprobrium of being one when he suggests in his funeral oration that Brutus has a heart of stone. Antony does not exactly say that Brutus is devoid of human emotion—after all, he had promised not to blame the conspirators—but he does say that everybody else has feelings. Dead Caesar, he says, was a man of compassion: "When that the poor have cried, Caesar hath wept; / Ambition should be made of sterner stuff" (III.ii.91–92). Antony himself chokes with emotion, an affliction he exploits oratorically: "My heart is in the coffin there with Caesar, / And I must pause till it come back to me" (106–7). He cleverly alleges that he does not wish the people to see Caesar's will:

> You are not wood, you are not stones, but men;
> And being men, hearing the will of Caesar,
> It will inflame you, it will make you mad.
>
> (142–44)

The insinuation that Brutus and his conspirators are men of wood and stone—and thus for the Elizabethans the worst of austere Stoics —is clear. To emphasize the contrast between Brutus and the Romans in general, Antony approvingly notes the "gracious drops" of pity on his listeners' faces. Ironically, however, these are the same people whom Marullus called for good reasons "You blocks, you stones, you worse than senseless things!" (I.i.36). It is equally ironic that the one character who feels that his constancy exempts him from the ranks of men who "are flesh and apprehensive" and makes him "unshaked of motion" is Caesar. In view of his previous wavering on whether to go to the Capitol, he does not appear to be totally immobile; but he sees himself at any rate as a super-Stoic. Brutus, who knows himself a flint that occasionally strikes a hasty spark, does not. And by giving way somewhat to grief and anger, he becomes indulgent with the human limitation of the boy Lucius in the next scene; he is gently protective when Lucius falls asleep. We should not succumb to stereotype notions about the Romans and Roman philosophy or to Antony's insinuation and call Brutus a Stoic.

If Brutus fails to satisfy in the end, it is not because he is a Stoic but because he does not experience his situation existentially enough. This, I think, is both an emotional and an intellectual failing, but of a different order from Stoic "apathy." If there is a shortcoming in Brutus's philosophy, it is not his failure to feel deeply enough in

general but his failure to react to the events in some way that makes
one think that he understands how insecure man is and how much
he sometimes becomes the prisoner of events he cannot control.

The failure of Brutus to examine his situation in some such
fashion is the more notable as the characters in the play comment
on man's inability to foresee the consequences of his actions. Even
the generally unreflective Cassius shows an awareness of man's predicament when he questions Brutus on what to do in case of defeat:
"But, since the affairs of men rest still incertain, / Let's reason with
the worst that may befall" (V.i.95–96). Cassius also has something
of a metaphysical shudder when he gives way to fear about unfavorable omens and "partly" credits them. This fear even makes
him give up his Epicurean philosophy, which denied their meaning
(V.i.76 ff.). Cassius, one might say, becomes a fideist. By contrast,
Brutus declares himself capable of judging the "tide in the affairs of
men"—although the wave images he uses should make him aware
of the erratic nature of the events on which man floats (IV.iii.216–
22).

But the most explicit statement by any character concerning man's
susceptibility to misjudging the tides is made earlier, during the
crucial period when Brutus is in the process of coming to his fateful
decision of murdering Caesar, and it is made by a character whose
role in the play is secondary, although it was primary in Roman
life: Cicero. In the tempestuous night full of strange happenings that
frighten the previously cynical and blunt Casca and make him believe
that they are portents of the events to come, the philosophic Cicero
comments:

> Indeed, it is a strange-disposed time;
> But men may construe things after their fashion,
> Clean from the purpose of the things themselves.
> (I.iii.33–35)

Cicero's ensuing question, "Comes Caesar to the Capitol to-morrow?"
associates his generalization in our minds with the plan of murdering Caesar—of which Cicero knows nothing. But one may apply
what he says to all the erroneous judgments made in the play, those
of Caesar, of the conspirators, and particularly of Brutus. As Lüthi
has shown, Cicero's statement characterizes the intellectual climate

of the play; its significance is enhanced by being assigned to the man whom the Renaissance recognized as its philosophical father.

The failure of Brutus, measured by Cicero's skepticism, lies in his taking a positive, idealistic attitude toward human actions in preference to a pragmatic and skeptic one. Rather than to incline toward the Old Academy (as Plutarch said Brutus did), he should favor the more skeptical New Academy (to which Cicero's *Academica* belonged and which, according to Plutarch, Brutus did not like). Instead, he remains an idealist; the world is his will and idea, not in the crude sense of his being arrogant, but in the sense of his believing that he can transform the world according to the ideal pattern of his mind. There may, of course, be a subtle sense of human pride in all philosophical idealism—at least, the skeptics thought so. The skeptic and fideistic atmosphere of the play is one reason more that we find the grave and sober words he continues to speak inappropriate to the occasion. In this respect, he resembles the human figures on mannerist canvases that include details that conflict with and contradict the proportions and the postures of these persons. Mannerist painters, as has been noted, often did not give to their major figures the same psychological language as that which they gave to the surroundings.[20]

Thus, in the final analysis, Brutus offers more of a contrast than a parallel to Henry V, of whom Shakespeare must have been reminded when he created him. Both, it is true, are men in whom the elements are mixed in perfect proportions. But, in the situation in which Henry finds himself, this temperance provides a sufficient basis for the kind of self-knowledge that leads to the deployment of the self for maximum success; in the situation of Brutus it does not. If my argument is accepted that the failure of Brutus lies in not considering sufficiently the baffling uncertainty between intention and execution, character and event, one must say that the pattern of perfection cannot escape some blame for this deficiency; it had no built-in provisions for considering such uncertainty. Intentionally or not, Shakespeare's treatment of the pattern in Brutus shows up its insufficiency and even irrelevance to actual life; and it does so in a manner like Montaigne's and the skeptics', for whom the self had to adapt itself to the changing human environment. A constancy and self-consistency like Brutus's seemed to Montaigne particularly inadequate. In *Julius Caesar,* Shakespeare appears to have felt the

winds of skepticism that are blowing much stronger in *Hamlet*. If
so, Montaigne hardly is responsible; not even the most fervent advocates of the influence of the essays have discovered parallels in
Julius Caesar. There were, after all, native fideistic sources of skepticism, and there was the moderate New Academy of Cicero, who in
the play becomes a spokesman for the skeptics' position of suspending
judgments. And, there was Plutarch, whose dispassionate treatment
of the events may have suggested to Shakespeare a need for rethink-
ing his ideas on the connection between character and fate, between
human agency and historical development.

But I must confess to a lingering doubt about my interpretation.
If, as I have claimed, Brutus's lack of flexibility and his idealistic
rigidity are fundamental flaws of his character and motivating
themes of the action, it must be said that they are not given altogether convincing dramatic expression and are, to say the least,
difficult to convey on the stage. What one does notice in performances
is that the later Brutus becomes more withdrawn and taciturn. As
Granville-Barker put it, "Having lifted his heroic Roman to this
height, . . . [Shakespeare] leaves him to stand rather stockishly
upon it." [21] Barker blamed Brutus's Stoicism for his "stockishness."
I believe that the explanation I have given of his inappropriate
"idealism" accords better with Shakespeare's intentions as they can
be ascertained from close reading of the source and the play. But to
make this philosophy of Brutus responsible for his lack of self-
discovery requires more arguments about what he does not do or say
than what he does or says. For an audience or reader to feel that the
tragic hero is denied an *anagnorisis,* they must expect one, or be told
by the dramatist that they should. To see a hero's self-certitude as
a failure to adopt a skeptic attitude, one must not only understand
that the other characters take such an attitude but he must also
sympathize with it (unless, of course, the hero himself confesses his
failure in an *anagnorisis*). My reader must judge for himself on
these points. In his tragedies, Shakespeare generally does seem to
provide some kind of *anagnorisis,* but it is sometimes a very rudi-
mentary one, such as Romeo's "O, I am fortune's fool!" and occasionally, as in *Hamlet,* it is so questionable as a diagnosis of the
hero's flaw and situation that the term does not appear appropriate.
But one can speak with greater assurance of a missed *anagnorisis*
when he analyzes himself wrongly than when he says nothing
at all. And we certainly do not know the percentage of skeptic-

fideists in Shakespeare's audience, people who would have been conditioned to interpret the play in the fashion I have suggested.

Perhaps our curiosity as to why Brutus is uncommunicative about what we consider the great psychological issue of the play is merely the result of an unhistorical and oversubtle approach to character interpretation. Perhaps my explanation that Brutus fails because he faces the world with philosophic certainty comes from too much reading of Montaigne. Perhaps Shakespeare wished merely to suggest that Brutus is isolated and lonely. But the fact remains that we are baffled about his behavior. So we are, of course, about Hamlet's; but in his case, we accept a much stranger behavior—although not verbal reticence—as dramatically right. In *Julius Caesar,* there is something dramatically not quite right. But if the play is—it seems a presumptuous judgment—something of a failure, it is an explicable one and one most beneficial for Shakespeare to have suffered. I know of no real precedent Shakespeare had for exploring the internal structure of a man like Brutus. The conventional *nosce teipsum* theories on which he had drawn for the *anagnorisis* of his earlier tragic heroes gave him no help; they were even hard to acclimatize to Rome. What he needed he could only obtain in the school of the skeptics and in the school of experience, and he had, perhaps, not yet progressed sufficiently in either. That he learned from *Julius Caesar* is evident in *Hamlet,* where the constraint of the source material and the complexity of issues created by Shakespeare himself are never allowed to detract from our fascination with, and belief in, Hamlet as a tragic human being. Shakespeare walked Hamlet's uncertain road with dramatic certainty. Shakespeare may have learned more from the relative artistic failure of *Julius Caesar* (it was an audience success) than from his previous triumphs. And only in comparison with his later and greater tragedies can one speak of a failure at all.

CHAPTER TEN

Hamlet:
Probing a Restless Self

I T IS APPROPRIATE that *Hamlet,* the play that poses so
many questions, begins with one, Bernardo's challenge to
Francisco: "Who is there?" This is the first of the many identity questions, and it is one that originates in a confusion, for not
the sentry at guard, Francisco, but the relieving officer, Bernardo,
asks for the watchword; he is immediately corrected by Francisco:
"Nay, answer me." A dozen lines later, the confusion repeats itself
when the relieved Francisco, rather than Bernardo, challenges the
newcomers, Horatio and Marcellus: "Who is there?"

The slight irregularities with which the play opens are symptomatic of the sinister threat to order in Denmark that gradually reveals itself in other questions of identity. The appearance of the
ghost on the dark platform of Elsinore throws an ominous shadow
over the beginning action. This ghost, being as like to the dead King
Hamlet, Horatio says to Marcellus, "as thou art to thyself," yet
defies Horatio's attempt at identification:

> What art thou that usurp'st this time of night
> Together with that fair and warlike form
> In which the majesty of buried Denmark
> Did sometimes march?
>
> (I.i.46–49)

Apprehensions about the ghost's identity and purpose carry over
from the first scene to the second, from the dark platform to the
lighted room of state, where the new king, Claudius, evokes the
memory of "Hamlet, our dear brother's death" with a "dropping
eye," and his marriage to his brother's wife with an "auspicious"
one. Claudius appears suave, efficient, and benevolent. The marriage

occurred with the approval of the counselors, but Shakespeare's audience, like Hamlet, would have considered it incestuous. There appears now, almost as disturbing as the ghost, the dark figure of the prince in all the warmth, color, and light. When Claudius, having attended to urgent external and domestic problems, turns to him in apparently fatherly concern, "But now, my cousin Hamlet, and my son—," the uncomfortable young man sets himself apart from the kindness and complacency around him in a riddling aside: "A little more than kin, and less than kind." He rejects the identity Claudius wishes to impose on him; he declines to be related to his "uncle-father." When his mother asks him to cast his mourning garments off because, as she innocently says, why should what is common seem so particular to him, Hamlet takes offense. He refuses to be identified with his garments or, indeed, with any observances of grief that merely *seem* and, by implication, with all that is common and merely seeming in Denmark. He is nauseated by the identities that the others assume and by that which they wish to thrust on him, and he thinks of suicide. In his first soliloquy, he betrays a desire to leave the unweeded garden of a world possessed by things rank and gross in nature. He is prevented only by the religious injunction against self-slaughter.

The subject of identity arises in a different key in the following scene, as in a narrower room the members of the family of Polonius lecture each other on their proper roles in family, society, and state. At the brink of his departure for France, Laertes warns Ophelia not to show favor to Hamlet: the prince's identity as designated heir to the throne will put him out of Ophelia's reach. Ophelia offers some reciprocal advice on her brother's virtuous conduct in France. Polonius then enters and dispenses to his son a string of maxims on morals and manners, capped with the admonishment to be true to himself. Such has not been the case with Ophelia, the loquacious counselor argues as he is left alone with her: "You do not understand yourself so clearly / As it behoves my daughter and your honour" (I.iii.96–97). Ophelia must give up Hamlet and isolate him further.

Hamlet's crisis of identity reaches its first climax when he confronts the ghost. Its relationship to him is even more problematic than that of Claudius; but whether or not it is "a spirit of health or goblin damn'd" he will call it king, father, and royal Dane. Hamlet's disposition is horribly shaken; his already restless mind is set into violent turbulence. He accepts the challenge with the same overheated reaching for the ultimate with which he earlier protested his devotion to truth above appearances. He will stir in this revenge, but, strangely, he will do so by putting on an antic disposition. Whatever Shakespeare may have thought was the reason for Hamlet's psychological self-disguise, and even if he had no particular reason at all, the device of playing the madman gives Hamlet's restless mind something to do. He can put this antic disposition on and off like a mask, play fast and loose with his enemies, and take time to explore his own identity and that of the others.

Hamlet's actions and behavior proceed from a highly agitated and complex state of mind, which, from the beginning of the play, makes him uncertain about his place in the world. His melancholy, his bitterness and disillusionment, his feigned madness and real nervous shock give additional impulses to his churning intellect that cannot identify itself totally with anything—not with the state of Denmark, not with the world, not with his revenge, not with his grief. Hamlet is thus driven not only to avenge his father, but also to explore the basis on which all actions, good and evil, rest. He becomes concerned with self-knowledge.[1]

That Hamlet considers self-knowledge an ultimate goal, we have his own words. The remark comes very late in the play, in the final scene when Osric invites the prince to the duel with Laertes (V.ii. 136 ff.).[2] The foppish courtier professes to give Hamlet a fair warning: "You are not ignorant of what excellence Laertes is—." Hamlet cuts him short: "I dare not confess that, lest I should compare with him in excellence; but to know a man well were to know himself." The remark is somewhat cryptic, and thus Dr. Johnson tried to straighten out its syntax and meaning. Hamlet, Dr. Johnson said, means "I dare not pretend to know Laertes lest I should pretend to an equality; but no man may completely know another but by knowing himself, which is the utmost of human wisdom."

But this paraphrase is not quite correct, for it ignores the inversion that gives the statement a more conditional turn: what Hamlet really says is that "to know Laertes were to pretend to know that I am as excellent as he; but I could do so only if it were possible to know myself." It will be said, of course, that this statement is part of Hamlet's game of puncturing Osric's turgid rhetoric, and it is; yet the phrasing of the interchange between Osric and Hamlet points to its having a philosophical significance worth recovering for the thoughtful reader of the play. The key words of Osric's invitation that excite Hamlet's rejoinder are "ignorant" and "excellence." They were common in Renaissance moral tracts dealing with self-knowledge; Pierre de la Primaudaye, for instance, began the first chapter of his *French Academy* by marveling at the "excellence of man" and by warning that "ignorance of ourselves [is] the cause of much evil." [3] Reacting as he does to Osric, Hamlet shows his sensitivity to the idiom of self-knowledge and proves himself aware of the importance and difficulty of the subject.

Hamlet's struggle for self-knowledge is a subject of utmost importance in this play, which, unlike any other of Shakespeare's, forces us to approach it through the hero's baffling and baffled consciousness. The pragmatic test of theater and of criticism proves that in *Hamlet* it is not, as in Aristotle's *Poetics,* plot before character but character before plot. And the greatness of the play does not derive from having as its hero a character most appropriate for the action, but rather one most inappropriate. *Hamlet,* the play, exhibits a mannerist tension between its form, that of a revenge tragedy, and its content, that of a drama of ideas. And Hamlet, the hero, suffers stresses and conflicts between one part of his nature and another, between himself and his task, between the real and the ideal. He is a much more deeply divided man than Brutus; his internal tensions are heightened beyond the normal scale. Eliot's observation that Hamlet is dominated by an emotion that is in the final analysis inexpressible was well made; Hamlet's passion is in excess of the facts as they appear.[4] But it does not follow, therefore, that the play is a failure; rather, the very incongruity between the facts and Hamlet's emotions is one of the reasons for its success. If Aristotle will forgive me, I shall say that one reason for the appeal of *Hamlet* is that through the actions and reactions of its unique hero it purges us of the guilt feelings we have about our own maladjustments to this inadequate world by magnifying them.

In no play of Shakespeare's have the hero's soliloquies greater importance for getting a feeling of its quality; yet from the point of view of action, they are almost negligible, and the plot can be summarized with very little reference to them. Hamlet's soliloquies, which have been the focus of most critical interpretations of the play, are fascinating and perplexing exercises in self-analysis. Without them, *Hamlet,* the play, would not rise as far above Elizabethan revenge tragedies as it does. Without them, Hamlet, the hero, would

look more like certain other characters and types we know from the
stage. The soliloquies are surely a major reason why descriptions of
him as an average young man fail to satisfy. No mere "young man's
unreasonable disgust when he discovers that elders are as strongly
sexed as himself" [5] accounts for the almost late-Tolstoyan sex nau-
sea of Hamlet's first soliloquy, "O, that this too too solid flesh would
melt." And surely, the self-flagellation of the second soliloquy, "O,
what a rogue and peasant slave am I!" goes beyond the customary
self-reproaches of a typical avenger.[6] Hamlet's most famous soliloquy, the third, which has been thought to show that he is a descendant of the medieval Everyman,[7] does not deal merely with the religious question of death and immortality, to be and not to be, but
also with the existential question, to act or not to act and thus to be
or not to be, and with the speculative question on the state of the
soul after death. Hamlet's fourth and short soliloquy " 'Tis now the
very witching time of night" betrays no Christian conscience and
makes him outwardly appear a typical bloodthirsty avenger; but the
action it introduces is not the killing of the king, but Hamlet's moral
lectures to his mother. The fifth soliloquy, "How all occasions do inform against me," is hard to reconcile with any of the three mentioned abstractions—the average young man, the Everyman, and the
avenger—and to designate him on its basis as a typical Elizabethan
nobleman contradicts his hatred of code and court.

Hamlet is extraordinary, and he possesses an extraordinary mind.
The quality and fascination of the play lie to a large degree in his
strange and complex mental states that take in and simultaneously
deny typical forms of experience. Whatever one may say about
Hamlet, he is not static; restlessness is a major ingredient of his
searching and suffering spirit.

Since the romantics at least, critics of very different persuasions
have found Hamlet agitated by a spirit of this kind even though they
have diagnosed his problem as due to divergent underlying causes.
Although the descriptions themselves are often astute, the alleged
causes are more indicative of cultural and critical climates than of
the roots of Hamlet's behavior. We realize now that the romanticists'
aversion to dramatic action, which made them incapable of writing
actable plays, also distorted their view of both *Hamlet* the play and
Hamlet the man. Coleridge's image—a kind of self-image of the
prince's enormous intellectual activity, accompanied by a proportionate aversion to real action—is irreconcilable with the Hamlet of

the stage, who is constantly in motion, most of the time in actions that have at least something to do with his revenge or with his plan to baffle and evade the king. But although the romanticists were unduly concerned with Hamlet's inaction, they did recognize his intellectual restlessness. Even though Goethe put the emphasis on Hamlet's shrinking from his task, he observed how he winds, turns, torments himself, advances and recoils. Although Schlegel thought Hamlet's power of action crippled, he noted his calculating consideration, which exhausts all the relations and possible consequences of the deed. Hazlitt, who believed Hamlet's capacity to act was eaten up by thought, yet granted him high enthusiasm and quick sensibilities.

The diagnosis of Hamlet's problem as melancholy—whether in a general sense or in that of the Elizabethan humor disease—has similarly produced engaging descriptions of a Hamlet that is unstable, emotionally unhinged, gyrating between fits of energy and spells of lassitude. Nobody has given a finer account of a Hamlet whose mind totters and reels under the blows to his existence than A. C. Bradley.[8] And even attempts to formulate Hamlet into a sterile prototype of a malcontent avenger have produced astute descriptions of the scintillating and contradictory nature that make him, as E. E. Stoll has it, "both vindictive and high-minded, active and reflective, ironic and pathetic, merry and melancholy, indecent and decorous, insolent and courteous, cruel and tender, both suspicious and crafty and also (as Claudius himself has noted) 'most generous and free from all contriving.' " [9]

Hamlet's mind is in restless agitation; he is propelled by a turbulent spirit, one we feel to be very much akin to our own. But this conception of the spirit was by no means unknown to the Renaissance.[10] The particular form it took in Hamlet owed, I believe, very much to a prevailing climate of mannerism and skepticism. The Renaissance skeptics described man as moved and distracted by a violently active spirit that is both his glory and his perdition. Pierre Charron, Montaigne's disciple, said that there was nothing so great in man as his spirit. Yet this precious gift was also "both to itself and to another a dangerous instrument, a ferret to be feared, a little trouble-feast, a tedious and importune parasite, and which, as a juggler and player fast and loose, under the shadow of some gentle motion, subtle and smiling forgeth, inventeth, and causeth all the mischiefs of this world; and the truth is, without it, there are none." [11] "Irresolution on the one part and afterwards inconstancy and instability," said Charron elsewhere, "are the most common and apparent vices in the nature of man." [12] And Montaigne: "What we even now purposed, we alter by and by and presently return to our former bias; all is but changing, motion, and inconstancy." [13] The player-king in *Hamlet* puts it similarly:

> Purpose is but the slave to memory,
> Of violent birth, but poor validity;
>
> .   .   .   .
>
> What to ourselves in passion we propose,
> The passion ending, doth the purpose lose.
> The violence of either grief or joy
> Their own enactures with themselves destroy.
> Where joy most revels grief doth most lament;
> Grief joys, joy grieves, on slender accident.
>
> (III.ii.183–94)

It is tempting to think that these lines belong to the mysterious "some dozen or sixteen" of his own composition Hamlet instructs the actors to insert in the performance of the "Mousetrap." But whether they do or not, they characterize not only Gertrude's behavior, as they are intended to do, but also, and more appropriately, Hamlet's. And the view of man expressed in them is that of the skeptics.

The confident German critic who claimed that Hamlet was Montaigne had, I believe, an inkling of the truth. Not that the prince is an impersonator of the skeptic philosopher; rather, he is the kind of man Montaigne described himself as being. Montaigne, as subjective as he seems, really displays himself as the true, not idealized, specimen of general man. Like Montaigne's self-portrait, Hamlet is both extraordinary and yet has most of the features the skeptics considered characteristic of all men. Self-contradictions, hesitations, and changes of opinion are among the most notable features of Montaigne's portrait, as they are of Hamlet's character. "If I speak diversely of myself," said Montaigne, "it is because I look diversely upon myself." [14] A man of the kind portrayed by the French essayist is driven to examine all things; he possesses a restless spirit and is often possessed by it. Thus again and again, he is derailed from his present purpose, particularly if he is a man of keen intellect. As Charron explained,

> It is easy to see how rash and dangerous the spirit of man is, espe-
> cially if it be quick and vigorous. . . . it will undertake to examine
> all things, to judge the greatest part of things plausibly received
> in this world to be ridiculous and absurd, and, finding for all an ap-
> pearance of reason, will defend itself against all, whereby it is to
> be feared that it wandereth out of the way and loseth itself.[15]

Hamlet is endowed with a vigorous and restless spirit that drives
him to exertions that change their purpose and direction. His
thoughts and actions, far-reaching as they are, often become periph-
eral or else lose all relation to the task of revenge.

It is not that Hamlet loses himself in passion. It is rather that, unlike other tragic heroes, such as Richard II and Othello, he cannot
lose himself in passion, or at least not in the kind of passion that
escapes the control of reason. Hamlet's passion and reason cannot be
easily distinguished; both drive him on to be the speculative, analytic,
restless, and tortured figure he is. The conflict between reason and
passion, as D. G. James has well said, is not joined in him.[16] Hamlet
speaks of the excitements of his reason *and* his blood that drive him
to revenge (IV.iv.58). His adoption of the antic disposition, his self-
comparisons with the actors and with Fortinbras, even his staging of
the mousetrap, all serve at least in part the purpose of putting himself in the right—that is to say, passionate—frame of mind for his
revenge. But these devices succeed in this purpose only temporarily,
if they succeed at all. His meddling intellect interferes; he remains
too conscious of himself, too much aware of the psychic resources
and the immediate stimuli from which his efforts come, and he loses
all spontaneity. He overshoots the mark or falls short of it. His first
soliloquy is limitless in its metaphysical despair, and the queen is not
altogether wrong when she claims that its occasion, the death of a
father, is "common." In comparing himself with the actors and with
Fortinbras, he thinks his passion too weak, although, in the first case,
we find it too strong, even if not properly focused, and, in the second,
too improperly related to the stimulant, Fortinbras's territorial ambition. Hamlet's whole design of producing passion intellectually is
unworkable: at best, it produces pyrotechnical discharges; but these
never give Hamlet relief from his tensions.

In all this self-conscious fretting about technique, there appears to
be a concern that is not only Hamlet's but also Shakespeare's.
Hamlet suffers and studies passion, and so does Shakespeare through
him. No other Shakespearean character examines so closely the

cause, nature, and expression of emotions, obeying in this and other
respects the demands of the *nosce teipsum* writers—but with a
vengeance! It is significant that the word "passion" occurs more
often in *Hamlet* (eleven times) than in any of the other tragedies,
even *Othello* (eight occurrences), in which a gigantic passion is
dramatized but not analyzed. Even more significant than the quantity of references to passion are the shifting connotations of the
word. Hamlet gives "passion" two meanings quite new in the time,
that of a sudden, violent emotion and that of the expression of this
emotion in speech.[17] In these senses, the word becomes equivalent
to "ecstasy," as it frequently does in the later, baroque tragedies.
Hamlet, however, who can give "passion" this meaning, finds it
difficult to supply the substance. Notably, "ecstasy" also occurs more
often (five times) in *Hamlet* than elsewhere. This too was a word in
the process of intensifying its meaning; in the earlier plays it denotes
a fairly light transport of emotion, whereas from *Hamlet* on, it is a
serious, violent derangement of the spirit, akin to madness, as when
Ophelia finds the form and feature of Hamlet's youth "blasted with
ecstasy" (III.i.160). The word is used on one of the two occasions
in which Hamlet's passion rises most vehemently, during his reproaches of his mother, when he protests that he is not afflicted by
"ecstasy" in the sense of madness (III.iv.139). During his second
most passionate explosion, in the grief contest with Laertes at
Ophelia's grave, the word as such is not mentioned, but the prince
seems to define the passion he evinces at this time as "ecstasy" when
he later explains to Horatio that he feels sorry that "to Laertes I
forgot myself; / . . . the bravery of his grief did put me / Into a
tow'ring passion" (V.ii.76 ff.). In Cooper's *Thesaurus, ecstasis* is
translated as "an astonying, a damp, a trance, when one forgetteth
himself."

But even on this occasion Hamlet does not really forget himself in
an uninhibited and spontaneous outbreak. The cause of his passion is
curious; it is certainly not the death of the unfortunate Ophelia.
Rather, Hamlet is annoyed with Laertes's hysterical ranting that
piles Pelion on Ossa. It is almost as if he were hurt that the young
man can achieve such a volume of passion—Hamlet's vanity about
his acting ability seems involved. At any rate, he sees in Laertes's
Herculean outbreak a histrionic effort that he himself must overtop
—this surely is implied in the seemingly cryptic words with which he
abandons his own effort: "Let Hercules himself do what he may, /

The cat will mew, and dog will have his day" (V.i.285–86). Hamlet's attempt to rival Hercules, the Renaissance model for hyperbolic passion, leaves him in the end with a feeling of absurdity. He uses an incident that has nothing to do with his revenge action in order to test his capacity for passion. His subsequent explanation to Horatio and his apology to Laertes show that he worries as much about his emotional reactions to the situations as he does about the situations themselves.

Whenever Hamlet concerns himself specifically with self-knowledge, his probing, restless mind involves itself as much with the technique of the process as with the goal. No Shakespearean hero uses more constantly the methods traditionally thought helpful for the attainment of self-knowledge. When he says to Osric "to know a man well were to know himself," he shows that he knows the most important of these methods, that of comparing oneself with others. Cicero, the philosophical mentor of the humanists, recommended in *De Officiis* (I.114, 146) that the virtuous man, who wishes to fulfill his duty to man and God, closely observe other men, and the Renaissance *nosce teipsum* literature propagated the idea that one's fellow man is the glass into which one must look in order to see oneself.[18]

Hamlet uses this method to madness: he lets no opportunity go by to measure himself by others. When, to Osric, he modestly compares his fencing skill with that of Laertes, he does so in the presence of Horatio, who is not only his confidant but also his avowed mirror and model. In comparing himself with Horatio, Hamlet follows the idea—dating back to Aristotle's *Magna Moralia* (II.15, 1213a)— that, in order to know himself, a person should study a friend whom he admires. Hamlet sees in Horatio the balanced man whose blood and judgment are well commingled; Horatio is Hamlet's pattern of perfection. He is "as just a man / As e'er my conversation cop'd withal" (III.ii.52–53). It is for Hamlet surely as significant that Horatio is a *man* as it is that he is just. The word *man* is for Hamlet a title of honor that he bestows sparingly; besides his friend, only his father qualifies: " 'He was a man, take him for all in all" (I.ii.187). A man is for Hamlet more than a father and a king. In comparing himself with Horatio and with his father, Hamlet is put in mind of general manhood.

But in spite of Hamlet's glowing tribute to the concept of ideal humanity in Horatio and in his father, these two representatives of the ideal remain strangely pale and indistinct. A good ghost, as

Shakespeare, but not some of his fellow dramatists, knew, must be elusive and mysterious, and the old king is a true specter of this kind.[19] He is a gigantic hero of the past, walking in armor; he is an emissary from some outer region, come to tell a horrible story and incite his son to revenge; yet, in housegown, he is gently protective of his guilty wife. This is about all one learns of him from his appearances in the play; in Hamlet's affectionate recollection, he is, it is true, much more. His father, says Hamlet, had Hyperion's curls, the front of Jove, the eyes of Mars, and the stature of Mercury (III.iv.55). But this does not bring the man to life. Hamlet's montage of excellences resembles the technique of some mannerist painters admired by Vasari, who copied "the most beautiful objects and afterwards combined the most perfect, whether the hand, head, torso, or leg, and joined them together to make *one* figure, invested with every beauty in the highest perfection." [20] Hamlet's father is something of a mannerist picture puzzle; the conglomeration of his excellences in his son's description blurs the portrait. Nor does it become more distinct when Hamlet sets himself and Claudius in relationship to it. Claudius, says Hamlet, is "no more like my father / Than I to Hercules" (I.ii.152–53). What exactly does this say about any of the three persons compared?

If, in spite of his high praises, Hamlet does not make his father into a clear and distinct figure, he distorts even more the image of Claudius, the non-man, who is for Hamlet a king of shreds and patches from everything he finds odious and despicable: he is a satyr, a moor, a "bloat king," a cutpurse of the empire, a vice of kings. Murderer and villain that Claudius is, he does not really deserve these epithets.

Perhaps it may be thought natural for Hamlet to brighten his father's image, whom he loves, and to blacken his uncle's, whom he hates, and thus to blur both. But it is certainly strange that there is so little in the play to bear out Hamlet's admiration for his living ideal man, Horatio. It is not in the play but in Hamlet's words that Horatio becomes the man who, in suffering all, suffers nothing and takes fortune's buffets and rewards with equal thanks (III.ii.65 ff.). The Horatio we know is merely the prince's shadow and mirror, a servant who goes no further than to advise his master against inquiring too curiously and to make the futile gesture of attempting to join him in death.

Hamlet, it will be said, aggrandizes Horatio in order to lower himself. It is indeed true that Hamlet's friendship with the "poor" Horatio ennobles the prince and makes him less an egotist than he would otherwise be. And it will be said that Hamlet sees in Horatio a master over passion and fortune because he feels himself to be their slave. But Hamlet's character does not reveal itself so simply and clearly by his obsessive comparisons with others when we examine these in their context and with reference to his behavior. Hamlet is not exactly passion's slave. It will not do to saddle him with the "vicious mole of nature" of which he speaks to Horatio (I.iv.24) and call it melancholy. Hamlet's censure arises from a specific occasion, the addiction of the Danes to drink; what corruption of individual men by particular faults he has in mind is a puzzle; but it is much more natural to apply the remark to Claudius's grossness and Gertrude's sensuality than to Hamlet. And even if Hamlet thought of himself, the words still would leave the question whether the vicious mole is an "o'ergrowth of some complexion" or a "habit" that "o'erleavens the form of plausive manners." And in the latter case, the possibilities are infinite. It has even been suggested that the vicious mole, the "dram of eale," is the effect of the original sin that affects all men.[21] Surely this is not a very helpful passage for an analysis of Hamlet's character.

And just what is the effect of the ghost's command on Hamlet? Is it really, as Bradley and Miss Campbell thought, that, were it not for his melancholy, Hamlet would have no problems? Hamlet never says so; he only asserts that the task is uncongenial to him: "The time is out of joint. O cursed spite, / That ever I was born to set it right!" (I.v.189–90). If Hamlet here accentuates the "I," as is likely, the question arises why he, in particular, feels out of sympathy with the task. What kind of man was he born? It is not sufficient, I think, merely to refer to Ophelia's testimony that the Hamlet before his father's death was an ideal nobleman, that he had "the courtier's, soldier's, scholar's, eye, tongue, sword" (III.i.151). Ophelia's characterization is quite unsatisfactory for the Hamlet of the play; it is quite unsatisfactory, that is, if one associates, as is natural and presumably intended, the tongue with the courtier, the sword with the soldier, and the eye with the scholar. If, however, one associates the epithets with their referents in Ophelia's order, the characterization becomes much more appropriate: the Hamlet we know moves through the court with the critical courtier's eye rather than the polite tongue; he measures himself against Fortinbras with a soldier's tongue rather than with the sword, and he reaches for the life of Claudius with a scholar's sword, searching for the truth even more than for the king's life. I do not mean to say that Ophelia's inversion of epithets is a Freudian slip rather than a rhetorical figure, but I suggest that Shakespeare could hardly have wished his audience to think that the obedient little Ophelia ever looked into the recesses of the heart of her enigmatic lover. Hers is at best a partial truth, that of Hamlet's outside. Can one really imagine him, who in his first speeches characterizes himself as a fanatic of truth and as a man who knows not seeming, to have ever been merely the "glass of fashion and the mould of form"?

The Hamlet of the play is not a glass of fashion but a frustrated seeker for an ideal human mould. He has a passion, a passion much stronger than his grief or his thirst for revenge, to seek for this form in himself and in others and to note its presence or absence. He compares and contrasts himself incessantly, with his father, with Claudius, with Horatio, with Laertes, with Fortinbras, with Polonius, with Rosencrantz and Guildenstern, with the player-king, with the gravediggers, and with dead Yorick. But wherever Hamlet gives way to this passion, his overactive mind introduces a subjective distortion. In Fortinbras, Hamlet admires the man who "greatly" finds "quarrel in a straw, / When honour's at the stake"—yet Fortinbras's particular quarrel is not even an argument of honor, but merely an expedition to Poland, arranged to take the place of that against Denmark. Fortinbras's bellicose energy hardly demonstrates by contrast Hamlet's lack of divine ambition.

Hamlet similarly misjudges Laertes. He takes a properly cautious attitude toward him as a fencer, but he throws discretion to the winds when he calls him a "noble youth" and never suspects him of being capable of using a poisoned sword. When Hamlet does see a parallel between himself and Laertes, the occasion and the subject are odd. At Ophelia's grave, he cannot stand Laertes's passionate protest of grief, but must outrant him to assume the role of next-of-kin himself: "This is I, / Hamlet the Dane!" In spite of the emphatic self-identification, Hamlet assumes here a role that does not fit. His protest that the love of forty thousand brothers cannot make up the sum of his love contrasts oddly with his earlier cruelty toward Ophelia. And his later explanation to Laertes that it was not Hamlet but Hamlet's madness that cried out at Ophelia's grave appears to be another instance of inappropriate role-playing.

Yet role-playing as such was a recommended procedure in acquiring self-knowledge. In *De Officiis* (I.113), Cicero said that each man, like an actor, should choose the part in life most suitable to himself. This, as we noted earlier, is the doctrine of individual *decorum,* on which the humanists founded their ideas of human individuality. Hamlet, a greater individualist than they, violates this doctrine; rather than choosing the role that suits him best, he tries, as Cicero said one should not do, whether other men's roles fit him.

Hamlet is by avocation an amateur actor who frequently mistakes the world for the stage. He feels compelled to vie with the actors; he begins to recite the speech about "rugged Pyrrhus" from the play that was "caviary to the general." One is somewhat puzzled as to why he admires this elaborately wrought speech. It has the vexing quality of making one scan it for parallels to Hamlet's predicament. Is the hellish Pyrrhus perhaps to evoke the murderous Claudius? Or is he Hamlet's wishful image of the avenger he himself would like to be? Neither identification seems quite appropriate. The cruel Pyrrhus, the "painted tyrant," gored with the blood of fathers, mothers, and sons, is wholly unlike the subtle and smooth Claudius. Pyrrhus, it is true, is like Hamlet an avenger for a father killed; but unlike Hamlet, Pyrrhus is the destroyer of hostile Troy, not the would-be reformer of his own state. And Hamlet's cruelty to Gertrude, unlike that of Pyrrhus to Hecuba, is not meant to go beyond speaking daggers. The actor's recital of the murder and bloodshed at the fall of Troy—a subject famous as an example of tragic πάθος in the Renaissance—ought to strike a listener with horror and pity rather than, as it does Hamlet, with self-reproach for delay in revenge. And Hamlet's subsequent soliloquy, which in its nervous and introspective complexities contrasts effectively with the balanced Renaissance turgidity of the actor's speech, begins, as noted, with Hamlet setting himself into quite a false relationship to the actor. Hamlet's comparison of the actor's passionate recital to his own situation is quite irrelevant. Hamlet's problem is not that he can *say* nothing. He knows the words and gestures of passion very well.

Hamlet's self-comparisons generally lead to self-laceration and self-humiliation. His keen, restless mind fails to strike the balance, and prevents him from becoming the impartial judge of his own and others' merits and defects that Cicero said the man of self-knowledge should be. But at least he does not overassess himself as Polonius does. It is ironic that the emphatic demand for proper self-identifica-

tion—that is, in Renaissance terms, for "individual *decorum*"—
should come from this humorous-pathetic conformer to court cus-
toms: "To thine own self be true." Hamlet's situation belies the
assumption that the man who is true to himself cannot be false to
any man. Hamlet must play the role of the avenger in order to be
true to himself, and therefore he must hide and dissimulate, be false
to almost everybody.

For Hamlet, role-playing does not provide the reassuring acquisition of *decorum* Cicero demanded it should have. And his failure cannot be merely blamed on improper methods. He tries to be true to
himself; but he finds it hard to reconcile this attempt with the more
important injunction to preserve general *decorum,* which, according
to humanistic ideas, directed and limited individuality. The man who
wishes to be true to himself—so general *decorum* decreed—must
regulate his behavior not by his own nature only; he must also act
in his proper character as a man, that is, as a moral being. He must
live in awareness of his fundamental difference from the animals.
But, for Hamlet, this easy and comforting back-reference to general
decorum is problematic. No Shakespearean character tries harder to
act according to the precepts of moral philosophy than Hamlet; none
seeks so much reference and support in the general condition of a
humanity ideally conceived. His admiration for Horatio as a man of
balance and virtue conforms to this tendency. And so does his
making Fortinbras's Polish expedition a reminder of the duties imposed on man by his privileged place in the universe: "What is a
man, / If his chief good and market of his time / Be but to sleep and
feed?" (IV.iv.33 ff.) This question and Hamlet's answer, that man
has a "capability and godlike reason" that must not "fust . . . un-
us'd," paraphrase a significant passage from the beginning of Cicero's
De Officiis (I.12; see Appendix A). Whether Shakespeare had it
from Cicero or elsewhere, the fact remains that he gave Hamlet an
authoritative humanistic statement of the doctrine of general *decorum,* of the demand that man's actions must come from his consciousness of being man. Yet this reference to the general duty of man
proves irrelevant as Hamlet questions whether the violation of this
duty is really the reason for his inaction: "Now, whether it be /
Bestial oblivion, or some craven scruple / Of thinking too precisely
on th' event. . . ." He also questions this second alternative: "I do
not know / Why yet I live to say 'This thing's to do.'" Hamlet is
enough of a skeptic to realize that the roots of actions or inactions lie

often too deep for thoughts. The traditional picture of man, at any rate, does not reveal them. Whenever Hamlet tries to draw on philosophical wisdom about man and on moral commonplaces of consolation in order to reconcile himself to this world and the world to come, he fails.

His most conspicuous effort and failure is his "to be or not to be" soliloquy. It is a variation in a different key of Montaigne's rhetorical question "Should I have died less merrily before I read the Tusculans?" and of his assertion that "I had rather understand myself well in myself than in Cicero." [22] The dramatic situation suggests that Hamlet in this scene enters book in hand—in Quarto 1, the king actually says: "See where he comes, reading upon a book." The particular book from which Hamlet takes the theme of his soliloquy, as Professor Baldwin has plausibly argued, is Cicero's *Tusculan Disputations,* or, in its customary Elizabethan title, *Tusculan Questions;* Hamlet ponders the first of these questions, that of death and immortality.[23] But even if Hamlet's book should have been not Cicero's *Tusculans* but Cardanus's *Comfort* [24] or Montaigne's *Essays,*[25] or if there was no book at all, the fact remains that he seeks consolation in a standard passage of moral philosophy. Like Socrates in Plato's *Apology,* he ponders his and man's fate in relation to death and the afterlife; but for him there can be no calm acceptance of his destiny: the question of mortality versus immortality becomes hopelessly entangled with the questions of action versus inaction, of death in struggle or death by suicide, of the sufferings of life on earth compared with the risks of the unknown, of the desirability of a dreamless sleep as against the horrible vision of tortures in the hereafter. Hamlet's soul-searching only heightens his feeling of self-loss, and he proceeds to agonize Ophelia as much as he agonized himself.

Hamlet's probing into the existential situation, as searching as it is, ends in dissonance, incongruity, irrelevance, and absurdity. Hamlet is not satisfied merely to assume a *contemptus mundi* pose as does Richard II. He deeply "considers" man's corruptible body, but, as Horatio says, he considers too curiously. In metaphysical clownery he makes the dead Polonius into an object lesson on the dietary habit of worms—the method is the same as that by which Montaigne deflated the claim of man to constancy: "Touching strength, there is no creature in this world open to so many wrongs and injuries as man. . . . The heart and life of a mighty and triumphant emperor is but the breakfast of a silly little worm." [26] In the churchyard, as he "reads" the skulls, Hamlet takes again this ironic view of metamorphosis; he pierces the absurdity of the human existence that transforms an Alexander into dust, earth, loam, and finally into the plug of a beer-barrel. Hamlet turns the graveyard into an excavation ground and a debating hall, and, in a final twist, into a wrestling arena where he grapples with Laertes over the cere-clothed body of Ophelia. It is a bizarre dance macabre in the style of mannerist painters like Tintoretto and El Greco.

Besides comparing himself to the general image of man, Hamlet also follows the *nosce teipsum* writers' recommendation to examine his proper place in the universe. And again, the theories Hamlet tests are orthodox even if he examines them under strange circumstances. One occasion is that in which Rosencrantz and Guildenstern attempt to extract from him the reason for his strange behavior (II.ii.221 ff.). He evades them by philosophical arguments on the prison that is Denmark and the world, on the reward that is an active imagination, on the curse that comes from bad dreams, and on the shadow that is ambition. Then, with one stab, the prince, who can be as brutally direct as frustratingly indirect, elicits from the courtiers the reason for their coming: they were sent for by the king. Whereupon Hamlet diverts them with another philosophic disquisition, this time on his present unhappiness about the ideal picture of the world and of man.

His appraisal is concocted by the best Renaissance recipes on how to write a commonplace on *homo* and *mundus,* and it is framed in the proper rhetorical balance. And yet, Hamlet dissociates himself from it. The picture has lost its attraction for him although, he says, with a touch that is surely not intended merely to confuse Rosencrantz and Guildenstern, he does not know why: "I have of late— but wherefore I know not—lost all my mirth, forgone all custom of exercises; and indeed it goes so heavily with my disposition that this goodly frame, the earth, seems to me a sterile promontory." After thus disclaiming any joy in the ideal macrocosm, Hamlet assesses the microcosm: "What a piece of work is a man! how noble in reason! how infinite in faculty! in form and moving, how express and admirable! in action how like an angel! in apprehension, how like a God! the beauty of the world! the paragon of animals!" [27] Hamlet finds this paragon as little to his liking as the frame that surrounds him: "And yet, to me, what is this quintessence of dust?"

One need not go so far as a German scholar who sees in Hamlet's speech a renunciation of the Renaissance [28] to find this a disturbing picture. By itself, as we have noted, the speech is quite traditional in subject and structure, and, in Shakespeare's theater, it had an appropriate setting; but it becomes disturbing—its very orthodoxy contributes to that—by the acutely felt tension between the ideal and the actual. The picture is beautiful; but it has lost its relevance. Hamlet's agitated mind, swaying from earth to heaven, from heaven to earth, from soul to body, and from body to soul, finds no assurance and resting place. Everything is a shifting semblance, a diffused world.

Hamlet's restless spirit is guided and incited by a glorious but heated imagination. In general humanistic thought, the imagination was an ambiguous gift, both a divine force and a danger to man's happiness.[29] For the skeptics, it was primarily the latter; its straying turbulence, which sidetracks both passion and reason, served them as a major argument that man was unstable. Intelligence and reason offered no protection: the more agile the mind, the greater the danger of derailment. "From the rarest and quickest agitation of our souls," said Charron, "[come] the most desperate resolutions and disorderly frenzies." [30] And so it is for Hamlet. When he first sees the ghost beckoning to him, he turns "desperate with imagination" (I.iv.87). He ceaselessly conjures up his task, his inadequacies for it, his father's greatness, his uncle's villainy, and his mother's sexuality. Yet he also knows the potential rewards of the imagination. He could, he says to Rosencrantz and Guildenstern, be bounded in a nutshell and count himself king of infinite space were it not that he has bad dreams (II.ii.255). He is acutely conscious of what the imagination does to him, awake and asleep, and how it both conjures up an ideal existence and prevents him from reaching it as he becomes oppressed with the sordid realities of his demanding task and uncertain life.

It is perhaps the most astonishing turn of the play that from his knowledge of the working of the imagination, observed on himself, Hamlet forges his most purposeful action of the play, that of catching the conscience of the king. Hamlet's self-awareness becomes, as it were, the design of his revenge. This is a most ingenious device, based on ancient theories about the imagination, specifically concerning the transfer of the power of the imagination from the poet through the actor to the audience. It seems to have been Shakespeare's own idea to have Hamlet use this stratagem; in the *Ur-Hamlet,* if it was Kyd's, the function of the play-within-the-play is not likely to have been different from *The Spanish Tragedy,* where it served the avenger to kill the criminal without exciting suspicion.[31] Hamlet's way of staging the play is characteristic of the way he conceives revenge as an intellectual and artistic problem.

The stratagem is so Hamletian as to make one forget that it is based on theories that enjoyed philosophical and rhetorical respectability. They go back to Plato's *Ion* (334–36), where Socrates asks the professional reciter of poetry whether he is in his senses or in ecstatic empathy with the events when he narrates incidents from Homer's epics, such as Odysseus's unmasking himself to Penelope's suitors or Achilles's attacks on Hector or one of the pitiful passages about Andromache, Hecuba, or Priam. Ion admits that in reciting tales of pity and horror his eyes are filled with tears, his hair stands on end with fear, and his heart leaps. Socrates elicits from him the explanation that he is divinely inspired; a spirit has entered the poet, and then, through the reciter or "actor," is conveyed to the audience. The poet is the "inner ring," the actor the "middle ring," and the audience "the outer ring"; the deity draws the spirit of men from the center toward the outside. Quintilian (VI.ii.34 ff.) and Cicero in *De Oratore* (II.xiv.189) applied the theory to the orator, comparing his task to that of the actor, who, as Quintilian said, leaves the theater still drowned in tears after the performance of a moving role.[32]

From Quintilian and Cicero, directly or indirectly, Shakespeare provided Hamlet with the theory for his plan. It is characteristic that the idea occurs to Hamlet at a moment when he observes the effect of the imagination and is himself most strongly oppressed by it. He has just noted how the "passionate speech" he requested puts its speaker, the actor, into the appropriate mood observable by outward signs. Just as Quintilian said, the actor grows pale, has tears in his eyes, speaks with a broken voice and suits his whole function "with forms to his conceit" (II.ii.50). Hamlet gives his own peculiar twist to this tradition when, by an act of the imagination, he puts the actor in the actual role of an avenger by asking what the actor would do if he had Hamlet's motive and cue for passion.

In reproaching himself for his lack of passion, Hamlet uses arguments that parallel Cicero's statement on the superiority of true to feigned grief.[33] Hamlet's particular application of the idea of emotional transfer to the unmasking of the king also has precedents. Notably, on this occasion Hamlet remembers having heard that "guilty persons at a play" were driven to confess their crimes. Montaigne, among others, reported just such an incident, an anecdote from Plutarch according to which Alexander, tyrant of Pheres, had to give up seeing tragedies for fear his subjects might see him sob at the misfortunes of Hecuba and Andromache.[34] Although Hecuba's tears did not stop Pyrrhus, they were effective enough to touch some hard hearts from the time of the ancients to the Renaissance!

The theory on which Hamlet bases catching the conscience of the king is founded on good authorities, and it works. We should note, however, that it arises from an act of self-analysis that is quite problematic and that the success of the device does not change Hamlet's attitude toward his task. In the soliloquy in which he concocts his stratagem, Hamlet applies a rhetorical argument to a psychological and moral situation with which it is not commensurate. When Hamlet asks himself what the actor would do if he had the motive and the cue for passion he himself has, he puts the problem of revenge in the wrong perspective. It is not that Hamlet lacks articulateness of word and gesture, "pronunciation" in Renaissance terms. It is rather that he has too much, and the unmasking of the king makes it no more possible for him to suit his actions to his words than it was before he sprang the mousetrap.

Hamlet's identification with his role as avenger is closest during and immediately after his stratagem. His imagination and his passion appear now synchronized with his spirit: here is finally an action that will directly promote his revenge. He succeeds temporarily in recovering the excitement with which he pledged himself to the execution of his task immediately after the appearance of the ghost. He anticipates with sarcastic elation the demasking of Claudius, and when the latter rises in horror, Hamlet triumphs and sings satirical verses to Horatio. With wild words he harries Rosencrantz and Guildenstern, who come to invite him to attend his mother; he pulls Polonius's leg, and, left alone, feels that he could drink blood.

Hamlet then proceeds to what he considers his first bitter business of the day: to convert his mother to virtue and abstinence. That, on his way, he should come across Claudius attempting to pray and fail to execute his major business is a supreme irony in which fate and Hamlet's character interact. It is not a failure due to passion; Hamlet rapidly scans the situation—no scene better demonstrates how rapidly he can look at a situation from several angles. He decides not to take the easy revenge that offers itself to him now because it would not be perfect retribution. He will fulfill the revenge code to the last letter and dispatch Claudius when he is engaged in some odious occupation. But ironically, Hamlet has thought too curiously; the king finds it impossible to pray and rises after Hamlet leaves. Hamlet's probing, circling thoughts have missed their target as much as Hamlet's hand, just at the moment when he is most in sympathy with his role.

The closet scene has the same air of futility. Although Hamlet is now at his most passionate in his role of reformer of Denmark—a role he cannot separate from his role as avenger—he is also at his most ineffective. For the first time he holds up the glass of self-recognition to somebody else, that is, to his mother, but his zeal makes it into a magnifying glass. His feverish imagination evokes such details as Claudius's and Gertrude's "rank sweat of an enseamed bed" and their "honeying and making love / Over the nasty sty" (III.iv.92–94). But while he is much concerned with "the black and grained spots" on his mother's soul, he forgets that the ghost warned him not to taint his own mind by conceiving aught against his mother. He is carried away by passion, an excessive passion for truth and moral reform, and he comes close to killing her; both Polonius and the ghost fear for her safety. Ironically, it is Hamlet's excited reaction to the appearance of the latter that convinces Gertrude of Hamlet's insanity. If Hamlet's stab at his mother's conscience fails, that which he directs at the man whom he mistakes for Claudius succeeds. And from now on the king is in ascendance, and Hamlet's moves are countermoves.

According to one school of interpretation, the Hamlet who returns from England is a new man who has learned to master his problems. He certainly does accept providence and fate as he describes his action in sending Rosencrantz and Guildenstern to their doom:

> Rashly,
> And prais'd be rashness for it—let us know,
> Our indiscretion sometime serves us well,
> When our deep plots do pall; and that should learn us
> There's a divinity that shapes our ends,
> Rough-hew them how we will.
>   (V.ii.6–11)

But as a guideline to action the principle Hamlet proclaims does not serve him well. The same "indiscretion" in which he will kill Laertes and the king did not serve Hamlet so well when he killed Polonius, and his success at sea owed something to an admixture of deliberation. Hamlet's acceptance of providence does, however, advance the tragic solution. In this spirit, he accepts the invitation to the fencing match that proves both a trap and a deliverance. But the exact nature of this spirit of acceptance is something of a puzzle. One finds it hard to call it Christian fortitude, or Stoic resignation, or a pragmatic acceptance of the skeptics' world in which all things are relative and uncertain. The special providence that is in "the fall of a sparrow" is biblical, the "readiness" that is all is stoical, and the concluding sentence is skeptic, at least in the preferable Quarto 2 version: "Since no man of ought he leaves knows, what is it to leave betimes?" (V.ii.216).[35]

This is a particularly interesting sentence because it is fashioned on the losing-finding antithesis, which since *Love's Labor's Lost* and *The Comedy of Errors* was for Shakespeare associated with the search for identity. But in the early plays, there was the promise that the search would be rewarded, that self-discipline would bring felicity and that brother would embrace brother in the end. Now the humanistic certainty is gone. Hamlet's search is vain; his mellowing in the end consists only in taking a somewhat calmer attitude toward what remains, in the final analysis, inscrutable. The best one can say is that Hamlet learns to adapt somewhat more easily to the restless behavior prescribed by his mind. He realizes that his situation is not quite as unique as it appeared to him, and he accepts—fideistic fashion—a providence that transcends rational explanations of his behavior and of human actions in general. But it is hard to think of this realization as self-discovery because it does not bring any particularly illuminating insight.

And it cannot be different. In the diffuse and corrupt world in which Hamlet lives, it is impossible for him to find his identity. In such a world, nobody knows what he leaves behind. And there may even be doubt about what he finds hereafter. It is anybody's guess whether, his task accomplished in the random action in which "indiscretion" serves him well, Hamlet sinks into silence or ascends to heaven. Shakespeare has left us even wondering whether Hamlet's silence is Stoic or Christian. Ironically, it is Horatio, the professed rationalist, and not Hamlet, the self-acknowledged fideist, who hopes for the chorus of angels to sweeten it.

The situation of the survivors appears no less problematic. To say that in the end all is well with the world and with Denmark is to substitute the conclusions of *Richard III* or *Henry IV* for that of *Hamlet*. What we actually witness in the end is not the supplanting of a tyrant by a man who has legitimized himself before God and the nation, as in *Richard III,* or the succession of a son who has overcome his fathers' handicaps, as in *Henry IV.* In *Hamlet,* it turns out quite unexpectedly that Fortinbras, only so far known as the foreign leader of a "list of lawless [F: 'landless'] resolutes" (I.i.98), will sit on the throne of Denmark. Somebody, one assumes, has to take over. One finds it hard to believe that Hamlet's last wish to clear his wounded name and to have his story told to the unsatisfied will provide Denmark with a legend through which it can become sane and healthy. Horatio's outline of Hamlet's story, at any rate, does not promise a very illuminating tale: it speaks of "carnal, bloody, and unnatural acts; / Of accidental judgments, casual slaughters; / Of deaths put on by cunning and forc'd cause; / And, in this upshot, purposes mistook / Fall'n on th' inventors' heads" (V.ii.373–77). The subsequent history of *Hamlet* criticism proves that Hamlet's story cannot be told so easily.

Hamlet is Shakespeare's most problematic hero, and it is impossible ever to pluck out his last mystery. But the mystery does not come from lack of self-explanation. Hamlet is aware, or overaware, of himself; but ironically, for this very reason he does not attain even the kind of self-knowledge that, on the level of evil, Claudius has, who is properly conscious of his villainy. Hamlet is profoundly disturbed by the discrepancies between what he is and what he would like to be, between what he purposes and what he accomplishes. His is the tragedy of a problematic self, a tragedy the more harrowing because it lacks a reassurance that is capable of any solution. It is not a tragedy of lack of self-knowledge so much as a tragedy of the problematic nature of the quest for self-knowledge.

The theme as such was not new to Shakespeare, who stated it in comic terms in *Love's Labor's Lost* and at least adumbrated its tragic possibilities in *Julius Caesar.* The fascination of its treatment in *Hamlet* arises in part from its use in the apparently incongruous setting of a revenge tragedy but even more from the fact that the hero in search of himself is a man of quick and wide sensibilities and of a keen and probing intellect. His restless spirit cannot separate the duty of being himself, which necessitates being an avenger as well as a human being, from the passionate desire of knowing himself. Although he finally fulfills his task of revenge, his search for himself leads nowhere.

CHAPTER ELEVEN

Troilus and Cressida:
Fragmenting a Divided Self

LTHOUGH SHAKESPEARE SEEMS to have written *Troilus and Cressida* very soon after *Hamlet,* the play does not at first sight appear to concern itself greatly with questions of identity and self-knowledge. The hero does not torture himself with the relationship of his self to others and the universe as does Hamlet. Yet he does ask the identity question once, in the first scene of the play, when he enters, sighing with love for Cressida. The ungracious clamors of the war emphasize the disharmony in his heart:

> Peace, rude sounds!
> Fools on both sides! Helen must needs be fair,
> When with your blood you daily paint her thus.
> I cannot fight upon this argument;
> It is too starv'd a subject for my sword.
> But Pandarus—O gods, how do you plague me!
> I cannot come to Cressid but by Pandar;
> And he's as tetchy to be woo'd to woo
> As she is stubborn-chaste against all suit.
> Tell me, Apollo, for thy Daphne's love,
> What Cressid is, what Pandar, and what we?
> (I.i.88–98)

Troilus addresses himself here to the god who was reputed to have demanded that man know himself, but obviously he does so with very special pleading when he asks the question in the manner of a courtly lover, "for thy Daphne's love." There is a curious mixture of skepticism and self-deception in these lines. Troilus cannot fight for Helen, or so he says, because she has no absolute value for him; he finds her fairness gored with blood. But at the same time, he elevates the value of the unpleasant and bawdy Pandarus and even more, in the subsequent lines, that of Cressida, who becomes a pearl, whose bed is India. From this hyperbole, Troilus descends to absurdity when he calls the space between her and his domicile "the wild and wand'ring flood," Pandar the sailing bark, and himself the merchant. We know about Pandar by now, we wonder about Cressida, whom Pandar's pleasantries have compared to Helen, and certainly most of all, we question Troilus's assessment of the world and of those around him. We distrust his taste when he says to Pandarus in an atrocious metaphor "Thou . . . / Pourest in the open ulcer of my heart— / Her eyes, her hair, her cheek, her gait, her voice . . ." (I.i.52–53).

Not only are his judgments strange and false; they also are inconsistent as when, later in the debate of the Trojans, he bestows on Helen, whom he devalued earlier, the title of pearl he deemed appropriate for Cressida. For Troilus, values fluctuate; they are dependent on time and on subjective needs: "What's ought but as 'tis valued." Troilus is a shallower man than Hamlet, but his skepticism is more apparent, and so is the skeptic strain that runs through the play. Hamlet has no brothers in spirit in his play; Troilus does. He is, of course, not as dominant a figure; we are not asked to view the action through his eyes and mind. The statement the play makes about self-knowledge depends almost as much on Ulysses, on Cressida, and on other characters as it does on him; and it depends more on the plot and on the discussion of ideas than it does in *Hamlet*.

The one character who appears to know himself and others clearly is Ulysses. And it is he who uses the most explicit pattern of self-knowledge in the play when he excites the vanity and jealousy of Achilles in an attempt to get him back to battle. Ulysses does so by reminding Achilles of the familiar comparison of the eye to the soul, by which the Renaissance liked to demonstrate the need and the difficulty of the soul's knowledge of itself. In *Julius Caesar,* Cassius transforms this comparison into a bait for Brutus; in *Troilus and Cressida,* Ulysses gives it an even more ironic and deceptive twist. That his purpose is not to enlighten Achilles about his true identity would be clear to anybody but that conceited and obtuse athlete. Ulysses enters, reading a book, in which, he says in answer to Achilles' question, a "strange fellow" claims that, no matter what man's qualities, he "cannot make boast to have that which he hath, / Nor feels not what he owes, but by reflection" (III.iii.98–99). The

position is not strange to Achilles, who, like any Elizabethan with
a modicum of education, knows that the eye cannot see itself:

> The beauty that is borne here in the face
> The bearer knows not, but commends itself
> To others' eyes; nor doth the eye itself—
> That most pure spirit of sense—behold itself,
> Not going from itself; but eye to eye opposed
> Salutes each other with each other's form;
> For speculation turns not to itself
> Till it hath travell'd, and is mirror'd there
> Where it may see itself.
>   (III.iii.103–11)

But Ulysses' author gives this familiar position an unusual drift,
one that appeals to Achilles because it explains why he is slighted by
his former admirers. This author proves

> That no man is the lord of anything,
> Though in and of him there be much consisting,
> Till he communicate his parts to others;
> Nor doth he of himself know them for aught
> Till he behold them formed in th' applause
> Where th'are extended; who, like an arch, reverb'rate
> The voice again; or, like a gate of steel
> Fronting the sun, receives and renders back
> His figure and his heat.
>   (115–23)

In Ulysses' Circean words, the mirror of self-knowledge becomes the
glass of self-love into which Achilles gazes amorously. Ulysses's unexpected revelation that he actually refers to "the unknown Ajax"
comes thus as a shock to him.

The "author" in whom Ulysses alleges to have read his reflection
simile is a minor puzzle. I know of no ancient writer who used the
image similarly, certainly not Plato, who has been claimed to be the
source. Ulysses gives a distinctly skeptical turn to the commonplace:
man is only what he is valued, subject to the vagaries of public whim.
No Renaissance skeptic is likely to have gone so far; this author is
indeed a "strange fellow," apparently invented by Ulysses to stir
Achilles into seeking the approval of his peers by rejoining the

battle. The pattern of self-knowledge thus turns into a *persuasio* of a narcissistic egotist; the alleged mirror of self-knowledge is merely a deceptive trick.

However, it is noteworthy that one English *nosce teipsum* book, Thomas Wright's *The Passions of the Mind in General* (1601), used the eye-mirror analogy in order to illustrate man's tendency to mistake self-love for self-knowledge and that it did so together with other images that play a role in the stultification of Achilles. Says Wright:

> The reason we judge more quickly other men's faults than our own partly proceeds from self-love, which blindeth us in our actions, partly because we see other men's defects directly and our own by a certain reflection; for as no man knoweth exactly his own face because he never sees it but by reflection from a glass, and other men's countenances he conceiveth most perfectly because he vieweth them directly and in themselves, even so by a certain circle we wind about ourselves whereas by a right line we pass into the corners of men's souls, at least by rash judgments and sinister suspicions.[1]

If this argument does not completely parallel that of Ulysses' author, it does explain why for men like Achilles the mirror of self-knowledge is the mirror of self-love. Interestingly, the supposition that Shakespeare derived Ulysses' argument from \The Passions of the Mind* is made more attractive by Wright's marginal note to the passage: "Non videmus id manticae quod in tergo est." This is exactly the *sententia* by which Ulysses explains why Achilles is being passed by and neglected:

> Time hath, my lord, a wallet at his back,
> Wherein he puts alms for oblivion,
> A great-siz'd monster of ingratitudes.
> Those scraps are good deeds past, which are devour'd
> As fast as they are made, forgot as soon
> As done.
>
>   (145–50)

Shakespeare gave the *sententia,* which Wright used in an abridged form, a meaning closer to its original source, Persius: "Ut nemo in sese temptat descendere, nemo / Sed praecedenti spectatur mantica tergo." [2] But Shakespeare put the wallet on the back of time rather than on that of a person; what in Persius and Wright is a figure that illustrates man's delusions about himself, his unwillingness to descend into his own soul, becomes in the words of Ulysses an illustration of the subjection of all worth and honor to "envious and calumniating Time" (174). Here again is a skeptical twist: the changes wrought by time have always been one of the skeptics' favorite proofs for the relativity of judgments and for the instability of man. As Charron put it,

> the greatest part of our actions are nothing else but eruptions and impulsions enforced by the occasions. . . . Our spirits also and our humors are changed with the change of time. Life is an unequal motion, irregular, and of many fashions.[3]

The touch of nature that, as Ulysses says, makes all men kin in their forgetfulness is also a touch that makes some men very obtuse, as he shows by his treatment of Achilles. The possibility that this touch came from Wright's palette is enhanced by Shakespeare's using at the end of the scene another figure associated with self-knowledge that occurs in *The Passions of the Mind*. Achilles, thoroughly shaken by Ulysses' clever commonplaces, laments finally, "My mind is troubled, like a fountain stirr'd; / And I myself see not the bottom of it." But Thersites has sounded the depth of this fountain: "Would the fountain of your mind were clear again, that I might water an ass at it. I had rather be a tick in a sheep than such a valiant ignorance" (III.iii.303–8). Wright depicted the fountains of men's minds, deeper fountains than that of Achilles, as waters of ignorance: "Only I will infer our extreme ignorance that few or none of these difficulties which concern us so near as our souls and bodies are thoroughly as yet in my judgment declared even of the profoundest wits; for I know not how their best resolutions leave still our understandings dry, thirsting for a clearer and fresher fountain." [4]

Thus a case can be made that Ulysses' "strange author" is Thomas Wright, the only English *nosce teipsum* author I know of that was much affected by skepticism. One must then assume that Shakespeare gave Wright's arguments a few still stranger twists. But regardless of whether Shakespeare followed Wright when he made Achilles' glass of self-recognition one of self-love and his fountain of the mind one of ignorance, the images he used are indicative both of his continuing interest in the patterns of self-knowledge and his skeptical look at humanistic "truths" about human nature in *Troilus and Cressida*.

If Ulysses is one character in the play who knows himself and others, he is also one of the least amiable. His knowledge of the souls of others is a realization of their lies, pretenses and self-deceptions. And that goes even for what he calls "the soul of state." As he says grandiloquently to Achilles:

> There is a mystery—with whom relation
> Durst never meddle—in the soul of state,
> Which hath an operation more divine
> Than breath or pen can give expressure to.
> (III.iii.201–4)

As it turns out, this mystery comes from a good spy system, which Ulysses calls the "providence" of a watchful state. Thus, not so mysteriously, Ulysses knows about the motivation that keeps Achilles away from battle: his love of Priam's daughter Polyxena. In Ulysses, a skeptic attitude toward values is combined with an eminently practical, Machiavellian view of furthering the aims of the state. There is perhaps a contradiction between his theoretical skepticism and his practical espousal of the state as an absolute value, but that was an inconsistency common to Renaissance skeptics.

The contradictions, disjunctions, and paradoxes with which the skeptics illustrated the ignorance and instability of man are ingrained in the texture of the play. From the chorus's words to the audience, "Like or find fault; do as your pleasures are; / Now good or bad, 'tis but the chance of war," the play takes a problematic attitude toward values. Good or bad, success or loss, truth or falseness, buying and selling are some of the oppositions that become relative. What is good may depend on the viewer, what is true, on the speaker. The validity of a statement is negated by its opposite. "Bifold authority," the phrase in which Troilus expresses his utter disbelief that Diomed's Cressida is the same woman who, a few hours before, swore to be eternally faithful, could well be the motto of this play with its peculiar dualism in plot, character, thoughts, and themes that leads to division and finally to dubiety and impotence.[5]

It is, of course, natural that the plot should be divided into two parts, the love intrigue and the war story; but Shakespeare went beyond necessity in creating a structural bipartition by making them nearly equal in length and, presumably, significance—or perhaps we should say insignificance. Each of the war parties is internally divided, although the Greeks are more deeply so. By and large, the Trojans are more sympathetically portrayed than the Greeks, but they too have flaws that soil their virtues. They espouse and partly embody the aesthetically pleasing ideals of chivalry, but they vitiate them by turning the pursuit of honor into an obsession. The Greeks, who are much coarser, have a more realistic view of war, but they tend to brutality and stupidity. Not even the best of heroes are totally sympathetic. It is as if Shakespeare endeavored to show them occasionally at their worst. What we first learn about Hector, as much a character of heroic stature as there is in the play, is that he has struck his armorer and scolded his wife although he is said to be generally a man "whose patience / Is as a virtue fix'd" (I.ii.4–5). Ulysses is certainly the shrewdest of the Greeks, yet his major actions are the perpetration of a hoax on Achilles and a rather unkind exposure of Troilus to the truth about Cressida.

Shakespeare's method of playing out favorable against unfavorable traits is most schematic in the characterization of Ajax, who, early in the play, is described as a bundle of contrarieties:

> This man . . . hath robb'd many beasts of their particular additions: he is as valiant as the lion, churlish as the bear, slow as the elephant—a man into whom nature hath so crowded humours that his valour is crush'd into folly, his folly sauced with discretion. There is no man hath a virtue that he hath not a glimpse of, nor any man an attaint but he carries some stain of it; he is melancholy without cause and merry against the hair; he hath the joints of everything; but everything so out of joint that he is a gouty Briareus, many hands and no use, or purblind Argus, all eyes and no sight.
>
> (I.ii.19–29)

One would be hard put to find any of the few glimpses of virtue here attributed to Ajax borne out by his actions in the play. Evidently, Shakespeare's mannerist view of men as composites of shreds and patches worked in favor of Ajax, providing him with a somewhat better reputation than he deserves. The man we get to know is mere joints and no brain, but it could be said that the joints have their duality; he is half-made of Hector's blood, a compositional fact to which he owes his survival—Hector would kill some of his single parts if he could identify any that are clearly and distinctly Greek.

The war plot proper begins with the debate in the Greek camp (I.iii), which leads to Ulysses' scheme against Achilles. This debate is paralleled by another one among the Trojan leaders (II.ii), in which Hector's challenge of a Greek hero to single combat is ratified. These debates and their consequences form, except for the inconclusive battle in the fifth act, all there is to the war plot. It is a story of frustrations and missed opportunities. The decisions taken in the debates prove utterly pointless. It is not Ulysses' ruse that brings Achilles back to the field, but the death of his friend Patroclus, dubbed by Thersites his "masculine whore." Nor does Hector's heroism and chivalry help the Greek cause, for, in what Troilus calls his "vice of mercy," he refuses to fight Ajax. Purpose is but slave to memory, of violent birth, but poor validity.

Yet the debates and their consequences are of significance for the thought of the play; they highlight the conflict between orthodox theory and refractory reality, as important a theme here as it is in *Hamlet;* they give us a feel for the intellectual and the moral qualities of the combatants; and they provide an important perspective on the hero, Troilus. In the Greek debate, Agamemnon's opening speech clearly strikes the theme of the incongruity of theory and practice: "The ample proposition that hope makes / In all designs begun on earth below / Fails in the promis'd largeness" (I.iii.3–5). The subsequent speeches of the Greek leaders breathe a similar frustration and disillusionment. But Ulysses succeeds in restoring the faith of his compeers in the high road of theory when he diagnoses the troubles as due to the neglect of "the specialty of rule."

This much-analyzed speech need not detain us long. Ulysses, as we have noted in examining his patterns of self-knowledge, is not addicted to humanistic principles. He is philosophically a skeptic, politically an absolutist. His clever manipulation of others has its equivalent in the specious way in which he makes ideas, even old humanistic commonplaces, subservient to his purposes. As Professor Elton has shown in detail, his degree speech is not a straightforward defense of hierarchical order but reflects the multiple ironies, ambivalent attitudes, and the skeptic tone of the play. For Ulysses, values have no purpose per se; they are subject to their daily quotation by the opinion brokers: "No man is the lord of anything . . . / Till he communicate his parts to others" (III.iii.115–17). In the degree speech, he does not defend the intrinsic values of an aristocratic hierarchical order—he would be no skeptic if he did. The external signs of this order, as he says in an ironic theatrical simile, must be maintained: "Degree being vizarded, / Th' unworthiest shows as fairly in the mask" (I.iii.83–84). The paraphernalia of degree must be maintained, or the system will collapse. The negative aspects of this defense of external values is highlighted by the unimpressiveness of Agamemnon, the "med'cinable" sun, on whose display of "priority and place" the maintenance of Ulysses' order depends. When Aeneas enters immediately after the Greek debate, he fails notably to recognize that the "god in office, guiding men," Agamemnon, for whom he asks, is actually the person to whom he addresses his question (I.iii.224 ff.). Subsequently, Thersites, not unjustly, demonstrates how foolish it is when one fool obeys another higher up the hierarchical ladder (II.iii.40 ff.). Ulysses' theories are proved to be shoddy most signally by his own action. His rhetorical effort is merely an introduction to his attempt to get Achilles back to the battlefield by stirring "the envious fever / Of pale and bloodless emulation" between Achilles and Ajax. Here and elsewhere, the actuality of men's behavior belies their references to idealistic principles that in themselves are shown to be flawed. The ironies of *Troilus and Cressida,* as Professor Elton has shown, go deep.[6]

As a diagnosis of the reasons for the stagnation of the war and the flaws of Greek society. Ulysses' speech is inadequate and one-sided, and it does not agree with any philosophy of order Shakespeare expressed in the history plays or elsewhere. Ulysses attributes the dragging out of the war to "oppugnancy," the conflict and tension in the Greek camp. But, as we noted in discussing the structural principles of the Renaissance macrocosm, Shakespeare seems to have thought of the tension of opposing forces as creative, at least up to a point. Of course, these forces were those of well-organized layers of society, not selfish cliques. Achilles' private grudge is as sterile as is Ulysses' skeptic authoritarianism, and the conflict between the two can bring no organic order. Neither does the mainspring of the philosophical and political dislocation lie in what Ulysses calls "appetite, an universal wolf" (I.iii.121)—this may be one of Achilles' problems, but it is certainly not one of Ulysses'. The stagnation of the Greeks is not oppugnancy but intellectual and moral inadequacy.

It looks at first sight as if the debate of the Trojans presented an alternative to the Greeks' sterility. The Trojans do discuss a more fundamental question, and they do so apparently in a spirit of greater seriousness, the question whether to continue a war that appears to some of them pointless. The opposing positions are clearly drawn up: Hector, seconded by Helenus, argues that reason decrees that

Helen should be returned to the Greeks and the war be ended;
Troilus, supported by Paris, attacks this argument with the claim
that such action would violate the national honor.

As we have noted earlier, Hector begins the debate with an announcement of his philosophical position as a moderate skeptic who
uses reason cautiously in determining the all-important issue of war
and peace; all calculations suggest that Helen must leave (II.ii.8–
25). He is passionately interrupted by Troilus, whose arguments are
enthusiastic, novel, and seemingly idealistic. We shall examine them
first.

Troilus's main point is that the king of the country and a foreign
queen who has become a national symbol (no matter how obtained)
cannot be evaluated rationalistically. Priam's honor and worth cannot be put on a "scale of common ounces" with reasons and fears
about war and peace (22–32), and Helen's value has been established as "inestimable" by the national effort of abducting and keeping her (69–96). Troilus, we say, is romantic and idealistic about
kingship and women. He does, of course, quite clearly flout the humanistic position of reasonable action when, like Tarquin in *Lucrece,*
he wafts away "reason and respect" as fit only for cowards (49–50).
If one defines "idealism" in its popular meaning (not to speak about
the philosophical one) as the desire to see the world as it should be
or as the attempt to create such a world, Troilus is merely an illustration of the inadequacies and fallacies that often lurk behind this
vision or endeavor. Idealism demands a belief in intrinsic values, in
absolutes, and Troilus is even less capable of such belief than Ulysses.
His ingrained skepticism shows itself best in his pivotal argument
on the value of Helen. For him, it is not, as in Marlowe, her "face"
—which he had earlier declared to be gory—but her "price"—that
of a "pearl"—which launched the thousand ships. The commercial
simile, one of the many in the play, here demonstrates his need of
values but also his habit of affixing variable prices to them. His odd
example of the man who "distastes" later the wife he has chosen
(61–68) is characteristic of him. Troilus, of course, argues that
honor demands that one must keep such a wife, just as the Trojans
must keep Helen—we shall not comment on the aptness of the analogue—but this example and his figure of the pricing of Helen show
that Troilus's value system is a shifting and changing one in which
pearls can be marked up and down according to the dictates of the
will, an instrument very much subject to envious and calumniating

time; the strongest love can become boredom and aversion. Troilus espouses absolutes because of what Hector calls "the hot passion of distemp'red blood" (169). As Derek Traversi has said, his "disembodied idealism covers a sensual impulse which he refuses to recognize." [7]

But the pseudo-idealism of Troilus is even more disintellectualized than disembodied. His need to have ideals, contradicted as it is by his skepticism about absolute values, leads him to embrace fervidly those that his will elects. One could speak here of a pseudo-fideism. Troilus, rejecting all measurements of his ideals, acclaims them as intuitively apprehended by his faith in an analogous way to that which the fideist said was the only method to know God. One might compare Troilus's ridicule of the idea that Priam's worth and honor can be measured and his acclaim of the "past-proportion" of the king's "infinite" (26–29) with Montaigne's rejection of the idea that God is measurable (from the strongly fideistic ending of "An Apology of Raymond Sebond") :

> It were a sin to say of God, who is the only that is, that he was or shall be; for these words are declinations, passages, or vicissitudes of that which cannot last nor continue in being. Wherefore we must conclude that only God *is,* not according to any measure of time, but according to an immovable and immutable eternity.[8]

Montaigne's call to "vile, abject man" to "raise himself above humanity" not by his reason but by faith in an infinite God has its secular analogue in Troilus's rejection of reason and adoption of faith in honor, king, and national symbol. Troilus's chivalry, patriotism, and glorification of the divinity of kings are articles of a pseudo-religion. Ironically, he, whose hot blood no "discourse of reason" can reach, mocks the "high strains of divination" of his sister Cassandra (101 ff.).

But even Hector, who analyzes his brother well, turns out to be less consistently reasonable than his initial position indicates. It is true that he does defend humanistic rules of social and political action that Shakespeare had elsewhere shown to be basic to civilized life; he evokes the traditional moral virtues and asks that they be applied to the law of nations. His argument is so technical as to seem fashioned on Cicero's *De Officiis,* the most authoritative source.[9] When he says that the law of nature and of nations demands that Helen be returned, he espouses the same moral-psychological prin-

ciple of temperance as did Cicero, who noted the inadmissibility of
theft on a private as well as an international scale (III.21–74). Like
Ulysses, Hector is an apologist of reason and order, and like Ulysses
he loses his credibility for us by his actions. In a surprising switch
during the debate, Hector abandons his theoretical principles and
adopts Troilus's hawkishness. On the intellectual issue, he does not
retract; what he has said is "in way of truth." But in practice, he will
side with Troilus and advocate keeping Helen because she represents
a cause "that hath no mean dependence / Upon our joint and several
dignities" (192–93). The cleavage between what men know to be
right and true and what they actually do, which opens up in *Hamlet,*
here becomes even wider. Shakespeare gave it dramatic emphasis by
the entrance, in the middle of the debate, of Cassandra, that symbol
of truth for which men have no ears. Her prophecies and tears are
not enough to keep Hector on the course of rational action; to
Troilus, they are merely brainsick raptures. But the raptures really
dangerous to Troy are those of Troilus, and even the more prudent
Hector is infected by the irrationality that is in the air. The Trojan
debate manifests not only an external division, that between hawks
and doves, but also more subtle and serious internal fissures between
one part of a disputant's nature and the other, between Hector's
rationality and obsessive sense of honor, and between Troilus's skepticism and his fideistic pseudo-idealism.

The scenes of battle (V.iv–x) that conclude the war plot and
the play (except for Pandarus's epilogue) are fragmentary, but they
are right for this play. The camera shifts, as it were, from one brief
individual action to the other. The glorious war dissolves into a
number of private feuds that give vent to personal jealousies and
grievances, but do not end them. Where human character might be
strong enough to execute intentions, the shadow of fate falls between
the conception and the execution. Those who have reasons for deadly
hatred of their opponents are denied the satisfaction of killing them.
Menelaus cannot slay Paris; Troilus cannot take his revenge on
Diomedes. Hector is indeed killed, but not in fair battle. When he
and Achilles confront each other, the cowardly Greek withdraws because his arms are "out of use." When Hector falls into his enemy's
hands, it is ironically just after he has succumbed to greed, an emotion that little suits his chivalry, by hunting and killing a Greek because of his sumptuous armor. Achilles, who does not have any

sense of chivalry, has him murdered by the cruel Myrmidons just when, unarmed, he takes a rest from the battle.

Hector's murder and the subsequent indignity inflicted on his body is a commentary on the ironic brutality of war. A warrior with the reputation of nobility becomes, just at the moment when his hands are stained, the victim of a gang led by a cowardly, conceited, and brutal half-wit. The episode is an illustration of the humanists' belief that war was the product of man's ignorance of himself, a belief shared by some skeptics. In his chapter "Of the military Profession," Charron neatly balanced the stereotype of war as the breeding place of nobility, ardor, glory, vigor, manliness, and courage with its horrible effects—hatred, fury, madness, destruction, and death. "And all this," Charron concluded, "to serve the passion of another, for a cause which a man knows not to be just, and which is commonly unjust." [10]

The battle scenes and much else in *Troilus and Cressida* lead one to a conclusion like Charron's about war; they use the skeptics' favorite method of negating man's illusionary ideals by pragmatic and brutal realities. And as if glimpses we get of the war action were not disillusioning enough by themselves, we see Thersites scouting the battlefield like an ubiquitous war correspondent, giving us sordid inside information not intended for the homefront. Those that have thought that these final scenes were written by Shakespeare in a hurry or added by somebody else are surely wrong; they are a powerful, if satiric and bitter, commentary on men at war. They pulverize the lie of war.

The war story is intertwined with the love plot, and the juxtaposition makes some ironic points about the congruity of the two most absorbing occupations of man.[11] In the one scene in which Helen appears—a scene difficult to assign to either the war plot or the love plot—she, the inadequate issue of the war, is also debunked as the queen of romance. She proves to be merely a sex-obsessed girl, entertained by Pandarus with what must be the most inane love songs in Shakespeare. Helen, it is true, had lost much of her romantic glamor for the Elizabethans; in *Lucrece,* Shakespeare called her "the strumpet that began this stir" (1471). But just before her appearance in *Troilus and Cressida,* he conjured up her old romantic value, ironically by the Clown, who introduces her as "the mortal Venus, the heart-blood of beauty, love's invisible soul" (III.i.31).

The Clown's pun on "stew" adds an obscene touch that contributes to the absurdity of Pandarus's seven-times repeated "fair" in his greeting of Helen. In the Platonizing language of the courtesy books, the "First Fair" was the highest kind of beauty, spiritual and invisible, the permanent and divine Idea.[12] Pandarus's play on "fair" accentuates the obtrusive visibility and earthiness of Helen, the "Nell" of the Trojans. The scene is thus a sardonic introduction to the love tryst of Troilus and Cressida, which follows immediately.

There would obviously be no place in this disintegrating moral climate for a hero like Romeo; youthful purity here would be merely incredible naïveté. There would also be no place for a tortured seeker of values like Hamlet; no such man could fall in love with Cressida. The Troilus that Shakespeare actually created is different from either and undoubtedly of smaller stature. But he is not a totally simple man, and one could argue that he is as modern, perhaps more modern but uncomfortably so, as these two tragic favorites have proved to be. His characterization of himself and those of him spoken by others contrast oddly with his actual character. Even the two seemingly conventional *laudes* of his person, the one by Pandar (I.ii.244 ff.) and the other by Ulysses (IV.v.96 ff.), are puzzling and unsatisfactory. Ulysses' appraisal comes via Aeneas and thus has a distancing quality that, by itself, is vexing; but even taken at face value, Ulysses' balanced antitheses leave one with some doubts about the young man. He is a "true knight," but "not yet mature"; he is "not soon provok'd," but, if provoked, not "soon calm'd." Other features given by Ulysses are untrue; his remark that Troilus does not dignify "an impair thought with breath" denies his voluptuous remarks to both Pandar and Cressida and can be understood only from the perspective of Aeneas, his fellow Trojan. Most disturbing is the statement that Troilus is as manly as Hector, but "more dangerous." The relative absence of "danger," of vindictiveness, is, after all, Hector's most amiable feature.

The other portrait, that drawn by Pandar, is a playful build-up intended to endear Troilus to Cressida; but it may contain some hidden truth. "Do you know what a man is?" Pandarus asks his niece—and we wonder how he should know. In Pandarus's culinary analogy, a man's "spice and salt" are birth, beauty, good shape, discourse, manhood, learning, gentleness, virtue (a term Pandarus can understand only imperfectly), youth, liberality, and so forth. A man with these spices, as Cressida wittily rejoins, is a "minc'd man."

And Troilus is divided and fragmented, even more deeply so than the other characters. His seasoning leaves much to be desired, and, by the end of the play, he has lost most of the moral qualities in Pandarus's recipe of manhood and become what one might call a minced man, a very imperfect man indeed, hitting blindly right and left, wildly attempting to take revenge for a slight he thinks the world has given him.

Shakespeare kept Troilus from becoming sympathetic even in moments when we could identify most clearly with him. His sensuous anticipation of the love tryst makes him a junior voluptuary. Pandarus becomes for him, in one of his juvenile lapses of taste, a Charon that wafts him to the Elysian fields where he will "wallow in the lily beds" (III.ii.12 ff.). He shows himself almost as much a devotee to sensations as Cressida when he fears that "th' imaginary relish" might prove so sweet as to make him "lose distinction" in his joys.[13] Troilus's anticipation is not only slightly soiled by an earthy ingredient but is also made subtly ironic by a skeptic awareness of the cleavage between desire and fulfillment, between the infinity of the will and the limitations of the act.[14] He knows that "we taste nothing purely," as Montaigne said in the title of one of his essays. He lacks the spontaneity of youth and love that radiates from Romeo. He cannot really lose himself totally in love before he loses Cressida by fate.

It is by an exercise of the will he acclaimed as the supreme arbiter of values that he makes Cressida a symbol of ideal love. We have seen the real Cressida in bawdy pleasantries with Pandarus, and we have heard the latter mistaking the Clown's effusions about Helen as applying to Cressida—the two are sisters in spirit, and their value is out of proportion to the price men pay for them. Yet in the tryst, Cressida attempts to rise to Troilus's ideal conception of her. It is a superb touch of Shakespeare's artistry when he makes her effort conspicuous as she tries to put her amorous technique aside in order to enter into the spirit of the moment. It is a violation of her strategic principles to admit that she only *seemed* hard to win (III.ii.114) and that, perchance, she may be using more "craft" than she feels "love" (149)—there is a double irony here, for she wishes Troilus to reject these absolutely true statements. But the most ironic of her remarks is when she divides herself into two selves, thus parodying Troilus's split personality: "I have a kind of self resides with you; / But an unkind self, that itself will leave / To be another's fool"

(144–46). She is not really so deeply split; her ideal self is very largely that of Troilus's imagination, which she feebly tries to re-create. Her actual self is the unkind self that acts deceptively as if she were reluctant to embrace Troilus, the self that will later act similarly toward Diomedes.

Here and elsewhere, much of what Cressida says forms a satiric commentary on the ironies of Troilus's exertions. If his protests of truth and faithfulness are immature and hyperbolical, hers are hysterical and theatrical: she enjoys "tasting" the grief of her sepa-ration from Troilus as much as she did their union. And if Troilus can be a skeptic and find man's will directed by his deceptive senses (II.ii.61 ff.), by the same token she can excuse her fickleness:

> Troilus, farewell! One eye yet looks on thee;
> But with my heart the other eye doth see.
> Ah, poor our sex! this fault in us I find,
> The error of our eye directs our mind.
> What error leads must err; O, then conclude,
> Minds sway'd by eyes are full of turpitude.
>   (V.ii.105–10)

This climactic scene, in which she reveals flagrantly her true nature, that of a "daughter of the game," is one of Shakespeare's most complex dramatic exposés. The flirtatious Cressida, the direct Diomede, the wily Ulysses, the deflating Thersites, all contribute to showing that not only has Troilus been deceived by Cressida but that he also has deceived himself and will continue to do so. It is the moment when Troilus most nearly rises to the stature of a tragic hero; it is his greatest passion as well as his closest approach to self-discovery. Yet it also shows him incapable of the full dignity and the passion that characterize Shakespeare's great tragic heroes. In some ways, the scene foreshadows the later over-hearing scene in *Othello,* when the Moor watches Iago and Cassio and then Cassio and Bianca in the belief that they ridicule his cuckoldry. Troilus, of course, has an ocular demonstration of Cressida's unfaithfulness, which Othello does not; yet he is much less passionate. One may compare, for in-stance, Othello's wild protestation of patience, "I will be found most cunning in my patience; / But—dost thou hear?—most bloody" with Troilus's feeble "I will be patient; outwardly I will" (V.ii.68). If Troilus does not have the temperament to rise to the passion of an

Othello, neither has he the intellectual strength of a Hamlet to hide pain by wit and sarcasm.

It is symptomatic of his self-deception that his immediate reaction is to try to cling, in spite of all appearances, to the romantic image of Cressida. He would like to listen to

> a credence in my heart,
> An esperance so obstinately strong,
> That doth invert th' attest of eyes and ears;
> As if those organs had deceptious functions
> Created only to calumniate.
>
> (118–22)

Troilus displays here the same inconsistent idealism as when he sought to revalue Helen on the basis of the price the Trojans paid for her. As he was then inflamed by the subjective need of having absolute ideals (although his skepticism should have denied such possibility), so now again his desperate need for them rings in his cry: "Let it not be believ'd for womanhood. / Think, we had mothers" (127–28). He even tries to refute the idea that the Cressida he has just observed is the real Cressida.

His pathetic attempt to reject the attest of eyes and ears parallels Cressida's excuse of being led by the error of the eye, according to her a congenital one with women. And in both cases the claim is deflated by Thersites, who calls Cressida's argument a proof of strength she could outdo only by claiming that her mind has turned whore and who wonders whether Troilus will swagger himself out of his own eyes. Troilus is here no closer to real self-knowledge than he was at the beginning of the play when he asked Apollo who he, Pandar, and Cressida were. He deceives himself with picturesque and unilluminating metaphors.

But even if Troilus's reaction to the great disillusionment of his life lacks in self-awareness, it leads to a supreme rhetorical exercise that draws on humanistic patterns of self-knowledge. The confused and pathetic speech in which he explains his state and feeling is, together with Ulysses' eye-soul analogy, symtomatic of the twist Shakespeare gave to these patterns in this deeply disturbing play. Troilus characteristically begins with another attempt to deny that the actual Cressida is the true one:

> If beauty have a soul, this is not she;
> If souls guide vows, if vows be sanctimonies,
> If sanctimony be the gods' delight,
> If there be rule in unity itself,
> This was not she.
>
> (136–40)

Troilus expresses the impossibility that his Cressida is disloyal by making her into a "soul," a familiar enough identification for a lover. As a soul, she is, in Renaissance terms, the most cohesive and unalterable of unities; Cicero called it a *semper idem,* and the Renaissance commentators insisted that its unity was self-evident—"plain to anybody who knows anything about physics," as Camerarius put it.[15] Troilus reaffirms this unity by logical demonstration; but he finds himself unable to deny what reality presents, and his own soul suffers a "madness of discourse, / That cause sets up with and against itself! / Bifold authority!" He thus tortures himself with a logical contradiction that a skeptic should be able to accept; as Charron put it, there is no reason, but has a contrary reason.[16] But Troilus's projection of the ideal unity, the "soul," into Cressida makes this position untenable for him. The split in this supposed soul becomes now a deepening split in his own:

> Within my soul there doth conduce a fight
> Of this strange nature, that a thing inseparate
> Divides more wider than the sky and earth;
> And yet the spacious breadth of this division
> Admits no orifex for a point as subtle
> As Ariachne's broken woof to enter.
>
> (145–50)

The seeming division of Cressida into two beings opens for him a macrocosmic cleavage:

> Instance, O instance! strong as Pluto's gates:
> Cressid is mine, tied with the bonds of heaven.
> Instance, O instance! strong as heaven itself:
> The bonds of heaven are slipp'd, dissolv'd, and loos'd.
>
> (151–54)

This cosmic extension of disintegration still arises from the soul concept with which Troilus identifies his ideal Cressida. The Renais-

sance commentators on the *semper idem* anchored its unity in that of
the macrocosmic spirit; Troilus quite appropriately sees Cressida's
"disunity" as well as his own reflected in the heavens. Yet with all
this rhetorical effort, in the end he has to resign himself to the
undeniable reality:

> And with another knot, five-finger-tied,
> The fractions of her faith, orts of her love,
> The fragments, scraps, the bits, and greasy relics
> Of her o'er-eaten faith, are bound to Diomed.
> (155–58)

Troilus has thus fragmented his supreme value, Cressida, and, in
the process, his inner fragmentation finds its outward expression.
He is now truly Cressida's "minc'd man." What comes from now
on is of no real consequence to him. And what happens to him
is of little consequence to us; it is dramatically significant only
by showing that his subsequent life is inconsequential. He continues
to live, seeking with "careless force and forceless care" some kind of
revenge (V.v.40). But the action does not give him this satisfaction;
it would be much too absolute an ending for this play of impotence
and sterility. Death would restore Troilus from fragmentation to
some kind of wholeness; therefore, it would be inconsistent with the
relentless disintegration of men and values.

The general finale of futility is thus appropriate both thematically
and dramatically. Inconclusive and seemingly irrelevant as the actions in the disrupted battle scenes are, they emphasize the theme of
the fragmentation of the self in a twilight world. And the concluding
episode, in which Pandarus enters in the throes of the Neapolitan
bone-ache he wishes to bequeath to the audience, is just the right
touch. Everything, like the bee in the pathetic little song of that
former troubadour of love, has lost its honey and its sting. Pandarus's insult is a final, futile, and unpleasant gesture, but it is
dramatically right.

The patterns of self-knowledge in *Troilus and Cressida* turn out
to be patterns of ignorance, deception, and self-deception. They are
imbued with a skeptical and satirical look at humanity. But I think
that for this very reason they are not as deeply disturbing as those
of *Hamlet*. They have a kind of built-in *reductio ad absurdum*.
When all men and values are shown to be defective, we sense the

author's satirical intention and are apt to attribute some of the implied social and philosophical criticism to the formal requirements of a satire. Also, the low intellectual and moral stature of the Greeks and Trojans lessens the significance of their ideas. Hamlet's skepticism has the ring of search and suffering; it is not the congenital inconsistency of a fragmented Troilus.

This lessening of the sting seems to me to have a considerable effect on the role skepticism plays as a philosophical theme. It is difficult to say which of the expressed skeptic attitudes are to be taken seriously; and Troilus's use of skeptic ideas is satirized, Cressida's is burlesqued. The humanistic position, theoretically taken by Hector, although in practice denied by him, comes off a little better. It is not deflated as such and has a somewhat better spokesman. *Troilus and Cressida* seems to indicate that Shakespeare was becoming more skeptic of skepticism and somewhat more tolerant of the humanistic absolutes he had questioned, ironically and sometimes bitterly, in *Hamlet*.

That this may have been so is made more likely by the way the play's greatest skeptic, Thersites, is portrayed. His skepticism about values and human nature has none of the inconsistencies of Troilus's. But Thersites is also one of the most unsympathetic characters. We cannot help accepting his comments on the degeneracy of the other characters and the rottenness of Greece and Troy as true even if they are unpleasant. It is Thersites who puts into words the overwhelming impression created by the play: "Lechery, lechery! Still wars and lechery! Nothing else holds fashion" (V.ii.194–95). Yet he, the deadly accurate fragmenter of men, is also a parasite and as such less than a full man; Achilles fittingly calls him a "fragment" (V.i.8). The character of Thersites shows that a presumed self-knowledge that questions all values, and does so in a spirit that reveals a lack of sympathy with humanity, is barren and odious; and it is also false because it denies the truth of the human condition that makes men dependent on one another.

CHAPTER TWELVE

Measure for Measure:
Looking into Oneself

IN THEIR WAYS, *All's Well That Ends Well* and *Measure for Measure* have proved to be as perplexing to critics as has *Troilus and Cressida*. It is true that, unlike the latter play, they do not pose a problem concerning the genre to which they belong—comedy, comical satire, tragedy, or history—since they are clearly comedies. But in exchange they offer even greater resistance to critics in search of their design; there is always some refractory detail that does not fit into the proposed scheme. But these plays appear more unified as well as deeper in their significance, I believe, if one understands them as being concerned with a subject that fascinated Shakespeare during the period in which they were written: the difficulty of gaining self-knowledge in situations unusually complicated and distressing.

It must be granted, however, that the perplexities of *All's Well* are not quite of the same order as those of *Measure for Measure*. The former play, although somewhat simpler, has something undeniably inadequate in its dramatic conception and execution; it may well be an insufficiently revised play of Shakespeare's earlier period, perhaps the mysterious *Love's Labor's Won.*[1] If so, Shakespeare may have decided to take up the story of *Measure for Measure* for dramatization because it allowed him to treat more successfully a pattern of self-knowledge he had attempted in *All's Well*. The two plays certainly do have similarities beyond their resistance to totally satisfying interpretations. Both have heroes who present to the world deceptive outsides, Bertram in his handsomeness, noble lineage, and martial accomplishment, Angelo in his judicial strictness and ethical rectitude. They are put in unusual and perplexing situations that test their moral fiber, and they fail, Bertram by first agreeing to marry and then rejecting the beautiful and deserving but socially inferior and poor Helena, Angelo by first enforcing an unnaturally strict law, then violating it by his lust for Isabella and compounding his failing by hypocrisy and villainy. Bertram and Angelo prove, in the words of Shakespeare's sonnet 94, that "lilies that fester smell far worse than weeds." [2] Just as in this sonnet apparently ideal men, who "inherit Heaven's graces," are slowly and subtly revealed to be unsympathetic, so with mannerist indirection and irony Bertram and Angelo are shown to be inwardly rotten and corrupt. Both are re-generated, largely through their interaction with heroines who, although apparently superior to them morally, are yet difficult to evaluate. To some critics, they have seemed to be less than the unspotted lilies they appear. It is true, their virtue is tested in more dubious ways than is that of Shakespeare's earlier and later heroines—in particular, their involvement in the "bed-trick" has offended some critics—but they also have character traits that have been found unattractive, such as the persistence of Helena—"predatory" it has been called—in pursuing her man, or the "coldness" of Isabella in being willing to see her brother die rather than surrender her chastity.

I shall not try to list all the similarities of the two plays that have been pointed out,[3] but in my subsequent discussion of *Measure for Measure* I should like to glance now and then at *All's Well*, for its indirect and ironic approach to the patterns of self-knowledge constitutes a significant new departure for Shakespeare. *All's Well*, at least in the form we have it today, which may be a revision, appears to be an experiment in a dramatic mode that Shakespeare developed further in *Measure for Measure*.[4] And what he did in the latter play, particularly by creating the characters of Angelo and the duke, points forward to the dramas of self-loss and self-discovery that were to come, most of all to *Lear* and to *The Tempest*.

Although self-knowledge is an issue in *All's Well*, particularly through the education of Bertram—which is the central theme, if the play can be said to have one—the issue is only imperfectly developed. It is true Bertram does learn something about himself and his deceptions in the end as his friend and trusted advisor, Parolles, is revealed as a coward and traitor and as he comes to recognize the strength of Helena's affection. But all this is rather perfunctorily handled. Bertram never sees himself, in the way we see him, as a young cad who may become a very odious old lecher and snob. We have to trust to Helena's continuing strength and will power, of which we have had formidable demonstrations, that he will remain on the right path. Angelo, however, does look into himself deeply once, even though he turns his eyes away too quickly. But this look makes a great deal of difference.

If, as a very competent student of the play has suggested, it was the problem of self-knowledge inherent in the story of the corrupt judge that induced Shakespeare to write *Measure for Measure*,[5] he decided to emphasize it by putting Angelo's failure and regeneration in a larger frame. Angelo's need to know himself is reflected in the similar, though less glaring, need of Isabella; it is paralleled, I should like to suggest, by a subtly hinted-at deficiency of the duke. At the end, not only is Angelo a better man, but Isabella is also more feminine and humane; and even the duke may have learned something about himself, although it is not what he set out to learn. And these patterns of self-knowledge evolve in a climate that poses fundamental questions, such as those of the price of chastity, the roots of self-discipline, the ethical bases of the law, and the ruler's obligations to punish and to be merciful. Only in *King Lear* are there more far-reaching implications in the ethical imperative "know thyself."

Shakespeare's Angelo is, to all appearances, a man of honor and rectitude. But he is a puzzling, contradictory character, quite different from the uncomplicated judge in Whetstone's *Promos and Cassandra*, on whom he is based. Promos is an ordinary, essentially decent, and apparently mature man with a clean record, who just happens to be overcome by lust; Angelo, though young, is reputed to be of such spectacular virtue and knowledge that everybody accepts him as a most appropriate substitute during the absence of the duke and as fit to translate the virtues he possesses into action. There is no sign that he assumes his great office with the excusable overeagerness of his prototype in Cinthio's *novella*, which formed the basis of Whetstone's play and was probably known to Shakespeare. Cinthio's young governor, appointed to administer Innsbruck, was "more pleased with the office to which the Emperor called him than sound in the knowledge of his own nature." [6] Angelo, by contrast, accepts his responsibility with apparent humility and even diffidence: "Let there be some more test made of my metal, / Before so noble and so great a figure / Be stamp'd upon it" (I.i.49–51).

In the slow, gradual disclosure of Angelo's nature, Shakespeare adopted a strategy quite contrary to his usual dramatic practice of firmly establishing the outlines of his major characters early, often immediately. Angelo's heart of darkness, like that of Kurtz in Conrad's famous story, is, at first, no more than hinted at. There is an irony, hardly suspected by the subtlest of first-time readers of the play, in the duke's seeming commendation: "Angelo, / There is a kind of character in thy life / That to th' observer doth thy history / Fully unfold" (I.i.28–30). The duke, who has observed this history, does not disclose it until he tells, in the third act, the story of Angelo's perfidy to Mariana; but questions about the true nature of Angelo begin in the second scene, as Claudio wonders what the reasons for his judicial severity may be: whether it be the "fault and glimpse of newness," or whether Angelo intends to let people know that he can command by making them "straight feel the spur" (I.ii.150 ff.).

In the following scene, the duke reveals that he expects severity from Angelo, "a man of stricture and firm abstinence" (I.iii.12), and has purposely installed him as deputy to bring about a change from his own lax administration of the laws. Duke Vincentio, on this occasion, calls Angelo "precise"—the regular term for Puritan—and a man that "scarce confesses / That his blood flows" (51–52). Lucio, in the next scene, joins in by calling Angelo

> a man whose blood
> Is very snow-broth, one who never feels
> The wanton stings and motions of the sense,
> But doth rebate and blunt his natural edge
> With profits of the mind, study and fast.
>   (I.iv. 57–61)

The general impression created by the Angelo of the first act is that of a virtuous, extremely disciplined man who is convinced that human nature can be controlled and that the affections can, Stoic fashion, be mastered by might. He is not the stage Puritan of the Elizabethans, murmuring pious phrases while pursuing a lustful or avaricious course of action. However, he does have some of the symptoms of the more dangerous, more inhuman elements of the Puritan syndrome, elements that, ignited, can lead to a dangerous explosion.

Angelo's legal absolutism arises from his conviction that his own mind is superior to that of others and can easily control his course of action. He has the kind of intellectual pride censured by Montaigne and the skeptical fideists. He thus rejects the argument of the older and wiser Escalus that mercy be applied to Claudio because of man's general vulnerability to temptation: " 'Tis one thing to be tempted, Escalus, / Another thing to fall" (II.i.17–18). The cool and studious Angelo does not convey the impression of ever having been really tempted; he never understood, as he later says, why men could be so foolish as to fall through passion. Angelo can therefore feel quite safe when, with dramatic irony, he declares himself willing to die should he ever commit the same fault as Claudio.

An audience trained to listen for dramatic ironies, as the Jacobeans must have been, may have sensed a significance on this occasion in Escalus's request that Angelo ask himself whether he would not have erred like Claudio at some time if circumstances had been similar. The irony of the hint becomes clear in Isabella's later pleading that Angelo imagine Claudio's fault his own (II.ii.136 ff.), for by now Angelo has fallen prey to lust. But not until the third act is the past deed revealed that counts most against him: his desertion of Mariana. Outwardly, this action resembles Claudio's failure to marry Juliet. But Angelo's breach of promise was a real act of villainy whereas Claudio's was not: Angelo abandoned his betrothed, Claudio merely delayed marriage. On the other hand, Angelo could think himself legally justified; his contract with Mariana was evidently not the stronger *de praesenti* contract of Claudio and Juliet, but the weaker *de futuro* agreement, thought binding only when consummated, as is done later in the play.[7] Despicable as his abandonment of Mariana was when she lost her dowry, he can reason that the conditions on which his promise was based have changed, and he can rationalize his villainy into an act of prudence. This exactly is his later defense (V.i.218). That he cast aspersions on her character when he deserted her makes him more odious, but does not seem to have dimmed his specious self-image as a man of virtue and temperance.

The image is shattered when he cannot resist his lust for Isabella. His two soliloquies, one immediately following his first conversation with her, the other preceding the second and decisive interview, show the change in his soul. Passion conquers the reason of which he prided himself, and he realizes now that the self-knowledge he imagined he possessed was merely self-delusion. He no longer knows himself: "What dost thou, or what art thou, Angelo?" (II.ii.173). It is the most fundamental question that any of Shakespeare's characters asks himself, and none had yet asked it in so direct and explicit a manner before *Measure for Measure*. Antipholus of Syracuse in

The Comedy of Errors came close to it; but for him the question was merely one of wonderment about the identity the Ephesians thrust on him. Richard II had looked into the mirror of self-knowledge, but vanity prevented him from looking beyond his grief deeply into himself. Brutus had overlooked the impurity of the mirror Cassius had held up to him. Hamlet had mystified and complicated the inquiry into the self by skeptically asking who he was and what man is. Troilus had altogether evaded the look into himself when his disillusionment through Cressida's betrayal gave him the opportunity. None of Shakespeare's tragic heroes had yet said simply, "what do I and what am I," as does Angelo. Lear was later to ask the question again.

Not that Angelo's answer is altogether clear and honest. In his first soliloquy, in which he poses the question, he tries to wriggle out of it by calling his temptation the work of the devil. Arrogantly, he thinks of himself as a saint baited by another saint. And there is a similar presumption in his second soliloquy when he regrets the loss of his gravity—the least of his losses—coyly remarking that he hopes nobody will hear him taking pride in his reputation for seriousness. Yet he cannot totally suppress the awareness that he, like others in high places, has lived with a lie:

> O place, O form,
> How often dost thou with thy case, thy habit,
> Wrench awe from fools, and tie the wiser souls
> To thy false seeming! Blood, thou art blood.
>   (II.iv.12–15)

The new Angelo is a man whose thoughts and prayers are at cross purposes. When Isabella appears for the second time before him, he speaks to her no longer in the clear, absolute idiom he used earlier, but he tortures her and himself with sexual allusions and innuendos. His attempt to trap her into accepting the act of lust as one of mercy for her brother and Isabella's misunderstanding of his meaning produce moments of psychological subtlety and high comedy.

A kind of incipient self-knowledge comes to Angelo through his self-loss, through the experience of "blood," that is, passion, in himself. Even though he now becomes worse, his evil is more accessible to cure. He is a conscious hypocrite rather than, as formerly, an unconscious one. Although he has fallen through passion, he has now become capable of a cathartic human emotion: lust is related to love, the greatest and most beneficial of man's feelings. There is something to the seemingly absurd argument with which Mariana in the end eagerly pleads for his life: "They say best men are moulded out of faults; / And, for the most, become much more the better / For being a little bad" (V.i.437–39). To use a figure from *All's Well*, the web of Angelo's life is a mingled yarn and his faults whip his virtues. His ideal image of himself as a saint, specious as it is, is yet of assistance in his change, giving him an ethical and religious awareness of his fall and making his later penitence somewhat more plausible.

Angelo's regeneration, however, is brought about in a most unusual manner: it hinges on his sexual fall, caused by his lust, and its medium is Mariana, whom he believes to be Isabella. Thus Angelo's marriage is completed and Mariana's wrong righted. He is pardoned and forgiven. Incredible as the story is, Shakespeare makes it, in various ways, psychologically most intriguing, not least by suggesting that there is a connection between Angelo's sexual knowledge of Mariana and his acquisition of a greater knowledge of himself. Hints of a connection between these two kinds of knowledge are given. There is, at a critical moment of the dialogue between Angelo and Isabella, a pun on the cognitive and sexual meaning of "knowing":

ISAB. I am come to know your pleasure.
ANG. That you might know it would much better please me
        Than to demand what 'tis.

                    (II.iv.31–33)

The pun is repeated during the denouement just before Mariana unveils herself:

                    that is Angelo,
        Who thinks he knows that he ne'er knew my body,
        But knows he thinks that he knows Isabel's.
                    (V.i.200–202)

Before getting to know himself, Angelo has unknowingly known (carnally, as Lucio says) the woman to whom he was engaged on a pre-contract; his marriage is ratified.

In giving a role to carnal knowledge in developing self-knowledge, *Measure for Measure* resembles *All's Well,* where on two similar junctures there are puns on "knowing." Bertram harps on the word when he demonstrates his aversion to marrying the poor Helena (II.iii.111 ff.) and again when he accepts her if she proves to have been his partner: "If she, my liege, can make me know this clearly, / I'll love her dearly, ever, ever dearly" (V.iii.309–10). But the passage also may be taken to imply that Bertram's love and, with it, his continued improvement depend on Helena's sexual power. If so, it raises the question whether a character change achieved by a fortunate fall into a bed can be lasting.

The idea that there was a connection between self-knowledge and sexual knowledge was playfully suggested by Ovid in *The Art of Love* (498–502). The Delphic Apollo here advises the lover that "only he who knows himself will love with wisdom and perform all his tasks according to his powers." [8] The idea was apt to be moralized in the Middle Ages and Christian-humanist Renaissance, but it was also understood in its true cynical meaning by the new Ovidian poets. Shakespeare used it in his Ovidian *Venus and Adonis* —and here already its significance is uncertain—by making Adonis reject the importunities of the amorous Venus: "Before I know myself, seek not to know me" (525). In contrast to Adonis, Shakespeare's problematic heroes, Bertram and Angelo, experience the knowledge of women—shall we say good or shall we say bad women? —before they discover whatever self-knowledge they gain.

It is not merely our overexposure to psychoanalysis that makes us speculate on the psychological significance of the events that occur in the dark chambers of Marseilles and Vienna. By drawing attention to the cognitive aspects of the bed tricks, Shakespeare prevents us from accepting them in the way some scholars say we should accept them, that is, merely as dramatized devices deriving from the romantic *novella,* in which they were used as a narrative convention. It has been pointed out that Elizabethan psychology allowed Shakespeare's contemporaries to entertain more easily the idea that sexual consummation had a regenerative power because of the way they explained the act physiologically. In intercourse, they thought, men and women exchanged their seeds and mingled them in a manner analogous to the way Platonic lovers fused their souls on an ideal plane; the seeds, in turn, were believed to enter the bloodstream. Yet this explanation would not have given an Elizabethan audience the certainty that Helena's and Mariana's influence wins out because the physiologists were at odds on the question whether a stronger woman could improve a weaker man in this fashion.[9] Moreover, there is the question whether Helena and Mariana really are morally superior; their consent to the bed trick makes this a debatable issue. The puzzling Helena does not really concern us here, and Mariana is so slightly sketched that she does not emerge clearly as an improving influence on Angelo. Her idyllic life at "the moated grange" may suggest her romantic possibilities, and her ardent plea for Angelo's life may prove her kindness (or is it her sexual interest in him?). All this is very little.

We therefore had better turn to the other and more carefully drawn woman, who is an important agent in the accomplishment of the bed trick and in the pardon of Angelo. Isabella is more properly Helena's counterpart in *Measure for Measure*. At least she does not suffer from Helena's handicap of directly practicing the deceitful substitution (a handicap that Helena well realizes). But although Isabella is saved from having to submit herself sexually and from other strenuous business that requires Helena to exert herself, she is a problematic heroine. Like Angelo and because of him, she is subjected to an intricate test of her character, first by his lust for her and later by the problem of how his transgression should be judged.

Shakespeare complicated her test by making her a novice of the convent of Saint Clare. For the heroine of Whetstone's play, there is no problem of which is dearer to her, her chastity or her brother. She opts for her brother, which presumably Shakespeare's contemporaries thought was the right choice for her. Isabella, however, is at the threshold of the convent; she is about to dedicate soul and body to God and thus is in a dilemma for which there is no easy answer; hers is a case of extreme moral delicacy. One can have different opinions about what she should do. The critics who lay aside this vexed question and concern themselves not with the rightness or wrongness of her decision but with the way it is given appear to have a more promising approach to her character. It is notable that she never hesitates for a moment and that she rises to the challenge almost with gaiety:

> Then, Isabel, live chaste, and, brother, die:
> More than our brother is our chastity.
> I'll tell him yet of Angelo's request,
> And fit his mind to death, for his soul's rest.
> (II.iv.184–87)

She is, as has been said, of the stuff of which martyrs are made; but it should make a difference to her that the martyrdom she accepts is not her own but her brother's. The test of her faith does not involve her soul only but also that of the human being closest to her.

Her reaction agrees with the impression she creates from the beginning. Her first eager question about the rules of the order of the convent of Saint Clare is motivated by her wish to live a life of even "more strict restraint" than prescribed by the austere order.[10] She parallels Angelo's ascetic temperament, and she has something of his bent for legal and ethical absolutism, for dividing the world into white and black. The two absolutists consequently react to each other like flint and stone, but the flame they produce is divided into a holy and a profane one.

Isabella's stony purity makes her a strong but rather cold pleader for her brother's life. She has really no quarrel with the anti-fornication law—she and Angelo are the only characters that think it entirely just—and she admits from the beginning that in pleading for Claudio she is "at war 'twixt will and will not" (II.ii.33). The allusion to Paul's account of the struggle of flesh and spirit indicates that she believes that the *caritas* that makes her plead has an element of carnality. Her inability to see the issue as one between law and justice leads her to highly abstract arguments on the magistrate's duty to be merciful—a concept as theoretical as is Angelo's of justice. But the religious intensity with which she demands that the mercy of man be brought in line with the forgiveness of God has been thought aesthetically pleasing; she burns, to use Walter Pater's famous phrase, with a hard, gemlike flame.

Pater, whose portrait of her forms a refreshing contrast to such Victorian sentimental gush as Mrs. Jameson's, admired her fiery eloquence that occasionally lights up in swift, vindictive anger. A famous example is when she turns her eyes upward toward heaven, pleading with Angelo not to judge more severely than God:

> Merciful Heaven,
> Thou rather, with thy sharp and sulphurous bolt,
> Splits the unwedgeable and gnarled oak
> Than the soft myrtle. But man, proud man,
> Dress'd in a little brief authority,
> Most ignorant of what he's most assur'd,
> His glassy essence, like an angry ape,

> Plays such fantastic tricks before high heaven
> As makes the angels weep; who, with our spleens,
> Would all themselves laugh mortal.
>   (II.ii.114–23)

Isabella's speech is occasioned by Angelo's immediately preceding metaphor of the law as a newly awakened prophet, who looks into a mirror to see what future evils must have their instantaneous end before they come to life—an ironic figure in view of Angelo's imminent temptation. Isabella holds up a mirror of her own to Angelo and to judging man in general. Like Angelo's earlier soliloquy, her speech is fraught with *nosce teipsum* implications of the kind Shakespeare developed in *Lear*. The diminution Isabella discerns in the image of man when seen from a divine perspective resembles Lear's vision of the world as a great stage of fools. She contrasts the brief robe of authority man proudly wears with his ignorance of himself— the "glassy essence" of which he feels assured but which he fails to understand as his fragile soul.[11]

The image, however, has some implications for Isabella's own soul. The law is not alone in being angry—in fact, its earthly representative is, at present, in the throes of a different passion; Isabella also speaks in anger or, as she presumes, in a divine indignation. The mirror had a general symbolic value for the angry and a special one for simians, particularly female ones, and both are most appropriate for Isabella. In his essay "Of Anger" (II.xxxvi.1–3), Seneca took note of the suggestion that it was good for people to look at themselves while angry; but he refuted the idea for various reasons: the mirror does not reveal the whole man, the man who goes to the mirror generally is already a changed man, and sometimes angry people even like their fiery image. There can be little doubt that the spirited Isabella likes hers; she holds up the *veritas* mirror (with its particular implication for magistrates) to Angelo, but ironically she does not realize that she looks into the *ira-vanitas* mirror herself.

We may use an early seventeenth-century emblem to illustrate the simian symbol used by Isabella as it applies to her. The emblem is a few years too late to have influenced Shakespeare, but it is based on a tradition with which Shakespeare must have been familiar, perhaps as early as grammar school. The emblem pictures an ugly ape— female, as the context implies—looking into a mirror. The picture banner explains that all are pleased with their own shape—an allusion to Ovid's *Art of Love* (I.614), where it is stated that every woman thinks herself lovable no matter how ugly her appearance. As the emblem motto explains, even the ugliest thinks of herself as a goddess.[12] The accompanying explanation refers to such classical illustrations as the mirror of self-love in Virgil's *Eclogues* II.25, where the infatuated Corydon asks the offish Alexis, whose love he wishes to gain, to be the "judge" in confirming the beauty of his self-image in the sea. This passage was one of those which the humanists thought demonstrated how wisdom was often dissociated from love. The prime Ovidian passage for this purpose was the story of Polyphemus in *Metamorphoses* XIII; here Polyphemus fancies that he "knows himself" (*novi me*, 840) when he admires his hairy image in a clear pool. Polyphemus also boasts on this occasion of being bigger than the thunderer Jove (as does Isabella's man of authority). It is possible that, in expounding these passages, Shakespeare's schoolmaster would have made the point, as does the motto of the emblem, that an inward ugliness is more deplorable than an outward one and offends God. Some words on self-knowledge and on self-love would then have been also natural. But it does not matter how Shakespeare acquired the associations of the *vanitas* mirror; this was familiar material and he used it with masterful allusiveness to create a superbly ironic image of Isabella.

The angels surely weep about the assurance with which Isabella, god-like, holds up the mirror to judging man. If she looked into herself, she would see that she too judges, and that she does so with angry severity. Her sympathy with the brittle, glassy nature of man is limited. This point is also suggested, and again by ironic mirror imagery, in her second interview with Angelo. She finds women as frail "as the glasses where they view themselves, / Which are as easy broke as they make forms" (II.iv.125–26). She exempts herself, and, indeed, her frailty does not have the softness of the feminine complexion. But it does have a touch of that intellectual pride which stains Angelo, a pride that was the main reason for the skeptics to characterize man as a stupid and histrionic animal.

Strangely, she does subsequently bend in some fashion by lending herself (and, more directly, Mariana) to the duke's plan of "the substitute bride." Her legalism—after all, the trick does constitute a "marriage"—her subjection to religious authority, and a curious conception of charity all appear to play a role in her enthusiasm for the questionable device. That the "image" of it pleases her is comical. The duke's rejoinder to her that this image "lies much in your holding up" (III.i.252) may indicate that we are to look upon this episode as merely preparatory for her later character development. There is certainly no bending here of the kind needed for self-knowledge.

It is the task of the duke, one of his several tasks, to bring about that change. Vincentio is himself a puzzling character, as changeable in his actions and psychological explanations as he is in his clothes. The play begins as his governmental experiment, an experiment, it appears, in which he will take no further hand. Yet from the third act on, his direction of events in the guise of a friar is powerful to a degree that he becomes something like the author of the play, the writer of its script, the director of the actors, and the main *dramatis persona*. The play proves to be what it did not appear at first, an intricate, controlled experiment, planned and supervised by the duke, or, more precisely, by Shakespeare through the duke.

In this respect, *Measure for Measure* resembles *The Tempest*. Duke Vincentio and Prospero are the two Shakespearean characters in whom even critics generally opposed to the biographical heresy have seen some measure of identification between the poet and his creature.[13] But Prospero's purpose is made much clearer, and his resources are supernatural and incontestible. Duke Vincentio's plan is, by contrast, never stated, and its execution depends on his ethically questionable disguise as a friar, which gives him a peculiarly intimate acquaintance with the thoughts and feelings of Claudio, Isabella, and Mariana. He uses his power as a spiritual adviser to keep Claudio in agony about his imminent execution, to arrange with Isabella and Mariana the dubious bed trick, and to lead Isabella to believe that her brother has been executed when, in fact, he is still alive. His secretiveness and indirection make Lucio's slur of him as "the old fantastical Duke of dark corners" (IV.iii.154) not totally inappropriate. On the other hand, his benevolent vigilance also gives credence to Angelo's later observation that the duke watched over him "like pow'r divine" (V.i.367).

The duke is, it appears to me, the key figure in a strategy of indirect presentation and ironic revelation; it is a strategy for which mannerism is noted. The method is not unlike that of sonnet 94. Just as here the poet, by intimation and irony, slowly reveals the true nature of the unmoved movers, so the duke only gradually allows us a look into his mind and heart. At first, it appears as if he had arranged a simple governmental experiment by putting in his place a man supposedly stronger than himself, a man who had inherited all of heaven's graces. No danger for him of becoming lax as has been the case with Vincentio! But then, the duke discloses that his deputy is a man whose self-control is dangerously taut, and the question arises what, if power change purpose, will our seemers be. Even as an answer comes to this question in Angelo's fall through passion, and he is exposed as a man that does not do the thing he most shows, the duke discloses that his experiment had another aspect or even a different direction: it is now to reveal that Angelo is a lily that smells far worse than a weed.

The political side of the experiment turns on a problem that Jean Bodin, theorist of absolutism, discussed in *The Six Books of a Commonweal,* which was translated in 1606, a few years after Shakespeare wrote *Measure for Measure* (1604?). In one of his chapters (IV.ii), Bodin dealt with the question "Whether it be convenient or expedient for the majesty of a sovereign prince to judge his subjects himself or be much conversant with them," and he came to the conclusion that, by and large, it was not convenient or expedient. Of course, in *Measure for Measure,* the question is bedevilled and made morally ambiguous by the fact that the duke's deputy is a dangerous character, a fact that may in part account for the surreptitious supervision and control Vincentio adopts. But even with a morally pure deputy, the experiment would smack of Machiavellism. As the duke explains, he sees in Angelo a convenient instrument to enforce laws that through his own fault have fallen into disuse. Angelo may "in th' ambush of my name, strike home, / And yet my nature never in the fight / To do in slander" (I.iii.41–43). Angelo thus becomes the duke's administrative tool—the figure of the ambush makes the idea particularly unpleasant—to enforce laws and let the duke escape the blame for them. This was exactly the method Gentillet's *Contre-Machiavel,* which was translated in 1602 —not long before the play was written—accused Machiavelli of advocating as a maxim: "A Prince ought to commit to another those affairs which are subject to hatred and envy and reserve to himself such as depend upon his grace and favor." [14] Jean Bodin, however, thought it entirely proper for the prince to reserve for himself the rewards, honors, graces, and favors and to leave to others the "condemnations, fines, confiscations, and other punishments" so as to acquire and maintain the love of his subjects.[15]

Vincentio is an exemplar of the theory and practice of political absolutism. In that surely lies the explanation for the resemblance he has to King James and for the parallels, mostly commonplaces, of some of his words and actions to passages in this monarch's *Basilicon Doron*.[16] A direct identification was hardly intended; that James would have considered it a compliment is doubtful. The similarities they have, such as their reluctance to show themselves to the people, can be most easily explained by their aura as absolute rulers. The wise prince, according to Bodin, "must but seldom times come into the sight of his subjects."[17] The rhymed tetrameters in which Vincentio explains his governmental theory (III.ii.243 ff.) state in quite general terms the requirements and functions of the absolute prince, who must be as holy as he is severe and distribute justice by weighing "self-offences." He is a ruler who has to apply craft against vice because he has to deal with men like Angelo, angels on the outer side who hide the darkness within.

The theory of absolutism was posited on the skeptics' view of man as an unstable, inconstant, and deceptive creature who needed to be ruled by a prince who radiated an ideal self but actually adapted himself in some fashion to his environment. Vincentio's Vienna is not the organic medieval-Renaissance state of the England in *Henry V,* but resembles the kind of late Renaissance state Charron saw as the norm, "wholly composed of lies, colored, counterfeit, and dangerous." In this state, it is required "of the sovereign, distrust, and that he keep himself close, yet so as he be still vertuous and just." A ruler of this kind, Charron says, expanding Machiavelli's serpentfox metaphor, must in turns be a lion, a fox, a serpent, and a dove.[18] There is a strain on the moral and psychic powers of a ruler who, like Vincentio, must frustrate a design of lust, save a condemned man, arrange a substitution of bedmates, and bring about conversions. There is also a strain on the credibility of a plot that allows all these manipulations to be successful. In the fifth act, this strain is almost unbearable when the duke turns from fox to dove and, intermittently, threatens to become a lion. And these protean changes seem a great deal of effort for exposing and improving Angelo, the main business of the act.

The climactic issue, the repentance of Angelo, is, however, much

better treated than the corresponding situation in *All's Well*. The
final turn-about is prepared in the fourth act by Angelo's realization
that he has fallen from grace (IV.iv.17 ff.). In the final scene,
Angelo once more shows his hypocrisy and his unfitness as a judge
when he allows himself to be put in judgment of Mariana and Isabella; also Vincentio proves his potential severity when he reveals
himself in all his majesty. Now Angelo faces his transgression without blanching. In agreement with the judgment he ironically found
just for a crime such as his, he begs immediate death. He does not
support the pleading of Mariana and Isabella for his pardon. But,
most important, he feels sorry, humanly sorry, for the grief he has
inflicted:

> I am sorry that such sorrow I procure;
> And so deep sticks it in my penitent heart
> That I crave death more willingly than mercy;
> 'Tis my deserving, and I do entreat it.
> (V.i.472–75)

Isabella too is being tested and, I think, found improved. She has
much reason to hate Angelo, and not only because of his lust for her;
the duke has made her believe that Claudio is dead—the explanation
he gives in soliloquy, that he will "make her heavenly comforts of
despair," is characteristic of his strategy of indirection. When
Angelo is exposed, we might expect Isabella, the ethical crusader, to
burn once more in ferocious indignation. We are in dramatic sus-
pense as Mariana, imploring the duke for her husband's pardon,
appeals for her help. Will she overcome her ethical absolutism and
become truly merciful? Will she plead for the man she assumes to be
her brother's murderer even though she must believe it to be the
duke's wish to make Angelo pay for Claudio, death for death? Mariana has to ask her twice; but then Isabella complies, kneeling down
next to her, and pleads with the duke:

> Look, if it please you, on this man condemn'd,
> As if my brother liv'd. I partly think
> A due sincerity govern'd his deeds
> Till he did look on me; since it is so,
> Let him not die. My brother had but justice,
> In that he did the thing for which he died;
> For Angelo,

His act did not o'ertake his bad intent,
And must be buried but as an intent
That perish'd by the way. Thoughts are no subjects;
Intents but merely thoughts.

(V.i.442–52)

For Isabella, the great debater, this is an almost unbelievably bad speech, "a string of palpable sophistry," as Quiller-Couch called it.[19] Since it is bad logic, one can argue, of course, that it is an insufficient guide for human conduct (but, from a skeptic-fideistic point of view, all logic was exactly that). The very conspicuousness of her bad logic suggests that she is highly emotional in a new way. She has lost —permanently, one hopes—her old absolutism of standards; before now, she certainly never thought of anything *partly*. In granting Angelo sincerity, she is, of course, partly right. The contrast she makes between her brother and Angelo, however, is quite dubious. When she says that her brother had but justice, she sounds like the old absolute Isabella, but she does not set Angelo in any logical relationship to this statement; the metrically defective line "For Angelo" points to confused and conflicting ideas and emotions as she looks into herself. The excuse she makes for Angelo, that he did not actually execute his crimes (through no fault of his own!) is legalistic enough, but it runs counter to Christian ethics in which intention counts as much as execution. A reason for her forgiveness is needed, and she supplies it, a bad reason for a good act. What one remembers better than these half-truths—and what an audience cannot miss— is the cry of her heart: "Let him not die." It is a salutary change from the callous sentence she had earlier for her brother: " 'Tis best thou diest quickly." Thus, her last speech is bad logic with a note of true compassion. To the duke's marriage proposal she says nothing, and that is better than a shout of joy. And Shakespeare hardly intended her to express her pleasure pantomimically as I have seen an actress do.

Yet the actresses' and the critics' difficulties with the role suggest that one should be somewhat tentative about all interpretations of her character. I do not think that this is because the workmanship of the scene is defective, but because the reverse is true. Too much certainty would be the wrong ending for a play that deals with such ambiguous situations and such complex and opaque characters. Isabella's is not the only notable silence in the end; we get no explanations of their feelings from Angelo—except for the "quickening" in his eye—and from Mariana. The pardoned Claudio never speaks a word. All have been through distressing situations; Claudio, of course, has suffered most. These are silences of uncertainty and, one hopes, of self-knowledge.

The duke's marriage proposal to Isabella is the second great surprise of the scene after the almost offhanded pardon of Angelo by the duke. (We shall pass by such minor surprises as the survival and pardon of Barnardine.) For Isabella, the proposal is a reward—unless we think she should have stayed in a nunnery. We may take it tentatively as an outward sign of her moral improvement and softened sensibility.

But the more important implications of the proposal may be those that concern the duke's character rather than Isabella's and the outcome of his experiment rather than her improvement. The duke's decision to marry is certainly unexpected. One of the first statements he makes in the play, in a bantering conversation with a friar, indicates how far from his thoughts is the search for a wife; he rejects the idea that "the dribbling dart of love / Can pierce a complete bosom" such as his (I.iii.1–3), and he explains that he has other reasons for desiring seclusion. His preference for the life removed—in Shakespeare, generally a danger for a ruler—points not only to a realization that emotions are dangerous—that was good Renaissance doctrine—but also to a fear of using emotions for beneficial purposes. His reluctance to stage himself to the eyes of his people, good absolutist theory as it may be, yet may also be taken to corroborate his distrust of all emotional commitments.[20] Vincentio, not unlike Angelo, has turned this deficiency into a self-acknowledged virtue by taking pride in his self-control; both suffer from a Puritanical suppression accompanied by the compensatory intellectual complaisance against which the skeptics warned. There is a slight comical touch in the duke's wounded pride at hearing himself slandered as a lecher by Lucio. He promptly seeks reassurance from Escalus that his self-image as a man of all temperance is true; and that old and benevolent counselor characterizes him as "one that, above all other strifes, contended especially to know himself" (III.ii.218).

The duke's marriage proposal, then, looks like an admission that self-knowledge requires him to become more human, just as Isabella has become more so. The embrace of a woman now seems more important to him than a certificate of temperance, just as an orgasm has proved more important for Angelo than his reputation of probity. When Vincentio marries Isabella, it is in the realization of an unfulfilled need. There is, I think, an indication of this in his words as he unmasks Claudio and proposes to Isabella:

> If he be like your brother, for his sake
> Is he pardon'd; and for your lovely sake,
> Give me your hand and say you will be mine,
> He is my brother too.
>
> (V.i.489–90)

Ironically, self-recovery, for Duke Vincentio just as for Angelo (and, for that matter, for Isabella), consists in becoming more like Claudio, the one character who has succumbed to a human impulse and, for that reason, has faced death. Thus, by marrying, Vincentio adds another stipulation to the conventional and stiff *desiderata* he had established for the ruler: he will not be only "holy and severe" and weigh others by "self-offences," but he will also put aside the subtle pride in his armor against human affections. What he calls the "pattern in himself to know" will include a recognition that it is through their nobler emotions that men become brothers.

In recognizing the significance of human brotherhood, the ending of *Measure for Measure* has a faint resemblance to that of *The Comedy of Errors*. But there is also a marked difference, symbolized by the way one must visualize the processional exits. No longer is there a graded order, determined by a design inherent in the world, according to which Antipholuses and Dromios march out hand in hand. The absolute ruler now determines to whom he extends his hand. Much is left to his arbitrary reordering; and, of the future disposition of such matters as marriages, much is left to heaven. But one need not be cynical with Lord Byron. The ending does affirm the importance of human values and of building units, even though it does affirm both significances in a somewhat tentative way. But there is no longer the intense questioning and debilitating uncertainty that there is in *Hamlet* and *Troilus and Cressida*. Theoretical humanism is shown to be subject to revision, but practical humanism is affirmed.

However, we had better look at what the ending does to the disposition of the major issues of the play. The apparent outcome of Duke Vincentio's experiment is certainly unexpected and ironic. The quest for self-knowledge has led him to measure his performance in the administration of the law; perhaps his psychological interest or perhaps his awareness of the advantages of the choice of Angelo for his own reputation as a merciful ruler has led him to select a flawed man as his deputy and as a medium for his self-comparison. He has sought answers to the questions on the right way to govern, on the human qualities needed for the ruler, and on the proportionate relationship of justice and mercy. All this is an oblique and complicated way to search for the self—not quite as obviously wrongheaded as the quest of the knights of Navarre in *Love's Labor's Lost,* but more subconsciously weighted in favor of a success flattering to the ego, much like the experiments we generally undertake with ourselves in real life, subtly biased and with a hoped-for answer predicated. But it turns out—again in a subtle way that is only half-acknowledged by the duke—that he shares in some measure the deficiency of his experimental medium. He rectifies the problem by wholesale pardons and by a marriage proposal. What these actions imply for the nature and result of the governmental experiment is uncertain, and if one wishes to give a tentative answer, he must infer what he can from a few hints and from the general quality of the ending. That the play's title is ironic would be obvious even if the irony were not driven home by the duke when he threatens to punish Angelo: "Like doth quit like, and Measure still for Measure." But in what this irony, followed as it is by Angelo's repentance and pardon, consists, is not so certain. We can say that retributive justice, as the duke realizes and—it appears by his previous laxity and his selection of the strict Angelo—has always realized, is no preventive to sin and crime. But it does not appear that he thinks or that we ought to think that the solution is to give up judging altogether and to just forgive. If this were true, there would have been no reason for Vincentio to test himself by instituting the experiment. And, by pardoning Angelo, the duke does make a judgment based on the predication that Angelo's repentance augurs a permanent reformation. One can, of course, say that the play proves that man must judge not by giving measure for measure but by judging with measure and thus proves the need for the *via media*.[21] But if so, it is strange that the ending puts more emphasis on mercy than on the moderation of punishment. One might even say that the play proves the difficulty of finding a *via media,* desirable as it would be to determine where it is. Nobody really seems to represent it. Escalus, wise man and old judge, is probably too easygoing. The duke, by his own confession, has veered too far toward lenity in the past and may just possibly have made the same mistake again by pardoning Angelo and Barnardine. In demonstrating the difficulty of judging according to a just measure, Shakespeare agreed with Bodin that it is "a most hard thing for a sovereign prince fitting himself in judgment to keep a mean between too much lenity and severity." [22] But Bodin thought such judgment possible, if difficult. Shakespeare appears to say that situations arise in which it is better to forget about judging and try to take up life as if it had a new beginning. It may even have occurred to Shakespeare, as it did not to Bodin, that absolutism, as the duke must practice it, does not really permit a true *via media*.

The play's last dialogue, that between the duke and Lucio, throws an ironic sidelight on the ethical and legal judgments debated and made in the last scene. Lucio is the only character who is not released into at least conditional happiness and the only one that is dissatisfied with the way measure has been meted out. For a moment it seems even as if the old reprobate, for whom we have acquired some liking because he has made us laugh, were to be punished severely by being forced to marry and by being whipped and hanged. The duke is spoofing, and he promptly remits Lucio's punishments except for the marriage. But, for Angelo and Claudio marriage is mercy; for Lucio it is not. As he says, establishing his own scale of what measure for measure means: "Marrying a punk, my lord, is pressing to death, whipping, and hanging" (V.i.520–21). Considering what we know of the lady in question—her name, Kate Keepdown, is symptomatic —he may be said to have a point if he feels punished rather than forgiven. Nor can his sentence be said to be correspondent to the nature of his crime: he is married to Kate not for fathering her child but for calumniating the duke. When the latter claims that slandering a prince deserves being punished by marriage to a punk, we might well wonder a little at the incongruity between punishment and crime. And as we compare Lucio's situation with that of the others, we experience a feeling for the relativity of all judgments: the same measure that offers the hope of a better life for Angelo, Claudio, and the duke threatens a dismal one for Lucio.

Thus, in a peculiar way, Lucio lives up to the symbolism inherent in his name: he brings some light to the play by showing in his own way how bewildering the human situation is. But if we sympathize with Lucio in his perplexing predicament, we do so only for a moment; then we laugh, and it seems all a little less painful. Of the rotten commentators that help to make the worlds of the problem comedies more rotten, he is the least noxious and most amiable and humorous. Thus Lucio's name is appropriate in still another sense: he adds a touch of badly needed lightness to the play and particularly to the ending, which otherwise is rather solemn.

Lucio's treatment is an amusing example of the oblique and indirect way in which Shakespeare presented the major theme of *Measure for Measure:* the dilemma of man who judges and who is being judged. The play shows up the difficulty of gaining and preserving self-knowledge in either role. The major characters, like men in general, are sometimes in the stand of the accused and sometimes on the bench of the judge; they are most severely tested when they are in judgment of themselves. The play does tell us that man must judge and, most of all, must judge himself, although such verdicts are difficult and may bring uncertain and unexpected results. In judging himself, as in all other judgments, man may err in quantity or quality, fall below what is needed or exceed it.

Does the play, then, say anything at all about the connection between self-knowledge and the judgment of others? I think it does in some fashion. It indicates that the law is apt to be administered poorly by those who have not looked into themselves and that there is at least hope of justice—and, even more, of mercy—from the hands of those who have looked into themselves and become more human. And, indeed, were one to be judged by an Angelo, would it not be better to be judged by him after, rather than before, he has repented?

PART FOUR

Achievement and Synthesis

CHAPTER THIRTEEN

Will and Passion:
Heightening the Self

THERE IS GOOD EVIDENCE that Shakespeare wrote *Measure for Measure* and *Othello* in the same year, 1604, and the two plays do indeed have some similarities in their patterns of self-knowledge. In both, man's lack of self-knowledge is one of the central issues. Angelo creates the illusion that he is a man of rectitude and attempts to live with it; Othello accepts the absolute lie that Desdemona is unfaithful that is pressed upon him by Iago. Both heroes change from men of signal self-control into slaves of passion. Yet these similarities are slight in comparison to the differences. In *Othello,* the indirect strategy of psychological development we noted in *Measure for Measure* has given way to a direct one; the Moor is a fascinating but not a puzzling character, and the play is one of the most simple, lucid, and direct of Shakespeare's. This is not merely due to a difference of genre, a shift from comedy or tragicomedy to tragedy, for even if *Hamlet,* which anticipates *Othello* by only two or three years, becomes the medium of comparison, the contrast remains. The dramatic hesitations and perplexities Shakespeare built into the plays of his mannerist period have given way in *Othello* to an energetic artistic affirmation, one that persists in the great tragedies and romances that were to follow.

Not that Shakespeare returned to the simpler patterns of his earlier, "Renaissance" period. The moral field of action of Shakespeare's later tragic and romantic heroes is wider than that of the earlier ones, and they move more dynamically in it. Ethically, Othello is, in the beginning, somewhere near the angelic Desdemona, but he turns from good to evil under the influence of the diabolic persuasion of Iago. In *Lear,* good and evil characters are even more strongly contrasted. The old king is somewhere in the middle ground between them; in his terrifying outbreak, however, he surrenders

himself to evil, and it takes a tremendous expiatory suffering for
him to realize the falsity of those he believed good and the goodness of those he believed evil. Macbeth opts from the beginning for
the evil world symbolized by the witches (and I shall argue that
he does not do so by way of a basic change in character); but his
soul is so strongly and progressively subjected to evil as to undergo
also a dynamic movement.

If the heroes of Shakespeare's later tragedies have a dynamic
ethical development, we cannot be in doubt about its direction, and
we can be sure about their orientation at any point of the action. In
the plays of Shakespeare's mannerist period, the question of who and
what is good is often posed but generally not definitely answered;
now it does not even arise because the moral positions are more
certain from the beginning. We debate how to place Hamlet, Troilus,
and Angelo morally, but we know that Iago is evil and that Othello,
good at the beginning, becomes evil, and we know just when this
transformation occurs. And we have no questions about Desdemona's
moral fiber, whereas we are puzzled about Ophelia, Gertrude, and
Isabella. This ethical placement is a major reason for our feeling
that Shakespeare's plays from *Othello* on—experiments and partial
failures like *Timon of Athens, Pericles,* and *Cymbeline* excluded—
have greater clarity and unity.

This unity is dynamic, comprising contrast and diversity and deriving primarily from the opposition and interplay of gigantic forces
of good and evil, or will and passion. *Othello* here provides the best
demonstration. Coleridge expressed the general feeling that this
tragedy has a conspicuous dramatic unity when he said that in it
everything assumes its due place and proportion and the mature
powers of Shakespeare's mind are displayed in admirable equilibrium.[1] This, however, is a different balance from the one achieved
in some pre-Hamletian plays, as is evident from a comparison of
Othello with *Henry V,* the model of a symmetrically balanced play
in Shakespeare's Renaissance period. The balance of *Othello* is dynamic; it derives not from a static view of an ideal hero but from
the interaction of polar forces of evil and good, passion and patience,
hate and love. The play pairs and antithesizes the most cold-blooded
of Shakespeare's villains with a strong and warm-hearted hero. It
also contrasts this most evil of villains with the one among Shakespeare's heroines most actively intent on doing good. Once the stage
is set, the force of evil attacks with purposive speed and awakens

in the seemingly self-assured Othello a dormant passion that tears him apart in a conflict of love and hate. Othello's passion explodes, most manifestly, in an epileptic fit and, most painfully, in the murder of the woman he deeply loves. Simultaneously, the force of evil, working through an Othello transformed into a slave of jealousy, turns Desdemona from a self-assured Venetian lady into a frightened and confused little girl who, without understanding the reason, becomes her husband's victim. All the contrasting dynamic forces are integrated into a unified dramatic structure unequaled in Shakespeare until *The Tempest,* the last of the romances.

I shall show in greater detail in the next chapter that the foregoing brief analysis of *Othello* describes accurately the essence of the play. I have given this account here because I believe it exposes a formula of dramatic construction that elucidates the patterns of self-knowledge in the plays I shall subsequently discuss. Each of these achieves or comes close to achieving a dynamic unity on the basis of the formula, modified and varied to suit the particular action. This is not to deny that each play has its unique human, social, or political concerns; but if one interprets it from the central dynamic placement of its hero, a similarity to the *Othello* formula emerges. The tragic heroes, and at least Leontes and Prospero among those of the romances, are greater than life-size; they are endowed with mighty wills and potentially violent passions that erupt as a consequence of the powerful evil that is at work from the outside or inside and destroys or threatens to destroy them. All these men are in the center of a general conflict of good and evil forces that draws into a vortex the innocent and guilty until the heroes die or, in the romances, until they are released from suffering and passion. Thus, in a sense, the plays ratify the humanists' warnings against evil and passion, but they also demonstrate humanity's dignity and greatness in its extraordinary capacity for suffering. The heightened selves of Shakespeare's later heroes are constructed on the paradox that what destroys or nearly destroys them also makes them great.

It should be said that the *Othello* formula, as I have called it, is not used in two later tragedies, *Antony and Cleopatra* and *Coriolanus.* Although the heroes of both have mighty wills and passions, these are not triggered by conspicuous forces of evil. Nor is the theme of lack of self-knowledge as prominent in them as in *Othello, Lear,* and *Macbeth;* it is transcended by other concerns, the conflict of love and power in *Antony and Cleopatra* and the rival demands of

pride and patriotism in *Coriolanus*. In a discussion of the dynamics
of will and passion in Shakespeare, these two plays would be
prominent, but in the present study, they do not urgently demand
treatment.[2]

Because the principle of the dynamism of will and passion affects
all patterns of self-knowledge in Shakespeare's later plays, we may
recall how much it reflects prominent political, spiritual, intellectual,
and artistic concerns of the dawning baroque age, an age that celebrated and practiced power and was at the same time fascinated with
intense feelings and states of mind.[3] Absolute monarchs and their
statesmen craved and achieved authority and adorned it with ceremonies and displays of luxury. In their desire to dominate their
subjects politically, the princes and their councilors were rivaled by
the eagerness of both Catholics and Protestants to dominate their
believers spiritually, and neither the efforts of the monarchs nor
those of the religious leaders were restricted to their respective political and religious spheres. Because there was a growing and justified
conviction among the intellectuals that these were trying times,
philosophers and moralists of various persuasions sought no less
arduously than the theologians to arm men for the battle of life,
particularly by giving rules on how to strengthen their wills and to
direct and, if necessary, to break the wills of others. Bacon combined this theoretical interest with a statesman's practical aim of
political domination. He went beyond these ethical and political
concerns to outline a system through which man would find it possible to subject and control nature.

An energy similar to that which made Bacon turn outward to
nature made itself felt in the turning inward in religious thought
and expression, in the mysticism and the mystical poetry that
flowered in the seventeenth century. Baroque painting and sculpture
translated this interest in the dynamics of feelings into works aflame
with emotions. These strike us often as excessive, but they give a
unity of movement to the total design. Bernini's Saint Theresa appears the victim of a religious transfiguration hardly distinguishable
from an erotic rapture, and she is aquiver with a synchronized emotion equally apparent in the expression of her face and the tremor
of her gown. And what was true for religious art also held good for
secular painting, sculpture, and architecture. The baroque, as art
historians have described it, was both more emotional and more
unified than the preceding styles. It overcame the mannerist uncer-

tainties by dynamic certainties. It worked with great masses of stone or color in motion, masses that were controlled and subordinated to the total design.[4] It is true that the English plastic arts had no real equivalent for this exuberant baroque, be it because of the restraining influence of Puritanism or because of the relative lack of patronage at the English court. But English poetry and drama of the early seventeenth century show evidence of a tendency analogous to that of continental art to intensify will and passion and make them central to a baroque unity of composition.

To ascribe the greater force and unity of Shakespeare's later tragedies to the baroque style is not to question that their artistic success was, first of all, due to his mature mastership of all stylistic and dramatic means. But these means and the strong integrative impulse with which he used them owed something, I would say a great deal, to artistic and cultural tendencies of the age. I have noted in an earlier part of this book that the concept of self-knowledge underwent considerable modifications and shifts in emphasis because of certain counter-humanistic tendencies. It is true that these originated before the seventeenth century, but they reached their full strength and had their greatest impact at this time. All shared a particular interest in the working of the will and, for the most part, of the passions, the two structural elements of the *Othello* formula. Even if Shakespeare was not attracted to any one of these political, religious, and philosophical movements and doctrines, he could not have escaped the aggregate of their influence, which promoted an interest in what one might call personality dynamics. The dialectics of ideas in Shakespeare's later plays, I believe, clearly shows that he was influenced.

One such influence, pervasive but difficult to pinpoint, was that of aristocratic tastes. Under absolutism, the expansive self of the courtier was becoming the inflated self of the royalist cavalier. This development tended to create two separate ethical standards, a religious-moral one for common men and a glorified antihumanistic one for aristocrats. For instance, Tommaso Buoni in *The Problems of Beauty and All Human Affections* (translated in 1606) extolled the superior constancy of great men in love and even explained as natural their greater talent for hatred and condoned it: princes "are endowed with a knowledge more than human" and therefore have greater insight into wickedness and conceive greater hatred against it; altogether, in noble men, who have "natures more divine, the affections, making deeper impressions, are of greater force." [5] Aristocratic tastes gained greater influence on drama as the interest of the court increased—as is evident in the much larger number of dramatic performances at court—and as the middle class began to desert the theaters that the Puritanical preachers condemned *in toto* as sinful. Aristocratic tastes were surely influential in promoting the popularity of the great-souled hero with superhuman will and passion, although a shoemaker's son from Canterbury had started the fashion and the learned and abstruse Chapman brought it to a culmination.

Will power was not cultivated only in aristocratic circles; it became not merely an attribute of status but also a requirement for economic aspiration. This is a subject even more impervious to literary analysis, and there is no space here to discuss economics. We may merely recall that, in the seventeenth century, England participated in a European economic crisis due to universal restructuring of society. The crisis indeed had been brewing in the sixteenth century, but only now did it lead to a recognizable conflict of economic classes. The possessive and increasingly wealthy bourgeoisie began to feel its strength and its economic superiority over the financially debilitated nobility in the capitalistic-absolutistic order.[6] The practical and acquisitive self of the bourgeois came into conflict with the courtly and inflated self of the aristocrat, who, in fact, was becoming economically dependent on the bourgeoisie. Shakespeare was sensitive to the trend toward acquisitiveness and its effect on morality; as William Elton has noted, *King Lear* and *Timon of Athens* condemningly explore "with more specific monetary allusions than usual in Shakespeare, the new acquisitive impulse." [7] Elton sees a connection between the rejection of ethical absolutes and natural law by a character like Edmund in *Lear* and the self-assertion of those who felt that they were the class who, because of its drive and freedom from conventional restrictions, had the right to rule.

We must take into consideration still another class, one that had no chance of exerting its will actively but was attracting more attention: the poor. Except for some preachers and a few satirists, the poor had no advocates in the sixteenth century, and even these generally did not diagnose poverty as the result of economic conditions but as due to misfortune or man's sinfulness (that of the poor as well as the rich). But now there were occasional attempts to see the world from the perspective of the poor. One of these was a two-part poem, *The Poor Man's Passions and Poverty's Patience,* by Arthur Warren (1605), written, according to the author, in prison (evidently a debtor's prison) as a kind of *nosce teipsum* poem for the poor. It paints a somber, unjust, upside-down, and degenerating world in which the poor can live only by adopting an extraordinary patience. This solution, to which the whole second part of the book is devoted, draws on conventional Christian and Stoic remedies. One of the consolations—"So low I am, lower I cannot fall" [8]—is shown as the fallacy that it is by Edgar in *Lear* (IV.i.26). What makes Warren's poetic pamphlet almost a manifesto of class pride is his acclaim of the superiority of the life of the poor, their primitive, simple, wholesome life, as compared with the luxurious, ostentatious, wasteful, and diseased life of the rich. Even if the elements of this contrast can be found in earlier literature, the author's angle of vision, tone, and emphasis gives them a certain novelty and conviction. There is here an urgency in the call for justice based on charity that can also be felt in *Lear.*

More open to literary analysis than the role of the economic and social conditions in creating an increased interest in the working and the use of the human will is the influence of the major religious and intellectual movements. Of course, there was a connection between these movements and the economic upheavals; if we believe the Marxists, the former caused the latter. But reverse relationships have also been pointed out, such as the function of Calvinism in promoting capitalism.[9] Even if we restrict ourselves to considering the ideological core of these movements, we shall see a fascination with will power, a fascination that transcended individual creeds and philosophies. In religion, it was fostered by the religious crisis. As the warfare of the Christian on earth became largely internecine, both parties, the Protestants as well as the Roman Catholics, sought to stiffen the determination of their followers. There was, of course, nothing new in the interest in the will as such. Medieval and Renaissance theologians saw it as the human faculty that subjected man to sin and yet was a significant instrument in bringing about his salvation. The Christian humanists restated this balanced account of the failure and the achievement of the will, and their position later became Anglican doctrine. As Richard Hooker pointed out in *The Laws of Ecclesiastical Polity* (Bk. I, Chap. vii), man sinned because he willed to sin; but his will also enabled him to make the right choices between good and evil if it followed the guidance of the understanding in adjusting itself to the divine order.

The two major theological movements that competed with Anglicanism in England, Roman Catholicism and Calvinism, gave still greater emphasis to the role of the will in man's conduct on earth and stressed his need for discipline. For the Roman Catholics, convinced as much as the Anglicans of the freedom of the will, this emphasis grew out of the aims and needs of the Counter-Reformation. Its main instrument, the Jesuit order, had been founded on the idea of gaining and retaining control over souls through a brotherhood trained in soldierly discipline. Naturally, they incurred much hostility. "Their holy exercise," said an English clergyman, was "but a mere Machiavellian device of policy only to make strong themselves in their busy preparations for a spiritual monarchy." [10] It is surely obvious that the English recusants were in need of bolstering their confidence in some more than ordinary way. It is not surprising that exhortations to constancy, firmness, application, resolution, and fortitude are recurrent notes in the popular little book of doctrine that the Jesuit Robert Parsons published for his fellow Catholics in England under the title of *The First Book of Christian Exercise* (1582). But it is astonishing that this book, later called *The Christian Directory,* was republished, in only slightly adapted form, by Anglican divines far into the seventeenth century. Parsons's call for an energetic religion evidently found response and echo in the Protestant camp.

The greater outward belligerence in religion was accompanied by a turning inward for renewed strength. The plentiful descriptions of the evil, degenerating world—in particular, of that new Jerusalem, London, with its fashions, vices, and sins—and the threats of an impending doom were intended to keep the faithful on the right path as much as to deter the wicked. In the new literature of exhortation and consolation, the believers were asked to despise the allurements of this world as much as they had been in the old *contemptus mundi.* For the writers of such tracts, self-knowledge meant primarily a realization of the world's evils, a repentance of sin, and a recognition of the need for patience. As the Spanish Jesuit Diego de Estella said in his *De Contemptu Mundi,* which was twice translated in Elizabethan times, once for the benefit of Roman Catholics at Douay and once by the Protestant clergyman Thomas Rogers: "Therefore, if thou seek to know thyself, it will cause thee neither to be proud nor ambitious nor disdainful; it will make thee bear injuries with a quiet mind in as much as thou shalt find thyself to be a miserable sinner, and worthy of all men to be hated and condemned." [11] This is exactly the kind of self-knowledge so painfully acquired by Cardinal Wolsey in Shakespeare's last play, *Henry VIII*. After his fall, Wolsey renounces his pride and ambition and, in his famous farewell, says, "I know myself now"; and he feels in himself "A peace above all earthly dignities, / A still and quiet conscience" (III.ii. 350 ff.). Not even so conspicuous a consumer of *contemptus mundi* as Shakespeare's Richard II espouses more strongly than Wolsey the concept of self-knowledge of this old tradition. In *Lear* and other later dramas, similar moral patterns occur that stress the danger of pride, the need for patience, and the connection between self-knowledge and the voice of conscience. An apocalyptic mood imbues parts of *Othello, Lear, Timon of Athens,* and *Macbeth;* and the romances have such strong religious strains as to have tempted many critics to interpretations in terms of Christian allegory. In some ways, the universes of these plays take on the coloring of the morality of the characters in them, as is true for the romantic and treacherous world of the Mediterranean in *Othello* and the usuring, decaying Athens that "wears as it grows" in *Timon* (I.i.3) ; but this connection— and it is often a problematic one—cannot console the characters about the existence of a benevolent purpose in the world. They must rely altogether on their own resources.

This greater inwardness of the later patterns of self-knowledge in Shakespeare's plays, fideistic as it is in a general way, does not allow us to claim Shakespeare's adherence to any particular creed. If the Roman Catholics assessed the human situation pessimistically and derived from this pessimism the need for a stronger faith, so did the Calvinists, whose number and assertiveness were increasing. Self-knowledge meant for Calvin primarily a recognition of man's fallen nature and a submission of the human will to the will of God. For Calvin, the role of the will was most crucial in drawing man to sin, for it did not have the understanding as its guide, as it did for the Christian humanists; the whole mind, understanding and will, of unregenerated man was for him corrupt, and in fact, mind was merely flesh in the biblical sense. Yet this corruption did not relieve man of his responsibility for his actions; his will was "voluntary" even though God was assumed to foresee and preordain its choices.

A paradox like Calvin's of basing a voluntaristic ethics on a providential metaphysics is, of course, common to deterministic theologies and philosophies, which are always interested in attracting believers to their system of determinism. Calvin's way out of the paradox of determinism and free will was to say that the will of man that obeyed God fulfilled necessity, but that the will of man opposing Him was responsible for its disobedience.

Of greatest interest in Calvin's theology for our present subject was his disparagement of the understanding and his elevation of the will to the role of guide for man's actions. Calvin brought the will in much closer conjunction with the passions than did the Christian humanists, for whom, according to the medieval faculty psychology they continued, it was the active part of the rational soul; man's successful life on earth depended on making the will serve the understanding in controlling the appetites, which belonged to the sensitive soul and thus were clearly segregated from reason. In Calvin's psychology, however, the will of unregenerated man was to all intents and purposes identical with the passions. And yet, paradoxically, this will was the human faculty most necessary for salvation.

In making little distinction between the will and the passions and in attributing to them greater significance in human conduct, Calvinism was paralleled by various current philosophical directions. The skeptics, whose affinity to fideism has been noted earlier, thought of reason as little as did Calvin. They decried the Christian humanists' trust in the ability of reason to keep the appetites under control, a trust founded on the Socratic equation of truth and virtue. By showing that the understanding was too weak to discern the truth and the will was too fickle to stick to what reason posited as a goal, the skeptics described man as a being motivated largely by nonrational factors. They attributed greater force to the will than to the understanding, basing their theory of ethical conduct on the former rather than on the latter. Self-knowledge thus became more closely associated with what man wants than with what he knows. As Charron said, "A man is neither good nor wicked, honest nor dishonest, because he understandeth and knoweth those things that are good, and fair, and honest, or wicked and dishonest; but because he loveth them and hath desire and will towards them." [12] Although the only partly skeptical Francis Bacon was generally confident in the ability of reason, freed from errors, to find the way to truth, he described the influence of passion and will on the understanding in terms very similar to those of the skeptics. In pointing out the "errors of the tribe," that is, mistakes of judgment due to the general human condition, he noted that reason cannot be tightly separated from the will and from the emotions; man often thinks that to be true which he wishes: "The human understanding resembleth not a dry light, but admits a tincture of the will and passions, which generate their own systems accordingly; for man always believes more readily that which he prefers . . . in short, the feelings imbue and corrupt his understanding in innumerable and sometimes imperceptible ways." [13]

Shakespeare's later villains and heroes exemplify the truth of Bacon's principle although, of course, they do so through their actions and the explanations they give for them rather than through philosophic inquiry. When they appeal to reason or believe to found their behavior on it, they often express only the dictates of their will. When Iago proclaims that "we have reason to cool our raging motions," he means that man by his will can control the direction of his desires. Iago appears so cool and rational that it is easy to forget that he is perverted and impelled by a destructive hatred that has corrupted his mind. Sometimes, when self-knowledge becomes a possibility for Shakespeare's later heroes, it remains a rational consideration powerless to combat the forces of will and passion that have infiltrated the understanding and pull it in the direction of what they prefer. Although Macbeth is at the threshold of self-knowledge, he refuses to act on its prompting because his will drives him to seek a knowledge of evil that promises power and domination. And even though Antony at one point realizes the effect of his abandonment to pleasure and publicly admits that "poisoned hours had bound me up / From mine own knowledge" (II.ii.93–94), this rational consideration does not help him to resist the magnetic attraction of Cleopatra. In the very next scene after this admission of having lacked in self-knowledge, he suddenly announces: "I will to Egypt; / . . . I' th' East my pleasure lies" (II.iii.39–41). Quite generally, in Shakespeare's later plays, the passions are even more powerful than in the Christian humanists' warnings against them because they are often indistinguishable from the will and together with it imbue and corrupt the understanding in innumerable and often imperceptible ways.

Of the ancient philosophies that came into vogue in the seventeenth century, Stoicism gave the greatest emphasis to the function

of the human will; it insisted on man's need to elevate himself by its
power over fortune and fate. Stoicism, it is true, had been an ingredient of the Christian-humanist synthesis. But, although some of
the humanists admired Seneca's ideas and culled commonplaces
from his essays, their preference for Cicero's style drew them to the
latter's eclectic ethics, which was only in part indebted to the Stoics.
Although Shakespeare surely read some of Cicero's philosophical
works in grammar school, it is extremely unlikely that he was exposed to anything more than a few commonplaces from Seneca's
essays, and there is nothing to show that he read these later. They
were not available in translations, except for two minor essays,
until Thomas Lodge's complete translation in 1614, and Shakespeare probably had no taste for reading moral philosophy in Latin
after leaving school. But some of the treatises of continental neo-
Stoic writers became available in English before the end of the
sixteenth century. Sir John Stradling translated Justus Lipsius's *De
Constantia* in 1595, and Thomas James rendered Guilleaume du
Vair's *La Philosophie morale des Stoiques* in 1598. The impact of
neo-Stoicism was increased by the fact that it was accompanied by a
change in English prose style from the imitation of Cicero's balanced
rhetoric to that of Seneca's racy and aphoristic sentences.[14] English
essayists like William Cornwallis and Francis Bacon imitated
Seneca's manner and echoed many of his ideas. So did Marston,
Webster, and Chapman.

In assessing the influence of Seneca on Jacobean drama, one
should not separate Seneca's essays from his tragedies, in which the
seventeenth century discovered a new interest. *Macbeth* has closer
parallels to Seneca's tragedies than any of Shakespeare's plays since
Titus Andronicus and *Richard III,* and some of these parallels are
so close as to give the impression that they come from a knowledge
of the Latin text.[15] Shakespeare, who is not likely to have encoun-
tered Seneca's tragedies in school, may well have preferred to read
them in the original language rather than in the antiquated early-
Elizabethan translations.

This interest of the age in both the essays and the tragedies testifies to a realization that they have a common substance. One could
say, indeed, that this substance has a striking similarity to the
Othello formula of violent contrasts that yet form a dramatic unity,
and one could even liken neo-Stoicism to Calvinism in this respect.
Like Calvin's theology, Stoicism is based on a paradoxical combina-

tion of a voluntaristic ethics with a deterministic metaphysics; it reconciles inexorable fate—in the Christian Stoics' terminology, the providence of God—with man's responsibility for his choices. As the neo-Stoics liked to say in an old Christian formulation, God knows man's choices, but it is the will of man that makes them. Seneca and the Stoics pointed up the opposites that constitute man, life, and the universe, that is, body and soul, passion and reason, vice and virtue, good and evil. They countered the variability of the world with the constancy of the mind and the violence and passions of ordinary mankind with the patience and the imperturbability of the saint-like Stoic sage. These contrasts were to encourage man to choose the latter alternatives and to make him aware that the choice was in the power of his will. Even more stridently than the essays, Seneca's dramas oppose evil and good, passion and patience. In the tragedies, hysterical and pathological outbreaks, like those of Medea, Oedipus, and Hercules, are set off by choruses of moderation, such as the second ode in *Medea,* the fourth in *Oedipus,* and the first in *Hercules Furens.* Hercules, Seneca's superman, unites in himself the antithesis of passion and patience through his blinding fury in which he kills his family (*Hercules Furens*) and through his endurance on Mount Oeta (*Hercules Oetaeus*).

In the dynamic relationship of violent contrasts, this dramatic Stoicism of Seneca had an affinity to a tendency in baroque art to set light and dark areas and contrasting bodily shapes in tension and energetic movement, a tendency we have noted in the dynamic contrasts of the *Othello* formula. Seneca's polarization of passion and patience could have served as a prototype for the dynamic tension of Iago and Othello. The evil in Iago, who is absolute in his patience because he is devoid of ordinary human emotions, is the force that sets in passionate motion the soul of the too-trusting Othello. Iago's patience is, of course, that of a villain, not that of a Senecan philosopher or Christian Stoic; but, in that it is based on the suppression of all emotions, it has a resemblance to the ironlike "apathy" the theologians accused the austere Stoics, new and old, of advocating.

Further, Stoicism may well have had something to do with the growing emphasis on the theme of salvation from passion and evil through patience, a patience purified through love, in Shakespeare's later tragedies and romances. It is now patience even more than temperance that becomes associated with self-knowledge. The achievement of self-knowledge through patience is the major theme

of the subplot of *Lear,* the Gloucester story. In *Lear* and the romances, the heroes who fall prey to passion are accompanied by, or
contrasted with, characters who come close to being embodiments of
patience and who aid them on the way to regeneration. Such are
Cordelia, Kent, and Edgar in *Lear,* Marina and Thaisa in *Pericles,*
Imogene in *Cymbeline,* Hermione and Paulina in *The Winter's
Tale,* and Gonzalo in *The Tempest.* Interestingly, in Shakespeare's
last play, *Henry VIII,* the dying Queen Katherine, a figure of
patience herself, is consoled by a maid named Patience—one of the
few overt allegorical touches Shakespeare ever allowed himself. It
is in most of these cases fruitless to debate the question whether the
patience of a character is Christian or Stoic because in practice there
was little difference. The Christian theologians tended to make less
of the power of reason to overcome passion than did Cicero and the
ancient Stoics, and they often denounced the Stoics' insistence that
all passions were evil; but Christian patience was in effect very
similar to the Stoic brand in being an active virtue that demanded
unusual strength and fortitude.

In any case, the Jacobean emphasis on man's need for patience
must in large part be attributed to the darkening moral climate, to
the growing belief that the world was more evil than good and becoming worse rather than better. When man is a feather to each
wind that blows, as it appeared to adherents of various creeds and
philosophies, he can be saved only by an extraordinary patience. The
neo-Stoics, the neo-Platonists, the austere Calvinists, the militant
Catholics, and conservative sympathizers with the poor, like Arthur
Warren, all thought so.

But there was also a more active method than the use of patience
to steel one's will for the conflict with an evil world, a method that
came to be fathered upon Machiavelli. As pessimism became more
widespread during the last decade of the sixteenth century, there
were occasional remarks that Machiavelli had been right, after all,
when he based his politics on the premise that men are by nature
inconstant, dissembling, and lacking in gratitude. Such statements
appeared at first in attacks on Machiavelli, as for instance, in Richard
Barckley's *A Discourse of the Felicity of Man* (1598):

> The time is so changed and men's manners with them so corrupted
> that the precepts heretofore given by wise men for the commodity
> of life, grounded upon virtue and honesty, will not serve the turn.
> Friendship is grown cold; faith is foolishness; honesty is in exile
> and dissimulation hath gotten the upper hand. That is effectually

done which is commonly spoken: he that cannot dissemble cannot live. Machiavel's rules are better followed in these days than those of Plato, Aristotle or Cicero; whose scholars have so well profited under him that many are able to teach their master.[16]

The querulous tone and the rhythm of Barckley's diatribe resemble quite notably Gloucester's complaint in *Lear* (I.ii.112) that he has seen "the best of our time": "Love cools, friendship falls off, brothers divide. In cities, mutinies; in countries, discord; in palaces, treason; and the bond crack'd 'twixt son and father." Ironically, Gloucester makes these comments to his Machiavellian son Edmund, who in his immediately following soliloquy adopts his father's analysis that this is the worst of times but who is happy to live in it, totally rejecting his father's contention that the stars determine man's fate and limit the freedom of the will.

As we have noted earlier, the claim of the anti-Machiavellians that *The Prince* served as a conduct book for his "scholars" appears justified. Although Machiavelli drew the portrait of a prince who by manipulation achieved political supremacy and retained it, the picture could inspire lesser mortals to think of themselves as men of potential prestige, influence, success, and power. Machiavelli seemed to describe so much better the actual world of power struggle and intrigue than the humanistic moralists with their sentimental picture of order, harmony, and degree. This, at any rate, was the conclusion drawn by Gabriel Harvey, who thought Machiavelli really knew the "fashion and cunning of the world" and could teach him to be wise for himself, to acquire the wisdom of the serpent, to be bold, to concentrate all his strength on the immediate purpose, to have a winning manner for achieving success, and to become a veritable combination of serpent, dove, and wolf. The method could not fail to bring results: "A grain of credit with other; and a dram of confidence in yourself is powerable to remove mountains and states and to work miracles, being politically applied with reasonful discretion." [17] Although the method did not actually produce miracles for Harvey, his words prove that Machiavelli taught his disciples (whose aspirations would have utterly surprised him) to associate self-knowledge with a tough-minded, utilitarian, and materialistic concept of man. He taught them to evaluate themselves in relationship to a world where only strength succeeded and to impose their wills subtly on those whose weakness could be exploited.

Bacon's discipleship of Machiavelli rested on the feeling that *The Prince* described more accurately than the humanistic conduct books what men actually do rather than what they say. And he had a point. One looks in vain into the *nosce teipsum* tracts, which continued to be written by the preachers and schoolmasters, of whose improving influence Bacon thought little, for a recognition that the humanistic recipes work only when people in general adopt them. The one tract I know of which proceeds beyond these recipes is Thomas Wright's *The Passions of the Mind* (1601), whose sympathy with skeptic ideas has been noted previously. In his Preface, Wright suggested that knowing oneself had the practical usefulness of equipping the honest against the dishonest. He advertised his book as helpful for good men to protect themselves against "inventions, fetches, sleights, and judgments." He found his countrymen in particular need of this protection because they lacked the "certain politic craftiness" of the Italians and Spaniards. Naïveté about villainy, he said in another passage, can be costly since "simple men . . . must first try and then trust, for their rule lieth in experience and practice more than in reading and speculation because their own harms or their neighbors must school them, for few are capable of practical rules in universal, or at least they cannot apply them to particular, subjects." [18]

Wright believed in the need for serpentine wisdom beneath columbine innocence. His chapters on "Prudence in Passion" and "Policy in Passion" presuppose that even for an honest man the end justifies the means in dealing with villainy. He advised "to conceal, as much as thou canst, thy inclinations or that passion thou knowest thyself most prone to follow." The prudent man must know that the way of evil men is to destroy others "by ministering matter to passions, to cast a bait with a hook to draw them into their own ruin." In this world of envy and deception "it importeth much to know how to second or cross other men's affections, how we may please them, make them out friends or foes." Because men are delighted with those whom they see affected by the passions they have themselves, it follows that "if thou wilt please thy master or friend, thou must apparel thyself with his affections and love where he loveth and hate where he hateth." [19] Wright expanded the discussion of these matters in his second edition of 1604, showing how the passions can be moved by various means, such as producing visual "appurtenances" for stimulation. [20]

I have, on purpose, quoted instructions showing that the techniques useful for honest men and those practiced by villains were often identical for Wright in order to point out how different Shake-speare is in this respect. Although Wright's arguments sometimes evoke parallels from Shakespeare, they do so mainly when it comes to his villains' attitude and strategy. These indeed draw Wright's moral that simplicity is foolishness in this evil world—and they accept this world gladly. Thus Iago sneers at the "free and open nature" of Othello (I.iii.393), at his "unbookish jealousy," which will make him construe falsely Cassio's conversation with Bianca (IV.i.101), and at "honest fools" like Cassio and Desdemona. Iago is a master in moving the passion of Othello, producing as the final irritant that visual appurtenance, the handkerchief. Edmund congratulates himself on having "A credulous father! and a noble brother, / . . . on whose foolish honesty / My practices ride easy!" (I.ii. 170 ff.). Wright's remarks on the shortcomings of honesty also recall Iago's hypocritical protests that "to be direct and honest is not safe" (III.iii.382) and that "I should be wise; for honesty's a fool, / And loses that it works for" (386–87). In reading Wright's remark that simple people must be schooled by their harms, one recalls Regan's saying that her father had ever but slenderly known himself (I.i.293) and her "moral" on his exposure to the storm: "to wilful men / The injuries that they themselves procure / Must be their schoolmasters" (II.iv.301–3). Wright's instructions on prudence and policy in passion bring to mind how Shakespeare's villains ensnare their victims, as, for instance, how Iago kneels next to his master and swears to devote "wit, hand, and heart" to Othello's service and how Edmund draws his sword against his brother "in defence" of his father. Both Edmund and Iago boast their self-knowledge, and, in the sense the word takes in *The Passions of the Mind,* they have a point.

Wright's book was more useful as practical psychology than the conventional *nosce teipsum* tracts because it had something of a new practical orientation. Shakespeare might indeed have found it helpful when he read it, as I think he did,[21] but he also must have thought distasteful the attitude taken in it that human beings can be managed and controlled. Although *Othello* and *Lear* may be said to demonstrate the danger of a lack of self-knowledge of the kind described by Wright, they do not point the moral that good characters must study rules and tricks of rhetoric for combatting evil. When a good character, such as Edgar in *Lear,* uses techniques of counter-strategy against evil, he is aware of the ambiguity of the situation, and thus

we become conscious that virtue and deviousness are uneasy bed-
fellows.

Just as Shakespeare had not succumbed to the stifling moralizing
of traditional *nosce teipsum* doctrines, so he did not espouse the
simplifications of the practical approach to self-knowledge. His
knowledge of "men as they really are" was deeper than that of the
"Machiavellian" psychologists of his time, and it was more sympathetic. One can well imagine him to have smiled at some of Wright's
generalizations, such as the one according to which resemblance in
nature causes love, and contrast, hatred.[22] Although Iago persuades
Othello of the truth of this principle, it is negated by Desdemona's
abiding affection for Othello. Nor did Shakespeare accept the
premise that men as a whole are ungrateful, inconstant, and dissembling. Although his later tragic world is dark, the gloom is
relieved by the brightness of the Desdemonas, Cordelias, Kents, and
Edgars. Timon's misanthropic tirades are disproved as an absolute
truth about human nature by the loyalty shown to him in misery by
a selfless steward. Shakespeare had less to learn from the moralists,
even from one as practically oriented as Wright, than they could
have learned from him had they desired to do so. He was conscious,
as they were not, that it is impossible to classify human nature. He
had a sense for the unexpected as well as expected actions of men,
for weaknesses that lie below surface strength, as in Coriolanus's
sudden reversals, and for subterranean psychic forces that break
through miraculously, as in Lear's self-discovery in suffering and
madness.

Shakespeare's essential humanity also saved him from the danger
of distortion inherent in the heightening of his heroes' selves. Out of
context, one might sometimes read a passage in his plays as an
adjustment to inflated aristocratic self-conceptions. In *The Winter's
Tale,* Polixenes, like Buoni and others, claims that the passions of
great men are part of their greatness:

> This jealousy
> Is for a precious creature; as she's rare,
> Must it be great; and as his person's mighty,
> Must it be violent . . .
>   (I.ii.451–54)

But in Shakespeare, we must understand the remark in its dramatic
context; Polixenes' words are the benevolent excuse of the weak-

ness of a friend. Even if they echo an aristocratic prejudice, it was
not Shakespeare's. And when Shakespeare created in Coriolanus an
aristocratic Herculean hero in the pattern of Chapman, he made his
inner weakness clear, and it is impossible to think of him as an apotheosis of superhuman will and violent passions.

Shakespeare's humanity, gentleness, and sanity did not leave him
as he fashioned the dynamic patterns of self-knowledge in his later
plays. His questioning of the rigid formulas during the *Hamlet*
period had evidently helped him to gain a more penetrating vision
of the varied and complex patterns of life; but he did not reject what
he found valuable in the humanists' concept of self-knowledge: their
call for self-control and for a reasonable assessment of the human
situation is audible in his later plays even more clearly than in his
earlier ones, although now his heroes have to face this call without
the assurance that it will give them a rational orientation to the
universe. And Shakespeare assimilated to these patterns the ideas of
the changed intellectual climate that were congenial to him, such as
the demand for social justice, a demand raised with particular
urgency in *Lear* and *Timon*. But since *Julius Caesar* at least, Shakespeare had a strong sense for the limitations of all theory. The heroes
from Brutus on are not insured against self-loss by possessing humanistically orthodox theories of self-knowledge. Othello has them;
he is very much aware of the hierarchy of psychic functions that
subordinates passion to reason, and yet he cannot control his passion.
He is even, à la Wright, conscious that the means of persuasion used
by Iago might be tricks of custom in a dishonest man, and yet he
succumbs to them. Macbeth knows that in order to live with his
deed, he will have to deny his former self, and yet he continues on
his path to crime. But the choice of the opposite direction, the acquisition of self-knowledge or of at least part of a knowledge of himself
in the humanistic sense is for Coriolanus a choice of death. When he
gives in to his mother's pleading to show mercy to Rome rather
than to continue his revenge—a choice we think is right although,
ironically, he feels it offends the gods—he speaks his death sentence.
Elsewhere, the humanistic injunction to self-knowledge is shown to
be a valid guideline for the reasonable conduct of a moral life, but
the injunction is transcended as a criterion for judging a hero's
character. One can condemn Antony by Christian-humanist standards, but such judgment is drawn into doubt by his romantic
charisma and the power of his love that, at times, makes Rome's
imperium seem paltry.

Although Shakespeare took from the creeds, doctrines, and fashions of his day what he found useful, he remained himself. He rejected what he could not reconcile with the immensely sane view of man that had become his, and he continued to draw on ideas that he found true and important, no matter whether they were conventional or fashionable. His deep and abiding humanity prevented him from adopting the simplifications in any of the particular concepts of man that vied for his allegiance. His good sense kept him from accepting and echoing what was exaggerated in the baroque; he was not tempted by it to create caricatures rather than characters. Instead we find that his later heroes' heightened selves intensify experiences and feelings that are true and genuine. Although Shakespeare's great characters are often more passionate or more patient, more virtuous or more infamous, more glorious or more unfortunate than we shall ever be and speak in a language more mighty and splendid than ours, we feel that they are essentially like us.

CHAPTER FOURTEEN

Othello:
Subjecting the Self

THE MOST CONCENTRATED, most tightly constructed, and fastest-moving of Shakespeare's tragedies, *Othello* has a kinetic unity that derives in large part from the impetus given to the action by Iago, who, although not the hero of the tragedy, is its prime mover. He is the controller and transformer of the characters and personalities of the others, particularly of Roderigo, Cassio, Desdemona, and Othello. It must be said, of course, that to move some of these he requires little effort because of an overt weakness in them and that circumstances and unconscious cooperation by his victims aid him. Roderigo is a born gull. Cassio has a low resistance to alcohol that makes it easy for Iago to compromise him and have him ousted from his office. The change of Desdemona from a self-assured Venetian lady and loving wife into a frightened little girl is only indirectly Iago's work, for it is effected by Othello's apparently inexplicable passion and cruelty, which are in turn fed by her kind solicitations to the Moor for the reinstatement of Cassio. It is the transformation of Othello from a calm and composed man, "whom passion could not shake," into a gull, a slave of jealousy, and the murderer of his wife that is Iago's hardest task, the one he accomplishes, with some help from others and from accidents it is true, essentially by himself. He convinces a man who has just married a woman who deeply loves him that she is a strumpet. This man is Iago's superior, a Moor with a romantic background and military distinction, a famous general of royal lineage, appointed by the Venetian state, which relies on him, to be governor of Cyprus, a man whose self Shakespeare heightened externally and internally.

There is a modern school of interpretation that would de-psychologize the influence Iago exerts on Othello and would attribute it to the stage convention of the "calumniator believed." Iago would thus become primarily a theatrical mechanism, a traditional evil, tacitly accepted by the audience. According to Bernard Spivack, he belongs to the family of the medieval Vice and carries on the function of seduction common to this type.[1] But whatever few touches Iago may owe to the Vice, he is surely not merely a type on whom a conventional human nature is grafted; he is a complex character, almost incredibly evil and yet totally believable, and his subjection of Othello is a subtle and accomplished performance. It is the play and not merely our interest in psychology that makes us ask the question what it is that gives him the strength to change and finally to destroy the initially calm and self-composed Othello.

The answer to this question is surely not that Iago has a superhuman intelligence because, as a reasoner, Iago does have limitations.[2] He lives in a lower world of the intellect, completely devoid of all feeling for the higher qualities of mankind: love, generosity, kindness are unknown to him. He has no full comprehension of a world in which husband and wife are faithful to each other and handsome young men do not habitually go to bed with other men's wives; his is a world in which animal instincts predominate. He believes, or appears to believe for a while, that it would be possible for him to seduce Desdemona and that she might fall in love with Cassio—even Roderigo finds that hard to accept! Nor is Iago a great strategist. At the outset, he has no very clear idea of what to do except to harm Othello, and he plays with two alternatives—either to seduce Desdemona or to make Othello insanely jealous. His success in the latter plan can be ascribed more to superior tactics than to strategy, to improvisation and clever exploitation of accidents rather than to a master plan. His best stroke, the use of the handkerchief, is due to Desdemona's accidentally dropping it at the time Othello demands an "ocular proof," and nothing could demonstrate Iago's weakness in strategy better, considering that the handkerchief becomes the incriminating evidence that brings him down. That he involves his wife in procuring it proves him to be less than a totally competent judge of people, for he underestimates her loyalty to Desdemona.

But yet the skill with which Iago makes his world, his thoughts, and his imagination dominate Othello is masterful. The process is not primarily an intellectual one, for neither agent nor victim are strong thinkers. Professor Jorgensen has pointed out that the two characters' deficiency in quality of thought is highlighted by the ironic use of keywords denoting knowing and thinking and that this motif illuminates the mind-control Iago exerts.[3] Iago, who uses words with cognitive meaning more than anyone else, understands how to make what he knows of others, incomplete as it is, the starting point of his design, and to create for them a pseudo-knowledge that they are not able to contradict. The first words of the play indicate how he uses what he *knows* in order to exploit Roderigo, and they hint that he may have used this method earlier. Says the latter:

> Tush, never tell me; I take it much unkindly
> That thou, Iago, who has had my purse
> As if the strings were thine, shouldst know of this.

In duping Othello, Iago uses a similar technique of making the most of bits of true knowledge he has about the Moor and others and of having these true items serve to support the putative knowledge he seeks him to accept. Thus, in the persuasion scene, he intimates, by references to Cassio's role in the wooing of Desdemona and to Brabantio's earlier prediction of Desdemona's unfaithfulness, that there has been a long, amorous relationship between her and the lieutenant and that she has a bent toward disloyalty.

Yet this clever technique is hardly sufficient to explain by itself the power Iago can achieve over the minds of others. And it does not account for his genius of destruction. We must look for other facets in his make-up. We may, I think, rule out supernatural sources.[4] Iago, it is true, shares with all Shakespeare's villains something of the eternal spirit that denies goodness and truth; he is a mocker, a cynic, who sneers at honesty as the weakness of fools. But he lacks the incandescence of mind that makes Goethe's Mephistopheles a believable antagonist of the deity, and he is surely not an allegorical figue representative of the Jacobeans' idea of the devil. Occasionally he glories in being of the devil's party, swears by the divinity of hell, and feels at home in the infernal darkness that will bring the monstrous child of his brain to light.But this self-elevation to the ultimate evil is belied by the pettiness of his personal grievances. His glorying in the imagery of damnation and hell demonstrates not his greatness in evil but his littleness as a person, his need to bolster his ego. Neither is the "diabolical" imagery associated with him alone; Othello uses it even more after he adopts Iago's habits of thought.[5] It is true that, in his final moments, Othello temporarily entertains the notion that Iago is a devil and that he looks for Iago's cloven foot. He charges at him and cries, "If that thou be'st a devil, I cannot kill thee," and he cannot. But the reason for this failure surely lies in the Moor's physical exhaustion. When, just after his futile attempt at Iago's life, he speaks metaphorically of Iago as having ensnared his body and his soul, he calls his seducer merely a "demi-devil" (V.ii.289–305).

Iago is too small a man to be the devil incarnate, as much as he would like to be. He is a man of multiple and petty resentments, a malcontent who sets himself apart from the social order and delights in the disorder he creates.[6] He is an envious man with an ingrained contempt and hatred for all that is worthy and good, one who resents the success of others. It is characteristic of him that he gives as one of the reasons why Cassio must die that "He hath a daily beauty in his life / That makes me ugly" (V.i.19–20). The reader or spectator is not likely to find such extraordinary beauty in Cassio's life and must conclude that its evocation by Iago is a symptom of his envious disposition.

Iago's motives are those of an envious man who must have subjects and objects for envy. As Thomas Rogers put it, "It is part of this envy like as fire to covet the highest places and to bark at those worthiest preferred."[7] He hates Cassio, whom he thinks "a mere arithmetician," but who is highly regarded in Venice, as his appointment as Othello's successor demonstrates. Most of all he hates the Moor, as we learn in the first lines of the play and hear again afterward. When he sneers at Roderigo's stupidity, he quickly reproaches himself for spending too much thought on this gull and reasserts his hatred of Othello (I.iii.376 ff.). This primacy of hatred, as Lily Campbell has pointed out, is quite characteristic for an envious man because envy was, in the thinking of the Renaissance, a species of hatred. When Iago explains his hatred of the Moor in the instance just noted, he gives as his reason his fear of having been cuckolded by Othello, a rumor, he says, he has heard. But he does not even care whether it is true; he says that he, "for mere suspicion in that kind, / Will do as if for surety" (I.iii.383–84). Iago's sexual jealousy is part of his all-inclusive envy of others; in Renaissance psychology, jealousy was generally considered a subspecies of envy and in Shakespeare's English, "jealous" could be used as synonymous with "envious."[8]

Iago's jealousy, which has been taken too seriously at times, is significant not really as a motive for his malignity, whose ultimate origin is probably as undiscoverable as the ultimate reasons for the existence of evil in the universe, but on other grounds. His search for motives, no matter how petty and specious, demonstrates his small, calculating mind. Moreover, his acquaintance with jealousy, slight as it is, gives him some familiarity with the passion he decides to produce in the Moor. One might even say that Iago's "jealousy" (in both the general and the specific sense of the word) furnishes him with the design for Othello's destruction. He ponders whether he should get even with the Moor, "wife for wife," but then he decides that he will put him into a jealousy so strong that judgment cannot cure it (II.i.293 and II.i.295). Iago's own jealousy *can* be cured by judgment. He does not writhe in passion as the moralists said an envious or jealous man does. Once, it is true, he says that he is tortured, that is, when he professes suspicion that Othello has cuckolded him, "the thought whereof / Doth like a poisonous mineral gnaw my inwards" (II.i.290–91). But this statement comes immediately after he disclaims interest in Desdemona, whom he "loves" merely because she will "diet" his revenge. The context gives his statement a peculiar flavor; it appears that in attributing a gnawing jealousy to himself, he is, as it were, trying out and heating up the emotion so he can transfer it to his victim.

Iago has a constitutional, but controllable, inclination to jealousy because of his endemic envy. The devouring effect of jealousy, which Iago claims he feels in himself, is very much the one that moralists like Thomas Rogers attributed to envy:

> This envy is compared unto the canker; for as the canker eateth and destroyeth iron, so doth envy eat and consume the hearts of the envious. . . . For another's prosperity is their poison, and another's adversity their comfort.[9]

And when Iago later inoculates Othello with jealousy, he gives him an imaginary picture of the tortures of this passion, a picture quite in the tradition of the moralists' warnings against envy:

> O, beware, my lord, of jealousy;
> It is the green-ey'd monster which doth mock
> The meat it feeds on.
>
> (III.iii.169–71)

In the central part omitted from the passage previously quoted from Rogers's tract, envy is described similarly: "The poets feign Envy to be one of the Furies of hell and to be fed with nothing but adders and snakes to show that envious persons do swallow down poison and likewise vomit up the same again." The *topos* of envy-jealousy as a monster that makes the food it mocks was common. Iago knows the trait and produces it in Othello, in whose poisoned imagination Desdemona becomes "a cistern for foul toads / To knot and gender in!" (IV.ii.62–63). Thus Iago is the preceptor of Othello; he teaches him a jealousy that has the worst features of envy and makes him eat out his heart. Othello is Iago's obedient disciple, who in turn applies ideas suggested to him most inappropriately—or, from Iago's point of view, appropriately—to Desdemona.

If Iago's "jealousy" is the primary one and Othello's the secondary, as Professor Heilman has said, Othello's is also the manifest, explosive passion, Iago's the submerged and controlled one. In fact, one forgets during the play that Iago is capable of hate, envy, and jealousy because he appears practically passionless. On his conciousness of self-control Iago builds much of his assurance of self-knowledge, an arrogant assurance, but one that is, in a sense, justified. In the second speech he has in the play, he asserts that he knows his "price." This knowledge makes him feel superior to others; he says sneeringly of Roderigo that "I mine own gain'd knowledge should profane / If I would time expend with such a snipe / But for my sport and profit" (I.iii.378–80). Until his exposure in the end, he never loses the assurance that he can master all situations. He is the only one of Shakespeare's major villains who has not a single moment of remorse. And in the end, when he is exposed and his knowledge of others is shown to be faulty, he still takes pride in his self-control: he announces that henceforth he will never speak another word. It is not important whether we believe him or Gratiano, who says that torture will open his lips; Iago's assurance matters, and what he says with it: "What you know, you know" (V.ii.306). His knowledge of himself, a knowledge synonymous with trust in the strength of his will, remains with him to the end.

In the sense in which the Christian humanists or the fideistic skeptics spoke of self-knowledge, Iago cannot be said to possess it, for he totally lacks any moral commitment or faith. Moreover, such presumption of self-knowledge was outrageous to them even when ethically or religiously oriented. Erasmus said in the sixth chapter of *Enchiridion* that nobody should hold the fantastic opinion that he knows himself well enough; even Paul did not dare judge himself. Iago's self-estimation is not only arrogant but also egotistic and immoral; he compounds the sin of pride with the sin of self-love. He never yet found a man who knew "how to love himself" (I.iii.315) —except, of course, himself. By following Othello, he follows but himself, and, in glaring perversion of the concept "soul," the first and primary object of self-knowledge, he declares those who act like him to be fellows that "have some soul."

In equally conspicuous contempt for the doctrine of moral *decorum,* which the humanists had thought central to self-knowledge, Iago espouses a philosophy of seeming:

> For when my outward action doth demonstrate
> The native act and figure of my heart
> In compliment extern, 'tis not long after
> But I will wear my heart upon my sleeve
> For daws to peck at: I am not what I am.
> (I.i.62–66)

This is a self-declaration underneath the surface meaning intended for Roderigo that Iago must disguise his true feelings for Othello. Iago's concluding boast, "I am not what I am," denies both the self-reflexive identification, "I am what I am," and the identification with the human race, "I am a man in the sense of a moral being." [10] He feels that he is a man apart, outside human and divine laws.

By standing outside, or believing to stand outside, the human race, Iago finds it possible to manipulate the others without really involving anything but his will in his contact with them. The student and teacher of jealousy is also a student and practitioner of the science of the will, and it is here that he is most competent. He observes the use of will-power by himself and by others, seeing himself as possessing a strong and effective will that gives him self-direction, aggressiveness, energy, and determination, and he finds the will of the others to be submissive, determined by wishful thinking, and dominated by appetite and lust. This attribution of weakness to others, however, is often merely another side of his inability to understand the higher provinces of thought and emotion. He has a consistently low opinion of Othello's will because Othello loves, an emotion that he equates with softness:

> His soul is so enfetter'd to her love
> That she may make, unmake, do what she list,
> Even as her appetite shall play the god
> With his weak function.
>
> (II.iii.334–37)

Iago has no such fetters. The "love" that he confesses for Desdemona is the attraction of the villain to the victim, the satisfaction of finding a human being whose destruction serves to destroy another. Although Iago's failure to understand man's nobler nature and his lack of capacity for love makes him an incomplete human being, it also gives him a liberty and scope denied to those who are ethically superior to him.

Thus we may say in answer to the question posed earlier, what quality enables Iago to be the powerful and destructive agent of Othello's tragedy, that this quality is his will. He succeeds because of his effective use of a strong, morally uninhibited will for the subjugation of the morally oriented and restricted wills of the others. For Iago, the exercise of his will is, as Bradley saw, the main motivation —if one can speak here of motivation. Joy in the triumph of his will is what he primarily gets out of doing what he does: he chuckles about making Roderigo his purse, and he anticipates turning Desdemona's virtue into pitch and leading Othello by the nose like an ass. The prospect of "pluming up" his will, not the desire for the lieutenancy, is the subject of his first soliloquy. Mere ambition, the main driving force of Shakespeare's earlier Machiavellian villains, is only a minor motive for him. He evinces no joy when he becomes Othello's lieutenant, and he goes forward without stop on his destructive path.

Iago understands how to estimate the quantity and quality of the wills of others, and he foresees what happens when different wills come together to reinforce or to oppose each other. He recognizes that by creating in the doting Roderigo's mind the hope of obtaining Desdemona he also has fashioned a completely subservient tool who does not shy away even from murder. He realizes that Cassio's low resistance to alcohol can be used to bring about disorder and thus to provoke Othello's will to preserve order. From the beginning, Iago is convinced that he can mastermind Othello. "These Moors," he says, "are changeable in their wills" (I.iii.348). This remark is to give Roderigo hope that Othello may stop loving Desdemona, but it is also symptomatic of Iago's confidence in his ability to control the Moor.

Even more than on the control of Roderigo, Cassio, and Othello, Iago counts on making Desdemona his tool. "Out of her own good- ness," he says, he will make "the net / That shall enmesh them all" (II.iii.350–51). It is a matter of his counting not on the weakness of Desdemona's will but rather on its strength, strength for the achieve- ment of good purposes. Desdemona's strength of will is, in fact, stressed repeatedly; by it, she, rather than Othello, appears to be at times Iago's opponent. This strength, which proved itself in her unconventional choice of a husband, permits Iago with a semblance of truth to argue that she is fundamentally perverted:

> Foh! one may smell in such a will most rank,
> Foul disproportion, thoughts unnatural.
> But pardon me—I do not in position
> Distinctly speak of her; though I may fear
> Her will, recoiling to her better judgment,
> May fail to match you with her country forms,
> And happily repent.
> (III.iii.236–42)

The argument can make the by-now weakened Othello feel that Desdemona must be unfaithful according to a kind of natural law. But Iago is right about the strength of her will although not about its perversion. When she takes up Cassio's cause, it is with an unfortunate tenacity: "I will have my lord and you again / As friendly as you were" (III.ii.6–7). She pledges to do more for Cassio than for herself: "What I can do I will; and more I will / Than for myself I dare" (III.iv.131–32). Her extraordinary energy shows itself most excruciatingly in her physiologically improbable revival from strangulation and in her pathetic last words that nobody killed her but herself, the white lie with which she at- tempts to help her husband. Her determination to do good has a symbiotic effect on Emilia, who, at the crucial moment of the action, acquires an obstinacy that even overcomes Iago's when she refuses to be silenced by him. It is ironic that Iago, who masterminds every- body else, finds it impossible to restrain his own wife, intent on salvaging her mistress's reputation. This is the only miscalculation Iago makes in judging the will of others; he succumbs here to his inability to understand higher emotions and loyalties.

An interest in the manipulation of the will, as we have noted, was in Shakespeare's air at the time he wrote *Othello*. Will and its triumphs were widely admired from the Machiavellians to the devout Catholics. Iago's view of man, as much as it differs from these movements in other respects, resembles them in seeing man's character as primarily a product of his will. Iago is, of course, much more extreme in this belief. This feature gives him his look of total emancipation from Christian humanism and makes him a "new man." Most revealing for this seventeenth-century "modernity" is his speech to Roderigo that precedes the soliloquy in which he expresses pleasure in "pluming up his will." This carefully worked-out speech constitutes a new pattern of self-knowledge in Shakespeare, one that travesties the old in some important aspects. Iago reacts to the simpering Roderigo's lament that it is not in his "virtue," that is, power, to amend his "fondness." Answers Iago:

> Virtue? a fig! 'Tis in ourselves that we are thus or thus. Our bodies are our gardens to the which our wills are gardeners; so that if we will plant nettles or sow lettuce, set hyssop and weed up thyme, supply it with one gender of herbs or distract it with many, either to have it sterile with idleness or manur'd with industry—why, the power and corrigible authority of this lies in our wills. If the balance of our lives had not one scale of reason to poise another of sensuality, the blood and baseness of our natures would conduct us to most preposterous conclusions. But we have reason to cool our raging motions, our carnal stings, our unbitted lusts; whereof I take this that you call love to be a sect or scion.
>
> (I.iii.320–31)

Iago proclaims here the need for psychic balance and does so by means of the field-garden imagery with which humanistic philosophy underlined the importance of education. A passage in La Primaudaye's *French Academy* is similar enough to be suspected as Shakespeare's source:

> The nature of man is like a pair of balance. For, if it be not guided with knowledge and reason unto the better part, of itself it is carried to the worse. And although a man be well born, yet if he have not his judgment fined and the discoursing part of his mind purged with the reasons of philosophy, it will fall often into gross faults and such as beseem not a prudent man. For in those men that are not induced with virtue ruled by certain knowledge, nature bringeth forth such fruits as naturally come from the ground without the manuring and helping hand of man.[11]

Iago's speech appears to carry the idea of balance even further than La Primaudaye by including the flora of the garden that is man: the two sets of plants, hyssop and nettle versus thyme and lettuce, balance each other, for according to the herbalists' botany the former were hot and dry, the latter cold and moist.[12] However, Iago's choices for the will are not the moral qualities of the humanistic use of the figure, good and evil, but the psychological ones, control and lack of control of desire. It may even be more significant that Iago equates will and reason; in effect, will is Iago's balancer or gardener rather than reason and knowledge as in La Primaudaye. In the latter's system, will is the agent, even the servant of reason, not its master; reason or (elsewhere) God is the gardener. Nowhere in Renaissance moral literature have I found will designated as balancer or gardener; if either role is assigned to man, it is always because he is divinely endowed with reason. Thus Iago's speech does not have the true Renaissance balance; rather, it advocates the supremacy of the "rude will" that in *Romeo and Juliet* Friar Lawrence calls the enemy of "grace." Iago's particular use of the garden imagery and the microcosmic analogy proclaims not the virtue of temperance but the gospel of the iron will, a gospel that the humanistically educated in Shakespeare's audience must have recognized as false, but that to some advanced thinkers of the time sounded sweet.

Iago's "Virtue! a fig!" disparages goodness and puts in its stead a concept of "virtue" as innate ability and powerful exertion of the will. Iago's speech has thus a general allusiveness to the intellectual trends in Shakespeare's time that in various ways emphasized the significance of will power. It may have made some in Shakespeare's audience uncomfortably aware of the evils of the acquisitive spirit that was around them and in themselves. To others it may have suggested the Machiavellian virtù in its vulgarized interpretation as the power to manipulate people and get ahead. For still others of Shakespeare's contemporaries, the argument may have cast Iago in the role of a "Jesuitical Machiavel" given to the machinations associated with a sinister brotherhood.[13] Perhaps some may have seen him as applying to psychology the new scientific rationale with its empirical methods and step-by-step procedure. Others may have identified him with one of the "new Stoics" about whom they had heard from the pulpit, men who were also sometimes, with that loosely applied term, called atheists.

The speech, in fact, does make this latter identification evident.

When, in conclusion, Iago denounces love as "merely a lust of the blood and a permission of the will," he associates himself with the rigorous Stoics, censured by Saint Paul as men "without affection" (2 Tim. iii: 3). As Bullinger said, "We Christians have nothing to do with the ironlike philosophy, since our Lord and Master hath not in words only but with his own example also utterly condemned it." [14] Iago's classification of love as lust would have struck Renaissance theologians as the worst kind of such Stoicism. Even the admired Cicero was thought to have erred in this matter when in *Tusculan Disputations* he declared *amor* to be an irrational emotion that fell under *libido* and was subject to voluntary control (III.12–13; IV.57, 65, 72). Cicero's method of devaluating love was so similar to Iago's that it may well have been in Shakespeare's mind: *libido* was, just like "lust," originally a neutral word, meaning desire in a general sense; but both words, by their authors' times, had depreciated in meaning. For Iago, new man and new Stoic, "love" is merely a raging and stinging lust of the blood and a permission of the will, just as *libido* was for Cicero.

Iago's affinity with the new Stoics also shows in his fondness for the word "patience," which is used more often in *Othello* (thirteen times) than in any other play of Shakespeare. Iago mocks those who, like Roderigo, are poor because "they have not patience" (II.iii.358). When Iago victimizes Othello, the sneer shows in his hypocritical advice: "Patience, I say; your mind perhaps may change" (III.iii. 456). "Patience" here counterpoints "passion," for immediately after this advice Othello's jealousy rises like "the Pontic Sea." Desdemona's method, innocently adopted to help Cassio, to "watch him [Othello] tame, and talk him out of patience" (III.iii.23), has the same effect. Iago's repeated admonitions to Othello to preserve patience are intended to kindle the latter's passion while giving him the delusion of control.

This is certainly Iago's technique as he makes Othello observe the confidences of Cassio and Bianca and induces him to believe that they concern an assignation between Cassio and Desdemona. Othello has just risen from a lethargy and acquired a new fury in demanding "ocular proof" of Desdemona's unfaithfulness. As Othello's passion rises, Iago admonishes his victim to confine himself "but in a patient list" (IV.i.75) and appeals to his sense of manhood: "Marry, patience; / Or I shall say you are all in all in spleen, / And nothing of a man" (87–89). Whereupon Othello chimes in with a bitterly ironic play on "patience": "I will be found most cunning in my patience; / But—dost thou hear?—most bloody" (90–91). Thus Iago, like a hypnotist, imprints on Othello a concept of manhood founded on a perverse and inhuman idea of patience while stirring his mounting passion.

We may note here how the idea of the victory of patience over passion becomes an ironic movement in the symphonic structure of *Othello* as the Moor, imagining himself to be an interrogating judge, "examines" Desdemona, who understands only the fury in his words but not their sense. The deluded Othello fancies that his habitual and exemplary patience has been lost because of the magnitude of Desdemona's "crime":

> Had it pleas'd heaven
> To try me with affliction, had they rain'd
> All kinds of sores and shames on my bare head,
> Steep'd me in poverty to the very lips,
> Given to captivity me and my utmost hopes,
> I should have found in some place of my soul
> A drop of patience.
>   (IV.ii.48–54)

Othello's model for self-comparison is the biblical Job, who lost his possessions and contracted boils and sores, and yet remained patient: his story in the words of the preamble in the Genevan Bible was "the example of a singular patience." But Othello goes even further by claiming that not even an angel's patience could endure his suffering:

> Turn thy complexion there,
> Patience, thou young and rose-lipp'd cherubin—
> Ay, here, look grim as hell!
>   (63–65)

This personification of patience evokes, in a highly ironic manner, the allegorical Christian portraits and descriptions of this virtue. Bullinger, for instance, when redrawing Tertullian's "lively image of Patience," sketched her with

> her countenance . . . calm and quiet, her forehead smooth without furrowed wrinkles, which are signs of sorrow or anger. Her brows are never knit, but slack in cheerful wise, with her eyes cast comely down to the ground, not for the sorrow of any calamities, but only

for humility's sake. . . . Her color is like to theirs that are nigh
no danger and are guiltless of evil. . . . For she sitteth in the
throne of that most meek and quiet spirit, which is not troubled
with any tempest nor overcast with any cloud but is plain, open,
and of a goodly clearness.[15]

The hellish grimness with which Othello endows his Patience is
incongruous with such serene portraits; it fits this virtue as little as
the accusation of adultery does Desdemona, who listens uncompre-
hendingly. Indeed, the maligned Desdemona is an image of the
patience extolled by Tertullian-Bullinger, but refurbished for grim
times. The sources of her fortitude are old, but her strength of will
makes this fortitude commensurate to times of exceptional tribula-
tion. If Iago is a new man, she is something of a new woman. She is
certainly a new kind of heroine in Shakespeare, heightened as she is
by her signal patience; and she foreshadows the heroines of the romances: Marina, "Like Patience gazing on kings' graves, and smiling
/ Extremity out of act" (*Pericles,* V.i.137–38), or Hermione, who
teaches the guilty Leontes a lesson in expiation by remaining in
hiding for sixteen years before revealing herself to him as a seeming
statue—a living monument to patience. Othello's grotesque image of
Patience with her clear brow darkened to look as grim as hell, points
up the exemplary patience of Desdemona—who takes her place
among the suffering and patient women in Shakespeare's later plays
—and it is also an ironic caricature of the changed self of Othello.

Iago's relatively easy success in achieving this distortion of
Othello's vision points to some weakness in the Moor that facilitates
the villain's task. Perhaps we should say that, in spite of appearances
to the contrary, Othello's character has an affinity with Iago's or, at
least, that there is something in Othello that desires such affinity.
Othello's subjugation by Iago is, in a sense, a seduction, and a
seduction requires not only a seducer but also a person who can be
seduced.[16] Surely it is not true that under Othello's circumstances
any man would become jealous, and Shakespeare provides occasions
where Othello very simply could test Iago's insinuations. Not that
Othello is naturally jealous or even, at first, notably passionate; his
calmness and composure at the beginning are extraordinary, and so
is the eloquence with which he demonstrates them. Such phrases as
"I fetch my life and being / From men of royal siege" and "my
parts, my title, and my perfect soul" ring in one's ear. Yet there is
something in these assertions that makes one distrust their confi-

dence. In a more melodious and elevated key, they echo Iago's protestations of self-knowledge, and they are, like his, underlined by
repeated uses of the word "know." And it is ironic that Othello's
claim of having a "perfect soul" follows Iago's declaration that those
fellows who, like him, do not follow their masters "have some soul."
Of course, Othello's perfect soul is one free from wrongdoing, Iago's
soul is one that gives him power to deceive the world; but in either
case there is a lack of humility. The humanists and, even more
strongly, the skeptics had enjoined this virtue as a prerequisite for
whatever self-knowledge a man can achieve, and Othello is almost as
conspicuously shown deficient in humility of mind as is Iago.

There is a hint at self-delusion in Othello's assertion that amorous
emotions are "defunct" in him as he supports Desdemona's request
to accompany him to Cyprus. The idea that her presence might dis-
tract him from his military duties is, to him, absurd:

> No, when light-wing'd toys
> Of feather'd Cupid seel with wanton dullness
> My speculative and offic'd instruments,
> That my disports corrupt and taint my business,
> Let huswives make a skillet of my helm,
> And all indign and base adversities
> Make head against my estimation!
> (I.iii.268–74)

Apart from the low estimate of the power of passion that these lines
betray, they are sound as theoretical psychology of the humanistic
kind: Othello's distinction between the speculative and the active
mind shows his awareness of the mental processes that the humanists
thought involved in moral action. But the lines also indicate Othello's
trust in his will, the one faculty in which Iago thinks him deficient.

Othello has, like Iago, a penchant for self-dramatizations. Othello's,
it is true, ring sonorously in one's ear; Iago's grate on it. I do not
think that self-dramatization is per se a tragic weakness; it is rather
a demonstration of the tragic hero's heightened self that makes us
feel his glory and suffering as extraordinary.[17] Yet Othello's manner
of self-dramatization is different from Hamlet's or Lear's. The
sensual lilt, the "Othello music," as Professor Knight has called it,
points to a sentimental temperament, and the subject matter is
generally Othello's romantic past. Not that he exaggerates its
glamor. As one listens to his account of his travels, one thinks of

Elizabethan adventurers' voyages to faraway lands. But it is notable that he dramatizes himself almost always in terms of his past. Iago, who practically never talks of the past, is his very opposite here; he has no romantic vein. He is colder, more efficient.

It may be natural for an older man to try to establish his identity by reference to the past, to define what he is in the present by what he has been before; but there is often something in Othello's recapitulations that inspires apprehension about his ability to cope with the present. The most notable example is his eloquent retrospective self-assessment in which he says farewell to the soldierly profession (III.iii.351 ff.). It is a hasty farewell, as precipitous as the despair of Richard II; Iago has not yet played his trump of the handkerchief. The premature defeatism is as unwise as his earlier boast of rational control; the speech bears some resemblance to those of earlier dramas in which erstwhile confident conquerors confess the subjugation of their souls by love, but Othello's ruination is more painful because it is due not to light-feathered Cupid but to the green-eyed monster of jealousy.

It will be said that the important difference between Iago and Othello is not that the one represents the present and the other the past, but that the one is a Negro and the other a Venetian. This, of course, is true; but the difference matters only because of what Iago makes of it. At the decisive moment of the seduction, he hints that he knows such supersubtle Venetians as Desdemona, and Othello does not. It is after having made Othello insecure that Iago suggests the significant difference between himself and Desdemona on the one hand and Othello on the other: the dissimilarities of "clime, complexion, and degree" (the first two imply race) make Desdemona's choice of Othello "unnatural" (III.iii.205–37). Iago's argument for the seduction of Othello hinges on an old commonplace of the mutual attraction of like natures and the repulsion of unlike ones.

As previously noted, Iago's method of arguing was paralleled in the procedures recommended for the "passion mover," that is, the person engaged in controlling other people's reactions, by Thomas Wright in *The Passions of the Mind*, which had its second, enlarged edition in the year Shakespeare presumably composed *Othello* (1604). We may recall that Wright takes a similarly protective attitude toward his well-meaning but naïve countrymen as Iago hypocritically does toward Othello: they must be shielded from the sleights and deceits of sophisticated foreigners (specified as Italians and Spaniards by Wright). Of course, Wright wanted his book to serve the defense of virtue; Iago's arguments are used in its defeat. But in the employment of psychological means, Wright and Iago have something in common; they have been to a new school, whereas Othello is "unbookish."

If Othello is overly trustful, he is certainly not a born dupe like Roderigo; even Iago does not call him an ass but predicts that he will, egregiously, make him one. Othello's trust is the abundance of a good quality and, as such, a fault, large enough for an Iago to exploit, small enough to warrant our sympathy. There is a subtle dramatic irony in Othello's speaking of Iago as a man "of honesty and trust" (I.iii.284) just after declaring his imperviousness to passion. Othello's confidence in himself thus becomes associated with a mistake of judgment of others. In his conversation with Roderigo, Iago has just blatantly demonstrated his unworthiness of the trust Othello puts in him, and one must conclude therefore that Othello's knowledge of himself and of other people is faulty. When it later becomes evident that his judgment of Iago is shared by others, one is not likely to judge that Othello really knows more of people than it appeared, but that Iago is an even more clever villain than it seemed.

The skillful transfer of envy and jealousy from Iago to Othello requires a peculiar closeness, almost a melting of the one into the other. The two become friends who swear eternal brotherhood; they are now, in an old humanistic commonplace, "one soul in bodies twain." In Wright's terms, the two form a "union of haters," which reinforces their strength.[18] But in this combined organism, they are still differentiated; Iago supplies the will and Othello the passion. Iago is thus, in Wright's term, the "passion mover." In one of his analogues Wright calls this agent the "doctor" who administers doses of passion or moderation according to the condition of his "patient"—the old metaphor of the passion as a disease thus assumes a new meaning: "The passion mover must look narrowly to this point and imitate herein the common practice of prudent physicians who apply their medicine to the same maladies with particular respect and consideration of the patient's temper."[19]

This is exactly the treatment Iago administers to Othello; he provides at all stages just the right dose of poison to stimulate Othello's passion and the right amount of a lenitive to keep it from exploding prematurely. He produces in Othello a progressive series of cumulative reactions, each of which is calculatingly determined and controlled by Iago, until Othello loses all self-direction and collapses. The first incident in this series is Iago's instigation of Cassio's drunkenness, which strains Othello's sense of discipline to the breaking point; the confusion of Cassio and Montano about the reasons for the disorder and the seeming reluctance of Iago to reveal them prevent Othello from making a rational inquiry, and passion threatens to overcome reason (II.iii.196 ff.). This is a prelude to the future turbulence. When Iago slowly injects jealousy into Othello's mind, the effect becomes audible and visible, and Iago himself registers the progress on the Moor's face, bearing, and speech. Othello now gyrates between love and hate, and between violence and exhaustion. In one sentence, he pities Desdemona and recalls her sweetness, in the next, he wants to tear her all to pieces; in one scene, he shouts at the perplexed Desdemona in highest passion, and in the next, he enters so fatigued and exhausted as to make it possible for Iago to anesthetize him with a few obscene insinuations.

The continued vexations engineered by Iago do not allow Othello to return to his former, composed self. Just before his epileptic breakdown, he does, however, make something of an attempt to shed the character imposed upon him by Iago. The latter's question, "Will you think so?" with which the fourth act opens, suggests that Othello has objected to Iago's report of a kiss between Cassio and Desdemona or tried to give it an innocent interpretation; but when Iago evokes the picture of Cassio and Desdemona naked in bed, Othello's passion rises again. Iago reminds him now of the handkerchief, and the memory of it comes over Othello's mind "as doth the raven o'er the infected house." When Iago now insinuates that Cassio has confessed to lying with Desdemona, the word "lie" hits Othello like a dagger, and his puns turn it around in his heart. His mind disintegrates, he stammers disjointed and incoherent phrases, trembles and shakes, sees in the darkening of his vision a foreshadowing of nature, loses consciousness, and falls to the ground.

This is the moment of Othello's greatest physical passion. Iago calls it "epilepsy" when Cassio appears on the scene. The fit is, I believe, modeled on Hercules's breakdown and madness in Seneca's *Hercules Furens,* which in the Renaissance was interpreted as epilepsy.[20] But the question whether it is this particular disease is of secondary importance; Othello's sprawling on the ground is certainly pathological, and represents the ultimate in the physical expression of passion. Only the presence of Iago, who stands triumphantly over his fallen master, makes this tremendous outbreak credible; the incident of Othello's highest passion is also the moment of the complete subjection of his self to Iago's will. Passion and will attain here a powerful baroque intensity. Iago can suggest now to Othello that self-knowledge requires the murder of Desdemona. Othello's case, he says, is better than that of those cuckolds who do not know they have been deceived:

> No, let me know;
> And knowing what I am, I know what she shall be.
> (IV.i.72–73)

Othello accepts this monstrous idea as wisdom: "O thou art wise; 'tis certain."

This, the climax of the action, falls into the fourth act, as is usual in Shakespeare's dramatic structure. In *Othello,* the impact is intensified by the three episodes in which the Moor is visibly blinded by passion; besides his collapse, there are his maddening commentary, accompanied by violent gestures, on Cassio's conversation with Bianca and his striking of Desdemona in Lodovico's presence. In each case, the provocation is great, but in each case it is also based on delusion—on the fantasy image of Desdemona and Cassio in bed, on a misinterpretation of the subject of Cassio's discourse, and on a misunderstanding of Desdemona's innocent remark that she is glad to see Cassio made governor of Cyprus for "the love" she bears him. By showing Othello so totally deluded, Shakespeare lessens the painfulness of his decision to kill Desdemona for the sake of "justice." The Othello who goes to kill Desdemona has been brainwashed by an expert and is no longer in control of himself. Lodovico's amazement about the change of the man whom passion could not shake draws attention to the accomplished change.

The answer to the question whether Othello ever emerges from his subjection to Iago is a difficult one.[21] It seems sentimental to claim that there is always something in Othello that resists the ultimate subjugation. But I think it is also not true that he remains in the end completely submerged. The crux is Othello's last, most important, and most problematic self-assessment in his charge to

Lodovico to report to the Venetian Senate the story of his life: "Speak of me as I am" (V.ii.345). The present tense should not blind us to the fact that this is another retrospective self-dramatization. However, it is not, I think, merely an exercise in *Bovarysm,* as T. S. Eliot claimed.[22] *Bovarysm* implies an ironic incongruity between the ideal and the actual arising from a congenital inability to face the truth about oneself; and as much as Othello may dramatize himself, he is not anywhere shown to be merely a romantic liar. He appears to be intent on telling his story aright to Lodovico so that it can be told to the unsatisfied in Venice—"nothing extenuate, / Nor set down aught in malice":

> Then must you speak
> Of one that lov'd not wisely but too well;
> Of one not easily jealous, but, being wrought,
> Perplexed in the extreme.
>
> (V.ii.345–49)

But this is too simple a formula. That Othello loved not wisely, one agrees; but that he loved too well is hardly true: surely the greatest kind of love is not one that leads to precipitous jealousy. When Othello calls himself "not easily jealous," he denies what in the course of little more than a day has taken place. But yet, the speech is not merely rationalization or self-pity. It is possible to read Othello's words in the explanatory way some critics do: "loving too well" may mean to be doting; it may be the kind of all-absorbing passion that, as does Othello's, becomes an obsession. "Not easily jealous" may mean "not naturally jealous," and Othello certainly is not a naturally jealous man in the sense in which Iago is one. Still, this interpretation is not immediately suggested by what Othello says, and, without it, Othello's self-explanation falls short of total illumination.

After all, it would be surprising if Shakespeare, after writing plays that demonstrate man's difficulty in attaining a true picture of himself, would have given one of his least intellectual heroes a clear and rational view of his situation. Moreover, the dim and partial recognition of the truth he gave to Othello is psychologically and dramatically appropriate. The man who once more looks back at his life has just murdered his wife and has experienced the chaos in himself that he ironically predicted would be the end of love. He has realized that both the nonjealous and the jealous Othello have ceased to exist. "That's he that was Othello—here I am," he says as his pursuers take him captive. In this simple phrase is contained perhaps a better *anagnorisis*—and note the juxtaposition of past and present tense—than in his last retrospective self-assessment, which cannot be totally successful if it is to be plausible. The words are those of a man who drops tears as fast as the "Arabian trees their med'cinable gum," who is still in the grip of passion although of a nobler one than that which motivated him to kill. And the words are the prelude to another passionate act: suicide. It is probably impossible ever to recapture the past completely; for Othello to formulate a rational self-explanation at this moment would be quite unconvincing.

If the intellectual truth of Othello's words is incomplete, there is something in the imagery of the speech that adds a glow of emotional, "fideistic" truth, to which the allusion to Othello's Christianity contributes. He now senses the value of the pearl that he, like the base Indian (or, should we read "Judean" with the Folio?), threw away. And his concluding description of the incident in Aleppo when he slew the Turk that "beat a Venetian and traduc'd the state" recalls that Othello hit another Venetian, Desdemona; and if he did not traduce the state, he certainly scanted its "serious and great business." Past and present merge in the magnificent metaphor in which Othello takes his own life: the hand that leads the knife is now, just as in Aleppo, Othello's; the same hand that killed Desdemona kills now himself. Othello is not only the executor of justice but also a criminal; he is the "dog" whom he once slew.

Although Othello's conscious judgment of himself is defective, it is nevertheless true that he is a victim who deserves pity. As he says, he was, "being wrought, / Perplexed in the extreme." Even granted the imperfections in Othello's character—his overconfidence, his rootedness in the past, his excessive trust, his premature defeatism, his obsessive love—without Iago's extraordinary skill of engendering jealousy in him, the Moor could not be thought to turn from an honorable general into what he grotesquely calls an "honorable murderer." One gets the impression that Othello's self-knowledge, defective as it is, would have been sufficient for all situations except the one in which Iago involves him. The subjection of Othello's self requires the skillful and relentless ministrations of a master deceiver. Iago's machinations interlock with Othello's reactions so that the latter always appear a plausible result of the former. In contrast to other Jacobean dramatists who also strove for strong effects, Shakespeare understood how to make great passion humanly credible: Othello's jealousy and violence strike us as plausible and awe-inspiring because of the strength of the begetter Iago. The effect is commensurate to the cause. The dynamic subjection of Othello's self is so masterfully treated that the intensity of Othello's passion produces not merely amazement but also compassion. Othello inflicts suffering; but he himself also suffers excruciatingly. It is primarily his capacity for suffering that, in spite of his lack of intellectual strength, makes him the powerful tragic hero he is.

CHAPTER FIFTEEN

King Lear:
Valuing the Self

THE LACK OF SELF-KNOWLEDGE is treated trag-
ically in *King Lear,* as it is in *Othello.* The theme is, of
course, the spring for most of Shakespeare's plays. Even the
comic plots generally evolve around men's failures to know themselves and their conditions; but they deal with this subject more
lightly, and the flaw is corrected in time. In the plays of Shakespeare's mannerist phase, the problem of man's understanding of
himself is associated with that of man's insecurity, and it is treated
in the larger frame of the difficulty of understanding the truth in
general. This context is also present in the baroque tragedies, but
the lack of self-knowledge is here intensified and shown to have
gigantic consequences because of the tremendous will and passion
of the heroes. Hamlet is puzzled, thwarted, and disillusioned as
he seeks for truth in an environment that hides and obscures it;
Othello, in a situation more open to rational solution, accepts an
absolute falsehood as truth, a falsehood that becomes the guiding
force of his whole being. Macbeth equally resolutely excludes the
possibility of facing the imperative of moral action and goes on to
violate it in one senseless murder after another. But Lear's lack of
self-knowledge even by comparison with Othello's and Macbeth's is
monumental and its consequences are devastating. With no outside
persuader or extraordinary temptation to blind and seduce him, the
king foolishly accepts his false daughters as true and his true
daughter as false, and, as a result, he is subjected to a gigantic
suffering of body and soul; he disintegrates while the world that
he once ruled trembles and shakes.

The first scene of *King Lear* makes the strongest statement about
lack of self-knowledge anywhere in Shakespeare, so strong a statement that it comes close to being psychologically improbable. A

man who arranges a contest of love protestations among his daughters and, as a result, disinherits his favorite at the spur of the moment may be thought, from the point of view of strict realism, to be
too foolish to be a tragic hero; and, indeed, the great realist Tolstoy
preferred the somewhat less irrational Leir of Shakespeare's source
play to him. Shakespeare disdained to give his king even the kind of
feeble motivation he has in the old play, where the rejection of the
favorite daughter is somewhat prepared for in the six scenes that
precede it. Here the idea of dividing the kingdom was not the old
king's but that of a trusted counselor, reluctantly agreed to by Leir
because it gave him an opportunity to provide dowries for his
daughters to make them marriageable. The contest had the special
purpose of tricking his favorite Cordella into marriage; she had so
far refused to marry, wanting to do so only if she could love. Confidently expecting Cordella to outdo her sisters in affirming her devotion, Leir plans to take the opportunity to elicit from her the promise
to marry the Duke of Brittany as a pledge of her love. His dis-
appointment, a mild passion compared to Lear's terrifying wrath, is
rooted in a father's frustration over his failure to provide for his
daughter.

By contrast, Shakespeare has his king commit a well-nigh inexplicable blunder, enhanced by a public display of gigantic wrath. The
love declarations, a private matter in the old play, become a ceremonious rite of kingship arranged for no better purpose than the
satisfaction of Lear's ego after the *fait accompli* of the division of his
kingdom. His outbreak of anger is punctuated by the violent oath
with which he disclaims propinquity and paternal care of Cordelia:

> . . . by the sacred radiance of the sun,
> The mysteries of Hecat and the night;
> By all the operation of the orbs
> From whom we do exist and cease to be.
> (I.i.108–11)

Lear's folly is underlined by his parallel reaction to Kent's cou-
rageous warning to "see better." When Lear swears "by Apollo," the
asseveration must have struck many in Shakespeare's audience as
ironic because the ancients had thought that *nosce teipsum* emanated
from this very Apollo. As Kent says, Lear swears his gods in vain.
The truth, which Lear says shall be Cordelia's dowry, is irreconcil-

able with the demands of his ego. His lack of self-knowledge is monumental.

The setting of the first scene is a ritual, ceremonious and splendid; but the public show is punctured by elemental passions. The moral and emotional coloring is heightened above realism. Goneril and Regan protest their loves in hyperbolically hypocritical ways; Cordelia, confessing her love for her father in asides, is uncompromisingly forthright in her insistence that she can say nothing to compete with her sisters; Kent minces no words when he calls Lear "mad" and "old man." Will impacts on will, and the clashing forces —evil and good, treachery and loyalty, self-seeking and altruism, hate and love—are irreconcilable. Between these stands Lear, as extreme in his passion as is Cordelia in her low-voiced patience. He is an elementary human force, a creature of a distant and pagan past; when he casts Cordelia from his heart as if she were a "barbarous Scythian," he characterizes himself as barbaric, primitively irrational in his hatred. But this hatred betrays an equally elemental love from which it springs, an unreasonable, egotistic love that demands what it has no right to ask. We cannot but accept Regan's judgment: he has ever but slenderly known himself.

Not enough is one such demonstration of folly; the second scene presents a similarly gigantic blunder (although put into a somewhat lower key because the scene is in prose, except for Edmund's soliloquy). On the basis of the forged letter given to him by his bastard son, the Earl of Gloucester concludes that his legitimate son is a villain who seeks to conspire against him to bring about his death. Edmund pushes the unbelievability of the situation to the degree that he alleges this letter was thrown into his window in what, from a realistic point of view, must appear to be an unnecessary and inexplicable conspiratorial furtiveness. But Gloucester accepts this monstrous lie as truth; he trusts where he should suspect and suspects where he should trust. Even on Edgar, who enters almost immediately after Gloucester leaves, the villainous practices of Edmund ride easily. The tragedy of Gloucester, which will vie in intensity with Lear's, has begun.

As *Lear* sharply contrasts good and evil, knowledge and ignorance, patience and passion, so it groups the major characters according to their capacity or incapacity to reevaluate, to suffer, and to learn. Obviously, the irremediably evil ones, Regan, Goneril, Edmund, and Cornwall, do not learn. They "understand themselves" in the sense in which Iago does; they cannot comprehend that feelings and thoughts beyond egotistic desires have beauty and value. Yet, Shakespeare was never simple and schematic, and he gave at least Edmund a last-minute change of mind and perhaps of heart when, against his "nature," he tries to save Cordelia, whose death he has ordered. Yet even this seeming inconsistency helps to point up the destructive consequences of learning nothing or learning too little and too late: Cordelia is already dead. Contrasted with the wicked who refuse to learn are those characters who are sent to school: Lear, Edgar, Gloucester, and Albany. Each of them can be said to fail a test: Lear and Gloucester that of recognizing truth and falsehood, loyalty and treachery; Edgar that of courage and cowardice; Albany that of decision and indecision. Yet each of them also progresses beyond the lowest point, most spectacularly Edgar, who becomes a teacher of patience to his father and, in the end, the prosecutor and judge of the wicked. Two characters need not learn since they already possess truth and goodness, the old Kent and the young Cordelia. They represent virtue by what they are.

The learning processes, which include partial discoveries, hesitations, reversals, and (in the case of Edgar) full achievement, take on a cosmic dimension through the characters' pagan theologies. This is a subject which has been fully explored in William Elton's painstaking study,[1] but we need to examine its bearing on the theme of self-knowledge. Incontrovertibly, *Lear* is a paganized version of the same story to which the old *Leir* had given a pious Christian coloring. Jupiter, Apollo, Hecate, and Nature are invoked, but not the Christian God. As the characters, in agony and despair, in horror and awe, in anger and grief, and (rarely) in hope and joy, view themselves and others, they express their reactions by addressing the gods, invoking, questioning, rejecting, and accepting them. Thus the theologies give the characters a metaphysical extension and help to place them into psychological and philosophical categories.

But I do not think that the views the characters express about the gods detract attention from the human predicament the play depicts; they do not do so for us, and neither, I think, would they have done so for the Christians (and these, from lukewarm to orthodox, surely constituted the overwhelming majority) of Shakespeare's audience. I shall argue that—paradoxical as it may sound—the pagan climate was likely to have increased their interest in the theme of self-knowledge. In order to understand the implications of a strongly pagan treatment of a story for the theme of self-knowledge in Shakespeare's time, one should realize that the theologians, regardless of their attitude toward possible salvation for pagans, found meritorious whatever moral excellence these possessed; in fact, they found it more meritorious than the virtue of Christians, who had the guidance of the true faith. And though pagans could not know the ultimate goodness, that is, God, they could understand the springs of virtue in the human soul. Deprived of the spiritual light as they were, they were examples of how far men may go by the light of reason alone in practicing virtue. If they demonstrated self-knowledge, they could serve as exemplars for Christians, whose faith provided them with much greater incentive. Thus, the theologian Thomas Rogers explained that he had illustrated his *Anatomy of the Mind* "with many examples of heathen men, to the bettering, I hope, of dissembling Christians, which—if not by wholesome sermons of godly men, yet by the notable example of others destitute of those gifts and graces which we are adorned with—may know themselves, be ashamed of their ungratefulness, embrace virtue, and increase in godliness." [2]

Thus the pagan frame of a story could serve to give *nosce teipsum* precedence over *nosce Deum,* as I think does *Lear.* It is the merit of Professor Elton's study to have shown that *Lear* is not a play about purification leading toward salvation in a benevolent world order, as it has often been interpreted, and to have demonstrated the characters' complex relationships to the gods as well as the analogies these relationships suggest to Christian conceptions of God. But the play is not an examination of pagan religion, or an examination of religious skepticism, or an evocation of the horror of existential nothingness, although it does contain such elements or keeps them at the edges of the characters' experiences. Neither, of course, is *Lear* a sermon, although it does contain much homiletic material. And I shall not claim that it is a program for the achievement of self-knowledge; but I shall argue that it draws on such programs and that they are a major constituent element in the tragic vision imprinted on the action and the thought.

I should like to go a step further and say that the program of self-knowledge inherent in this tragic vision is humanistic in the two major, and not always compatible, senses in which the word is used for Shakespeare's period. The program is humanistic in the sense of this study inasmuch as it contains values championed by the Christian humanists; but it is also humanistic in the sense that

the way to self-knowledge is not illuminated by a theologically conceived universe that cooperates in man's plan. The *Deus absconditus*
who, according to Mr. Elton, is enthroned over Lear's England, does
not reveal his design. Some time before *Lear,* as we have noted,
Shakespeare had dissociated the search for self-knowledge from the
purposes of the universe and the dispositions of heaven. But *Lear,*
like other plays of Shakespeare, does measure men, not with a
divine measurement but with one obtained by a sympathetic and yet
firm view of humanity. Much of this measuring is done by the way
the characters are compared and contrasted with one another. Man,
in *Lear,* is as he values himself and others and is valued by them.

In *Lear,* more than elsewhere, the measuring and valuing proceeds
by way of paradoxes. The most sympathetic characters often take positions that contrast with common opinion, and they make us take their
perspective. The action itself is constructed on the pattern of a huge
paradox that tests the characters by turning them into the opposites
of what they were or appeared to be at first. A powerful king, whose
every word is a command, becomes a despised old man subjected to
the inclemencies of the weather. From the center of his kingdom, he
is thrust to its periphery; from a demigod, he plunges to being hardly
more than a naked animal. Analogous paradoxical transformations,
arising from Lear's and Gloucester's follies, are undergone by others.
The two daughters whom Lear has enriched turn against him in
boundless cruelty, and the one he has deprived and rejected becomes his last joy. Cordelia, at first Lear's most-loved daughter, then
his most hated, is, in his deprivation, his consoler and temporary
healer. Kent, the king's favorite nobleman, is made into an outlaw;
then, in disguise, he becomes the faithful companion of the king who
outlawed him. Gloucester, who like Lear is part-agent of his downfall, descends from a mighty duke to a blind old man, pursued by the
bastard son whom he has made his heir, but saved and guided by the
legitimate son whom he has disinherited. Edmund, the treacherous
bastard, becomes "the legitimate," and, at least briefly, Earl of
Gloucester. Edgar, the true and loyal son, finds himself a man without a name, a fugitive who masquerades as a crazed beggar. Yet
when all seems lost, he turns into an executor of justice who, although he cannot prevent the death of innocents, exposes the evil-
doers and brings about their punishment. This outcast of society,
Edgar, becomes in the end the ruler of England.

These outward paradoxes are associated with, and accompanied

by, inner ones. To these even critics who deny that the physical sufferings of Lear and Gloucester are accompanied by, or bring about,
ethical or religious purification react in some fashion. Although
Swinburne wanted to have nothing to do with finding atonement,
reconciliation, requital, redemption, amends, equity, explanation,
pity, and mercy in *Lear,* he saw its pessimism as carrying a paradoxical message: "Nature herself, we might say, is revealed—and
revealed as unnatural." [3] L. L. Schücking, who wished to see *Lear*
as a play of the stage only and thought the king attains few insights
in madness, yet found him a paradox: his weaknesses are comple-
ments of his strength; what makes him so majestic and powerful,
that is, his consciousness of authority and greatness, are the main
elements in the rigidity that brings about his downfall through
wrath. [4]

Swinburne responded to the paradoxical uses of "nature" in the
play, and other critics, notably Robert Heilman, have uncovered
similar language and image clusters that force statements in terms
of thematic paradoxes. As Heilman has shown massively, the method
of underlining meaning by symbols and images embraces the play;
each of these is a restatement of the central theme on a reduced scale
—a restatement that never merely repeats, but amplifies, enriches,
supports, and gives a new perspective to the central theme. [5] Thus the
paradoxes of *Lear* go beyond the Renaissance concern with rhetorical
devices; they are not merely verbal and formal like the sophistical
wit of a Berowne in *Love's Labor's Lost* or the sentential warnings
of a Lucrece to Tarquin. The paradoxes of *Lear* enter into the plot
structure, the character delineation, the thematic strands, the fiber of
thought. They are paradoxes of significance, intrinsic to a dramatic
and moral strategy that negates in order to affirm, plunges Lear into
madness to give him a sense of the human condition, deprives
Gloucester of sight to make him see feelingly, causes fools to speak
more wisely than the sane and intellectually keen, and strips those
that wear gorgeous clothes more revealingly naked than those that
have nothing but blankets to hide their skins. These thematic paradoxes turn opinion upside-down, not merely in order to prove it
wrong, but also to make us evaluate the characters' actions against a
higher truth and wisdom. In this respect, the paradoxes of *Lear*
resemble the technique of baroque artists who created a spatial
perspective by taking the viewers' eyes backward and forward from
foreground to background and from background to foreground and

who thus achieved "first negation, then strong affirmation, which gives a special illusion of release into 'distance' and 'infinity.' " [6]

In creating this perspective, which combines a most painful tragic experience with a profound ethical and metaphysical suggestiveness, Shakespeare drew on a tradition of Renaissance moral paradoxes, which in their Christian-pagan syncretism suited the particular intellectual and spiritual atmosphere of the play. The general indebtedness of *Lear* to this convention has been well recognized, and Professor Colie has sketched engagingly the paradoxical thought of the play in the context of her work on the Renaissance paradoxical tradition; [7] but in this study we shall do well to reexamine briefly the general sources of Shakespeare's patterns in order to extract the raw materials they rendered to him for the design of his tragedy.

Both the classical and the Christian traditions of self-knowledge were ingrained with paradoxes. Renaissance prescriptions of *nosce teipsum* generally pointed to Socrates's modest interpretation of the Delphic oracle's pronouncement that he was the wisest of men: he was aware of his own ignorance. And man in general was depicted in Renaissance psychology as a paradox of body and soul, of animal and spirit, as simultaneously the weakest and most conceited being, the most glorious and most abject of earthly creatures. His physical and psychic organisms were composed of antithetical qualities: hot against cold, moist against dry in his humorial constitution; animal passion against angelic reason in his soul; speculative understanding against angelic reason in his mind. He needed to realize that the stars influenced in some way his condition and action, but that his free will made him responsible for his actions. The humanistic school exercises acquainted all educated men with the Stoic paradoxes of the slavery of the supposedly free man and the freedom of the apparently enchained. And educated and uneducated alike were nourished with the biblical, particularly Pauline, paradoxes of the value of the goods of the faith as compared with the riches of the world, of the blindness of those that think they see and the foolishness of those that believe they know.

Eager collectors of the pearls of wisdom hidden in the shell of rhetorical figures as the humanists were, they gathered paradoxes from various sources, adding to them by their own ingenuity and making them subservient to their non-doctrinaire but ethically charged Christianity. They drew into this context even the paradoxes that began as rhetorical sleights of hand, the paradoxical

encomiums, that is, ironical eulogies of minute, or apparently un-
worthy, or trifling subjects. One large collection of paradoxes, some
merely clever, some seriously probing man's condition, was the
Italian humanist's Ortensio Landi's *Paradossi* (1543). It was translated, paraphrased, and augmented by Charles Estienne as *Paradoxes*
(1553). Twelve of Estienne's twenty-six paradoxes were in turn
translated into English by Antony Munday under the title of *The
Defence of Contraries: Paradoxes Against Common Opinion* (1593).
Some of these paradoxes are of the kind Shakespeare wove into
Lear: besides the ubiquitous ones that extol foolishness over wisdom
and blindness over seeing, there are those that claim the preference
of banishment to liberty, of illness to health, of scarcity to abundance,
of sterility to fertility (because of the ingratitude of children), and
(this latter paradox is merely listed, not developed into an essay) of
bastardy to legitimacy.[8]

Although the primary purpose of *The Defence* was to provide
young minds with rhetorical exercises, a secondary one, as the
Epistle to the Reader explained, was to teach that truth is a matter
of perspective:

> Even as contrary things, compared one with another, do give en-
> deavor of their value and virtue, so the truth of any matter whatso-
> ever appeareth most clearly when the different reasons against the
> same is equaled or neighbored therewith. . . . For this intent, I
> have undertaken in this book to debate on certain matters which
> our elders were wont to call paradoxes, that is to say, things con-
> trary to most men's present opinions, to the end that by such dis-
> course as is held in them opposed truth might appear more clear
> and apparent.[9]

I am tempted to think that Shakespeare read *The Defence* and was
impressed by its strategy of moral perspective before writing *Lear;*
but whether he ever saw the book or not, he was surely familiar
with the tradition it reflected.

As Professor Jorgensen has shown, there is yet another kind of
paradox that plays a very special role in *Lear,* an offshoot of the
genre of paradoxical encomiums, the praise of that subject of least apparent value, of "nothing." [10] A sixteenth-century French poet, John
Passeratti, may have started the fashion in a Latin poem, "Nihil."
An Italian, Francesco Beccuti (Il Copetta), wrote a series of prose
reflections in the same vein, *Capitolo ne quale si lodano le Nonce-*

velle. This exercise also produced an English offshoot when an E. D., variously identified as Edward Dyer or Edward Daunce, adapted the idea in a small prose pamphlet, *The Praise of Nothing* (1585). E. D.'s attempt at a comico-serious tone is not totally successful, but he does manage to collect an impressive list of the significant "nothings" on which depend all things. Central to his design is the rejection of the claim that "nothing comes from nothing." To refute this axiom is a "mean to attain to the true knowledge of God and of ourselves; of God, who, making all things for man of nothing, is preached to us by the architecture of this mighty engine of the world; of ourselves, who, being made of reasonable souls and bodies, partake of both the nature of angels and brute beasts." [11] Similar statements can be found elsewhere outside of the paradoxical genre. In the light of this commonly held belief, it is clear that Lear's "nothing will come of nothing" would have struck Shakespeare's audience as a falsehood. It is, I think, no less than a symbolic statement of Lear's *hamartia,* which consists of a gigantic lack of self-knowledge.

Because the phrase has become overlaid with commentary, it will be salutary to recall its primary meaning: Lear says that where nothing is given, that is, no declaration of love, there will be no dowry, no land. Lear's axiom is based on a hardheaded, materialistic attitude toward a world in which everything has its price. The phrase symbolizes Lear's procedure in the first scene: he metes out lands and possessions according to protestations of love he expects as a return on his own investment in his daughters. He speaks according to what he thinks is a realistic assessment of the world, of the kind of world described by the Stoic Guillaume du Vair, who says bitterly that those who wish to have honors, favors, and riches must flatter and cheat, suffer injuries, and lose their liberty: "For as the world goeth now, there is nothing to be gotten for bare nothing." [12]

However, the nothing-from-nothing phrase had a metaphysical and ethical suggestiveness. Many in Shakespeare's audience would have remembered from grammar school Persius's third satire, in which the ignorant are ridiculed who refuse to be enlightened about "what we are" and who laugh at the axiom *gigni de nihilo nihil, in nihilum posse reverti.* But the Renaissance commentators, and thus the pedagogues, proved Persius himself ignorant in this matter, and with him such materialistic philosophers as Democritus,

Epicurus, and Lucretius. The commentators opposed to them the ecclesiastical dogma that God had created the universe as well as man's
soul from nothing.[13] When Shakespeare studied Persius in grammar
school, he was very likely told that all important things came from
nothing. Besides, the antinomies of "all" and "nothing" were ingrained in the language into which he grew; they were the antipodes
to underline the eternal significances of life and death, immortality
and mortality.

Lear's "nothing will come of nothing" highlights in its context his
ignorance of spiritual and ethical values, in particular his ignorance
of the nature of the "all" that arises from man's soul. As Shakespeare's audience knew, God created that sublime essence, man's soul,
of nothing. To quote only one of the many statements, from *The
Anatomy of Sin* (1603), "When God inspired a soul into Adam, he
made a blast not of his own nature, nor the air round about him,
but even of nothing." [14] And E. D. was "persuaded that this
latter age cannot but acknowledge sundry benefits which rise of
nothing, as that which nurseth the godly in the love of virtue and
punisheth the transgressors of good laws." [15] Lear takes a squarely
materialistic attitude in a matter that concerns the most immaterial
of substances and its qualities. By contrast, Cordelia, Kent, and
France take an ethical-spiritual stance in their low opinion of material
comforts and possessions valued by the world. Cordelia is ready to
live as the nothing that paternal rejection makes her; Kent takes on
himself the nothing he must be in exile; and the King of France accepts the Cordelia who, according to Lear, is nothing without her
dowry. All three understand that some nothings must be accepted
for the sake of keeping and obtaining greater values.

France most strongly denies the truth of nothing from nothing
when he refuses to believe in Cordelia's wickedness, a belief, as he
paradoxically puts it, which would be "a faith that reason without
miracle / Should never plant in me" (222–23). The point, of course,
is that he has faith in miracles like Cordelia, a point enlarged upon
in the paradoxes in which he acclaims the ideal nothingness of
Cordelia, "most rich, being poor; / Most choice, forsaken; and most
lov'd, despis'd" (250–51). This speech suggests clearly the Pauline
attitude toward the things of this world which are "nothing" (1
Cor. 1) and toward the materially poor but spiritually rich, who,
"having nothing," yet possess all things (2 Cor. 6:10). The Genevan
sidenote to the former passage explained that the "vile things"

chosen by God are "in man's judgment almost nothing, but taken for abjects and castaways." When France accepts Cordelia in marriage and takes up, as he says, "what's cast away" (253), he shows that he understands, pagan though he is, the quality of nothing. In his contrasting ignorance, Burgundy rejects her on Lear's principle that nothing can come from nothing. This thematic use of the paradox thus points up symbolically Lear's and Burgundy's failures of self-knowledge as rooted in their inability to understand the values of the human soul, and it contrasts this ignorance with the wisdom of Cordelia, Kent, and France.

The resulting suffering of Lear and his painful and thwarted groping toward an understanding of himself and of others will be the subject of the following chapter; at present I shall turn to the subplot, the Gloucester story, a subplot unique in Shakespeare by being of an importance almost equal to that of the main plot. It is indeed possible that the idea of treating the Cordelia-Lear story tragically in contrast to the sources, where it ended happily, came to Shakespeare through the source of the Gloucester plot, the story of the Paphlagonian king in Sir Philip Sidney's *Arcadia*. For Sidney, the story was a lesson in self-knowledge, demonstrating the danger of breaking the marriage bond and with it the laws that keep man within the bounds of humanity.[16] But the story also was an example of the alleviating influence of true sympathy on suffering. Sidney's king falls prey to the deceit of his wicked bastard son, Plexirtus, who slanders the legitimate son, Leonatus, and makes his father reject him. In "wretched ungratefulness," Plexirtus has his father blinded, usurps his place, and causes him to stray helplessly through the country. In this misery, Leonatus, endowed with "true natural goodness," becomes his father's helper and guide, the king's acknowledged "glass even to my blind eyes." [17] Here was the nucleus for the moral significance of the subplot and for the seeing-in-blindness paradox, which, together with that of wisdom-in-folly, is the major structural paradox of the play.

The two paradoxes of blindness and folly were generally thought to be related. In *The Defence of Contraries,* the claim that ignorance is better than knowledge (Declamation 3) is followed by the assertion that blindness is better than sight, and both make the point that the states of deprivation entail greater wisdom and insight. Thus blindness "gives men leasure and commodity of power, at their own ease, to contemplate celestial beauties and excellencies divine." But

The Defence quickly lapses into absurdity: one of the "advantages" the blind have over the seeing is that the former "have no need of spectacles wherewith to see small things nor of eyeglasses, otherwise called barnacles, when they travel in windy weather." [18]

It is possible that this painful jest gave Shakespeare the idea of connecting, by means of the "nothing" leitmotiv, Gloucester's *hamartia* with that of Lear. As Edmund pretends to be surprised by Gloucester and alleges to have been reading "nothing," the Duke queries: "No? What needed then that terrible dispatch of it into your pocket? The quality of nothing hath no such need to hide itself. Let's see. Come, if it be nothing, I shall not need spectacles" (I.ii.32–35). Gloucester's comment plays a variation on Lear's "nothing from nothing" phrase and symbolizes, by its expression of optic myopia, his spiritual blindness. There is also an echo of Lear's materialistic interpretation of "nothing" in Gloucester's order to pursue Edgar: "Find out this villain, Edmund; it shall lose thee nothing" (I.ii.115). This charge follows immediately upon Gloucester's wholesale acceptance of judicial astrology ("These late eclipses in the sun and moon portend no good to us"), which corroborates both Gloucester's bent to credulousness, evidenced in his trust of Edgar, and his delusion of knowing all about the ways of the world.

That Gloucester thinks of himself as worldly-wise is evident from the nonchalance with which, at the opening of the play, he speaks to Kent about the pleasant faux pas that produced Edmund. Such inclination to pleasure and lust was, as Lodowyck Brysket explained, a kind of blindness:

> And this ignorance concerning the knowledge of a man's self is the cause that he [the voluptuous man] cannot tell how to use himself. For these unreasonable affections do so darken the light of reason that he is a blind man and giveth himself over to be guided, as one that hath lost the right way, to as blind a guide as himself and so wandereth astray which way soever his bad guide doth lead him.[19]

Gloucester's credulousness, which is intellectual blindness, and his sensuality, which is moral blindness, make his later loss of sight an external manifestation of his human flaws. Gloucester's blinding parallels and emphasizes Lear's madness, which in turn arises from anger (a passion that, according to the much-quoted Horatian dictum, was a "short madness"). One revolts against considering

Gloucester's blindness and Lear's madness as "punishments" because this idea seems so much like taking the part of Edmund, Goneril, and Regan; yet these afflictions have a relationship—if not in degree, at least in kind—to the nature of the follies to which they succeed. Thus Shakespeare conveyed the impression that there are sometimes cause-and-effect relationships between conduct and fate; but, by making the effects excessive, he avoided the false moral that in this world one receives exactly what one deserves.

The act of blinding, even more importantly, demonstrates the sadistic urges of those who in this world set themselves up as the judges of morality but whose hands are stained with greater vices than those whom they condemn. In its questioning of worldly justice, *Lear* recalls *Measure for Measure,* but it proceeds from a probing into an accusing mood. Gloucester's torture is the more painful and raises the greater horror because it is occasioned by his acts of sympathy for his old sovereign, when he shelters him and communicates with Cordelia's party. In this most wantonly cruel act of the play, Shakespeare demonstrated climactically the boundless cruelty of the wicked who seek to achieve the satisfaction of their egos by naturalistic self-seeking. We identify with the servant's and with Albany's horror of this unnatural act and feel that humanity so directed must at least eat up itself. We also identify, momentarily at least, with Albany's feeling that there are justicers above when the servant kills that most contemptible of villains, Cornwall.

The blindness of Gloucester, first spiritual and then actual, serves to underline the folly of Lear in wrath and in madness. The play encourages continual cross-references between Gloucester and Lear; what one of them does or experiences is in an analogous mode done or suffered by the other. Lear's rejection of Cordelia can be looked upon as a kind of ethical and spiritual blindness; the imagery of darkness and light, which accompanies the rejection, encourages the analogy. Similarly, Gloucester's failure to discern truth and falsehood is not only blindness but also foolishness bordering on madness. And as Lear's insensitivity to "nothing" extends his ignorance of himself, so Gloucester's superstition gives his spiritual myopia a cosmic dimension. It is not Gloucester but Lear who actually brings up blinding and ironically foreshadows what will happen to the duke (I.iv.301). And while Gloucester never mentions sexuality and its effects again after his initial allusion to the "sport" that went into Edmund's making, Lear is obsessed with the subject from his denunciation of Goneril—"Into her womb convey sterility . . ." (I.iv. 278 ff.)—to the terrifying Centaur speech (IV.vi.111–31), the latter being delivered in the presence of Gloucester, *homo sensualis.*

Since Lear's earlier imprecations immediately precede the threat of blinding and are a reaction to Goneril's demand that he disquantity his train, an association between ingratitude, sterility, and blindness is created. This is one of the most pervasive thematic links, and it is therefore worth noting that the same linking occurs in the paradox "that a barren woman is more happy than a bearing" of *The Defence of Contraries* (Declamation 8). With heavy irony, *The Defence* recommends sterility as "a sovereign medicine against the private malice of children" and suggests that those who wish to bear children should procure "the divine plant, called *Hermetiae,* which whosoever useth—if Democritus be not a liar—not only shall engender honest children and well disposed, but likewise fair and gracious." But, says *The Defence,* this herb may be lost, or Democritus imagined it, or dreamed of it, "after he had put out his own eyes to become thereby the better philosopher."[20] But, regardless of whether there is any influence of *The Defence* on *Lear* in this point, the Democritus exemplum serves to remind one that there were precedents for the symbolic meaning of the Gloucester story that physical blindness can mean better spiritual vision. Tiresias, Oedipus, Samson, and Saint Paul come to mind; their blindness was apt to be moralized in the Renaissance as showing that this affliction can bring about understanding and insight.

But perhaps the most relevant example was that of Tobit in the Apocrypha because it pointed a moral much like that Edgar wishes to instill in his father when he asks him to "bear free and patient thoughts" (IV.vi.80). In the words of the Genevan side-note, Tobit was "made blind as an example of patience to his posterity." As Estella put it, "By afflictions . . . assure thyself that thou shalt recover the inward sight as Tobit did by the gall of the fish."[21] The dung that deprived Tobit of his eyesight was generally interpreted to represent the filth of the world and to symbolize punishment for worldly pleasures—a parallel to Edgar's moral that "the dark and vicious place" where Gloucester begot Edmund "cost him his eyes" (V.iii.172–73). Also, Tobit's physical recovery, like the moral regeneration of Gloucester, was aided by a good son, Tobias, who, like Edgar, was believed to have been lost. Tobias's faith, symbolized by the gall of the fish, makes this miracle possible. The story was well-known; one place among many in which Shakespeare may have been reminded of it was that old Stratford building which is now the Swan Hotel. The message of the mural it harbors was not lost to him as it is to the modern tourist.

But before Gloucester can approach a pattern of patience like that of Tobit, he falls prey to the temptation of his suicide attempt at Dover Cliff, which leads to the pseudo-miracle engineered by Edgar. Shakespeare fashioned the incident from a one-sentence statement in Sidney's *Arcadia* in which the Paphlagonian king asks Leonatus to lead him to the top of a rock so he can take his life by throwing himself down, a demand that Leonatus understandably denies. Shakespeare made Gloucester take a leap; but since it is on level ground and, as a fall from height exists only in Gloucester's imagination (which is aided by Edgar's description), the incident is complex, inaccessible to realistic interpretations, and somewhat baffling in its bearing on the ethical issues.

The lesson Edgar teaches his father at Dover Cliff does not only include the jump but also what immediately precedes and what follows. It is a lesson in visual and spiritual perspective; Edgar becomes the glass to Gloucester's eyes. The elaborateness of Edgar's description of the dizzy height (IV.vi.11 ff.) goes certainly beyond what is required by the dramatic need to create for Gloucester the illusion of standing at the edge of a precipice. In a very similar description in *Cymbeline* (III.iii.11 ff.), the speaker draws the conclusion that "it is place [that is, status and rank] which lessens and sets off." In *Lear,* the moral is more subtle. At first sight, it may appear fanciful to connect Gloucester's downward look with the arguments of skeptic philosophers that the human eye fails to see things truly, that the same objects seen from different sides, or from different angles, or at different places, appear different objects— proof of the unreliability of the senses. Yet a passage in Montaigne's "Apology of Raymond Sebond" developing this topic has been plausibly claimed to have been Shakespeare's source for Edgar's description.[22] Montaigne argued that the senses can dominate a man's imagination and inspire him with such fear as he cannot counteract with his reason: even a philosopher put in a cage on top of Notre Dame could not keep his composure, "but the sight of that exceeding height must needs dazzle his sight and amaze or turn his senses." Montaigne then reported his own experiences in the Alps in words that have some resemblance to Edgar's.

But Montaigne's conclusion is perhaps of even greater interest since it makes the point of the superiority of insight over sight:

> And that we cannot, without some dread and giddiness in the head, so much as abide to look upon one of those even and downright precipices: *"Ut despici sine vertigine simul oculorum animique non possit:* So as they cannot look down without giddiness both of eyes and minds." . . . Therefore was it that a worthy philosopher pulled out his eyes that so he might discharge his soul of the seducing and diverting he received by them and better and more freely apply himself unto philosophy.[23]

Edgar, like Montaigne, will "look no more; / Lest my brain turn, and the deficient sight / Topple down headlong" (IV.vi.22–24). The deficient sight becomes associated with Gloucester's lack of moral perception. He stumbled when he saw, and he walks unsteadily even now. After the Dover Cliff episode, he will walk a little more steadily.

Gloucester's suicide attempt is an outgrowth of the pessimism and fatalism of the we-have-seen-the-best-of-our-time speech of the beginning (I.ii.100 ff.)—a speech associated with his optic and ethical blindness. Up to the moment of his leap, Gloucester believes that his fate is due to the "great opposeless wills" of the gods; in their sight, he seeks to "Shake patiently my great affliction off" (IV.vi.34 ff.). From a Christian point of view (one valid also when it came to judging meritorious pagans), Gloucester's self-knowledge fails him when he assumes his act to be a deliverance. In Brysket's words, he is like a man who is so overcome by happy or unhappy incidents that he does not realize that his passion proceeds from the nature of his mind:

> For their cowardice, who suffer themselves to be overcome by such passions, persuades them that such things happen of necessity and through the immutable order of things, and so they make themselves wittingly slaves where they were free, wanting either will or power to use that liberty of their mind, either in the one fortune or the other.[24]

The thoughts Edgar wishes his father to bear are significantly not merely "patient" but also "free" (80). The most obvious lesson of the incident is thus a rejection of the idea that suicide is permissible under certain circumstances and then constitutes a patient acceptance of the inexorable laws of the universe—an idea attributed to some extreme Stoics. Edgar teaches his father that suicide is really despair and submission to fate rather than to the will of the gods.[25] He makes Gloucester believe that his life is due to a miracle, a supernatural event that breaks the apparently unbreakable enchainment of causes. And Gloucester indeed does assume a fideistic attitude now; he thinks that the gods, who, as Edgar prompts him, "make them honours / Of men's impossibilities," have preserved him.

However, the incident is also fraught with the implications human engineering generally has in Shakespeare: it is a deceit, even though a benevolent one in the manner Thomas Wright recommended it to the "passion mover." Edgar has a faint similarity to an Iago imprinting his will on Othello by administering to him a dose of "medicine"; it is a calculated dose because it is restricted to an attempt at curing his father from his suicidal urge. Edgar does not reveal his identity to him and thus does not free him from the ignorance this lack of information entails. Why he does not do so is one of the several puzzles of the play. Perhaps he thinks his father's heart too weak to sustain this truth as, indeed, it proves to be when he reveals it to him. However, by then, this heart has been subjected to further suffering.

But whatever moral ambiguity is attached to Edgar's conduct in the episode of Dover Cliff is relieved by the irony that this incident and his subsequent guiding of Gloucester is as much or more a testing of the psychic and ethical resources of Edgar than it serves to restructure Gloucester's philosophy. Edgar cannot prevent his father from subsequently relapsing into despair and from dying in a highly uncertain state of soul—between joy and grief. And the eye-piercing sight of the meeting between the mad king and the blind earl proves almost too much for Edgar himself. He is not "stoical" like Iago, and neither is he superhuman; as he intimates later, he, too, has been tempted to take his own life (V.iii.184–86). But Edgar's general capacity for feeling and his strength to translate it into sympathetic action make him the most conspicuous learner and teacher; and, in the end, he can be said to have passed all tests. He tries to teach his father how to see "feelingly" and he keeps to the very end his awareness of the alleviating power of human emotion, asking us in the last lines of the play to say what we feel, not what we ought to say.

The transformation of Edgar from an apparently minor figure at the beginning to a dominant one at the end is one of the most

surprising dramatic developments in Shakespeare. The introduction
of Edgar by his maliciously histrionic brother—"Pat! he comes like
the catastrophe of the old comedy" (I.ii.128)—carries a strong
irony. Edgar does indeed become the medium for whatever allevia-
tion there is in the end; he provides a "comic catastrophe" at least
to the degree of bringing about the punishment of the villains and
taking the reins in his hand.

Edgar's vitality and protean role-changes give him a tremendous
vitality on the stage, but he assumes even greater significance in
thematic analysis. His various roles unite all the important paradoxes
that form the schematic pattern of the evaluation of men in *Lear*. In
playing a half-crazed beggar, he shows that foolishness is better than
arrogant knowledge, poverty better than unfeeling wealth, scarcity
better than careless abundance, and humility better than proud greatness. In his first soliloquy, he declares that he must be a near-nothing
in this world; he has become a man without a name, "the basest and
most poorest shape / That ever penury in contempt of man / Brought
near to beast" (II.iii.7–9). The pricks he puts in his bleeding flesh
manifest his physical suffering, which, like Lear's, is stifled by the
overwhelming mental pain.

Edgar tries to adjust to the "something" he has now become;
he adopts a Stoic resignation somewhat in the tenor of the paradox
"that a man ought not to be grieved though he be despoiled of his
goods and honors" (*The Defence,* Declamation 6). As he reasons
in his second soliloquy, the lowest and most dejected thing in nature
has the advantage of expecting a change for the better (IV.i.1–9).
There is a touch of Pollyannaism in this Stoic self-consolation, and
Edgar's concluding defiance of the unsubstantial air to whose blast
he owes "nothing" reads like a *hybris* in the light of the simultaneous
entrance of his blind father led by an old man. Edgar is forced to
revise his Stoicism: "The worst is not / So long as we can say 'This
is the worst' " (IV.i.27–28). Mere theory, no matter how well intended, breaks down in the inferno of life. Man must feel, suffer, and
act rather than theorize. Edgar's empathetic initiation into the
human tragedy is marked by his awe at the "mutations" of this world
(IV.i.11).

Only after being theoretically negated does Edgar's acceptance of
"nothing" prove itself in the heat of fire. He can now assume a new
and exemplary identity as a thing first to be wondered at, then to be
imitated. When his voice sounds from the tempest-shaken hovel, he

provokes Kent's amazed question: "Who's there? . . . What art
thou that dost grumble there i' th' straw?" (III.iv.41 ff.). Lear, himself at the threshold of madness, interrogates him on the reason for
his deprivation: "What, has his daughters brought him to this pass?
/ Could'st thou save nothing? Would'st thou give 'em all?". Immediately following, Lear strips himself naked in emulation to become, like Edgar, a quintessential man ("Consider him well"). And
this uncovering takes place during an identity crisis that focuses on
Edgar; Lear asks "What hast thou been? . . . What's he?", and
Kent and Gloucester join in: "Who's there? What is't you seek?
. . . What are you there? Your names?" When Lear subsequently
calls Edgar a philosopher, he is mad, but there is a touch of sanity
in this madness: if Edgar does not exactly philosophize on some of
the big questions, he poses them by what he is. He represents the
self-sufficient man, unencumbered by an adulterating civilization;
he is the incarnation of the value of "nothing."

At the crucial point of the inception of Lear's madness, Edgar thus
becomes for the old king a teacher of the essentials of nature, a kind
of Cynic philosopher. Shakespeare's contemporaries were fascinated
by this austere sect, whose insistence on frugality and the simple life
suggested *contemptus mundi* attitudes with which they were familiar;
Christian asceticism and ancient Cynicism had much in common.
Yet since the Middle Ages some theologians thought that the Cynics'
asceticism went too far and that they missed the purpose of the
effort, which was to demonstrate faith in the true God; they were
peculiar combinations of saints and madmen.

One of Lear's titles for Edgar, "good Athenian," would, for
Shakespeare's audience, have suggested the Cynic Diogenes, who
had a signal place in Renaissance moral thought. He had been put
on the stage in Lyly's *Campaspe,* where his way of life was much
like that assumed by Edgar: "A crumb for thy supper, an hand for
thy cup, and thy clothes for thy sheets. For *Natura paucis contenta"*
(I.ii.4–5).[26] Lear's other title for Edgar, "learned Theban," also has
significant associations. As has been suggested, the address most
likely would have evoked the Theban philosopher Crates, a disciple
of Diogenes, who loomed almost as large in the anecdotage of the
Renaissance as did his teacher.[27] The anecdote of Crates' throwing
his patrimony into the sea in order not to be hampered in the study
of philosophy was for Thomas Nashe an example of the contrast
between the frugal and sensible life of a true man and the luxurious-

ness and wantonness of courtiers who were intent on nothing but "the feeding of their mistress' fancy and the fostering of their lawless lusts, showing under their purple robes and embroidered apparel a heart spotted with all abuses." [28] One is reminded of the way Edgar describes his alleged career as a serving man, "proud in heart and mind; that curl'd my hair; wore gloves in my cap; serv'd the lust of my mistress' heart and did the act of darkness with her" (III.iv.84 ff.). This is the state of average sophisticated depravity Edgar asserts to have overcome in order to be the Crates of Lear. Crates's attacks on women's luxuriousness and inordinate desires would make him also the pattern for Lear in his ragings against the female sex, but the king in his madness exceeds the model in savagery.

Lear's identification of Edgar with a Cynic like Crates also gives Edgar the structural role of exemplifying the paradox that it is better to be a fool than to be wise. The titles "philosopher" and "fool" were sometimes treated as interchangeable in the paradoxical tradition. In *The Mirror of Madness* (1576), Dame Madness demonstrated that she was the "notablest philosopher" by the argument that "by reason of madness—that is to say, the matter—philosophers' books are esteemed and accounted most excellent" and that "whatever maketh a thing such, the thing whereby it is made is of necessity more such." [29] When Lear comes to mistaking Edgar for a famous philosopher, he does so according to the principle that a philosopher may look like a madman; and there is a justification in his nominating Edgar, who, feigning madness, has actually become the most notable philosopher of the play. Crates, the learned Theban, was a salient example of the wise madness of philosophers; in philosopher's madness he vied with Diogenes, whom Lyly called "a Socrates furious." As Robert Greene said in *The Debate Between Folly and Love*, "What kind of people that hath been in greater credit than philosophers, and who more fools? . . . Did not Crates in casting his treasure into the sea commit a wise deed?" [30]

The "Cynicism" assumed by Edgar and sensed by Lear becomes an important issue in the paradox that scarcity is better than abundance—an issue touched on in Gloucester's temptation and central to Lear's change of values. Lyly's Diogenes already knew that one should not give nature more than nature needs. And Nashe upheld Crates as exemplifying the axiom that "no *vestis sed virtus hominem evehit,*" and he hoped that the courtiers "would reject all superfluity" as sinful and "betake themselves to a more temperate moderation in each degree of excess." [31] Edgar's affiance to poverty makes him a catalyst for both Gloucester's and Lear's questioning of themselves on essential human needs in their struggle to gain a perspective on human life. When Gloucester gives money to his disguised son so he will lead him to Dover, he comments on the relativity of a fate that creates happiness for the poor from the wretchedness of the rich, and he commends the heavens for creating greater economic quality in this fashion (IV.i.66–72). A similar note is sounded by Lear, just before he finds Edgar, in his prayer to "naked poverty":

> Take physic, pomp;
> Expose thyself to feel what wretches feel,
> That thou mayst shake the superflux to them,
> And show the heavens more just.
> (III.iv.33–36)

On one level, this prayer is a call for greater social justice, a call of the kind increasingly being raised in England during the time of the first performances of *Lear*. Thus in *The Poor Man's Passions and Poverty's Patience* (1605), Arthur Warren asked Virtue to protect him with her "sacred providence" by not giving him too much or too little:

> Give not abundance lest I should forget
> The Giver where such surplusage I see;
> The golden mediocrity I crave
> To quit the world and me conduct to grave.[32]

But Lear's is not merely a call for social justice; it is also an anguished outcry against an unjust cosmic order. Out of Lear's suffering, questioning of necessities, and his quarrel with his gods comes a proclamation of human fellowship for the achievement of a distribution more nearly equal of the means for happiness. And yet, as I shall argue in the next chapter, our understanding of the meaning of this prayer would be incomplete without some sense of what it does for Lear's own soul.

But we must return to the major agent of this development. Edgar, who aids the others in their search for self-knowledge, also has to pursue his own quest, and strenuously so. It does not, I think, lead to a certainty of achieving self-knowledge. It does lead, of course, to success in an outward sense by his finding of himself in a significant role, a greater one, indeed, than could have been envisaged before. He resembles the traditional hero of a legend, who has lost his inheritance and suffered much, but who has won a greater gain. Thus he embodies the paradox of *The Defence* that "it is better for a man to lose his worldly estates and dignity than himself to be lost and destroyed forever." [33] But when it comes to describing what Edgar has won, internally, the skeptic reader of the play can hardly be certain. It may be said, perhaps, that he has won "ripeness," the goal that he holds out to his father when the latter falls once more into his fatalistic despair after the lost battle: "Men must endure / Their going hence, even as their coming hither: / Ripeness is all" (V.ii.9–11). But the content of this ideal ripeness is hard to define; it varies according to the perspective from which we approach it. We must think of it presumably as a concept that merges the best of paganism and Christianity, as do other of the values suggested by the play. We may say that ripeness includes a patient but not fatalistic endurance of life, an altruistic conception of man's role in the world, and a sympathy with all suffering humanity. Admittedly, this is vague; but to go much beyond it is to risk substituting one's own goals for the vaguer, but also more provocatively suggested, ideals of the play. In Edgar, Shakespeare did not portray a pattern that embodies all the wisdom self-knowledge could be made to include, but he created a dramatic character who struggles, in a particular context and under particular circumstances, for the achievement of such wisdom. It would be presuming too much to say that he achieves it; but his career implies that the struggle does avail. A man may find himself, as much as he ever can be said to, even in the naturalistic world of *Lear* when character and fortune cooperate. The success of Edgar brightens the otherwise somber and tragic ending and increases the feeling created by the play that learning how to evaluate oneself and others justly is important.

By drawing a lesson of this kind, we respond to tragedy with a moral reaction; we experience a feeling of tragic pleasure (some would call it a *catharsis*). And this is a paradoxical feeling. As Edith Hamilton has noted, our reaction to great tragedy expresses itself in the way we speak about it: we call pain, sorrow, and disaster depressing, but never tragedy; we say "lift us to tragic heights." We speak of the depth of pathos, but always of the height of tragedy.[34]

It has been the argument of this chapter that the paradoxes embedded in *Lear* have much to do with the feeling of tragic pleasure created by this greatest of Shakespeare's tragedies. These paradoxes stimulate us to seek for a meaning in life even at its most cruel. And they suggest that a way to self-knowledge may be found by applying a paradoxical perspective: we should consider the possibility that what appears to be pride is really humility, what seems weakness is really strength, what looks like foolishness is yet wisdom, and what we believe to be misfortune is beneficial to our souls; and we should ponder many similar apparent paradoxes. At the same time, *Lear* also warns us against simplifying all statements about ourselves and our situations, including paradoxical statements; it invites us to view characters, situations, and incidents from unexpected angles and to revise our opinions in the light of later insights; and it creates the hope that the whole picture eventually will become intelligible. Thus the paradoxes ingrained in *Lear* help to promote the illusion that this play is like life itself, which forces us to evaluate ourselves and our situations with whatever wisdom we are able to acquire.

King Lear:
Stripping the Self

EAR IS A KING born to command, not to ask questions. His first words give the order that the King of France and the Duke of Burgundy are to attend the ceremonious division of the kingdom. The questions Lear asks in the beginning of the play could just as well be put as imperatives. The fateful "Which of you shall we say doth love us most?" is not really an inquiry but an order to his daughters to protest their quantity of love. But love is a subject in which quality means everything, and therefore Cordelia, as she announces in an aside, will not answer a question so wrongly posed: "What shall Cordelia speak? Love, and be silent." When asked by Lear what she can say "to draw / A third more opulent than your sisters," she replies, "Nothing." This is the first unexpected answer Lear receives; unbelievingly, he asks Cordelia to repeat it. It is an answer that strikes at his value system, and similarly upsetting answers are to follow. Thus, contrary to Lear's expectation, the King of France replies affirmatively to the question whether he will accept Cordelia in marriage without dowry; he disregards the absence of a quantitative endowment because of her possession of a qualitative one, her lack of riches for her owned sincerity.

After Lear has divested himself of power, he receives a different kind of unexpected answers. Lear's questions tend to become rhetorical now, based as they are on the conception of himself as a powerful monarch and beloved father. Only the faithful Kent, banished by Lear but still ready to serve him in disguise, accepts the king on these terms. When Lear asks him, "Dost thou know me, fellow?" he answers, "No, sir; but you have that in your countenance which I would fain call master" (I.iv.27). Those that go the way the world goes do not assess Lear any longer by the authority imprinted on his face. The disrespectful Oswald answers Lear's question "Who

am I?" with the insolent "My lady's father" (I.iv.78). Lear's evil
daughters give him an identity entirely different from the one he
gives himself; they call him a weak old man who should adjust to his
age and become wise, and they do not accept his self-image of a
powerful king surrounded by a large troop of retainers. With a hint
at Lear's lack of self-knowledge, Goneril suggests that he should have
only such men around him "which know themselves and you" (I.iv.
251). Goneril and Regan apply the kind of quantitative reasoning to
their father that he had demonstrated in arranging the love protest;
they wish him to "disquantity" his train and to know himself for
what he is, that is, in measurable terms, "nothing." With a semblance
of truth on her side, Goneril asks her father to "put away / These
dispositions which of late transport you / From what you rightly
are" (I.iv.220–22). But the Fool, with his remark about the ass's
not knowing when the cart draws the horse, puts the situation in a
different perspective and induces Lear's first identity crisis: "Does
any here know me? This is not Lear. / . . . Who is it that can tell
me who I am?" (I.iv.225–29). The rhetorical questions have led to
an existential one.

The answers the others give to Lear's questions place them in a
moral scheme. Kent answers as a loyal courtier, Oswald as a time-
server and opportunist, and Goneril and Regan as ungrateful and
disloyal daughters. The valuing of the selves has begun. And with it,
Lear begins to re-evaluate. The process is speeded up but also made
more bitter for Lear by the Fool, who rubs his wounds with the
salve of truth, a simple commonsense truth in rhymes, songs, and
sayings. Lear first threatens to whip him; but he nevertheless listens
to him. When the disrespectfully treated king asks who can tell him
who he is, the Fool's ready answer, "Lear's shadow," does not
produce another threat of whipping from Lear but the relatively
gentle remark that he would fain learn why he should be a shadow
since he has daughters. The Fool becomes a teacher for Lear: "Lad;
teach me" (I.iv.138), Lear says. And so the Fool does, setting his
master to the school of men, fools, and ants.

Lear's progress in education that began with imperative questions,
to which he thought the answers self-evident but found them totally
unexpected, and continued with rhetorical questions, to which the
answers were impertinent, has led to a profoundly disturbing existential question. His educational progress will lead finally to questions on the nature of man, questions that he had never posed in his

life and of which the answers involve moral and metaphysical values. As Lear becomes unsure of his identity, he loses his certainty of the identity of men and gods. He becomes an alien in the world he once dominated, and man appears to him an alien in the world he claims to rule. In the storm on the heath, feeling no better than a naked animal and worse equipped to defy the elements, he poses his culminating question: "Is man no more than this?" (III.iv.101 ff.). As he strips himself naked, he exposes the naked self of man.

From his first question on his personal identity to this question on the identity of man, Lear follows unconsciously a program of self-examination as it was implied for the humanists in the injunction *nosce teipsum*. The general process has been well described by Professor Jorgensen.[1] Lear's is not a consistent, clearly progressive procedure, and the insights he attains are momentary and partial; they come to him at the threshold of madness, in lucid intervals, and as lightning-strokes in the night of madness. But there is yet behind them a method and a philosophy that bring to fruition the concepts in Shakespeare's earlier plays. In order to illuminate this method and this philosophy, I shall examine Lear's self-questioning by reference to a book that makes schematic and explicit what Lear does tentatively and unsystematically. This work, which has been previously mentioned, is Sir James Perrott's *The First Part of the Consideration of Human Condition* (1600). It is a slender book of sixty pages; but, in the words of its subtitle, it promises no less than "the moral consideration of man's self as what, who, and what manner of man he is."[2]

"Consideration" is for Sir James a program of the total assessment of man as a species and as an individual in relationship to everything that is under him, next to him, and above him. The program thus aims at gaining wisdom by perspective, one that comes from seeing man in the place he takes in the total picture of the universe. To consider man in this fashion means to meditate on his human, political, and divine nature and his relationship to the material and spiritual domains; it means to ask the right questions. Sir James not only poses these but also answers them unequivocally. In his scheme, all questions man must ask are subsumed under three major ones: what is man, who is man, and what manner of man is he. The answers to these questions require subsidiary questions. To know what man is, one must ask what his main components are, where he takes his origin and how he ends, and what the purpose of a life is that leads from one of these stations to the other. Perrott answers in orthodox humanistic fashion with a strong touch of *contemptus mundi:* man is primarily a soul chained to a body for a short period; his beginning and end are painful; and the in-between is short and uncertain. Only death is certain, but it also offers the hope of immortality. Sir James's second main question, who man is, requires an examination of his material condition; the state of his body, its health or sickness; the nature of his possessions, his wealth or poverty; and his worldly status, his calling, profession, and authority. The answer to this question must be given with the understanding that all these material qualities depend on the impermanent parts of man, which are inferior to those deriving from his immortal soul. To understand who man is, one must take into consideration what he is so as not to over-estimate the importance of temporal achievements. The answer to Perrott's final question, what manner of man somebody is, probes the differences in intellect, character, and temperament by which men become individuals. The doctrine of the humors and the system of the virtues are here evoked, but with a hortatory note: no inclinations, complexions, and traits must negate the demand that man fulfill his essence and be what he ought to be. That means he must search for wisdom and control the perturbations of his mind.

If the questions of *The Consideration* are used as a standard test for humanistic self-examination, as, I believe, they can be, they show how woefully deficient the early Lear is in self-knowledge. In the first scene of the play, the king fails all three questions. His "nothing can come of nothing" shows that he does not know *what* man is, that is, he does not know his origin. Truth and Scripture, as Perrott explained, said "that the world was made of nothing . . . and of this nothing, made something, was man at the first created, as Holy Writ doth testify; for he was made of no other mould than of the dust of the earth, a weak and slender beginning for a high and haughty mind, but most fit to set forth the great might of the almighty creator" (p. 11).

But Lear also shows immediately that he does not know *who* he is because he is unmindful of the warning given to the great of the earth:

> If thou be noble-born, then commonly pride and presumption catch hold and lay such violent hands on thy will, thy affection, and thy understanding that they can hardly be removed from thee till they have removed thee from the knowledge of thyself, who thou art.

For thy presumptuous pride and self-liking affection will make thee believe that thou art much better than indeed thou art. (p. 29)

Obviously, Lear is also ignorant of *what manner of man* he is. His anger against Cordelia and Kent, instances of the wilfullness that, according to Regan, has always been characteristic of him, violates the postulates of self-control and wisdom; Kent's calling him mad and foolish punctuates his temperamental and intellectual weakness. Lear is of the choleric temperament that Perrott, in the wake of the physicians, describes at length; his anger is of the kind *The Consideration* warns of as against reason when a man is angry with himself "because he cannot do that which he would or cannot have that which he desireth, being things either impossible or unprofitable to be performed, or else unlawful or unmeet to be desired" (p. 58).

Goneril, who is blind to the larger aspects of Lear's lack of self-knowledge because they have an affinity to her own, yet recognizes the physical component of Lear's self-ignorance, his excess of choler; in conformance with the humors theory, she predicts that he will grow more wrathful with increasing age. And it appears that her prediction will be fulfilled as the king's wrath waxes in volume and intensity until in the storm he vies with the raging elements. This anger expresses itself against all kinds of persons and objects; it assumes the spectrum analyzed in *The Consideration* according to which there are five shades: the anger of man against himself, of man against man, of man against God, of man against inferior beings, and of man against things without life (pp. 57–58). And Lear's anger explodes into madness, as Perrott warned unprofitable and unmeet anger would. But, and here Shakespeare's portrayal differed from that of Perrott, Lear's wrath is also an impetus to self-discovery. It has, perhaps, an element of what the theologians called "just anger"; at any rate, Lear's questions ride on a tide of wrath, and as it rises, advances his progress not only toward madness but also toward self-awareness. Lear does not gain whatever self-knowledge he acquires primarily through an intellectual process, but through a predominantly volitional and emotional one. In his baroque plays, as we have had occasion to observe, Shakespeare presented men not as beings whose pysche can be divided into neat categories but as dynamic organisms in whom intellectual and emotional powers are inextricably mixed.

After Lear meets with neglect and disrespect, his questions are as much outcries as inquiries. His reactions are generally much more vehement than the situation warrants; until Goneril and Regan exclude Lear from shelter in the storm, they show themselves as egotistic and callous, but not as the cruel monsters Lear calls them and they later turn out to be. Yet from his excessive anger about lack of respect come Lear's first questions about his identity: "Who am I, sir?" "Who can tell me who I am?" This is not as yet a serious inquiry, and the answer he receives serves as much to increase his irritation as his curiosity. From anger with himself and others, Lear turns to attacking the gods and their injustice and what Perrott calls "things without life"; in the storm, he curses the raging elements, to whom he feels enslaved, as "servile ministers" of his ungrateful daughters. Yet with his increasing irrationality comes also an advance in the kind of questions he asks about man; from questions that fall under Perrott's "who is man" category, he proceeds to those of the "what is man" type: "Is man no more than this?" "Is there any cause in nature that make these hard hearts?" "What, art mad? A man may see how this world goes with no eyes."

Lear never explicitly asks Perrott's third question, what manner of man he is; but he begins to answer it, together with the "what is man" question, in the storm. His ignorance about this latter subject was directly responsible for his outbreak of anger against Cordelia and Kent, and it appears now to him that the question he did not ask himself is being demanded of him by the raging elements that arrogate to themselves the roles of judges by joining with his two pernicious daughters: "Here I stand, your slave, / A poor, infirm, weak, and despis'd old man" (III.ii.19–20).

But, as much as he approaches an answer to the question of what manner of man he is, he lacks the humility a man must have who knows who and what he is. Defiantly, he wrestles with his gods, and they keep silent. And when he calls himself "a man / More sinn'd against than sinning" (59–60), self-pity is in his voice. Just as it is not Edgar's theorizing about misfortune but his empathy with his father that takes him a step further, so it is Lear's genuine concern for the welfare of the Fool, a concern that grows out of his own deprivation, which advances his reeducation. As the Fool feels cold, so does Lear; it is his first altruistic emotion. The last step in Lear's progress to the answer of what manner of man he is comes much

later, in the lucid interval when he kneels before Cordelia and
acknowledges humbly:

> I am a very foolish fond old man,
> Fourscore and upward, not an hour more nor less;
> And, to deal plainly,
> I fear I am not in my perfect mind.
>
> (IV.vii.60–63)

For an audience that was acquainted with the general method of
self-examination implied in the Renaissance injunction of *nosce
teipsum,* there were implications in what Lear says that we are apt
to miss. The Renaissance attitude toward self-knowledge was, for
one thing, determined by the basic postulate to understand the nature
of body and soul, of matter and spirit, and of their relationship. In
the first scene of the play, Lear showed his ignorance of these
fundamentals. His "nothing from nothing" axiom denies the existence of a spiritual realm in which the greatest somethings come
from nothing. Lear is ignorant of the love that arises from the soul.
But it turns out that he does not even realize what the axiom means
in the limited, material field to which it applies. In a world in which
physical nature reigns, such as the world of Goneril and Regan,
nothing comes from nothing: where there is no power there is no
respect and authority. The Fool, with his needling, childish songs
and commonplace wisdom, drives home this lesson:

> Can you make no use of nothing, nuncle?
> *Lear.* Why, no, boy; nothing can be made out of nothing.
> *Fool.* [To *Kent.*] Prithee tell him, so much the rent of his land
> comes to.
>
> (I.iv.130–32)

And again:

> Now thou art an O without a figure. I am better than thou art now:
> I am a fool, thou art nothing. [To *Gon.*] Yes, forsooth, I will hold
> my tongue; so your face bids me, though you say nothing.
>
> (192–94)

Lear gradually learns what it is to be materially nothing; he is
taught a lesson about the physical needs of the body. This initiation

into wisdom is quite in agreement with his nature; from the beginning he has a strong sense for, one might say even an obsession with, the physical nature of man. He severs, for instance, his ties with Cordelia by disclaiming his "propinquity and property of blood" in her (I.i.113). In his horror about Goneril's ingratitude, he calls her a disease in his flesh and prays to nature to make her womb sterile (I.iv.278). But Lear has to realize that he shares this property of blood with all humanity, that, to speak with Sir Thomas Elyot, a gentleman and a carter are made of the same clay.[3] And he learns. As in the storm he is subjected to deprivation, he experiences on his own body what *The Praise of Nothing* calls "the affinity . . . between nothing and the poverty of men." Poverty, says the author of this tract, is "necessary for the knowledge of ourselves that are by the contrary most insolent and intolerable."[4] The suffering Lear acquires an empathy with his fellow sufferers, with the naked Edgar and with the houseless poverty of other poor wretches. He feels now the same needs that others have, the basic needs of human beings badly equipped for the struggle with nature.

Lear's concern with the needs of nature points from the physical to the psychic realm and is foreshadowed earlier in the play. When Goneril and Regan dispute Lear's idea about his need of retainers and Regan bests her sister in asking him why he wants even one attendant, Lear reacts with the outcry, "O reason not the need!" If one allows nature no more than nature needs, he lectures her, man's life is as cheap as that of a beast and her gorgeous clothes are therefore superfluous. Rage makes him choke in the middle of this disquisition, and he realizes that he too has needs: "patience, I need" (II.iv. 270). Although Lear appears to be thinking here only of the necessity of controlling himself, he touches on one of the most basic permanent psychic needs the moralists of Shakespeare's age proclaimed. To quote two of the *Disticha Catonis* by which Shakespeare was introduced to this postulate early in grammar school:

> The commodity of nature thee never faileth
> If thou be content with that that need requires.
> If thou be in poverty, see patiently that thou take it,
> And think how, into the world, you came all naked.[5]

Lear is in the process of learning a lesson on the physical and moral needs of man, of which patience is one of the greatest, and that

presumably makes him feel darkly in his madness that he is no longer
a mere learner, but can be now a teacher of patience to Gloucester:
"Thou must be patient" (IV.vi.179). Gloucester has been deficient
in patience, but it is Lear who has the greatest need.

It is through the inquiry into physical needs that Lear advances
most toward self-knowledge. In agreement with the moralists'
program of self-consideration, Lear probes both theoretically and
practically the essential nakedness of man. When the boundless
cruelty of man makes him the equal of the lowest of mankind, he
defiantly rejects his coverings as symbolic of all the trappings of the
civilization he has come to loathe. This moment is emphasized by his
most dramatic gesture in the play, his stripping himself naked. He
thus imitates Edgar, his quintessential man. The speech that accompanies Lear's gesture is his last clearly sane one before he mis-
identifies Edgar as a philosopher; in it, he gives the needs-of-nature
theme its most pessimistic accent: man's life is as cheap as a beast's
but it is more miserable, and man, natural man, is worse equipped to
cope with his condition than an animal:

> Is man no more than this? Consider him well. Thou ow'st the worm
> no silk, the beast no hide, the sheep no wool, the cat no perfume.
> Ha! here's three on's are sophisticated! Thou art the thing itself:
> unaccommodated man is no more but such a poor, bare, forked
> animal as thou art. Off, off, you lendings! Come, unbutton here.
>
> (III.iv.104–8)

Pessimistic as Lear's assessment of the physical condition of man
is, it is quite in the tradition of humanistic self-consideration, which
had pagan as well as Christian precedents. These are amply rehearsed
by Perrott, according to whom a man wanting to know what he is
must first answer the question of "what thou art in thy conception
and natural constitution." And here one must start with the body
and consider it in comparison with the animals—the passage is worth
quoting at some length:

> But if thou wilt enter farther into the consideration of thy natural
> constitution of body after thou art born, thou shalt find that, as thou
> art born naked, so thou dost still of thyself remain naked, having
> by nature no other covering or any defense save only thy bare body,
> but that thou dost borrow helps of other creatures, which thou ac-
> countest but as base and vile. For thou clothest and keepest thyself
> warm with the garments made of wool, being but the covering of

silly sheep; with skins, the natural garments of brute beasts; thou
deckest thyself with silk, being but the excrements of poor worms.
. . . all which the needy, naked man doth borrow of beasts and of
other creatures to cover, to maintain, and to adorn his weak and
all-wanting body. But thou, not being content to use the help of
those natural creatures, for the supply of thy natural defects, dost
yet therewith take occasion to be proud, like the beggar, who, having borrowed a new coat, should therewith presently fall into liking
of himself and scorn all the rest of his fellow beggars. So doth the
naked unconsiderate man borrow, of birds, feathers; of beasts,
skins, wool, with other coverings. . . . And, having all these helps
not of himself but of other creatures, he useth them as instruments
to increase his pride rather than to sustain his necessities.

(pp. 12–13)

Perrott's contrasting comparison of man and animals derives from
Pliny.[6] Shakespeare, it has been suggested, read it in a passage of
Montaigne, beginning, "Truly when I consider man all naked." [7] It
might be noted, however, that Perrott's version of the commonplace
has equivalents for the "worm," "sheep," and "hide" of Shakespeare's
version, but Montaigne does not; Perrott, it is true, lacks an
equivalent for "perfume," which Montaigne has. In this as in other
significant statements of man, Shakespeare, just like Perrott and
Montaigne, seems to have made his own commonplace from various
sources of the particular *topos*. These, besides Pliny, included a
biblical-theological tradition of consideration in which to "consider"
is the key word, deriving from Hebrews 2:6: "What is man that
thou shouldst be mindful of him? or the son of man that thou
wouldst consider him!" (Genevan only; Bishops has "thou visitest
him.") The likening of man's condition to beasts comes from a related passage, Ecclesiastes 3:18–19: "I considered in mine heart
the state of the children of men that God had purged them; yet to
see too they are in themselves as beasts. For the condition of the
children of men and the condition of beasts are even as one condition
unto them. As the one dieth, so dieth the other; for they have all one
breath, and there is no excellence of man above the beast; for all is
vanity." When Lear says to Edgar—it is this sentence that sets him
off on his consideration of man—that he were better in his grave, he
refers to this temporal condition of man.

This condition was deeply probed in the *contemptus mundi* tradition and in the new naturalism of the later sixteenth and earlier
seventeenth centuries, which borrowed some of its colors from tradi-

tional Christian pessimism. "Let man then, with tears, consider whereof he is made, what he doth and what he meaneth to do" is George Gascoigne's rendering of one of the first sentences of Pope Innocent's *De Humanae Miseriae Conditione.*[8] Pierre Boaistuau's *Theatrum Mundi,* a later product of this tradition, "considered" man very similarly, repeatedly using this key word. In one passage it serves to introduce the same Plinian commonplaces used by Shakespeare:

> Now therefore—having well considered the universal state of man —it is requisite to make a most ample discourse of this matter and to contemplate man more near, to the end that he learn to humble himself under the hand of his God. . . . among all the heathen, Pliny, as me seemeth, hath most worthily philosophied of our nature. . . . Let us consider a little, saith he, how it behooveth a man to cover his body at the dispensation of beasts, who, being favorable of their natural liberality, bring even from the belly of their dams some, feathers; others, hair, skin, scales; and others, wool.[9]

Thus, to sum up this discussion of the general sources of Lear's consideration-of-man speech, it uses a pagan's, that is, Pliny's images on the physical insufficiency of man, images that were thought appropriate for illustrating Christian ideas. When Lear asks the question whether man is no more than this, he introduces a familiar *topos,* which he labels by exhorting himself to "consider" man well. This prefix was expected in a pessimistic account of the material condition of man, just as Hamlet's "what a piece of work is a man" was expected to introduce a balanced assessment of man, body and soul. As a statement on the *teipsum* that is the body, Lear's consideration exposes, according to approved recipes, the naked self of man. And the presence of Edgar, as we have noted, makes the consideration of what man is into an object lesson.

In terms of self-search, Lear's stripping on the heath can be said to lead only to a partial discovery. It might even be said that in seeing himself as animal-like, he approaches the naturalistic basis from which Edmund proceeds. But that would be stressing the mere outward likeness; there are indications, as in his struggle for patience even when it ironically highlights his impatience ("I will be the pattern of all patience; I will say nothing"), that Lear reaches toward a higher wisdom.

According to humanistic prescriptions of self-knowledge, Lear could not be said to have attained a sufficient perspective unless he gained some understanding of the nature of the soul. Virtuous pagans were expected to realize the immortality of the soul and its role in the achievement of human happiness. If Lear's questioning is to bear fruit in the sense in which the moralists thought it should, his concern with the flesh must lead to an understanding of the nature of the soul and its relationship to the body. The full spiritual significance of these matters could hardly be revealed to a pagan like Lear, but even pagans could attain good parts of this knowledge. Aristotle had developed theories about the natural soul that were approved of, and Plato, Cicero, and others had anticipated Christians in understanding the immortality of this divine essence.

I think it can be shown that Lear does concern himself in a dim, tentative way with his soul, and that this concern is the most subtle and allusive part of Lear's quest for self-knowledge. In the same sense in which Lear's initiation to poverty can be said to be the beginning of his understanding of the nature of the flesh and the body, his realization of what it is to be ill is the key to his understanding of the soul. That affliction and sickness could promote such knowledge was often noted by moralists. As Thomas Rogers said, "Sickness is necessary to bring a man to the mindfulness of himself when health hath brought forgetfulness. . . . Plato is reported never to have favored philosophy before sickness made him to know himself." [10] And *The Defence* illustrated by this notable example the paradox "That it is better to be sick than always healthful" (Declamation 10) :

> Plato, the philosopher, because he felt himself strong and overmighty in nature to follow his study as he ought, chose for his place of abiding a watery, marshy ground, a discontented air, where heaven showed none other but dark and pitchy clouds, that thereby he might become sick and so have means to refrain the tedious and perilous assaults of the flesh wherewith he felt himself sometimes pricked and moved. For his advice was that a good mind could not flourish if first of all the flesh was not overmastered.[11]

Lear demonstrates early in the play an interest in illness, conceiving it as a dominance of the flesh; but later in the storm, suffering grievously in his own body, he contradicts this explanation with one that more nearly approaches that of *The Defence*. When— this is the first instance—Cornwall refuses to receive him, the old man protests furiously that as a king and father he deserves better treatment, but then he seeks to excuse the earl by what he thinks he knows of physical matters:

> May be he is not well.
> Infirmity doth still neglect all office
> Whereto our health is bound; we are not ourselves
> When nature, being oppress'd, commands the mind
> To suffer with the body.
>
> (II.iv.103–7)

Although this may seem a simple statement, it touches on the much-discussed problem of the interaction of body and soul, and it does so in highly technical language. There were, one might say, two divergent attitudes: that of Aristotle and the Aristotelians, according to which the body influences the mind; and that of Plato and the Stoics, supported by *The Defence,* according to which the mind must reject such influence. The wording of Lear's excuse reflects these two attitudes though siding with Aristotle. From Plato comes the idea that "nature commands the mind" (although the Platonic "nature" commands the mind to control the body rather than to suffer with it). As George Gascoigne translated (without acknowledgment) the well-known passage from *Phaedo* (86 A), "The body and the mind being in one, nature doth yet command the body to be governed, to serve, and to be subject. But it commandeth the mind or the soul to rule and bear dominion." [12] Lear uses the first part of this statement, that nature commands the mind, but he disregards the Platonic injunction that the mind should rule the body. Instead, he finishes his explanation by borrowing from the Aristotelian (or, as it is now assumed, pseudo-Aristotelian) *De Physiognomica.* This work begins with a sentence that John Woolton translated as follows:

> For there is such a sympathy between the body and soul that the inclination of the soul followeth the constitution of the body and is affected with the motions thereof, as it may be evidently seen in gluttony, drunkenness, and diseases of the body, when the mind is oppressed with dullness and sorrow. [13]

On the following page, Woolton paraphrased "sympathy" as "compassions and suffering of the soul and body together," a phrase that resembles Lear's "the mind to suffer with the body." Clearly, Lear's words show Shakespeare's knowledge, in whatever way acquired, of the psychological terminology that goes back to Plato and Aristotle.

But the point is not that Lear is accurate in his terminology, nor even that the application of the Aristotelian doctrine of the sympathy of body and soul to Cornwall is quite meaningless, since Cornwall is not physically ill—like Regan and Goneril, of course, he does suffer from a worse illness, that of the soul. The point is rather that Lear before the storm signally stresses the physical above the psychic and spiritual elements, and that Aristotle's conception of the soul as a physically oriented phenomenon was, to the moralists, one-sided. Brysket explained that

> Aristotle in his books *De Anima* spoke of the soul as she was nat-
> ural and the form of the body, performing her operations together
> with the body, and as she was the mover of the body and the body
> moved by her, but not as she was distinct or separate from the
> body. And right true it is that, while she is tied to the body, she
> cannot understand but by the means of the senses; but, that being
> free and loosed from the body, she has not her proper operations,
> that is most false.[14]

Lear could hardly be expected to realize the freedom of the soul in its immortality, the sense in which Brysket uses the word "free"; but it is significant that in the storm he discovers the distinctness and separateness of the soul in a way that directly contradicts what he said at Cornwall's door—an indication that he has, in the words of *The Defence,* "overmastered the flesh." Exposed to the elements, but yet suffering even more cruelly mentally, Lear learns how much worse psychic pain is than physical torture. His mental strain reaches such intensity that it all but obliterates his physical discomfort. In raging with the elements, he denies what he said about Cornwall and proclaims the dominance of the mind:

> Thou think'st 'tis much that this contentious storm
> Invades us to the skin; so 'tis to thee,
> But where the greater malady is fix'd
> The lesser is scarce felt. . . .
>   When the mind's free
> The body's delicate; the tempest in my mind
> Doth from my senses take all feeling else,
> Save what beats there.
>   (III.iv.6–14)

Sir John Davies said similarly, "when the body's strongest sinews slake, / Then is the soul most active, quick, and gay." [15] And Lear's advocacy of the hegemony of the soul is the same Platonic one as in Tommaso Buoni's *Problems of Beauty and All Human Affections* (trans. 1606), where the body-soul interactions are discussed in a series of "problems" (numbers 101–7). Buoni asked and tentatively answered such questions as why the grief of the body is communicated to the mind, and the grief of the mind to the body, and why grief in general is "more sensible and violent in soft and delicate bodies." And, again apropos of Lear, Buoni asked in problem 103: "Why are the griefs of the mind far greater than those of the body?" What Buoni took for granted, Lear discovers through suffering.

A recognition of the immortality of the soul might have come next in Lear's discovery, but Shakespeare did not provide it, or, he did not quite provide it. However, I believe that Lear's prayer on the heath does have some intimations of immortality, that is, some indications in the wording and the imagery that he dimly feels the soul's immortality. He approaches the notion through a widening of his sympathies, through a realization that there is something in others, even in the lowest of mankind, that deserves protection and help. The boundless cruelty of those from whom he had most right to expect gratitude frees him from the human and social limitations of his position, from the arrogance into which he grew and which was fed by the flattery around him. When the winds in their fury catch his white hair and make "nothing" of it, he experiences the paradox of nothing, of being nothing in the eyes of the world, but yet being much better than he was before. He becomes the equal of the lower, suffering part of mankind; he feels the needs of others. He urges Kent and the Fool to enter the protection hovel first, quite contrary to the order of rank of which Shakespeare's audience was more conscious than we are. Gloucester, interestingly, makes a similar altruistic gesture and directly associates it with the care of the soul when he asks that clothes be given to the almost naked Edgar: "And bring some covering for this naked soul" (IV.i.45). And Gloucester, like Lear, follows his act with a prayer for a better distribution of commodities.

Lear's prayer, at first sight, seems to be lacking any indication that he seeks for a spiritual meaning, addressed as it is to physical needs and to the establishment of social justice. But the first part of the prayer contains some subtle spiritual notes:

> Poor naked wretches, wheresoe'er you are,
> That bide the pelting of this pitiless storm,
> How shall your houseless heads and unfed sides,
> Your loop'd and window'd raggedness, defend you
> From seasons such as these?
>
> (III.iv.28–32)

For an audience brought up on the Bible, as the Jacobeans were, this house-garment imagery would surely have provided an intimation that Lear is groping his way toward an understanding not merely of the body but also of the soul. In 2 Corinthians 5 : 2–5, Paul described naked man as sighing for being "clothed with our house, which is from heaven." Elizabethan moral literature accustomed Shakespeare's contemporaries to associate house-garment metaphors with the body, the earthly house and covering of the soul, and with heaven, its ultimate home and garment. These were metaphors that, with warnings against luxury, must have sounded from many an Elizabethan pulpit.[16] Although Lear's prayer has no explicit Christian reference, it uses evocatively a traditional religious imagery associated with the soul and thus makes Lear's prayer significant not only in his struggle for social justice but also for a greater awareness of the needs of his soul.

Lear must, after all, seek to establish his own measure of the soul, as he must seek to gauge the depth of hell and the distance of heaven; he is not in the possession of Perrott's reassuring handbook. His probing of these outer limits is beyond the confines of this study. But we may touch, at least for a moment, on the awesome Centaur speech, which has implications not only for Lear's hell but also for that of man in general. It is a mad speech, with its virulent attack on the lasciviousness of women and their simpering hypocrisy, and, most of all, with the reference to that hell beneath their girdle— that "sulphurous pit— / Burning, scalding, stench, consumption" (IV.vi.128–29). The vivid image suggests that this hell has always been a disturbing reality in Lear's imagination; the ounce of civet he asks now to sweeten it is an ironically inadequate means. Lear, it appears, has never been able to love wisely either paternally or sexually (but to be wise and love exceeds man's might). What the speech may imply about Lear's earlier sexuality or his conception of heaven and hell we can only guess; as Lear is raving, we can be sure only that it is a continuation, in a more strident key, of the crusade against the flesh that he began when he was still sane.

We are on safer, more conventional *nosce teipsum* grounds when Lear probes the condition of man between birth and death—what man is. In the voice of the preacher, he harangues Gloucester:

> Thou must be patient; we came crying hither.
> Thou know'st the first time that we smell the air
> We wawl and cry. I will preach to thee. Mark.
> *Glou.*   Alack, alack the day!
> *Lear.*   When we are born, we cry that we are come
> To this great stage of fools.

(IV.vi.179–84)

Shakespeare here has Lear turn a simple moral commonplace into a reason-in-madness lesson on the wisdom that comes from seeing mankind in perspective. Lear's "text" is biblical, one often quoted by the moralists to illustrate what man is by his natural condition: "And when I was born, I received the common air and fell upon the earth, which is of like nature, crying and weeping at the first as all the others do. . . . For there is no king that has any other beginning of birth. All men have one entrance unto life and a like going out" (Wisdom 7:3–6). Lear's metaphor of the world as a stage, a Renaissance *topos*, evolves naturally from the biblical figure of the entrance and exit of life. If the actors on Lear's stage are fools, so were they for Erasmus's Stultitia: "Good Lord, what a theater is this world? How many and diverse are the pageants that fools play therein." [17] Lear's, like Stultitia's, is a peculiar perspective on life, but one that has analogues in the moral literature concerned with self-knowledge. Pierre Boaistuau, for instance, explained at length in his Preface that men, born naked and crying, develop many different roles for themselves in the theater of life until death comes and "maketh an end of this bloody tragedy. . . . And then the Lord that is in Heaven laugheth at their foolish enterprises and vanities—as the Prophet David witnesseth—but with such a dreadful laughter that he maketh us quake for fear and the earth to shake." [18] What looks like a tragedy from below is a comedy, albeit a bitter one, when seen from above as by Boaistuau's God. And the mad Lear forcefully tries out the divine perspective.

Only for one short moment does Lear's vision of truth become sane and strong, in the fourth act, as he awakens from the curative sleep imposed upon him by the doctor. Lear is on the rack of this tough world; he feels as if he came out of a grave and were bound

upon a wheel of fire. As he dimly sees Cordelia before him, he thinks
of her as "a soul in bliss." And when she asks him the identity
question, "Sir, do you know me?" Lear answers, "You are a spirit,
I know. / Where did you die?" (IV.vii.48–49). He is in the
twilight zone between sanity and insanity; he is still "far wide,"
as Cordelia says, but he is also never closer to the truth. Man is but a
soul or a spirit and that divine creature is most poignantly one.
Lear's visionary insight is accompanied by a new and true humility,
in which he kneels and confesses to be a foolish, fond old man. For a
moment, a precious moment, Lear knows—or, better, feels—who,
what, and what manner of man he is. This is his *anagnorisis* and the
summa epitasis of the play.

    In its inward turn, Lear's anagnorisis is a much less intellectual
process than the self-recognition of Perrott's *Consideration*. Of all
those in Shakespeare's plays, it is the most dream-like and precarious. It demonstrates Shakespeare's turn toward fideism, a turn
that also agreed with the baroque tendency to see the strongest kind
of experience as an emotional condition. Of the descriptions of states
of the soul by Renaissance moralists and physicians, Lear's self-
discovery approaches most that of the supersanity of a trance. In such
a state, the soul was said to rely on its "inward sense" with little
help from the outer ones. As Sir John Davies put it, the soul sees
with "a power above the senses." [19] Timothy Bright argued that this
state was an anticipation of the separation of soul and body. The soul
could also experience this anticipation in some dreams that are "a
kind of ecstasy or trance and separation of the soul from this bodily
society, in which it hath been in old time instructed of God by
revelation and mysteries of secrets revealed unto it, as then more fit
to apprehend such divine oracles than altogether enjoying awake the
corporal society of these earthly members." [20]

    If the diagnosis be accepted that Lear's self-recognition is an
initiation into a "mystery of secrets" in the sense that Lear's soul
intuitively grasps its needs and experiences the value of goodness,
something can also be said in explanation of the state of his soul when
he sinks into madness again, without attributing to him either a
blabbering idiocy or a vision of an impending salvation for himself
and Cordelia. As Lear and Cordelia are led captive onto the stage,
the latter asks whether they shall now see "these sisters and these
daughters," and Lear shrinks from the evil reality. The fourfold
"no," which anticipates the fivefold "never" just before his death, be-

trays his desire to cling to his happy vision. He would rather withdraw to the prison as to a birdcage and warble, birdlike, an escapist
dream :

> No, no, no, no! Come, let's away to prison.
> We two alone will sing like birds i' th' cage.
> When thou dost ask me blessing, I'll kneel down
> And ask of thee forgiveness; so we'll live,
> And pray, and sing, and tell old tales, and laugh
> At gilded butterflies, and hear poor rogues
> Talk of court news; and we'll talk with them too—
> Who loses and who wins; who's in, who's out—
> And take upon's the mystery of things
> As if we were gods' spies; and we'll wear out,
> In a wall'd prison, packs and sects of great ones
> That ebb and flow by th' moon.
>
> (V.iii.8–19) [21]

Lear's speech has an almost surrealistic quality. The curious idea of
singing with Cordelia like birds in a cage hints that for Lear the
prison will be the house of madness from which even laughing at
gilded butterflies can bring no deliverance; Lear craves in vain for
the happiness of a bird. But there is still a soft echo of his former
search for more important goals. The prison or cage was after all
the conventional symbol of the body that fettered the soul—it is so
in Richard's speech at Pomfret Castle—and birds were symbolic of
the imprisoned soul. There is, for instance, a plethora of such images
in Thomas Walkington's *The Optic Glass of Humors* (1606), in
which the body is described as a "darksome cage" and the soul as
"not so blind as a bat; yet is it like an owl," and, freed from its
prison, like "a high-soaring eagle." [22] For Palingenius, the soul,
"Like as the goldfinch while in cage, her doleful destiny / With
sundry sorts of pleasant tune doth seek to pacify." [23]

When Lear would like to beguile his time in this bird-like existence
by taking upon himself and Cordelia "the mystery of things," the
irony between his expectation and the hope of its fulfillment appears
overwhelming. I doubt that the words have blasphemous overtones,
as Professor Elton suggests; [24] Lear is not concerned with an over-
curious inquiry, thought unlawful by some, into the mystery of
nature. It is more natural to associate this wish with his happy,
dream-like state at his reunion with Cordelia. In dreams, said John

Davies of Hereford, the soul often "doth wakeful thoughts conceive, / Making the mind beyond itself to spy" [25]—an analogue that serves Davies to support the legitimacy of visionary experiences of the soul. Whatever the mystery is Lear seeks to spy into, it is clear that in its permanence it contrasts with the pseudo-achievements of "packs and sects of great ones / That ebb and flow by th' moon." There is a hint here of Lear's desire to leave the world of mutability for the higher regions above the moon. Palingenius, speaking about the soul in the prison of the body, asked his readers to "mind these mysteries I tell: / All things are good and never fade above the moon that dwell." [26] But Lear cannot fly to this region; he must live below the moon where all is "naught and ill." Just when Lear appears to be at the point of establishing a saving intercourse with his true self, madness irrevocably engulfs him. His desire to learn of "the mystery of things" is merely a pathetic echo of his former search for self-knowledge.

His last entrance with the dead Cordelia in his arms is heartbreaking, and one wishes with Kent that one might let him pass and vex not his ghost. Surely no futher revelation of either self-knowledge or divine knowledge can be read into his speeches. He has passed beyond them. Neither Gloucester nor he dies into love, joy, or knowledge. Gloucester's heart breaks in a conflict it is too weak to sustain. If one took the usual position of Renaissance moralists, one might call his death a warning against excessive joy as well as grief. But that would be mere pedantry. The ending is stark, tragic—an apocalyptic vision that conjures up an image of the end of a decaying world. Lear tortures himself as much with the vain hope that Cordelia may be alive as with the conviction that she is "dead as earth" (V.iii.261). Why a dog, a horse, a rat should have life and Cordelia no life at all is finally unanswerable. Lear's despair is cosmic, and his five-times repeated "never" denies any consolation. Whatever he may see on Cordelia's face when he utters his final "look there," even if it were a sign of life or an escaping breath, does not matter; it is at best an illusion; at worst, the reality. In either case, our normal reaction is to feel heartbroken that now, when he has fathomed the value of Cordelia, he cannot live with her. His final pathetic request, "Pray you undo this button," recalls in ironic contrast his earlier defiant divesture of his clothes in the storm. Once he could strip the self of man; now he has to seek help to breathe more easily.

What this starkly tragic ending does to the meaning of the play is a much-debated question. Perhaps no universally valid answer can be given; we are addressed here too personally and individually. We may say with Kent—and it appears to be the first and most natural reaction—that all is cheerless, dark, and deadly. Or we may say something similar by quoting Gloucester's earlier words that men are like flies to the gods, who kill them for their sports. Certainly, if one is affected by this play at all, he cannot come away from it "feeling good" about man and his place in the scheme of things. But somehow, an unlimited pessimism is an incomplete reaction to the ending and to the play; taking this attitude means accepting the point of view of a character who has grown prematurely old in his sympathetic suffering with the greatest of the play's sufferers and who is destined soon to depart on another "journey," and it means echoing the passionate outcry of an old man driven into temporary despair by the pain inflicted on him by man's cruelty. These are partial reactions, and they are only partially valid. For these characters, pessimism is a personal response; for us, it is a much too external one like counting the dead, commenting on the absurdity of fate, and going about our business. Somehow, we are asked to say (I am almost tempted to say "do") more: we are asked to say what we *feel,* and thus to assimilate our attitude in some manner to the speaker's, Edgar's, sympathetic humanity. And what we have come to feel about Lear is very much influenced not only by his suffering but also by the ethical transformation, however incomplete and finally negated, we have seen him undergo. The material values on which he put his trust, his power and authority, have proved insubstantial; the spiritual values, which he rejected as nothings, have given him whatever small and dim consolation he achieves. And we have seen him suffer and, in his suffering, have gauged the potential greatness of his soul. We have experienced a similar regenerative movement in the weaker Gloucester's struggle for patience. Lear's plunge into madness and death and the cracking of Gloucester's heart make their moments of sanity and strength stand out even more saliently.

Shakespeare does not permit his characters to spy into the mystery of things, if by that is meant the way of the gods or of God with men, nor does he explain this mystery to us. Neither does he altogether explain some human mysteries. Palingenius said that man cannot know God's mysteries, he can only know himself.[27] But by the time of *Lear,* Shakespeare had grown away from the definiteness of the "know" in this statement. Not only the design of the universe but also the springs of man's actions had become more mysterious to him. I have contended that Lear does spy a little into the inner mystery, that of the human soul; but it is certainly much more significant that both he and Gloucester and other characters in the play have *experienced* a mystery in themselves and in others: the mystery of evil and good. If we are to say what we *feel* at the end of the play, we must speak of the mystery of evil; but we must also pay tribute to the mystery of goodness: to the miraculous goodness of Cordelia, the loyal goodness of Kent, the just goodness of Albany, the active goodness of Edgar, and, not the least, the growing toward goodness of Lear. That there is so much goodness in the darkest and greatest tragedy of Shakespeare is one of the most remarkable paradoxes.

CHAPTER SEVENTEEN

Macbeth:
Losing the Self

O MOVE FROM *Lear* to *Macbeth* is to move into a different but related tragic world. Like *Lear, Macbeth* is the tragedy of a man who loses himself in the crisis of his life. The danger of such self-loss, as we have noted, is present in all of Shakespeare's dramatic designs and is, even in the comedies, often at or near their center; but in the tragedies, it is more ominous and becomes in the end a destructive reality. The heroes are isolated, lost in a world they had taken for granted, but which suddenly takes on a menacing look and becomes an illusional landscape or enemy territory; as they lose themselves, they find death, whether at their own hand or that of others. All Shakespeare's tragedies are in some sense tragedies of self-loss;[1] but those generally considered his greatest, *Hamlet, Othello, Macbeth,* and *Lear,* have the best claim for this designation. They are tragedies of self-loss not merely in the sense that they depict it in the fate of their heroes but also in that they present patterns for the self-losses of men in general, address themselves to deep-seated fears and anxieties, and give us, so to speak, metaphysical shudders. Shakespeare's earlier tragedies and their heroes do not have quite this effect. The wholesale murders and at times grotesque horrors of *Titus Andronicus* alternately numb and bewilder our sensitivities and make it difficult to accept the individual sufferings of its hero as psychologically convincing and truly tragic; moreover, it is not even clear which, if any, of his actions are to be attributed to moral failure. The serious self-losses in *Romeo and Juliet* are not those of the lovers, whatever their responsibility for falling precipitously in love and marrying without their parents' consent; these losses are those of the quarreling Montagues and Capulets who create a world in which the lovers cannot live together and must, crossed by fate, die together. *Richard III* is the tragedy of a villain's self-loss, but the moral issue is somewhat perfunctorily treated. *Richard II* appears so much more tragic in the Shakespearean way because the play dwells on the hero's state of mind and soul when he experiences grief and anxiety about his place in his kingdom and in the world. If one hesitates to mention the play in one breath with the great tragedies, it is because Richard is and remains too immature and self-pitying to attract full tragic sympathy and because the play is too lyrical and not sufficiently intense dramatically. Nor does *Julius Caesar* appear to be in the first rank of Shakespeare's tragedies; although the political issues of the play are handled brilliantly, the hero, Brutus, does not permit a look into himself that shows us that his fortune has engendered a human reaction deep enough to experience vicariously. Hamlet, however, does attract tragic sympathy; he lives in an agony of uncertainty and expresses it hauntingly—a condition that is understandable to audiences and readers of all kinds and times because it goes beyond Hamlet's particular problem of revenge to include a general anxiety about the human condition. In the major tragedies that I have called baroque, the application of the heroes' particular situation to mankind's general predicament comes about, I believe, in a somewhat different fashion. Their follies, passions, and crimes are so monumental and at the same time so convincingly depicted that Shakespeare's art persuades us to accept them as symbolically heightening the self-losses all mankind is subject to. The huge and commanding Othello is turned into a tortured slave of jealousy and a wife-murderer in a way so convincing on the stage that it excites awe and fear about the destructive nature of human passions. Lear, who loses himself in incredibly foolish anger, gives a gigantic demonstration of the effects of blinding emotion, and his pain and madness are so agonizing as to create an empathy for not only his own suffering but that of mankind in general, which he and we come to feel him as symbolizing. In their destructive effects on others, the consequences of Lear's self-loss go even beyond those shown in *Othello*.

Nowhere, however, did Shakespeare dramatize the phenomenon of self-loss more emphatically, explore it with greater seriousness, than in *Macbeth*, where he showed the effect of self-loss on the hero's soul, that of his wife, and the fortune of a whole nation. Macbeth's first crime, the murder of Duncan, is invested with a supernatural horror because of Macbeth's temptation by the witches, and it drains his moral being, losing him all relationships, including the association with his wife who urged him to commit the deed. Although the murder brings him the crown, it robs him of all peace of mind. To regain it and secure himself, he commits crime after crime and divests himself of the remnants of his human feelings. He attempts to replace his moral self by an amoral one and seeks to draw assurance and strength from the powers of evil. But he gains no satisfaction as either a man or a king, and, with the loss of his humanity, comes spiritual nihilism. Macbeth's self-loss is the greater because Shakespeare, after the murder of Duncan, never allows him to repent and acknowledge his responsibility as do Othello and Lear after their falls. And Macbeth's self-loss gains a spectacular national significance as it threatens the loss of Scotland's self when he throws the cloak of his bloody tyranny over her. Only his death rescues the country from total chaos.[2]

The tragedy of self-loss thus has two aspects, a personal and a public one. The weight of interest of the personal tragedy lies in the earlier parts of the play, in Macbeth's state of mind before and after the murders of Duncan and Banquo; the public drama comes to the fore in the later parts when Macbeth recedes into the background and the spotlight is on the suffering of the Scots, most excruciatingly dramatized in the murder of Lady Macduff and her children. In the earlier parts, Macbeth suffers in struggling with his fear and guilt; in the later parts, Scotland groans under oppression and tyranny. The one suffering follows logically and consistently from the other.

Near the beginning of his career, in *Lucrece,* Shakespeare had dealt with the consequences that a crime committed by a public figure has on the psyche of the criminal and on the order and well-being of a state. If one makes allowance for the differences between narrative poetry and tragedy, *Lucrece* adumbrates much of the outer structure of *Macbeth.*[3] The first half of the poem is devoted to the conception, preparation, and execution of Tarquin's crime, the second to the suffering of the violated heroine; but neither crime nor suffering is described as a merely personal act. The criminal is the son of the king of Rome, and his deed brings about a lack of political stability and threatens chaos. The core of *Lucrece* as well as that of *Macbeth* lies in the personal tragedy, in the harm the crime does to the souls of criminal and victim; the public consequences flow from that. But in *Macbeth* they flow more quickly and more naturally. In order to underline the public aspects of Tarquin's crime,

Shakespeare resorted to the far-fetched device of making the heroine recall a painting of the fall of Troy and reflect on the connection between personal guilt and general suffering. The political allegory is tenuous, and rather than explaining the connection, it tends to make it less plausible. With obvious application to Tarquin, Lucrece asks at one point, "For one's offence why should so many fall, / To plague a private sin in general?" (1483–84), and indeed one wonders why they should. In *Macbeth,* there can be no such question, and that is not merely because Macbeth becomes king while Tarquin is a prince. Macbeth's crime is speedily reflected in the public chaos that, with tragic irony, he predicts immediately after the deed. The death of Duncan, so he intones elegiacally, has led to the loss of everything worthwhile: renown and grace are dead and the wine of life is drawn. The hypocritical dirge is proved to be prophetic not only by Macbeth's later weariness with life but also by Scotland's loss of all happiness. It is dramatically significant that this note of loss is struck in the presence of Duncan's sons, who are most directly affected. Donalbain's question "What is amiss?" and Macbeth's answer "You are, and do not know't" (II.iii.95) transfer the theme of self-loss from him to them. Donalbain's subsequent remark, "the near in blood, / The nearer bloody" (139–40), makes of this transfer almost a physical law. The conversation between Ross, Macduff, and the old man, which follows in the next scene, shows how doubts and fears spread further afield. Before Macbeth's death, all Scotland will be plunged into uncertainty and horror.

Scotland thus becomes an extension of the self of Macbeth, a motif that is underlined by thematic echoes. In a moment of near-repentance after Duncan's murder, Macbeth admits, "To know my deed, 'twere best not know myself" (II.ii.73). Later, when Ross comes to inform Lady Macduff of her husband's flight, he expresses his fear for Scotland and himself in words that seem to echo Macbeth's: "But cruel are the times, when we are traitors / And do not know ourselves" (IV.ii.18–19). The continuation of the speech also recalls an earlier sentiment of Macbeth's. We lose the knowledge of ourselves, according to Ross,

> when we hold rumor
> From what we fear, yet know not what we fear,
> But float upon a wild and violent sea
> Each way and none.
>
> (19–22)

This recalls Macbeth's agitated state of mind at the witches' prophecy:

> Present fears
> Are less than horrible imaginings.
> My thought, whose murder is yet but fantastical,
> Shakes so my single state of man
> That function is smother'd in surmise,
> And nothing is but what is not.
>
> (I.iii.137–42)

Macbeth's fear of facing his deed and knowing himself is once more echoed by Ross when he joins Malcolm and Macduff in England and reports on the condition of Scotland: "Alas, poor country, / Almost afraid to know itself!" (IV.iii.164–65). Ross's description of the suffering of the Scottish people, whose "violent sorrow seems / A modern ecstasy" (169–70), recalls the tortures of the mind, of which Macbeth speaks earlier, in which he lies in "restless ecstasy" (III.ii.22). Macbeth overcomes the affliction of his terrible dreams only by inflicting similar anxieties on Scotland. He makes the macrocosm a reflection of his chaotic microcosm; he tyrannizes Scotland in a kind of attempt to purge himself from fear by creating fear, just as Iago purges his jealousy by creating it in Othello.

Such forceful projection of the self as that of Macbeth is a feature inherent in the heightening of the heroes and villains in Shakespeare's later plays. Analogies between man and the universe on this basis differ in their one-sidedness from the structural dependence Renaissance moralists saw between microcosm and macrocosm. When Lear in his anger "Strives in his little world of man to outscorn / The to-and-fro conflicting wind and rain" (III.i.10–11), he makes the storm of nature into a symbolic projection of the power of his own tempestuous soul. And Prospero, as we shall note, succeeds by his will to make his island realm a reflection of his own painfully achieved self-control. In *Macbeth*, it is the negative aspect of the hero that imprints itself in such fashion on the country that he rules.

Personal and public self-loss are more strongly interlinked in *Macbeth* than in *Lucrece* for still another reason besides the dynamic way in which the latter loss is shown to be the result of the former. In *Macbeth*, both individual and general affliction arise more believably from a substance of evil that suffuses the universe. In *Lucrece*,

Shakespeare seems to have been hard put to it to explain how suddenly evil springs up in Tarquin's soul: "Why should the worm intrude the maiden bud?" (848). And indeed one might wonder why. In *Macbeth,* ones does not wonder; one feels horror and awe. Yet the reason for the existence of evil is hardly different: it is a metaphysical fact and a mystery. The "explanation" given in *Lucrece* is that "no perfection is so absolute / That some impurity does not pollute" (853–54)—the perfection being the human soul, created divine and immortal. But in *Macbeth,* there is no bald statement of this kind, which can only be intellectually unsatisfactory; rather, the hero is dramatically confronted with the horrifying shapes of the weird sisters, creatures of destiny and symbols of evil. They predict the outcome of Scotland's battle and the future glory of Macbeth; they tempt him to shape his fate to his own and his country's undoing. In addition, Macbeth is urged on by a wicked wife who invokes spirits of evil to unsex her and fill her with direst cruelty. Later he draws reassurance from a visit to the weird sisters. The supernatural forces that tempt and support Macbeth do not cause his murderous thoughts or his oppressive reign, but their presence adds an element of cosmic mystery to Macbeth's submission to, and persistence in, evil. We may speak of the greatness of his temptation, of the bad influence of his wife, of his anxiety to secure his position; but we cannot help feeling that there is something mysterious, an element that defies final analysis, in the urge that drives him to kill and kill again and that his nature has a subhuman or superhuman stratum that responds powerfully to the suggestion of evil.

Because Macbeth's infection with evil is quasi-demonic, it is much more serious than that of Tarquin, and the evil with which he infects Scotland is too pervasive to be healed by human power alone. It is not accidental that the forces destined to heal the sickness of the body politic of Scotland gather at the English court, where the saintly Edward cures the scrofula by touch. At the end of the play when "the time is free," Malcolm acknowledges the "grace of Grace" that has helped him to restore order and, he prays, will help him to perform his royal duties.

The story of personal self-loss, which will be examined in the remainder of this chapter, can have no such happy ending. The soul of Scotland can be cleansed; that of Macbeth, which has incurred mortal sin, cannot. Here again, the basic pattern is that adumbrated in *Lucrece.* Although Tarquin feels sorry for what he has done whereas Macbeth does not, what is at stake in both cases is quite similar. One might say that the formula on which Shakespeare constructed the two personal tragedies is the winning-losing antithesis of Mark viii.36: "For what shall it profit a man if he win all the world and lose his own soul?" The Genevan side-note explained this question in words that are echoed by both Tarquin and Macbeth: "They are the most foolish of all men, which purchase the enjoying of this life with the loss of everlasting bliss." Tarquin senses even before his crime the foolishness of what he seeks to win—"A dream, a breath, a froth of fleeting joy"—and yet goes on to sell "eternity to get a toy" (211–14). Macbeth realizes his bad bargain after his first murder:

> For Banquo's issue have I fil'd my mind;
> For them the gracious Duncan have I murder'd;
> Put rancours in the vessel of my peace
> Only for them, and mine eternal jewel
> Given to the common enemy of man
> To make them kings—the seeds of Banquo kings!
>
> (III.i.64–69)

Tarquin conquers the body of Lucrece, but loses his soul. Macbeth wins the crown, and also loses his soul.

Yet, quite apart from the fact that for most of us murder is a more serious crime than rape, the case of Macbeth is not quite the same as that of Tarquin. Macbeth does not face up to what he loses as does Tarquin; he never attains Tarquin's recognition of the greatness of his crime or the immensity of his responsibility before heaven. Macbeth regrets the loss of his "eternal jewel" only because it has not brought him the full gain he expected, a firmly held crown. Moreover, he hesitates to admit the seriousness of his loss and covers it through a semantic ambiguity. What exactly is the "eternal jewel" whose loss he laments? One might take it to mean "soul," but the preceding "vessel of my peace," which the image varies, suggests that Macbeth means merely his peace of mind.[4] And even "common enemy of man" is an evasive phrase for whatever power of evil Macbeth has in mind.

By having Macbeth express a sense of indefinite anxiety but punctuate it with traditional ethical and religious images, Shakespeare emphasized the moral consequences of Macbeth's fall without having him confess them. Macbeth is thus a much more believable

criminal than Tarquin, who is a "heavy convertite" and knows his
soul indelibly spotted when he steals away from Lucrece. For that
matter, Macbeth is a much more believable human being. We know
only too well that it is human nature to embellish faults and only
half-admit guilt and responsibility if admit them at all. There is just
a little of Macbeth in all of us so as to make us understand his eva-
sions if not to sympathize with them.

If the winning-losing formula is used with greater psychological
subtlety in *Macbeth* than in *Lucrece,* it nevertheless enters more
prominently into the texture of the language. The antithesis is immediately struck in the first scene, so atmospheric and foreboding,
when the witches appear only to agree to meet again "when the battle's lost and won." What winning and losing means to these evil
creatures is inhuman; for them "fair is foul and foul is fair"—as the
immediately following paradox suggests. This suggestion of a reversal of values tinges with irony the words of Duncan that immediately precede the reappearance of the witches: "What he [Caw-
dor] hath lost, noble Macbeth hath won" (I.ii.68). Macbeth is to
win from the Thane of Cawdor not only his title of thane but also
his evil nature and the title of traitor, and for whatever he wins, he
loses his soul. Macbeth's first appearance when he approaches the
witches, but does not yet see them, associates him with their topsy-
turvy values: "So foul and fair a day I have not seen" (I.iii.38).
It is a day of victory in battle and a dark day not only in weather
but also in the hero's life.[5]

The relevance of the winning-losing formula to Macbeth is emphasized by the contrast between his and Banquo's reactions to the
witches' prophecies. Although Banquo too is given expectations of
future glory, at least for his family, he realizes at once the seductive
danger of the promise:

> And oftentimes to win us to our harm,
> The instruments of darkness tell us truths,
> Win us with honest trifles, to betray's
> In deepest consequence.
>   (I.iii.123–26)

Banquo appears to fear from the beginning that the witches'
prophecy might enkindle Macbeth to gain the crown by foul play.
This is surely the reason for his brief conversation with Macbeth

just before the murder of Duncan when he broaches the subject of the witches by saying that he dreamed of them. When he notes on this occasion that to Macbeth they have brought some truth, he does so evidently in order to elicit from Macbeth an indication as to whether he is affected by temptation. Macbeth first evades the implied question; but then the idea of testing Banquo in return occurs to him. He says that he will later discuss the matter with Banquo when it will "make honor" for him if he "cleaves" to Macbeth's consent. But Banquo rules himself out as a possible ally; he rejects the idea of winning dishonestly and sets himself unequivocally in contrast to Macbeth:

> So I lose none [honor]
> In seeking to augment it, but still keep
> My bosom franchis'd and allegiance clear.
> (II.i.26–28)

Duncan's death makes into near-certainty Banquo's suspicion that Macbeth has succumbed to the witches' lure, has played "most foully" for what they promised (III.i.1–3). If Banquo does not openly oppose Macbeth now but rather professes loyalty, the reason is surely not (as Bradley thought) Banquo's hope to make the witches' prediction for his children come true. Only lack of opportunity and time prevents him from opposing the tyrant. That even Banquo must give "mouth-honor," must lie and prevaricate, is symptomatic of the falseness that Macbeth has injected into the life of Scotland. For men whose intentions are fair this country has become an alien place, where, as Lady Macduff later says, "to do harm / Is often laudable, to do good sometime / Accounted dangerous folly" (IV.ii.74–76). But in Banquo's conscience, fair is still fair and foul is foul. He is the foil of Macbeth, and he represents the positive case of the winning-losing formula. Although he does not actively seek to make the witches' prediction come true, he reaps the profit and becomes the ancestor of a royal dynasty.

Macbeth recognizes the fundamental contrast between Banquo and himself when he details the reasons why Banquo must die. He fears Banquo not merely because his designation as the ancestor of future kings limits his own power and glory but also because in Banquo's "royalty of nature / Reigns that which would be fear'd." Macbeth feels that by him "My genius is rebuk'd, as it is said /

Mark Antony's was by Caesar" (III.i.49 ff.). The remark not only anticipates *Antony and Cleopatra* but also looks back to the struggle of Brutus's "genius" with his "mortal elements" in *Julius Caesar* (II.i.66) ; yet neither Antony nor Brutus feels threatened because he thinks himself morally inferior to his adversary. To adapt a phrase Iago applies to Cassio, Banquo has a daily beauty in his life that makes Macbeth feel ugly. And thus Banquo must die.

This hatred of Banquo's moral superiority marks Macbeth as an envious and an evil man. He does not appear to me ever really to show the essential or original nobility so many critics and actors have read into his character, misled, I think, by the attribution of nobility to him early in the play and perhaps also by some general ideas about what a tragic hero is or should be, notions on which Aristotle's definition has had considerable influence. We all know, theoretically at least, that Aristotle's model of a noble and above-average character is not properly applicable to Macbeth—for Aristotle a villain did not make a fitting tragic hero anyway—but we find it in practice difficult to get away from the generalizations of *The Poetics*. If Macbeth is greater than the average, it is not because of his nobility but because of the magnitude of his crime and through what is at stake in his grasp for power—not only his kingdom but also his immortal soul. And, I think, Macbeth is tragic not because of the ruination of his alleged nobility but because of the intensity of his emotional states that, in heightened form, depict the self-loss sin and crime bring with it.

More than one critic has found the idea of nobility hard to reconcile with Macbeth's criminal nature. Some, like Robert Bridges, have seen here an inconsistency that cannot be psychologically resolved and is explainable only by Shakespeare's sacrificing character consistency to theatrical effect.[6] The reputation of nobility, it should be said, rests on Macbeth's martial courage, which is notably contrasted with his private insecurity. L. L. Schücking has noted that "Macbeth is certainly a lion in the field of battle; open and visible dangers leave him unmoved. But this is not compatible with the fact that, at heart, he is greatly dependent on other people, is always prey to fear and feels himself helpless in every moral conflict into which his actions lead him." [7] Schücking came to see in this contradiction an antithetical character construction, peculiar to the baroque.[8] However this may be, I do not think that the character of Macbeth lacks in psychological consistency, provided one realizes the limited nature of the nobility attributed to him. Richard Moulton appears to me to have seen his nature clearly when he described it as a "union of superficial nobility with real moral worthlessness . . . connected with the purely practical bent of his mind." [9]

Macbeth's nobility is shown to be superficial quite early in the play in one of the kind of indirect and ironic revelations of character that Shakespeare practiced since *Measure for Measure*. Indeed, it comes in that famous phrase of the "milk of human kindness" of which the Lady says her husband is too full (I.v.14)—a phrase we have often heard applied benevolently to Macbeth. But of that milk, nothing is evident in him; it is a measure of the Lady's perversion of standards that she should consider whatever reluctance to murder exists in Macbeth as due to kindness and holiness. What she actually says about her husband's morals is quite damaging if one makes allowance for her peculiar definition of terms:

> Thou wouldst be great;
> Art not without ambition, but without
> The illness should attend it. What thou wouldst highly,
> That wouldst thou holily; wouldst not play false,
> And yet wouldst wrongly win.
> Thou'dst have, great Glamis, that which cries
> "Thus thou must do," if thou have it;
> And that which rather thou dost fear to do
> Than wishest should be undone.
>
> (I.v.15–22)

The Lady does not really credit her husband with a moral nature, but sees in him a lack of determination to execute evil by "catching the nearest way." There is irony in her calling him "great Glamis," and, significantly, she says that he would "wrongly win." Banquo makes it clear that he would not. What the Lady appears to have in mind is not that Macbeth is too kind but that he has a residual consciousness of being of humankind and subject to its laws. This is a far cry from the nobility some commentators have seen in him and rather bears out Moulton's characterization, old-fashioned as it may appear in its moral tone, that Macbeth has no "real love of goodness for its own sake, founded on intelligent choice or deep affection." [10]

Macbeth's residual consciousness of belonging to humanity does indeed contribute to his suffering and makes him at times appear less evil than Richard III or Iago. But it should be said that neither

of these villains ever quite designs and personally executes a murder
as Macbeth does Duncan's; neither of them, therefore, is quite
tested in his commitment to evil as he. Nor, for that matter, is the
Lady, who prides herself on her superior strength. Although she
entertains the notion of killing Duncan herself and grandiloquently
announces that he may leave everything to her, she cannot actually
do the deed.

One should resist the temptation of constructing a character for
Macbeth before he appears and confronts the evil sisters; but given
the man presented in the play, it is difficult to think of him as ever
having been positively good and noble. He is certainly not merely
duped by superior demonic forces and an evil, scheming wife. Even
though the witches are at least partially prescient, knowing as they
do that Macbeth will become Thane of Cawdor and king, they are
not executors of fate; they do not decree how he is to become king,
whether by fair means or foul. Macbeth himself considers the possibility that he might be crowned without any effort of his own.
Presumably the witches know that he will become king because he
is ready to get the crown by foul means. Although their prophecy
stirs the thought of murder in Macbeth's brain, the thought is still
his own. And he appears to have had it even earlier; the Lady's
question, what made him "break this enterprise" to her when he
now seems reluctant to execute it, indicates that Macbeth considered
murdering Duncan when there were no evil spirits yet to tempt
him.

Macbeth's intense fascination with evil (accompanied as it often
is by weak recoils) is unparalleled among Shakespeare's villains. On
his first appearance, he reacts with a kind of a psychic shock to the
witches' greetings, but Banquo remains calm and unperturbed. The
latter notes how Macbeth "starts" and seems "rapt withal" (I.iii.57).
He recovers temporarily, only to be again "rapt" (142) when he is
promptly awarded the title of Thane of Cawdor. Banquo is as much
surprised by his partner's extraordinary reaction as he is by the
appearance of the witches. Macbeth is given to states of feverish
excitement in which he is attracted to evil as much or more than
he shrinks from it. These psychic states are not absorptions in
thought, but "raptures," that is, turmoils of the spirit in which
thought, imagination, and passion circle wildly around the events;
they are neurotic anxieties, transportations of fear, hallucinations,
and strange obsessions. They are not reactions to stimuli commen-

surate with them. Macbeth is as profoundly affected by the illusion of the dagger he knows to be merely in his mind as he is by the ghost of Banquo that is for him—and was for Shakespeare's audience—real enough. If he did not almost crave the fright that the specter produces, he would hardly repeat the name of Banquo that brought about its first appearance. Lady Macbeth's explanation at the banquet that he has been subject to seizures since his youth (III.iv.54) has a ring of truth. Associated from the beginning with a "bloody execution" as Macbeth is and reacting emphatically to the suggestion of evil as he does, he is destined by character and temperament to do a gigantically monstrous deed.

But Macbeth's "raptures" represent not only a psychological phenomenon but are also a dramatic device comparable to similar dramatic devices in Shakespeare's baroque plays. The moments of Macbeth's greatest attraction to evil have an outward resemblance to Lear's penetration to goodness in his intuitive realization of his and Cordelia's true values in that both Macbeth and Lear are in trance-like states. Different as the inner conditions of these two heroes are, both of them achieve the strongest emotional expression of their characters by at least partial removal from their surroundings. And we may also recall Othello's passionate breakdown, which is called a "trance" by the Folio stage direction, and by Iago (to Cassio) an "epilepsy" and (to Othello) an "ecstasy" (IV.i.43,50, 78). We shall observe a similar tendency of heightening passion into ecstasy in *The Tempest* when Prospero takes leave of his island spirits. The strong movements toward self-loss or self-finding by the heroes of Shakespeare's later plays are given an extraordinary emotional emphasis.

I think that the psychological and dramatic movement of the earlier parts of *Macbeth* derives not, as is frequently explained, from a conflict between ambition and conscience in Macbeth but from his intense reaction to evil and from the impact of the strong will of the Lady on his weaker but also criminal will. Of the dynamic interplay of these two characters' wills something must be said later. As to the matter of Macbeth's conscience, it is surprising that, in view of the role it has played in the analysis of his character, Macbeth himself never speaks of "conscience." It is notable that there is something inexplicable for him (and, as I have argued, also for us) in why he acts as he does; and that puzzlement includes for him also why he feels as he does. He cannot explain why the appear-

ance of the weird sisters shakes him so violently and sets his whole
being adrift. He is dimly aware that he violates human and divine
laws, and yet he is compelled to commit his crimes. The imaginary
dagger terrifies him and yet draws him to Duncan's chamber. He
appears to know that he cannot rely on the evil sisters—"damn'd all
those that trust them," he says to Lennox (IV.i.139)—and yet
he is reaffirmed by them in his evildoing. But though he never
speaks of conscience, he often speaks of, and evinces, fear. Of course,
one may see in this fear and its accompanying phantasmagoria a
subconscious reassertion of his conscience; but then one must also
acknowledge Macbeth's conscience to be a fear-inspired psychic
state, a conscience of the most conventional and unexamined kind
and one difficult to distinguish from neurosis. Marlowe's reputed
utterances concerning religion indicate that some free Renaissance
spirits wanted to relegate all manifestations of conscience to a con-
ditioning in fear. But the orthodox, then as now, attempted to distinguish between conscience and fear. They contrasted the "honest
fear" of conscience, which included some intellectual considerations,
focusing on a moral view of man and a reverence of God and his
laws, with a "dishonest," that is, practical and cowardly, fear. The
latter could become pathological, and, as such, it interested not only
the moralists but also doctors like Timothy Bright, for whom it was
a form of the all-inclusive psychological illness of melancholy (by
which, in this case, he meant neurotic disorders). Admitting the
difficulty of distinguishing between conscience and fear-melancholy,
Bright saw the latter characterized by vivid conceits, fearful apparitions, imagined voices, and frightful dreams.[11] Macbeth is affected
by evil in this fashion.

In regard to the kind of conscience with which Macbeth is endowed, a comparison with Tarquin in *Lucrece* is illuminating.
Shakespeare almost appears to invite a comparison when Macbeth
"With Tarquin's ravishing strides, towards his design / Moves like
a ghost" (II.i.55–56). But the Tarquin of Shakespeare's poem
goes through a long debate between reason and passion before he
strikes, and the former is given a hearing even if its arguments are
rejected. Macbeth's internal conflict never leads to a real weighing
of alternatives, not even in the first aside after the witches' prophecy
when, as Coleridge surmised, the decision to kill or not to kill is still
in his power. But I believe it is clear that Macbeth is already yield-
ing to the evil in his heart:

> This supernatural soliciting
> Cannot be ill; cannot be good. If ill,
> Why hath it given me earnest of success,
> Commencing in a truth? I am Thane of Cawdor.
> If good, why do I yield to that suggestion
> Whose horrid image doth unfix my hair
> And make my seated heart knock at my ribs
> Against the use of nature? Present fears
> Are less than horrible imaginings.
>
> (I.iii.130–38)

These lines do reflect Macbeth's struggle with good and evil; but they depict a morally confused struggle that betrays the tremendous impact the suggestion of evil has on him. Macbeth is confused about what is "good" and "ill." The fulfillment of the first part of the witches' prophecy is "good" because it is a happy prologue to the imperial theme of which he dreams. Good is what brings power. What is "ill" is less clear. Is it the "horrid image," the personified imaginary murder of his thought, or is it the fear that makes him shrink from the image? Certainly, if "present fears / Are less than horrible imaginings," a good way to go about restoring the "smothered function" is to commit the murder. The reason Macbeth kills Duncan is surely not merely that he wants to become king. That wish is the one Lady Macbeth has for her husband; she appears to have no other motive. The traditional roles of man and woman are here reversed: it is she who has the acquisitive urge and he who has the scruples, weak and confused as they are. Macbeth, who mentions ambition only once, compares it to a horse that overleaps itself under the spur of the human will and declares it to be an insufficient motivation (I.vii.25–27).

What then, if not ambition, drives Macbeth to kill? To the degree that an answer can be given, it must be sought in the nature of the fear that both drives him on and makes him recoil. One need not subscribe to Lily Campbell's thesis that the whole of Macbeth is a study in fear in order to accept her arguments on the significance of this emotion in the hero's psychological constitution.[12] The man who is introduced as "brave Macbeth" and "valor's minion" and who is called "valiant cousin" by Duncan and "Bellona's bridegroom" by Ross before we even meet him is, during much of the action of the play, under the spell of fear. Shakespeare surely intended the irony and wished to make some statement concerning the nature of courage and fear.

Miss Campbell explains, I think correctly, Macbeth's courage in battle as what the moralists called "false courage" or "rashness," a passion devoid of reason and opposite to fear. True courage was the Aristotelian mean between the excesses of rashness and fear. Macbeth veers from one of these excesses to the other. There is something excessive in that first action reported of this minion of valor when he slew Macdonwald, not desisting "Till he unseam'd him from the nave to th' chaps, / And fix'd his head upon our battlements" (I.ii. 22–23). Although this deed is applauded, it gives the impression of being committed by a man who is easily carried away. And when Macbeth says he killed the sleeping grooms because the expedition of his violent passion (his alleged love for Duncan) outran "the pauser, reason" (II.iii.109), the explanation sounds most appropriate for a man with a reputation of rashness. Later, Macbeth contrasts himself enviously with Banquo: "And to that dauntless temper of his mind / He hath a wisdom that doth guide his valour / To act in safety" (III.i.51–53). Banquo's is the true courage.[13]

The combination of military courage and moral cowardice in Macbeth, antithetically baroque as it has been thought, is yet plausible in our psychology as well as that of the Renaissance. According to humanistic moralists, excessive courage or rashness could be the expression of an underlying fear. Charron noted that some military courage was of this kind:

> This military valor is pure and natural in beasts, with whom it is as well in females as in males. In men it is often artificial, gotten by fear and the apprehension of captivity, of death, of grief, of poverty; of which things, beasts have no fear. Human valor is a wise cowardliness, a fear accompanied with foresight to avoid one evil by another; choler is the temper and file thereof. Beasts have it simply.

The driving force of Macbeth is well characterized by Charron when he describes the "dishonest fear" that impels man to evil as

> that vicious fear that troubleth and afflicteth, which is the seed of sin, the twin of shame, both of one womb, sprung from that close and cursed marriage of the spirit of man with a diabolical persuasion. . . . It is a deceitful and malicious passion and hath no other power over us, but to mock and seduce us. It serves its turn with that which is to come; where though we seem to foresee much, we

see nothing at all . . . for fear seemeth not to other end than to make us find that we fly from. Doubtless, fear is of all other evils the greatest and most tedious, for other evils are no longer evils than they continue and the pain endureth no longer than the cause; but fear is of that which is and that which is not and that perhaps which never shall be, yea, sometimes of that which cannot possibly be.[14]

Charron's is the perfect explanation of the feverish state of the imagination in which Macbeth's function is smothered in surmise, and "no thing is but what is not." Charron elsewhere shows how false fear can drive a man to violent deeds. This fear, he says,

ariseth from dangers and many times casteth us into dangers; for it engendereth in us such an inconsiderate desire to get out that it astonisheth, troubleth, and hindreth us from taking that order that is fit to get out. It bringeth a violent kind of trouble whereby the soul, being affrighted, withdraweth itself into itself and debateth with itself how to avoid the danger that it presented. Besides that great discouragement that it bringeth, it seizeth on us with such an astonishment that we lose our judgement, and there is no longer reason or discourse in us.[15]

The fear described by Charron is the kind of emotion that besets Macbeth when his soul withdraws into itself during his raptures. It vitiates his attempts to assess his situation rationally and makes him prefer the quick solution to the moral and prudent one.

This urge to extricate himself from trouble by a quick action prevents Macbeth from ever fully probing his condition. His nervous, disjointed, and equivocal soliloquy before he murders Duncan—"If it were done when 'tis done, then 'twere well / It were done quickly"—is an example how Macbeth approaches the great moral issue at stake, but then quickly evades it. The residual compunction and weak recoil from the deed are overcome by his leap forward, not in courage but in cowardice, so he can catch what the Lady calls "the nearest way":

> If th' assassination
> Could trammel up the consequence, and catch,
> With his surcease, success; that but this blow
> Might be the be-all and the end-all here—
> But here upon this bank and shoal of time—
> We'd jump the life to come.
>
> (I.vii.2–7)

Macbeth in this speech does not make clear to himself and to us what he really fears, whether it is the possibility of failing and with it the punishment of worldly justice, or, in spite of success, the punishment of God. The logic of the argument, such as it is, favors the former interpretation; some of the terms and images, it is true, the latter. "The life to come" echoes the prayer-book phrase for the after-life, "the life of the world to come." Yet Macbeth continues with "we still have judgment *here*. . . ." And even if one assumes him to be vaguely afraid of spiritual consequences, the question is still whether he thinks of these as a risk to be taken or a threat to be evaded—"jump" could have either meaning. In both cases, the energetic action suggested by the image contrasts sharply with the vague if imaginatively beautiful evocation of the retardative forces. The "even-handed justice" Macbeth fears seems to be temporal punishment; but when he says that it "Commends th' ingredience of our poison'd chalice / To our own lips," he appears to think of a spiritual affliction. When he imagines that the old king will attract pity to himself because of his meekness in office, Macbeth thinks in a very practical way about the murder and its consequences; but when he likens pity to a "naked, new-born babe" and to "heaven's cherubin hors'd" and sees Duncan's virtues plead like angels "against / The deep damnation of his taking-off," the religiously tinged language evokes a hazy, child-like picture of divine vengeance. However, Macbeth uses these images merely as analogies, and the specific reasons he marshals against killing Duncan are not in themselves particularly spiritual: Duncan is his kinsman and his lord as well as his guest, and the laws of family loyalty and hospitality demand that he should be protected rather than murdered. Never does Macbeth face directly the commandment "Thou shalt not kill." If his argument against the killing were that murder, heinous by itself, is still more heinous in this case, it would be strong; but because Macbeth evades the main moral issue, the wrongness of murder, the reasons he gives do not serve to underline his recoil as much as they bring his monstrous ingratitude to our minds.

When, after this soliloquy, the Lady enters, the reasons Macbeth gives her for wanting to desist are even weaker than those he gives to himself. They are strictly prudential rather than ethical, and they demonstrate, as Moulton has it, his practical mind rather than his moral nature: Duncan has honored him of late and he has gathered golden opinions from others. The Lady could easily refute these objections by reminding him that the murder of Duncan will bring him even greater honor: the crown. But she does not choose to reason with her husband in this fashion; rather, she accuses him of cowardice and admonishes him to be a man. She makes him afraid of being thought afraid. And surely she does so because she thinks that he is at heart a coward who is willing to silence his humanistic conscience if he is assured of success. That she is proved right proceeds from Macbeth's last and weakest objection to the murder, "If we should fail" (59). To demonstrate her own superiority to such weakness as his, she proclaims her readiness to dash out her child's brain had she sworn to execute this deed as he has the murder—a remark that elicits from Macbeth the half-admiring, half-horrified exclamation "Bring forth men-children only." Her "undaunted mettle" dissuades him from the fear that they might fail, and her "example" energizes him: "I am settl'd, and bend up / Each corporal agent to this terrible feat" (79–80). Earlier, the Lady had asked him to "look like th' innocent flower, / But be the serpent under't" (I.v.62–63). Macbeth now accepts this Machiavellian principle and reciprocates with the advice: "Away, and mock the time with fairest show; / False face must hide what the false heart doth know" (I. vii.81–82).

For the ideological and dramatic pattern of the drama, it is significant that in the clash between Macbeth and the Lady two concepts of manhood are evoked, the one humanistic, the other antihumanistic and tinged with Machiavellism as it was understood in Shakespeare's time.[16] Manhood and its relationship to courage and fear is a major issue of the play; all through the action, Macbeth feels challenged in his status as a man. There is something in him that requires him to prove himself as such. At the Lady's charge of cowardice in that moment of hesitation before the murder of Duncan, he seeks to take refuge in the notion that being a man means to accept moral limitations: "I dare do all that may become a man; / Who dares do more is none" (I.vii.46–47). Sarcastically, the Lady retorts: "What beast was't then / That made you break this enterprise to me?" Her specious contrast of man and beast flouts the humanistic doctrine of moral decorum based on the distinction of man and beast. For her, Macbeth can prove himself "more the man" if he can throw off his moral fetters. She sees man as an exclusive product of his will, a will strong enough to impose its laws on the world.

Here, as before, the Lady assumes the traditionally masculine role; she resembles the kind of "new man" embodied by Iago. Her acceptance of the philosophy of seeming and her glorification of the will as the victorious agent in a battle that has to be fought by assuming the "condition of the beast" make her a "Machiavellian." She prides herself in possessing the psychic strength that some of Machiavelli's disciples identified with their master's concept of virtù and that they thought free of all ethical limitations. Gabriel Harvey, as we observed, was one of the stealthy Machiavellians; and his secret acclaim of man's psychic resources is worth quoting in full:

> *Quicquid est in deo, est deus;*
> *Quicquid est in viro, sit virtus et vis;*
> *Quicquid cogitat, vigor;*
> *Quicquid loquitur, emphasis;*
> *Quicquid agit, dynamis;*
> *Quicquid patitur, alacritas.*
> *Totus vita entelechia, furor, zelus, ignis.*[17]

Force in thought, emphasis in speech, dynamism in action, courage in suffering—qualities characteristic of the baroque age of energy—were traits that fascinated Shakespeare when he created the heroes and villains of his later tragedies. But unlike Harvey, he did not identify a collection of such traits with manhood, as is evident by his representing them, strongly and in an unalloyed manner, in his villains. An Iago and an Edmund are deficient as human beings because they possess much force, emphasis, dynamism, and courage, and very little else.

In *Macbeth,* the psychological dynamics bears a certain resemblance to that in *Othello:* one of the two major characters supplies the ethically unrestricted will that triggers the passionate action of the other—or so, at least, it is for Macbeth's first crime. But there are major differences. In *Macbeth,* the process is not a seduction away from good and toward evil, for Macbeth is already under the spell of evil; it is merely an infusion of energy to keep him on his path. Macbeth's "humanism" is halfhearted; it gives the impression of having been learned by rote rather than ever deeply felt. He has an old-fashioned sense—one that, by now, is quite unusual in Shakespeare—that the world should have a firm, "framed" order that comprises matter and spirit, microcosm and macrocosm:

But let the frame of things disjoint, both the worlds suffer,
Ere we will eat our meal in fear and sleep
In the affliction of these terrible dreams
That shake us nightly.

(III.ii.16–19)

Yet this humanistic assertion of a universal cohesiveness (earlier, he speaks of the "single state of man") only springs to his mind when he ponders murder. It is an acquired, mechanical reaction accompanying the ambiguous fear that both makes him shudder and drives him on; it is not a deeply felt conviction.

Different from *Othello* also is the profoundly ironic effect of the infusion of energy that takes place in *Macbeth*. The man of passion does indeed succeed in suppressing his disturbing emotionalism, and he acquires the qualities of *vis* that Harvey admired (although he does not, I shall argue, retain his most aspired-to acquisition, courage, to the very end); but this gain comes at a terrible price: he loses all humanity and becomes alienated from himself, his wife, and the world. And the Lady breaks under the strain of her absorption of these qualities. She, no less than he, is a most conspicuous example of the folly and tragedy of trying to force human nature into a mould of superhuman hardness.

The irony of the Lady's self-proclaimed dehumanization becomes apparent first: she fancies herself to have derived her strength from evil spirits and to have divested herself of all womanly and motherly feelings; yet her influence on her husband, diabolical as one might call it, is not exerted in any supernatural way. No superhuman force is needed to dispel the compunctions of this mechanical humanist. Moreover, although the Lady rises in words to demonic power, her deeds do not carry the same conviction.[18] She does not actually make the wound in Duncan's body with her keen knife as she envisaged that she would (I.v.49). Her spirit buoyed up by alcohol, she is bold enough to smear the grooms with the blood from the daggers Macbeth thoughtlessly brought back with him. But there is some lack of logic in her reproach of him for refusing to return to the place of his crime: "the sleeping and the dead / Are but as pictures; 'tis the eye of childhood / That fears a painted devil" (II. ii.53–55). It was with the eye of childhood that she looked at the sleeping Duncan and found herself incapable of murdering him. A substratum of human nature that she mistakenly thought did not exist in her comes to the surface when she faints during her husband's account of his murder of the grooms. Ironically, her composure leaves her just when he excuses his act as inspired by courage to make known his love (II.iii.117)—she appears to have overrated her own courage and demonic strength; the alternate explanation that she is merely feigning here has no support in the text or in the stage directions.[19] She does recover temporarily from this failure of her nerves, and even acts once more as her husband's support when he is unnerved by fear at the appearance of Banquo's ghost and quite "unmanned in folly" (III.iv.74); and once more she urges her concept of manhood on him. But she has the advantage of not seeing the ghost. Notably, she now conjures up no more evil spirits to help herself or him.

This is the last time she appears as her husband's monitor. As he becomes increasingly self-directed, the embodiment of *vis* in Harvey's Machiavellian sense, he needs her less and less. He keeps the details of his plan to murder Banquo from her; in the killing of Lady Macduff and her children she has no role at all. She drops from sight after the banquet, and when she reappears in the sleepwalking scene, nature has taken its revenge. When Macbeth was obsessed with the notion that an ocean could not wash Duncan's blood from his hand, she scoffed at his distraction; a little water, she thought, would clear them both of the deed. Now all the perfumes of Arabia cannot wipe the spot from her hand. But her insanity and death, presumedly by suicide, are merely side issues of the story.

The main issue, to which the Lady is a mere contributor, is the loss of Macbeth's self, a loss that consists in a progressive self-reduction to nothingness. This movement is the main psychological one of Macbeth in the later parts of the play; but it begins with his neurotic self-alienation immediately after the murder of Duncan when Macbeth is frightfully shaken and, in his fearful anxiety, looks at himself, as it were, from the outside: the man who committed the deed is a man whom he does not know. The voice he hears cry "sleep no more" addresses him as a triple stranger: "Glamis hath murder'd sleep; and therefore Cawdor / Shall sleep no more—Macbeth shall sleep no more" (II.ii.42–43). He views in horror his own bloody hands as if they did not belong to him: "What hands are here? Ha! they pluck out mine eyes" (59). When the Lady now admonishes him "be not lost / So poorly in your thoughts," Macbeth answers in a sentence pregnant with meaning: "To know my deed, 'twere best not know myself" (II.ii.73).

This sentence is deceptively simple, and hard to paraphrase. On the primary level, it can be read (as does Kenneth Muir) to show Macbeth's shrinking from reality: "It were better for me to remain permanently 'lost' in thought, i.e., self-alienated, than to be fully conscious of the nature of the deed." [20] But the disjunctive syntax of Macbeth's sentence supports an interpretation that makes it another instance of his evasion of moral responsibility and of his unwillingness to admit the existence of a conscience. One might expect Macbeth, that is, a stronger, moral Macbeth, to have said, "To know, i.e., fully acknowledge, my deed would mean to feel repentance." Instead, Shakespeare's Macbeth gives the sentence the cognitive meaning recognized by Professor Muir. But the disjunctive syntax also makes the second part of the sentence a kind of answer to the first, an answer that draws a balance, such as in Una Ellis-Fermor's paraphrase: "If I am to live on terms with this deed, I must break with my real—my former—self." [21] The sentence is thus a diagnosis of Macbeth's state of mind, an evasion of his guilt, and a program for the future.

With regard to Macbeth's evasion of the name and idea of conscience, it is interesting to note that, according to an old theological definition, the conscience could be described as the soul's knowledge of itself. William Worship noted the definition in *The Christian's Jewel* (1617):

> *Conscientia,* saith Saint Bernard, soundeth as much as *cordis scientia* because it [i.e., the soul] knows itself and many other things. *Conscientia,* saith Aquinas, is *scientia cum alio,* a knowledge with another; which combination hath either reference to the soul, reflecting upon itself, or else to God, who is privy to her inmost contents. . . . What man knows the things of man, saith Saint Paul, save the spirit of man which is in him? [22]

There is no indication, however, that Macbeth uses the phrase "know myself" in Worship's sense; and in the seventeenth century, as we have noted, an ethical-religious definition of self-knowledge was no longer taken for granted. But by shrinking from such a definition and from acknowledging his guilt, Macbeth stops far short of self-discovery. The vague and ill-defined way in which he uses the term indicates that he tries to transfer the awareness of his guilt from the ethical sphere to the intellectual one. Macbeth's "to know my deed, 'twere best not know myself" thus marks a missed *anagnorisis,* paradoxically by invoking the idea of self-knowledge.

For a self-knowledge with an ethical basis, Macbeth tries to find a substitute in an arcane knowledge of evil he need not share with others, not even with his wife. The term of endearment he has for her when he refuses to satisfy her inquiry into his plans for Banquo ironically emphasizes the distance that begins to separate him from her: "Be innocent of the knowledge, dearest chuck, / Till thou applaud the deed" (III.ii.45–46). However, the "knowledge" he keeps from her is actually quite indebted to her teaching; when he goads the murderers to kill Banquo, he does so by questioning whether they are men, ready to avenge wrongs: the strategy of questioning the manhood of the two daredevils is the same the Lady applied to him. A common "manhood" associates him now with the two villains, for whom he feels such contempt.

He is, however, not immediately successful in his attempt to break with his former self. Banquo's ghost shocks him once more into fear. But since he alone sees the specter, this event contributes to his isolation and self-alienation:

> You make me strange
> Even to the disposition that I owe,
> When now I think you can behold such sights
> And keep the natural ruby of your cheeks,
> When mine is blanch'd with fear.
>   (III.iv.112–16)

But he determines to readjust his values to his new self and calls the brief resurgence of fear his "strange and self-abuse," which is only "the initiate fear that wants hard use" (142–43). He decides to visit the weird sisters in order to obtain the knowledge he needs to still his fear and harden his heart: "For now I am bent to know / By the worst means the worst" (134–35). Again, Macbeth follows the method he had seen the Lady use; she, too, called upon the spirits of evil to fill her with direst cruelty.

Macbeth's visit to the weird sisters is the dramatic climax of the play, the *summa epitasis.* Structurally, it introduces the counter-movement, the revenge action of Malcolm and Macduff, through the apparitions of the armed head, the bloody child, and the crowned child, bearing a tree. Macduff's flight to Malcolm, which is reported immediately afterwards, confirms the success of the countermovement and highlights Macbeth's increasing isolation. But, deluded by false knowledge, he takes the witches' warnings about the man of no woman born and about the moving of the wood to Dunsinane Castle as assurance of his invulnerability. His desire to know finds thus its specious gratification in equivocations that he takes to be certificates of security. The visit to the witches does indeed produce the "new Macbeth," formed in the image of manhood proclaimed by the Lady, the man free from fear and from the remnants of his moral self. But the visit also emphasizes the barrenness of this achievement by the show of the eight kings symbolizing the succession of Banquo's line. Macbeth is isolated not only in his time, but also in history. He wears a useless crown. He reacts in passion; once more he is in the throes of one of the raptures through which threatening events register on his nervous system: he stands "amazedly" (IV.i.126). But he has no moral recoil now even while he recognizes the horror of the event: "Let this pernicious hour / Stand aye accursed in the calendar" (133–34). As in Job iii.5, to which Macbeth's words form a kind of ironic parallel, this is the hour of darkness stained by the shadow of death. There is no substitute for self-knowledge; the knowledge of evil Macbeth seeks is a denial of the principle of life.

Because Macbeth never acknowledges what was at stake, he never admits what he has lost. He does subsequently deplore the side-effects of his self-loss when he speaks of having lost the comforts of life:

> My way of life
> Is fall'n into the sear, the yellow leaf;
> And that which should accompany old age,
> As honour, love, obedience, troops of friends,
> I must not look to have; but in their stead,
> Curses, not loud but deep, mouth-honour, breath,
> Which the poor heart would fain deny, and dare not.
>
> (V.iii.22–28)

These lines are not an appeal to sympathy; they are a demonstration of the moralists' warnings against the suppression of all fear. As Coeffeteau says,

There is a kind of people which fear nothing, that is to say, such as have renounced all feeling of things whereof we have just cause to apprehend the loss, as they which have lost all honor, abandoned all shame, wasted their fortunes and their goods, and those whose lives are tedious unto them. For what can they fear who have nothing remaining to trouble them.[23]

Macbeth is now a symbol of the emptiness of life and of the inanity of trying to impose an amoral self on the world. He had envisaged the even-handed justice of temporal punishment, and he had even glanced at the risks in the life to come; but he had not thought of what actually becomes his fate: his reduction to a meaningless existence. In this progressive loss of his self in this life, not in his death or in any consequences to his soul in the hereafter, lies his tragic predicament.

As the others lose all trust in him, so he loses all trust in them, clinging only to the hope of survival given him by the weird sisters. While he goes through the motions of activity, fortifying Dunsinane, he does so without any sense of the significance of his actions either for himself or for Scotland:

> Some say he's mad, others, that lesser hate him,
> Do call it valiant fury; but for certain,
> He cannot buckle his distemper'd cause
> Within the belt of rule.
>
> (V.ii.13–16)

With the loss of his fear, he loses also all power to feel compassionate. The women's shriek that heralds his wife's death elicits from him the boast that he has almost forgotten what fear tastes like. When the cry is interpreted as due to his wife's death, he has no word of sympathy and pity; he expresses no sense of loss at the news of her death, only annoyance at the untimely event and disgust with the monotony and uselessness of life. With the loss of his moral self, Macbeth has gained only a meaningless life: it is a tale told by an idiot, signifying nothing. The utter impersonality of this most pessimistic passage in all Shakespeare marks it not as the poet's *ipse dixit*, but as a dramatic expression of the price of self-loss. The generalization is grand and false.

After the exhaustion of his life substance, to have provided Macbeth with even a shred of repentance would have weakened the impression of the tragic consequences of self-loss and sentimentalized his character. Shakespeare did not make this mistake. Macbeth never admits his responsibility for his fall; as he begins to realize the danger threatening him, he blames the witches, not himself. The final change in Macbeth's psyche—and another ironic turn in the play—is provided not by a repentance but by a reemergence of that fear Macbeth thought he had extinguished.

The first blow falls when Birnam Wood actually comes to Dunsinane. "I pull in resolution," says Macbeth, "and begin / To doubt th' equivocation of the fiend / That lies like truth" (V.v.42–44). Interestingly, when he now remembers the witches' prophecy, it is not quite in the form it was given. *"Fear* not, till Birnam wood / Do come to Dunsinane" (44–45) is his version, but the witches said: "Macbeth shall never vanquish'd be until / Great Birnam wood to high Dunsinane hill / Shall come against him" (IV.i.92–94). Yet he does not admit fear but evinces disgust with the world: "I gin to be aweary of the sun, / And wish th' estate o' th' world were now undone." And he actually recovers temporarily his heroic stance: "At least we'll die with harness on our back" (V.v.49–52).

But stark, naked fear breaks out in Macbeth when he confronts Macduff. His puzzling refusal to fight Macduff even before the latter reveals that he was untimely ripped from his mother's womb may be a combination of weariness and of that instinctive fear of the Thane of Fife he had expressed earlier (IV.i.74). He had surely not avoided Macduff "of all men else" because of what he gives as the reason for his refusal to fight: "My soul is too much charg'd / With blood of thine already" (V.viii.5–6). To read into this sentence a repentance is to disregard the meaninglessness of the concept of soul for the Macbeth who has lost his self. And undisguised fear is his reaction to Macduff's revelation of himself as the man of no woman born: "Accursed be the tongue that tells me so, / For it hath cow'd my better part of man!" (17–18). His belief of having won a new self, free from fear, is shown to be an illusion. Thus again, just before the catastrophe, Macbeth avoids a true self-discovery; he fails to "know himself" in the ethical-religious sense of the humanists, although he knows himself as a coward well enough. We are the more aware of his moral failure because of the great number of explicit *nosce teipsum* references—*Macbeth* can be said to have more of these than any other play of Shakespeare. The tragedy that presents self-loss on the largest scale also reasserts most strongly the value and significance of the humanistic concept of self-knowledge.

In its last scenes, the play points up the self-destructiveness of a manhood such as Macbeth's that lacks all ethical considerations. Macbeth's cry of fear when he faces Macduff demonstrates that the acquired *vis, emphasis,* and *dynamis* are not enough to preserve Macbeth's *alacritas,* that painfully acquired courage. The phrase "better part of man," generally used to refer to the soul, has an ironic ring in the mouth of the man whom Macduff calls hell-hound and traitor; the phrase might well be transcribed as "hope for survival." Macbeth's last fear is the fear of death. Macduff has to shock him into fighting by threatening to display him as a monster for public show, as a beast rather than a man. That Macduff on this occasion calls him "coward" may also awaken that old fear in Macbeth of being thought fearful—so potent in him, as the Lady knew—and help to lash him into a last desperate action.

Macduff's fight with Macbeth takes place behind the stage, so we never really learn whether Macbeth's last stand (or is it a run?) is as determined as he would have it; but the last words we hear, "And damn'd be him that first cries, 'Hold, enough!' " sound like a self-pronounced epitaph. Also, the episode intervening between his cry and Macduff's return with the head of Macbeth would lose its significance if it were not intended as a contrast to the death of a coward. In this episode, Ross reports the death of young Siward to his father:

> Your son, my lord, has paid a soldier's debt.
> He only liv'd but till he was a man;
> The which no sooner had his prowess confirm'd
> In the unshrinking station where he fought
> But like a man he died.
>
> (V.viii.39–43)

There is an irony in young Siward's dying like a man whereas Macbeth, who had so strenuously sought to be what the Lady suggested to him, "more than man," has become no better than a beast. The "unshrinking station" where the young man ends his life evokes by contrast the shrinkage of Macbeth's world; and old Siward's acclaim of his son's prowess points up the cowardice of the tyrant. The father takes consolation in his son's bearing his wound in front: "Had I as many sons as I have hairs, / I would not wish them to a fairer death" (48–49). We are not told whether Macbeth receives his fatal wound in front or in back; nobody asks Macduff, and Macduff merely presents "the usurper's head" without comment. At any rate, Macbeth's end, however exactly it comes about, is not "fair." Nothing is falser to the spirit of the play than the final bravado performance often given by actors of the role. Macbeth's death is not even worthy of the epitaph usually bestowed on the hero at the close. In his concluding speech, Malcolm merely refers in passing to "the dead butcher and his fiend-like queen." We realize in the flash of the reference that even the memory of the man who lost his self will soon be lost in Scotland.

CHAPTER EIGHTEEN

The Tempest:
The Mastered Self

N EAR THE END of Shakespeare's career stands a simple play not of self-loss but of self-gain. Shakespeare may well have intended it to have been his final one; it is difficult to think of *Henry VIII* as anything but an afterthought. A comedy or a tragicomedy, of course, was expected to present an action that moved toward self-gain; and the romances Shakespeare wrote during his last phase, *Pericles, Cymbeline, The Winter's Tale,* and *The Tempest,* all conclude happily with their heroes' self-recoveries. But *The Tempest* differs from the other romances in notable ways: the hero's self-loss has taken place before the beginning of the play, as we are told by him in the second scene; during the action, he is in command of himself and in control of the events. Further self-loss is a continuing threat to Prospero—a somewhat more serious threat, I think, than is usually realized—but because it is avoided and because the play never really approaches tragedy, it is not quite in the same category as are its immediate predecessors. It probably deserves to be called a comedy rather than a tragicomedy.

Indeed *The Tempest* continues and perfects the comic treatment of the themes of self-loss, self-search, and self-recovery on which Shakespeare structured his early comedies; it gives this structure a new and more festive polish. But a reading of *The Tempest* against the background of Shakespeare's developing patterns of self-knowledge suggests resemblances also to most other preceding plays, even to that signal tragedy of self-loss *Macbeth*. Reading *The Tempest* in such fashion, as I propose to do in this concluding chapter, will allow us to glance back at Shakespeare's earlier patterns as well as to see in perspective Shakespeare's final achievement in giving dramatic form to the ideas that have been the concern of this study.

To call *The Tempest* a simple play, as I have done, is to invite contradition in view of the diversity of interpretations it has produced; yet simplicity seems to me one of its most notable qualities. The story is, admittedly, a trifle fantastic; some of its credibility depends on the acceptance of magic, which for us, contrary to the Jacobeans, requires a suspension of disbelief. But the fine web of fantasy Shakespeare spun in the play lessens the problem; we give our hearts to *The Tempest* much as we do to fairy tales. And perhaps for this reason critics become fanciful and imaginative when they analyze it; its outlines become vast, wavering, and infinite, and we are told that "any interpretation, even the wildest, is more or less plausible." [1]

Actually, no play of Shakespeare's has a clearer dramatic structure, one more closely tied up with the nature of its hero and the major strands of its thought than this, and few have as simple a thematic content. That *The Tempest* observes the unities of time, place, and action—the only play of Shakespeare after the early *Comedy of Errors* to do so—is well known. The action is fitly digested into five acts—they are accurately marked in the Folio text—according to the formula derived from the comedies of Terence, modified in the epitasis by a movement that comes from revenge tragedy. In its act structure, composite but yet composite on a simple plan, *The Tempest* could be compared with *Love's Labor's Lost* (for the simple formula) and with *Hamlet* (for the revenge plot).

There is, of course, room for disagreement on the place of details in this pattern and even more on the meaning of the action. But no legitimate interpretation can avoid speaking of the losses and their recoveries and of the material, moral, and spiritual transformations that give movement to the action. On a very simple level, this idea is articulated in an almost liturgical tone by the good old counselor Gonzalo in the comic catastrophe of the last act. Recalling that he and the other Neapolitans set out to attend the wedding of the King of Naples' daughter at Tunis, Gonzalo hails the journey's unexpected outcome:

> O, rejoice
> Beyond a common joy, and set it down
> With gold on lasting pillars: in one voyage
> Did Claribel her husband find at Tunis;
> And Ferdinand, her brother, found a wife

Where he himself was lost; Prospero his dukedom
In a poor isle; and all of us ourselves
When no man was his own.

(V.i.206–13)

The losing-finding antithesis that forms the text of Gonzalo's hymn
to joy recalls the rhythm of the paradox of salvation Shakespeare
had used in previous plays to emphasize the importance of self-
knowledge and to give structural patterns to his plays. Because the
adaptation of the losing-finding formula in *The Tempest* grows out
of these earlier instances, a glance back will serve to demonstrate
Shakespeare's reliance on this pattern of self-knowledge for recurring
as well as changing thematic ideas and to point up its particular configuration in the present play.

The formula, as we noted, was basic to the thematic structure of
Shakespeare's two earliest comedies, *The Comedy of Errors* and
Love's Labor's Lost. Although *The Comedy of Errors* primarily
exploits the outward possibilities and impossibilities of mistaken
identities, it at least implies the danger of self-loss and depicts the
joy of self-recovery. When Antipholus of Syracuse arrives in
Ephesus to search for his brother, he feels like a drop of water
searching for another drop in the vast ocean. "So I," he says, "to
find a mother and a brother, / In quest of them, unhappy, lose myself" (I.ii.39–40). Antipholus's search starts a chain reaction of
errors, making the twin-masters and twin-servants doubt at times
that they know who they are. *The Comedy of Errors* attains whatever thematic depth it has by the comic horror Shakespeare injected
into the threatening loss of identities, and its happy finale comes
about through a universal finding. The movement from self-loss to
self-recovery is very similar to that of *The Tempest;* but in the later
play, both the seriousness of the one and the joy of the other are
heightened: Prospero's enemies are restrained only by his magic
power from doing harm to each other and to themselves, and his
forgiveness has a sacerdotal quality that brings about a more spectacular recovery. But in the endings of both plays, the resumption of
true identities and relationships creates the hope that a better order
will evolve when the respective sets of hostile cities, Ephesus and
Syracuse, Milan and Naples, are leagued in marriage; *The Tempest,*
however, makes this point more strongly through a marriage of
the heirs of the rulers. On the other hand, the ending of *The Tem-*

pest does not depict merely a finding of brother by brother but the reconciliation of two sets of formerly hostile brothers; and the question—one we must postpone for the moment—of the completeness and permanence of this reconciliation has been raised by critics.

Closer to the thematic structure of *The Tempest* than *The Comedy of Errors* is *Love's Labor's Lost*. It is essentially a comedy of self-loss and self-recovery that turns on the problem of self-search. King Ferdinand and his three courtiers are shown to be mistaken in their belief that they can find their true selves by withdrawing into an academy that bars influences disturbing to study, particularly women and love. When the princess and her ladies-in-waiting arrive on the scene, nature promptly takes its course and Cupid his revenge. The love-stricken courtiers are in a dilemma that even the astute Berowne cannot solve with his quibble on the losing-finding antithesis: "Let us once lose our oaths to find ourselves, / Or else we lose ourselves to keep our oaths" (IV.iii.358–59). This ingenious turn of the formula Shakespeare may have borrowed from the Genevan-Tomson side-note to Matthew 16:25: "they that deny Christ to save themselves do not only not gain that which they look for but also lose the thing they would have kept, that is, themselves, which loss is the greatest of all." If "losing oneself" is the greatest loss of all—as the side-note says and Berowne implies—"finding oneself," in the sense of becoming a human being who attains his greatest moral potential and assumes his proper role in society, is the greatest gain. The endings of both *Love's Labor's Lost* and *The Tempest* pay tribute to the precious goal of "finding" as well as to the difficulty of achieving it. The courtiers of Navarre, who have thoughtlessly sworn vows contrary to nature and who have shown no compunction about breaking these vows, ill-advised as they were, must, on the princess's orders, expiate their transgressions in a year of penitence and service; the gayest of the courtiers, Berowne, who had sworn against his better knowledge, must prove his regeneration by serving his term of penitence in a hospital. There is good reason to believe that he and his fellow sinners will eventually find their true selves as both honorable gentlemen and men of flesh and blood since the princess and her ladies-in-waiting have promised to marry them if they pass their tests. In *The Tempest*, Prospero arranges the finding of the others and of himself. He resembles in this respect, as in some others, Duke Vincentio in *Measure for Measure*. Prospero, in the end, forgives transgressions as great as does Vincentio—and certainly much greater ones than does the princess—and he forgives, as do the arrangers of these two comedies, in order to make humane values triumph. However, as I shall argue, *The Tempest,* particularly through the character of its hero and the nature of its ending, makes the point even more strongly that self-finding must be accomplished through a discipline based on a realistic understanding of the nature of man.

When we turn to the tragedies, we find self-loss to be the main theme and self-gain to be implied as a desirable goal. The self-losses of the tragic heroes and villains arise from serious moral failures, from passion, sin, and crime, and they lead to the destruction of the heroes and of other characters, innocent and guilty. The nuanced value system Shakespeare infused into the tragedies from *Hamlet* on gave the losing-finding formula a subtler, more existential meaning. The Danish prince exercises his probing mind on all questions about his own role and the function of man in the world, and yet he loses himself more and more in the web of his destiny. Once during his probing for certainty in the world of shifting realities, Hamlet touches on the biblical losing-finding formula. Just before his fatal duel with Laertes, a test that to Hamlet appears one of self-knowledge as well as of physical skill, he asks the perplexing question: "Since no man of ought he leaves knows, what is't to leave betimes?" (V.ii.216). If this version of the passage, that of Quarto 2, is correct, as I think it is, Hamlet here gives a skeptical turn to the paradox of salvation; for him, life has no recognizable pattern, and man profits little by retaining it. But Hamlet's preceding reference to the special providence in the fall of a sparrow suggests that, at least to God, the pattern is meaningful. A similar skepticism-fideism, emphasized by a view of the world as illusionary and temporary, is beautifully expressed in Prospero's end-of-revels speech; but the detachment with which Prospero views the transcience of all earthly things has some drops of soothing serenity that are completely absent from Hamlet's tentative acceptance of the divinity that shapes all ends.

Although self-losses occur in all the tragedies and the importance of self-recovery is suggested somehow in all of them, the losing-finding formula rings particularly strongly in *Lear* and *Macbeth*. In *Lear,* the paradox of what the world seeks and what it loses becomes a tragic agony. The King of France weaves from this paradox the beautiful speech in which he accepts the disinherited Cordelia, who is "most rich, being poor; / Most choice, forsaken; and most lov'd, despis'd" (I.i.250–51). In the course of the play, Lear, who has let evil develop in himself and in others, has fleeting glimpses of his and man's true nature as he loses himself in anger, grief, and madness. By contrast, Edgar, from being a man whose name is lost, comes to find himself in the end; and he assumes a more significant role than he has in the beginning. But even if Edgar's self-recovery anticipates, in some fashion, Prospero's, it is more painfully achieved and at greater loss. Neither—since Edgar is not the hero—did Shakespeare focus on the state of his soul as he did on Prospero's.

Macbeth is as relentless a tragedy of self-loss as *The Tempest* is a consistent comedy of self-gain. Macbeth's self-loss is pointed up by the evasiveness with which he speaks about losing the "eternal jewel" of his soul. But by his negative example and by his oppression of Scotland, this tragedy makes a strong point that a man must seek to find himself and that a country can find itself only when it is ruled morally. "The time is free" when Scotland shakes off the oppressor's yoke in the end. Though the benevolent Prospero and the murderous Macbeth are worlds apart, *The Tempest* not only dramatizes self-finding but also demonstrates the danger of self-loss. An evil similar to that of Macbeth (although it is not examined in its origin or spotlighted in its manifestation) dwells in the soul of Prospero's brother Antonio, who plots the murder of King Alonso with the help of Alonso's own brother, Sebastian. Prospero's firm direction keeps these wicked plotters and would-be regicides from succumbing to the total self-loss that engulfs Macbeth. To Prospero himself, nothing worse seems to happen in the play than a temporary threat to his peace of mind; but I shall argue that this threat does present a danger, particularly because we know that he has harmed himself years ago by becoming lost in his studies and by thus facilitating Antonio's usurpation of his throne. Prospero's self-recovery from this evil of omission is the main plot of *The Tempest*.

However, evil is a less serious threat in *The Tempest* than in the other romances, which veer toward tragedy. In *The Winter's Tale,* for instance, Leontes's unfounded accusation and condemnation of Hermione brings about the death of his son Mamilius. If these heroes do not suffer permanent self-losses, the reasons lie in the extraordinary efforts of recovery through penitence and faith they make or in the powerful help, human and divine, they receive. The romances, with their stories of shipwreck, of broken and reunited families, of deep self-losses and strong, sometimes miraculous, recoveries, make the losing-finding formula even more prominent than do the early comedies, but the formula is now pregnant with moral and spiritual associations.

However, none of the romances or any other play of Shakespeare gives greater prominence to the losing-finding formula and extols self-finding more melodiously than does *The Tempest*. No other play makes the presence of the formula as strongly felt; "lose," "lost," "loss," "search," "find," and "found" are key words that occur at significant junctures of the action and provide clues to the placement of the characters in the total design. These words are also constant reminders that the action presented brings a long story to a climax: losses are to be remedied, ills to be healed, and blessings to be gained.

The spectacular tempest that opens the play and furnishes its title is an example of this fusion of past and present. Apparently it brings about the loss of a ship, its passengers, and its crew. But the second scene makes it clear that this storm is also a reenactment of that earlier storm, twelve years past, in which Prospero and his infant daughter, Miranda, expelled from Milan by the evil Antonio, were cruelly exposed to the roaring of the waves; by firmly controlling the effect of the present storm and preventing harm to human lives, Prospero recoups his loss and makes it possible for all to be themselves. Renaissance rhetoric had taught the Jacobeans to think of storms as metaphorical for the gusts of passion and the blows of fortune. The initial storm may thus be taken to symbolize the passions of the ship's guilty passengers, the passions that brought about Prospero's expulsion and continue to threaten violence on the island. But this storm may also be understood to symbolize the passions of Prospero, slumbering as they are during most of the play. We learn of his potentially passionate nature by his account of that earlier, intellectual ecstasy, when, "transported / And rapt in secret studies," he let his brother usurp his place (I.ii.76–77). Most of all, we experience Prospero's one, if muted, outbreak of anger when, at the decisive moment of the play, disgust with Caliban's revolt wells up in him and threatens to make him prefer revenge to mercy.

Shakespeare's audience would have especially relished the story of the shipwreck and the miraculous preservation of its passengers and crew because of the similar fate of his majesty's ship *Sea Adventure*, wrecked on the reefs of Bermuda in 1609. Shakespeare exploited the interest created by the incident; he had Ariel remember how Prospero once awakened him, while sleeping at the same nook where now the Neapolitan ship is safely hidden, in order to have him "fetch dew / From the still-vex'd Bermoothes" (I.ii.228–29). But if Shakespeare could count on his audience's familiarity with this topical incident, he could and did rely even more on their knowledge of a moral tradition that made shipwreck a prime test of human reaction to fate and fortune. Narratives of the Bermuda wreck, particularly that in the Council of Virginia's apologetic *True Declaration of the State of the Colony of Virginia* (1610), were tinged with this moral tradition.[2] It was one that, derived from Homer's *Odyssey,* was continued in Virgil's *Aeneid* and became familiar in the Renaissance to many a grammar-school boy, including William Shakespeare, through Erasmus's colloquy *Naufragium.* As Professor Baldwin has noted, Erasmus presents a tempest that recalls Shakespeare's in many respects, although Erasmus was more obviously interested in the moral make-up of his characters.[3] But even so, one could well expect Shakespeare's audience to have concluded from the extremely vivid first scene of *The Tempest* that the shipwreck represents a moral-psychological test for the passengers and crew and that nearly all fail it as they are thrown into utter confusion, get into each other's way, curse, and despair: "All lost! . . . All lost!" (I.i.48).

There is one notable exception: the old counselor Gonzalo, who keeps his humor and, though in vain, admonishes the others to be patient; by contrast, Sebastian laments that he is "out of patience" (51). From the beginning, Gonzalo's role in the play is crucial. Throughout, he is the voice of charity and patience. This is a voice frequent in Shakespeare; but, as we have noted, it became more insistent from *Lear* onward. It is embodied sometimes in a young man like Edgar, more often in an old man, like Gonzalo and his fellow counselor Helicanus in *Pericles,* but most often in suffering women, in Cordelia, Marina, Imogene, Hermione, Perdita, and Paulina. In view of the customary identification of Prospero with Shakespeare, it is intriguing to ponder that, judging by the fact that his name appears in fourth and fifth position of the actors of his company, Shakespeare is more likely to have thought of himself when writing the part of Gonzalo than when writing that of Prospero. But Shakespeare probably did not act in *The Tempest,* and one should realize that the voice of Gonzalo, that of patience—important as it is for articulating the virtue that was becoming the most important one for the achievement of self-knowledge in Shakespeare's later plays—is still only one of his many voices. The aging Shakespeare may have felt greater need for patience; but he knew also of many other needs.

The patient Gonzalo is an instrument of the power of good and demonstrates how man may endure and even master his fate. When the storm of fortune raged hardest for Prospero, it was Gonzalo who gave him the means to regain control over his fate by furnishing the bark in which he and Miranda were set adrift with the books from which Prospero gained his knowledge of magic. On the island, Gonzalo constantly tries to cheer and comfort his companions. He finds that they have cause for joy, as he says in his first words after the miraculous rescue: "for our escape / Is much beyond our loss" (II.i.2–3). It is Gonzalo who, awakened by Ariel, cries out and thus unknowingly saves the king and himself from being murdered by Antonio and Sebastian. His cry, "good angels / Preserve the King" (II.i.298–99), is symptomatic of his reliance on heavenly help; he is the only one among the Neapolitans to invoke it. Gonzalo becomes at times a choric commentator, registering the transformations that take place, noting the outward signs of the effect of guilt on the others, and rejoicing about the completed changes in the end. His tears, shed for the suffering of the others, engender "fellowly" drops in Prospero —"holy Gonzalo" Prospero calls him then (V.i.62). His example makes Prospero in the end reaffirm patience as an abiding virtue. When Alonso laments what he thinks is the irreparable loss of his son and claims that "Patience / Says it is past her cure," Prospero (thinking of losing Miranda through marriage) answers: "For the like loss I have her sovereign aid / And rest myself content" (V.i. 140–44).

Thus Gonzalo becomes a pattern of patience and charity for all, even for Prospero. It is a patience anchored in faith—Christian in a general sense (although the pagan Cordelia has it too); it is tempered by sympathy and pity rather than hardened into suppression of the emotions as the Stoics recommended. Gonzalo's orientation toward one dominant trait is a feature he shares with other characters in Shakespeare's baroque plays and makes critics speak of allegory. But Gonzalo has other, if less important, traits; we simply are made more aware of the one that is primary for the function he has in the thematic movement.

Of the traits that prevent him from becoming a mere symbol of patience, his garrulity and whimsicality help to take the edge off some of his moral commentary. Shakespeare allows him a holiday of the spirit on the "poor isle" whose enchanting airs encourage all kinds of extravaganzas. Crudely derided by the others, Gonzalo paraphrases the famous passage in Montaigne's essay "Of the Cannibals" that describes in glowing colors an anarchistic utopia of universal happiness. Gonzalo would like to make the island into such a state and govern, somewhat illogically, as a king "with such perfection . . . / T' excel the golden age" (II.i.161–62). But the island turns out to be a quite different country from the idealized Brazil of Montaigne's essay—Shakespeare was aware that travelers' tales like those glorified by Montaigne do lie. Although the spirits commanded by Prospero appear to Gonzalo to be islanders of monstrous shapes but of manners kinder than civilized men's, the banquet they serve to the starved Neapolitans proves a cruel mirage; it is snatched away by Ariel in the guise of a harpy. From now on, the Neapolitans' life is a nightmare. Thus, in his utopian dream, Gonzalo, after a fashion, loses himself; but his self-loss is of the mildest kind, a fantasy of what cannot be and must not be. The island of dreams, the forest of Arden, the golden age are never more than temporary retreats in Shakespeare's plays. Man who knows himself must accept the actual world and assume his proper role in it. Gonzalo cannot live in a benevolent anarchy, but must again be a counselor of princes. Prospero cannot remain on the island that he rules so well, but has to return to Milan to govern as duke. And all others must resume their destined functions and offices.

If a positive and sympathetic reaction to the storm and shipwreck characterizes Gonzalo, so it does Miranda. As she watches the events from the shore, she sympathizes with the suffering of the people whom she fears to be lost: "O, I have suffer'd / With those that I saw suffer" (I.ii.5–6). Miranda is blessed with that active patience, a species of fortitude as well as a religious virtue in the humanistic system of values. Like the patience of Marina in *Pericles,* hers smiles "extremity out of act." As a child, she instilled her groaning father with "fortitude from heaven" when she helped him to bear up in the storm-tossed boat that carried the two to the island (I.ii.154). But Miranda also plays a part in the thematic movement from self-loss to self-recovery. Like the Neapolitans and like Prospero, she is the victim of "sea-sorrow." The earlier storm that drove her to the island has wiped out her identity; she has lost her privileged place in the

world. She still remembers vaguely that she was once favored by
her birth; her only childhood recollection is that she was tended by
four or five women (I.ii.46). She is now ignorant of what she is,
as her father says (I.ii.18), both in the sense of knowing neither her
exact position nor the real world that surrounds her. But directed by
her instincts and guided by Prospero, she will find herself in the
end as the future wife of Ferdinand and as the prospective queen of
Naples.

Before she can find herself, she must suffer another "sea change"
through the impact of the outside world on her sheltered existence.
Because she has never seen a man besides her old father and the semi-
devil Caliban, she idealizes the creatures of the brave new world,
particularly the handsome Ferdinand. Miranda's innocence is, baroque fashion, heightened by being spectacularly contrasted with the
evil of the world. Unacquainted with this evil—her bad experience
with the only half-human Caliban evidently does not count—she
equates appearance with reality. She objects to Prospero's calling
Ferdinand a spy: "There's nothing ill can dwell in such a temple"
(I.ii.457). She happens to be right in this case, but she is quite
wrong when she hails the checkered company of the Neapolitans:
"How beauteous mankind is! O brave new world / That has such
people in't." Prospero's comment is sobering: " 'Tis new to thee"
(V.i.183–84). She mistakes the old world for the new, and she is too
innocent and idealistic to realize that both contain much evil. She
will have to acquire some prudence and practical wisdom if she is
not to be lost in the world in which she must play a stellar part. But
she is virtuous and she can inspire—and does in Ferdinand—virtuous behavior.

In her innocence, bordering on naïveté, Miranda bears some
resemblance to the pastoral maidens of Fletcher's tragicomedies. The
whole idea of such pristine innocence as hers is precarious to a degree
that one step further will lead to absurdity. Dryden and Sir William
Davenant took this step in their adaptation of *The Tempest* when
they made out of Miranda two white virgins shrouded in ignorance
but not devoid of human instincts and confronted them with a young
man much more naïve than the pellucid Ferdinand because he had
never seen a woman. Dryden thought this triplication of ignorance
an "excellent contrivance," and the situations arising from it are indeed pleasantly risqué; but Shakespeare would never have succumbed to the temptation inherent in the baroque to paint with

strong colors by applying false ones as did his adapters. Miranda's naïveté is bearable because her case is singular; and, besides, she has an appealing vitality that makes her take a refreshingly active role in courtship. Her father's vigilance—or so at least he thinks— is required to prevent her from further self-loss by throwing herself on Ferdinand. But we may trust her power of recovery when in the final scene she is revealed as playing with her fiancé that game of intellectual patience *par excellence,* chess. We feel that she is bound to become Ferdinand's support and comfort as she was Prospero's.

It appears that Ferdinand will need her. The young man of the beginning of the play who is the first to jump from the burning ship with the cry "Hell is empty, / And all the devils are here" (I.ii.214– 15), is evidently in need of some improvement. But Ferdinand is not burdened with guilt as is his father, and he has positive virtues. He demonstrates his filial affection when he grieves for the loss of his father whom he believes to be drowned (I.ii.487, III.i.58). He is the first of Alonso's party to feel the power of regeneration as Ariel's music creeps by him on the waters, "Allaying both their fury and my passion / With its sweet air" (I.ii.392–93). Cheered on by Miranda, he demonstrates a newfound patience in the emblematic log-carrying task and proves his equilibrium at chess.

Of the older Neapolitans, King Alonso is relatively sympa- thetically portrayed. Although he abetted the usurpation of Prospero's dukedom by Antonio, Alonso is clearly not a soul totally lost. He has a capacity for human sentiments; he suffers deeply from the loss of his son, following hard upon that of his daughter (e.g., II.i. 103, 116, 129, 313; III.iii.75, 100; V.i.137). In violent despair, he seeks to drown himself in the sea "deeper than e'er plummet sounded / And with him there lie mudded" (III.iii.101–2). His sorrow, the self-destructive grief of which the humanists and theologians warned, is in part punishment for his complicity in Antonio's crime. But grief as such is still a noble passion, and Alonso's basic goodness shows itself in his repentance in the end. Although the marriage of Ferdinand and Miranda makes him "twice lose" his son (V.i.177), he says "amen" when Gonzalo wishes them a blessed crown, and he adds his voice to the old counselor's hymn to joy (V.i.204 ff.).

The two arch-plotters, Sebastian and Antonio, are so perverse as to be moved by Alonso's grief not to sympathy but to a murder plot. With Alonso and Ferdinand removed, Antonio wickedly suggests, Sebastian may seize power without interference. Antonio's influence on Sebastian and their Machiavellian plotting has a distinct resemblance to Lady Macbeth's incitement of Macbeth before the murder of Duncan. Poetic justice requires that these two criminals be harshly treated. Consequently, they are sorely struck by Prospero's magic: in madness they wander through the island in search of an invisible enemy and are in danger of killing each other. "And even with such-like valour men hang and drown / Their proper selves," comments Ariel (III.iii.59–60). The tempest in their hearts, threatening self-loss, is at its climax. One must assume them to rave in frenzy through the fourth act while the masque is performed and Prospero makes his nostalgic farewell speeches. Not until the fifth act are Sebastian and Antonio released, together with the despairing Alonso, by Prospero's heavenly music.

Some critics have been disturbed because neither Sebastian nor Antonio manifests repentance, and they have seen in this omission Shakespeare's lack of confidence in the way he brought *The Tempest* to a conclusion.[4] But conscience is, after all, at work in their self-threatening fury just as it is in Alonso's despair. "Their great guilt," comments Gonzalo, "Like poison given to work a great time after, / Now gins to bite the spirits" (III.iii.105–6). There is some indication that a moral transformation has taken place in Sebastian when he hails the reappearance of Ferdinand and his union with Miranda as "a most high miracle" (V.i.177). Sebastian now acknowledges the divine power that he derided when Gonzalo attributed to it the preservation of the travelers after the shipwreck. True, there is not even such a sign of a change of heart in Antonio, and this silence is alarming. But would not a declaration of repentance, which Shakespeare could easily have provided, be even more disturbing? Such profession, which could hardly be very long and very eloquent in the pressure of the ending, would scarcely have been convincing.

Antonio is the most wicked character of the play; the influence he wields over Sebastian is almost comparable to that of Iago over Othello. We may on this basis surmise that he will plot again; but it is vain to predict what any of Shakespeare's characters will do after they leave the stage, whose illusion is their only reason for existence. (That we are constantly tempted into guessing is a tribute to Shakespeare's power to make us believe in the reality of his creations.) We cannot really know whether Antonio will or will not plot again. What we can say is that in Shakespeare's conception "every man with his affects is born, / Not by might mast'red, but

by special grace" (*Love's Labor's Lost,* I.i.149–50). Antonio, born
with more passions than most men, surely needs both uncommon
strength, vigilant supervision, and a strong dose of heavenly grace
if he is to master them. But when even a Caliban, brought up in
Setebos-worship, promises in the end of the play to "be wise hereafter / And seek for grace" (V.i.294–95), one may discern some
hope also for Antonio. The emphasis of Shakespeare's ending, at any
rate, is not on the miraculous efficacy of conversions but on Prospero's power of forgiveness. If we are left with the impression that
Antonio will require Prospero's supervision in Milan, we may take
that as a tribute to Prospero's strength—a purely human strength
after his renunciation of magic.

Of Ariel and Caliban one can hardly speak in the same analytical
terms as one speaks of human characters. The two are creatures of a
brilliant fantasy that tempts a scholar to become a poet. Shakespeare's empathetic imagination triumphs when it rides on the
curled clouds, swims through the water, and dives into the fire with
Ariel, and when it creeps on the ground, listens to the noises of the
island, and breathes its sweet airs with Caliban. *The Tempest,* like
the other romances, has levels of movement that leave the dull
brain behind. But the scholar can say at least that Ariel belongs to a
Platonic realm of the spirit that lies beyond the sensual and rational
one. Crawling on the ground with Caliban is no more comfortable
an intellectual experience; one must assimilate himself to a quite
different realm and a no less strange one, that of half-human
monsters. Caliban, too, is a fantastic and unique creature, sketchily
but evocatively drawn so as to leave much to the imagination in
which such as he must live if they are to live at all.

But it is to my purpose in elucidating the thematic structure of
The Tempest to recall that Caliban and Ariel, different as they are,
have something in common that is important for the movement of
the play: they suffer from a similar sense of dislocation and depend
on Prospero for their release from servitude. They thirst for the
freedom they have lost, and we cannot help sympathizing a little
even with Caliban's pathetic desire; but we should not forget that he
seeks freedom to avenge himself, freedom to hurt and to kill. He
lacks both gratitude and sense when he exchanges his benevolent
master, Prospero, for the braggadocio, Stephano, and the raga-
muffin, Trinculo. When the noblemen lose themselves in dreams,
conspiracy, and grief, Caliban and the two clowns whom he deifies

lose themselves in the bottle. The apocalypse that strikes the noblemen dumps the servants in the pool, where they drop their bottle—an
infinite loss for Stephano (IV.i.207). Prospero has his spirits
administer a thorough drubbing to the three, and Caliban, at least,
comes to realize his stupidity. Whether he will be able to remain wise
as he promises depends on the "grace" he seeks and on strong
guidance. Appropriately, he and his two companions are released not
into immediate freedom but into temporary servitude so that they
may find their proper subordinate place in society: they are ordered
by Prospero to trim his island cave, whereas Ariel receives immediately his deserved freedom. The humorous Caliban subplot thus
adds a scherzo movement to the symphonic theme of self-loss and
self-recovery that reaches its purest notes in the soprano voice of
Ariel.

   The subhuman Caliban and the superhuman Ariel are the poles
between which Prospero is placed. He shares a reason aided by grace
with the former and the world of the senses and passions with the
latter; the two creatures indicate the directions, evil and good, into
which Prospero can move. In a way, all of Shakespeare's characters
are placed between two such poles, but none is so visibly and, at the
same time, symbolically assigned to a field of action in which he must
move, a field that reaches from almost beneath the earth to just below the heavens. And, from the beginning, Prospero moves with
energy and determination. The concentration and speed of the action
result from his vigorous and firm control. He makes use of the
advantage offered to him by providence and brings the moment to its
crisis:

> by my prescience
> I find my zenith doth depend upon
> A most auspicious star, whose influence
> If now I court not, but omit, my fortunes
> Will ever after droop.
>
> (I.ii.180–84)

   One could say even that the classical unities the play possesses
are due to Prospero's direction. Divine providence brought Alonso's
ship to the island, but it is Prospero who makes the work of punishment, redemption, and reconciliation happen in the last four hours
of his island residence. Almost as if he had a stopwatch in his hand,

he says to Ariel: "The time 'twixt six and now / Must by us both
be spent most preciously" (I.ii.240–41). All through the play, there
is a sense of speed, starting with the first cries of the mariners,
"bestir, bestir," a feeling maintained by frequent expletives like
"here" and "now" and by the several references to Ariel's impending
release and the completion of Prospero's work.[5] The movement of
the action, including its temporary relaxation in the more idyllic
fourth act, is rigorously controlled by him. His energy infuses itself
into everything and everybody, produces the storm and the rescue
of the Neapolitans, sends Ariel about his work, separates Ferdinand
from the others, engineers his meeting with Miranda, keeps the two
from too precipitous a union, confounds and punishes his enemies,
puts on a mask in celebration of the coming wedding, and finally
effects the universal recovery and reconciliation.

Prospero's control is the more impressive as it requires only a
minimum of his magic skill. That he possesses great occult powers is
suggested, but very little of what he actually does on the stage
violates the laws of nature.[6] He is not a very professional magician,
as critics have noted. He has no magic cauldrons, no witches' brew,
no squeaking ghosts. The passage in which he evokes most nearly the
traditional image of the sorcerer is his speech beginning with "Ye
elves of hills, brooks, standing lakes, and groves" (V.i.33 ff.).
These lines are adapted from Medea's incantation in Ovid's *Metamorphoses;* but some of Ovid's lurid details are left out, and the
speech serves only to abjure "this rough magic." [7]

Prospero exerts his power largely through Ariel, whom he has
learned to understand and to control evidently by the study of the
books he prized above his dukedom; at times, Ariel appears to be
an extension of his mind and imagination.[8] Prospero practices white
magic or theurgy, that is, magic in the service of good and performed
by benevolent spirits. He appears to have derived it from a study of
natural philosophy and its excrescences astrology and alchemy, and
also from a knowledge of the properties of music—one of the liberal
arts in which, as he says, he immersed himself in Milan. Prospero
uses music by drawing on its generally acknowledged hypnotic and
medicinal effects. Through his music, he stirs up emotions and allays
them: a melody in the winds and in the thunder threateningly sings
like an organ pipe the name of Prospero to the conscience-stricken
Alonso, and gentler strains sound in the tune that assuages the
Neapolitans' grief and fury. Music here has a transforming power on

the self; it has the kind of influence that interested Thomas Wright, the *nosce teipsum* author most concerned with the moving of the passions. (The section on the moving through music was added in the second edition of 1604, which had some new material on the control of the emotions.) Prospero's particular use of magic testifies to the fascination with human engineering Shakespeare evinced in his baroque plays. Like an Iago, Prospero knows how to make men lose themselves; but like an Edgar, although more successfully, he makes men find themselves.

Generally, Prospero dispenses even with his gentle magic and prefers the schoolmaster's apple and rod. He is the teacher of Miranda and Caliban, and, occasionally, of Ariel. After he has created the initial storm, he doffs his magic mantle and lectures Miranda on her past, observing in the process the degree of her attention and giving her, as it were, good and bad marks. If this be weakness, it is one with which Shakespeare may have had some personal experience and sympathy if, as Aubrey says, he was in his younger years a schoolmaster in the country. But if Prospero is at times the impatient pedagogue, he also has trained himself to be a patient researcher; he does not despise to learn even from Caliban, who curses himself for having shown Prospero the fresh springs, brine pits, and barren and fertile places.

One can look upon Prospero's activity as a kind of experiment for which the island provides the laboratory. If he is to be successful, he must show in this smaller setting that he will prevail in the greater world of Milan. His exile, except for being forced rather than voluntary, resembles the temporary experimental withdrawal of Duke Vincentio from the government of Vienna. Both dukes have a preference for the "life removed," a preference they find it hard to reconcile with the demands of their office. Both become engaged in experiments the nature of which is not evident in the beginning, experiments that involve their own self-knowledge, the government of their countries, and the relationship between their knowledge of themselves and the proper conduct of their political affairs. But *Measure for Measure* treats these problems with mannerist opaqueness and indirection. The questions, it turns out, are obliquely posed because of Vincentio's choice of the corrupt Angelo to give a demonstration of the difficulty man has in meting out judgments; and, as we noted, the outcome of it all is something of a question mark. It is true that the full nature of Prospero's experiment is not revealed until its results are established at the beginning of the fifth act when Prospero forgives his enemies and renounces his magic; but his experiment never has the psychological complications of Vincentio's, and the outcome, toward which the action develops logically and consistently, is much more neat and conclusive than that of the earlier play.

Because Prospero is the ruler over forces of nature, his experiment concerns not only psychology (or in the term of Shakespeare's time, moral philosophy) and politics but also natural science and raises the question of their relation. It is interesting in this respect that, on the connection and analogy between natural science and politics, Sir Francis Bacon based an appeal he addressed to King James in the first year of his reign. In *A Brief Discourse Touching the Happy Union of the Kingdoms of England and Scotland* (1603), Bacon argued that James should study nature in order to reign well and bring about the harmonious fusion of his two kingdoms. Bacon's Preface opens with the statement that the king should not find it strange that a certain book by Heraclitus, now lost, was regarded by some readers as a discourse on nature and by others as a treatise on politics, "because there is a great affinity and consent between the rules of nature and the true rules of policy, the one being nothing else but an order in the government of the world; and the other, in the government of an estate." Therefore, Bacon claimed, the education of the kings of Persia was called an education in "magic": "For the Persians, magic, which was the secret literature of their kings, was an observation in the contemplation of nature and an application there to a sense politic, taking the fundamental laws of nature, with the branches and passages of them, as an original and first model, whence to take and describe a copy and imitation for government." [9]

This curious reference to magic certainly does not prove that Shakespeare read the *Brief Discourse* and was influenced by it in writing *The Tempest*. By evincing an interest in the control of nature through human energy, Shakespeare showed that, like Bacon, he belonged to a period that was fascinated with the search for power, which, as a modern historian has said, was the common ground of the baroque age. [10] But, as we have noted at the beginning of this study, in their ideas about self-knowledge and its place in human endeavor, Bacon and Shakespeare differed fundamentally. In the *Brief Discourse* and elsewhere, Bacon looked upon natural science as the field under which to subsume all other human

ACHIEVEMENT AND SYNTHESIS

knowledge and activity, whereas Shakespeare even in his late
Tempest paid tribute to the humanistic view of man according to
which a knowledge of moral nature is the initiation to all other
human knowledge and endeavor. For Shakespeare-Prospero, the harmony of nature becomes secondary to the harmony of the self, which
must be established if the body politic is to be ordered and governed.
And the power over nature is much less important than the power
over the self for Prospero: he abandons his control over the forces
of nature voluntarily and returns to Milan as a ruler over himself and
his dukedom.

It is only from the point of view of the centrality of the moral self
and in the context of the play's movement from losing to finding that
the events of the fourth and the beginning of the fifth acts, together
with the most important speech of the play, the end-of-revels speech,
make sense. Already Prospero's admission of his failure as a duke,
which he makes to Miranda in the second scene, indicates how
personally he is involved in the losing-finding movement that underlies the action. His account of his rapture and transport during his
secret studies shows that he is a man of passionate dedication and has
an explosive temperament. He has mastered this earlier weakness;
but in the fourth act, he is beset by an inner turmoil that makes it at
least possible that he may lose again the stability of mind and the
control over himself and others he has gained in his twelve years of
island residence.

Shakespeare gave Prospero's disturbance strong dramatic emphasis
by having it occur in the midst of the most idyllic episode, the performance of the masque. For no apparent reason, Prospero suddenly
starts to speak. Instantaneously, his spirit-actors disperse, "to a
strange, hollow, and confused noise," as the Folio stage direction
says. In an aside, Prospero explains his vexation as due to his
remembering Caliban's rebellion. Both Ferdinand and Miranda
punctuate Prospero's distemper by astonished exclamations. Prospero then begins to speak haltingly, addressing Ferdinand, until his
emotion channels itself into the powerful visionary images of the
end-of-revels speech. But he stops abruptly, apologizes for his
weakness and infirmity, and announces that he will walk a turn or
two to "still" his beating mind. The force of his passion makes itself strongly felt, although Shakespeare softened its visual impression by taking him off the stage soon after its inception. Before
he goes, he expresses in a soliloquy his despair about the educability

of Caliban, a despair underlined by the repetition of the key-word "lost":

> A devil, a born devil, on whose nature
> Nurture can never stick; on whom my pains,
> Humanely taken, all, all lost, quite lost;
> And as with age his body uglier grows,
> So his mind cankers. I will plague them all,
> Even to a roaring.
>
> (IV.i.188–93)

When Prospero reappears, there is no apparent sign that his passion has lessened. He and Ariel unleash the spirits in the shape of dogs against the rebels, and Prospero's last words in the fourth act have an ominous ring: "At this hour / Lies at my mercy all mine enemies" (261–62). Prospero's enemies were at his mercy from the beginning of the play; his present awareness of his power over them raises the suspicion that he is tempted to avenge himself. Prospero is at the point where he must finally show that he is not made of the stuff of littleness that produces the villain who avenges himself but of the stuff of greatness that characterizes the hero who can forgive.

The significance of Prospero's anger and its connection with the end-of-revels speech has frequently been misunderstood. Theodore Spencer thought that "in Prospero there is no conflict; in his control of the world, internal conflict has no place." [11] But this opinion disregards both Prospero's obvious anger and the peculiar nature of this tension-fraught speech, of which something will have to be said later. Prospero's agony, it is true, takes a very different form from similar phenomena in heroes of earlier plays. It is largely intellectual; but it differs also from the melancholy cerebration of a Hamlet, which would be out of spirit with a festival play like *The Tempest* and would not be in agreement with the tendency in Shakespeare's later plays to punctuate strong movements toward man's losing or finding himself with ecstatic states of his soul. Such climaxes in Shakespeare's baroque tragedies and romances manifest themselves in rapture, epilepsy, dream-like experiences, and, in Prospero's case, in an apocalyptic vision, not in a discourse of reason or in a rhetorical expression of passion.

Frank Kermode, who is among the critics that are at least surprised by Prospero's strong perturbation, yet thinks it "apparently unnecessary" and surmises that it "may be the point in which an

oddly pedantic concern for classical structure causes it [the distur-
bance] to force its way through the surface of the play." [12] Far from
it, Prospero's anger is very important for the play, and it is not entirely unmotivated. The rebellion of Caliban threatens the loss of twelve
years of Prospero's educational labors with him and thus the failure
of one half of the strictly educational side of his experiment (the
success of the other half depends on Miranda's chastity). Further,
the boorish ingratitude of Caliban recalls the graver ingratitude of
Antonio, and Caliban's threat to Prospero's order mirrors the more
portentous threat to all order in Antonio's and Sebastian's plot
against Alonso. In a sense, Caliban's revolt can be taken as symbolic
of the recalcitrance and rebelliousness inherent in all human nature
owing to its being weighed down by its earthly ingredients. Thus
Caliban's rebellion can be thought to externalize an internal threat—
a threat as all men face it—to Prospero's stability, whose preservation is necessary for the happy outcome. In this respect, Caliban
becomes representative of the lower forces of Prospero's soul, of
his worse self. This interpretation is supported by Prospero's later
recognizing a kind of kinship with Caliban, "this thing of darkness,"
which he acknowledges as his own (V.i.275). Ariel, who in the
denouement sympathizes with Prospero's enemies, becomes symbolic
of Prospero's better self; but he is also superhuman—he has no
senses, as Shakespeare reminds us—and Prospero's problem is a
human one. Significantly, we hear of Ariel's sympathy after Prospero
has made his decision strictly as a human being (V.i.1 ff.).

Prospero's anger occurs at the structural climax of the play, the
summa epitasis, but it is a mistake to assume that the play's structure
produces the anger; it would be more appropriate to say that
Prospero's vexation creates the crisis. His present understandable
urge to avenge himself and his even more understandable temptation
to cling to his magic powers could be as costly to him as his earlier
intellectual fervor that deprived him of a dukedom. If Prospero is to
demonstrate that he knows himself and that he can bring the action
to a happy conclusion, he must once and climactically show that he
can exorcise the ghost of potential self-loss and resist the attraction
of superhuman power. This is the acid test of the long and painful
struggle Prospero has waged on his island; everything depends on
winning it. Only after he has shown convincingly that he has found
himself can he help his enemies to find themselves. When he does, the

revenge movement of the plot turns into a movement of reconciliation. Threatening loss becomes confirmed recovery.

Prospero's end-of-revels speech has to be understood in the dramatic and thematic context that I have just sketched. It is not Shakespeare's leave-taking from life and art or a soothing commonplace—although it has a glow of sunset and a touch of serenity—but it breathes Prospero's struggle with his intemperance and impatience. Blended of nostalgia and vexation as the speech is, it rises to a consideration of life that envelops and yet transcends Prospero's particular problem and general unhappiness.

Dramatically, the speech arises from Prospero's stormy mood that interrupts the masque. It is not in sober reflection but in a near-breakdown of his self-control that Prospero, his spirits scattered in fear, turns to the astonished Ferdinand and begins to speak haltingly: "You do look, my son, in a mov'd sort, / As if you were dismay'd; be cheerful, sir, / Our revels now are ended" (IV.i.146–48). If this assurance is not apt to console Ferdinand, neither is the panoramic prediction of the disappearance of all earthly things which follows. The spirit-actors, Prospero says,

> Are melted into air, into thin air;
> And, like the baseless fabric of this vision,
> The cloud-capp'd towers, the gorgeous palaces,
> The solemn temples, the great globe itself,
> Yea, all which it inherit, shall dissolve,
> And, like this insubstantial pageant faded,
> Leave not a rack behind. We are such stuff
> As dreams are made on; and our little life
> Is rounded with a sleep.
> (IV.i.150–58)

We are so familiar with the speech that we forget how full of tension, how puzzling and ambiguous it is.

Prospero seemingly disparages the masque, the "baseless fabric of this vision," with which he compares the fragile and unreal show of life. His imagination wings itself above the modest masque when he considers the analogous evanescence of the earth and the unreality of life; temporary as he knows the dream of existence to be, it is yet beautiful with its cloud-capped towers, gorgeous palaces, and solemn temples. There is here an aesthetic transfiguration of what, alas, is so fugitive, a transfiguration that envelops both life and the masque. The real and the artificial realms become indistinguishable: life is a vision and a pageant, and the masque becomes the great, dissolving globe. The beauty of the double evocation of transcience suggests Prospero's difficulty in distancing himself from both worlds, the natural and the supernatural one, as he must as an old man who approaches the end of his life and as a mere man who must divest himself of powers that are not man's to wield.

The two final images of Prospero's speech are evidence of his struggle for detachment by taking refuge in conventional ideas on life and death; they are an attempt to console himself and find equilibrium. The idea of Prospero's concluding sentence was and is commonplace, and Shakespeare's pregnant expression has made it more so to us. Yet, in their context, these lines are charged with an ambiguity that goes beyond the traditional nature of the sentiment they express. The comparison of life to a dream was typical of *contemptus mundi* attitudes; it was intended to prevent man from taking life on earth as the purpose of man. As Calderón's drama *La vida es sueño* shows, the concept appealed also to the baroque imagination. In Prospero's reflection, just as in Calderón's play, fragile man is still the maker of his dreams, and Prospero's has a seductive glory that makes one almost forget the evanescence that is its subject. Prospero's final image of sleep rounding off life evokes the proverbial figure of sleep as the image of death, which Shakespeare would have met in *Sententiae Pueriles* of early grammar school—*somnum imago mortis,* a proverb that was thought to accustom man to the idea of death. But the notion of the dream of life and perhaps also that of the sleep of death becomes tinged with the aesthetic and kinetic associations of the preceding stage-and-world images so as to suggest that the quality of the dream and possibly that of the sleep have something to do with man's performance in life. This, at most, is a suggestion conveyed through the images; but, perhaps, I have merely read it into the speech.

This is not a speech of certainty—if it were, it would not fit Prospero's humility as he expresses it in his epilogue. And the uncertainty is highlighted by the ambiguous meaning of "sleep": we cannot be sure whether it "rounds off" life merely by bringing it to a conclusion or by coming before and after. Perhaps, as has been suggested, Shakespeare wished his audience (did he also have in mind such skeptical readers as us?) to supply their own answers.[13]

When it comes to what Shakespeare believed, we cannot even be sure that he really envisaged a final dissolution of the earth, although the recurrence of the idea in his plays makes it likely that he did. But Shakespeare expressed here the nostalgia and vexation of Prospero. And from the point of view of Prospero's approach to self-knowledge, it is most important that he concern himself with the fact of mortality, universal mortality, and not with the hope of immortality. Prospero anchors his renunciation of magic on a self-knowledge humanly achieved and not on the reward of heaven. In *The Tempest,* as in Shakespeare's later plays generally, it is apparent that man cannot seek to find himself by guessing at the designs of heaven but only by using his own resources; he can, of course, pray that these be increased by divine aid, as Prospero does in the end.

The recognition of human limitations makes Prospero not a weak but a strong man. "In der Beschränkung zeigt sich erst der Meister," Goethe says somewhere. Prospero's role in *The Tempest* is comparable to the one Henry V, Shakespeare's Renaissance pattern of perfection, has in his play; but it exceeds it, given the somewhat different attitude toward self-knowledge operative in the two plays. The extension of his influence through his magic gives Prospero, of course, a power of action that other Shakespearean heroes do not have (even though, as we have noted, he uses this power gently, humanly). Nothing happens in the play of which he does not have knowledge, and he instigates everything except Antonio's plot and Caliban's rebellion; and even these provide no real difficulty for him. Not even Duke Vincentio, whom Angelo likens to "providence divine," manages events so flawlessly. There is no such imperfection in Prospero's direction as is created by the reluctance of the rogue Barnardine in *Measure for Measure* to have himself executed when Vincentio expects it of him.

But Prospero is also a strong man because he has to win what Shakespeare always considered the hardest battle, that against the passion and presumption in oneself; and in his case, the battle is the harder because Prospero's self is heightened much above the normal scale by his supernatural powers. His passions by themselves are potent, as is generally true for the heroes of Shakespeare's baroque plays; but their potential destructiveness is increased. Some neo-Platonic practitioners of theurgy claimed that magic could elevate man to the level of the gods; [14] but Prospero rejects this presumption and accepts his limitations as a human being. This is not because he is a serene sage, as he is sometimes portrayed on the stage. As Edward Dowden has said, "Shakespeare has shown us his quick sense of injury, his intellectual impatience, his occasional moment of keen irritability, in order that we may be more deeply aware of his abiding strength and self-possession, and that we may perceive how these have been grafted upon a temperament not impassive or unexcitable." [15] Given this temperament, Prospero demonstrates his victory over his passions as much as does Henry V, who says that they are as subject to him as are "our wretches fetter'd in our prisons." Henry's passions serve life sentences, but they were from the beginning lesser criminals. Prospero has the passionate nature of a baroque hero like Othello; but he also has the will-power commensurate with it, a will-power cleansed from egotistical motives. His passion and his control have the force and strain of baroque art.

Prospero owes his present strength to his consciousness of having overcome his intemperance and impatience. He could, in this respect too, be compared with Henry V, who, as a prince, had indulged himself—not in study, like Prospero, but in reveling. But, in doing so, he was conscious of his future glory and set his indulgence in contrast to it, so that to some critics his licentiousness has appeared to be a proper preparation for his later success. This is not quite so; Henry, as the ending of *The Second Part of Henry IV* and the beginning of *Henry V* make clear, goes through a "consideration" in which he sheds his offending Adam. But Henry always has control over himself, and his indulgence is a controlled indulgence; Prospero's victory over himself comes from an imperfection overcome and conquered by will power. His is a mastered self.

But Shakespeare took care not to make him priggish. He does not assume the voice and tone of perfection. Considering the echoes of the *Aeneid* in *The Tempest*—a drama that takes place in the general location of Virgil's epic—it is remarkable that Prospero is so unlike the stately Roman *vir perfectus*. Although Aeneas, Dido, and Carthage are referred to in the play, Prospero has a quite un-Virgilian humanity and humility. Even in comparison to Henry V, who has a touch of Aeneas, Prospero appears extremely modest. The portrait of Prospero, pattern of perfection that it represents in its particular way, breathes a much stronger awareness of human imperfection than does the figure of Henry V. But then, *The Tempest* also contains a strong echo of Montaigne, who, as we have noted, criticized the Renaissance pattern of perfection as unrealistic and unattainable. Prospero has some obvious human weaknesses: he is impetuous; he coaxes, lectures, blusters, and threatens. He is irritated not only with Caliban and the Neapolitans but also occasionally with Ariel, Ferdinand, and Miranda. Prospero's is a changeable, adaptable self of the sort Montaigne saw and observed in himself and others. Prospero's attitudes and moods range widely: he is fervent at one moment and wise at the next; he detaches himself from the world at one time and, at another, immerses himself in it with excitement. His Protean personality is, for instance, exemplified in the long second scene with Miranda, when he is, in turns, a loving father, a narrator of past events, a coaxing schoolmaster, a preacher of faith, and a mighty magician. Such quick changes of roles put actors to a severe, perhaps an impossible, test.

In the end, he affirms his temperance, patience, and humility. He does not here or elsewhere become a "close replica to Christ," as Professor Wilson Knight says in pardonable enthusiasm for his character.[16] Neither does he show himself as weak and prone to further disasters, as some critics would have it. Prospero, says Northrop Frye, "appears not to be promising much improvement after he returns."[17] One suspects that the major reasons for this doubt about Prospero's continuing strength lie in his prediction that in Milan "every third thought shall be my grave" (V.i.311) and in the acknowledgment of his final prayer that from now on he will have only human strength. But in concerning himself with death and its requirements, he follows a long-standing stipulation of self-knowledge. "To philosophize is to learn to die" was the title of one of Montaigne's essays, which echoed a long tradition that, in its Christian form, went back to the *ars moriendi*. For Prospero, the preparation for death is, because of his age, a governmental and a human sine qua non; but it does not exclude other important considerations. If one wanted to be mathematical, he could say that, in turning every third thought toward the grave, Prospero will be using merely that part of his time made free by giving up Miranda, whom he earlier called "a third of mine own life" (IV.i.3). But it will be sufficient to say that Prospero's success as an island ruler bodes well for his strength as a duke in Milan.

The ending of *The Tempest* does suggest that self-control and political control are an unfinished and continuing business, for which human might and divine grace are needed; but it does not show that Prospero is tired of his work or defeated by it. Neither, I think, is there anything in *The Tempest* that shows it to be the work of a tired Shakespeare who had too many third thoughts, be it thought illness or religious preoccupation or both, as has been suggested. The tight structure and the sweep of ideas do not support Lytton Strachey's claim that Shakespeare, when writing his romances, was bored with nearly everything, with life, and even with drama, with all but poetic dreams.[18] And I cannot, with Clifford Leech, detect in this play a Shakespeare weakened by the Puritan impulse. Though for Leech *The Tempest* is still "the fullest and most ordered expression" of this impulse, it shows signs that Shakespeare had grown "tired of disciplining human nature and recognized it as impossible to execute." [19] A certain fideism, as I have suggested, is notable in Shakespeare's plays long before *The Tempest;* but it is not, in any specific sense, Calvinistic or Puritan. In Calvin's *Institutes* life may have the evanescence of Prospero's vision, but it altogether lacks its glory.

Shakespeare, of course, did acknowledge in *The Tempest* that the disciplining of human nature has its limits. For these, Caliban, on whose nature "nurture" has not so far taken, is the most obvious example. But even he becomes in the end somewhat of an educational success when he promises to "be wise hereafter, / And seek for grace" (V.i.294–95). Undoubtedly, Caliban will need much grace if he is to reach a normal level of intelligence and morality, but the fact that now he recognizes the fundamental difference between the scoundrels whom he adored as gods and his kind master whom he caused anguish provides grounds for hope. Caliban's pledge to change his ways is a delayed reaction to Prospero's pains taken with him and provides an ever so slight support for the expectation of general improvement.

Prospero, his final humility and the tentativeness of the conversion of his enemies notwithstanding, is a very strong hero, perhaps Shakespeare's strongest. He has achieved self-knowledge in terms of the definition of the Christian humanists. "Nothing," said Erasmus in *Enchiridion,* "is more hard than that a man should overcome himself; but, then, there is no greater reward than is felicity." [20] This reward is promised to Prospero when he controls his passions and renounces the magic of unlimited power. But Prospero has also come as close as possible to achieving self-knowledge in terms of those who, like Montaigne, thought that the Christian humanists' program was simplified and in need of revision. He does not seek self-knowledge by lessons on body and soul and on the nature of the passions, but he realizes that it is an on-going process that ends only with death. He will base his life in Milan on this realization, which includes an acknowledgement of his weakness, the weakness of being human. His future power to transform the world and to master others will lie not in the magician's wand, not in a power over nature, not in Machiavellian schemes, but in a strength that radiates from a mastered self. There are good reasons to believe that Prospero will retain his mastery and become the fortunate man that his name implies—good *human* reasons, at least. And for the rest, Prospero prays for divine grace (a supplication that Shakespeare combined with a compliment to that deity of the dramatists, the audience).

Whether Prospero's reliance on a political control that centers on self-control is fantastic or prophetic must be decided by the future of mankind, not by the reader or writer of this book. Perhaps it is unrealistic to expect man to act like a Prospero. Perhaps it is merely a humanistic dream that the strength of man develops by self-conquest and that felicity ensues when man limits his power and abandons the idea of dominating others through social and scientific means. But it is not an implausible dream, and its fulfillment, which will require a most propitious star, is still one of mankind's happier expectations.

APPENDIXES

Hamlet:
"What Is a Man?"

This passage (IV.iv.33 ff.) is one of the several in *Hamlet* that show Shakespeare's literacy in the lore of body and soul and its application to self-knowledge. As Hamlet reflects on Fortinbras's march against Poland, he sees man and himself as part animal, part rational being. In agreement with the demands of moral *decorum,* as the Renaissance derived them from Cicero's *De Officiis,* Hamlet argues that man must set his course of action by overcoming his animal nature and by listening to the dictates of reason:

> How all occasions do inform against me,
> And spur my dull revenge! What is a man,
> If the chief good and market of his time
> Be but to sleep and feed? A beast, no more!
> Sure he that made us with such large discourse,
> Looking before and after, gave us not
> That capability and godlike reason
> To fust in us unus'd.
>
> (IV.iv.32–39)

Hamlet's words have a close resemblance to a passage from the beginning of Cicero's *De Officiis* (I.11), the *locus classicus* for the special obligation of man, as contrasted with animals, to fulfill his duties. But the parallel becomes even closer when one consults a sixteenth-century edition of *De Officiis,* such as the Paris edition of 1560, which has the traditional headings, marginal notes, and commentaries. In this edition, Erasmus introduced the passage as being from the *sententiae* that concern the chief good that proceeds from nature: "Ex veteris Academiae & Stoicorum sententiae, qui summum bonum a natura proficisci putant" (Cf. Hamlet's "the chief good and markets of his time"). The text follows:

Principio generi animantium omni est a natura tributum, ut se vitam, corpusque tueatur, declinetque ea quae nocitura videantur, omniaque quae sint ad vivendum necessaria anquirat & paret: ut pastum ut latibula, ut alia generis eiusdem. Commune item animantium est coniunctionis ap-petitus, procreandi causa, & cura quaedam eorum quae procreata sunt. Sed inter hominem & beluam hoc maxime interest, quod haec tantum quantum sensu movetur, ad id solum quod adest, quodque praesens est, se accommodat, paulum admodum sentiens praeteritum aut futurum: Homo autem quod rationis est particeps (per quam consequentia cernit, causas rerum videt, earumque progressus, & quasi antecessiones non ignorat, similitudines comparat, rebusque praesentibus adiungit atque annectit futuras) facile totius vitae cursum videt ad eamque degendam praeparat res necessarias.[1]

Quid intersit inter hominis propria & beluarum

Ratonandi vis hominis propria

The obvious similarities between the two texts are heightened by the marginal notes in the 1560 edition, which provide the structure of Hamlet's reflection: Hamlet poses the question, What is man? (*quid intersit inter hominis propria & beluarum*); and he answers that man's possession of reason sets him off from the animals (*rationandi vis hominis propria*)—the *rationandi vis* of the note designates more specifically the mental process Hamlet calls "dis-course" than does the *ratio* of the text.[2] The properties of animals in Cicero are *ut pastum ut latibula ut alia generis eiusdem;* in *Hamlet* they are "but to sleep and feed" (in the balanced structure of the passage, Shakespeare used hendiadys and mentioned only these two major "good and markets"). Hamlet's phrase "large discourse, looking before and after" summarizes Cicero's *homo autem quod rationis est particeps . . . totius vitae cursum videt;* "large," in particular, glances at *totius vitae cursum;* for looking, Cicero has *videt* and *cernit;* for "before and after," *praeteritum aut futurum.* Hamlet's "god-like reason" is accounted for by *rationis est particeps* and by the note *cujus* (*ut alio loco ait Cicero*) *prima homini cum Deo conjunctio est.* This note would also account for Hamlet's making God rather than nature the source of man's reason, but such change was to be expected in the appropriation of pagan wisdom in the Christian Renaissance. It may be added that Betuleius's com-mentary interprets the whole passage in the sense of a reproach for man as Hamlet applies it: "To our shame we must say that no animal neglects the law prescribed by its kind, nor does it have to be goaded to it; man, however, cannot be provoked even by the spur of conscience." [3]

There were other versions of the commonplace available to Shakespeare in English.[4] But I have yet to see a passage that in general drift, structural correspondence, and verbal parallels comes as close to Hamlet's words as that in *De Officiis*. Shakespeare, I believe, must either have remembered it very clearly from his grammar-school days or consulted Cicero for the purpose of penning Hamlet's speech. Certainly no passage was more relevant in the Renaissance than Cicero's for emphasizing the conflict between the rational man of theory and the bestial man of experience—a conflict Theodore Spencer has called an essential part of Hamlet's conscience.[5]

Lucrece: "Why Should the Worm Intrude the Maiden Bud?"

More than one critic has claimed that Shakespeare's poem *Lucrece* was a most important preparatory work for his later tragic art.[1] It should also be noted that the poem is suffused with theoretical patterns of self-knowledge as hardly any other of Shakespeare's works. These attach, in particular, to Tarquin, who is an early example of a Shakespearean hero prompted by passion to commit a spectacular act of folly and crime; he is a very general model for the later Othello, Lear, Antony, and, most of all, Macbeth. A brief demonstration may here suffice to show how this conception arose from Shakespeare's study of humanistic ideas of self-knowledge, especially as they concerned the virtue of temperance and the obligation of moral decorum.

The story was ready-made for a tragic interpretation that stressed Tarquin's self-loss. In *De Legibus* (II.iv.10), Cicero depicted Tarquin as a public figure whose lack of self-knowledge brought about a dangerous political situation, and La Primaudaye summarized the story of Tarquin's crime and fall as an illustration of a particularly serious manifestation of intemperance because committed by a prince.[2] The tragedy of Lucrece presented a more difficult problem because of Christian objections to suicide in general and to the glorification of hers, in particular, by Saint Augustine in *The City of God* (I.19). But in the literature with which Shakespeare is likely to have had direct acquaintance, sympathetic accounts prevailed. Renaissance moralists, particularly those that concerned themselves with the education of women, noted her as an example of chastity, which she demonstrated in her fidelity to her husband. Thus the theologian Thomas Rogers thought her an example from which Christians could learn self-knowledge and lauded her chastity, a major ingredient in the complex of virtues represented by temperance as it applied to women.[3]

I believe that Shakespeare presented her sympathetically; but she need not concern us here except for the contrast she offers to Tarquin in the earlier parts of the poem, when she becomes an almost personified temperance. The contrast between temperance and intemperance is here woven into the poem's fabric, most notably in the pervasive juxtaposition of light and dark tones. Thus when Tarquin hears of Lucrece's beauty, envy "taints" his heart (38). By contrast, "silver-white" virtue stains the blushing beauty of Lucrece (56). The dark pigments of envy, greed, hate, hypocrisy, and deceit blend into the blackness of intemperance; the luminous hues of beauty, honor, chastity, and holiness softly encircle the whiteness of temperance.[4]

In this atmosphere of color symbolism, the lengthy internal conflict in Tarquin proceeds. It is a "debate" in the Elizabethan sense of the word as not only an intellectual argument but also a contention of opposing forces. In Tarquin's case, the concupiscible appetite, leagued with his will, is locked in a deadly combat with his reason. The vehemence of the struggle is such that Tarquin's soul, as Shakespeare says in an image frequent among the moralists, resembles a tempest-tossed ship (171, 279). In La Primaudaye's words, "as the winds torment and toss that ship which they have seized upon now here, now there and will not suffer it to be guided by her master, so intemperance, moving and compelling the soul to disobey reason, suffereth her not to enjoy tranquillity and rest, which is an assured heaven of harbor from all the winds" (p. 81). Tarquin is allured by the pleasures that, as La Primaudaye said, "flatter us with disguised visage and, when they depart, they leave us full of sorrow and sadness" (p. 224). The "honest fear" that attempts to pull him back is the shame or shamefacedness allied with temperance: "There is, saith Cicero, a certain shame and bashfulness in temperance, which is the guardian of all vertues and deserveth great commendation, being also a most goodly ornament of the whole life, as that which fashioneth it according to the pattern of decency and honesty" (p. 242).

Temporarily, Tarquin's "honest fear," the ally of his conscience, makes him see his evil purpose in the right perspective; he asks himself in the biblical losing-finding antithesis: "What win I if I gain the joy I seek?" and he answers appropriately that the prize is nothing but a dream, a breath, a fleeting joy, and a toy (211–13). But Tarquin acts against his better knowledge; although reason has irrefutable arguments to make him desist, will, which has already become "reprobate desire," wins out, and he stamps out "reason's weak removing" (243). "There is," says La Primaudaye, "no kind of dissoluteness wherein the intemperate man plungeth not himself, no wickedness or cruelty which he executeth not for satisfying of his unclean desires and insatiable lusts, no fear or imminent danger which can draw him back" (p. 182). Tarquin thus braces himself: "Who fears a sentence or an old man's saw / Shall by a painted cloth be kept in awe" (244–45). He rationalizes his moral weakness into martial courage like La Primaudaye's intemperate man, who "laboreth oftentimes to procure that glory and honor should be given to his most cursed and execrable misdemeanors, imagining and fancying with himself dreams answerable and agreeable to that he most desires" (p. 182). Tarquin pleads the superiority of love and beauty over moral scruples and extols the glory that is attached to conquering the object of love. Instead of ruling appetite by reason as the moralists demanded, Tarquin enlists under the banner of passion and makes affection his "captain" (271 ff.). Like the oath-breaking courtiers of Navarre in *Love's Labor's Lost,* he becomes one of "affection's men-at-arms," but with the difference that the affection he calls love is lust and has tragic consequences. Instead of keeping the frail part of his mind bound as Cicero demanded, Tarquin "heartens up his servile powers" (295). The psychology of this disastrous subversion is traditional: on the prompting of the eye, affection corrupts the heart and inveigles it to revolt against reason. Tarquin implicitly acknowledges the moral disaster when he pretends to fear no "sinking"; this is the imagery in which the moralists warned against the subjugation of the will: to make affection the pilot is to provoke a storm of passion that wrecks the ship of the soul.[5]

From a rationalizer, who speciously attempts to persuade himself that evil is good, Tarquin turns into a perverter of values. When he contends that "sad pause and deep regard beseems the sage" (278), he states the important moral doctrine Cicero placed in the center of the teaching of temperance, the doctrine of *decorum,* or the rule of what beseems a man. "In temperance," said La Primaudaye, "a man may behold modesty, with the privation of every perturbation in the soul, as also a way how to frame all things according to that which is decent or seemly, which the Latins call *decorum,* being a convenience meet for the excellence of man and that wherein his nature differeth from other living creatures" (p. 171).

A kind of dramatic examination of this *decorum* is central to the Tarquin part of the poem, first in the rapist's perversion of the doctrine, then in Lucrece's counterarguments that restate it in orthodox fashion. Tarquin's insistence that what "beseems" him is the part of youth that beats "sad pause and deep regard" from the stage applies the rules not of moral but of aesthetic *decorum,* which derived from literary criticism.[6] The image itself may actually have come to Shakespeare through a line in Horace in which the poet, speaking as an old roué, orders himself to make place for youth "lest he be beaten away by this age, for which wantonness is more becoming." [7] But Tarquin also can be said to see himself quite generally in the stereotyped role of the young lover of comedy with the *temeritas, appetitus, libido,* and *cupiditas* proper to the part. However, Tarquin does not beat off the stage the competitor of *juventus* in Roman comedy, that is, the *senex amans* with his *timiditas, tristitia,* and *severitas,* which are temporarily muted by his *libido,* but rather he rejects the qualities of aged prudence that both the commentators of Terence and the moralists admired and associated with *ratio:* respect, pause, and regard. These were high up in the humanistic scale of values espoused by Shakespeare.[8] Tarquin's choice of the role of a lascivious youth is definitely perverse from the point of view of moral *decorum,* which decreed temperance and thus the control of the appetites. For Cicero, the law of nature was violated when the appetites escaped the rein of reason and galloped away to overleap all bounds of measure.[9] For Tarquin, "nothing can Affection's course control, / Or stop the headlong fury of his speed" (500–501).

This rejection of all hindrances makes Tarquin very much the intemperate man the moralists described. In La Primaudaye's words, "Thus we see that intemperance, as Cicero saith, is the mother of all perturbations in the soul and causeth man, as Socrates said, to differ nothing from a beast because he never thinketh upon that which is best but only seeketh how to satisfy and content the unbridled desires of pleasure and lust, having no more use of reason than beasts have" (p. 181). Lucrece's attempt to dissuade Tarquin from his nefarious intention must therefore fail: "Like a white hind under the grype's sharp claws," she "Pleads, in a wilderness where are no laws, / To the rough beast that knows no gentle right"—a beast that obeys nothing but "his foul appetite" (543 ff.). Like Edmund and Iago, Tarquin recognizes only the law of the jungle.

Yet Lucrece continues to plead in this wilderness—for fifteen long stanzas—before Tarquin stops her. She becomes here the mouthpiece of temperance, proclaiming, at times quite abstractly, the greatness of this virtue and refuting Tarquin's specious arguments for passion and crime. Temperance is for her La Primaudaye's virtue that comprehends all others and through which "a harmony, concordance, and conjunction of them all is made" (p. 172). She implores Tarquin by what was dear to him before he became passion's slave, by knighthood, friendship, holy human law, common loyalty, heaven and earth, sacred hospitality, and human pity. But her climactic argument, like Tarquin's, turns on the doctrine of *decorum*. Shakespeare made her unconsciously answer Tarquin's treatment of the subject that provided the rationale for his attack. Lucrece now asks him to desist for his own sake and become again the man in whose "likeness" she entertained him (596). With this appeal, she admonishes Tarquin to observe the individual *decorum* that he perversely distorted when he saw himself in the role of a young lover. But her final appeal turns on what Cicero called the *decorum* of circumstance, the proper behavior according to profession and age. She asks him to envisage the shame that will be "seeded in thine age," when "thus thy vices bud before thy spring!" (604) —an argument that refutes Tarquin's adoption of the "part of youth." She goes on to remind him of his obligation to be an example for the people: "For princes are the glass, the school, the book, / Where subjects' eyes do learn, do read, do look" (615–16). Her admonishment echoes the humanists' demand that the prince must be the moral example, the pattern of his people. So, for instance, Chelidonius: "The prince . . . is, as it were, a theatre and glass that the world should behold." [10]

Lucrece subsequently backs up her argument on the *decorum* of circumstance by admonishing Tarquin to realize the paradoxical nature of his situation, in which he, a prince, is enslaved by passion. This is another strain of reasoning conventional in the teaching of temperance. In the same chapter on voluptuousness and lechery in which La Primaudaye summarized the story of Tarquin's fall, he asked the question whether the incontinent man can be called free and answered that nobody can be called a master that is a slave to pleasure and lust (p. 226). Lucrece tries to restrain Tarquin with moral paradoxes of this kind, generally based on the fifth paradox in Cicero's *Paradoxa Stoicorum,* that "all wise men are free and all fools are slaves," but I shall forbear to list the commonplace parallels. The paradoxes that do not stop Tarquin have a way of inundating the reader.

Of the rape itself, we are offered only the sparsest account—Lucrece's stifled cry and her tears, in which Tarquin bathes his hot face, are the only physical details. At the climactic moment of the poem, Shakespeare concentrated on the effect of the act on Tarquin's, the criminal's, soul. And that was quite in agreement with the theme of temperance and intemperance, of which, according to La Primaudaye, the soul is the proper subject (p. 170). We are by the winning-losing antithesis (689) reminded of what is at stake and are told that Tarquin's psychic forces revert from joy to pain, from desire to disdain, and that his self-will has become tired like a jade. The struggle of passion and reason in Tarquin has led to the spiritual collapse that La Primaudaye described to be the final result of intemperance: "The sensual and unreasonable part of the soul contendeth no more with reason—which then is, as it were, stark dead and suffereth itself to be carried to ugly and unnatural vices and to all fleshly desires—because the divine part of the soul is weakened in such sort that she hath no more strength nor feeling of her essence, which is an enemy to vice" (p. 181). Shakespeare put the idea in words that, like La Primaudaye's, echoed the Pauline terminology of the battle of flesh and spirit: "The flesh being proud, Desire doth fight with Grace, / For there it revels; and when that decays, / The guilty rebel for remission prays" (711–14).

Shakespeare symbolized the collapse of Tarquin's reason in an allegory familiar from Spenser's *Faerie Queene* (II.ix,xi).[11] Like Spenser's Alma, Tarquin's soul is mistress of a castle beleaguered by sins and vices. In agreement with the pagan context of *Lucrece,* the soul is a priestess inhabiting a "temple" and through Tarquin's act deprived of her power of prescience; the "consecrated wall" of her dwelling is now pulled down. But the most dire effect is that Tarquin's soul has lost its immortality and become "thrall / To living death and pain perpetual" (725–26).

This concern not only with Lucrece's but also with Tarquin's soul (in fact, more with Tarquin's) is, at first sight, astonishing. But the poem is conceived as not merely depicting the tragedy of the heroine but also, at least as poignantly, that of the hero. It is the latter's tragedy, one of subjection to intemperance, that effects the former's. This connection is imaginatively underlined by the pervasive siege imagery that has one of its climaxes in the account of the defeat of Tarquin's soul.[12] This strain of images begins with Tarquin's setting out to attack the "never-conquered fort" of Lucrece (482), is continued in some details of the account of the rape, as in the likening of Lucrece's breasts to ivory towers, and carried over into the Lucrece part of the poem. Here the heroine considers the tapestry depicting the fall of Troy and draws the analogy between Sinon and Tarquin: "As Priam him did cherish, / So did I Tarquin; so my Troy did perish" (1546–47). And again the trope of the siege appears when Lucrece ponders suicide because she feels her soul's "mansion batter'd by the enemy: / Her sacred temple spotted, spoil'd, corrupted" (1171–72). The act of intemperance unites violator and victim and gives the whole poem a unity of imagery and tone that modern readers interested in psychology but impatient of soul analysis, the original concern of this science, may easily miss.

Incidentally, Shakespeare has been criticized for making Tarquin disappear so suddenly after his crime by dropping him from the picture and barely reporting his banishment at the end of the poem. But this immediate departure is quite in agreement with the moralists' description of gratified lust. "The repentance of an incontinent man," said La Primaudaye, "followeth hard at the heels of his sin and transgression" (p. 170).[13] And thus Tarquin speeds away, "a heavy convertite." The external catastrophe, in this case Tarquin's perpetual banishment, is a natural consequence of the internal catastrophe, the destruction of his soul. Tarquin's deed, however, remains in the reader's mind throughout the remainder of the poem, not only because of Lucrece's lamentations and veiled references, such as the analogy to the lust that felled Troy, but also because of the continuing imagery of staining and polluting. The stain on Tarquin's soul has infected Lucrece and it spreads beyond into Rome. It is in order to remove this blemish in her soul and to restore her reputation that Lucrece commits suicide.

I shall touch briefly on Lucrece's pollution images because they constitute her main commentary on Tarquin's tragedy. The series of these images is introduced by the question "Why should the worm intrude the maiden bud?" and concludes with the generalization "But

no perfection is so absolute / That some impurity does not pollute"
(848–54). Lucrece appears to ask here the question why there is
such a thing as a tragic flaw and, in some sense, to give an answer.
But the question is not clearly and directly posed, and neither is it,
I think, satisfactorily answered from a philosophic point of view.
That would have meant to write a philosophic disquisition, for which
Shakespeare was hardly prepared and which would have taken something away from the final mystery that enshrouds all evil—a mystery
that Shakespeare later found an effective dramatic device. In Lucrece's questions, the images have ambiguous referents. Although
the cankerworm settled in the maidenbud is logically associated with
the "tyrant folly" that lurks in "gentle breasts" (851) and thus with
the lust that vitiated Tarquin's rationality, the vivid figure also
brings to mind the thrust of the rapist at the victim, and the maidenbud suggests the actual excellence of Lucrece even more than the
deceptive one of Tarquin. The figure supports the generalization of
the vulnerability of all perfection, which, however, raises in turn
the question why evil has such a destructive force. Lucrece does ask
the latter question without answering it when she censors the
treacherous Sinon while she views the wall painting of Troy: "For
one's offence why should so many fall, / To plague a private sin in
general?" (1483).

All this resembles the explorations of the nature of evil and crime
one finds in Seneca's dramas, from which, indeed, it appears, Shakespeare borrowed here, perhaps, as has been suggested, via a commonplace book such as *Illustrium Poetarum Flores* of Octavianus
Mirandola.[14] Seneca, the tragedian (as opposed to the philosopher),
gave no answer to the question of the involvement of the innocent
in guilt; and neither did Shakespeare in *Lucrece,* whatever he may
have thought privately on the subject. In her apostrophes to Night,
Time, and Opportunity, and in her comments on the Troy painting,
Lucrece does not seek to explain what exactly the tragic flaw is
and how it comes about except for saying that it is an imperfection
in a universe constructed to allow, for whatever reason, such imperfection to become destructive. Without the help of Night, Opportunity, and Time, Tarquin could not have accomplished his deed;
they "blew the fire when temperance was thawed" (838), and the
fall of Troy shows by the most famous historical example that the
world has always had its Tarquins and Lucreces. A universe such
as Lucrece sees it—she may be said to assume a choric function—is

eminently brittle and mutable. Tragedy in it is abetted by fortune and accident, and the chastest bodies like the greatest citadels are not able to control the forces of rape and destruction.

Lucrece's consideration of the destructiveness of evil, of course, does not excuse Tarquin nor does it modify the analysis of Tarquin's imperfection as intemperance in the way it is given in the poem. And this analysis bore its fruit in the subtler dramatic presentation of Shakespeare's later tragic heroes. Like Tarquin, these suffer a moral failure that has spiritual consequences; they fall prey to passion, let their wills and passions pander their reason, pervert individual and general *decorum*, struggle in the grip of conflicting emotions and have temporary recoils before they finally damage their souls. As is true for Tarquin, the evil these heroes commit radiates outward, enthralls their victims' souls, and makes the whole state a scene of woe. But if these heroes lose themselves in a fashion similar to Tarquin, the processes of thought and emotion they undergo are less schematic and more plausible. When Macbeth loses himself, he is not conscious, as is Tarquin, of the deep moral consequences, even if we are. If *Lucrece* was for Shakespeare, as he called it in the Dedication, a "pamphlet," it was such in the sense of presenting a program for his later dramatic practices, but a program that he modified considerably.

Hamlet:
"What a Piece of Work Is a Man!"

This, the most explicit statement of Hamlet on what man is (II.ii. 295 ff.), is constructed on the same principle of the antithesis of man and animal as the passage investigated in Appendix A. It is more complex philosophically, for it draws on the various aspects of the *conjunctio oppositorum* in man. Hamlet's assessment forms a cryptic answer to Rosencrantz's and Guildenstern's probing for the secret of his melancholy: "I have of late—but wherefore I know not—," the prince explains, "lost all my mirth, forgone all custom of exercise." And Hamlet goes on to paint a picture of the world and of man that delights him no longer. The humanistic orations on the dignity of man that have been cited as analogues prove Hamlet's speech—and the orations themselves—to be a web of commonplaces; the correspondence of its structure to that of the eighth psalm and the parallels to exegeses of the biblical account of creation that have been pointed out demonstrate the theological orthodoxy.[1] One must realize that the eighth psalm was for the humanists and theologians a major source for the theme of "the dignity of man"—the heading the psalm has in the Genevan Bible—and that it suggested descriptions of man according to his creation. But since the indebtedness of Hamlet's words to theological patterns has been expertly examined by others, I shall stress their conformity to the philosophical background.

When Hamlet looks first at the universe before considering man, he follows not only the structure of the psalm but also the demand of Cicero in *Tusculan Disputations* (V.69–70) to study first the revolution of the spheres so that the soul might know its own self and feel its union with the divine mind.[2] This macrocosm-microcosm sequence was almost automatic in Renaissance treatises. Pierre de La Primaudaye, for instance, began his chapter "Of Man" with a rotund praise of the heavens,[3] and Guillaume du Vair turned his eyes upward before asking man to "look into himself." [4] The familiar sequence, "this great world," followed by "man that is so glorious a creature," is about all that is left of Hamlet's speech in the doggerel verse of the First Quarto (1603); the adapter, whoever he was, that mangled some of Shakespeare's best philosophical passages knew at least enough not to tamper with the order!

When Hamlet appraises the macrocosm, he does so by paraphrasing the biblical account of creation as did, with slightly different details, La Primaudaye and du Vair. Hamlet first considers the earth: "this goodly frame, the earth, seems to me a sterile promontory." Then he appraises the heavens, which appear nothing to him "but a foul and pestilent congregation of vapours." In the descriptions of the heavens, modern editors generally prefer the version of Quarto 2: "this most excellent Canopie the ayre, look you, this braue orehanging firmament, this maiesticall roofe fretted with golden fire." This version, however, obscures the essential bipartition of the creation: first God created the earth, then the "firmament." The latter was, as the Genevan sidenote to Genesis 1:6 explained, again bipartitioned into "spreading over, and air." The version of the Folio corresponds to the biblical dualism: [1] "this most excellent Canopy the Ayre, look you," [2] "this braue o'erhanging, this Maiesticall Roofe, fretted with golden fire." The "overhanging" is thus in turn partitioned into a "roof" and its upper adornment, the sphere of golden fires.

Some recent editors' preference for the version of Quarto 2 has created havoc with the interpretation of Hamlet's assessment of the microcosm and has led one commentator to sense a lack of balance, an abruptness, and repudiation of the traditional world picture.[5] But the Folio version, which appears to me distinctly preferable, is clearly balanced. It will be instructive to set the two side by side:

Quarto 2 (1604):	Folio (1623):
What peece of worke is a man, how noble in reason, how infinit in faculties, in forme and moouing, how expresse and admirable in action, how like an Angell in apprehension, how like a	What a piece of worke is a man! how Noble in Reason? how infinite in faculty? in forme and mouing how expresse and admirable? in Action, how like an Angel? in apprehension, how like a

God: the beautie of the world; the paragon of Animales; and yet to me, what is this quintessence of dust: man delights not me, nor women neither, though by your smilling, you seeme to say so.	God? the beauty of the world, the Parragon of Animals; And yet to me, what is this Quintessence of Dust? Man delights not me; no nor Woman neither; though by your smiling you seeme to say so.

Hamlet's topic sentence, "What a piece of work is a man," echoes the "what is man" of the psalm. As the Genevan side-note explained, man, "touching his first creation," was lower than God. Hamlet's phrase, "piece of work," is a reminder that man was created by God of the earth, and thus differed fundamentally from God. As John 3 : 31, puts its, "He that is from on high is above all; he that is of the earth is of the earth and speaketh of the earth. He that is come from heaven is above all." The Genevan-Tomson side-note explained that he that is of the earth is "nothing else but man, a piece of work made of the slime of the earth."

Hamlet then pays tribute to the nobility of man's reason—both theologians and philosophers saw in it man's greatest gift—but he balances the praise by also admiring the powers of the soul in general: "how noble in reason? how infinite in faculty?" The Quarto's "how infinite in faculties" is surely incorrect; the soul could be considered infinite in its power or potentiality, but not in the number of its faculties. As a unit, it had one "faculty." For instance, Timothy Bright explained that the soul "is able, with one universal and simple faculty, to perform so many varieties of actions as the instrument by which it performeth them carrieth an apt inclination thereto." [6]

Because man was created in the image and likeness of God primarily through his soul and secondarily through his body, Hamlet now considers the body: "In form and moving how express and admirable?" I fail to understand the sense of "how infinite in faculties, in form and moving," as some editors, in agreement with the Quarto, divide. (To introduce "faculty" from the Folio into this confusion does not improve it.) Shakespeare, in the Folio version, speaks in terms of the creation of man in the "image" of God. "Form" and "express" go particularly well with "image," for the latter word, as John Woolton explained, for some theologians meant anything that is

either in painting or graving or by another means expressed after
the example of another matter. . . . The word "image" therefore
appertaineth unto the form, and "similitude" unto nature. . . . An
"image" is an outward bodily form or fashion, expressing or representing any man.[7]

Man thus expresses the divine form, but no matter how "express and
admirable" his body is, it is still—as is implied in "form and moving"—his animal part, for animals as well as men possessed the
faculties of sense and motion.

But Genesis 1:26 said that man was created not only in the
"image," but also in the "likeness" (or "similitude") of God; and
in Woolton's definition "a similitude is a quality of the mind which
we imitate and follow." Hamlet therefore turns once more to the
primary resemblance of man to God: "in action, how like an angel?
in apprehension how like a God?" The twofold evocation "angel"
and "God" may well have come from the psalm, which in one version, that of the prayerbook, reads, "thou madest him lower than
the angels," and in another, that of the Genevan, "a little lower than
God." But the angels also fitted into the hierarchical Elizabethan
world picture; and "angel . . . God" was another balanced doublet. This action of the angels has disturbed some commentators;
but in the general Christian tradition, angels have always been
vigorous ministers of God's will, swift of motion, like flames of
fire, riding the moving clouds. The "form and moving" of Hamlet's preceding sentence offers indeed an excellent transition to the
"action" of the angels. An Elizabethan who had been told that angels were incapable of action might have retorted with Barckley
that man could well take the example of the angels for his action:

> If felicity, as the philosophers affirm, be the proper action of man,
> . . . it must be an action peculiar and proper to him alone. And
> seeing that man is made of two distinct natures, . . . it is more
> reason that this felicity should be agreeable with the best part of
> his nature, which is a reasonable soul, and resembleth the angels
> that are made after the image of God, than with the worst part of
> his nature, which resembleth and is of the like substance to brute
> beasts.[8]

The "action" of the angels, of which Hamlet speaks, is a spiritual
activity, and the idea is rhetorically balanced by the "apprehension"
of God. And not only rhetorically. The division of action and apprehension corresponds to the ultimately Aristotelian division of the

mind into an active and a speculative or contemplative part, or, simply, into judgment and will.[9] Shakespeare knew this division, as can be inferred from Desdemona's "my speculative and active instruments" (Quarto 1), or (in the Folio) "my speculative and offic'd instrument" (I.iii.270). "Offic'd" (which I prefer) is a particularly appropriate term for the active mind because it has an association with the angels, whom Shakespeare elsewhere called "offic'd" (*All's Well*, III.ii.125)—the office of the angels, of course, being to serve God. As Peter Martyr explained: "They execute the office committed to them by God, both wisely and speedily, which two things are most worthily commended in ministers and ambassadors. For then they rightly execute their office if they join celerity with wisdom." [10] There could be no more appropriate way to praise the active part of the mind than to liken it to the action of the angels. And "apprehension" is similarly appropriate for the contemplative mind because it designated the highest activity of the rational mind, completely abstracted from the body, that draws man closest to God. As Calvin said, "we have no apprehension of the heavenly life when we are tied to this world." [11] Hamlet thus proceeds properly from the action of the angels to the apprehension of God; by contrast, the Quarto's "how like an angel in apprehension, how like a God," makes the angels inactive and ends in a direct comparison of man and God that to the Elizabethans must have sounded less than proper, if not blasphemous.

In the concluding section of his appraisal, Hamlet considers once more man's physical nature, and he does so in a characteristically balanced antithesis: man is "the paragon of animals" but also "the quintessence of dust." The Genevan side-note to the psalm expressed a similar contrast when it reminded man that he owed his existence to God, for whom "it had been sufficient . . . to have set forth His glory by the heavens though he had not come so low as to man, which is but dust." Man is a proud and yet a wretched thing.

The phrase "quintessence of dust" is something of a *discordia concors* itself. Man was "quintessenced" because, as the duke in *Measure for Measure* explained, he existed "on many a thousand grains / That issue out of dust" (III.i.20–21). The process of quintessencing was the attempt to distill a fifth essence or element from the other four; Aristotle was thought to have identified this fifth essence with man's mind.[12] But this idea was generally declared to be theologically unsound. As Sir John Davies noted, no air, fire, earth, or water can be found in the operations of the soul, which operations are excellent beyond anything found in the elements: "What alchemist can draw with all his skill / The quintessence of these out of the mind?" [13] Yet the idea lingered, and Du Bartas, although he denied Aristotle's account, still thought of the soul as a certain kind of fifth essence, even though not a chemical one, when it rises in a mystic flight from the dull earth and, mounting to heaven, "quintessences" man in God.[14] The phrase "quintessence of dust" that strikes one as so Shakespearean in its intensity thus has an overtone of admiration; it is the deprecating yet transcendent touch that completes Hamlet's picture of man.

But with all its beauty and complexity, Hamlet's picture of man is essentially a conventional picture, put together according to humanistic formulas. If Shakespeare ever wrote an essay on *homo* in grammar school, he was likely to have used some or all of the ideas in Hamlet's speech; even a modern scholar's little Latin allows him to put together a fair approximation of the content of Hamlet's speech by selecting appropriate quotations under such rubrics as *mundus, homo,* and *anima* in commonplace books like Nannus Mirabellius's *Polyanthea.* Shakespeare was certainly familiar with the technique of "finding out" pertinent "places" for philosophical themes and putting them together in rhetorical patterns. In composing his *Oration on the Dignity of Man,* Pico presumably used the same method, as the beginning of his speech indicates: "It is a commonplace of the schools that man is a little world, in which we may discern a body mingled of earthly elements, an ethereal breath and the vegetable life of the plants, and the intelligence of the angels and a likeness to God." [15] The basic learning of the Renaissance was available at Stratford-on-Avon as well as in Florence.

The Elizabethans were taught by their humanistic schoolmasters to admire and imitate philosophical *topoi.* They had not yet lost what Douglas Bush has called "the courage of the commonplace." Shakespeare had this quality to the highest degree, and he had the skill to practice it. He who, according to Francis Meres, distilled in his poetry "the sweet witty soul of Ovid," also knew how to quintessence philosophic commonplaces. In doing so, he imprinted his poetic genius on material, conventional in kind, with which the labors of theologians and humanists and, more directly, of preachers and schoolmasters had provided him in the hope that he might thus learn to know himself.

Notes

For full references, see the first mention of books. Where not otherwise indicated, the place of publication of sixteenth- and seventeenth-century books is London.

INTRODUCTION

1. For uses of *nosce teipsum* references in English literature, see Albert W. Fields, *"Nosce Teipsum:* The Study of a Commonplace in English Literature, 1500–1900 (Ph.d. diss., University of Kentucky, 1967); and Eliza G. Wilkins, *The Delphic Maxims in Literature* (Chicago, Ill., 1929). For the classical sources, see Helen North, *Sophrosyne: Self-Knowledge and Self-Restraint in Greek Literature* (Ithaca, N.Y., 1966).

2. Sir Philip Sidney, *An Apology for Poetry* (1595), sig. Cᵛ.

3. Arthur Miller, "Tragedy and the Common Man," *New York Times,* Feb. 27, 1949, rpt. *Theater Arts* 35, no. 3.

4. *Venus,* 525; *R. III,* II.iii.2; *Merch.,* I.i.7; *A.Y.L.,* III.v.57; *Ham.,* V.ii.139; *Meas.,* III.ii.219; *Lear,* I.i.293, I.iv.251; *Macb.,* II.ii.73, IV.ii.19, IV.iii.165; *Ant.,* II.ii.95; *Cor.,* II.i.62; *H. VIII,* II.ii.208; III.ii.378.

5. The first, and so far only, systematic use of *nosce teipsum* tracts for Shakespeare interpretation is by Paul A. Jorgensen, *Lear's Self-Discovery* (Berkeley, Calif., 1967).

6. For Shakespeare's education and classical background, I have particularly relied on T. W. Baldwin, *William Shakspere's Small Latine and Lesse Greeke,* 2 vols. (Urbana, Ill., 1944); *Shakspere's Five Act Structure* (Urbana, Ill., 1947); *On the Compositional Genetics of THE COMEDY OF ERRORS* (Urbana, Ill., 1965).

7. Wilhelm Dilthey, "Weltanschauung und Analyse des Menschen seit Renaissance und Reformation," in *Gesammelte Schriften* (Leipzig, 1914), 2:18. For an argument on the *vis inertia* of the earlier Renaissance, see Herschel Baker, *The Dignity of Man* (Cambridge, Mass., 1947). Simplistically, Shakespeare's thought was identified with the medieval humanistic synthesis by E. M. W. Tillyard, *The Elizabethan World Picture* (London, 1943). Tillyard himself came to modify this position somewhat, admitting that "it is then, on balance, no fiction that the conception of man changed from the Middle Ages to the Renaissance" (*The English Renaissance: Fact or Fiction?* [Baltimore, Md., 1951], p. 20). That the pendulum has swung away from the medievalizing of Shakespeare is indicated by the recent *A*

New Companion to Shakespeare Studies, ed. Kenneth Muir and Samuel Schoenbaum (Cambridge, Mass. 1971). Cf. particularly the essay by William R. Elton, "Shakespeare and the Thought of His Age," pp. 180–98.

8. L. J. Potts, *Comedy* (London, 1948), p. 16.

9. Maurice Charney, *Style in Hamlet* (Princeton, N.J., 1969), p. xx. Charney's book contains many valuable insights, but suffers, I think, from his reluctance to generalize on character and theme.

CHAPTER ONE

1. Andreas Alciatus, *Emblemata* (Lyon, 1550), p. 200; Geoffrey Whitney, *A Choice of Emblems* (1586), p. 130. The use of the mirror for gaining self-knowledge had a number of classical precedents. The idea was associated with Socrates, who recommended that young men take frequent looks into a mirror so that handsome men acquire a behavior corresponding to their appearance and ugly onces conceal their defects by the development of their inner beauty. See Diogenes Laertius, *Vitae Philosophorum,* 2:33. A similar contrast is made in Phaedrus, III.8. The recommendation to use the mirror for self-knowledge was also ascribed to the Seven Sages of Greece; their sayings were often attached to the sentence collection called *Cato,* a standard book for parsing in Renaissance grammar schools. Seneca has some remarks on the use of the mirror for self-knowledge, introduced by "Inventa sunt specula ut homo se ipse nosceret" (*Naturales Quaestiones,* I.xvii.4).

2. Desiderius Erasmus, *Enchiridion Militis Christiani,* trans. [William Tyndale?] (1533), sig. C7ʳ. Cf. Sol. 1:7. The Elizabethan English bibles do not convey the idea of self-knowledge here (and neither does the King James version), but the Genevan side-note explains that Christ commands those who "are ignorant to go to the pastors to learn"—an injunction that may be taken as a plea for self-education. The idea of self-examination is expressed in 2 Cor. 13:5. Seneca, *De Providentia,* iv,3 ff., compares the acquisition of self-knowledge to the testing of a soldier in battle.

3. Francis Seager, *The School of Virtue* (1957), sig. B8ᵛ–C1ʳ.

4. See S. Blach, "Shakespeare's Latein-Grammatik," *SJ* 44 (1908):70.

5. Leonhardus Culman, *Pueriles* (Augsburg, 1546), sigs. A2ʳ, A2ᵛ, A6ʳ, etc.; *Catonis Disticha* (1562), sigs. H1ʳ, H5ʳ, etc.

6. Jodocus Willichius, Commentary, *Publii Terentii Afri Fabulae* (Zürich, 1550), p. 402: "Physici quoque hinc tamquam ex exemplo iracundiae causas, signa, effectiones, et eventa recte docerent."

7. Michel de Montaigne, *Essays,* trans. John Florio (1603), ed. George Saintsbury [Tudor Edition] (1893), 2:97 [chap. 10]. All subsequent references to Montaigne are to this edition.

8. Arthur Golding, "To the Reader," in Ovid, *Metamorphoses,* trans. Arthur Golding (1567), sig. A2ʳ.

9. For an analysis of the book, see Foster Watson, *The ZODIACUS VITAE of Marcellus Palingenius Stellatus* (London, 1908), and Rosemond Tuve's introduction to *The Zodiac of Life,* trans. Barnabe Googe, Scholars' Facsimiles and Reprints (New York, 1947). For the influence of Palingenius on Shakespeare, see John E. Hankins, *Shakespeare's Derived Imagery* (Lawrence, Kans., 1953). Sources other than Palingenius for Sir John Davies's *Nosce Teipsum* have been suggested by G. T. Buckley, "The Indebtedness of Sir John Davies' *Nosce Teipsum* to Philip Mornay's *Trunesse of the Christian Religion*", *MP* 25 (1927):67–78, and

Louis Bredvold, "The Sources Used by Davies in *Nosce Teipsum*", *PMLA* 38 (1923) : 745–69. Sir John was traveling a familiar route. He may, as T. W. Baldwin has suggested, have been putting his lecture notes to good use during his penitential year at Oxford when he composed the poem.

10. M. T. Cicero, *Four Several Treatises* [*De Amicitia, De Senectute, Paradoxa, Somnium Scipionis*], trans. Thomas Newton (1577), fol. 130. Cf. Girolamo Cardano, *Cardanus's Comfort*, trans. Thomas Bedingfield (1576), sig. A8^r: "A man is nothing but his mind." Thomas Pritchard, *The School of Honest and Virtuous Life* (1579), sig. J4^r: "Man is as his mind is." The *locus classicus* of the idea is Plato, *Alcibiades* (130).

11. Heinrich Bullinger, *Fifty Godly Sermons* [*Decades*], trans. Miles Coverdale (1577; 3d ed., 1587, p. 755 [Dec. 4, Serm. 10].

12. For "mind" or "soul," see *Caes.*, I.ii.310, II.i.322; *Ham.*, III.i.100, 150; *I H. IV*, V.iv.20; *R. II*, II.i.57; *H. VIII*, I.i.146; *Sonn.*, 115, 116. For "self," see *Err.*, II.ii.122; *Per.*, II.iv.37; *Ant.*, IV.xii.47; *W. T.*, I.ii.79, IV.iv.7; *H. VIII*, II.ii.92, III.ii.336.

13. The first to notice the parallel appears to have been Charles Wordsworth, *On Shakespeare's Knowledge and Use of the Bible* (London, 1864), pp. 111–12.

14. Rolf Soellner, "Prudence and the Price of Helen: The Debate of the Trojans in *Troilus and Cressida*," *SQ* 20 (1969) : 255–63.

15. The difference between these two kinds of *decorum* is noted by Marvin T. Herrick, *Comic Theory in the Sixteenth Century* (Urbana, Ill., 1950), p. 140.

16. Cicero, *De Officiis*, I.110–14.

17. Cicero, *Three Books of Duties* [*De Officiis*], trans. Nicholas Grimald (1556), fol. 45.

18. John Woolton, *A Treatise of the Immortality of the Soul* (1576). Concerning Woolton's claim to have been the first to have written on the soul in English, it should be said that the subject had not been passed by in theological works, e.g., in John Rastell's *A New Book of Purgatory* (ca. 1530), and in John Calvin's *Institution of Christian Religion*, trans. Thomas Norton (1561). Woolton appears to borrow from Bullinger's sermon on the soul in *Decades* (which had its first English translation in 1577). There were many Latin humanistic works in the *de anima* tradition; a long list is in Conrad Gessner's *Pandectarium* (Zürich, 1574).

19. Thomas Rogers, *A Philosophical Discourse Entitled the Anatomy of the Mind* (1576). Probably induced by Rogers's book, John Woolton published *A New Anatomy of Whole Man: As Well His Body as His Soul* (1576). The equation of self-knowledge with knowledge of mind *and* body was general; e.g., it is in Timothy Bright, *A Treatise of Melancholy* (1586) ; Juan Huarte de San Juan, *Examen de Ingenios: The Examination of Men's Wits*, trans. Richard Carew (1594) ; Sir John Davies, *Nosce Teipsum* (1599) ; Thomas Walkington, *The Optic Glass of Humors* (1607) ; and Pierre Charron, *Of Wisdom*, trans. Samson Lennard (1612).

20. See G. P. Conger, *Theories of Macrocosms and Microcosms in the History of Philosophy* (New York, 1922). Cf. Aristotle, *Phys.*, VIII.2(252b).

21. See Paul H. Kocher, *Science and Religion in Elizabethan England* (San Marino, Calif., 1953). For the general background of Renaissance atheism and the reaction to it, see Don C. Allen, *Doubt's Boundless Sea* (Baltimore, Md., 1964).

22. Deut. 32 : 29; Psalms 8 : 4; Isa. 1 : 3; Jer. 23 : 20, 30 : 24; Eccl. 3 : 18; Heb. 2 : 6. Some Elizabethan and Jacobean tracts were still very much in the tradition of *consideratio*, e.g., Andrew Kingsmill, *A View of Man's Estate* (1574) and *The Anatomy of Sin* (1603), attributed to Thomas Lodge.

23. Sebastian de Covarrubias Orosco, *Emblemas Morales* (Madrid, 1610), I, Emblem 82: "Consideravit seipsum et abiit."

24. *Certain Sermons,* Scholars' Facsimiles & Reprints, ed. M. E. Rickey and Thomas Stroup (Gainsville, Fla., 1968), p. 10.

25. Full treatments of Calvin's attitude toward man are in T. F. Torrance, *Calvin's Doctrine of Man* (Grand Rapids, Mich., 1947), and Leroy Nixon, *John Calvin's Teaching on Human Reason* (New York, 1960).

26. Calvin, *Institution,* I.5.3.

27. See L. L. Schücking, *The Puritan Family* (New York, 1969; German edition, 1929); for the Elizabethan manuals, see Louis B. Wright, *Middle Class Culture in Elizabethan England* (Chapel Hill, N.C., 1935), part 2, chap. 8: "Guides to Godliness."

28. Thomas Wright, *The Passions of the Mind in General* (1601), p. 2.

29. See Ruth Kelso, *The Doctrine of the English Gentleman in the Sixteenth Century* (Urbana, Ill., 1929).

30. Sir Thomas Elyot, *The Book Named the Governor* (1531), fol. 176 [Bk. III, chap. 3].

31. See Ruth Kelso, *The Doctrine of the Lady in the Renaissance* (Urbana, Ill., 1956).

32. Giovanni Bruto, *The Necessary, Fit, and Convenient Education of a Young Gentlewoman,* trans. W. P. (1598), sig. G8ᵛ.

33. Tigurinus Chelidonius, *The Institution and First Beginning of a Christian Prince,* trans. Sir James Chillester (1571), p. 107. The actual author of this tract was presumably its French "translator," Pierre Boaistuau; see J. Brunet, *Manuel du Libraire* (Paris, 1860), 1 : 983.

34. Sir James Perrott, *The First Part of the Consideration of Human Condition* (Oxford, 1600). My attention was drawn to this very rare book by Professor Robert Dent at the Huntington Library. I have found it very useful for illustrating the patterns of self-knowledge in *Lear.* Sir James's ambitious plan was to follow up the *First Part,* devoted to moral consideration, with three more parts on political, natural, and metaphysical consideration. He seems to have had in mind a kind of "English Academy" to rival the *French Academy of La Primaudaye.* But Sir James became involved in politics and abandoned his philosophic consideration.

35. Pierre Boaistuau, *Theatrum Mundi* (1566), trans. John Alday, sig. A4ᵛ.

36. William Baldwin, *A Treatise of Moral Philosophy* (1564; 1st ed. 1547), fol. 76. These verses appear to be Thomas Palfreyman's, who competed with Baldwin in augmenting the *Treatise.* The 1564 edition has a long section, "Of Man and What he is," full of notable *nosce teipsum* sayings, some of them credited to certain philosophers without foundation in fact. The medieval wisdom literature, from which Baldwin's collection descends, was evidently under pressure from the humanistic *nosce teipsum* trend.

Chapter Two

1. "Counter-humanism," as Paul Kristeller has suggested, is a more appropriate term for the intellectual tendencies incongruous with the Erasmian synthesis than "counter-Renaissance," which has been given currency by the provocative study of Hiram Haydn, *The Counter-Renaissance* (New York, 1950).

2. Robert Chambers, "A Christian Reformation of *Nosce Teipsum,*" MS, British Museum, Royal 18, A6g. This manuscript is discussed and quoted by R. H. Bowers, "An Elizabethan Manuscript 'Continuation' of Sir John Davies' *Nosce Teipsum,*" *MP* 58 (1960) : 11–19.

3. See Robert Hoopes, "Fideism and Scepticism during the Renaissance: Three Major Witnesses," *HLQ* 14 (1951): 319–47. On the fallacy of equating Renaissance philosophical skepticism with religious skepticism, see Ernest A. Strathmann, *Sir Walter Ralegh: A Study in Renaissance Scepticism* (New York, 1951). Renaissance skepticism in general is discussed by Richard Popkin, *The History of Scepticism from Erasmus to Descartes* (Assen, Holland, 1960). On Montaigne's conception of self-knowledge, see Donald M. Frame, *Montaigne's Discovery of Man* (New York, 1955).

4. *Essays*, 2:250 [chap. 12].

5. Ibid., 1:48 [chap. 10].

6. Ibid., 3:297 [chap. 12].

7. Ibid., 3:339 [chap. 13].

8. Roger Ascham, *English Works*, ed. W. A. Wright (Cambridge, 1904), p. 111.

9. Baldassare Castiglione, *The Courtier*, trans. Sir Thomas Hoby (1561; ed. 1588), sig. M3^v [Bk. II].

10. See Felix Raab, *The English Face of Machiavelli* (London, 1964); also, Irving Ribner, "The Significance of Gentillet's *Contre-Machiavel*," *MLQ* 10 (1949): 153–57. One of the Elizabethan manuscript translations was published by Hardin Craig (Chapel Hill, N.C., 1949).

11. "The old-fashioned and simple opinion, according to which Machiavelli was a teacher of evil," is very effectively defended by Leo Strauss, *Thoughts on Machiavelli* (Glencoe, Ill., 1958).

12. Niccolo Machiavelli, *The Prince*, trans. Edward Dacres (1640), p. 111 [chap. 11].

13. Ibid., p. 136 [chap. 18].

14. Ibid., 137 [chap. 18].

15. Ibid., 140 [chap. 18].

16. *Gabriel Harvey's Marginalia*, ed. G. C. Moore Smith (Stratford-upon-Avon, 1913), p. 147. Harvey was "Machiavellian" about Machiavelli; he publicly satirized him; but he mentioned him numerous times approvingly in his *marginalia*. Cf. T. H. Jameson, "The Machiavellianism of Gabriel Harvey," *PMLA* 56 (1941): 645–56.

17. Ibid., p. 148.

18. Christopher Marlowe, *Tamburlaine Part I*, II.vii.18–29, in *The Complete Plays of Christopher Marlowe*, ed. Irving Ribner (New York, 1963), p. 75.

19. Thomas Hobbes, *Leviathan*, ed. Michael Oakeshott (Oxford, 1946), p. 6.

20. Bacon's ideas of self-knowledge are discussed by Sidney Warhaft, "Bacon and the Renaissance Ideal of Self-Knowledge," *Personalist*, 44 (1963): 454–71. I am indebted to Warhaft's analysis. For a precedent to Bacon's utilitarian interpretation of self-knowledge, one could point to the ancient Sophists, who thought that to know oneself was to know his need.

21. Sir Francis Bacon, *Advancement of Learning*, in *The Philosophical Works of Francis Bacon*, ed. J. M. Robertson (London, 1905), p. 140. Subsequent references to this edition are in the text.

22. When Bacon spoke in the corresponding passage of *De Augmentis* (IV.i), of the theme of the "triumphs of man," which had not been sufficiently investigated, he evidently thought of a subject different from the humanists' orations on the "dignity of man"; he presumably wanted to see man's control over his environment glorified.

CHAPTER THREE

1. Guillaume de Saluste du Bartas, *The Divine Weeks and Works,* trans. Sir Joshua Sylvester (1605), p. 205 [Sixth Day of First Week].

2. Bacon criticized the microcosmic theories of Paracelsus and the alchemists; see Conger, *Macrocosms and Microcosms,* p. 67. For the criticism by Calvin and Montaigne, see above, chap. 2.

3. See C. S. Lewis, *The Discarded Image* (Cambridge, 1964); Paul H. Kocher, *Science and Religion in Elizabethan England;* Herschel Baker, *The Wars of Truth: Studies in the Decay of Christian Humanism in the Earlier Seventeenth Century* (Cambridge, Mass. 1952).

4. The earliest unmistakable meaning of "frame" in the sense of border or case listed in *OED* is from 1660. It is true, *OED* cites "frame" in Shakespeare's sonnet 24 as an example, but, as I am arguing in the present chapter, the word should be taken to refer to the structure of man.

5. *Batman upon Bartholomew* [Bartholomaeus Anglicus, *De Proprietatibus Rerum*], trans. Stephen Bateman (1582), Bk. 10: "De Materia et Forma."

6. Sir Thomas More, *Utopia,* trans. Ralph Robinson (1551; 3d ed. 1597), sig. D^v.

7. Arthur Golding, Epistle Dedicatory, *Metamorphoses,* sig. B^v.

8. Nevill Coghill, *Shakespeare's Professional Skills* (Cambridge, 1964), pp. 8-9.

9. *Divine Weeks,* p. 231 [Seventh Day of First Week].

10. *Courtier,* sig. H5^r [Bk. I].

11. For the pictorial conception of Hamlet's speech on man (II.ii.295 ff.), see Baldwin, *Compositional Genetics,* pp. 301 ff. Cf. below, Appendix C.

12. Sir Thomas Elyot, *Of the Knowledge Which Maketh a Wise Man* (1533), fols. 44-46.

13. John Dee, "Mathematical Preface," in Euclid, *The Elements of Geometry,* trans. H. Billingsley (1570), sig. C3^r. Cf. C. A. Patrides, "The Numerological Approach to Cosmic Order during the English Renaissance," *Isis* 49 (1958): 391-97.

14. "Ne meritum praelustre tuum, dignissima mundi / Pars Homo, servili conditione premas; / In te tota patet coelorum atque orbis imago, / Hinc decus, hinc dotes noscere disce tuas" (Florentius Schoonhovius, *Emblemata* [Gouda, 1618], Emblem 1).

15. *All's W.,* III.i.12, IV.ii.4; sonnet 59; *R. III,* I.ii.243; *Oth.,* II.iii.330.

16. "Homo natus de muliere brevi vivens tempore repletur multis miseriis" (Laurens van Haecht Goidtsenhoven, μικροκόσμος, *Parvus Mundus* [Frankfurt, 1618], Emblem 1). This is the emblem depicted on the dust jacket. Courtesy of the British Museum.

17. See Victor Harris, *All Coherence Gone* (Chicago, Ill., 1949); Don C. Allen, "The Degeneration of Man and Cosmic Pessimism," *SP* 35 (1938): 207-27. Cf. C. A. Patrides, "Renaissance and Modern Thought on the Last Things: A Study in Changing Conceptions," *Harvard Theological Review* 51 (1958): 170-85.

18. Abraham Fleming, *A Bright Burning Beacon* (1580), sigs. H4^r, I2^v.

19. See Harris, *All Coherence Gone,* pp. 106-48. Jacobean pessimism is cautiously assessed by F. P. Wilson, *Elizabethan and Jacobean* (Oxford, 1945).

20. Richard Barckley, *A Discourse of the Felicity of Man* (1598), p. 353.

21. The pregnant phrase "muddy vesture of decay" strikes one as a Christian

accent. Yet it might be noted that, in a passage on the soul's knowledge of itself, which may well be a source of Lorenzo's speech, Cicero asks the rhetorical question whether the soul was formed out of this "earthy, mortal, and decaying" substance (*terrena mortalique natura caduca*). See *Tusculan Disputations*, I.62.

22. John Davies of Hereford, *Mirum in Modum* (1602), sig. A3ʳ. For the use of the analogy of the circle in the Renaissance and its disappearance under the impact of the Copernican revolution, see Marjorie H. Nicolson, *The Breaking of the Circle* (Evanston, Ill., 1950).

23. "Shakespeare and the Thought of His Age," p. 188.

24. See Kocher, *Science and Religion*, pp. 88, 171; James Winny, *The Frame of Order* (New York, 1957), p. 17.

25. *Felicity of Man*, p. 354.

26. Ibid., p. 6. Cf. Homer, *Iliad*, VIII. The *aurea catena* was identified with a chain of order, reaching from God to the bottom of the universe, in the Commentary of Macrobius on Cicero's *Somnium Scipionis*. For the development of this idea, see Arthur O. Lovejoy, *The Great Chain of Being* (Cambridge, Mass., 1936). There is much to object to in the popularization of the concept in Tillyard's *The Elizabethan World Picture*. Tillyard's claim that it would be easy to accumulate texts describing the great chain of being in Elizabethan literature is misleading. The Elizabethans seem to have been reluctant to use the metaphor in the manner of Macrobius. One reason appears to be that the Stoics identified the golden chain with an inexorable fate that transcended even the will of the gods, a notion that conflicted with the Christian idea of divine providence (see Baldwin, *Compositional Genetics*, p. 139).

27. Wylie Sypher, *Four Stages of Renaissance Style* (Garden City, N.Y., 1954), p. 62. Sypher here summarizes the concepts of artistic composition basic to the Renaissance style according to the fundamental study of Heinrich Wölfflin, *Kunstgeschichtliche Grundbegriffe* (1915), translated as *Principles of Art History* (New York, 1922). Wölfflin's concepts are: (1) linear vision: the stress is on the outlines, the "limits" of things; (2) plane organization: the parts of a total form are reduced to a sequence of planes; (3) closed form: a clear, "tectonic" form is established by rules and ratios that govern the relations of the parts; (4) multiple unity: the parts maintain a certain independence in a composition that aims at a harmony based on multiplicity.

28. For an exposition of Renaissance natural law and its influence on drama, see George C. Herndl, *The High Design: English Renaissance Tragedy and the Natural Law* (Lexington, Ky., 1970). Herndl sees Shakespeare as an apologist of natural law; but I shall in later parts of this book argue that Shakespeare developed doubts about this concept as he did also of other Renaissance orthodoxies.

29. E.g., Sir John Fortescue, *De Natura Legis Naturae*, in *Works*, ed. Thomas Clermont (London, 1869), chap. 59: "The Judge First Shows How the Woman Is Subordinated to Man in the Order of the Universe."

30. *Nosce Teipsum* (1599), p. 11.

31. Marcellus Palingenius, *The Zodiac of Life*, trans. Barnabe Googe (1567; 2d ed., 1588), p. 120 [*Libra*].

32. E.g., Boethius, *De Consolatione*, II, m. 8; III, m. 10; *Romance of the Rose*, 1685–88; Chaucer, *Knight's Tale*, A 2985–88; *Troilus and Criseyde*, III, 1744–72; Spenser, *Colin Clouts*, 841–52; *Faerie Queene*, IV.i.xxx; *An Hymne in Honour of Love*, 85–92.

33. *French Academy* (1589), p. 18.

34. Sig. A2ʳ.

35. *Zodiac*, p. 110 [*Libra*].

36. See Albert W. Fields, "Milton and Self-Knowledge," *PMLA* 83 (1968): 392–99.

37. Philippus Beroaldus, Commentary on Cicero's *Quaestiones Tusculanae* (Paris, 1562), fol. 34: "Homo autem cognoscit seipsum, si originis natalisque exordia prima respexerit: . . . et hoc intelligi vult esto in loco M.T. . . . anima cognoscit semetipsam, quando scrutamur utrum corporea vel incorporea, utrum simplex an ex pluribus composita, utrum facta an omnino a nullo sit facta, utrum origo ejus pariter cum origine corporis traducatur, quod se traducem fieri dicitur an perfecta extrinsecus veniens parato jam et formato inter viscera muliebra corpore inducatur et multa hoc genus."

38. "Participate" apears to have here a more active meaning than indicated in Schmidt's paraphrase "to have in common with others." In its transitive use, the verb has the connotation of the translation of *participere* in Thomas Cooper's *Thesaurus* (1578) : "to give part, to make partner or of counsel."

39. Bartholomaeus Anglicus, *De Proprietatibus Rerum* (Nürnberg, 1519), sig. 3ʳ.

40. *Oth.,* III.iii.378; *T. N.,* IV.iii.9.

41. *Rom.,* I.iii.28; *Caes.,* II.i.66.

42. Sir John Davies, *Nosce Teipsum,* p. 86.

43. Hallett Smith, "Tamburlaine and the Renaissance," *Elizabethan Studies and Other Essays in Honor of G. F. Reynolds,* University of Colorado Studies (1945). pp. 126–31.

44. See Ernest W. Talbert, *The Problem of Order* (Chapel Hill, N.C., 1962).

45. It could be said, of course, that the universe was "full" in a physical sense at least below the moon because all voids were filled with air; but theologians objected to the idea that no world more filled with objects and creatures was conceivable. This objection to plenitude is the same as noted for the Middle Ages by Arthur Lovejoy, *The Great Chain of Being* (Cambridge, Mass., 1936), pp. 99 ff. Thus one of the key concepts of the "great chain of being," as some modern critics have used the term, was decidedly unorthodox in Shakespeare's time. Lovejoy, contrary to Tillyard, does not claim that the great chain of being was a familiar image or idea for the Elizabethans.

46. Richard Hooker, *Of the Laws of Ecclesiastical Polity* [I.2], ed. Hanbury (London, 1830), 1 : 114.

47. Annibale Romei, *The Courtier's Academy,* trans. J. Kepler (1598), pp. 25–26.

48. *Laws* [VIII.2], ed. Hanbury, 3 : 263.

49. William Elton, "Shakespeare's Ulysses and the Problem of Value," *ShakS* 2 (1966) : 95–111.

CHAPTER FOUR

1. The themes of the play and their derivation are meticulously examined by T. W. Baldwin, *Compositional Genetics.* I reached my conclusions before his study came out, but I have taken a few suggestions from him in presenting them. The serious elements of the play are emphasized by Harold Brooks, "Themes and Structure in *The Comedy of Errors,*" in *Early Shakespeare,* Stratford-upon-Avon Studies, 3 (1961), pp. 52–72; by R. A. Foakes, Introduction to the New Arden Edition (London, 1962) ; and by Gwyn Williams, "*The Comedy of Errors* Rescued from Tragedy," *REL* 5 (1964) : iv, 63–71.

2. A. E. Housman, *The Name and Nature of Poetry* (New York, 1933), p. 35.

3. Cf. sonnet 74; *Macb.* V.viii.18.

4. See Laurence J. Mills, *One Soul in Bodies Twain* (Bloomington, Ind., 1937).

5. Cicero, *Tusculan Disputations,* I.67: "Non valet tantum animus, ut se ipse videat: at ut oculus, sic animus se non videns alia cernunt." Cf. *Caes.* I.ii.51 ff., *Troi.* III.iii.104 ff.

6. *Immortality* (1576), fol. 74.

7. For the five-act formula, see T. W. Baldwin, *Five Act Structure.* An example of a strong passion in Terence analyzed as being close to *tragicus furor* is Geta's outbreak of anger in *Adelphoe* III.ii; the term is that of Willichius in his commentary on Terence, *Fabulae* (Zürich, 1550), pp. 401–2.

8. Williams, "The *CE* Rescued," p. 63.

9. See Richard Henze, "*The Comedy of Errors:* A Freely Binding Chain," *SQ* 22 (1971) : 35–41. This metaphorical use of the chain has nothing to do with the great chain of being; see above, chap. 3, n. 26.

10. Baldwin, *Compositional Genetics,* pp. 166 ff.

11. *A New Anatomy* (1576), fol. 4. Woolton's "enclosures of nature" translates *lex naturae.* Cf. Cicero, *Tusculan Disputations,* V.xiii.38.

12. E.g., Peter Martyr [Pietro Vermigli], *Commonplaces,* trans. Antony Marten (1583), I, 124: ". . . woman, compared unto man, as touching the actions and affairs of this life, she is not in the image of God, because she was created to be the helper of man." Luciana's argument was also a properly legal one. See above, chap. 3, n. 29.

13. Epistle, *Metamorphoses* (1567), sig. B2ʳ.

14. *A New Anatomy* (1576), fols. 12–13.

15. Cf. *Rom.,* II.vi.37, *Caes.,* II.i.273, *H. V,* V.ii.357.

16. Stefano Guazzo, *Civil Conversation,* trans. George Pettie (1581; ed. 1586), fol. 132 [Bk. III].

17. *Zodiac,* p. 127 [*Libra*]. Cf. Hankins, *Shakespeare's Derived Imagery,* chap. 11, "Earth."

18. *Nosce Teipsum,* p. 13. Chelidonius, *Institution* (1571), p. 158.

CHAPTER FIVE

1. Edward Dowden, *Shakspere: A Critical Study of His Mind and Art* (1872; rpt. New York, 1962), pp. 62 ff. The significance of the theme of self-knowledge in *Love's Labor's Lost* has been noted briefly by Cyrus Hoy, "*Love's Labor's Lost* and the Nature of Comedy," *SQ* 13 (1962) : 31–40.

2. Cf. Theodore Spencer, *Shakespeare and the Nature of Man,* 2d ed. (New York, 1961), p. 87.

3. Lodovico Guicciardini, *Hours of Recreation,* trans. James Sanford (1576), p. 70.

4. Virgil Whitaker, *Shakespeare's Use of Learning* (San Marino, Cal., 1953), p. 84.

5. Sigs. Aᵛ–A2ʳ. Subsequent references to this edition in this chapter are in the text.

6. *Zodiac,* p. 9 [*Virgo*]. On the contradictions created by the fusion of classical, medieval, and Christian-humanist notions of honor, see Curtis B. Watson, *Shakespeare and the Renaissance Concept of Honor* (Princeton, N.J., 1960).

7. Cf. J. S. Reid, "Shakespeare's Living Art," *PQ* 1 (1922) : 226–27.

8. *French Academy,* p. 41. For an example of the transmission of the distinction

between active and contemplative philosophy in a grammar school of Shakespeare's time, see Baldwin, *Shakspere's Small Latine,* 1 : 325: a Winchester student recorded the division in his notebook from the dictation of his master.

9. Rom., 8 : 13, Col., 3 : 5.

10. Cicero, *De Officiis,* I.19.

11. *Zodiac,* p. 97.

12. Ibid., 96, 98.

13. Ibid., p. 98.

14. Castiglione, *Courtier,* sig. Cc3ʳ [Bk. IV].

15. Alexander Nowell's *Catechism* warns against abusing the name of God "either with forswearing or with swearing rashly, unadvisedly, and without necessity" (*A Catechism,* trans. Thomas Norton [1571], sig. D2ᵛ).

16. Beroaldus, Commentary, *Quaestiones Tusculanae* (Paris, 1549), fol. 257: "Caeterum Hieronymus, Lactantius, Augustinus, ecclesiastici doctores reprobant aegritudinem Stoicorum, approbantes mediocritatem Peripateticorum: quod et ratio demonstrat, & sensus communis exposcit: namque extirpare radicitus affectus est hominem ex homine tollere, et in corpore constitutum esse sine corpore, et optare potius quam docere. Meritoque scripsit Flaccus in satyra: 'Nam vitiis nemo sine nascitur. . . . Naturalia enim haec sunt, non voluntaria quae peripatetici providenter et necessaria nobis insita esse demonstrant." The Horace quotation is from *Satires,* I.iii.69. In Drant's translation, it reads: "For faultless, doubtless, born is none, / And he is even best / Whose life sincere admitteth few / And with the least is pressed" (*Horace,* trans. Thomas Drant [1567], sig. k 4ᵛ).

17. Cf. La Primaudaye, *French Academy,* p. 30: "Reason, by the means of God's grace, can both easily constrain, master, and compel all passions in such sort that they take no effect and also bring to pass that whatsoever is rashly desired shall be overcome by the discourse of prudent counsel." Also, Woolton, *Anatomy* (1576), fol. 31: "The devil . . . without God's especial and wonderful grace is able to do much against silly and weak man." Similarly, Barckley, *Felicity of Man,* p. 472: "A contented and quiet mind, void of sorrow and fear, . . . cannot be obtained without God's special grace and gift and his alliance to our endeavors."

18. "Facile precor gelida quando pecus omne sub umbra / Ruminat" (IV.ii.89–90). Most modern editions, including Alexander, restore Holofernes's "Facile" to the "Fauste" of "good old" Mantuan. This emendation eliminates a joke: the pedagogue's Latin is a little rusty.

19. For an examination of the recurring speculation that this passage is a satirical barb at an alleged "School of Night," see Ernest A. Strathmann, "The Textual Evidence for 'the School of Night,'" *MLN* 56 (1941) : 176–86. Among the emendations suggested, "suit of night" is attractive. On the basis of the Palingenius passage quoted above, "owl of night" might be appropriate, but it would be difficult to believe that it could lead to the misreading of "school of night." At any rate, the object of comparison must be of a dark hue and must fit into the context of contrasts between dark and light, night and day, which is conventional for the twin themes of spiritual warfare and courtly love. A satirical reference of the kind suggested by the adherents of the "School of Night" theory would be merely confusing.

20. Berowne's words echo as late as *The Tempest* (IV.i.52–53) : "The strongest oaths are straw / To th'fire i'th' blood." Cf. also *Merch.,* I.ii.20.

21. The repetitive nature of the subsequent lines indicates that Shakespeare revised the passage and that both the original version (IV.iii.291–313) and the revision (314–61) remained standing. In my analysis, I shall use this latter passage, which Shakespeare presumably wanted to take the place of the earlier lines.

22. Cf. Pierre de la Primaudaye, *The Second Part of the French Academy,* trans.

Thomas Bowes (1594), p. 8: 'All things created have their proper motion, which they follow according to that love that every one of them beareth to his natural disposition. . . . And as the fire and air naturally love to be above and therefore draw thitherward without ceasing, so the water and earth love to keep below so that they always bend that ways." Shakespeare developed this idea at length in a conceit he carried through two of his sonnets (44 and 45).

Chapter Six

1. This Tudor opinion is illustrated by Irving Ribner, *The English History Play in the Age of Shakespeare* (Princeton, N.J., 1957), p. 161, and by Lily B. Campbell, *Shakespeare's "Histories": Mirrors of Elizabethan Policy* (San Marino, Calif., 1958), pp. 168 ff.

2. Some key images are earth, blood, weeping, tongue, sickness, blot, sun, and moon; see Richard Altick, "Symphonic Imagery in *Richard II,*" PMLA 62 (1942) : 339–65. Most of these illustrate grief or give it cosmic dimensions. The up-and-down movement in the imagery has been noted by Paul Jorgensen, "Vertical Patterns in *Richard II,*" *Shak. Ass. Bull.* 23 (1948) : 119–34. Again, this imagery illustrates grief, considered by the physiologists a "heavy" passion, dragging down the afflicted person. For the variations of the theme of grief in contrasting patterns, see Rolf Soellner, "The Four Primary Passions: A Renaissance Theory Reflected in the Works of Shakespeare," SP 55 (1958) : 549–67.

3. Raphael Holinshed, *The Chronicles of England, Ireland, and Scotland,* in *Narrative and Dramatic Sources of Shakespeare,* ed. Geoffrey Bullough (London, 1960), 3 : 388.

4. See Bullough's Introduction to the sources of the play, and Willard Farnham, *The Medieval Heritage of Elizabethan Tragedy* (Berkeley, Calif., 1956). Froissart, whose Chronicle Shakespeare may have read in the translation of Lord Berner, expressed considerable pity for Richard. Other French sources, such as, for instance, the *Chronique de la Traïson et Mort de Richard Deux Roy Dangleterre,* were even more decidedly anti-Lancastrian.

5. *Chronicles,* 3 : 401.

6. Ibid.

7. For an excellent argument on Shakespeare's relatively gentle treatment of Richard, see Peter Ure, Introduction, *Richard II,* New Arden Edition (London, 1956).

8. *Governor,* fol. 177 [Bk. III, chap. 3].

9. I disagree with the argument that Shakespeare conceived Richard as a "mercurial humor" made by J. W. Draper, "The Character of Richard II," *PQ* 21 (1942) : 228–36. Mercurial humors were thought to be of Protean instability, changing from one mood to another. But the earlier Richard is not quite as unstable or "stupid" as Professor Draper finds him.

10. Levinus Lemnius, *The Touchstone of Complexions,* trans. Thomas Newton (1565; 3d ed. 1581), fol. 98.

11. Ibid., fol. 148.

12. Ibid.

13. Ibid., fols. 90–91.

14. These features are noted by Timothy Bright, *Treatise* (1586), pp. 100–101.

15. *Consideration of Human Condition,* p. 5.

16. Pope Innocent III, *The Mirror of Man's Life* [*De Humanae Miseriae Conditione*], trans. Humphrey Kerton (1576), sig. B3ʳ.

17. On the elements of this passage, cf. Baldwin, *Compositional Genetics,* pp. 326 ff.

18. The first to suggest that Holbein's woodcut influenced Shakespeare seems to have been Francis Douce, *Illustrations of Shakespeare* (London, 1807), 1 : 140.

19. The well-worn commonplace of the theater of the world was, in its association with *consideratio,* familiar to the Elizabethans by the titular image of Boaistuau's popular *Theatrum Mundi,* in its first and longest part, a *contemptus mundi* tract.

20. *Institution,* p. 114.

21. Richard's inability to separate his sacral role from his profane existence is discussed by Ernst H. Kantorowicz, *The King's Two Bodies: A Study in Medieval Political Theology* (Princeton, N.J., 1957).

22. *Catonis Precepta Moralia,* ed. Erasmus (Strasbourg, 1515), sig. Cʳ: "In speculo teipsum contemplare, et si formosus apparebis, age quae deceant formam. Sin deformis, quod in facie minus est, id morum pensato pulchritudine." Cf. chap. I, n. 1.

23. Diego de Estella, *A Method unto Mortification* [*De Contemptu Mundi*], trans. Thomas Rogers (1586; ed. 1608), pp. 381–82. Peter Ure, in the introduction to the New Arden edition, examines the *veritas-vanitas* convention and gives further references. Ure notes that Queen Elizabeth is said to have asked for a mirror on her deathbed, then rejected the "flattering glass" and demanded a "true" one. Cf. also Shakespeare, sonnet 62.

24. *Nosce Teipsum,* p. 63.

25. The association between the mirror symbol and books conducive to self-knowledge was well established. Thomas Bowes introduced his translation of *The French Academy,* Pt. II, by calling the book a "mirror" so the reader could "know himself the better" by it (La Primaudaye, *Second Part,* sig. A5ʳ). Pierre Charron, *Of Wisdom,* said in his preface to Part I, that "we have no clearer looking glass, no better book, than ourselves." There was of course, above all, *The Mirror for Magistrates,* into which Elizabethans might have wished Richard II to have looked.

26. *Mirror,* sig. D3ᵛ. Similarly, La Primaudaye, *French Academy* (1589), p. 576.

27. *Anatomy,* fol. 33.

28. Plutarch, *Morals,* trans. Philemon Holland (1603), p. 1182 ["Of the Face Appearing in the Moon"]. The parallel was noted by Reinhold Sigismund, "Übereinstimmendes zwischen Shakespeare und Plutarch," *SJ* 18 (1883) : 156–82.

29. *Mirror,* sig. D2ʳ. Cf. Matth. 19: 21–26, 2 Cor. 6: 10.

30. John Middleton Murry, *Shakespeare* (London, 1936), p. 142.

31. The incomplete self-awareness of Richard is well described by Robert Heilman, *Tragedy and Melodrama* (Seattle, Wash., 1968), pp. 180 ff. Heilman suggests that this lack of completeness is a major reason why the play is a melodrama rather than a tragedy. But I do not think that intellectual self-awareness is a prerequisite for a tragic hero; Othello and Lear (not to speak of Macbeth) possess little of this commodity, and I shall subsequently argue that the processes of self-knowledge in Shakespeare's later tragedies are not primarily intellectual. For *Richard II* setting a pattern for Shakespeare's tragedies, see Peter G. Philias, "*Richard II* and Shakespeare's Tragic Mode," *TSLL* 5 (1963) : 344–55, and Travis Bogard, "Shakespeare's Second Richard," *PMLA* 70 (1955) : 192–209.

CHAPTER SEVEN

1. For a review of unsympathetic reactions to *Henry V*, see Paul A. Jorgensen, "Accidental Judgments, Casual Slaughters, and Purposes Mistook: Critical Reactions to Shakespeare's *Henry V*," *Shak. Ass. Bull.* 22 (1947) 51–61. Hazlitt was an earlier critic who anticipated the modern antipathy to the play.

2. Lemnius, *Touchstone* (1581), fols. 33 ff.

3. Huarte, *Examen de Ingenios*, pp. 239 ff.

4. See J. H. Walter, Introduction, *Henry V*, New Arden Edition (London, 1954), and above, chap. 1.

5. Erasmus, *The Education of a Christian Prince* [*Institutio Principis Christiani*], trans. Lester K. Born (New York, 1936), p. 189. Similarly, Aristotle, *Politics*, VII, xiv.

6. Edward Hall, *The Union of the Noble and Illustrious Families of York and Lancaster* (1542; ed. 1548), fol. 49.

7. *Chronicles*, in *Narrative and Dramatic Sources of Shakespeare*, ed. Geoffrey Bullough (London, 1962), 4: 406–8.

8. *Prince*, pp. 153, 203.

9. Lemnius, *Touchstone*, fols. 34–36.

10. See Leslie Freeman, "Shakespeare's Kings and Machiavelli's Prince," *Shakespeare Encomium* [The City College Papers, I] (New York, 1964), pp. 25–43.

11. See Baldwin, *Shakspere's Small Latine*, 2: 323 ff., and William McAvoy, "Shakespeare's Use of the *Laus* of Aphthonius," (Ph.D. diss., Urbana, Ill., 1952).

12. As is noted by Walter in the introduction, Henry's "consideration" is religious as well as secular and amounts to a total change of personality. The program is of the kind outlined by Perrott, *Consideration of Human Condition*. Cf. below, chap. 16.

13. Ronald S. Berman, "Shakespeare's Alexander: Henry V," *CE* 23 (1962): 523–38. Berman seems to me to overstate the similarities between Shakespeare's Henry and Plutarch's Alexander.

14. Henry N. Hudson, Introduction, *Henry V*, New Hudson Shakespeare (Boston, 1908), pp. xlvi–xlix.

15. Una Ellis-Fermor, *The Frontiers of Drama*, 2d ed. (Oxford, 1947), p. 45.

16. Mark van Doren, *Shakespeare* (New York, 1939; rpt. Garden City, N.Y., n.d.), p. 149.

17. Cf. Albert H. Tolman, "The Epic Character of *Henry V*," *MLN* 34 (1919): 7–16.

18. *Governor*, fols. 176–77 [Bk. III, chap. 3].

19. This is the judgment of E. M. W. Tillyard, *Shakespeare's History Plays* (New York, 1944), p. 308.

20. Peter Martyr, for instance, went so far in his metaphysical optimism as to prove the wisdom of the divine plan by the argument that "there would be no life of lions if there were no slaughter of sheep wherewith the lions be fed; neither would there be patience of martyrs unless the cruelty of tyrants were permitted by God" (*Commonplaces* [1583], I, 200).

21. *Touchstone*, fol. 51.

22. *Prince*, pp. 162, 184.

23. Van Doren, *Shakespeare,* p. 149.

24. Harold Goddard, *The Meaning of Shakespeare* (Chicago, 1951), 1 : 263.

25. H. A. Evans, Introduction, *Henry V,* Old Arden Edition (London, 1903), pp. xl–xli.

26. For the principles of Renaissance composition that underlie the structure of *Henry V,* see above, chap. 3, n. 27.

CHAPTER EIGHT

1. *Julius Caesar* is considered Shakespeare's first problem play by Ernest Schanzer, *The Problem Plays of Shakespeare* (1963; rpt. New York, 1965), p. 10. There has been no unanimity on the definition of "problem play" and on the question of which particular plays should be thus designated. F. S. Boas, who applied the term for the first time to Shakespeare (in analogy to Ibsen's social dramas), included *Hamlet, Troilus and Cressida, All's Well That Ends Well,* and *Measure for Measure* (*Shakespeare and his Predecessors,* New York, 1896). E. M. W. Tillyard accepted the same grouping (*Shakespeare's Problem Plays,* London, 1949). W. W. Lawrence restricted the term to the three comedies and found *Cymbeline* to have similar qualities (*Shakespeare's Problem Comedies,* New York, 1931). Peter Ure took Boas's group, but added *Timon of Athens* (*William Shakespeare: The Problem Plays.* Writers and Their Work, Pamphlet No. 140, London, 1961). Schanzer's choices are *Julius Caesar, Measure for Measure,* and *Antony and Cleopatra.* Schanzer points out the difficulty of defining what a problem play is, but his own definition is also open to criticism. A problem play is for him one "in which we find a concern with a moral problem which is central to it, presented in such a manner that we are unsure of our moral bearings, so that uncertain and divided responses to it in the minds of the audience are possible or even probable." Moral centrality is too subjective a term to bear such heavy weight in deciding the designation of genre.

2. The discussion of the use and the limitations of "mannerism" in art and literature is inextricably tied up with the controversy about the baroque. For the application of the latter term to literature, see René Wellek, "The Concept of the Baroque in Literary Scholarship," in *Concepts of Criticism* (New Haven, Conn., 1963). Wellek makes an appeal for the use of "baroque" in "more general terms of a philosophy or a world-view or even merely an emotional attitude toward the world" (p. 63). This general principle seems to me also valid for "mannerism." It is basic to Wylie Sypher's use in *Four Stages of Renaissance Style;* but unfortunately Sypher mars his literary analyses by metaphorical uses of terminology more proper to art history. Discussions on the literary side of the controversy are in *Colloquia Germanica,* 1 (1967) and in *Literaturwissenschaftliches Jahrbuch,* N. F., 2 (1961) : 174 ff. Major accounts of mannerism that also include literary analyses are: Jacques Bousquet, *Mannerism: The Painting and Style of the Late Renaissance* (New York, 1964); Arnold Hauser, *The Social History of Art,* vol. 2 (New York, 1960), and *Mannerism,* 2 vols. (London, 1965); John Shearman, *Mannerism* (New York, 1967). My claim for the occurrence of mannerist features in Shakespeare is more limited than that of most others who have used the term. Hauser considers all of Shakespeare mannerist, and so, it appears, does Freiherr Kleinschmit von Lengefeld, "Der Manierismus in der Dichtung Shakespeares," *SJ* 97 (1961) : 62–99. Sypher finds *Hamlet, Measure for Measure, Lear,* and the romances mannerist. Some stimulating ideas on *Julius Caesar* and *Hamlet* as transitional plays between Renaissance and baroque are in Max Deutschbein, "Individ-

uum und Kosmos in Shakespeares Werken," *SJ* 69 (1933) : 6–26. For the applicability of "mannerism" to the problem plays (defined as the three comedies), see Jewell K. Vroonland, "Mannerism and Shakespeare's Problem Plays: An Argument for Revaluation" (Ph.d. diss., Kansas State University, 1969).

3. It is arguable that the contradiction between the title of the play and the person of its protagonist stems from Shakespeare's still writing in the pattern of the histories. See Moody E. Prior, "The Search for a Hero in *Julius Caesar*," *Renaissance Drama* N. S., 2 (1969) : 81–101. But the histories that are clearly tragedies, *Richard II* and *Richard III,* have both their heroes and their centers of gravity in the same person, and there is no question about the appropriateness of their titles.

4. *Shakespeare's Problem Comedies,* p. 233.

5. E.g., Brian Morris, "The Tragic Structure of *Troilus and Cressida*," *SQ* 10 (1959) : 481–91.

6. Ernst Gombrich, "Zum Werke Giulio Romanos," *Jahrbuch der Kunsthistorischen Sammlungen in Wien,* N. F., 8, 9 (1934 / 35) : 79–104, 121–49. Julio Romano is, of course, the artist referred to in *WT.,* V.ii.95, as the alleged creator of the statue that turns out to be Hermione. Shakespeare was familiar with more homely forms of mannerist art, such as in late Elizabethan costumes and portraits.

7. *Shakespeare's Problem Plays,* p. 3.

8. See B. L. Joseph, *Elizabethan Acting* (London, 1951).

9. The distinction of πάθος and ἦθος is made by Quintilian, *Institutio Oratoria,* VI.ii.9 ff. In *De Oratore,* II.liii.212, Cicero argued, much like Hamlet, that the more vehement emotions should be mingled with the milder ones in temperate speech; some inflow of mildness should reach the fiercest passion, and some energy must also kindle this mildness.

10. Cf. Leonard Goldstein, "On the Transition from Formal to Naturalistic Acting in the Elizabethan and Post-Elizabethan Theater," *Bulletin of the New York Public Library* 62 (1958) : 330–49.

11. Arnold Hauser, *Social History,* 2 : 100–101.

12. *Mannerism,* p. 28.

13. Justus Lipsius, *Six Books of Politics,* trans. William Jones (1594), p. 59.

14. *Essays,* 2 : 137 [chap. 12].

15. Sypher, *Four Stages,* p. 120. The literary style of Montaigne is defined as "mannerist" by Helmut Hatzfeld, "Per una definizione dello stile di Montaigne," *Convivium* 22 (1953) : 284–90, and in *Estudios sobre el Barocco* (Madrid, 1964), pp. 308–17.

16. The first systematic attempt to connect Shakespeare and Montaigne was made by J. M. Robertson, *Montaigne and Shakespeare* (London, 1897). Robertson ascribed much of Shakespeare's intellectual growth to his reading of Montaigne. Less far-reaching claims are made by Elizabeth R. Hooker, "The Relation of Shakespeare to Montaigne," *PMLA* 17 (1902) : 312–66; G. C. Taylor, *Shakespeare's Debt to Montaigne* (Cambridge, 1925); W. B. D. Henderson, "Montaigne's *Apologie of Raymond Sebond* and *King Lear*," *Shak. Ass. Bull.* 14 (1939) : 209–25. It has been argued that Shakespeare saw Florio's translation in manuscript prior to its publication in 1603. Some translation was circulating by 1600, judging from a remark in Essay 12 of William Cornwallis's *Essays.*

17. *Essays,* I : 288 [chap. 10].

18. Palingenius states the position emphatically : "But yet it forceth not if that the dunghill cock do guess / A precious stone as nothing worth, this makes not it the less / Of value" (*Zodiac* [1588], p. 99 [*Virgo*]).

19. See Don C. Allen, *Doubt's Boundless Sea;* George T. Buckley, *Rationalism in Sixteenth Century English Literature* (Chicago, 1933); Paul H. Kocher, *Christopher Marlowe* (Chapel Hill, N.C., 1946).

20. Cf. Woolton, *Anatomy,* fol. 2: "The philosophers, entreating of the excellence of man's nature, did guess and, as it were, dream of the divine qualities and operations of man's soul in the state of innocence." Quoting Luther, Woolton (fol. 5) says that Genesis gives "an evident and plain description of perfect nature, whereof the philosophers did rather divine and dream than know anything effectually."

21. See Rolf Soellner, "Hang up Philosophy: Shakespeare and the Limits of Knowledge," *MLQ* 23 (1962) : 135–49.

22. *Essays,* 2 : 141 [chap. 12].

23. Ibid., 2 : 144 [chap. 12].

24. M. Johann Mannich Diaconus, *Sacra Emblemata* (Nürnberg, 1624), "Nosce Teipsum": "Ales, Juno, tuus gemmantes explicat alas, / Conspectis vero, dejicit has pedibus. / Dotibus ingenii fisus sic tollit in altum / Cristas: ac meditans, deprimit has, homo, humum." ("Your bird, Juno, extends its brilliant feathers; but when it has seen its feet, it lets them fall to the ground. So man, trusting his mental powers, lifts his crest up in the air; but when he meditates, he lowers it to the earth.")

25. *Essays,* 3 : 361 [chap. 13].

26. Ibid., 2 : 6 [chap. 1].

27. Cf. Friedrich Piel, "Zum Problem des Manierismus in der Kunstgeschichte," *Literaturwissenschaftliches Jahrbuch,* N. F., 2 : 207 ff.

28. Cf. George Wilson Knight, *The Wheel of Fire* (1930; rpt. Oxford, 1965), pp. 73–96.

29. See Nicholas A. Sharp, "Shakespeare's Baroque Comedy: *The Winter's Tale*" (Ph.D. diss., Ohio State University, 1971), chap. 2.

CHAPTER NINE

1. Cf. *H.V,* III.i.19, IV.vii.20 ff., V.Prol.27 ff.

2. On the ambiguities in the character portrayals, see Schanzer, *The Problem Plays,* pp. 14 ff. Schanzer delineates well Shakespeare's technique of engaging and disengaging the sympathies of the audience; he seems to me, however, somewhat too generous to Caesar. The difficulties critics have had in interpreting the play and its charatcers are surveyed by Mildred Hartsock, "The Complexity of *Julius Caesar,*" *PMLA* 81 (1966) : 56–57.

3. Plutarch, "The Life of Marcus Brutus," in *Narrative and Dramatic Sources of Shakespeare,* ed. Geoffrey Bullough, 5 (1964) : 110.

4. Michael Drayton, *The Barons' Wars* (1603), p. 61 [Bk. III], echoed this passage in characterizing Mortimer: "Such one was he . . . / In whom in peace th'elements all lay / So mixed as none could sovereignty impute / . . . His lively temper was so absolute, / That't seemed when heaven his model first began, / In him it show'd perfection in a man." The edition of 1619 (which has slight alterations in the text of the passage) has the marginal note: "In the person of Mortimer, the pattern of an excellent man." Drayton recognized a pattern of perfection when he saw one.

5. This is a biblical term. Cf. Rom. 6 : 12–13 (Bishops): "Let not sin reign therefore in your mortal body that ye should thereunto obey by the lusts of it. Neither give you your members as instruments of unrighteousness unto sin."

6. Cf. Cooper's *Thesaurus* (1578): "*Genius:* The good or evil angel that pagans thought to be appointed to each man; the spirit of man."

7. Cf. Bernard Breyer, "A New Look at *Julius Caesar*," in *Essays in Honor of Walter Clyde Curry* (Knoxville, Tenn., 1954), pp. 161–80.

8. Plutarch, "Life of Julius Caesar," in Bullough, *Sources,* 5 : 78.

9. "Life of Brutus," in Bullough, *Sources,* 5 : 96.

10. Cicero, *Tusculan Disputations*, I.67. Beroaldus's commentary associates this figure explicitly with self-knowledge: "Animus seipsum modo quodam videre dicitur, quando scilicet noscit seipsum" (*Quaestiones Tusculanae* [Paris, 1562], fol. 43).

11. Sir Mungo W. MacCallum, *Shakespeare's Roman Plays* (London, 1935), pp. 245 ff.; John Palmer, *Political Characters of Shakespeare* (London, 1945), pp. 1 ff.

12. Plutarch, "The Comparison of Dion with Brutus," in Bullough, *Sources,* 5 : 133.

13. J. Dover Wilson, Introduction, *Julius Caesar*, New Shakespeare (Cambridge, 1949).

14. Max Lüthi, *Shakespeares Dramen* (Berlin, 1957), pp. 32–33.

15. Gordon R. Smith, "Brutus, Virtue, and Will," *SQ* 10 (1959) : 367–79.

16. "Life of Brutus," in Bullough, *Sources,* 5 : 90.

17. *Shakspere,* p. 283.

18. *Caes.,* IV.iii.142 ff.: For the opinion that there was no revision and that the text as it stands is correct, see Warren D. Smith, "The Duplicate Revelation of Portia's Death," *SQ* 4 (1953) : 153–61. The argument appears strained, particularly in view of the fact that there is not only a repetition of the news of Portia's death, but there are *two* very admiring comments by Cassius on Brutus's fortitude. One of them is surely redundant.

19. In *De Amicitia*, Cicero said, "Take away the motions of the mind, and tell me what difference there is—I will not say, between a beast and a man, but even—between a man and a stone or a log or any other such like thing?" (*Four Several Treatises*, fol. 22). Bullinger spoke of the Stoics as men who "of patience do make a kind of senselessness and, of a valiant and constant man, a senseless block or a stone without passions" (*Sermons*, 1587, p. 302). Cf. *Shrew*, I.i.31.

20. Sypher, *Four Stages,* p. 176.

21. Harley Granville-Barker, *Prefaces to Shakespeare,* 1 (1927) : 61.

CHAPTER TEN

1. The question of self-knowledge and self-identity in *Hamlet* has received some consideration in recent years, e.g., by D. G. James, *The Dream of Learning* (Oxford, 1951); Maynard Mack, "The World of Hamlet," *YR* 41 (1951/52) : 503–23, and "The Jacobean Shakespeare," in *Jacobean Theater* (Stratford-upon-Avon Studies, I), pp. 11–41; Harry Levin, *The Question of Hamlet* (New York, 1959); L. C. Knights, *An Approach to Hamlet* (London, 1960); Barbara Burge, "*Hamlet*: The Search for Identity," *REL* 5 (1964) : ii, 58–71; Robert Heilman, "To Know Himself: An Aspect of Tragic Structure," *REL* 5 (1964) : ii, 36–57. However, none of these studies examines the question in the frame of the meaning of *nosce teipsum* in the Renaissance.

2. *Ham.,* V.ii.136–38: these lines are only in Quarto 2, not in the Folio; but since they dovetail with the rest, one can assume that they are not extraneous additions.

3. La Primaudaye, *French Academy,* pp. 10–12. Similarly, Castiglione, *Courtier,* sig. o6ʳ⁻ᵛ [Bk. II].

4. T. S. Eliot, "Hamlet and His Problems," *The Sacred Wood* (London, 1920).

5. G. B. Harrison, *Shakespeare's Tragedies* (New York, 1951), pp. 88 ff.

6. Cf. E. E. Stoll, *Hamlet: An Historical and Comparative Study* (Minneapolis, Minn., 1919). Stoll also makes the claim in other studies.

7. Irving Ribner, *Patterns in Shakespearean Tragedy* (New York, 1960), pp. 68 ff.

8. A. C. Bradley, *Shakespearean Tragedy* (1904; rpt. New York, 1960), pp. 102–3.

9. E. E. Stoll, *Shakespeare and Other Masters* (Cambridge, Mass., 1940), p. 128.

10. On the general motif, see Paul A. Jorgensen, "Hamlet and the Restless Renaissance," *Shakespearean Essays,* ed. A. Thaler and Norman Sanders, University of Tennessee Studies in Literature (Knoxville, Tenn., 1964), pp. 131–34.

11. *Of Wisdom,* p. 56 [Bk. I, chap. 14].

12. Ibid., p. 136 [Bk. I, chap. 38].

13. *Essays,* 1 : 7 [chap. 1].

14. Ibid., 2 : 10 [chap. 1]. The vacillations of Hamlet's character are reflected in his way of speaking and gesturing. As Maurice Charney notes, Hamlet has no single identifiable style (*Style in Hamlet,* p. 258). Charney distinguishes four major styles used by the prince : self-conscious, witty, passionate, and simple.

15. *Of Wisdom,* p. 61 [Bk. I, chap. 14].

16. *The Dream of Learning,* p. 96.

17. See *OED,* "Passion." Richard Lever, *The Art of Reason* (1573), p. 172, noted : "Some take passion for affection, be it great or small; but in our English speech we use the term when we express a vehement pang, either of the body or the mind." The first example of "passion" as a passionate speech or outburst quoted in *OED* is from 1582.

18. Cf. Estella, *Mortification* (1608) : "If thou have a desire to know who thou art, take a glass and behold thyself in it. The glass that a man may best behold himself in is another man." Similarly, Thomas Wright, Preface, *Passions of the Mind* (1601). The humanists generally assumed that man could see in this glass the general features of humanity; with his *contemptus mundi* emphasis, Estella thinks of the dead body of man.

19. The ghost's lack of specificity is discussed by Robert H. West, *Shakespeare and the Outer Mystery* (Lexington, Ky., 1968), chap. 4. As West argues, this lack is not due to Shakespeare's ignorance of ghost lore but rather to dramatic reasons.

20. Quoted in Sypher, *Four Stages,* p. 108.

21. Ribner, *Patterns,* p. 83. Ribner speaks of a "symbolic" level on which this is true. But the context of the passage is secular and not symbolically Christian.

22. *Essays,* 3 : 297, 339 [chaps. 12, 13].

23. See Baldwin, *Shakspere's Small Latine,* 2 : 601 ff.

24. See Hardin Craig, "Hamlet's Book," *Huntington Lib. Bull.* 6 (1934) : 17–37.

25. See D. G. James, *The Dream of Learning,* pp. 58 ff.

26. *Essays,* 2 : 157 [chap. 12].

27. *Ham.,* II.ii.293 ff : I have followed the Folio version rather than Alexander and Quarto 2. For a defense of this preference and an analysis of the speech in general, see below, Appendix C.

28. Max Deutschbein, "What Is This Quintessence of Dust," *SJ* 70 (1934) : 525. E. M. W. Tillyard, however, thought it in the purest medieval tradition (*The Elizabethan World Picture,* p. 1). Others have seen similarities to orations on the dignity of man by Renaissance humanists. See K. Clark, "Alberti and Shakespeare," *TLS,* March 26, 1931 ; cf. Roy W. Battenhouse, "Hamlet's Apostrophe on Man : Clue to the Tragedy," *PMLA* 66 (1951) : 1073.

29. E.g., La Primaudaye, *Second Part,* pp. 155 ff.

30. *Of Wisdom,* p. 62 [Bk. I, chap. 14].

31. A contrary claim—that is, that the play-within-the-play already served the purpose of discovery in *Ur-Hamlet*—is made by Fredson Bowers, *Elizabethan Revenge Tragedy 1587–1642* (Princeton, N.J., 1940), pp. 85 ff. But Bowers's argument seems to me unconvincing; the genesis and the execution of the device of the play in Shakespeare is all of a piece, and Kyd is not generally noted for inventing refined psychological stratagems.

32. This form of audience reaction to tragedy was much discussed in the Renaissance. O. B. Hardison calls it "moral catharsis": "Three Types of Renaissance Catharsis," *Renaissance Drama,* N. S., 2 (1969) : 3–22.

33. The resemblance of Hamlet's words to the commentary of Lambinus is notable: "Aliquando vere dolemus, aliquando ficte. Si vere, commovemus et aptius et fortius; si ficte, nihil aut parum concitamus auditorem. . . . Dicet aliquis: fictus est dolor tragoediorum, tamen saepe universum theatrum movet, cum sit genus orationis excogitatum, in quo falsum dicitur, atque imitatione similatum, de Antiopa, de Hecuba, de Polyxena, de Oreste, de figmentis. Illud quidem verum, sed major ars in hoc genere quaeritur et agendo commovendus est animus. Et histriones quidam aliquando in scena flere visi sunt; testis est Quintilianus. Praestat igitur vere dolere. Qui fieri potest? transformando animum in causam. Quomodo? apprehendendo rem alienam perinde atque nostram" (*De Oratore* [Paris, 1557], fol. 163). Shakespeare earlier associated Hecuba's madness through sorrow with "Tully's Orator" in *Tit.,* IV.i.18–21.

34. *Essays,* 2 : 428 [chap. 27].

35. *Ham.,* V.ii.216: I am following Q2; the Folio has "Since no man has ought of what he leaves." This sentence looks like a simplification of Hamlet's skeptic thought according to the losing-finding antithesis in I Tim. 6:7 (a verse read in the burial service). Alexander emends: "Since no man owes of aught he leaves." But Hamlet's problem does not lie in any possessions he has or may leave behind.

CHAPTER ELEVEN

1. P. 261. This use of the figure is related to the *vanitas* as well as *veritas* convention. See above, chap. 6.

2. Persius, *Satires,* IV.23–24 : "Not a soul is there—no one—who seeks to get down into his own self; all watch the wallet on the back that walks before" (*Juvenal and Persius,* ed. and trans. G. G. Ramsey, Loeb Classical Library [Cambridge, Mass., 1940], p. 360). For Shakespeare's evolving the figure from Persius, see Baldwin, *Shakspere's Small Latine,* 2 : 544–45. Wright's version is from Erasmus's *Adagia,* which in turn derives from Catullus, xxii, 21 : "Sed non videmus manticae quod in tergo est."

3. *Of Wisdom,* pp. 136–37 [Bk. I, chap. 38].

4. *Passions,* p. 253.

5. See Una Ellis-Fermor, "Discord in the Spheres," in *The Frontiers of Drama* (London, 1945), p. 64. For the internal conflicts of Troilus, see also Richard C. Harrier, "Troilus Divided," in *Studies in English Renaissance Drama* (New York, 1959), pp. 142–56. A sense of "fragmented experience and diffused identity" is felt in the play and demonstrated particularly in the sexual attitudes of Troilus and Cressida by Charles Lyon, "Cressida, Achilles, and the Finite Deed," *Etudes Anglaises* 20 (1967) : 233–42. The inner division and disunity in the characters and

in society are shown to lead to sterility by Arnold Stein, *"Troilus and Cressida: the Disjunctive Imagination," ELH* 36 (1969) : pp. 145–67.

6. William Elton, "Shakespeare's Ulysses and the Problem of Value," *ShakS* 2 (1966) : 95–111.

7. D. A. Traversi, *An Approach to Shakespeare* (2d ed.; Garden City, N.Y., 1956), p. 53.

8. *Essays,* 2 : 332 [chap. 12].

9. See Soellner, "Prudence and the Price of Helen."

10. *Of Wisdom,* p. 208 [Bk. I, chap. 57].

11. Cf. Norman Rabkin, *"Troilus and Cressida:* The Uses of the Double Plot," *ShakS* 1 (1965) : 265–82.

12. For the concept of invisibility as the highest kind of beauty, cf. Tommaso Buoni, *Problems of Beauty and All Human Affections,* trans. Samson Lennard (1606), p. 48: "Why doth the beauty of the mind make us like unto things heavenly, and that of the body many times like unto earthly? Perhaps because the chief good, which is the First Fair, is invisible like a fair mind."

13. Losing distinction was thought to be a danger inherent in *voluptas,* as Lambinus (Commentary to Horace, Ode I.18) explained: "Libido enim omnium rerum discrimen ac delectum tollit resque maxime inter se disjunctas ac diversas conjungit et exaequat" (Horatius Flaccus, *Satyrae* [Paris, 1568], p. 57).

14. In Montaigne's "Of the Force of the Imagination" (*Essays,* 1 : 9 ff. [chap. 10]), the discrepancy between desire and execution is illustrated by the sexual act to which Troilus also alludes (III.ii.79).

15. Joachimus Camerarius, *Quaestiones Tusculanae* (Paris, 1562), p. 641 : "Quae mox de animis dicit manifesta esse omnibus nisi qui sint plane in physicis plumbei. . . . Diversa integra corpora duo aut plura unum esse quiddam intelligi non potest."

16. *Of Wisdom,* p. 59 [Bk. I, chap. 14]. The contradictions of human logic were, of course, commonly attacked by the skeptics.

CHAPTER TWELVE

1. See T. W. Baldwin, *Shakspere's LOVE'S LABOR'S WON* (Carbondale, Ill., 1957).

2. The relevance of sonnet 94 to *All's Well* and *Measure for Measure* has, in passing, been noted for Angelo by L. C. Knights, "The Ambiguity of *Measure for Measure," Scrutiny* 10 (1942) : 222–33; for Bertram, by Geoffrey Bullough, *Narrative and Dramatic Sources of Shakespeare,* 2 (London, 1958) : 386. On mannerist ambiguities in *Measure for Measure,* see Wylie Sypher, "Shakespeare as Casuist: *Measure for Measure," SR* 58 (1950) : 262–80. The critical issues of the play are reviewed by Jonathan R. Price, *"Measure for Measure* and the Critics: Towards a New Approach," *SQ* 20 (1969) : 179–204. Price ends with a question: "How has Shakespeare made us care so passionately about the drama of *Measure for Measure?"* That, indeed, is the greatest of the play's puzzles.

3. See G. K. Hunter, Introduction, *All's Well That Ends Well,* New Arden Edition (London, 1959), and J. W. Lever, Introduction, *Measure for Measure,* New Arden Edition (London, 1965).

4. I am assuming that *Measure for Measure* followed rather than preceded *All's Well.* Since *Measure for Measure* improves some of the themes of *All's Well,* this sequence is probable. See Lever's Introduction.

5. Mary Lascelles, *Shakespeare's Measure for Measure* (London, 1953), p. 162.

6. G. B. Giraldi Cinthio, *Hecatommithi* (De. 8, Nov. 5) trans. in Bullough, *Sources*, 2 : 421.

7. On the legal and human aspects of the marriages in the play, see Ernest Schanzer, "The Marriage Contracts in *Measure for Measure*," *ShS* 13 (1960) : 81–89. A counterargument to Schanzer is made by S. Nagarajan, "*Measure for Measure* and Elizabethan Betrothals," *SQ* 14 (1963) : 115–19. Nagarajan claims that Claudio's and Juliet's is a *de futuro* promise, Angelo's and Mariana's a *de praesenti* betrothal. But clearly, Claudio and Juliet consider their pledge to each other binding in a way that Angelo and Mariana do not, and the ratification of the latter couple's marriage depends on its consummation.

8. Ovid, *Ars Amatoria*, 498–502: "'Preceptor of wanton love,' he [Apollo] said to me, 'come, lead my pupils to my shrine, where there is a saying renowned in fame all over the world, which bids each to be known by himself. Only he who knows himself will love with wisdom and perform all his tasks according to his powers'" (*The Art of Love and Other Poems*, ed. and trans. J. H. Mozley [London, 1929], p. 101).

9. A physiological explanation of the coitus is in Huarte, *Examen de Ingenios* (1594), p. 314. Huarte thought that often, but not always, the seed of the stronger female would win out. The transforming power, both psychic and physical, of sexual love is discussed by Nicolas Coeffeteau, *A Table of Human Passions*, trans. Edward Grimestone (1621), pp. 157 ff. Cf. James L. Calderwood, "Styles of Knowing in *All's Well*," *MLQ* 25 (1964) : 272–94.

10. I do not think that Shakespeare showed Isabella as "idealistic" in contrast to a society that is not, as is argued by Eileen Mackay, "*Measure for Measure*," *SQ* 14 (1963) : 109–13. There is certainly no suggestion that the order she is about to join is corrupt.

11. The term "glassy essence," according to J. V. Cunningham, "Essence and the Phoenix and Turtle," *ELH* 19 (1952) : 265, describes man's intellectual soul, which is in the image of God; hence "glassy" because it reflects Him. Mary Lascelles, "'Glassie Essence': *Measure for Measure*, II.ii.120," *RES* 2 (1951) : 140, notes the medieval tradition of the soul as a vessel of glass.

12. Orosco, *Emblemas Morales*, I, Emblem 96. The inscription on the banner: "Nulli non sua forma placet" is from Ovid, *Ars Amatoria*, I.614. For the line of the motto, "la mal carada, se tendra por dea," cf. *Metamorphoses*, XIII, 838 ff., Virgil's *Eclogues*, II, 25. L. S. Hall, "Isabella's Angry Ape," *SQ* 15 (1964) : 157–72, draws attention to the traditional association of apes and looking glasses, dating back to the thirteenth century, in which the mirror is associated with vanity.

13. For a comparison of the roles of Vincentio and Prospero, see Harold S. Wilson, "Action and Symbol in *Measure for Measure* and *The Tempest*," *SQ* 4 (1953) : 375–84. Wilson assumes, however, that Shakespeare adopted identical designs for both plays, which, I think, is not true. See below, chap. 18.

14. Innocent Gentillet, *A Discourse Upon the Means of Well Governing and Maintaining in Good Peace a Kingdom or Other Principalities [Contre-Machiavel]*, trans. Simon Patrick (1602), p. 349. Cf. Machiavelli, *The Prince*, chap. 19; Aristotle, *Politics*, 1315A.

15. Jean Bodin, *Six Books of a Commonweal*, trans. Richard Knolles (1606), p. 512 [Bk. IV, chap. 2]. Charron, *Of Wisdom*, p. 387 suggests a similar procedure.

16. Strong claims have been made for the resemblance of the duke to James and for the influence of *Basilicon Doron*. Schanzer, *Problem Plays*, pp. 123 ff., asserts that the play deliberately turns on themes that were of special interest to James. The parallels, for all they are worth, are emphasized by David L. Stevenson, *The Achievement of MEASURE FOR MEASURE* (Ithaca, N.Y., 1966), pp. 144 ff., and by Josephine W. Bennett, *MEASURE FOR MEASURE as Royal Entertainment* (New York, 1966), pp. 78–104.

17. *Six Books,* p. 505.

18. *Of Wisdom,* pp. 354 ff. [Bk. III, chap. 2].

19. Sir Arthur Quiller-Couch, *Measure for Measure,* New Shakespeare (London, 1922), p. xxxii.

20. On the duke's unsatisfactory self-image, cf. Hal Gelb, "Duke Vincentio and the Illusion of Comedy, or All's Not Well That Ends Well," *SQ* 22 (1971) : 25–34. Gelb also observes that the duke's theory of being "absolute for death" clashes with his lack of empirical understanding of the world. It is amusing to ponder the possibility that, if Shakespeare thought of the duke as analogous to King James, he had discerned in this monarch some of the weaknesses modern historians have seen in him.

21. Cf. J. W. Lever, Introduction, *Measure for Measure.*

22. Bodin, *Six Books,* p. 511.

Chapter Thirteen

1. S. T. Coleridge, *Table Talk* (1812), in *Coleridge's Writings on Shakespeare,* ed. Terence Hawkes (New York, 1959), p. 167.

2. For the conception of the heroes of the two plays, the dramatic pattern of Hercules was influential; see Eugene M. Waith, *The Herculean Hero in Marlowe, Chapman, and Dryden* (New York, 1962). For remarks on the connection between the grandiose character of Antony and the baroque style, see E. M. Roerecke, "Baroque Aspects of *Antony and Cleopatra*," in *Essays on Shakespeare,* ed. Gordon R. Smith (University Park, Pa., 1965), pp. 182–95.

3. See Carl J. Friedrich, *The Age of the Baroque* (1952; rpt. New York, 1962), pp. 43 ff. Also, Carl J. Friedrich and Charles Blitzer, *The Age of Power* (Ithaca, N.Y., 1957).

4. Hauser, *Social History,* 2 : 178. For general works on baroque and mannerism, see above, chap. 8, n. 2. The criteria of distinction between Renaissance and baroque were established by Wölfflin, *Kunstgeshichtliche Grundbegriffe;* but some of Wölfflin's criteria for the baroque are better applicable to mannerism. Stimulating ideas on the baroque style in Shakespeare's tragedies are in L. L. Schücking, *Shakespeare und der Tragödienstil seiner Zeit* (Bern, 1947), and in Schücking's earlier *The Baroque Character of the Elizabethan Tragic Hero,* Annual Shakespeare Lecture of the British Academy (London, 1938). Some of the features I have labeled "baroque" could also be called "anti-humanist" or "counter-Renaissance," but baroque appears to me a more useful term for literary analysis because it is free from the misleading implication that there was a conscious reaction to the Renaissance and because it applies better to artistic matters and is also becoming increasingly accepted for ideological phenomena.

5. P. 145.

6. Cf. L. C. Knights, *Drama and Society in the Age of Jonson* (1937; rpt. New York, 1968). For the general European crisis, see Hugh Trevor-Roper, *Religion, the Reformation, and Social Change* (London, 1967).

7. "Shakespeare and the Thought of His Age," p. 193.

8. Arthur Warren, *The Poor Man's Passions and Poverty's Patience* (1605), sig. F3ᵛ.

9. Cf. Max Weber, *The Protestant Ethics and the Spirit of Capitalism* (London, 1930) ; Richard H. Tawney, *Religion and the Rise of Capitalism* (London, 1929).

10. Cf. Felix Raab, *The English Face of Machiavelli,* p. 69. Shakespeare's inter-

est in Jesuit techniques is shown by the reference to equivocation in the porter scene in *Macbeth* and in other allusions to equivocation and prevarication in the play. See Frank L. Huntley, *"Macbeth* and the Background of Jesuitical Equivocation," *PMLA* 79 (1964), 390–400.

11. Estella, *A Method unto Mortification,* p. 208.

12. *Of Wisdom,* p. 69 [Bk. I, chap. 17].

13. Francis Bacon, *Novum Organum,* trans. Joseph Devey (New York, 1901), p. 26.

14. See various essays on baroque prose style by Morris W. Croll, collected in *Style, Rhetoric and Rhythm,* ed. Max Patrick et al. (Princeton, N.J., 1967). The connection of seventeenth-century prose styles with varying concepts of life is examined by Joan Webber, *The Eloquent I: Style and Self in Seventeenth Century Prose* (Madison, Wis., 1968).

15. See Francis R. Johnson, "Shakespearian Imagery and Senecan Imitation," *Joseph Quincy Adams Memorial Studies,* ed. James G. McManaway et al. (Washington, D.C., 1948), pp. 33–53.

16. Pp. 536–37.

17. *Marginalia,* pp. 108, 147.

18. Wright, *Passions* (1601), p. 195, sigs. A4ʳ, A5ʳ.

19. Ibid., pp. 136–48.

20. Wright, *The Passions of the Mind* (2d ed., 1604), p. 152.

21. Cf. the parallels between Shakespeare and Wright quoted above, chap. 11, and below, chap. 14. Wright dedicated the second edition of *The Passions of the Mind* to the earl of Southampton, Shakespeare's patron. Because John Florio, the Montaigne translator, was also one of the earl's protégés, the chances are good that Shakespeare knew two leading propagators of anti-humanistic ideas of self-knowledge in England.

22. *Passions* (1604), p. 261.

CHAPTER FOURTEEN

1. Bernard Spivack, *Shakespeare and the Allegory of Evil* (New York, 1958). For a judicious criticism of Spivack's claim that Iago is a descendant of the Vice, see Robert H. West, *Shakespeare and the Outer Mystery,* chapter 7: "Iago and the Mystery of Iniquity."

2. Terence Hawkes, *Shakespeare and the Reason* (London, 1964), p. 107.

3. See Paul A. Jorgensen, " 'Perplex'd in the Extreme': The Role of Thought in *Othello," SQ* 15 (1964) : 265–75.

4. Coleridge proposed that Iago was a kind of Satan incarnate, an idea taken up by modern theologically oriented critics, e.g., Paul Siegel, "The Damnation of Othello," *PMLA* 68 (1953) : 1068–78. A classic criticism of this approach is Sylvan Barnet, "Some Limitations of the Christian Approach to Shakespeare," *ELH* 22 (1955) : 81–92.

5. S. L. Bethell, "Shakespeare's Imagery : Diabolic Images in *Othello,"* ShakS 5 (1952) : 62–80. The watershed, Bethell points out, is in III.iii, the scene in which Iago imposes his way of thinking on Othello. The transfer of such images is shown in the comprehensive study of Robert Heilman, *Magic in the Web: Action and Language in "Othello"* (Lexington, Ky., 1956), pp. 38–39.

6. See Theodore Spencer, "The Elizabethan Malcontent," *Joseph Quincy Adams Memorial Studies* (Washington, D.C., 1948), pp. 523–35.

7. *Anatomy,* fol. 45.

8. L. B. Campbell, *Shakespeare's Tragic Heroes* (Cambridge, 1930), chap. 13.

9. *Anatomy,* fol. 44.

10. *Oth.,* I.i.66: as has often been pointed out, Iago suggests that he is a kind of anti-God by denying the "I am that I am" (Ex. 3 : 14).

11. Pp. 161–62.

12. La Primaudaye, *Second Part,* p. 361. For the balance figure, cf. Justus Lipsius, *Two Books of Constancy,* trans. John Stradling (1595), pp. 15–16: "For whereas the quietness and constancy of the mind resteth, as it were, in an even balance, these affections do hinder this upright poise and evenness" [Bk. I, chap. 7].

13. Daniel Stempel, "The Silence of Iago," *PMLA* 84 (1969) : 252–63.

14. *Sermons,* p. 301 [Dec. 3, Serm. 1]. Cf. Calvin, *Institutes,* III.viii.9. One would have difficulty in finding an advocate of such unrestrained voluntarism among the neo-Stoics of the Renaissance. Even Lipsius, who in *Of Constancy* extols the power of man's will to overcome passions and fortune, adds the proviso that the will of man must aim at virtue and be made to conform to the will of God. William Elton notes that Iago's insistence on complete freedom of will parallels the Pelagian heresy (see *King Lear and the Gods* [San Marino, Calif. 1966], p. 137). Interestingly, Bacon, an eminent student of the will, appears to have echoed Iago's imagery; among the 1625 additions of his essay "Of Nature in Men" is the following ending: "A man's nature runs either to herbs or to weeds; therefore let him seasonably water the one and destroy the other."

15. *Sermons,* p. 303 [Dec. 3, Serm. 3].

16. This cause-effect relationship is developed by Burton Russel, "The Monstrous Birth," *Dickinson Review* 2 (1969) : 5–13.

17. The self-dramatization of Othello is considered to be the tragic flaw of Othello as well as that of other tragic heroes by Matthew N. Proser, *The Heroic Image in Five Shakespearean Tragedies* (Princeton, N.J., 1965). But if Shakespeare's later tragic heroes did not dramatize themselves, we would not take such extraordinary interest in them.

18. *Passions* (1604), p. 230.

19. Ibid., p. 184.

20. Cf. Rolf Soellner, "The Madness of Hercules and the Elizabethans," *CL* 10 (1958) : 306–24.

21. To quote two extreme positions on Othello's subjection to Iago: G. Wilson Knight goes so far as to say that the Iago spirit never envelops Othello (*The Wheel of Fire* [London, 1930], p. 118); F. R. Leavis claims that Othello is an egotist, whose nature is not shaped, but merely stimulated by Iago (*The Common Pursuit* [London, 1952], pp. 136 ff.).

22. T. S. Eliot, *Shakespeare and the Stoicism of Seneca,* The Shakespeare Association (London, 1927).

Chapter Fifteen

1. *King Lear and the Gods.*

2. Sig. Aa4^r. The even more orthodox William Baldwin thought similarly; cf. *A Treatise of Moral Philosophy,* fol. 73.

3. A. C. Swinburne, *A Study of Shakespeare* (1876; rpt. London, 1902), p. 172.

4. L. L. Schücking, *Character Problems in Shakespeare's Plays* (London, 1922), pp. 176 ff.

5. Robert Heilman, *This Great Stage: Image and Structure in "King Lear"* (Seattle, Wash., 1963), p. 277.

6. Sypher, *Four Stages*, p. 184.

7. Rosalie Colie, *Paradoxa Epidemica: The Renaissance Tradition of the Paradox* (Princeton, N.J., 1966). Professor Colie works out some of the major paradoxical strands of *Lear* (pp. 461–81); my intention is to show Shakespeare's indebtedness to specific patterns associated with the self-knowledge of perspective.

8. That the paradox of the preference of bastardy in Landi's version is the source of Edgar's speech "Thou, Nature, art my goddess" (I.ii.1 ff.) has been argued by Warner G. Rice, "The *Paradossi* of Ortensio Landi," *Michigan Essays and Studies in English and Comparative Literature* 8 (1932): 59–74.

9. Charles Estienne, *The Defence of Contraries: Paradoxes against Common Opinions* [partial translation of *Paradoxes*], trans. Antony Munday (1593), sig. A4^{r-v}.

10. Paul A. Jorgensen, "Much Ado about Nothing," *SQ* 5 (1954), 287–95, rept. in *Redeeming Shakespeare's Words* (Berkeley, Calif., 1962), pp. 22 ff.

11. E. D. [Edward Dyer or Edward Daunce?], *The Praise of Nothing* (1585), sig. B^v.

12. Guillaume du Vair, *The Moral Philosophy of the Stoics*, trans. Thomas James (1598), pp. 96–97.

13. Commentaries on the materialistic and the ecclesiastical attitudes toward "nihil ex nihilo" are, for instance, in Persius, *Satyrae* (Cologne, 1522), fol. 32, and *Satyrae* (Basel, 1551), p. 497.

14. *The Anatomy of Sin* (1603), Part II: "The Genealogy of Virtue," sig. B8^v.

15. *Praise*, sig. H^v.

16. See Fitzroy Pyle, "*Twelfth Night, King Lear,* and *Arcadia*," *MLR* 43 (1948): 449–55.

17. Sir Philip Sidney, *The Countess of Pembroke's Arcadia*, ed. A. Feuillerat (Cambridge, 1962), p. 210.

18. Pp. 34, 39.

19. Lodowick Brysket, *A Discourse of Civil Life* (1606), pp. 189–90.

20. P. 73.

21. *Mortification*, p. 134.

22. See W. B. D. Henderson, "Montaigne's *Apologie of Raymond Sebond* and *King Lear*."

23. *Essays*, 2: 321 [chap. 12].

24. *Discourse*, p. 217.

25. Lipsius sought to defend the Stoics against the accusation that they believed in an "indissoluble chain and linking of causes which bindeth all persons and things," but he had to admit that some such phrase may have passed from some of them in the vehemence of their disputes and writings. Cf. *Of Constancy* (1595), p. 45.

26. John Lyly, *Campaspe*, I.ii.4–5, ed. Bond: Lyly's Diogenes, like Lear, discusses not only the question of necessity, but also illustrates it with the superfluity of clothes and speculates on the origin of thunder. *The Praise of Nothing*, p. 98, says paradoxically that Diogenes had "near equality in nothing" with Alexander. On the general esteem of Diogenes in the Renaissance, see John L. Lievsay, "Some Renaissance Views of Diogenes the Cynic," *Joseph Quincy Adams Memorial Studies* (Washington, D.C., 1948), pp. 447–53.

27. See E. M. M. Taylor, "Lear's Philosopher," *SQ* 6 (1955) : 364–65.

28. Thomas Nashe, *The Anatomy of Absurdity* (1589), in *Works,* ed. R. B. McKerrow (Oxford, 1904), 1 : 34.

29. *The Mirror of Madness or a Paradox Maintaining Madness to be Most Excellent,* trans. from the French by James Sanford (1576), sig. Aᵛ.

30. Robert Greene, *The Debate between Folly and Love* (1584), in *Works,* ed. Alexander Grosart (London, 1881), 4 : 217. Cf. Thomas Rogers, *Anatomy,* p. 66: "I know also that Lactantius . . . judged Crates and such like a madman for flinging his substance and treasure into the sea, with which he might have relieved many's want."

31. Nashe, *Works,* 1 : 34.

32. Sig. G1ᵛ.

33. Pp. 58–59.

34. Edith Hamilton, *The Greek Way to Western Civilization* (1930; repr. New York, 1963), p. 166.

CHAPTER SIXTEEN

1. *Lear's Self-Discovery.* See also Winifred M. T. Nowottny, "Lear's Questions," *ShS* 10 (1957) : 90–97.

2. Sir James Perrott, *The First Part of the Consideration of Human Condition* (Oxford, 1600). References to this work in this chapter are in the text.

3. Elyot, *Governor,* fol. 176 [Bk. II, chap. 3].

4. E. D., *The Praise of Nothing,* sigs. E1ᵛ–E2ʳ.

5. *Precepts of Cato* [*Disticha Catonis*], trans. Richard Burrant (1560), sigs. F8ᵛ, L6ʳ.

6. Pliny, *Historia Naturalis,* vii.1–6.

7. Montaigne, *Essays,* 2 : 184–85 [chap. 12]: "Truly, when I consider man all naked . . . and view his defects, his natural subjection, and manifold imperfections, I find we have had so much more reason to hide and cover our nakedness than any creature else. We may be excused for borrowing those which nature had therein favored more than us with their beauties to adorn us and under their spoils of wool, of hair, of feathers, and of silk, to shroud us. . . . Whereas in other creatures there is nothing but we love and pleaseth our senses, so that even from their excrements and ordure we draw not only dainties to eat but our richest ornaments and perfumes." Montaigne uses "sophisticated" in a different passage, but in similar context: "Wherewith [with nature] men have done as perfumers do with oil; they have adulterated her with so many argumentations and sophisticated her with so diverse far-fetched discourses that she is become variable and peculiar to every man" (*Essays,* 3 : 310 [chap. 12]).

8. Innocent III, "The View of Worldly Vanities" [part translation of *De Humanae Miseriae Conditione*], trans. George Gascoigne, in *The Drum of Doomsday* (1576), sig. Aʳ.

9. Sig. B5.

10. *Anatomy* (1576), fol. 75.

11. P. 86.

12. *Drum,* sig. S2ᵛ. In Latin form the statement is in a collection of Platonic commonplaces, *Divinae Platonis Gemmae* (Paris, 1556), p. 80: "Quandiu in eodem

sunt anima atque corpus, hoc quidem servire atque subesse natura jubet, hanc vero praeesse atque dominari."

13. *Immortality,* fol. 80.

14. *Discourse,* pp. 125–26.

15. *Nosce Teipsum,* p. 11.

16. A long list of house-garment images for the body is in a book intended for preachers by Robert Cawdrey, *A Treasury or Storehouse of Similes* (1600), pp. 35–36.

17. Erasmus, *The Praise of Folly,* trans. Sir Thomas Chaloner (1549), sig. K2r.

18. *Theatrum Mundi,* sigs. A4v–A5r. Similarly, Chelidonius, *Institution* (1571), p. 115.

19. *Nosce Teipsum,* p. 17. Similarly, Palingenius, *Zodiac,* p. 129.

20. *Treatise,* p. 115.

21. *Lear,* V.iii.17 : I have substituted the more likely reading "gods'" for Alexander's "God's."

22. Pp. 20–21.

23. *Zodiac,* p. 162 [*Sagittarius*]. The idea of ebbing and flowing, which is in Lear's speech, occurs briefly before in Palingenius.

24. *King Lear,* pp. 249 ff.

25. *Microcosmos* (1603), p. 71. "Mystery" and "gods' spies" evoke biblical echoes. Cf. Dan. 2:29, Psalm 139:2–3, and Richmond Noble, *Shakespeare's Knowledge of the Bible and Book of Common Prayer* (London, 1935), p. 231.

26. *Zodiac,* p. 161 [*Sagittarius*].

27. Ibid., p. 24 [*Gemini*] ; p. 191 [*Capricornus*].

CHAPTER SEVENTEEN

1. Cf. Max Lüthi, *Shakespeares Dramen,* p. 385 : "Shakespeares Tragik ist wesentlich eine Tragik des Selbstverlustes." For the roots of this conception in Shakespeare's comic art, see above, chaps. 4 and 5.

2. For the political implications of Macbeth's tragedy, see E. M. W. Tillyard, *Shakespeare's History Plays* (New York, 1944), and Henry N. Paul, *The Royal Play of Macbeth* (New York, 1950). The cosmic implications of the tragedy have often been studied, e.g. by Roy Walker, *The Time Is Free* (London, 1949) and L. C. Knights, *Some Shakespearean Themes* (London, 1959), pp. 120 ff. For previous criticism of the character of Macbeth, see Kenneth Muir, Introduction, *Macbeth,* New Arden Edition (London, 1951). For Macbeth's moral confusion and ensuing self-loss, see C. C. Clarke, "Darkened Reason in Macbeth," *Durham University Journal* 53 (1960) : 11–18.

3. See M. C. Bradbrook, "The Sources of *Macbeth,*" *ShS* 4 (1951) : 35–47. For verbal and thematic parallels between *Lucrece* and *Macbeth,* see Kenneth Muir, *Macbeth,* New Arden Edition, Appendix C.

4. *Macb.,* III.i.66–68: "Jewel" signified the peace of mind provided by a clear conscience in William Worship's *The Christian's Jewel* (1617). In the Dedication to Francis Bacon, Worship said: "This peace of God, so much magnified in Scripture, is better known by feeling than by discourse; and, being the fairest jewel under heaven, is peculiarly given to the elect" (sig. A3r). Worship's chapter 29 is entitled "That Peace of Conscience is an Inestimable Jewel."

5. *Macb.*, I.iii.14–25: The sailor's story told by the first witch appears to foreshadow ironically the fate of Macbeth and of Scotland. Her prediction that the sailor's bark cannot be lost seems to refer to Scotland. The "pilot," Macbeth, will be lost, but the "bark" will be saved.

6. Robert Bridges, *The Influence of the Audience on Shakespeare's Drama* (London, 1926), pp. 12 ff.

7. *Character Problems*, p. 75.

8. *Baroque Character*, pp. 21–22.

9. Richard G. Moulton, *Shakespeare as a Dramatic Artist* (3d ed., Oxford, 1893), p. 135.

10. Ibid., p. 148.

11. *Treatise*, pp. 189–96.

12. L. B. Campbell, *Shakespeare's Tragic Heroes* (Cambridge, 1930), chap. 15.

13. *Macb.*, III.i.51–53: Macbeth's lack of true courage may also be implied by "courage" being among the "king-becoming graces" listed by Malcolm (IV.iii.91). Macbeth lacks such graces.

14. *Of Wisdom*, p. 500 [Bk. III, chap. 19]. Similar arguments are in La Primaudaye, *Academy*, pp. 279–80, and Coeffeteau, *A Table*, p. 440.

15. *Of Wisdom*, pp. 99–100 [Bk. I, chap. 33].

16. See Eugene M. Waith, "Manhood and Valor in Two Shakespearian Tragedies," *ELH* 18 (1950) : 262–73. Cf. Robert Heilman, "Manliness in the Tragedies: Dramatic Variations," in *Shakespeare 1564–1964*, Brown University Bicentennial Publications (Providence, R.I., 1964).

17. *Marginalia*, p. 148. Cf. above, chaps. 2 and 13.

18. Lady Macbeth evidently aims at a total self-transformation through the evil power of magic. This was believed to be possible, as is evidenced by Woolton, *Immortality* (1576), fol. 75. The fact that the Lady models herself on Medea also suggests transformation through magic as her aim. Cf. Inga-Stina Ewbank, "The Fiend-like Queen: A Note on *Macbeth* and Seneca's *Medea*," *ShS* 19 (1966) : 82–94.

19. The fallacy of the argument that the Lady feigns the fainting spell is pointed out by Schücking, *Character Problems*, pp. 228 ff.

20. Muir, *Macbeth*, p. 59.

21. Una Ellis-Fermor, quoted by Muir, ibid.

22. P. 6.

23. *A Table*, pp. 453–54.

CHAPTER EIGHTEEN

1. Mark van Doren, *Shakespeare*, p. 281.

2. For the possible influence of *True Declaration of the State of the Colony of Virginia* (1610) on *The Tempest* and for other connections of the play with the Bermuda wreck, see Frank Kermode, Introduction, *The Tempest*, New Arden Edition (1954). Also, D. G. James, *The Dream of Prospero* (Oxford, 1967).

3. *Shakspere's Small Latine*, I, 742.

4. Cf. Clifford Leech, *Shakespeare's Tragedies* (Oxford, 1950), p. 144.

5. The sense of speed in the play is discussed by Ernest Gohn, "*The Tempest*: Theme and Structure," *ES* 45 (1964) : 116–25.

6. See Nelson S. Bushnell, "Natural Supernaturalism in *The Tempest*," *PMLA* 47 (1932) : 684–98, and C. J. Sisson, "The Magic of Prospero," *ShS* 11 (1958) : 70–71.

7. See Baldwin, *Shakspere's Small Latine*, pp. 443 ff.

8. Since Ariel is at times immanent in the elements, he can be thought of as representing Aristotle's *quinta essentia*, the "quintessence" or fifth element extracted from the other four and identified with the mind. For this concept, see Appendix C.

9. Sir Francis Bacon, *A Brief Discourse Touching the Happy Union of the Kingdoms of England and Scotland* (1603), sig. A3^{r-v}.

10. Carl Friedrich, *The Age of the Baroque*, p. 45.

11. Theodore Spencer, *Shakespeare and the Nature of Man* (Cambridge, 1943), p. 200.

12. Kermode, Introduction, p. lxxv. The structural significance of Prospero's anger is well recognized by F. D. Hoeniger, "Prospero's Storm and Miracle," *SQ* 7 (1956) : 33–38. For a similar climax of an outbreak of passion in a comedy, see above, chap. 4.

13. Herbert R. Courson, Jr., "Prospero and the Drama of the Soul," *ShakS* 4 (1968) : 316–33.

14. See W. C. Curry, *Shakespeare's Philosophical Patterns*, 2d ed. (Baton Rouge, La., 1959), pp. 196 ff.

15. *Shakspere*, p. 418.

16. *The Crown of Life*, 2d ed. (London, 1948), p. 242.

17. Northrop Frye, Introduction, *The Tempest*, Pelican Shakespeare (1959), p. 20.

18. Lytton Strachey, "Shakespeare's Final Period," in *Books and Characters* (New York, 1922), p. 64.

19. Clifford Leech, *Shakespeare's Tragedies* (Oxford, 1950), p. 155.

20. Sig. D7^v.

Appendix A

1. Fol. 14.

2. Cf. Ambrosius Calepinus, *Dictionarium* (Lyon, 1550) under *Ratio:* "Accipitur et pro ipsa rationatione, hoc est, pro discursu animi ad investigandum rerum."

3. Xystus Betuleius, Commentary, Cicero, *De Officiis*, fol. 15: "Nefandumque dictu est, animantium quodque in suo genere legem sibi a natura praescriptam, sine exactore non negligere; hominem vero ne conscientiae quidem stimulis ad officium excitari."

4. Hankins, *Shakespeare's Derived Imagery*, pp. 121–23, cites Palingenius (*Zodiac*, 1588), p. 114. Robertson, *Montaigne and Shakespeare*, pp. 62–63, cites Montaigne, whose version he preferred to Cicero because he thought there were no parallels between Shakespeare and Cicero, but many between Shakespeare and Montaigne. Yet the parallel to Cicero is much closer.

5. Theodore Spencer, *Shakespeare and the Nature of Man*, p. 94.

APPENDIX B

1. Harold Walley, *"The Rape of Lucrece* and Shakespearean Tragedy," *PMLA* 76 (1961) : 480–87. Cf. also Roy W. Battenhouse, *Shakespearean Tragedy* (Bloomington, Ind., 1969), pp. 3 ff. I do not accept Professor Battenhouse's contention that Shakespeare was expounding the Augustinian attitude toward Lucrece.

2. La Primaudaye, *Academy* (1589), p. 229. Further references in the text to La Primaudaye are to this edition.

3. *Anatomy,* p. 122. The theological tradition about Lucrece was conflicting. Augustine dispraised her, but Tertullian and Jerome praised her chastity. Cf. Don C. Allen, "Some Observations on *The Rape of Lucrece," ShS* 15 (1962) : 89–92.

4. E.g., 13, 117, 176, 225, 372, 448, 674.

5. Cf. Bullinger, *Sermons,* p. 589 [Dec. 4, Serm. 10] : "Since this will doth follow a blind guide, God wot, that is to say, corrupt affection, it is unknown to no man what foolish choice it maketh and whereunto it tendeth. And although the understanding be never so true and good, yet is the will like to a ship tossed to and fro with stormy tempests, that is, of affections."

6. Cf. Marvin T. Herrick, *Comic Theory in the Sixteenth Century,* p. 140.

7. *Epistles,* II.ii.216: "Tempus abire tibi est, ne potum largius aequo / Rideat et pulset lasciva decentius aetas." Cf. also *Epode,* XIII.4–5: "dumque virent genua / Et decet, obducta solvatur fronte senectus." Lambinus here notes that *senectus* stands for sadness and severity: "tristitiamque ac severitatem senilem significat." Horatius Flaccus, *Opera* (Paris, 1568), p. 308.

8. In his commentary on *De Officiis* (Paris, 1560), fol. 90, Betuleius lists the following factors of prudence: *ratio, intellectus, circumspectio, providentia, docilitas, cautio.* Cooper's *Thesaurus* (1578) gives "regard" and "respect" as translations of *ratio.* For Shakespeare's association of these terms with prudence and temperance, see *Caes.* III.i.224, *Ham.* III.i.66–69, *Macb.* II.iii.114–17.

9. *De Officiis,* I.102. The image is Plato's in the parable of the horse-drawn chariot of reason in *Phaedrus,* 253–54.

10. *Institution,* p. 55.

11. For the general convention, see C. L. Powell, "The Castle of the Body," *SP* 16 (1919) : 197–205. Powell cites analogues to Spenser's allegory from medieval and Renaissance works, that is, Robert Grosseteste's *Le Château d'Amour, Sawles Warde, Piers Plowman,* and Du Bartas's *Divine Weeks.* In his preface to *The Second Part of the French Academy* (1594), Thomas Bowes, the translator, explained self-knowledge as a knowledge of body and soul and illustrated it by a lengthy allegorical description in the tradition of the castle of the body.

12. On the centrality of the siege imagery, see Sam Hynes, "The Rape of Tarquin," *SQ* 10 (1959) : 451–53.

13. La Primaudaye distinguished theoretically between incontinence and intemperance, but, like most moralists, disregarded the distinction in practice.

14. James M. Tolbert, "A Source of Shakespeare's *Lucrece," NQ* 198 (1953) : 14–15. Cf. Seneca's *Phaedra,* 565: "Cur omnium fit culpa paucarum scelus?"

Appendix C

1. See Baldwin, *Compositional Genetics*, pp. 297 ff.

2. Similarly, Cicero, *De Natura Deorum*, II.iv.15, 90, 98. Cf. Plato, *Timaeus*, 47, 49.

3. *French Academy*, p. 9.

4. Guillaume du Vair, *The Holy Love of Heavenly Wisdom* [*De la sainte Philosophie*] (1594), p. 82.

5. Hiram Haydn, *The Counter-Renaissance*, p. 655.

6. *Treatise*, p. 41. Bright's chapter 13 explains "How the soul by one simple faculty performeth so many and diverse actions."

7. *Anatomy*, fols. 6–7.

8. *Discourse*, p. 10.

9. Aristotle, *De Anima*, 432b.

10. *Commonplaces*, II, 358.

11. *Serm. Tim.*, 7632. Cf. *OED*: "Apprehension."

12. Cf. Cicero, *Tusc. Disp.*, I.22. This explanation was sometimes used by Renaissance moralists to illustrate the essential difference of body and mind.

13. *Nosce Teipsum*, p. 21.

14. *Divine Weeks*, pp. 285–86 [First Day of the Second Week].

15. Walter Pater's translation of Pico della Mirandola's *Oratio Dignitatis Homini*, in *The Renaissance* (rpt. London, 1924), p. 24.

Index

References to characters in Shakespeare's plays are given only for passages in the text outside of the chapters on the specific plays in which the characters appear. Sixteenth- and seventeenth-century works are indexed by title as well as by author, others by author only. Translators are listed merely when a special signficance is attached to them.

Absolutism, political, 35, 59, 118, 202, 205, 233, 235; and skepticism related, 200, 229; and baroque style, 242-43

Adagia. *See* Erasmus, Desiderius

Advancement of Learning. See Bacon, Sir Francis

Affection. *See* Passions

Alciatus, Andreas, *Emblemata,* 406 n.1

Alexander the Great, 120, 121-22, 150, 188, 417 n.13, 429 n.26

Alienation. *See* Self-alienation

Allegory, 247, 363-65

Allen, Don C., *Doubt's Boundless Sea,* 407 n.21

All's Well That Ends Well, xviii, xix, 30, 63-64, 76, 77, 131, 134, 137, 143, 144, 148, 215-17, 221, 222, 230, 403, 418 n.1, 424 n.4

Altick, Richard D., "Symphonic Imagery in *Richard II,*" 415 n.2

Anagnorisis. See Self-discovery

Anatomy of Absurdity. See Nashe, Thomas

Anatomy of Sin. See Lodge, Thomas

Angelo (*Measure for Measure*), 76, 95, 137, 140, 147, 148-49, 240

Anger: as short madness, 68, 293; and the mirror image, 225; Lear's, as choler, 309; Lear's, as stimulus to self-search, 309

Anglicanism. See Church of England

Antihumanism. *See* Christian humanism: trends counter to

Antipholus of Syracuse (*Comedy of Errors*), 219-20, 338

Antonio (*Merchant of Venice*), 36

Antony (*Antony and Cleopatra*), 249, 257, 390

Antony (*Julius Caesar*), 336

Antony and Cleopatra, xix, 77, 241, 336, 418 n.1, 426 n.2

Aphthonius, *Progymnasmata,* 118-19

Apology For Poetry. See Sidney, Sir Philip

Aquinas, Saint Thomas, 144

Arcadia. See Sidney, Sir Philip

Aristocracy: conduct books for, 19-21, 30-31; and the honor code, 20, 82-83; self-expansion of, 20, 30-31, 243-44, 256-57

Aristotle, 88, 318, 342, 403, 404, 433 n.8; *De Anima,* 318, 402-3; *De Physiogonomica,* 317; *Magna Moralia,* 181; *Poetics,* xii-xiii, 105, 110-11, 175

Art of War. See Machiavelli, Niccolo

Asceticism: fails in *Love's Labor's Lost,* 87-88, 92, 95; fails in *Measure for Measure,* 218-20, 224, 226-27, 232-33. *See also* Puritanism; Stoicism

Ascham, Roger, *Schoolmaster,* 30

As You Like It, xiv, 137

Atheism: of Renaissance doctors, 15; and skepticism, 142, 409 n.3; and new Stoicism, 269

Aubrey, John, 372

Augustine, Saint, 16, 434 n.1; *City of God,* 390

Bacon, Sir Francis, 36-40, 43, 242, 248-49, 250, 255, 409 n.20, 410 n.2, 431 n.4;

Bacon, Sir Francis (*continued*)
    Advancement of Learning, 36-38;
    *Brief Discourse . . . of England and
    Scotland*, 373-74; *De Augmentis*, 409
    n.22; *Essays*, 39, 428 n.14; *Novum
    Organum*, 39, 249
Baker, Herschel, *Dignity of Man*, 405
    n.7
Baldwin, T. W., xvi, 407 n.9; *Compo-
    sitional Genetics of THE COMEDY
    OF ERRORS*, 64, 405 n.6, 410 n.11,
    411 n.26, 412 n.1, 416 n.17; *Shakspere's
    Five Act Structure*, 405 n.6, 413 n.7;
    *Shakspere's Small Latine and Lesse
    Greek*, 187, 363, 405 n.6, 414 n.8, 423 n.2
Baldwin, William, *Treatise of Moral
    Philosophy*, 24, 408 n.36, 428 n.2
Baldwin, William, et. al., *Mirror for
    Magistrates*, 22, 99, 416 n.25
Baptismal Service. *See* Church of Eng-
    land: Book of Common Prayer
Barckley, Sir Richard, *Discourse of the
    Felicity of Man*, 50, 51-52, 252-53, 402,
    414 n.17
Barnet, Sylvan, "Some Limitations of
    the Christian Approach to Shake-
    speare," 427 n.4
Barons' War. See Drayton, Michael
Baroque: dramatic unity in, 239-43,
    259, 357, 370-71; definitions of, 242-
    43, 373, 418 n.2, 426 n.4, 427 n.14;
    heightened self of heroes in, 240-41,
    243-44, 256-58, 273, 328, 366, 379,
    382-83, 426 n.2; fascination with
    power in, 242, 253-54, 372-74; will and
    passion intensified in, 242-43, 258, 277,
    281, 309, 322, 339, 346; parallels to, in
    art, 242-43, 251, 287-88, 378; anti-
    thetical character construction in, 336-
    37, 342
Bartholomaeus (Anglicus), *De Proprie-
    tatibus Rerum*, 56. *See also* Bateman,
    Stephen
Bateman, Stephen, *Batman Upon Bar-
    tholomew* [translation and adaptation
    of Bartholomaeus (Anglicus), *De
    Proprietatibus Rerum*], 45.
Battenhouse, Roy W., "Hamlet's Apos-
    trophe on Man," 422 n.28; *Shake-
    spearean Tragedy*, 434 n.1
Beaumont, Francis, 136
Beccuti, Francesco (Il Copetta), *Capi-
    tolo ne quale si lodano le Noncevelle*,
    289-90
Bennet, Josephine W., *MEASURE
    FOR MEASURE as Royal Enter-
    tainment*, 425 n.16

Berman, Ronald S., "Shakespeare's
    Alexander: Henry V," 417 n.13
Bernard of Clairvaux, Saint, 349; *De
    Consideratione*, 16
Bernini, Giovanni Lorenzo, 242
Beroaldus, Philipus [humanist], Com-
    mentary on Cicero's *Quaestiones Tus-
    culanae*, 56, 88, 421 n.10
Bertram (*All's Well*), xviii, 76, 134,
    137, 144, 146-47, 148, 215, 216, 222,
    424 n.2
Bethell, S. L., "Shakespeare's Imagery:
    Diabolic Images in *Othello*," 427 n.5
Betuleius, Xystus [humanist], Commen-
    tary on Cicero, *De Officiis*, 388-89,
    434 n.8
Bible: texts used, ix; Colossians, 142;
    Corinthians, 92, 143, 291, 320, 406 n.2;
    Daniel, 431 n.25; Ecclesiastes, 314;
    Ephesians, 92; Genesis, 72, 402, 420
    n.20; Hebrews, 314; Job, 49, 103,
    351; John, 64, 401; Luke, 64; Mark,
    333; Matthew, 64, 149, 359; Psalms,
    6, 72, 399, 402, 431 n.25; Romans,
    420 n.5; Timothy, 270, 423 n.35; Tobit
    (Apocrypha), 295; Wisdom (Apoc-
    rypha), 321
Boaistuau, Pierre, 408 n.33; *Theatrum
    Mundi*, 23-24, 321, 416 n.19. *See also*
    Chelidonius, Tigurinus
Boas, F. S., *Shakespeare and His Pre-
    decessors*, 418 n.1
Bodin, Jean, *Six Books of a Common-
    weal*, 228-29, 235
Body and soul; imagery of, 5-7, 66-67,
    102-3, 107-9, 319-20, 323; knowledge
    of self as knowledge of, 6-7, 14, 54-58,
    123, 387-89, 407 n.19, 410 n.21, 434
    n.11; in Richard II's self-examination,
    100, 102-3, 107-9; Lear's probing of,
    311-24. *See also* Man; Soul
Bogard, Travis, "Shakespeare's Second
    Richard," 416 n.31
Bousquet, Jacques, *Mannerism*, 138, 418
    n.2
Bowers, Fredson T., *Elizabethan Re-
    venge Tragedy*, 423 n.31
Bowers, R. H., "An Elizabethan Manu-
    script 'Continuation' of Sir John
    Davies' *Nosce Teipsum*," 408 n.2
Bowes, Thomas, Preface to trans. of
    French Academy (La Primaudaye),
    416 n.25, 434 n.11
Bradley, A. C., *Shakespearean Tragedy*,
    177, 183, 266, 335
Bredvold, Louis, "Sources Used by
    Davies in *Nosce Teipsum*," 407 n.9

Bridges, Robert, *Influence of the Audience on Shakespeare's Drama,* 336
Brief Discourse . . . of England and Scotland. See Bacon, Sir Francis
Bright, Timothy, *Treatise of Melancholy,* 322, 340, 401, 407 n.19
Brooks, Harold, "Themes and Structure in *The Comedy of Errors,*" 412 n.1
Brunet, J., *Manuel du Libraire,* 408 n.33
Bruto, Giovanni, *Education of a Young Gentlewoman,* 20
Brutus, 133, 134, 137, 139, 141, 145, 146, 147, 148, 220, 328, 336
Brysket, Lodowyck, *Discourse of Civil Life,* 293, 297, 318
Buckley, George T., "Indebtedness of Sir John Davies' *Nosce Teipsum* to Philip Mornay's *Trunesse of the Christian Religion,*" 406 n.9
Bullinger, Heinrich, *Decades,* 10, 270, 271-72, 407 n.18; *Sermons,* 421 n.19, 434 n.5
Buoni, Tommaso, *Problems of Beauty and All Human Affections,* 208, 243-44, 256, 319
Burckhardt, Jakob, xvi
Burge, Barbara, "*Hamlet:* The Search for Identity," 421 n.1
Bush, Douglas, 404
Byron, George Gordon Lord, 233

Calderón de la Barca, Pedro, *La vida es sueño,* 378
Calepinus, Ambrosius [medieval scholar], *Dictionarium,* 433 n.2
Calvin, John, 16-20, 27, 28, 43, 126, 247-48, 250, 410 n.2; *Institutes,* 18, 382, 407 n.18; *Sermons,* 403
Calvinism: and self-knowledge, 17-19, 27-28; and function of will, 245, 247-48; paradoxes of, 250-51; *Tempest* and, 382. See also Puritanism
Camerarius, Joachimus [humanist], Commentary on Cicero's *Quaestiones Tusculanae,* 212
Campaspe. See Lyly, John
Campbell, Lily B., *Shakespeare's "Histories",* 415 n.1; *Shakespeare's Tragic Heroes,* 183, 262, 341, 342
Capitolo ne quale si lodano le Noncevelle. See Beccuti, Francesco
Cardano, Girolamo, *Cardanus's Comfort,* 187
Cardinal virtues. See Fortitude; Justice; Prudence; Self-knowledge, as knowledge of cardinal virtues; Temperance

Castiglione, Baldassare, *Courtier,* 30-31, 46, 52, 87
Catechism. See Church of England: Cathechism; Nowell, Alexander
Catharsis: alleged, at end of tragedies, 77; Hamlet's use of theory of, on Claudius, 189, 423 n.32; as "tragic pleasure" produced by *Lear,* 303-4
Cato. See *Disticha Catonis*
Catullus, 423 n.2
Cawdrey, Robert, *Treasury or Storehouse of Similes,* 431 n.16
Chain of Being, 51-52, 411 n.26, 412 n.45, 429 n.25. See also Degree
Chambers, Robert, "A Christian Reformation of *Nosce Teipsum*" [Elizabethan manuscript], 27-28
Chapman, George, 244, 250, 257
Characters, dramatic: significance for patterns of self-knowledge, xix-xx; in mannerist plays, 146-48; indirection and irony in presentation of, 216-18, 337, 341-42; in baroque plays, 239-42, 255-58
Charney, Maurice, *Style in HAMLET,* xix, 422 n.14
Charron, Pierre, *Of Wisdom,* 177-78, 178-79, 189, 199, 207, 212, 229, 248, 342-43, 407 n.19, 416 n.25, 425 n.15
Chelidonius, Tigurinus (Pierre Boaistuau?), *Institution and First Beginning of a Christian Prince,* 21-22, 104, 394
Choice of Emblems. See Whitney, Geoffrey
Christ, 114, 381
Christian Directory. See Parsons, Robert
Christian dogma, 4, 142, 231, 284-85, 303, 314-15, 381, 390. See also Aquinas, Saint Thomas; Augustine, Saint; Bernard of Clairvaux, Saint; Bullinger, Heinrich; Calvin, John; Estella, Diego de; Innocent III, Pope; Martyr, Peter; Tertullian
Christian humanism: and the image of man, 3-25, 55, 58-61, 127, 307-8, 353-54, 382-83; grammar and rhetoric in, 6, 53; trends counter to, 26-40, 59, 134-35, 139-49, 193, 243-57, 288-89, 345, 408 n.1, 426 n.4; reflected in Hooker and Shakespeare, 59-61; and the paradox of salvation, 64-65 (*see also* Salvation, paradox of); war criticized in, 121, 342; practical, in *Measure for Measure,* 233; and general humanism in *Lear,* 285-86; Macbeth's residual,

Christian humanism (*continued*)
337-38, 346-47; Prospero's reaffirmed,
382-83. *See also* Shakespeare, William: and Christian humanism; Shakespeare, William: between Christian humanism and counter-humanism
Christianity. *See* Bible; Calvinism; Christian dogma; Christian humanism; Church of England; Fall of Man; Fideism; God; Grace, divine; Roman Catholicism; Shakespeare, William: and religion
Christian's Jewel. See Worship, William
Chronicles. See Holinshed, Raphael
Chronique de la Traïson et Mort de Richard Deux Roy Angleterre, 415 n.4
Church of England, 17, 59-60, 245-46; Book of Common Prayer, 80, 84, 402; Catechism, 6, 80, 84, 88; *Certain Sermons* [Elizabethan Homilies], 17, 18, 59
Cicero, 3, 8, 9-13, 83, 170, 250; *Academica*, 141-42, 169; *De Amicitia*, 9, 66, 421 n.19; *De Divinatione*, 143; *De Legibus*, 390; *De Officiis*, 9, 10, 12, 52, 85, 181, 185, 186, 205, 206, 387-89, 392, 393, 394, 433 n.3, 433 n.4, 434 n.8; *De Oratore*, 190, 419 n.9, 423 n.33; *De Senectute*, 9; *Paradoxa Stoicorum*, 9, 395; *Somnium Scipionis* [*De Republica* VI], 9, 10, 411 n.26; *Tusculan Disputations*, 9, 10, 28, 56, 73, 88, 157, 158, 166, 187, 212, 270, 399, 411 n.21, 413 nn.5 and 11, 435 n.12
Cinthio, G. B. Giraldi, *Hecatommithi*, 217
Civil Conversation. See Guazzo, Stefano
Clark, Kenneth, "Alberti and Shakespeare," 422 n.28
Clarke, C. C., "Darkened Reason in Macbeth," 431 n.2
Climax, dramatic (*summa epitasis*): at height of passion, 68, 78, 276-77, 374-77, 433 n.12; in Richard II's emotional *anagnorisis*, 105; in Lear's dream-like *anagnorisis*, 322; in Macbeth's self-loss, 350; in Prospero's visionary *anagnorisis*, 374-79
Coeffeteau, Nicolas, *Table of Human Passions*, 351-52, 425 n.9, 432 n.14
Coghill, Nevill, *Shakespeare's Professional Skills*, 46
Coleridge, S. T., 108, 176, 340, 427 n.4; *Table Talk*, 240
Colie, Rosemary, *Paradoxa Epidemica*, 288
Colloquia. See Erasmus, Desiderius

Comedy of Errors, xviii, 22, 29, 52, 53, 62-77, 154, 193, 220, 233, 357, 358, 407 n.12
Commonplaces. See Martyr, Peter
Conger, G. P., *Theories of Macrocosms and Microcosms in the History of Philosophy*, 407 n.20, 410 n.2
Conrad, Joseph, *Heart of Darkness*, 217-18
Conscience: Macbeth's and Tarquin's, contrasted, 332-34, Macbeth's and neurotic states, 339-41. *See also* Self-knowledge: as voice of conscience; Repentance
Consideration (*consideratio*): literature of, 16-17, 23, 407 n.22; of Richard II, 103-4; of Henry V, 119-20, 417 n.12; Hamlet's, 187-88; Lear's 307-15. *See also* Contempt of the world
Consideration of Human Condition. See Perrott, Sir James
Contempt of the world (*contemptus mundi*): medieval and Renaissance, 5, 15-18, 49, 51, 103-11, 300, 308; baroque, 246-47, 314-15, 378. *See also* Consideration
Contre-Machiavel. See Gentillet, Innocent
Cooper, Thomas, *Thesaurus*, 45, 52-53, 180, 412 n.38, 420 n.6, 434 n.8
Cordelia, 36, 252, 256, 363
Coriolanus, 256, 257
Coriolanus, xix, 241, 242
Cornwallis, Sir William, *Essays*, 250, 419 n.16
Cosmos. *See* World
Counter-humanism. *See* Christian humanism: trends counter to
Counter-Renaissance. *See* Christian humanism: trends counter to
Courage. *See* Fortitude
Courtesy books. *See* Aristocracy: conduct books for
Coverdale, Miles, 4
Courtier. See Castiglione, Baldassare
Courtier's Academy. See Romei, Annibale
Craig, Hardin, 409 n.10
Crates [Cynic philosopher], 300, 301, 430 n.30
Cressida, 139
Croll, Morris W., *Style, Rhetoric and Rhythm*, 427 n.14
Culmannus, Leonhardus, *Sententiae Pueriles*, 3, 6, 378
Cunningham, J. V., "Essence and the Phoenix and the Turtle," 425 n.11
Cymbeline, 240, 296, 356

Cynicism: Edgar's affinity to, 300-302. *See also* Crates; Diogenes

D., E. [Edward Dyer or Edward Daunce?], *Praise of Nothing*, 290, 291, 312, 429 n.26
Davenant, Sir William, 366
Davies, John (of Hereford), *Microcosmos*, 19, 26, 39, 51, 324; *Mirum in Modum*, 50-51
Davies, Sir John, *Nosce Teipsum*, 8, 27, 54, 55, 57, 75, 106, 319, 322, 404, 406 n.9, 407 n.19
Death: preparation for, 16-17, 94, 96, 106, 303, 379, 381; and the prince, 103-4, 187-88
De Augmentis. See Bacon, Sir Francis
Debate Between Folly and Love. See Greene, Robert
Decades. See Bullinger, Heinrich
De casibus tragedy, 22, 99, 103-4
De Conscribendis Epistolis. See Erasmus, Desiderius
De Constantia. See Lipsius, Justus
De Contemptu Mundi. See Estella, Diego de.
De Copia Verborum ac Rerum. See Erasmus, Desiderius
Decorum, dramatic, 11-12, 127, 393
Decorum, moral: doctrine of, 11-12; and general man, 12, 186, 387-89; and individual man, 12, 30, 185; as theme in *Lucrece,* 12-13, 392-95; Richard II's lack of, 110; Hamlet's probing of, 185-86; Iago's perversion of, 265
Dee, John, Preface to Euclid, *Elements of Geometry,* 47
Defence of Contraries. See Munday, Antony.
Degree: in Renaissance order, 53-54, 59, 61, 71-73; ironies in Ulysses' speech on, 61, 146, 202-3; in absolutist order, 233. *See also* Chain of Being; Order
De Humanae Miseriae Conditione. See Innocent III, Pope
Democritus, 290, 295
De Natura Legis Naturae. See Fortescue, Sir John
Dent, Robert, 408 n.34
De Ratione Studii. See Erasmus, Desiderius
Desdemona, 36, 240, 241, 256
Deutschbein, Max, "Individuum und Kosmus in Shakespeares Werken," 418 n.2; "What Is This Quintessence of Dust," 189
Dictionarium. See Calepinus, Ambrosius

Dilthey, Wilhelm, "Weltanschauung und Analyse des Menschen seit Renaissance und Reformation," xvi-xvii
Diogenes, 300, 301, 429 n.26
Discourse of Civil Life. See Brysket, Lodowyck
Discourse of the Felicity of Man. See Barckley, Sir Richard
Disticha Catonis [medieval-Renaissance school book], 3, 6, 106, 312
Divinae Platonis Gemmae [collection of commonplaces from Plato], 430 n.12
Divine Weeks. See Du Bartas, Guillaume de Saluste
Donne, John, 51
Dostoevski, Feodor Mikhailovich, 127
Douce, Francis, *Illustrations of Shakespeare,* 416 n.18
Dowden, Edward, *Shakspere: A Critical Study of His Mind and Art,* 79, 165, 380
Drant, Thomas [translator of Horace], 9
Draper, J. W., "Character of Richard II," 415 n.9
Drayton, Michael, *Baron's Wars,* 420 n.4
Drum of Doomsday. See Gascoigne, George.
Dryden, John, 366
Du Bartas, Guillaume de Saluste, *Divine Weeks,* 43, 44, 45, 46, 48, 52, 404, 434 n.11
Dürer, Albrecht, 47, 52; *Knight, Death, and Devil,* 79, 80, 82, 85, 87, 94
Du Vair, Guillaume, *Holy Love of Heavenly Wisdom,* 400; *Philosophie Morale des Stoiques,* 250, 290
Dyer, Edward. See D., E.

Ecstasy: in *Comedy of Errors,* 67-68; Hamlet's definition of, 180-81; and baroque, 242, 339, 375; Othello's breakdown as, 276-77; in Lear's self-discovery, 322; in Macbeth's reaction to evil, 338-40; Prospero's intellectual, 362; Prospero's visionary, 374-75
Edgar, xviii, 245, 252, 255, 256, 361, 372
Edmund, 36, 39, 244, 253, 255, 346, 394
Egotism. *See* Self-love
El Greco (Domenicos Theotocopoulos), 123, 188
Eliot, T. S., "Hamlet and His Problems," 175; *Shakespeare and the Stoicism of Seneca,* 278
Elizabeth I, Queen, 59, 118, 416 n.23
Elizabethan Homilies. *See* Church of England: *Certain Sermons*

Elizabethan psychology. See Psychology, Elizabethan

Elizabethan world picture. *See* World picture, Elizabethan

Ellis-Fermor, Una, 349; *Frontiers of Drama*, 123

Elton, William, *King Lear and the Gods*, 284, 285, 286, 323, 428 n.14; "Shakespeare and the Thought of His Age," 51, 244; "Shakespeare's Ulysses and the Problem of Value," 202-3

Elyot, Sir Thomas, *Of the Knowledge Which Maketh a Wise Man*, 46-47; *Governor*, 20, 100, 123, 312

Emblemata. See Alciatus, Andreas; Schoonhovius, Florentius

Emblems. See *Nosce teipsum:* emblems

Emotions. *See* Ecstasy; Passion; Psychology, Elizabethan; *and names of individual emotions*

Empiricus, Sextus, *Hypotyposes*, 141

Enchiridion Militis Christiani. See Erasmus, Desiderius

Encomium Moriae. See Erasmus, Desiderius

Envy. *See* Jealousy

Epicureanism: of Cassius, 163, 168

Epicurus, 291

Epilepsy. *See* Ecstasy: Othello's breakdown as

Erasmus, Desiderius, 27, 144; *Adagia*, 3, 423 n.2; *Colloquia*, 6, 363; *De Conscribendis Epistolis*, 6; *De Copia Verborum ac Rerum*, 6; *De Ratione Studii*, 5; *Enchiridion Militis Christiani*, 3-4, 31, 79-94 passim, 144, 264-65, 382; *Encomium Moriae (In Praise of Folly)*, 86, 321; *Institutio Principis Christiani*, 21, 114, 115, 120, 121, 125; *Parabolae Sive Similia*, 6

Essays. See Bacon, Sir Francis; Cornwallis, Sir William; Montaigne, Michel de

Estella, Diego de, *De Contemptu Mundi*, 16, 106, 246-47, 295, 422 n.18

Estienne, Charles, *Paradoxes* (trans. of Ortensio Landi's *Paradossi*), 289. *See also* Munday, Antony

Evans, H. A., Introduction to *Henry V*, 126

Examination of Men's Wits. See Huarte, Juan de San Juan

Faith. *See* Fideism

Fall of Man: disorder since, 51-52; difficulty of self-knowledge since, 55

Famous Victories of Henry V [anon. Elizabethan play], 125

Faulconbridge (*King John*), 113-14

Fear: and courage in *Macbeth*, 336, 341-48, 350, 353-55; "honest" vs. cowardly, 343-45, 353-55, 391-92

Fideism, 193, 218, 279, 298, 382; and skepticism, 28, 142, 169; of Cassius, 168; in problem plays, 142-46, 148-49, 360; Troilus's pseudo-, 205-6; in later plays, 247, 322; in *Tempest*, 382

Fifty Godly Sermons. See Bullinger, Heinrich

First Book of Christian Exercise. See Parsons, Robert

Fleming, Abraham, *Bright .Burning Beacon*, 49

Fletcher, John, 136, 366

Florentine History. See Machiavelli, Niccolo

Florio, John, 419 n.16, 427 n.21

Foakes, R. A., Introduction to *Comedy of Errors*, 412 n.1

Folly: of Lear, 282-83, 294-95. *See also* Wisdom: of folly

Fortitude: of Henry V, 115, 121; emphasized by Jacobeans, 245, 252; of later heroines, 272. *See also* Patience

Frame, Donald, *Montaigne's Discovery of Man*, 409 n.3

French Academy. See La Primaudaye, Pierre de

Froissart, Jean, 415 n.4

Frye, Northrop, Introduction to *The Tempest*, Pelican Shakespeare, 381

Galen, 114

Gascoigne, George, *Drum of Doomsday*, 315, 317. *See also* Innocent III, Pope [Part I translates Innocent's *De Humanae Miseriae Conditione*]

Gelb, Hal, "Duke Vincentio and the Illusion of Comedy," 426 n.20

Gentillet, Innocent, *Contre-Machiavel*, 31, 228

Gertrude (*Hamlet*), 240

Gessner, Conrad [humanist], *Pandectarium*, 407 n.18

Gloucester (*Lear*), 252, 253

God: knowledge of self and, 8, 10, 16, 17, 18, 37, 144-45, 285, 290, 325

Goddard, Harold, *Meaning of Shakespeare*, 125

Goethe, Johann Wolfgang von, 177, 379; *Faust*, 261

Gohn, Ernest, *"The Tempest:* Theme and Structure," 432 n.5
Goidtsenhoven, Laurens van Haecht [emblematist], *Parvus Mundus,* 410 n.16
Golding, Arthur, Epistle to Ovid's *Metamorphoses,* 7, 45, 73
Gombrich, Ernst, "Zum Werke Giulio Romanos," 134
Goneril, xiv
Gonzalo (*Tempest*), 252
Governor. See Elyot, Sir Thomas
Grace, divine: need for, 19, 28, 57, 87, 369-70, 382, 414 n.17
Granville-Barker, Harley, *Prefaces to Shakespeare,* 170
Great Chain of Being. *See* Chain of Being
Greene, Robert, *Debate Between Folly and Love,* 301
Grief: as theme of *Richard II,* 98-99, 101-12; as stimulus for Richard II's self-search, 110. *See also* Melancholy
Grimald, Nicholas, 12
Grosseteste, Robert, *Le Château d'Amour,* 434 n.11
Guazzo, Stefano, *Civil Conversation,* 74
Guiccardini, Lodovico, *Hours of Recreation,* 81

Hal, Prince, 111, 113, 120, 122, 133, 147
Hall, Edward, *Union of the Noble and Illustrious Families of York and Lancaster,* 114-15
Hall, L. S., "Isabella's Angry Ape," 425 n.12
Hamartia. See Tragic flaw
Hamilton, Edith, *Greek Way to Western Civilization,* 303
Hamlet, xiv, 46, 48, 76, 126, 134-37, 139, 141, 142, 144, 145, 146, 147, 148, 164, 171, 196, 208, 211, 214, 220, 273, 281, 328, 360, 375, 387-89, 399-404, 410 n.11, 419 n.9
Hamlet, xvii, xix, 50, 68, 76, 131, 133, 134-37, 138, 140, 141, 144, 150, 170, 171, 173-94, 195, 196, 206, 213, 214, 233, 239, 257, 327, 357, 360, 387-89, 399-404, 407 n.12, 418 nn.1 and 2, 434 n.8
Hankins, John E., *Shakespeare's Derived Imagery,* 406 n.9, 433 n.4
Hardison, O. B., "Three Types of Renaissance Catharsis," 423 n.32
Harrier, Richard C., "Troilus Divided," 423 n.5
Harrison, G. B., *Shakespeare's Tragedies,* 175

Hartsock, Mildred, "Complexity of *Julius Caesar,*" 420 n.2
Harvey, Gabriel, *Marginalia,* 34, 253, 346, 347, 348
Hatzfeld, Helmut, "Per una Definizione dello stile di Montaigne," 419 n.15; *Estudios sobre el Barocco,* 419 n.15
Hauser, Arnold, *Mannerism,* 418 n.2; *Social History of Art,* 418 n.2
Haydn, Hiram, *Counter-Renaissance,* 400, 408 n.1
Hazlitt, William, 177, 417 n.1
Hecatommithi. See Cinthio, G. B. Giraldi
Hector (*Troilus and Cressida*), 141-42
Heilman, Robert B., *Magic in the Web,* 264, 427 n.5; *This Great Stage,* 287; "To Know Himself," 421 n.1; *Tragedy and Melodrama,* 416 n.31
Helena (*All's Well*), xviii, 134, 215, 222-23
Helicanus (*Pericles*), 363
Henderson, W. B. D., "Montaigne's *Apologie of Raymond Sebond* and *King Lear,*" 419 n.16
Henry IV, 111, 113, 114
Henry IV, Pt.1, 113, 122, 133, 193-94, 407 n.12
Henry IV, Pt. 2, 51, 113, 122, 133, 193-94
Henry V, 25, 53, 111, 146, 147, 153, 161, 169, 379, 380
Henry V, xviii, 51, 113-128, 131, 140, 229, 240
Henry VI, 97, 113, 128
Henry VIII, 113, 247, 252, 356, 407 n.12
Heraclitus, 79, 373
Hercules: as model of a heightened self, 180-81, 251, 257, 276, 426 n.2
Hermione (*Winter's Tale*), 252, 272, 363
Herndl, George C., *High Design,* 411 n.28
Heroines: self-knowledge of Shakespeare's 21, 71, 89-90
Herrick, Marvin T., *Comic Theory in the Sixteenth Century,* 407 n.15
Hierarchy. *See* Degree
Hobbes, Thomas, 33; *Leviathan,* 35
Hoeniger, F. D., "Prospero's Storm and Miracle," 433 n.12
Holbein, Hans (the Younger), 104
Holinshed, Raphael, *Chronicles,* 98, 99, 100, 101, 115, 117, 150
Holy Love of Heavenly Wisdom. See Du Vair, Guillaume
Homer, 190; *Iliad,* 51; *Odyssey,* 363
Honor: vs. humanism, 20, 82-83; Henry

Honor (*continued*)
V's moderate sense of, 121-22; Hamlet's craving for, 184; as obsession in *Troilus and Cressida*, 205-7.
Hooker, Elizabeth R., "Relation of Shakespeare to Montaigne," 419 n.16
Hooker, Richard, *Laws of Ecclesiastical Polity*, 17, 52, 59-60, 61, 144, 245-46
Horace, 7; *Epistles*, 7, 393; *Epodes*, 434 n.7; *Satires*, 88
Horatio (*Hamlet*), 142, 146
Hotspur, 17, 121
Hours of Recreation. See Guiccardini, Lodovico
Housman, A. E., *Name and Nature of Poetry*, 64-65
Hoy, Cyrus, "*Love's Labor's Lost* and the Nature of Comedy" 413 n.1
Huarte, Juan de San Juan, *Examen de Ingenios*, 114, 407 n.19, 425 n.9
Hudson, Henry N., Introduction to *Henry V*, 122
Humanism. *See* Christian humanism
Humility: man's need for, 3, 91, 264-65; woman's need for, 20-21
Humors. *See* Melancholy; Psychology, Elizabethan; Self-knowledge: as humorial balance
Humphrey, Laurence, *Nobles and of Nobility*, 20
Hunter, G. K., Introduction to *All's Well*, 424 n.4
Huntley, Frank L., "*Macbeth* and the Background of Jesuitical Equivocation," 427 n.10
Hynes, Sam, "Rape of Tarquin," 434 n.12

Iago, 36, 39, 240, 249, 255, 256, 298, 331, 336, 337-38, 346, 368, 372, 394
Ibsen, Henrik, 418 n.1
Idealism: of Brutus, 160-62, 167-71; pseudo-, of Troilus, 204-5, 211
Ideal man: Renaissance, 15, 25, 136; Christ as, 15, 114; Renaissance, questioned, 29, 146-48; and ideal frame, 47-48; Henry V as, and ideal king, 113-27; Brutus as, 146, 150-55, 165; Hamlet's search for, 146, 181-89; Vincentio as, 146-47, 233; Prospero as, 370-71, 379-82. *See also* Ideal prince
Ideal prince: and ideal Renaissance man, 15, 21, 115, 394; in Machiavelli, 33-34; in theory of absolutism, 228-29, 232-33
Identity: problems of, in *Errors*, 65-71; questions in *Hamlet*, 172-74, 193-94, 421 n.1; crisis in *Lear*, 299-300;

questions of Lear, 305-7; questions of Troilus, 195-96
Illustrium Poetarum Flores. See Mirandola, Octavianus
Imagination: Richard II's deranged, 109; Hamlet's ambiguous, 189-90; Macbeth's feverish, 343-44
Imogene (*Cymbeline*), 252, 363
Innocent III, Pope, *De Humanae Miseriae Conditione*, 15-16, 103, 108, 109, 315
Institutes of Christian Religion. See Calvin, John
Institution and First Beginning of a Christian Prince. See Chelidonius, Tigurinus
Institutio Principis Christiani. See Erasmus, Desiderius
Intemperance: as lack of self-knowledge, 11, 98, 120; Tarquin as embodiment of, 390-98
Isabella (*Measure for Measure*), 240

James, D. G., *Dream of Learning*, 179, 421 n.1; *Dream of Prospero*, 432 n.2
James I, King, 59, 229, 373, 425 n.16, 426 n.20; *Basilicon Doron*, 229, 425 n.16
Jameson, Anna B., 224
Jameson, T. H., "Machiavellianism of Gabriel Harvey," 409 n.16
Jealousy: Iago's, as species of envy, 262-64; Othello's, 278-79
Johnson, Samuel, 174
Jonson, Ben, 141
Jorgensen, Paul A., "Accidental Judgments, Casual Slaughters, and Purposes Mistook," 417 n.1; "Hamlet and the Restless Renaissance," 422 n.10; *Lear's Self-Discovery*, 307, 405 n.5; "Much Ado about Nothing," 289; "'Perplex'd in the Extreme': The Role of Thought in *Othello*," 260-61; "Vertical Patterns in *Richard II*," 415 n.2
Julius Caesar, 133, 141
Julius Caesar, xvii, xix, 30, 57, 76, 131, 133, 134, 137, 139, 140, 141, 150-71, 194, 196, 257, 328, 336, 407 n.12, 418 nn.1 and 2, 434 n.8
Justice: of Henry V, 115; vs. law in *Measure for Measure*, 219, 224-26, 230-36; social, and the Jacobeans, 245; social, questioned in *Lear*, 294, 302-3

Kafka, Franz, 65
Kantorowicz, Ernst H., *King's Two Bodies*, 416 n.21

Katherine (*Henry VIII*), 252
Keats, John, 39
Kent (*Lear*), 252, 256
Kermode, Frank, Introduction to *The Tempest*, 376, 432 n.2
King John, 114
King John, 30, 113
King Lear, 28, 49, 77, 220, 239-40, 256, 273, 329, 361, 390
King Lear, xviii, xix, 35, 77, 111, 134, 217, 225, 239, 241, 245, 247, 252, 253, 255, 257, 281-326, 327, 360, 408 n.34, 416 n.31, 418 n.2, 419 n.16
King Lear and the Gods. *See* Elton, William
King Leir (anon. play), 282, 284
Kingsmill, Andrew, *View of Man's Estate*, 407 n.22
Knight, G. Wilson, *Crown of Life*, 381; *Wheel of Fire*, 273, 428 n.21
Knights, L. C., "Ambiguity of *Measure for Measure*," 424 n.2; *Approach to Hamlet*, 421 n.1; *Some Shakespearean Themes*, 431 n.2
Kristeller, Paul, 408 n.1
Kyd, Thomas, 31; *Spanish Tragedy*, 190
Kyd, Thomas (?), *Ur-Hamlet*, 189-90, 423 n.31

Lack of Self-knowledge. *See* Self-knowledge: lack of
Lady Macbeth, 368
Lafeu (*All's Well*), 143
Laertes, Diogenes, *Vitae Philosophorum*, 406 n.1
Lambinus, Dionysius [humanist], Commentary on Cicero's *De Oratore*, 423 n.33; Commentary on Horace, 424 n.13, 434 n.7
Landi, Ortensio, *Paradossi*, 289, 429 n.8. *See also* Estienne, Charles; Munday, Antony
Langland, William, *Piers Plowman*, 434 n.11
La Primaudaye, Pierre de, *French Academy*, 20, 54, 79, 83, 175, 268, 269, 390-96, 399-400, 408 n.34, 414 nn.17 and 22, 416 nn.25 and 26, 432 n.14. See also Bowes, Thomas
Lascelles, Mary, *Shakespeare's MEASURE FOR MEASURE*, 217; " 'Glassie Essence': *Measure for Measure*," 425 n.11
Lawrence, W. W., *Shakespeare's Problem Comedies*, 133, 418 n.1
Laws of Ecclesiastical Polity. *See* Hooker, Richard

Laws of nature, 54-55, 72-73, 373, 393, 421 n.28
Leavis, F. R., *Common Pursuit*, 428 n.21
Leech, Clifford, *Shakespeare's Tragedies*, 382
Lemnius, Levinus, *Touchstone of Complexions*, 9, 15, 101-2, 114, 116-17, 123, 125
Lengefeld, Freiherr Kleinschmit von, "Der Manierismus in der Dichtung Shakespeares," 418 n.2
Leontes (*Winter's Tale*), 241, 361
Leroy (Regius), Louis [humanist], *De la Vicissitude*, 58-59, 60
Lever, J. W., Introduction to *Measure for Measure*, 234, 424 n.4
Lever, Richard, *Art of Reason*, 422 n.17
Leviathan. *See* Hobbes, Thomas
Levin, Harry, *Question of Hamlet*, 421 n.1
Lievsay, John L., "Some Renaissance Views of Diogenes," 429 n.26
Life, warfare of: in Erasmus, 4; in Calvin, 18; in Machiavelli, 32-34; in Hobbes, 33, 35; in Marlowe, 34-35; vs. romantic love in *Love's Labor's Lost*, 79-96, 81, 86-88, 91-94; and the theme of self-search in Shakespeare, 95-96
Lipsius, Justus, *De Constantia*, 250, 428 n.14, 429 n.25; *Six Books of Politics*, 138, 139, 428 n.12
Lodge, Thomas (?), *Anatomy of Sin*, 291, 407 n.22
Losing and finding. *See* Self-loss to self-recovery, movement from
Love: vs. philosophy in *Love's Labor's Lost*, 80-81, 88-90, 94; earthly and heavenly, 86, 91; as self-loss, 81, 88-96; as self-gain, 94, 232-33; vs. asceticism in *Measure for Measure*, 232-33
Lovejoy, Arthur O., *Great Chain of Being*, 411 n.26, 412 n.45
Love's Labor's Lost, xviii, 22, 40, 78-96, 193, 194, 234, 287, 357, 359, 368-69, 392
Love's Labor's Won, 215
Lucrece, 21, 330, 390-98, 434 nn.1 and 3
Lucrece, 12, 207, 287, 329-30, 331-34, 390-98, 431 n.3, 434 nn.1 and 14
Lucretius, 291
Lust: and love, 20-21, 220-21, 270; as spiritual blindness, 293
Luther, Martin, 27, 420 n.20
Lüthi, Max, *Shakespeares Dramen*, 163, 431 n.1
Lyly, John, *Campaspe*, 300, 301

Lyon, Charles, "Cressida, Achilles, and the Finite Deed," 423 n.5

Macbeth, xiv, 28, 49, 240, 249, 250, 257, 281, 361, 390, 398
Macbeth, xix, 35, 138, 241, 257, 327-55, 357, 361, 416 n.31, 426 n.10, 434 n.8
McCallum, Sir Mungo W., *Shakespeare's Roman Plays*, 160
Machiavelli, Niccolo, 31, 118, 252, 409. n.11, 409 n.16; *Art of War*, 31-32; *Florentine History*, 31-32; *Prince*, 21, 31-37, 118, 229, 253
Machiavellian *virtù*, 31, 34, 269, 346-48
Machiavellism, 34, 45, 59, 253, 268; in Elizabethan England, 31-32; in Bacon, 36, 37-38; Bolingbroke's, 97-98; Henry V's alleged, 118-19; of Cassius, 157-58, 161; of Ulysses, 200; in *Measure for Measure*, 228-29; "Jesuitical," 246, 269, 426 n.10; in Jacobean England, 252-56; in later plays, 255-56; in *Macbeth*, 345-48
Mack, Maynard, "Jacobean Shakespeare," 421 n.1; World of Hamlet," 421 n.1
Mackay, Eileen, *"Measure for Measure,"* 425 n.10
Macrobius, 411 n.26
Macrocosm. *See* Microcosm and macrocosm
Madness. *See* Folly
Magic: self-transformation through, 67, 347, 432 n.18; Prospero's limited, 371-74
Magna Moralia. See Aristotle
Man: duties of Renaissance, 9-11, 387-89; image of, for Christian humanists, 22-25; misery of Renaissance, 23, 49; paradox of Renaissance, 24, 288; Machiavelli's image of, 32-34; Marlowe's image of, 34-35, 59; Renaissance, and the cosmic frame, 46-54; according to Creation, 46, 291, 399, 401-3; symmetry of Renaissance, 47-48; dignity of Renaissance, 48, 399, 404, 409 n.20, 422 n.28; as conjunction of opposites, 54-56, 399, 401-4; and beast contrasted, 68, 387-89; skeptic view of, 144-48, 177-78, 197-98; insecurity of, in *Julius Caesar*, 168-69; fragmentation of, in *Troilus and Cressida*, 201, 208-14; as judge in *Measure for Measure*, 224-26, 233-36; Iago as a "new", 268-70, 272, 274; nakedness of, in *Lear*, 312-15; "new", in *Macbeth*, 345-47, 351. *See also* Ideal man;

Microcosm and macrocosm; Life, warfare of; Self; *and compounds of Self-*
Manhood: issue of, in *Macbeth*, 345-51, 354-55
Mannerism: and the problem plays, 30, 131-34, 148-49, 215, 240, 281; definition of, 133, 418 n.2; parallels to, in art 133-34, 138, 144-45, 147, 169, 182, 188, 201, 419 n.6; and innovation, 134-35; theory vs. reality in, 135-37, 145-47, 202-3, 205-7; theory vs. experience in, 137, 389; and skepticism related, 138-40, 177, 419 n.15
Mannerist: strategy of indirection in *Measure for Measure*, 227-28, 230, 236, 239, 372; tension in Hamlet, 174, 177, 179
Mannich, M. Johann (Diaconus), *Sacra Emblemata*, 145
Marginalia. See Harvey, Gabriel
Marina (*Pericles*), 252, 272, 363, 365
Marlowe, Christopher, 31, 244; *Edward II*, 97, 99, 100; *Tamburlaine*, 34-35, 59
Marston, John, 136, 141, 250
Martyr, Peter (Pietro Vermigli), *Commonplaces*, 403, 413 n.12, 417 n.20
Measure For Measure, xvii, xix, 30, 63-64, 76, 77, 131, 134, 137, 140, 148, 149, 215-36, 239, 294, 337, 372, 379, 403, 410 n.21, 418 nn.1 and 2
Melancholy, 65, 67, 74-75, 103, 340; Richard II's change from sanguine to, 101-3, 108, 415 n.9; Hamlet's, 177, 183. *See also* Grief
Merchant of Venice, 29, 50, 137, 414 n.20
Meres, Francis, 98, 404
Metamorphosis. *See* Transformation
Method unto Mortification. See Estella, Diego de
Microcosm and macrocosm, 43-61 passim, 108-9, 203, 212-13, 346-47, 399-400; origin of Renaissance concept of, 14-15; concepts of, questioned in later Renaissance, 18, 28, 37, 43, 410 n.2; Richard II's disordered, 108-9; scrutinized by Hamlet, 134-35, 188-89, 399-403; Brutus's dissonant, 153-55, 163-64; relationship of, in baroque plays, 331. *See also* Man; World
Microcosmos. See Davies, John (of Hereford)
Middle Ages: and Renaissance, xi, 54, 405 n.7. *See also* Consideration; Contempt of the world; Christian dogma; *De casibus* tragedy
Midsummer Night's Dream, 29

Miller, Arthur, "Tragedy and the Common Man," xiii

Milton, John, 55

Mind: as harmony, 57; and genius, 154-55; Hamlet's restless, 174, 176-79, 181, 185-86, 189, 194; speculative and active, 273, 402-3. *See also* Soul

Mirabellius, Mannus [Renaissance scholar], *Polyanthea,* 404

Mirandola, Octavianus, ed., *Illustrium Poetarum Flores,* 397

Mirror: of self-knowledge, 3, 7, 24-25, 38, 106, 181, 406 n.1, 416 n.25, 422 n.18; of death, 16, 106; prince as, 21, 394; for princes (*speculum principis*), 21, 99, 416 n.25; of grief, 105-6; of truth and vanity, 105-7, 158-59, 225-26, 416 n.23; of nature and drama, 136; of vanity and ignorance, 197-99; of anger, 224-25

Mirror for Magistrates. See Baldwin, William, et al.

Mirror of Madness, 301

Mirror of Man's Life [trans. of *De Humanae Miseriae Conditione*]. *See* Innocent III, Pope

Mirum in Modum. See Davies, John (of Hereford)

Montaigne, Michel de, *Essays,* 7, 28-31, 43, 138-39, 141, 142, 144, 146, 169, 170, 171, 178, 187, 190-91, 205, 209, 218, 296-97, 314, 365, 380-81, 382, 409 n.3, 410 n.2, 419 nn.15 and 16, 424 n.14, 433 n.4

More, Sir Thomas, 126; *Utopia,* 45

Mornay, Philip de, *Trueness of the Christian Religion,* 406 n.9; *True Trial and Examination of a Man's Own Self,* 9

Moulton, Richard G., *Shakespeare as a Dramatic Artist,* 337, 344

Muir, Kenneth, Introduction to *Macbeth,* 349, 431 nn.2 and 3

Muir, Kenneth, and Samuel Schoenbaum, *New Companion to Shakespeare Studies,* 405 n.7

Munday, Antony, *Defence of Contraries* [partial trans. of Charles Estienne's *Paradoxes*] 289, 292-93, 295, 299, 303, 316, 317, 318

Murry, John Middleton, *Shakespeare,* 110

Nagarajan, S. "*Measure for Measure* and Elizabethan Betrothals," 425 n.7

Narcissism. *See* Self-love

Nashe, Thomas, *Anatomy of Absurdity,* 300-301, 301-2

Nature: and man in Bacon and Shakespeare, 37, 373-74; in *Lear,* 287; Lear on needs of nature, 312-14

New Anatomy. See Woolton, John

New Book of Purgatory. See Rastell, John

Newton, Thomas [Elizabethan humanist and translator], 9

Nicolson, Marjorie H., *Breaking of the Circle,* 411 n.22

"Nihil." *See* Passeratti, John

Nixon, Leroy, *John Calvin's Teaching on Human Reason,* 408 n.25

Nobility: Macbeth's alleged, 336-37. *See also* Aristocracy

Nobles and of Nobility. See Humphrey, Laurence

North, Helen, *Sophrosyne: Self-Knowledge and Self-Restraint in Greek Literature,* 405 n.1

Nosce teipsum, xi, 47, 51, 256, 288, 321; origin of, 3, 195, 282; Apollo as patron-god of, 3, 195, 282; as slogan in grammar school, 3, 6; in the classics, 3, 7, 9-12, 222, 226, 290, 405 n.1; literature in the Renaissance, 3-24, 26, 180, 181, 188, 199, 254-55, 321, 372; emblems, 3, 16, 48, 49, 106, 144-45, 225-26; in sermons, 17; in courtesy books, 19-20; in literature for princes, 21-22; in Hobbes, 35; in Bacon, 37-39. *See also* Self-discovery; Self-image; Self-knowledge; Self-search

Nosce Teipsum. See Davies, Sir John

Nothing, quality of: in *Richard II,* 105, 109; in *Lear,* 289-92, 294, 299-300, 304, 308, 311-12, 319, 429 n.13, 429 n.26

Novum Organum. See Bacon, Sir Francis

Nowell, Alexander, *Catechism,* 87

Oedipus, 110, 295

Of the Knowledge Which Maketh a Wise Man. See Elyot, Sir Thomas

Of Wisdom. See Charron, Pierre

Ophelia, 240

Optic Glass of Humors. See Walkington, Thomas

Optimism: humanistic balance of, and pessimism, 23-24; Machiavelli's worldly, 34, 252-54; Henry V's ironic, 124-25, 417 n.20

Oration on the Dignity of Man. See Pico della Mirandola, Count Giovanni

Order: Christian-Platonic, vs. Aristo-

Order (*continued*)
telian, 59; Renaissance, 71-73; at end
of comedies, 75-77, 233; at end of
tragedies, 76-77, 193-94, 325-26. *See
also* Degree; Man; Microcosm and
macrocosm; Society; Shakespeare,
William: and Renaissance order;
World
Orosco, Sebastian de Covarrubias, *Emblemas Morales,* 16, 225-26
Othello, 49, 95, 126, 137, 179, 210, 211,
240, 241, 251, 255, 256, 257, 281, 328,
339, 380, 390
Othello, xvii, xix, 35, 132, 180, 210, 239-
43, 247, 250, 251, 255, 259-80, 281, 327,
346, 347, 403, 416 n.31
Ovid, 3, 7; *Art of Love,* 222, 226,
425 n.12; *Metamorphoses,* 7, 45, 226,
425 n.12

Palfreyman, Thomas [contributor to
Treatise of Moral Philosophy],
408 n.36
Palingenius, Marcellus, *Zodiacus Vitae,*
8, 54, 55, 74, 80, 83, 85, 86, 87, 323,
324, 325, 414 n.19, 419 n.18
Palmer, John, *Political Characters of
Shakespeare,* 160
Pandectarium. See Gessner, Conrad
Parabolae Sive Similia. See Erasmus,
Desiderius
Paracelsus, 410 n.2
Paradossi. See Landi, Ortensio
Paradoxes : of self-evaluation, 24; in the
thematic structure of *Lear,* 286-303;
of tragedy, 303-4. *See also* Nothing,
quality of; Salvation, paradox of
Paradoxes. See Estienne, Charles
Parolles (*All's Well*), 143, 216
Parsons, Robert, *First Book of Chris-
tian Exercise* [*Christian Directory*],
246
Parvus Mundus. See Goidtsenhoven,
Laurens van Haecht
Passeratti, John, "Nihil," 289
Passion : problem of control of, xiv, 5,
7, 10, 14, 87-88, 251-52, 262-64, 268-71,
309, 376-77; Hamlet's rhetorical, 135-
36, 179-80, 419 n.9; Hamlet's analysis
of, 179-81, 183, 185, 190-92; intensified,
in baroque, 243-44, 250-51, 256-58, 270,
276-77; moving of, 254-55, 274-75,
279-80. *See also* Ecstasy; Psychology,
Elizabethan; Self-knowledge : as control of passion; *and names of individual passions*

Passions of the Mind. See Wright,
Thomas
Pater, Walter, 224; *Renaissance,* 435
n.15
Patience : of women, 20-21, 272, 365,
367; and poverty, 224-45; Stoic, 251-
52; Christian, 252, 271-72; emphasis
on, in Shakespeare's later plays, 252;
as ironic keyword in *Othello,* 270-72;
and blindness in *Lear,* 295-97; false,
of suicide, 297-98; Lear's need for,
312-13; Gonzalo as embodiment of,
363-65; Miranda's, 355-67
Patrick, Max. *See* Croll, Morris W.
Paul, Henry N., *Royal Play of Mac-
beth,* 431 **n.2**
Paul, Saint, 80, 84, 224, 295, 349
Paulina (*Winter's Tale*), 252, 363
Perdita (*Winter's Tale*), 363
Pericles, 64, 240, 356, 407 n.12
Perrott, Sir James, *Consideration of
Human Condition,* 23, 103, 307-22
passim, 417 n.12
Persius, *Satires,* 3, 198, 290, 291, 429 n.13
Pessimism : humanistic balance of, and
optimism, 23-24; Elizabethan and
Jacobean, 35-36, 48-49, 51-52, 252-53;
Macbeth's nihilistic, 352
Philias, Peter G., "*Richard II* and
Shakespeare's Tragic Mode," 416 n.31
Philosophie Morale des Stoiques. See
Du Vair, Guillaume
Philosophy : active vs. passive, 83, 85.
See also Shakespeare, William : phi-
losophy of
Pico della Mirandola, Count Giovanni,
Oration on the Dignity of Man, 404
Piers Plowman. See Langland, William
Plato, 144, 165, 197, 316; *Alcibiades,*
158, 407 n.10; *Apology of Socrates,*
187; *Ion,* 190; *Phaedo,* 317; *Phaedrus,*
93, 406 n.1, 434 n.9
Platonism, 14, 317-19, 369, 379; and the
religion of beauty, 31, 60, 87, 207-8
Plautus, *Menaechmi,* 62-75 passim
Pliny, *Historia Naturalis,* 314, 315
Plutarch, *Lives,* 121-22, 140-41, 150-70
passim, 191; *Morals,* 108
Politics : as execution of the divine plan,
10; as dubious pursuit in *Julius
Caesar,* 139, 155, 160-61, 169-70
Polixenes (*Winter's Tale*), 256
Polonius, 50
Polyanthea. See Mirabellius, Nannus
*Poor Man's Passions and Poverty's
Patience. See* Warren, Arthur

Popkin, Richard, *History of Scepticism from Erasmus to Descartes,* 409 n.3

Poverty: idealization of, 146, 182-83; and patience, 244-45; and need for social justice, 302

Powell, C. L., "Castle of the Body," 434 n.11

Power: baroque fascination with, 242, 373-74; problem of, in *Tempest,* 373-83

Praise *(laus)*: characterization through, 118-20, 208-9

Praise of Nothing. See D., E.

Prayerbook. *See* Church of England, Book of Common Prayer

Precepts of Cato. See Disticha Catonis

Price, Jonathan R., "*Measure for Measure* and the Critics," 424 n.2

Pride: in learning deflated, 91; in reason deflated by fideists, 144-46; Brutus's idealism as concealed, 169; in self-discipline punctured in *Measure for Measure,* 218-19, 226, 232-33

Prince. *See* Death: and the prince; Ideal prince; Mirror: for princes; Mirror: prince as

Prince. See Machiavelli, Niccolo

Prior, Moody E., "Search for a Hero in *Julius Caesar,*" 419 n.3

Pritchard, Thomas, *School of Honest and Virtuous Life,* 407 n.10

Problem play: definition of, 131, 418 n.1. *See also* Mannerism

Problems of Beauty and All Human Affections. See Buoni, Tommaso

Progymnasmata. See Aphthonius

Proser, Matthew N., *Heroic Image in Five Shakespearean Tragedies,* 428 n.17

Prospero, 36, 77, 241, 339, 425 n.13

Providence: Hamlet's acceptance of, 192-93; in *The Tempest,* 364, 368, 370, 383

Prudence: of Henry V, 117-18

Psychology, Elizabethan: humors theory, 15; health of body and mind, 124-25; operation of the mind, 153-54, 268; the sexual act, 222-23, 425 n.9; hatred, envy, and jealousy, 262; man's antithetical composition, 288; anger and choler in old age, 309; functions of body and soul, 317-18; courage, rashness, and fear, 342; conflict of passion and reason, 391-96. *See also* Melancholy; Microcosm and macrocosm; Mind; Passion; Soul; Will

Puritanism: self-analysis in, 19; and the sobriety of Henry V, 126-27; of Angelo, 218-19, 232; alleged, in *Tempest,* 382. *See also* Asceticism; Calvinism

Pythagoras, 66, 67

Quaestiones Tusculanae. See Cicero, *Tusculan Disputations*

Quiller-Couch, Sir Arthur, Introduction to *Measure for Measure,* 231

Quintilian, *Institutio Oratoria,* 190, 419 n.9

Raleigh, Sir Walter, 85

Raphael (Sanzio), 52

Rapture. *See* Ecstasy

Rastell, John, *New Book of Purgatory,* 407 n.18

Reason: disparaged by skeptics and fideists, 18, 27, 28, 248-49; limited role of, in self-knowledge, 19, 309, 322, 248-49, 279, 309, 322, 375, 416 n.31. *See also* Passion; Psychology, Elizabethan

Regan, xiv, 255

Renaissance: nature of, xv-xviii, 43-44, 132-33; education, xvi, 3-13, 53, 291; style in literature and art, 44, 47-48, 52, 79-96 passim, 104, 123, 127-28, 138, 411 n.27; rhetoric, 53, 127, 135, 185, 191, 288-89, 362. *See also* Christian humanism; *Nosce teipsum:* literature in the Renaissance; World: frame of, in the Renaissance

Repentance: Angelo's, and self-recovery, 229-30; Macbeth's failure of, 351-53; Antonio's failure of, in *The Tempest,* 368; of Tarquin, 395-96

Ribner, Irving, *English History Play in the Age of Shakespeare,* 415 n.1; *Patterns in Shakespaerean Tragedy,* 176, 183

Rice, Warner G., "*Paradossi* of Ortensio Landi," 429 n.8

Richard II, 25, 53, 96, 113, 121, 127, 179, 187, 220, 247, 323

Richard II, xviii, 15, 17, 30, 76, 97-112, 114, 128, 139, 158, 328, 407 n.12, 419 n.3

Richard III, 113, 114, 147, 156, 337-38

Richard III, 145, 193-94, 250, 328, 419 n.3

Robertson, J. M., *Montaigne and Shakespeare,* 419 n.16, 433 n.4

Roerecke, E. M., "Baroque Aspects of *Antony and Cleopatra,*" 426 n.2

Rogers, Thomas, *Anatomy of the Mind,* 14, 54, 262, 263, 264, 285, 316, 390-91, 430 n.30

Role-playing: for assuming identity in Cicero, 12, 185; Hamlet's, 180, 184-86, 191-92; Prospero on man's, 378

Roman Catholicism, 245-46, 252

Romano, Julio, 419 n.6. *See also* Gombrich, Ernst

Romei, Annibale, *Courtier's Academy,* 60

Romeo, 208

Romeo and Juliet, xviii, 57, 76, 137, 148, 170, 327

Rosalind (*As You Like It*), 71

Russel, Burton, "Monstrous Birth," 428 n.16

Salvation, paradox of, 64-65, 78, 193, 332-34, 359, 360, 391

Samson, 295

Sanford, James. *See Mirror of Madness*

Sawles Warde, 434 n.11

Schanzer, Ernest, "Marriage Contracts in *Measure for Measure*," 425 n.7; *Problem Plays of Shakespeare,* 164, 418 n.1, 420 n.2, 425 n.16

Schlegel, August Wilhelm von, 177

Schoenbaum, Samuel. *See* Muir, Kenneth, and Samuel Schoenbaum

School of Honest and Virtuous Life. See Pritchard, Thomas

"School of Night," 87, 414 n.19

School of Virtue. See Seager, Francis

Schoonhovius, Florentius *Emblemata,* 48

Schücking, L. L., *Baroque Character,* 336, 426 n.4; *Character Problems in Shakespeare's Plays,* 287, 336, 432 n.19; *Shakespeare und der Tragödienstil seiner Zeit,* 426 n.4

Seager, Francis, *School of Virtue,* 5-6

Sebastian (*Twelfth Night*), 55-56

Sebond, Raymond, *Theologia Naturalis,* 138

Self: balanced and organic, in Erasmus, 4-5; corrupted, in Calvin, 18-19, 27; expansive, of aristocrats, 20, 30-31, 83, 243-44; variable, of Montaigne, 29; class-conscious, of courtiers, 30-31; assertive, in Machiavelli, 31-35, 253; arriviste, of Harvey, 34, 253, 346; psychological and time-bound, in Bacon, 38; circumscribed, of Christian humanists, 44, 83; problematic, in mannerism, 145, 194; restless, of Hamlet, 176-79, 181, 184, 189, 194;

divided, of Troilus, 204-5, 209-13; heightened, of later heroes, 241-42, 256-58, 259, 283, 328, 370-71; 382-83; acquisitive, of bourgeois, 243; lost, of Macbeth, 351-53; mastered, of Prospero, 362, 370-83

Self-alienation: in *Comedy of Errors,* 65, 73-75; Macbeth's, 348-49, 350

Self-analysis. *See* Self-discovery; Self-knowledge; Self-search

Self-control. *See* Self-knowledge: as control of passion

Self-discovery: in Aristotle and Shakespeare, xii-xiii, 104, 110-11; Richard II's limited, 105-11, 416 n.31; as confession of sin, 110, 246-47; Brutus's lacking of, 164-65, 170-71; Hamlet's problematic, 193; Troilus's avoided, 210-13; Othello's disputed, 277-80, 428 n.21; Edgar's tentative, 302-3; Lear's visionary, 309, 321-22; Macbeth's lacking of, 349-50, 353-54

Self-dramatization: Othello's romantic, 272-74; of other tragic heroes, 428 n.17

Self-evaluation. *See* Self-discovery; Self-knowledge; Self-search

Self-image: Christian humanists' conception of, 24-25; Richard II's changing, 99-104; Brutus's ambiguous, 157-59; specious, of Angelo, 219, 221; ironic, of Isabella, 224-26. *See also* Mirror

Self-knowledge: ancient, modern, and Shakespearean, xi-xv; explicit references to, in Shakespeare, xiii-xv, 106, 157, 174, 247, 264, 309, 330, 349-50, 353; as control of passion, xiv, 4-21 passim, 87-88, 115-16, 120, 122, 126, 251-52, 268-70, 309, 375-88; Christian, and pagan, 4-5, 284-85, 292, 297, 303, 315; as knowledge of cardinal virtues, 10-11, 15, 114-17; through study of others, 12, 16, 33, 37-39, 181-86, 254-56; as humorial balance, 15, 122, 151-52, 309; as knowledge of man's misery, 15-18, 23, 49-50, 103-9; practical, in courtesy books, 20-21, 30-31; as knowledge of man's equality, 21-22, 24-25, 100, 109, 123, 302, 308, 312-15; as knowledge of man's dignity, 23-24, 47-48; theories of, questioned, 28-29, 144-49, 174, 181-89, 104, 214; egoistic and utilitarian, in Machiavelli, 33-35; used for the manipulation of others, 33-39, 196-97, 200, 227-29, 253-56, 264-66, 298, 345-47; toughminded, of Gabriel Harvey, 34, 253,

346; utilitarian, in Bacon, 36-39, 253-54; arrogant, of Shakespeare's villains, 39-40, 255, 264-66, 283-84; Renaissance, and the cosmic frame, 43-61, 72, 76-77, 98, 127-28, 144, 188-89; practical, of Thomas Wright, 253-56; as voice of conscience, 247, 349-50, 368; achieved by Prospero, 379-83. *See also* Body and soul; Consideration; *Decorum;* Ideal man; Ideal prince; Microcosm and macrocosm; Mirror; *nosce teipsum;* Self-discovery; Self-image; Self-search; Soul; Temperance

Self-knowledge, lack of: according to Aristotle and Shakespeare, xii-xiii; according to Arthur Miller and Shakespeare, xiii; Ferdinand's in *Love's Labor's Lost,* 79, 82-83; by excessive self-assurance, 3, 82, 166-70, 218-19, 272-73, 275, 305; Adriana's in *Comedy of Errors,* 73-75; Richard II's, 98-101, 111; Troilus's, 195-96, 211-13; Angelo's, 219-20; Othello's, 272-75; of tragic heroes, 281; Lear's, 281-83, 290-91, 308-10; Gloucester's, 283, 293-95, 297-98. *See also* Tragic flaw

Self-loss: comic, 66-70, 81, 93; in tragedies, 327-28; in *Macbeth,* 328-55 passim; threatened in *Tempest,* 356-83 passim

Self-loss to self-recovery, movement from: in comedy and tragedy, xvii-xviii; in comedies and tragicomedies, 63-64, 358-60, 361-62; in *Comedy of Errors,* 64-65, 70-71, 75-76; in *Love's Labor's Lost,* 88-97; in *Richard II,* 110-11; Hamlet's problematic, 192-94; in *Measure for Measure,* 220-21, 233; in *Lear,* 298-303, 306-22; in *Macbeth,* 332; in *Tempest,* 362-83 passim. *See also* Salvation, paradox of

Self-love: and self-awareness of Richard II, 105-10; in Brutus's self-image, 157-58; in Achilles' ignorance, 196-98; in Isabella's pleading, 224-26; in Iago's self-control, 264-65. *See also* Mirror; Vanity

Self-search: by questioning oneself, 22-23, 70, 219-20, 305-15; in La Primaudaye and *Love's Labor's Lost,* 79; in Erasmus and *Love's Labor's Lost,* 79-94; Hamlet's unsuccessful, 175-76, 179-89, 193-94

Seneca [philosopher and dramatist], 250 [dramatist], 397; *De Providentia,*

406 n.2; *Hercules Furens,* 251, 276; *Hercules Oetaeus,* 251; *Medea,* 251, 432 n.18; *Naturales Quaestiones,* 406 n.1; *Oedipus,* 251; "Of Anger," 225; *Phaedra,* 434 n.14

Sententia Pueriles. See Culmannus, Leonhardus

Shakespeare, William: texts used, ix; First Folio, 166, 279, 400-403, 421 n.2; Quartos, 98, 193, 400-403, 421 n.2; phases of artistic development, xii, 29-30, 35-36, 76-77, 127-28, 131-33, 239, 243, 256-58; and grammar-school education, xvi, 4-13, 404-5; philosophy of, xx-xxi, 39, 143-44, 165; and man's potential greatness, 10; and Christian humanism, 13, 22, 25, 40, 57-58, 126, 382-83; and religion, 17, 19, 80, 142-44, 148-49, 247, 325, 378-79, 381-82; and the aristocracy, 19-21, 243-44, 256-57; and Montaigne, 29, 142, 419 n.16, 427 n.21; and skepticism, 29-30, 139-42, 169-70, 214, 378-79; and Bacon contrasted, 36, 39-40, 373-74; sympathy with humanity dramatically expressed by, 39-40, 214, 232-33, 298, 303, 319, 325-26, 383; and Renaissance order, 60-61, 111-12, 127-28; identified with Henry V, 126; and Stratford, 126, 296; on theatrical conditions, 134; as actor and playwright, 136-37; and the Essex rebellion, 140; between Christian humanism and counter-humanism, 149, 189, 214, 243, 256-58; identified with Hamlet, 179-80; and Thomas Wright, 198-99, 254-57, 427 n.21; identified with Vincentio, 227; identified with Prospero, 227, 363, 374; and the bourgeoisie, 244; and Seneca, 251; identified with Gonzalo (*Tempest*), 363-64

Shearman, John, *Mannerism,* 418 n.2

Sidney, Sir Philip, Apology for Poetry, xi; *Arcadia,* 292, 296

Siegel, Paul, "Damnation of Othello," 427 n.4

Sigismund, Reinhold, "Übereinstimmendes zwischen Shakespeare und Plutarch," 416 n.28

Sin. *See* Self-discovery: as confession of sin

Six Books of a Commonweal. See Bodin, Jean

Skepticism: and fideism, 28, 142-45, 148-49, 189, 218, 248; and the Copernican revolution, 44, 50-51; in problem plays, 139-49; moderate vs. Pyrrhonic,

Skepticism (*continued*)
141-42, 204-5; in *Julius Caesar*, 167-71; rampant in *Troilus and Cressida*, 196-200; 202-5, 212-14; Hamlet's, 177-79, 189, 193, 360; on war, 207; and political absolutism, 228, 235; in the ending of *Measure for Measure*, 233-38; and baroque emphasis on will, 248-49; Prospero's, 378-79. *See also* Montaigne, Michel de; Charron, Pierre

Smith, Gordon R., "Brutus, Virtue, and Will," 156

Smith, Warren D., "Duplicate Revelation of Portia's Death," 421 n.18

Society: and self in Bacon, 37-38; corrupt, in problem plays, 137, 145; under absolutism, 233, 235, 242-44; and capitalism, 244-45. *See also* Order; Poverty; World: frame of, in the Renaissance

Socrates, 158, 187, 190, 406 n.1

Soellner, Rolf, "Four Primary Passions," 415 n.2

Solomon, 114

Somnium Scipionis. See Cicero

Sonnets: *24, 47,* 410 n.4; *44,* 415 n.22; *45,* 414 n.22; *62,* 416 n.23; *94,* 216, 227, 424 n.2; *115,* 407 n.12; *116,* 407 n.12; *146,* 57-58

Sophocles, *King Oedipus,* xii

Soul: immortality of, 8, 57, 187, 395; and self in Renaissance *nosce teipsum,* 9-10, 13-14, 407 n.18; hegemony of, in the body, 14; division of, 56-57, 73, 153-54; imagery, 6-67, 74-75, 212-13; and eye analogous, 67, 157, 196-99; Brutus's dissonant, 152-55, 163-64; of state, 200; as symbol of unity, 212-13; as glassy essence, 225-26, 228-31, 425 n.11; perverted use of, by Iago, 265, 273; creation of, from nothing, 291; and self in *Lear,* 315-26; mystery of, 322-26; intemperance and death of, 395-96. *See also* body and soul; Psychology, Elizabethan

Southampton, Henry Wriothesley, earl of, 421 n.21

Spanish Tragedy. See Kyd, Thomas

Speculum principis. See Mirror: for princes

Spencer, Theodore, *Shakespeare and the Nature of Man,* 375, 389

Spenser, Edmund, *Faerie Queene,* 395, 434 n.11; *Hymne of Love,* 54

Spivack, Bernard, *Shakespeare and the Allegory of Evil,* 260

Stein, Arnold, "*Troilus and Cressida:* the Disjunctive Imagination," 423 n.5

Stevenson, David L., *Achievement of MEASURE FOR MEASURE,* 425 n.16

Stoicism: 10, 83, 317; and suppression of emotions, 87-88, 166-67, 218, 269-70, 364; Hamlet's problematic, 192-93; in Seneca's tragedies, 251; Brutus's alleged, 164-68; Julius Caesar's boastful, 167; will-power emphasized in, 249-52, 428 n.14; patience acclaimed by, 251-52, 270; Iago as a disciple of new, 269-70; Edgar's testing of, 298-99. *See also* Seneca

Stoll, E. E., *Hamlet,* 422 n.6; *Shakespeare and Other Masters,* 177

Strachey, Lytton, *Books and Characters,* 382

Strathmann, Ernest A., *Sir Walter Ralegh: A Study in Renaissance Scepticism,* 409 n.3; "Textual Evidence for 'the School of Night,'" 414 n.19

Strauss, Leo, *Thoughts on Machiavelli,* 409 n.11

Summa epitasis. See Climax, dramatic

Swinburne, A. C., *Study of Shakespeare,* 287

Sylvester, Sir Joshua [translator of Du Bartas], 43, 45

Sypher, Wylie, *Four Stages of Renaissance Style,* 139, 169, 411 n.27, 418 n.2; "Shakespeare as Casuist," 424 n.2

Table of Human Passions. See Coeffeteau, Nicolas

Taming of the Shrew, 72, 421 n.19

Tarquin (*Lucrece*), 12, 98, 114, 329-30, 332-34, 340, 390-98, 434 n.12

Taylor, G. C., *Shakespeare's Debt to Montaigne,* 419 n.16

Temperance, 6, 11-13, 151-52, 205-6, 232; as balance of humors, 15; Henry V's exemplary, 115-17, 120; embodied by Lucrece, 390-94

Tempest, 36, 40, 64, 77, 149, 339, 356-83, 414 n.20, 425 n.13

Terence, 357; *Adelphoe,* 7, 413 n.7

Tertullian, 271

Thaisa (*Pericles*), 252

Theatrum Mundi. See Boaistuau, Pierre

Thesaurus. See Cooper, Thomas

Three Books of Duties [trans. of Cicero's *De Officiis*]. *See* Cicero

Tillyard, E. M. W., *Elizabethan World Picture*, 405 n.7, 411 n.26, 412 n.45, 422 n.28; *English Renaissance: Fact or Fiction?*, 405 n.7; *Shakespeare's History Plays*, 417 n.19, 431 n.2; *Shakespeare's Problem Plays*, 134, 418 n.1

Timon, 256

Timon of Athens, xix, 240, 247, 257, 418 n.1

Tintoretto, 188

Tiresias, 295

Titus Andronicus, xviii, 76, 250, 327, 423 n.33

Tolbert, James M., "Sources of Shakespeare's *Lucrece*," 434 n.14

Tolstoy, Count Leo Nikolaevitch, 127, 176, 282

Torrance, T. F., *Calvin's Doctrine of Man*, 408 n.25

Touchstone of Complexions. See Lemnius, Levinus

Tragic flaw: in Aristotle and Shakespeare, xii-xiii; Hamlet's elusive, 182; Othello's sufficient, 272-75; Gloucester's and Lear's, connected, 292-95; Lear's gigantic, 290; examined in *Lucrece*, 396-98; self-dramatization of hero as, 428 n.17

Trance. *See* Ecstasy

Transformation: of selves threatened in *Comedy of Errors*, 66-70; Hamlet and physical, 188

Traversi, D. A., *Approach to Shakespeare*, 205

Treasury or Storehouse of Similes. See Cawdrey, Robert

Treatise of Melancholy. See Bright, Timothy

Treatise of Moral Philosophy. See Baldwin, William

Treatise of the Immortality of the Soul. See Woolton, **John**

Trevor-Roper, Hugh, *Religion, the Reformation, and Social Changes*, 426 n.6

Troilus, 137, 139, 141-42, 145, 146, 148, 220, 240

Troilus and Cressida, xvii, xix, 30, 61, 63-64, 76, 131, 133, 134, 137, 140, 141, 143, 145, 146, 148, 195-214, 215, 233, 413 n.5, 418 n.1

Tuve, Rosemond, Introduction to *Zodiac of Life*, 406 n.9

Twelfth Night, 55, 63

Two Gentlemen of Verona, 78

Tyndale, William, 4

Ulysses (*Troilus and Cressida*), 134, 145, 146

Universe. *See* World

Ure, Peter, Introduction to *Richard II*, 415 n.7, 416 n.23; *William Shakespeare: The Problem Plays*, 418 n.1

Ur-Hamlet. See Kyd, Thomas (?)

Van Doren, Mark, *Shakespeare*, 123, 124, 125, 357

Vanity. *See* Self-love

Vasari, Giorgio, 182

Venus and Adonis, 222

Vermigli, Pietro. *See* Martyr, Peter

View of Man's Estate. See Kingsmill, Andrew

Vincentio, Duke (*Measure for Measure*), 17, 140, 145, 147, 148, 359, 372, 379, 403

Viola, 55, 71

Virgil, 7; *Aeneid*, 123, 363, 380; *Eclogues*, 226, 425 n.12

Virginia, Council of, *True Declaration of the State of the Colony of Virginia*, 363, 432 n.2

Vroonland, Jewell K., "Mannerism and Shakespeare's Problem Plays," 418 n.2

Waith, Eugene M., *Herculean Hero*, 426 n.2

Walker, Roy, *Time is Free*, 431 n.2

Walkington, Thomas, *Optic Glass of Humors*, 323, 407 n.19

Walter, J. H., Introduction to *Henry V*, 417 nn.4 and 12

Warhaft, Sidney, "Bacon and the Renaissance Ideal of Self-Knowledge," 409 n.20

Warren, Arthur, *Poor Man's Passions and Poverty's Patience*, 245, 252, 302

Watson, Curtis B., *Shakespeare and the Renaissance Concept of Honor*, 413 n.6

Watson, Foster, *ZODIACUS VITAE of Marcellus Palingenius Stellatus*, 406 n.9

Webber, Joan, *Eloquent I*, 427 n.14

Webster, John, 250

Wellek, René, "Concept of the Baroque in Literary Scholarship," 418 n.2

West, Robert H., *Shakespeare and the Outer Mystery*, 422 n.19, 427 n.1

Whetstone, George, *Promos and Cassandra*, 217, 223

Whitaker, Virgil, *Shakespeare's Use of Learning*, 81

Whitney, Geoffrey, *Choice of Emblems,* 406 n.1

Wilkins, Eliza G., *Delphic Maxims in Literature,* 405 n.1

Will: and passion intensified in baroque, 239-57, 277, 280; Iago's subjugation of Othello's, 265-67, 270-80; Desdemona's strength of, 267; Othello's weakness of, 273; dynamics of, in *Macbeth,* 341-48; and passion in *Lucrece,* 392

Williams, Gwyn, "*The Comedy of Errors* Rescued from Tragedy," 68, 412 n.1

Willichius, Jodocus [humanist], Commentary on Terence, *Comoediae,* 7

Wilson, F. P., *Elizabethan and Jacobean,* 410 n.19

Wilson, Harold S., "Action and symbol in *Measure for Measure,*" 425 n.13

Wilson, J. Dover, Introduction to *Julius Caesar,* New Shakespeare, 160

Winter's Tale, 149, 256, 356, 361, 407 n.12, 419 n.6

Wisdom: as ultimate goal, 4, 80; of folly, 86, 300-301, 309, 321; as elusive goal in *Hamlet,* 174, 194; of perspective in *Lear,* 287, 289, 296-97, 303-4, 321; Prospero's final, 377-83

Wölfflin, Heinrich, *Principles of Art History,* 411 n.27, 426 n.4

Wolsey, Cardinal (*Henry VIII*), 247

Women: education of noble, 20-21; subjection of, 53-54, 59, 71-75; "new"

in Shakespeare's later plays, 272

Woolton, John, *New Anatomy,* 72, 73, 108, 401-2, 407 n.19, 414 n.17, 420 n.20; *Treatise of the Immortality of the Soul,* 13-14, 24, 67, 317, 432 n.18

Wordsworth, Charles, *On Shakespeare's Knowledge and Use of the Bible,* 407 n.13

World: frame of, in the Renaissance, 43-54, 58-61, 71-73, 75-77; as stage, 46, 104, 225, 321, 377-78, 416 n.19; decay of, 49-50, 144, 247, 324; frame of, and tragedy of Richard II, 111-12; frame of, skeptically viewed, 138, 145; frame of, and Henry V, 127; diffuseness of, for Bodin, 138; diffuseness of, for Hamlet, 188-89; natural and supernatural, in Prospero's vision, 377-78; upside-down Jacobean, 244-45; supernatural, in Macbeth, 322, 334-35, 347-48. See also Microcosm and macrocosm

World picture, Elizabethan, 44, 405 n.7

Worship, William, *Christian's Jewel,* 349, 431 n.4

Wright, Louis B., *Middle Class Culture in Elizabethan England,* 408 n.27

Wright, Thomas, *Passions of the Mind,* 15, 19, 198, 199, 254-55, 256, 274-75, 298, 372, 422 n.18, 423 n.2, 427 n.21

Zodiacus Vitae. See Palingenius, Marcellus